INTERNATIONAL HANDBOOK OF
EDUCATIONAL EVALUATION

Kluwer International Handbooks of Education

VOLUME 9

A list of titles in this series can be found at the end of this volume.

International Handbook of Educational Evaluation

Part Two: Practice

Editors:

Thomas Kellaghan
Educational Research Centre, St. Patrick's College, Dublin, Ireland

Daniel L. Stufflebeam
The Evaluation Center, Western Michigan University, Kalamazoo, MI, U.S.A.

with the assistance of

Lori A. Wingate
The Evaluation Center, Western Michigan University, Kalamazoo, MI, U.S.A.

KLUWER ACADEMIC PUBLISHERS
DORDRECHT / BOSTON / LONDON

Library of Congress Cataloging-in-Publication Data is available.

ISBN 1-4020-0849-X

Published by Kluwer Academic Publishers
PO Box 17, 3300 AA Dordrecht, The Netherlands

Sold and distributed in North, Central and South America
by Kluwer Academic Publishers,
101 Philip Drive, Norwell, MA 02061, U.S.A.

In all other countries, sold and distributed
by Kluwer Academic Publishers, Distribution Centre,
PO Box 322, 3300 AH Dordrecht, The Netherlands

Printed on acid-free paper

Printed and bound in Great Britain by MPG Books Limited, Bodmin, Cornwall

Table of Contents

SECTION 5: THE SOCIAL AND CULTURAL CONTEXTS OF EDUCATIONAL EVALUATION

PART TWO: PRACTICE

SECTION 6: NEW AND OLD IN STUDENT EVALUATION

SECTION 10: LOCAL, NATIONAL, AND INTERNATIONAL LEVELS OF SYSTEM EVALUATION

Section 6

New and Old in Student Evaluation

Introduction

MARGUERITE CLARKE

Boston College, Center for the Study of Testing, Evaluation and Educational Policy, MA, USA

GEORGE MADAUS

Boston College, Center for the Study of Testing, Evaluation and Educational Policy, MA, USA

Student evaluation involves making judgments about the merit or worth of student achievement in a particular area. Tests, assessments, and examinations are commonly used to collect the information on which these judgments are based. The result may be a decision about an individual student or students, or about the way in which instruction takes place. The four chapters in this section cover several key topics in this area of educational evaluation. Robert Mislevy, Mark Wilson, Kadriye Ercikan, and Naomi Chudowsky discuss psychometric principles in student assessment; Peter Airasian and Lisa Abrams provide an overview of evaluation in the classroom; Caroline Gipps and Gordon Stobart consider alternative assessment; and Thomas Kellaghan and George Madaus describe external (public) examinations.

While the term "evaluation" has been defined elsewhere in this volume, it is also worth looking at some definitions of the terms "assessment," "test," and "examination" since they figure prominently in the chapters that follow. The Oxford English Dictionary (OED) (1989) reveals interesting etymologies for the terms. While "assessment," modified by the adjectives "authentic," "alternative," or "performance," has only become popular in educational discourse in recent years, the OED reveals that the word, meaning estimation or evaluation, actually dates back to 1626. However, its first link to education, according to the OED, did not occur until 1956 when it was used in England in contradistinction to the more traditional term "examination." The term "test" is considered an Americanism by the OED. The first education-related reference is from 1910 when the term was used to imply a "simpler, less formal, procedure than an examination." "Examination" is the oldest of the three terms and the one preferred in Europe. The first reference to an academic examination (defined as the process of testing, by questions oral or written, the knowledge or ability of pupils) identified by the OED was in 1612, and reads as follows: "Which worke of continuall examination, is a notable quickner and nourisher of all good learning." There are a number of subtle and interesting differences between the OED definitions of the verbs "examine," "test," and "assess." To "examine" implies an

International Handbook of Educational Evaluation, 485–488
T. Kellaghan, D.L. Stufflebeam (eds.)
© *2003 Dordrecht: Kluwer Academic Publishers. Printed in Great Britain.*

attempt to investigate, inquire, and probe; to understand and learn about the capacity or knowledge of a student. To "test" implies putting students through an ordeal or trial designed to reveal their achievements. To "assess" implies determining or fixing an amount; the process or means of evaluating academic work.

Whichever term is used, certain fundamental principles underpin the process of collecting and evaluating information on students (AERA, APA, NCME, 1999; Madaus, Raczek, & Clarke, 1997; National Research Council, 1999). Mislevy, Wilson, Ercikan, and Chudowsky lay out these principles in the first chapter in this section. The authors describe the assessment situation as one in which information is gathered on what a student says, does, or makes in a few particular circumstances in order to make inferences about what the student knows or can do more generally. Whether this situation involves a teacher asking questions to find out if a student is ready to move on to the next page in her reading book, or policymakers mandating a national assessment of fourth grade students' reading ability, the assessment can be viewed as an evidentiary argument, of which the principles of *validity, reliability, comparability*, and *fairness* are regarded as desirable properties. While the focus of the Mislevy et al. chapter is on the statistical tools and techniques used to establish these properties in large-scale standardized testing, the authors note that the properties – since they are also social values – apply to other forms of student evaluation, although their operationalization may vary with context.

The three chapters that follow look at some of the contexts in which student evaluation takes place, as well as some of the uses to which information may be put. Airasian and Abrams describe evaluation in the classroom. Five areas of evaluation, which have as their common purpose to aid the teacher in making decisions about teaching and learning processes and outcomes, are outlined. The evaluation activities discussed include not only tests – either teacher-made or externally developed – but also more informal activities such as questioning or monitoring of a class during a lesson or activity. External examinations, as described by Kellaghan and Madaus, provide a strong contrast to these classroom-based evaluation practices, since they represent a form of evaluation in which control over purpose, content, length, timing, and scoring is external to the classroom. Furthermore, the data obtained are often used to make important decisions about students, including ones relating to entry to the next level of education, graduation, and certification. Given the high stakes that are attached to these decisions, issues of validity, reliability, comparability, and fairness are of greater concern than in many other kinds of student evaluation. The focus of the chapter by Gipps and Stobart is on alternative forms of assessment. While the purposes (i.e., assessment *for* learning) and characteristics of these forms (i.e., an integral part of the teaching/learning process, tends to take place under relatively uncontrolled conditions, seeks evidence of best rather than typical performances) seem more in tune with classroom-based student evaluation, the drive to include these kinds of information-rich approaches in large-scale assessment systems has given them, in these contexts, characteristics, purposes, and effects similar to those of external (public) examinations.

As Kellaghan and Madaus note, student evaluation has a long history. External testing systems can be traced back to the Western Zhou Dynasty in China (1027–711 BC). In addition to longevity, these kinds of evaluation activities affirm Ecclesiastes' moral (i.e., "What has been is what will be, and what has been done is what will be done; and there is nothing new under the sun") in terms of the formats used for collecting information on student achievement (Madaus, Raczek, and Clarke, 1997). For example, supply-type items were used by the medieval guilds and universities in Europe. The former required apprentices to supply a product as proof of competence; the latter used the viva voce, or oral disputation, to evaluate a student's knowledge and determine whether he was worthy of being included in the community that the judge had been authorized to represent (Hoskins, 1968). Selection-type items have a similarly long lineage. For example, the true-false test is believed to have forerunners in the Chinese civil service examination system (Loewe, 1986).

Student evaluation is a paradox. In some ways, it remains the same; in others, it is constantly evolving. Reflecting the latter reality, the chapters in this section refer to several developments in the areas of computer technology, cognitive psychology, and psychometrics that suggest exciting new possibilities and improvements (see also Pellegrino, Chudowsky, & Glaser, 2001). Despite these advances, it is important to keep in mind that while the tools, and even the functions, of student evaluation may change, certain key principles remain the same. These include the need to attend to issues of validity, reliability, comparability, and fairness; the need to balance instructional (usually classroom-based) and accountability uses of evaluation information; and the key role of the teacher as an influence on the context and outcomes of the evaluation process.

REFERENCES

American Educational Research Association, American Psychological Association, and National Council on Measurement in Education (1999). *Standards for educational and psychological testing.* Washington, DC: Author.

Hoskins, K. (1968). The examination, disciplinary power and rational schooling. *History of Education,* **8**, 135–146.

Loewe, M. (1986). The former Han dynasty. In D. Twitchett, & M. Loewe (Eds.), *The Cambridge history of China* (pp. 103–198). Cambridge: Cambridge University Press.

Madaus, G., Raczek, A., & Clarke, M. (1997). The historical and policy foundations of the assessment movement. In A. Lin Goodwin (Ed.), *Assessment for equity and inclusion: Embracing all our children* (pp. 1–33). New York: Routledge.

National Research Council (1999). *High stakes: Testing for tracking, promotion, and graduation.* Washington, DC: National Academy Press.

The Oxford English dictionary (1989) (2nd ed.). Oxford: Oxford University Press.

Pellegrino, J., Chudowsky, N., & Glaser, R. (2001). *Knowing what students know: The science and design of educational assessment.* Washington, DC: National Academy Press.

24
Psychometric Principles in Student Assessment[1]

ROBERT J. MISLEVY

University of Maryland, MD, USA

MARK R. WILSON

University of California, Berkeley, CA, USA

KADRIYE ERCIKAN

University of British Columbia, BC, USA

NAOMI CHUDOWSKY

National Research Council, Washington DC, USA

"Validity, reliability, comparability, and fairness are not just measurement issues, but *social values* that have meaning and force outside of measurement wherever evaluative judgments and decisions are made" (Messick, 1994, p. 2).

What are psychometric principles? Why are they important? How do we attain them? We address these questions from the perspective of assessment as evidentiary reasoning; that is, how we draw inferences about what students know, can do, or understand from the handful of particular things they say, do, or make in an assessment setting. Messick (1989), Kane (1992), and Cronbach and Meehl (1955) show the deep insights that can be gained from examining validity from such a perspective. We aim to extend the approach to additional psychometric principles and bring out connections with assessment design and probability-based reasoning.

Seen through this lens, validity, reliability, comparability, and fairness (as in the quotation from Messick, above) are properties of an argument – not formulae, models, or statistics per se. We will do two things before we even introduce statistical models. First, we will look at the nature of evidentiary arguments in assessment, paying special attention to the role of standardization. And secondly, we will describe a framework that structures the evidentiary argument in a given assessment, based on an evidence-centered design framework (Mislevy, Steinberg, & Almond, in press). In this way, we may come to appreciate psychometric principles without tripping over psychometric details.

International Handbook of Educational Evaluation, 489–532
T. Kellaghan, D.L. Stufflebeam (eds.)
© *2003 Dordrecht: Kluwer Academic Publishers. Printed in Great Britain.*

Of course in practice we do use models, formulae, and statistics to examine the degree to which an assessment argument possesses the salutary characteristics of validity, reliability, comparability, and fairness. Thus, it will be necessary to consider how these issues are addressed when one uses particular measurement models to draw particular inferences, with particular data, for particular purposes. To this end we describe the role of probability-based reasoning in the evidentiary argument, using classical test theory to illustrate ideas. We then survey some widely used psychometric models, such as item response theory and generalizability analysis, focusing on how each is used to address psychometric principles in different circumstances. We cannot provide a guidebook for using all this machinery, but we will point out some useful references along the way for the reader who needs them.

This is a long road, and it may seem to wander at times. We commence by looking at examples from an actual assessment, so that the reader will have an idea of where we want to go, in thinking about assessment in general, and psychometric principles in particular.

AN INTRODUCTORY EXAMPLE

The assessment design framework provides a way of thinking about psychometrics that relates what we observe to what we infer. The models of the evidence-centered design framework are illustrated in Figure 1. The *student model*, at the far left, concerns what we want to say about what a student knows or can do – aspects of the student's knowledge or skill. Following a tradition in psychometrics, we label this "θ" (theta). This label may stand for something rather simple, such as a single category of knowledge (e.g., vocabulary usage), or something much more complex, such as a set of variables relating to the strategies that a student can bring to bear on mixed-number subtraction problems, and the conditions under which particular strategies are selected and used. The *task model*, at the far right in the figure concerns the situations we can set up in the world, in which we will observe the student say or do something that gives us clues about the knowledge or skill that we have built into the student model. Between the student and task model are the scoring model and the measurement model, through which we reason from what we observe in performances to what we infer about a student.

These models may be illustrated with a recent example – an assessment system built for a middle school science curriculum, "Issues, Evidence and You" (IEY) (SEPUP, 1995). Figure 2 describes variables in the student model upon which both the IEY curriculum and its assessment system, called the BEAR Assessment System (Wilson & Sloane, 2000) are built. The student model consists of four variables, at least one of which is the target of every instructional activity and assessment in the curriculum. The four variables are seen as four dimensions on which students will make progress during the curriculum. The dimensions are correlated (positively, we expect), because they all relate to "science," but are quite distinct educationally. The psychometric tradition would use a diagram like Figure 3 to illustrate this situation. Each of the variables is represented as a circle, with the intention of indicating that they are unobservable or "latent" variables. They are connected by curving lines to indicate that they are not necessarily causally related to one another (at least as far as we are modeling that relationship), but that they are associated (usually we use a correlation coefficient to express that association).

The student model represents what we wish to measure in students. These are constructs, that is, variables that are inherently unobservable, but which we propose as a useful way to organize our thinking. They describe aspects of students' skill or knowledge for the purposes of, say, comparing programs, evaluating progress, or planning instruction. We use them to accumulate evidence from what we can actually observe students say and do.

Now look at the right hand side of Figure 1. This is the task model. This is how we describe the situations we construct in which students will actually perform. Particular situations are generically called "items" or "tasks."

In the case of IEY, the items are embedded in the instructional curriculum, so much so that students would not necessarily know that they were being assessed unless the teacher tells them. An example task is shown in Figure 4. It was

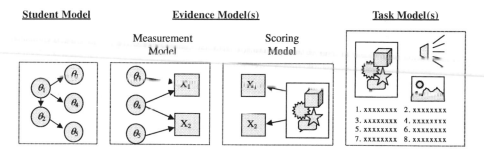

Figure 1: General Form of the Assessment Design Models

Understanding Concepts (U) – Understanding scientific concepts (such as properties and interactions of materials, energy, or thresholds) in order to apply the relevant scientific concepts to the solution of problems. This variable is the IEY version of the traditional "science content", although this content is not just "factoids".

Designing and Conducting Investigations (I) – Designing a scientific experiment, carrying through a complete scientific investigation, performing laboratory procedures to collect data, recording and organizing data, and analyzing and interpreting results of an experiment. This variable is the IEY version of the traditional "science process".

Evidence and Tradeoffs (E) – Identifying objective scientific evidence as well as evaluating the advantages and disadvantages of different possible solutions to a problem based on the available evidence.

Communicating Scientific Information (C) – Organizing and presenting results in a way that is free of technical errors and effectively communicates with the chosen audience.

Figure 2: The Variables in the Student Model for the BEAR "Issues, Evidence, and You" Example

designed to prompt student responses that relate to the "Evidence and Tradeoffs" variable defined in Figure 2. Note that this variable is a somewhat unusual one in a science curriculum; the IEY developers think of it as representing the sorts of cognitive skills one would need to evaluate the importance of, say, an environmental impact statement, something that a citizen might need to do that is directly related to science's role in the world. An example of a student response to this task is shown in Figure 5.

How do we extract from this particular response some evidence about the unobservable student-model variable we have labeled Evidence and Tradeoffs? What we need is in the second model from the right in Figure 1 – the *scoring model*. This is a procedure that allows one to focus on aspects of the student response and assign them to categories, in this case ordered categories, that suggest higher levels of proficiency along the underlying latent variable. A scoring model can take the form of what is called a "rubric" in the jargon of assessment, and in IEY does take that form (although it is called a "scoring guide"). The rubric for the Evidence and Tradeoffs variable is shown in Figure 6. It enables a teacher or a student to recognize and evaluate two distinct aspects of responses to the questions related to the Evidence and Tradeoffs variable. In addition to the rubric, scorers have exemplars of student work available to them, complete with adjudicated scores and explanations of the scores. They also have a method (called "assessment moderation") for training people to use the rubric. All these elements together constitute the scoring model. So, what we put in to the scoring model is a student's performance; what we get out is one or more scores for each task, and thus a set of scores for a set of tasks. In additoin to embedded tasks, the IEY assessments also include so-called "link-items", which are more like regular achievement test items (though scored with the same scoring guides).

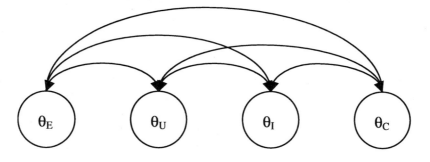

Figure 3:   Graphical Representation of the BEAR Student Model

2. You are a public health official who works in the Water Department. Your supervisor has asked you to respond to the public's concern about water chlorination at the next City Council meeting. Prepare a written response explaining the issues raised in the newspaper articles. Be sure to discuss the advantages and disadvantages of chlorinating drinking water in your response, and then explain your recommendation about whether the water should be chlorinated.

Figure 4:   An Example of a Task Directive from the BEAR Assessment

As an edjucated employee of the Grizzelyville water company, I am well aware of the controversy surrounding the topic of the chlorination of our drinking water. I have read the two articles regarding the pro's and cons of chlorinated water. I have made an informed decision based on the evidence presented the articles entitled "The Peru Story" and "700 Extra People May bet Cancer in the US". It is my recommendation that our towns water be chlorine treated. The risks of infecting our citizens with a bacterial disease such as cholera would be inevitable if we drink non-treated water. Our town should learn from the country of Peru. The article "The Peru Story" reads thousands of inocent people die of cholera epidemic. In just months 3,500 people were killed and more infected with the diease. On the other hand if we do in fact chlorine treat our drinking water a risk is posed. An increase in bladder and rectal cancer is directly related to drinking chlorinated water. Specifically 700 more people in the US may get cancer. However, the cholera risk far outweighs the cancer risk for 2 very important reasons. Many more people will be effected by cholera where as the chance of one of our citizens getting cancer due to the water would be very minimal. Also cholera is a spreading disease whereas cancer is not. If our town was infected with cholera we could pass it on to millions of others. And so, after careful consideration it is my opinion that the citizens of Grizzelyville drink chlorine treated water.

Figure 5:   An Example of a Student Response from the BEAR Assessment

What now remains? We need to connect the student model on the left hand side of Figure 1 with the scores that have come out of the scoring model. In what way, and with what value, should these nuggets of evidence affect our beliefs about the student's knowledge? For this we have another model, which we will call the *measurement model*. This single component is commonly known as a *psychometric model*. Now this is somewhat of a paradox, as we have just explained that the framework for psychometrics actually involves more than just this one model. The measurement model has indeed traditionally been the focus of psychometrics, but it is not sufficient to understand psychometric principles. The complete set of elements, the full evidentiary argument, must be addressed.

Figure 7 shows the relationships in the measurement model for the sample IEY task. Here the student model (first shown in Figure 3) has been augmented with a set of boxes. The boxes are intended to indicate that they are observable rather than latent, and these are in fact the scores from the scoring model for this task. They are connected to the Evidence and Tradeoffs student-model variable with straight lines, meant to indicate a causal (though probabilistic) relationship between the variable and the observed scores, and the causality is posited to run from the student model variables to the scores. Put another way, what the student knows and can do, as represented by the variables of the student model, determines how likely it is that students will make right answers rather than wrong ones, carry out sound inquiry rather than founder, and so on, in each particular task they encounter. In this example, both observable variables are posited to depend on the same aspect of knowledge, namely Evidence and Tradeoffs. A different task could have more or fewer observables, and each would depend on one or more student-model variables, all in accordance with the knowledge or skills the task is designed to evoke.

It is important for us to say that the student model in this example (indeed in most psychometric applications) is not proposed as a realistic explanation of the thinking that takes place when a student works through a problem. It is a piece

Score	Using Evidence:	Using Evidence to Make Tradeoffs:
	Response uses objective reason(s) based on relevant evidence to support choice.	Response recognizes multiple perspectives of issue and explains each perspective using objective reasons, supported by evidence, in order to make choice.
4	Response accomplishes Level 3 AND goes beyond in some significant way, such as questioning or justifying the source, validity, and/or quantity of evidence.	Response accomplishes Level 3 AND goes beyond in some significant way, such as suggesting additional evidence beyond the activity that would further influence choices in specific ways, OR questioning the source, validity, and/or quantity of evidence & explaining how it influences choice.
3	Response provides major objective reasons AND supports each with relevant & accurate evidence.	Response discusses *at least two* perspectives of issue AND provides objective reasons, supported by relevant & accurate evidence, for each perspective.
2	Response provides *some* objective reasons AND some supporting evidence, BUT at least one reason is missing and/or part of the evidence is incomplete.	Response states at least one perspective of issue AND provides some objective reasons using some relevant evidence BUT reasons are incomplete and/or part of the evidence is missing; OR only one complete & accurate perspective has been provided.
1	Response provides only subjective reasons (opinions) for choice and/or uses inaccurate or irrelevant evidence from the activity.	Response states at least one perspective of issue BUT only provides subjective reasons and/or uses inaccurate or irrelevant evidence.
0	No response; illegible response; response offers no reasons AND no evidence to support choice made.	No response; illegible response; response lacks reasons AND offers no evidence to support decision made.
X	Student had no opportunity to respond.	

Figure 6:   The Scoring Model for Evaluating Two Observable Variables from Task Responses in the BEAR Assessment

of machinery we use to accumulate information across tasks, in a language and at a level of detail we think suits the purpose of the assessment (for a more complete perspective on this see Pirolli & Wilson, 1998). Without question, it is selective and simplified. But it ought to be consistent with what we know about how students acquire and use knowledge, and it ought to be consistent with what we see students say and do. This is where psychometric principles come in.

What do psychometric principles mean in IEY? Validity concerns whether the tasks actually do give sound evidence about the knowledge and skills the student-model variables are supposed to measure, namely, the four IEY progress variables. Or are there plausible alternative explanations for good or poor performance? Reliability concerns how much we learn about the students, in

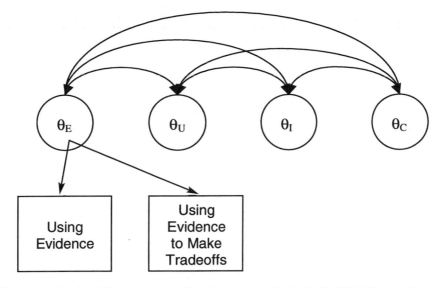

Figure 7:   Graphical Representation of the Measurement Model for the BEAR Sample Task for the item in Figure 2

terms of these variables, from the performances we observe. Comparability concerns whether what we say about students, based on estimates of their student-model variables, has a consistent meaning even if students have taken different tasks or been assessed at different times or under different conditions. Fairness asks whether we have been responsible in checking important facts about students and examining characteristics of task-model variables that would invalidate the inferences that test scores would ordinarily suggest.

PSYCHOMETRIC PRINCIPLES AND EVIDENTIARY ARGUMENTS[2]

We have seen, through a quick example how assessment can be viewed as evidentiary arguments, and that psychometric principles can be viewed as desirable properties of those arguments. Let's go back to the beginning and develop this line of reasoning more carefully.

Educational Assessment as Evidentiary Argument[1]

Inference is reasoning from what we know and observe to explanations, conclusions, or predictions. Rarely do we have the luxury of reasoning with certainty; the information we work with is typically incomplete, inconclusive, amenable to more than one explanation. The very first question in an evidentiary problem is: "evidence about what?" *Data* become *evidence* in some analytic problem only when we have established their relevance to some conjecture we are considering.

And the task of establishing the relevance of data and its weight as evidence depends on the chain of reasoning we construct from the evidence to those conjectures.

Both conjectures and an understanding of what constitutes evidence about them arise from the concepts and relationships of the field under consideration. We use the term "substantive" to refer to these content- or theory-based aspects of reasoning within a domain, in contrast to structural aspects such as logical structures and statistical models. In medicine, for example, physicians frame diagnostic hypotheses in terms of what they know about the nature of diseases, and the signs and symptoms that result from various disease states. The data are patients' symptoms and physical test results, from which physicians reason back to likely disease states. In history, hypotheses concern what happened and why. Letters, documents, and artifacts are the historian's data, which she/he must fit into a larger picture of what is known and what is supposed.

Philosopher Stephen Toulmin (1958) provided terminology for talking about how we use substantive theories and accumulated experience (say, about algebra and how students learn it) to reason from particular data (Joe's solutions) to a particular claim (what Joe understands about algebra). Figure 8 outlines the structure of a simple argument. The *claim* is a proposition we wish to support with *data*. The arrow represents inference, which is justified by a *warrant*, or a generalization that justifies the inference from the particular data to the particular claim. Theory and experience provide *backing* for the warrant. In any particular case we reason back through the warrant, so we may need to qualify our conclusions because there are alternative hypotheses, or *alternative explanations* for the data.

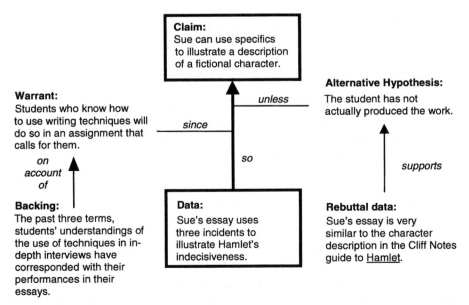

Figure 8:   A Toulmin Diagram for a Simple Assessment Situation

In practice, of course, an argument and its constituent claims, data, warrants, backing, and alternative explanations will be more complex than the representation in Figure 8. An argument usually consists of many propositions and data elements, involves chains of reasoning, and often contains dependencies among claims and various pieces of data. This is the case in assessment.

In educational assessments, the data are the particular things students say, do, or create in a handful of particular situations – written essays, correct and incorrect marks on answer sheets, presentations of projects, or explanations of their problem solutions. Usually our interest lies not so much in these particulars, but in the clues they hold about what students understand more generally. We can only connect the two through a chain of inferences. Some links depend on our beliefs about the nature of knowledge and learning. What is important for students to know, and how do they display that knowledge? Other links depend on things we know about students from other sources. Do they have enough experience with a computer to use it as a tool to solve an interactive physics problem or will it be so unfamiliar as to hinder their work? Some links use probabilistic models to communicate uncertainty, because we can administer only a few tasks or because we use evaluations from raters who do not always agree. Details differ, but a chain of reasoning must underlie an assessment of any kind, from classroom quizzes and standardized achievement tests, to coached practice systems and computerized tutoring programs, to the informal conversations students have with teachers as they work through experiments.

The Case for Standardization

Evidence rarely comes without a price. An obvious factor in the total cost of an evidentiary argument is the expense of gathering the data, but figuring out what data to gather and how to make sense of it can also be expensive. In legal cases, these latter tasks are usually carried out after the fact. Because each case is unique, at least parts of the argument must be uniquely fashioned. Marshalling evidence and constructing arguments in the O.J. Simpson case took more than a year and cost prosecution and defense millions of dollars.

If we foresee that the same kinds of data will be required for similar purposes on many occasions, we can achieve efficiencies by developing standard procedures both for gathering the data and reasoning from it (Schum, 1994, p. 137). A well-designed protocol for gathering data addresses important issues in its interpretation, such as making sure the right kinds and right amounts of data are obtained, and heading off likely or pernicious alternative explanations. Following standard procedures for gathering biological materials from crime scenes, for example, helps investigators avoid contaminating a sample and allows them to keep track of everything that happens to it from collection to testing. Furthermore, merely confirming that they have followed the protocols immediately communicates to others that these important issues have been recognized and dealt with responsibly.

A major way to make large-scale assessment practicable in education is to think these issues through up front: laying out the argument for what data to gather from each of the many students that will be assessed and the reason for gathering them. The details of the data will vary from one student to another, and so will the claims. But the same kind of data will be gathered for each student, the same kind of claim will be made, and, most importantly, the same argument structure will be used in each instance. This strategy offers great efficiencies, but it allows the possibility that cases that do not accord with the common argument will be included. Therefore, establishing the credentials of the argument in an assessment that is used with many students entails the two distinct responsibilities listed below. We shall see that investigating them and characterizing the degree to which they hold can be described in terms of psychometric principles.

Establishing the Credentials of the Evidence in the Common Argument

This is where efficiency is gained. To the extent that the same argument structure holds for all the students it will be used with, the specialization to any particular student inherits the backing that has been marshaled for the general form. We will discuss below how the common argument is framed. Both rational analyses and large-scale statistical analyses can be used to test its fidelity at this macro level. These tasks can be arduous, and they can never really be considered complete because we could always refine the argument or test additional alternative hypotheses (Messick, 1989). The point is, though, that this effort does not increase in proportion to the number of examinees who are assessed.

Detecting Individuals for Whom the Common Argument Does Not Hold

Inevitably, the theories, the generalizations, the empirical grounding for the common argument will not hold for some students. The usual data arrive, but the usual inference does not follow, even if the common argument does support validity and reliability in the main. These instances call for additional data or different arguments, often on a more expensive case-by-case basis. An assessment system that is both efficient and conscientious will minimize the frequency with which these situations occur, but routinely draw attention to them when they do.

It is worth emphasizing that the standardization we are discussing here concerns the structure of the argument, not necessarily the form of the data. Some may think that this form of standardization is only possible with so-called objective item forms such as multiple-choice items. Few large-scale assessments are more open-ended than the Advanced Placement (AP) Studio Art portfolio assessment (Myford & Mislevy, 1995); students have an almost unfettered choice of media, themes, and styles. But the AP program provides a great deal of information about the qualities students need to display in their work, what they need to assemble as work products, and how raters will evaluate them. This structure allows for a common argument, heads off alternative explanations about unclear evaluation standards in the hundreds of AP Studio Art classrooms across the country, and, most happily, helps the students come to understand the nature of good work in the field (Wolf, Bixby, Glenn, & Gardner, 1991).

Psychometric Principles as Properties of Arguments

The construction of assessment as an argument from limited evidence may be taken as a starting point for understanding psychometric principles. In this section, the key concepts of validity, reliability, comparability, and fairness are discussed in this framework.

Validity

Validity is paramount among psychometric principles, since it speaks directly to the extent to which a claim about a student, based on assessment data from that student, is justified (Cronbach, 1989; Messick, 1989). Establishing validity entails making the warrant explicit, examining the network of beliefs and theories on which it relies, and testing its strength and credibility through various sources of backing. It requires determining conditions that weaken the warrant, exploring alternative explanations for good or poor performance, and feeding them back into the system to reduce inferential errors.

   In the introductory example we saw that assessment is meant to get evidence about students' status with respect to a construct, some particular aspect(s) of knowledge, skill, or ability – in that case, the IEY variables. Cronbach and Meehl (1955) said "construct validation is involved whenever a test is to be interpreted as a measure of some attribute or quality that is not operationally defined" – that is, when there is a claim about a person based on observations, not merely a statement about those particular observations in and of themselves. Earlier work on validity distinguished a number of varieties, such as content validity, predictive validity, convergent and divergent validity, and we will say a bit more about these later. But the current view, as the *Standards for Educational and Psychological Testing* (American Educational Research Association, American Psychological Association, National Council of Measurement in Education, 1999) assert, is that validity is a unitary concept. Ostensibly different kinds of validity are better viewed as merely different lines of argument and different kinds of evidence for a single kind of validity. If you insist on a label for it, it would have to be *construct* validity.

   Embretson (1983) distinguishes between validity arguments that concern why data gathered in a certain way ought to provide evidence about the targeted skill knowledge, and those that investigate relationships of resulting scores with other variables to support the case. These are, respectively, arguments about "construct representation" and arguments from "nomothetic span." Embretson noted that validation studies relied mainly on nomothetic arguments, using scores from assessments in their final form or close to it. The construction of those tests, however, was guided mainly by specifications for item format and content, rather than by theoretical arguments or empirical studies regarding construct representation. The "cognitive revolution" in the latter third of the 20th century provided both scientific respectability and practical tools for designing construct meaning into tests from the beginning (Embretson, 1983). The value of both lines of argument is appreciated today, with validation procedures based on nomothetic span tending to be more mature and those based on construct representation still evolving.

Reliability

Reliability concerns the adequacy of the data to support a claim, presuming the appropriateness of the warrant and the satisfactory elimination of alternative hypotheses. Even if the reasoning is sound, there may not be enough information in the data to support the claim. Later we will see how reliability is expressed quantitatively when probability-based measurement models are employed. It may be noted here, however, that the procedures by which data are gathered can involve multiple steps or features, each of which can affect the evidentiary value of data. Depending on Jim's rating of Sue's essay rather than evaluating it ourselves adds a step of reasoning to the chain, introducing the need to establish an additional warrant, examine alternative explanations, and assess the value of the resulting data.

How can we gauge the adequacy of evidence? Brennan (2001) has noted that, since the work of Spearman (1904), the idea of repeating the measurement process has played a central role in characterizing an assessment's reliability much as it does in physical sciences. If you weigh a stone ten times and get a slightly different answer each time, the variation among the measurements is a good index of the uncertainty associated with that measurement procedure. It is less straightforward to know just what repeating the measurement procedure means, though, if the procedure has several steps that could each be done differently (different occasions, different task, different raters), or if some of the steps cannot be repeated at all (if a person learns something by working through a task, a second attempt is not measuring the same level of knowledge). We will see that the history of reliability is one of figuring out how to characterize the value of evidence in increasingly wider ranges of assessment situations.

Comparability

Comparability addresses the common occurrence that the specifics of data collection differ for different students or for the same students at different times.

Differing conditions raise alternative hypotheses when we need to compare students with one another or against common standards or when we want to track students' progress over time. Are there systematic differences in the conclusions we would draw when we observe responses to Test Form A as opposed to Test Form B, for example? Or from a computerized adaptive test instead of the paper-and-pencil version? Or if we use a rating based on two judges, as opposed to the average of two, or the consensus of three? We must extend the warrant to deal with these variations, and we must include them as alternative explanations of differences in students' scores.

Comparability overlaps with reliability, as both raise questions of how evidence obtained through one application of a data-gathering procedure might differ from evidence obtained through another application. The issue is reliability when we consider the two measures interchangeable; which measure is used is a matter of indifference to the examinee and assessor alike. Although we expect the results to differ somewhat, we do not know if one is more accurate than the other, whether one is biased toward higher values, or if they will illuminate different aspects of knowledge. The same evidentiary argument holds for both measures, and the obtained differences are what constitute classical measurement error. The issue is comparability when we expect systematic differences of any of these types, but wish to compare results obtained from the two distinct processes nevertheless. A more complex evidentiary argument is required. It must address the way that observations from the two processes bear different relationships to the construct we want to measure, and it must indicate how to take these differences into account in our inferences.

Fairness

Fairness is a term that encompasses more territory than we can address in this paper. Many of its senses relate to social, political, and educational perspectives on the uses to which assessment results are put (Willingham & Cole, 1997). These all give rise to legitimate questions, which would exist even if the chain of reasoning from observations to constructs contained no uncertainty whatsoever. Like Wiley (1991), we focus our attention here on construct meaning rather than use or consequences, and consider aspects of fairness that bear directly on this portion of the evidentiary argument.

Fairness in this sense concerns alternative explanations of assessment performances in light of other characteristics of students that we could and should take into account. Ideally, the same warrant backs inferences about many students, reasoning from their particular data to a claim about what each individual knows or can do. This is never quite truly the case in practice, since factors such as language background, instructional background, and familiarity with representations surely influence performance. When the same argument is to be applied with many students, considerations of fairness require us to examine the impact of such factors on performance, and to identify the ranges of their values beyond which the common warrant can no longer be justified. Drawing the usual inference from the usual data for a student who lies outside this range leads to inferential errors. If they are errors we should have foreseen and avoided, they are unfair. Ways of avoiding errors involve the use of additional knowledge about students to condition our interpretation of what we observe under the same procedures, and the gathering of data from different students in different ways, such as providing accommodations or allowing students to choose among ways of providing data (and accepting the responsibility as assessors to establish the comparability of data so obtained!).

A FRAMEWORK FOR ASSESSMENT DESIGN

In this section, a schema for the evidentiary argument that underlies educational assessments, incorporating both its substantive and statistical aspects, is presented. It is based on the "evidence-centered" framework for assessment design illustrated in Mislevy, Steinberg, and Almond (in press) and Mislevy, Steinberg, Breyer, Almond, and Johnson (1999, in press). We will use it presently to examine psychometric principles from a more technical perspective. The framework formalizes another proposition from Messick (1994):

> A construct-centered approach [to assessment design] would begin by asking what complex of knowledge, skills, or other attributes should be assessed, presumably because they are tied to explicit or implicit objectives of instruction or are otherwise valued by society. Next, what behaviors or performances should reveal those constructs, and what tasks or situations should elicit those behaviors? Thus, the nature of the construct guides the selection or construction of relevant tasks as well as the rational development of construct-based scoring criteria and rubrics (p. 16).

Figure 1, presented with the introductory example, depicts elements and relationships that must be present, at least implicitly, and coordinated, at least functionally, if an assessment is to effectively serve an inferential function. Making this structure explicit helps an evaluator understand how to first gather, then reason from, data that bear on what students know and can do.

In brief, the *student model* specifies the variables in terms of which we wish to characterize students. *Task models* are schemas for ways to get data that provide evidence about them. There are two components of the evidence model, which act as links in the chain of reasoning from students' work to their knowledge and skill. The *scoring component* contains procedures for extracting the salient features of student's performances in task situations (observable variables), and the *measurement component* contains machinery for updating beliefs about student-model variables in light of this information. These models are discussed in more detail below. Taken together, they make explicit the evidentiary grounding of an assessment and guide the choice and construction of particular tasks, rubrics, statistical models, and so on. An operational assessment will generally have one student model, which may contain many variables, but may use several task and evidence models to provide data of different forms or with different rationales.

The Student Model: What Complex of Knowledge, Skills, or Other Attributes Should be Assessed?

The values of student-model variables represent selected aspects of the infinite configurations of skill and knowledge real students have, based on a theory or a set of beliefs about skill and knowledge in the domain. These variables are the vehicle through which we determine student progress, make decisions, or plan instruction for students. The number and nature of the student model variables depend on the purpose of an assessment. A single variable characterizing overall proficiency in algebra might suffice in an assessment meant only to support a pass/fail decision; a coached practice system to help students develop the same proficiency might require a finer grained student model, to monitor how a student is doing on particular aspects of skill and knowledge for which we can offer feedback. When the purpose is program evaluation, the student-model variables should reflect hypothesized ways in which a program may be more or less successful or promote students' learning in some ways as opposed to others.

In the standard argument, then, *a claim about what a student knows, can do, or has accomplished is expressed in terms of values of student-model variables.* Substantive concerns about, for example, the desired outcomes of instruction, or the focus of a program evaluation, will suggest what the student-model variables might be and give substantive meaning to the values of student-model variables. The student model provides a language for expressing claims about students, restricted and simplified to be sure, but one that is amenable to probability-based reasoning for drawing inferences and characterizing beliefs. The following section will explain how we can express what we know about a given student's values for these variables in terms of a probability distribution, which can be updated as new evidence arrives.

Task Models: What Tasks or Situations Should Elicit Those Behaviors?

A task model provides a framework for constructing and describing the situations in which examinees act. We use the term "task" in the sense proposed by Haertel and Wiley (1993) to refer to a "goal-directed human activity to be pursued in a specified manner, context, or circumstance." A task can thus be an open-ended problem in a computerized simulation, a long-term project such as a term paper, a language-proficiency interview, or a familiar multiple-choice or short-answer question.

A task model specifies the environment in which the student will say, do, or produce something; for example, characteristics of stimulus material, instructions, help, tools, and so on. It also specifies the work product, or the form in which what the student says, does, or produces will be captured. But again it is substantive theory and experience that determine the kinds of situations that can evoke behaviors that provide clues about the targeted knowledge and skill, and the forms in which those clues can be expressed and captured.

To create a particular task, an assessment designer, explicitly or implicitly, assigns specific values to task model variables, provides materials that suit the specifications there given, and sets the conditions that are required to interact with the student. A task thus describes particular circumstances meant to provide the examinee an opportunity to act in ways that produce evidence about what they know or can do more generally. For a particular task, *the values of its task model variables constitute data for the evidentiary argument, characterizing the situation in which the student is saying, doing, or making something.*

It is useful to distinguish task models from the scoring models discussed in the next section, as the latter concern what to attend to in the resulting performance and how to evaluate what we see. Distinct and possibly quite different evaluation rules could be applied to the same work product from a given task. Distinct and possibly quite different student models, designed to serve different purposes, or derived from different conceptions of proficiency, could be informed by performances on the same tasks. The substantive arguments for the evidentiary value of behavior in the task situation will overlap in these cases, but the specifics of the claims, and thus the specifics of the statistical links in the chain of reasoning will differ.

Evidence Models: What Behaviors or Performances Should Reveal the Student Constructs, and What is the Connection?

An evidence model lays out the part of the evidentiary argument that concerns reasoning from the observations in a given task situation to revising beliefs about student model variables. Figure 1 shows there are two parts to the evidence model.

The *scoring component* contains "evidence rules" for extracting the salient features of whatever the student says, does, or creates in the task situation – i.e., the "work product" that is represented by the jumble of shapes in the rectangle at the far right of the evidence model. A work product is a unique human production, perhaps as simple as a response to a multiple-choice item or as complex as repeated cycles of treating and evaluating patients in a medical simulation. The squares coming out of the work product represent "observable variables," or evaluative summaries of what the assessment designer has determined are the key aspects of the performance (as captured in one or more work products) to serve the assessment's purpose. Different aspects could be captured for different purposes. For example, a short impromptu speech contains information about a student's subject matter knowledge, presentation capabilities, or English language proficiency; any of these, or any combination of them, could be the basis of one or more observable variables. As a facet of fairness, however, the student should be informed of which aspects of her/his performance are being evaluated, and by what criteria. Students' failure to understand how their work will be scored is an alternative hypothesis for poor performance which can and should be avoided.

Scoring rules map unique performances into a common interpretative framework, thus laying out what is important in a performance. These rules can be as simple as determining whether the response to a multiple-choice item is correct, or as complex as an expert's holistic evaluation of multiple aspects of an unconstrained patient-management solution. They can be automated, demand human judgment, or require both. *Values of the observable variables describe properties of the particular things a student says, does, or makes. As such, they constitute data about what the student knows, can do, or has accomplished as more generally construed* in the standard argument.

It is important to note that substantive concerns drive the definition of observable variables. Statistical analyses can be used to refine definitions, compare alternatives, or improve data-gathering procedures, again looking for patterns that call a scoring rule into question. But it is the conception of what to observe that concerns validity directly, and raises questions of alternative explanations that bear on comparability and fairness.

The *measurement component* of the Evidence Model tells how the observable variables depend, in probabilistic terms, on student model variables, another essential link in the evidentiary argument. This is the foundation for the reasoning that is needed to synthesize evidence across multiple tasks or from different performances. Figure 1 shows how the observables are modeled as depending on some subset of the student model variables. The familiar models from test theory that we discuss in a following section, including classical test theory and item response theory, are examples. We can adapt these ideas to suit the nature of the student model and observable variables in any given application (Almond & Mislevy, 1999). Again, substantive considerations must underlie why these posited relationships should hold; the measurement model formalizes the patterns they imply.

It is a defining characteristic of psychometrics to model observable variables as probabilistic functions of unobservable student variables. The measurement model is almost always a probability model. The probability-based framework model may extend to the scoring model as well, as when judgments are required to ascertain the values of observable variables from complex performances. Questions of accuracy, agreement, leniency, and optimal design arise, and can be addressed with a measurement model that includes the rating link as well as the synthesis link in the chain of reasoning. The generalizability and rater models discussed below are examples of this.

PSYCHOMETRIC PRINCIPLES AND PROBABILITY-BASED REASONING

The Role of Probability-Based Reasoning in the Assessment

This section looks more closely at what is perhaps the most distinctive characteristic of psychometrics, namely, the use of statistical models. Measurement models are a particular form of reasoning from evidence; they provide explicit, formal rules for how to integrate the many pieces of information that may be relevant to a particular inference about what students know and can do. Statistical modeling, probability-based reasoning more generally, is an approach to solving the problem of "reverse reasoning" through a warrant, from particular data to a particular claim. Just how can we reason from data to claim for a particular student, using a measurement model established for general circumstances – usually far less than certain, typically with qualifications, perhaps requiring side conditions that may or may not be satisfied? How can we synthesize the evidentiary value of multiple observations, perhaps from different sources, often in conflict?

The essential idea is to approximate the important substantive relationships in some real world problem in terms of relationships among variables in a probability model. A simplified picture of the real world situation results. A useful model does not explain all the details of actual data, but it does capture the significant patterns among them. What is important is that in the space of the model, the machinery of probability-based reasoning indicates exactly how reverse reasoning is to be carried out (specifically, through Bayes theorem), and how different kinds and amounts of data should affect our beliefs. The trick is to build a probability model that both captures the important real world patterns and suits the purposes of the problem at hand.

Measurement models concern the relationships between students' knowledge and their behavior. A student is modeled in terms of variables (θ) that represent the facets of skill or knowledge that suit the purpose of the assessment, and the data (X) are values of variables that characterize aspects of the observable behavior. We posit that the student-model variables account for observable variables in the following sense: We do not know exactly what any student will do on a particular task, but for people with any given value of θ there is a probability distribution of possible values of X, say $p(X|\theta)$. This is a mathematical expression of what we might expect to see in data, given any possible values of student-model variables. The way is open for reverse reasoning, from observed Xs to likely θs, as long as different values of θ produce different probability distributions for X. We do not know the values of the student-model variables in practice; we observe "noisy" data presumed to have been determined by them and, through the probability model, reason back to what their values are likely to be.

Choosing to manage information and uncertainty with probability-based reasoning, with its numerical expressions of belief in terms of probability distributions, does not constrain one to any particular forms of evidence or psychological frameworks. That is, it says nothing about the number or nature of elements of

X, or about the character of the performances, or about the conditions under which performances are produced. And it says nothing about the number or nature of elements of θ such as whether they are number values in a differential psychology model, production-rule mastery in a cognitive model, or tendencies to use resources effectively in a situative model. In particular, using probability-based reasoning does not commit us to long tests, discrete tasks, or large samples of students. For example, probability-based models have been found useful in modeling patterns of judges' ratings in the previously mentioned AP Studio Art portfolio assessment (Myford & Mislevy, 1995), which is about as open-ended as large-scale, high-stakes educational assessments get, and in modeling individual students' use of production rules in a tutoring system for solving physics problems (Martin & vanLehn, 1995).

It should be borne in mind that a measurement model is not intended to account for every detail of data; it is only meant to approximate the important patterns. The statistical concept of *conditional independence* formalizes the working assumption that if the values of the student model variables were known, there would be no further information in the details. The fact that every detail of a student's responses could in principle contain information about what a student knows or how he/she is thinking underscores the constructive and purposive nature of modeling. We use a model at a given grainsize or with certain kinds of variables, not because we think that is somehow "true," but rather because it adequately expresses the patterns in the data in light of the purpose of the assessment. Adequacy in a given application depends on validity, reliability, comparability, and fairness in ways we shall discuss further, but characterized in ways, and demanded in degrees, that depend on that application: the purpose of the assessment, the resources that are available, the constraints that must be accommodated. We might model the same troubleshooting performances in terms of individual problem steps for an intelligent tutoring system, in terms of general areas of strength and weakness for a diagnostic assessment, and simply in terms of overall success rate for a pass/fail certification test.

Since we never fully believe the statistical model we are reasoning through, we bear the responsibility of assessing model fit, in terms of both persons and items. We must examine the ways and the extent to which the real data depart from the patterns in the data, calling attention to failures of conditional independence – places where our simplifying assumptions miss relationships that are surely systematic, and possibly important, in the data. Finding substantial misfit causes us to re-examine the arguments that tell us what to observe and how to evaluate it.

Probability-Based Reasoning in Classical Test Theory

This section illustrates the ideas from the preceding discussion in the context of classical test theory (CTT). In CTT, the student model is represented as a single continuous unobservable variable, the true score θ. The measurement model simply tells us to think of an observed score X as the true score plus an error term. If a CTT measurement model were used in the BEAR example, it would address the sum of the student scores on a set of assessment tasks as the observed score.

Figure 9 pictures the situation in a case that concerns Sue's (unobservable) true score and her three observed scores on parallel forms of the same test; that is, they are equivalent measures of the same construct, and have the same means and variances. The probability distribution p(θ) expresses our belief about Sue's θ before we observe her test scores, the Xs. The conditional distributions p($X_j | \theta$)$_3$ indicate the probabilities of observing different values of X_j if θ took any given particular value. Modeling the distribution of each X_j to depend on θ but not the other Xs is an instance of conditional independence; more formally, we write p($X_1, X_2, X_3 | \theta$) = p($X_1 | \theta$) p($X_2 | \theta$) p($X_3 | \theta$). Under CTT we may obtain a form for the p($X_j | \theta$)s by proposing that:

$$X_j = \theta + E_j, \qquad (1)$$

where E_j is an "error" term, normally distributed with a mean of zero and a variance of σ_E^2.[4] Thus $X_j | \theta \sim N(\theta, \sigma_E)$. This statistical structure quantifies the patterns that the substantive arguments express qualitatively, in a way that tells us exactly how to carry out reverse reasoning for particular cases. If p(θ) expresses belief about Sue's θ *prior* to observing her responses, belief *posterior* to learning them is denoted as p($\theta | x_1, x_2, x_3$) and is calculated by Bayes theorem as:

$$p(\theta | x_1, x_2, x_3) \propto p(\theta)\, p(x_1 | \theta)\, p(x_2 | \theta)\, p(x_3 | \theta).$$

(The lower case xs denote particular values of Xs.)

Figure 10 gives the numerical details for a hypothetical example, calculated with a variation of an important early result called Kelley's formula for estimating

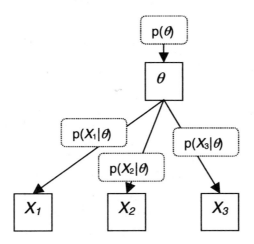

Figure 9:   Statistical Representation for Classical Test Theory

true scores (Kelley, 1927). Suppose that from a large number of students like Sue, we have estimated that the measurement error variance is $\sigma_E^2 = 25$, and for the population of students, θ follows a normal distribution with a mean of 50 and a standard deviation of 10. We now observe Sue's three scores, which take the values 70, 75, and 85. We see that the posterior distribution for Sue's θ is a normal distribution with mean 74.6 and standard deviation 2.8.

The additional backing that was used to bring the probability model into the evidentiary argument was an analysis of data from students like Sue. Spearman's (1904) seminal insight was that if their structure is set up in the right way[5], it is

---

Theorem

Let $N(\mu,\sigma)$ denote the normal (Gaussian) distribution with mean μ and standard deviation σ. If the prior distribution of θ is $N(\mu_0,\sigma_0)$ and the X is $N(\theta,\sigma_E)$, then the distribution for θ posterior to observing X is $N(\mu_{post},\sigma_{post})$, where $\sigma_{post} = (\sigma_0^{-2}+\sigma_E^{-2})^{-1}$ and $\mu_{post} = (\sigma_0^{-2}\mu_0+\sigma_E^{-2}X)/(\sigma_0^{-2}+\sigma_E^{-2})$.

Calculating the posterior distribution for Sue

Beginning with an initial distribution of $N(50,10)$, we can compute the posterior distribution for Sue's θ after seeing three independent responses by applying the theorem three times, in each case with the posterior distribution from one step becoming the prior distribution for the next step.

a) *Prior distribution:* $\theta \sim N(50,10)$.

b) *After the first response:* Given $\theta \sim N(50,10)$ and $X_1\sim N(\theta,5)$, observing $X_1=70$ yields the posterior $N(66.0,4.5)$.

c) *After the first response:* Given $\theta \sim N(66.0,4.5)$ and $X_2\sim N(\theta,5)$, observing $X_2=75$ yields the posterior $N(70.0,3.3)$.

d) *After the third response:* Given $\theta \sim N(70.0,3.3)$ and $X_3\sim N(\theta,5)$, observing $X_3=85$ yields the posterior $N(74.6,2.8)$.

Calculating a fit index for Sue

Suppose each of Sue's scores came from a $N(\theta,5)$ distribution. Using the posterior mean we estimated from Sue's scores, we can calculate how likely her response vector is under this measurement model using a chi-square test of fit:

$$[(70-74.6)/5]^2 + [(75-74.6)/5]^2 + [(85-74.6)/5]^2 = .85+.01+4.31 = 5.17.$$

Checking against the chi-square distribution with two degrees of freedom, we see that about 8-percent of the values are higher than this, so this vector is not that unusual.

Figure 10:   A Numerical Example Using Classical Test Theory

possible to estimate the quantitative features of relationships like this, among both variables that could be observed and others which by their nature never can be. The index of measurement accuracy in CTT is the *reliability coefficient* ρ, which is the proportion of variance in observed scores in a population of interest that is attributable to true scores as opposed to the total variance (which is composed of true score variance and noise). It is defined as follows:

$$\rho = \frac{\sigma^2_\theta}{\sigma^2_\theta + \sigma^2_E} ,$$ (2)

where σ^2_θ is the variance of true score in the population of examinees and σ^2_E is the variance of the error components, neither of which is directly observable! With a bit of algebra, though, Spearman demonstrated that if Equation 1 holds, correlations among pairs of Xs will approximate ρ. We may then estimate the contributions of true score and error, or σ^2_θ and σ^2_E, as proportions ρ and $(1-\rho)$ respectively of the observed score variance. The intuitively plausible notion is that correlations among exchangeable measures of the same construct tell us how much to trust comparisons among examinees from a single measurement. As an index of measurement accuracy, however, ρ suffers from its dependence on the variation among examinees' true scores as well as on the measurement error variance of the test. For a group of examinees with no true-score variance, the reliability coefficient is zero no matter how much evidence a test provides about each of them. We will see how item response theory extends the idea of measurement accuracy.

What is more, patterns among the observables can be so contrary to those the model would predict that we suspect the model is not right. Sue's values of 70, 75, and 85 are not identical, but neither are they surprising as a set of scores (Figure 10 shows how to calculate a chi-squared index of fit for Sue). Some students have higher scores than Sue, some have lower scores, but the amount of variation within a typical student's set of scores is in this neighborhood. But Richard's three scores of 70, 75, and 10 *are* surprising. His high-fit statistic (a chi-square of 105 with 2 degrees of freedom) says his pattern is very unlikely from parallel tests with an error variance of 25 (less than one in a billion). Richard's responses are so discordant with the statistical model that expresses patterns under the standard argument that we suspect that the standard argument does not apply. We must go beyond the argument to understand what has happened, to facts the standard data do not convey. Our first clue is that his third score is particularly different from both the other two and from the prior distribution.

Classical test theory's simple model for examinee characteristics suffices when one is interested in only a single aspect of student achievement, when tests are only considered as a whole, and when all students take tests that are identical or practically so. But the assumptions of CTT have generated a vast armamentarium of concepts and tools that help the practitioner examine the extent to which psychometric principles are being attained in situations when the assumptions are adequate. These tools include reliability indices that can be calculated from multiple items in a single test, formulas for errors of measuring individual students, strategies for selecting optimal composites of tests, formulas for approximating how long a test should be to reach a required accuracy, and methods for equating tests. The practitioner working in situations that CTT encompasses will find a wealth of useful formulas and techniques in Gulliksen's (1950/1987) classic text.

The Advantages of Using Probability-Based Reasoning in Assessment

Because of its history, the very term "psychometrics" connotes a fusion of the inferential logic underlying Spearman's reasoning with his psychology (trait psychology, in particular intelligence which is considered an inherited and stable characteristic) and his data-gathering methods (many short, "objectively-scored," largely decontextualized tasks). The connection, while historically grounded, is logically spurious, however. For the kinds of problems that CTT grew to solve are not just Spearman's problems, but ones that ought to concern anybody who is responsible for making decisions about students, evaluating the effects of instruction, or spending scarce educational resources, whether or not Spearman's psychology or methodology is relevant to the problem at hand.

And indeed, the course of development of test theory over the past century has been to continually extend the range of problems to which this inferential approach can be applied: to claims cast in terms of behavioral, cognitive, or situative psychology[6] to data that may be embedded in context, require sophisticated evaluations, or address multiple interrelated aspects of complex activities. We will look at some of these developments in the next section. But it is at a higher level of abstraction that psychometric principles are best understood, even though, in practice, they are investigated with particular models and indices.

When it comes to examining psychometric properties, embedding the assessment argument in a probability model offers several advantages. First, using the calculus of probability-based reasoning, once we ascertain the values of the variables in the data, we can express our beliefs about the likely values of the student estimates in terms of probability distributions – given that the model is both generally credible and applicable to the case at hand. Second, the machinery of probability-based reasoning is rich enough to handle many recurring challenges in assessment, such as synthesizing information across multiple tasks, characterizing the evidentiary importance of elements or assemblages of data, assessing comparability across different bodies of evidence, and exploring the implications of judgment, including different numbers and configurations of raters. Third, global model-criticism techniques allow us not only to fit models to data, but to determine where and how the data do not accord well with the models. Substantive considerations suggest the structure of the evidentiary argument, while statistical analyses of ensuing data through the lens of a mathematical model help us assess whether the argument matches up with what we actually see in the world. For instance, detecting an unexpected interaction between performance on an item and students' cultural backgrounds alerts us to an alternate explanation of poor performance. We are then moved to improve the data gathering methods, constrain the range of use, or rethink the substantive argument. Fourth, local model-criticism techniques allow us to monitor the operation of the reverse-reasoning step for individual students even after the argument, data collection methods, and statistical model are up and running. Patterns of observations that are unlikely under the common argument can be flagged (e.g., Richard's high chi-square value), thus avoiding certain unsupportable inferences, and drawing attention to cases that call for additional exploration.

Implications for Psychometric Principles

Validity

Some of the historical "flavors" of validity are statistical in nature. Predictive validity is the degree to which scores in selection tests correlate with future performance. Convergent validity looks for high correlations of a test's scores with other sources of evidence about the targeted knowledge and skills, while divergent validity looks for low correlations with evidence about irrelevant factors (Campbell & Fiske, 1959). Concurrent validity examines correlations with other tests presumed to provide evidence about the same or similar knowledge and skills.

The idea is that substantive considerations that justify the conception and construction of an assessment can be put to empirical tests. In each of the cases mentioned above, relationships are posited among observable phenomena that would hold if the substantive argument were correct, and whether or not they hold is determined by exploring the nomothetic net. Potential sources of backing for arguments for interpreting and using test results are sought in conjunction with explorations of plausible alternative explanations.

Consider, for example, assessments designed to support decisions about whether a student has attained some criterion of performance (Ercikan & Julian, 2002; Hambleton & Slater, 1997). The decisions, typically reported as proficiency or performance level scores, which are increasingly being considered to be useful in communicating assessment results to students, parents, and the public, as well as for evaluation of programs, involve classification of examinee performance to a set of proficiency levels. It is rare for the tasks on such a test to exhaust the full range of performances and situations users are interested in. Examining the validity of a proficiency test from this nomothetic-net perspective would involve seeing whether students who do well on that test also perform well in more extensive assessment, obtain high ratings from teachers or employers, or succeed in subsequent training or job performance.

Statistical analyses of these kinds have always been important after the fact, as significance-focused validity studies informed, constrained, and evaluated the use of a test, but they rarely prompted more than minor modifications of its contents.

Rather, as Embretson (1998) noted, substantive considerations have traditionally driven assessment construction. Neither of the two meaning-focused lines of justification that were considered forms of validity used probability-based reasoning. These are content validity, which concerns the nature and mix of items in a test, and face validity, which is what a test appears to be measuring on the surface, especially to non-technical audiences. We will see in our discussion of item response theory how statistical machinery is increasingly being used in the exploration of construct representation as well in after-the-fact validity studies.

Reliability

Reliability, historically, was used to quantify the amount of variation in test scores that reflected "true" differences among students, as opposed to noise (Equation 2). Correlations between parallel test forms used in classical test theory are one way to estimate reliability in this sense. Internal consistency among test items, as gauged by the KR-20 formula (Kuder & Richardson, 1937) or Cronbach's (1951) alpha coefficient, is another. A contemporary view sees reliability as the evidentiary value that a given realized or prospective body of data would provide for a claim. That is, reliability is not a universally applicable number or equation that characterizes a test, but an index that quantifies how much information test data contain about specified conjectures framed in terms of student-model variables (e.g., an estimate for a given student, a comparison among students, or a determination of whether a student has attained some criterion of performance).

A wide variety of specific indices or parameters can be used to characterize evidentiary value. Carrying out a measurement procedure two or more times with supposedly equivalent alternative tasks and raters will not only ground an estimate of its accuracy, as in Spearman's original procedures, but will demonstrate convincingly that there is some uncertainty to deal with in the first place (Brennan, 2001). The KR-20 and Cronbach's alpha apply the idea of replication to tests that consist of multiple items, by treating subsets of the items as repeated measures. These CTT indices of reliability appropriately characterize the amount of evidence for comparing students in a particular population with one another. This is indeed often an important kind of inference. But these indices do not indicate how much information the same scores contain about other inferences, such as comparing students against a fixed standard, comparing students in other populations, or estimating group performance for purposes of evaluating schools or instructional programs.

Since reasoning about reliability takes place in the realm of the measurement model (assuming that it is both correct and appropriate), it is possible to approximate the evidentiary value of not only the data in hand, but the value of similar data gathered in somewhat different ways. Under CTT, the Spearman-Brown formula (Brown, 1910; Spearman, 1910) can be used to approximate the reliability coefficient that would result from doubling the length of a test:

$$\rho_{\text{double}} = \frac{2\rho}{1 + \rho}. \tag{3}$$

If ρ is the reliability of the original test, then ρ_{double} is the reliability of an otherwise comparable test with twice as many items. Empirical checks have shown that these predictions can hold up quite well, but not if the additional items differ in content or difficulty, or if the new test is long enough to fatigue students. In these cases, the real-world counterparts of the modeled relationships are stretched so far that the results of reasoning through the model fail.

Extending this thinking to a wider range of inferences, generalizability theory (g-theory) (Cronbach, Gleser, Nanda, & Rajaratnam, 1972) permits predictions of the accuracy of similar tests with different numbers and configurations of raters, items, and so on. And once the parameters of tasks have been estimated under an item response theory (IRT) model, one can even assemble tests item by item for individual examinees on the fly, to maximize the accuracy with which each is assessed. (Later we will point to some "how-to" references for g-theory and IRT.)

Typical measures of accuracy used in CTT do not adequately examine the accuracy of decisions concerning criteria of performance discussed above. In the CTT framework, the classification accuracy is defined as the extent to which classification of students based on their observed test scores agree with those based on their true scores (Traub & Rowley, 1980). One of the two commonly used measures of classification accuracy is a simple measure of agreement, ρ_0, defined as

$$p_0 = \sum_{l=1}^{L} p_{ll},$$

where p_{ll} represents the proportion of examinees who were classified into the same proficiency level ($l = 1, \ldots, 5$) according to their true score and observed score. The second is Cohen's (1960) κ coefficient, which is similar to the proportion agreement p_0, except that it is corrected for the agreement that is due to chance. The coefficient is defined as:

$$\kappa = \frac{p_0 - p_c}{1 - p_c},$$

where

$$p_c = \sum_{l=1}^{L} p_{l.} \, p_{.l}.$$

The accuracy of classifications based on test scores is critically dependent on measurement accuracy at the cut-score points (Ercikan & Julian, 2001; Hambleton & Slater, 1997). Even though higher measurement accuracy tends to imply higher classification accuracy, higher reliability such as indicated by KR-20 or coefficient alpha does not imply higher classification accuracy. While these measures give an overall indication of measurement accuracy provided by the test for all examinees they do not provide information about the measurement accuracy provided at the cut-scores. Therefore, they are not accurate indicators of classification decisions based on test performance.

On the other hand, measurement accuracy is expected to vary for different score ranges, resulting in variation in classification accuracy. This points to a serious limitation of interpretability of single indices that are intended to represent classification accuracy of a test given a set of cut-scores. Ercikan & Julian (2002) study found that classification accuracy can be dramatically different for examinees at different ability levels. Their results demonstrated that comparing classification accuracy across tests could be deceptive, since it may be high for one test for certain score ranges and low for others. Based on these limitations, it is recommended that classification accuracy be reported separately for different score ranges.

Comparability

Comparability concerns the equivalence of inference when different bodies of data are gathered to compare students, or to assess change when the same students are assessed at different points in time. Within a statistical framework, we can build models that address quantitative aspects of questions such as these: Do the different bodies of data have such different properties as evidence as to jeopardize the inferences? Are conclusions about students' knowledge biased in one direction or another when different data are gathered? Is there more or less weight for various claims under the different alternatives?

A time-honored way of establishing comparability has been creating parallel test forms. A common rationale is developed to create collections of tasks which, taken together, can be argued to provide data about the same targeted skills and knowledge, which, it is hoped, will differ only in incidentals that do not accumulate. This may be done by defining a knowledge-by-skills matrix, writing items in each cell and constructing tests by selecting the same numbers of tasks from each cell for every test form. The same substantive backing thus grounds all the forms.

But it would be premature to presume that equal scores from these tests constitute equivalent evidence about students' knowledge. Despite care in their construction, possible differences between the tests in difficulty or in the amount of information covered must be considered as an alternative explanation for differing performances among students. Empirical studies and statistical analyses enter the picture at this point in the form of equating studies (Petersen, Kolen, & Hoover, 1989). Finding that similar groups of students systematically perform better on Form A than on Form B confirms the alternative explanation. Adjusting scores for Form B upward to match the resulting distributions addresses this concern, refines the chain of reasoning to take form differences into account when drawing claims about students, and enters the compendium of backing for the assessment system as a whole. We shall see below that IRT extends comparability arguments to test forms that differ in difficulty and accuracy, if they can satisfy the requirements of a more ambitious statistical model.

Fairness

The meaning-focused sense of fairness we have chosen to highlight concerns a claim that would follow from the common argument, but would be called into question by an alternative explanation sparked by other information we could and should have taken into account. When we extend the discussion of fairness to statistical models, we find macro-level and micro-level strategies to address this concern.

Macro-level strategies of fairness fall within the broad category of what the assessment literature calls validity studies, and are investigations in the nomothetic net. They address broad patterns in test data, at the level of arguments or alternative explanations in the common arguments that are used with many students. Suppose the plan for the assessment is to use data (say, essay responses) to back a claim about a student's knowledge (e.g., the student can back up opinions with examples) through an argument (e.g., students in a pretest who are known to be able to do this in their first language are observed to do so in essays that ask for them to), without regard to a background factor (such as a students' first language). The idea is to gather from a group of students data that include their test performances, but also information about their first language and higher quality validation data about the claim (e.g., interviews in the students' native languages). The empirical question is whether inferences from the usual data to the claim (independently evidenced by the validity data) differ systematically with first language. In particular, are there students who can back arguments with specifics in their native language, but fail to do so on the essay test because of language difficulties? If so, the door is open to distorted inferences about argumentation skills for limited-English speakers, if one proceeds from the usual data through the usual argument, disregarding language proficiency.

What can we do when the answer is "yes"? Possibilities include improving the data collected for all students, taking their first language into account when reasoning from data to claim (recognizing that language difficulties can account for poor performance even when the skill of interest is present), and preidentifying students whose limited language proficiencies are likely to lead to flawed inferences about the targeted knowledge. In this last instance, additional or different data could be used for these students, such as an interview or an essay in their primary language.

These issues are particularly important in assessments used for making consequential proficiency-based decisions, in ways related to the points we raised concerning the validity of such tests. Unfair decisions are rendered if (i) alternative valid means of gathering data for evaluating proficiency yield results that differ systematically from the standard assessment, and (ii) the reason can be traced to requirements for knowledge or skills (e.g., proficiency with the English language) that are not central to the knowledge or skill that is at issue (e.g., constructing and backing an argument).

The same kinds of investigations can be carried out with individual tasks as well as with assessments as a whole. One variation on this theme can be used with assessments that are composed of several tasks, to determine whether individual tasks interact with first language in atypical ways. These are called studies of differential item functioning (DIF) (Holland & Wainer, 1993).

Statistical tools can also be used to implement micro-level strategies to call attention to cases in which a routine application of the standard argument could produce a distorted and possibly unfair inference. The common argument provides a warrant to reason from data to claim, with attendant caveats for unfairness associated with factors (such as first language) that have been dealt with at the macro level. But the argument may not hold for some individual students for other reasons, which have not yet been dealt with at the macro level, and perhaps could not have been anticipated at all. Measurement models characterize patterns in students' data that are typical if the general argument holds. Patterns that are unlikely can signal that the argument may not apply with a given student on a given assessment occasion. Under IRT, for example, "student misfit" indices take high values for students who miss items that are generally easy while correctly answering ones that are generally hard (Levine & Drasgow, 1982).

SOME OTHER WIDELY-USED MEASUREMENT MODELS

The tools of classical test theory have been continually extended and refined since Spearman's time, to the extensive toolkit by Gulliksen (1950/1987), and to the sophisticated theoretical framework of Lord and Novick (1968). Lord and Novick aptly titled their volume *Statistical Theories of Mental Test Scores*, underscoring their focus on the probabilistic reasoning aspects in the measurement-model links of the assessment argument rather than the purposes, substantive aspects, and evaluation rules that produce the data. Models that extend the same fundamental reasoning for this portion of assessment arguments to wider varieties of data and student models include generalizability theory, item response theory, latent class models, and multivariate models.

Each of these extensions offers more options for characterizing students and collecting data in a way that can be embedded in a probability model. The models do not concern themselves directly with substantive aspects of an assessment argument, but substantive considerations often have much to say about how one should think about students' knowledge, and what observations should contain evidence about it. The more measurement models that are available and the more kinds of data than can be handled, the better assessors can match rigorous models with their theories and needs. Models will bolster evidentiary arguments (validity), extend quantitative indices of accuracy to more situations (reliability), enable more flexibility in observational settings (comparability), and enhance the prospects of detecting students whose data are at odds with the standard argument (fairness).

Generalizability Theory

Generalizability theory (g-theory) extends classical test theory by allowing us to examine how different aspects of the observational setting affect the evidentiary value of test scores. As in Classical Test Theory (CTT) the student is characterized by overall proficiency in some domain of tasks. However, the measurement model can now include parameters that correspond to "facets" of the observational situation such as features of tasks (task-model variables), numbers and designs of raters, and qualities of performance that will be evaluated. An observed score of a student in a generalizability study of an assessment consisting of different item types and judgmental scores is an elaboration of the basic CTT equation:

$$X_{ijk} = \theta_i + \tau_j + \varsigma_k + E_{ijk} ,$$

where now the observed score is from Examinee i, to Item-Type j, as evaluated by Rater k; θ_i is the true score of Examinee i; and τ_j and ς_κ are, respectively, effects attributable to Item-Type j and Rater k.

Researchers carry out a generalizability study to estimate the amount of variation associated with different facets. The accuracy of estimation of scores for a given configuration of tasks can be calculated from these variance components, the numbers of items and raters, and the design in which data are collected. A "generalizability coefficient" is an extension of the CTT reliability coefficient: it is the proportion of true variance among students for the condition one wishes to measure, divided by the variance among observed scores among the measurements that would be obtained among repeated applications of the measurement procedure that is specified (how many observations, fixed or randomly selected; how many raters rating each observation; different or same raters for different items, etc.). If, in the example above, we wanted to estimate θ using one randomly selected item, scored as the average of the ratings from two randomly selected raters, the coefficient of generalizability, denoted here as α, would be calculated as follows:

$$\alpha = \frac{\sigma_\theta^2}{\sigma_\theta^2 + \sigma_\tau^2 + (\sigma_\varsigma^2 + \sigma_E^2)/2} ,$$

where σ_θ^2, σ_τ^2, σ_ς^2, and σ_E^2 are variance coefficients for examinees, item-types, raters, and error respectively.

The information resulting from a generalizability study can thus guide decisions about how to design procedures for making observations; relating for example, to the way to assign raters to performances, the number of tasks and raters, and whether to average across raters, tasks, etc. In the BEAR Assessment

System, a generalizability study could be carried out to see which type of assessment, embedded tasks or link items, resulted in more reliable scores. It could also be used to examine whether teachers were as consistent as external raters.

G-theory offers two important practical advantages over CTT. First, generalizability models allow us to characterize how the particulars of the evaluation rules and task model variables affect the value of the evidence we gain about the student for various inferences. Second, this information is expressed in terms that allow us to project these evidentiary-value considerations to designs we have not actually used, but which could be constructed from elements similar to the ones we have observed. G-theory thus provides far-reaching extensions of the Spearman-Brown formula (Equation 3), for exploring issues of reliability and comparability in a broader array of data-collection designs than CTT can.

Generalizability theory was developed by Lee Cronbach and his colleagues, and their monograph *The Dependability of Behavioral Measurements* (Cronbach et al., 1972) remains a valuable source of information and insight. More recent sources such as Shavelson and Webb (1991) and Brennan (1983) provide the practitioner with friendlier notation and examples to build on.

Item Response Theory (IRT)

Classical Test Theory and generalizability theory share a serious shortcoming: measures of examinees are confounded with the characteristics of test items. Difficulties arise in comparing examinees who have taken tests that differ by even as much as a single item, or comparing items that have been administered to different groups of examinees. Item Response Theory (IRT) was developed to address this shortcoming. In addition, IRT can be used to make predictions about test properties using item properties and to manipulate parts of tests to achieve targeted measurement properties. Hambleton (1989) gives a readable introduction to IRT, while van der Linden and Hambleton (1997) provide a comprehensive though technical compendium of current IRT models. IRT further extended probability-based reasoning for addressing psychometric principles, and it sets the stage for further developments. We will present a brief overview of key ideas.

At first, the student model under IRT seems to be the same as it is under CTT and g-theory, involving a single variable measuring students' overall proficiency in some domain of tasks. Again the statistical model does not address the nature of that proficiency. The structure of the probability-based portion of the argument is the same as shown in Figure 9, involving conditional independence among observations given an underlying, inherently unobservable, proficiency variable θ. But now the observations are responses to individual tasks. For Item j, the IRT model expresses the probability of a given response x_j as a function of θ and parameters β_j that characterize Item j (such as its difficulty):

$$\text{Prob}(X_j = x_j | \theta, \beta_j) = f(x_j; \theta, \beta_j). \tag{4}$$

Under the Rasch (1960/1980) model for dichotomous (right/wrong) items, for example, the probability of a correct response takes the following form:

$$\text{Prob}(X_{ij}=1\,|\,\theta_i,\beta_j) = f(1;\theta_i,\beta_j) = \Psi(\theta_i - \beta_j), \tag{5}$$

where X_{ij} is the response of Student i to Item j, 1 if right and 0 if wrong; θ_i is the proficiency parameter of Student i; β_j is the difficulty parameter of Item j; and $\Psi(\cdot)$ is the logistic function, $\Psi(x) = \exp(x)/[1+\exp(x)]$. The probability of an incorrect response is then:

$$\text{Prob}(X_{ij}=0\,|\,\theta_i,\beta_j) = f(0;\theta_i,\beta_j) = 1-\Psi(\theta_i - \beta_j), \tag{6}$$

Taken together, Equations 5 and 6 specify a particular form for the item response function, Equation 4. Figure 11 depicts Rasch item response curves for two items, Item 1 an easy one, with $\beta_1 = -1$ and Item 2 a hard one with $\beta_2 = 2$. It shows the probability of a correct response to each of the items for different values of θ. For both items, the probability of a correct response increases toward one as θ increases. Conditional independence means that for a given value of θ, the probability of Student i making responses x_{i1} and x_{i2} to the two items is the product of terms like Equations 5 and 6:

$$\text{Prob}(X_{i1}=x_{i1}, X_{i2}=x_{i2}\,|\,\theta_i,\beta_1,\beta_2) = \text{Prob}(X_{i1}=x_{i1}\,|\,\theta_i,\beta_1)\,\text{Prob}(X_{i2}=x_{i2}\,|\,\theta_i,\beta_2). \tag{7}$$

All this is reasoning *from* the model and given parameters *to* probabilities of not-yet-observed responses; as such, it is part of the warrant in the assessment argument, to be backed by empirical estimates and model criticism. In applications we need to reason in the reverse direction. Item parameters will have been estimated and responses observed, and we need to reason *from* an examinee's *x*s, to the value of θ. Equation 7 is then calculated as a function of θ with x_{i1} and x_{i2} fixed at their observed values; this is the likelihood function. Figure 12 shows the

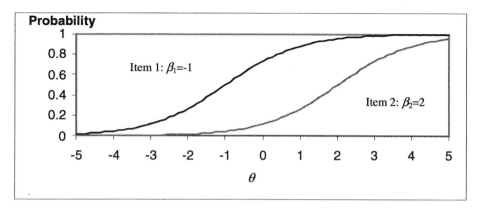

Figure 11:   Two Item Response Curves

likelihood function that corresponds to $X_{i1} = 0$ and $X_{i2} = 1$. One can estimate θ by the point at which the likelihood attains its maximum (around 0.75 in this example), or use Bayes theorem to combine the likelihood function with a prior distribution for θ, $p(\theta)$, to obtain the posterior distribution $p(\theta|x_{i1}, x_{i2})$.

The amount of information about θ available from Item j, $I_j(\theta)$, can be calculated as a function of θ, β_j, and the functional form of f (see the references mentioned above for formulas for particular IRT models). Under IRT, the amount of information for measuring proficiency at each point along the scale is simply the sum of these item-by-item information functions. The square root of the reciprocal of this value is the standard error of estimation, or the standard deviation of estimates of θ around its true value. Figure 13 is the test information curve that corresponds to the two items in the preceding example. It is of particular importance in IRT that once item parameters have been estimated ("calibrating" them), estimating individual students' θs and calculating the accuracy of those estimates can be accomplished for any subset of items. Easy items can be administered to fourth graders and harder ones to fifth graders, for example, but all scores arrive on the same θ scale. Different test forms can be given as pretests and posttests, and differences of difficulty and accuracy are taken into account.

IRT helps assessors achieve psychometric quality in several ways

Concerning Validity

The statistical framework indicates the patterns of observable responses that would occur in data if it were actually the case that a single underlying profi ciency did account for all the systematic variation among students and items. All the tools of model criticism from five centuries of probability-based reasoning can be brought to bear to assess how well an IRT model fits a given data set and

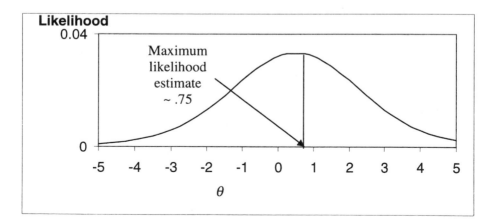

Figure 12:   **The IRT Likelihood Function Induced by Observing $X_{i1}=0$ and $X_{i2}=1$**

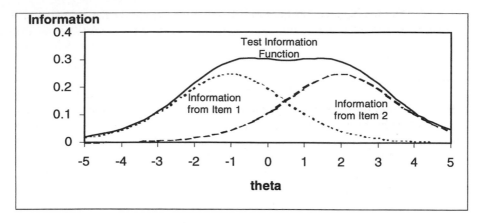

Figure 13:   An IRT Test Information Curve for the Two-Item Example

where it breaks down, now item by item, student by student. The IRT model does not address the substance of the tasks, but by highlighting tasks that are operating differently than others, or proving harder or easier than expected, it helps test designers improve their work.

Concerning Reliability

Once item parameters have been estimated, a researcher can gauge the precision of measurement that would result from different configurations of tasks. Precision of estimation can be gauged uniquely for any matchup between a person and a set of items. We are no longer bound to measures of reliability that are tied to specific populations and fixed test forms.

Concerning Comparability

IRT offers strategies beyond the reach of CTT and g-theory for assembling tests that "measure the same thing." These strategies capitalize on the above-mentioned capability to predetermine the precision of estimation from different sets of items at different levels of θ. Tests that provide optimal measurement for mastery decisions can be designed, for example, or tests that provide targeted amounts of precision at specified levels of proficiency (van der Linden, 1998). Large content domains can be covered in educational surveys by giving each student only a sample of the tasks, yet using IRT to map all performances onto the same scale. The National Assessment of Educational Progress, for example, has made good use of the efficiencies of this item sampling in conjunction with reporting based on IRT (Messick, Beaton, & Lord, 1983). Tests can even be assembled on the fly in light of a student's previous responses as assessment proceeds, a technique called adaptive testing (see Wainer et al., 2000, for practical advice on constructing computerized adaptive tests).

Concerning Fairness

Differential item functioning (DIF) analysis, based on IRT and related methods, has enabled both researchers and large-scale assessors to routinely and rigorously test for a particular kind of unfairness (e.g., Holland & Thayer, 1988; Lord, 1980). The idea is that a test score, such as a number correct or an IRT θ estimate, is a summary over a large number of item responses, and a comparison of students at the level of scores implies that they are similarly comparable across the domain being assessed. But what if some items are systematically harder for students from a group defined by cultural or educational background, for reasons that are not related to the knowledge or skill that is meant to be measured? This is DIF, and it can be formally represented in a model containing interaction terms for items by groups by overall proficiency, an interaction whose presence can threaten score meaning and distort comparisons across groups. A finding of significant DIF can imply that the observation framework needs to be modified or, if the DIF is common to many items, that the construct-representation argument is oversimplified.

DIF methods have been used in examining differential response patterns for gender and ethnic groups for the last two decades and for language groups more recently. They are now being used to investigate whether different groups of examinees of approximately the same ability appear to be using differing cognitive processes to respond to test items. Such uses include examining whether differential difficulty levels are due to differential cognitive processes, language differences (Ercikan, 1998), solution strategies and instructional methods (Lane, Wang, Magone, 1996), and skills required by the test that are not uniformly distributed across examinees (O'Neil & McPeek, 1993).

Extensions of IRT

We have just seen how IRT extends statistical modeling beyond the constraints of classical test theory and generalizability theory. The simple elements in the basic equation of IRT (Equation 4) can be elaborated in several ways, each time expanding the range of assessment situations to which probability-based reasoning can be applied in the pursuit of psychometric principles.

Multiple-Category Responses

Whereas IRT was originally developed with dichotomous (right/wrong) test items, the machinery has been extended to observations that are coded in multiple categories. This is particularly useful for performance assessment tasks that are evaluated by raters on, say, 0–5 scales. Samejima (1969) carried out pioneering work in this area. Thissen and Steinberg (1986) explain the mathematics of the extension and provide a useful taxonomy of multiple-category IRT models, and Wright and Masters (1982) offer a readable introduction to their use.

Rater Models

The preceding paragraph mentioned that multiple-category IRT models are useful in performance assessments with judgmental rating scales. But judges themselves are sources of uncertainty, as even knowledgeable and well-meaning raters rarely agree perfectly. Generalizability theory, discussed earlier, incorporates the overall impact of rater variation on scores. Adding terms for individual raters into the IRT framework goes further, so that we can adjust for their particular effects, offer training when it is warranted, and identify questionable ratings with greater sensitivity. Recent work along these lines is illustrated by Patz and Junker (1999) and Linacre (1989).

Conditional Dependence

Standard IRT assumes that responses to different items are independent once we know the item parameters and examinee's θ. This is not strictly true when several items concern the same stimulus, as in paragraph comprehension tests. Knowledge of the content tends to improve performance on all items in the set, while misunderstandings tend to depress all, in ways that do not affect items from other sets. Ignoring these dependencies leads one to overestimate the information in the responses. The problem is more pronounced in complex tasks when responses to one subtask depend on results from an earlier subtask or when multiple ratings of different aspects of the same performance are obtained. Wainer and his colleagues (e.g., Bradlow, Wainer, & Wang, 1999; Wainer & Keily, 1987) have studied conditional dependence in the context of IRT. This line of work is particularly important for tasks in which several aspects of the same complex performance must be evaluated (Yen, 1993).

Multiple Attribute Models

Standard IRT posits a single proficiency to "explain" performance on all the items in a domain. One can extend the model to situations in which multiple aspects of knowledge and skill are required in different mixes in different items. One stream of research on multivariate IRT follows the tradition of factor analysis, using analogous models and focusing on estimating structures from tests more or less as they come to the analyst from the test developers (e.g., Reckase,

1985). Another stream starts from multivariate conceptions of knowledge, and constructs tasks that contain evidence of that knowledge in theory-driven ways (e.g., Adams, Wilson, & Wang, 1997). As such, this extension fits in neatly with the task-construction extensions discussed in the following paragraph. Either way, having a richer syntax to describe examinees within the probability-based argument supports more nuanced discussions of knowledge and the ways it is revealed in task performances.

Incorporating Item Features into the Model

Embretson (1983) not only argued for paying greater attention to construct representation in test design, she argued for how to do it: Incorporate task model variables into the statistical model, and make explicit the ways that features of tasks impact on examinees' performance. A signal article in this regard was Fischer's (1973) linear logistic test model (LLTM). The LLTM is a simple extension of the Rasch model shown above in Equation 5, with the further requirement that each item difficulty parameter β is the sum of effects that depend on the features of that particular item:

$$\beta_j = \sum_{k=1}^{m} q_{jk} \eta_k ,$$

where η_k is the contribution to item difficulty from Feature k, and q_{jk} is the extent to which Feature k is represented in Item j. Some of the substantive considerations that drive task design can thus be embedded in the statistical model, and the tools of probability-based reasoning are available to examine how well they hold up in practice (validity), how they affect measurement precision (reliability), how they can be varied while maintaining a focus on targeted knowledge (comparability), and whether some items prove hard or easy for unintended reasons (fairness). Embretson (1998) walks through a detailed example of test design, psychometric modeling, and construct validation from this point of view. Additional contributions along these lines can be found in the work of Tatsuoka (1990), Falmagne and Doignon (1988), Pirolli and Wilson (1998), and DiBello, Stout, and Roussos (1995).

Progress on Other Fronts

The steady extension of probability-based tools to wider ranges of assessment uses has not been limited to IRT. In this section we will mention some other important lines of development, and point to work that is bringing these many lines of progress into the same methodological framework.

Latent Class Models

Research on learning suggests that knowledge and skills in some domains could be characterized as discrete states (e.g., the "production rule" models John Anderson uses in his intelligent tutoring systems [Anderson, Boyle, & Corbett, 1990]). Latent class models characterize an examinee as a member of one of a number of classes, rather than as a position on a continuous scale (Dayton, 1999; Haertel, 1989; Lazarsfeld, 1950). The classes themselves can be considered ordered or unordered. The key idea is that students in different classes have different probabilities of responding in designated ways in assessment settings, depending on their values on the knowledge and skill variables that define the classes. When this is what theory suggests and purpose requires, using a latent class model offers the possibility of a more valid interpretation of assessment data. The probability-based framework of latent class modeling again enables us to rigorously test this hypothesis, and to characterize the accuracy with which observed responses identify students with classes. Reliability in latent class models is therefore expressed in terms of correct classification rates.

Models for Other Kinds of Data

All of the machinery of IRT, including the extensions to multivariate student models, raters, and task features, can be applied to data other than just dichoto-mous and multiple-category observations. Less research and fewer applications appear in the literature, but the ideas can be found for counts (Rasch, 1960/1980), continuous variables (Samejima, 1973), and behavior observations such as incidence and duration (Rogosa & Ghandour, 1991).

Models that Address Interrelationships among Variables

The developments in measurement models we have discussed encompass wider ranges of student models, observations, and task features, all increasing the fidelity of probability-based models to real world situations. This contributes to improved construct representation. Progress on methods to study nomothetic span has taken place as well. Important examples include structural equations models and hierarchical models. Structural equations models (see, e.g., Jöreskog & Sörbom, 1979) incorporate theoretical relationships among variables and simultaneously take measurement error into account, so that complex hypo-theses can be posed and tested coherently. Hierarchical models (see, e.g., Bryk & Raudenbush, 1992) incorporate the ways that students are clustered in class-rooms, classrooms within schools, and schools within higher levels of organization, to better sort out the within- and across-level effects that correspond to a wide variety of instructional, organizational, and policy issues, and to growth and change. Clearer specifications   and   coherent   statistical   models   of   the relationships among variables help researchers frame and critique "nomothetic net" validity arguments.

Progress in Statistical Methodology

One kind of scientific breakthrough is to recognize situations previously handled with different models, different theories, or different methods as special cases of a single approach. The previously mentioned models and accompanying computer programs for structural equations and hierarchical analyses qualify. Both have significantly advanced statistical investigations in the social sciences, validity studies among them, and made formerly esoteric analyses more widely available. Developments taking place today in statistical computing are beginning to revolutionize psychometric analysis in a similar way.

These developments comprise resampling-based estimation, full Bayesian analysis, and modular construction of statistical models (Gelman, Carlin, Stern, & Rubin, 1995). The difficulty of managing evidence leads most substantive researchers to work within known and manageable families of analytic models; that is, ones with known properties, available procedures, and familiar exemplars. All of the psychometric models discussed above followed their own paths of evolution, each over the years generating its own language, its own computer programs, its own community of practitioners. Modern computing approaches, such as Markov Chain Monte Carlo estimation, provide a general approach to construct and fit such models with more flexibility and see all as variations on a common theme. In the same conceptual framework and with the same estimation approach, we can carry out probability-based reasoning with all of the models we have discussed.

Moreover, we can mix and match components of these models and create new ones to produce models that correspond to assessment designs motivated by theory and purpose. This approach stands in contrast to the compromises in theory and methods that result when we have to gather data to meet the constraints of specific models and specialized computer programs. The freeware computer program BUGS (Spiegelhalter et al., 1995) exemplifies this building-block approach. These developments are softening the boundaries between researchers who study psychometric modeling and those who address the substantive aspects of assessment. A more thoughtful integration of substantive and statistical lines of evidentiary arguments in assessment will further the understanding and the attainment of psychometric principles.

CONCLUSION

These are days of rapid change in assessment.[7] Advances in cognitive psychology deepen our understanding of how students gain and use knowledge (National Research Council, 1999). Advances in technology make it possible to capture more complex performances in assessment settings, by including, for example, simulation, interactivity, collaboration, and constructed response (Bennett, 2001). Yet as forms of assessment evolve, two themes endure: the importance of psychometric principles as guarantors of social values, and their realization through sound evidentiary arguments.

We have seen that the quality of assessment depends on the quality of the evi-- dentiary argument, and how substance, statistics, and purpose must be woven together throughout the argument. A conceptual framework such as the assessment design models of Figure 1 helps experts from different fields integrate their diverse work to achieve this end (Mislevy, Steinberg, Almond, Haertel, & Penuel, in press). Questions will persist. How do we synthesize evidence from disparate sources? How much evidence do we have? Does it tell us what we think it does? Are the inferences appropriate for each student? The perspectives and the methodologies that underlie psychometric principles (validity, reliability, comparability, and fairness) provide formal tools to address these questions, in whatever specific forms they arise.

ENDNOTES

[1] This work draws in part on the authors' work on the National Research Council's Committee on the Foundations of Assessment. The first author received support under the Educational Research and Development Centers Program, PR/Award Number R305B60002, as administered by the Office of Educational Research and Improvement, U.S. Department of Education. The second author received support from the National Science Foundation under grant No. ESI-9910154. The findings and opinions expressed in this report do not reflect the positions or policies of the National Research Council, the National Institute on Student Achievement, Curriculum, and Assessment, the Office of Educational Research and Improvement, the National Science Foundation, or the U.S. Department of Education.

[2] We are indebted to Professor David Schum for our understanding, such as it is, of evidentiary reasoning. This first part of this section draws on Schum (1987, 1994) and Kadane & Schum (1996).

[3] $p(X_j | \theta)$ is the probability density function for the random variable X_j, given that θ is fixed at a specified value.

[4] Strictly speaking, CTT does not address the full distributions of true and observed scores, only means, variances, and covariances. But we want to illustrate probability-based reasoning and review CTT at the same time. Assuming normality for θ and E is the easiest way to do this, since the first two moments are sufficient for normal distributions.

[5] In statistical terms, if the parameters are identified. Conditional independence is key, because CI relationships enable us to make multiple observations that are assumed to depend on the same unobserved variables in ways we can model. This generalizes the concept of replication that grounds reliability analysis.

[6] See Greeno, Collins, & Resnick (1996) for an overview of these three perspectives on learning and knowing, and discussion of their implications for instruction and assessment.

[7] *Knowing What Students Know* (National Research Council, 2001), a report by the Committee on the Foundations of Assessment, surveys these developments.

REFERENCES

Adams, R., Wilson, M.R., & Wang, W.-C. (1997). The multidimensional random coefficients multino mial logit model. *Applied Psychological Measurement*, **21**, 1–23.

Almond, R.G., & Mislevy, R.J. (1999). Graphical models and computerized adaptive testing. *Applied Psychological Measurement*, **23**, 223–237.

American Educational Research Association, American Psychological Association, & National Council on Measurement in Education. (1999). *Standards for educational and psychological testing.* Washington, DC: American Educational Research Association.

Anderson, J.R., Boyle, C.F., & Corbett, A.T. (1990). Cognitive modeling and intelligent tutoring. *Artificial Intelligence*, **42**, 7–49.

Bennett, R.E. (2001). How the internet will help large-scale assessment reinvent itself. *Education Policy Analysis*, **9**(5). Retrieved from http://epaa.asu.edu/epaa/v9n5.htlm.

Bradlow, E.T., Wainer, H., & Wang, X. (1999). A Bayesian random effects model for testlets. *Psychometrika*, **64**, 153–168.

Brennan, R.L. (1983). *The elements of generalizability theory.* Iowa City, IA: American College Testing Program.

Brennan, R.L. (2001). An essay on the history and future of reliability from the perspective of replications. *Journal of Educational Measurement*, **38**(4), 295–317

Brown, W. (1910). Some experimental results in the correlation of mental abilities. *British Journal of Psychology*, **3**, 296–322.

Bryk, A.S., & Raudenbush, S. (1992). *Hierarchical linear models: Applications and data analysis methods.* Newbury Park: Sage.

Campbell, D.T., & Fiske, D.W. (1959). Convergent and discriminant validation by the multitrait–multimethod matrix. *Psychological Bulletin*, **56**, 81–105.

Cohen, J.A. (1960). A coefficient of agreement for nominal scales. *Educational and Psychological Measurement*, **20**, 37–46.

Cronbach, L.J. (1951). Coefficient alpha and the internal structure of tests. *Psychometrika*, **17**, 297–334.

Cronbach, L.J. (1989). Construct validation after thirty years. In R.L. Linn (Ed.), *Intelligence: Measurement, theory, and public policy* (pp. 147–171). Urbana, IL: University of Illinois Press.

Cronbach, L.J., Gleser, G.C., Nanda, H., & Rajaratnam, N. (1972). *The dependability of behavioral measurements: Theory of generalizability for scores and profiles.* New York: Wiley.

Cronbach, L.J., & Meehl, P.E. (1955) Construct validity in psychological tests. *Psychological Bulletin*, **52**, 281–302.

Dayton, C.M. (1999). *Latent class scaling analysis.* Thousand Oaks, CA: Sage.

Dibello, L.V., Stout, W.F., & Roussos, L.A. (1995). Unified cognitive/psychometric diagnostic assessment likelihood based classification techniques. In P. Nichols, S. Chipman, & R. Brennan (Eds.), *Cognitively diagnostic assessment* (pp. 361–389). Hillsdale, NJ: Erlbaum.

Embretson, S. (1983). Construct validity: Construct representation versus nomothetic span. *Psychological Bulletin*, **93**, 179–197.

Embretson, S.E. (1998). A cognitive design systems approach to generating valid tests: Application to abstract reasoning. *Psychological Methods*, **3**, 380–396.

Ercikan, K. (1998). Translation effects in international assessments. *International Journal of Educational Research*, **29**, 543–553.

Ercikan, K., & Julian, M. (2002). Classification accuracy of assigning student performance to proficiency levels: Guidelines for assessment design. *Applied Measurement in Education.* **15**, 269–294.

Falmagne, J.-C., & Doignon, J.-P. (1988). A class of stochastic procedures for the assessment of knowledge. *British Journal of Mathematical and Statistical Psychology*, **41**, 1–23.

Fischer, G.H. (1973). The linear logistic test model as an instrument in educational research. *Acta Psychologica*, **37**, 359–374.

Gelman, A., Carlin, J., Stern, H., & Rubin, D.B. (1995). *Bayesian data analysis.* London: Chapman & Hall.

Greeno, J.G., Collins, A.M., & Resnick, L.B. (1996). Cognition and learning. In D.C. Berliner, & R.C. Calfee (Eds.), *Handbook of educational psychology* (pp. 15–146). New York: Macmillan.

Gulliksen, H. (1950/1987). *Theory of mental tests.* New York: John Wiley/Hillsdale, NJ: Lawrence Erlbaum.

Haertel, E.H. (1989). Using restricted latent class models to map the skill structure of achievement test items. *Journal of Educational Measurement*, **26**, 301–321.

Haertel, E.H., & Wiley, D.E. (1993). Representations of ability structures: Implications for testing. In N. Frederiksen, R.J. Mislevy, & I.I. Bejar (Eds.), *Test theory for a new generation of tests.* Hillsdale, NJ: Lawrence Erlbaum.

Hambleton, R.K. (1989). Principles and selected applications of item response theory. In R.L. Linn (Ed.), *Educational measurement* (3rd ed.) (pp. 147–200). Phoenix, AZ: American Council on Education/Oryx Press.

Hambleton, R.K., & Slater, S.C. (1997). Reliability of credentialing examinations and the impact of scoring models and standard-setting policies. *Applied Measurement in Education*, 10, 19–39.

Holland, P.W., & Thayer, D.T. (1988). Differential item performance and the Mantel-Haenzsel procedures. In H. Wainer, & H.I. Braun (Eds.), *Test validity* (pp. 129–145). Hillsdale, NJ: Lawrence Erlbaum.

Holland, P.W., & Wainer, H. (1993). *Differential item functioning*. Hillsdale, NJ: Lawrence Erlbaum.

Jöreskog, K.G., & Sörbom, D. (1979). *Advances in factor analysis and structural equation models*. Cambridge, MA: Abt Books.

Kadane, J.B., & Schum, D.A. (1996). *A probabilistic analysis of the Sacco and Vanzetti evidence*. New York: Wiley.

Kane, M.T. (1992). An argument-based approach to validity. *Psychological Bulletin*, 112, 527–535.

Kelley, T.L. (1927). *Interpretation of educational measurements*. New York: World Book.

Kuder, G.F., & Richardson, M.W. (1937). The theory of estimation of test reliability. *Psychometrika*, 2, 151–160.

Lane, W., Wang, N., & Magone, M. (1996). Gender-related differential item functioning on a middle-school mathematics performance assessment. *Educational Measurement: Issues and Practice*, 15(4), 21–27, 31.

Lazarsfeld, P.F. (1950). The logical and mathematical foundation of latent structure analysis. In S.A. Stouffer, L. Guttman, E.A. Suchman, P.R. Lazarsfeld, S.A. Star, & J.A Clausen (Eds.), *Measurement and prediction* (pp. 362–412). Princeton, NJ: Princeton University Press.

Levine, M., & Drasgow, F. (1982). Appropriateness measurement: Review, critique, and validating studies. *British Journal of Mathematical and Statistical Psychology*, 35, 42–56.

Linacre, J.M. (1989). *Many faceted Rasch measurement*. Doctoral dissertation, University of Chicago.

Lord, F.M. (1980). *Applications of item response theory to practical testing problems*. Hillsdale, NJ: Lawrence Erlbaum.

Lord, R.M., & Novick, M.R. (1968). *Statistical theories of mental test scores*. Reading, MA: Addison-Wesley.

Martin, J.D., & VanLehn, K. (1995). A Bayesian approach to cognitive assessment. In P. Nichols, S. Chipman, & R. Brennan (Eds.), *Cognitively diagnostic assessment* (pp. 141–165). Hillsdale, NJ: Erlbaum.

Messick, S. (1989). Validity. In R.L. Linn (Ed.), *Educational measurement* (3rd ed.) (pp. 13–103). New York: American Council on Education/Macmillan.

Messick, S. (1994). The interplay of evidence and consequences in the validation of performance assessments. *Education Researcher*, 32, 13–23.

Messick, S., Beaton, A.E., & Lord, F.M. (1983). National Assessment of Educational Progress reconsidered: A new design for a new era. *NAEP Report 83-1*. Princeton, NJ: National Assessment for Educational Progress.

Mislevy, R.J., Steinberg, L.S., & Almond, R.G. (in press). On the structure of educational assessments. *Measurement: Interdisciplinary Research and Perspectives*. In S. Irvine, & P. Kyllonen (Eds.), *Generating items for cognitive tests: Theory and practice*. Hillsdale, NJ: Erlbaum.

Mislevy, R.J., Steinberg, L.S., Almond, R.G., Haertel, G., & Penuel, W. (in press). Leverage points for improving educational assessment. In B. Means, & G. Haertel (Eds.), *Evaluating the effects of technology in education*. Hillsdale, NJ: Erlbaum.

Mislevy, R.J., Steinberg, L.S., Breyer, F.J., Almond, R.G., & Johnson, L. (1999). A cognitive task analysis, with implications for designing a simulation-based assessment system. *Computers and Human Behavior*, 15, 335–374.

Mislevy, R.J., Steinberg, L.S., Breyer, F.J., Almond, R.G., & Johnson, L. (in press). Making sense of data from complex assessment. *Applied Measurement in Education*.

Myford, C.M., & Mislevy, R.J. (1995). *Monitoring and improving a portfolio assessment system* (Center for Performance Assessment Research Report). Princeton, NJ: Educational Testing Service.

National Research Council (1999). *How people learn: Brain, mind, experience, and school*. Committee on Developments in the Science of Learning. Bransford, J.D., Brown, A.L., & Cocking, R.R. (Eds.). Washington, DC: National Academy Press.

National Research Council (2001). *Knowing what students know: The science and design of educational assessment.* Committee on the Foundations of Assessment. Pellegrino, J., Chudowsky, N., & Glaser, R. (Eds.). Washington, DC: National Academy Press.

O'Neil, K.A., & McPeek, W.M. (1993). Item and test characteristics that are associated with Differential Item Functioning. In P.W. Holland, & H. Wainer (Eds.), *Differential item functioning* (pp. 255–276). Hillsdale, NJ: Erlbaum.

Patz, R.J., & Junker, B.W. (1999). Applications and extensions of MCMC in IRT: Multiple item types, missing data, and rated responses. *Journal of Educational and Behavioral Statistics*, **24**, 342–366.

Petersen, N.S., Kolen, M.J., & Hoover, H.D. (1989). Scaling, norming, and equating. In R.L. Linn (Ed.), *Educational measurement* (3rd ed.) (pp. 221–262). New York: American Council on Education/Macmillan.

Pirolli. P., & Wilson, M. (1998). A theory of the measurement of knowledge content, access, and learning. *Psychological Review*, **105**, 58–82.

Rasch, G. (1960/1980). *Probabilistic models for some intelligence and attainment tests.* Copenhagen: Danish Institute for Educational Research/Chicago: University of Chicago Press (reprint).

Reckase, M. (1985). The difficulty of test items that measure more than one ability. *Applied Psychological Measurement*, **9**, 401–412.

Rogosa, D.R., & Ghandour, G.A. (1991). Statistical models for behavioral observations (with discussion). *Journal of Educational Statistics*, **16**, 157–252.

Samejima, F. (1969). Estimation of latent ability using a response pattern of graded scores. *Psychometrika Monograph No. 17*, **34**, (No. 4, Part 2).

Samejima, F. (1973). Homogeneous case of the continuous response level. *Psychometrika*, **38**, 203–219.

Schum, D.A. (1987). *Evidence and inference for the intelligence analyst.* Lanham, MD: University Press of America.

Schum, D.A. (1994). *The evidential foundations of probabilistic reasoning.* New York: Wiley.

SEPUP (1995). *Issues, evidence, and you: Teacher's guide.* Berkeley: Lawrence Hall of Science.

Shavelson, R.J., & Webb, N.W. (1991). *Generalizability theory: A primer.* Newbury Park, CA: Sage.

Spearman, C. (1904). The proof and measurement of association between two things. *American Journal of Psychology*, **15**, 72–101.

Spearman, C. (1910). Correlation calculated with faulty data *British Journal of Psychology*, **3**, 271–295.

Spiegelhalter, D.J., Thomas, A., Best, N.G., & Gilks, W.R. (1995). *BUGS: Bayesian inference using Gibbs sampling, Version 0.50.* Cambridge, MRC Biostatistics Unit.

Tatsuoka, K.K. (1990). Toward an integration of item response theory and cognitive error diagnosis. In N. Frederiksen, R. Glaser, A. Lesgold, & M.G. Shafto, (Eds.), *Diagnostic monitoring of skill and knowledge acquisition* (pp. 453–488). Hillsdale, NJ: Erlbaum.

Thissen, D., & Steinberg, L. (1986). A taxonomy of item response models. *Psychometrika*, **51**, 567–77.

Toulmin, S. (1958). *The uses of argument.* Cambridge, England: University of Cambridge Press.

Traub, R.E., & Rowley, G.L. (1980). Reliability of test scores and decisions. *Applied Psychological Measurement*, **4**, 517–545.

van der Linden, W.J. (1998). Optimal test assembly. *Applied Psychological Measurement*, **22**, 195–202.

van der Linden, W.J., & Hambleton, R.K. (1997). *Handbook of modern item response theory.* New York: Springer.

Wainer, H., Dorans, N.J., Flaugher, R., Green, B.F., Mislevy, R.J., Steinberg, L., & Thissen, D. (2000). *Computerized adaptive testing: A primer* (2nd ed). Hillsdale, NJ: Lawrence Erlbaum.

Wainer, H., & Keily, G.L. (1987). Item clusters and computerized adaptive testing: A case for testlets. *Journal of Educational Measurement*, **24**, 195–201.

Wiley, D.E. (1991). Test validity and invalidity reconsidered. In R.E. Snow, & D.E. Wiley (Eds.), *Improving inquiry in social science* (pp. 75–107). Hillsdale, NJ: Erlbaum.

Willingham, W.W., & Cole, N.S. (1997). *Gender and fair assessment.* Mahwah, NJ: Lawrence Erlbaum.

Wilson, M., & Sloane, K. (2000). From principles to practice: An embedded assessment system. *Applied Measurement in Education*, **13**, 181–208.

Wolf, D., Bixby, J., Glenn, J., & Gardner, H. (1991). To use their minds well: Investigating new forms of student assessment. In G. Grant (Ed.), *Review of Educational Research, Vol. 17* (pp. 31–74). Washington, DC: American Educational Research Association.

Wright, B.D., & Masters, G.N. (1982). *Rating scale analysis.* Chicago: MESA Press.

Yen, W.M. (1993). Scaling performance assessments: Strategies for managing local item dependence. *Journal of Educational Measurement*, **30**, 187–213.

25
Classroom Student Evaluation

PETER W. AIRASIAN

Boston College, School of Education, MA, USA

LISA M. ABRAMS

Boston College, Center for the Study of Testing, Evaluation and Educational Policy, MA, USA

Four classroom realities which define the richness and complexity of classrooms and teachers' lives provide a useful context for considering the nature and dimensions of classroom evaluation. First, classrooms are both social and academic environments. To survive and succeed, teachers need to know their students' social, personal, linguistic, cultural, and emotional characteristics, as well as their academic ones, since decisions about managing, monitoring, and planning require knowledge of a broad range of student characteristics. Second, the classroom is an ad hoc, informal, person-centered, and continually changing environment that calls for constant teacher decision-making about classroom pace, instruction, learning, and the like (Doyle, 1986). Third, many of the decisions that confront teachers are immediate, practical ones that focus on particular students and particular contexts. Fourth, teachers are both evaluators and participants in the classroom society, both of which can influence their objectivity in planning, implementing, and applying classroom evaluations (Airasian, 2001).

The general, overriding purpose of evaluation in the classroom is to help teachers make decisions in the complex social and instructional context in which it takes place (see AFT/NCME/NEA, 1990). In this chapter, five areas of classroom evaluation are described which encompass evaluations that take place before, during, and after instruction, and represent the vast majority of evaluations that a teacher will carry out. The areas are: evaluation in establishing and maintaining social equilibrium in the classroom; evaluation in planning instruction; evaluation during instruction; evaluation of assessments and tests; and evaluation for judging and grading academic learning.

International Handbook of Educational Evaluation, 533–548
T. Kellaghan, D.L. Stufflebeam (eds.)
© *2003 Dordrecht: Kluwer Academic Publishers. Printed in Great Britain.*

EVALUATION IN ESTABLISHING AND MAINTAINING SOCIAL EQUILIBRIUM IN THE CLASSROOM

A classroom is more than a group of students who are together in the same place. It is a complex social situation characterized by rules and routines that foster order, discipline, civility, and communication. At the start of each school year, teachers learn about their new students by gathering information and making judgments about their individual cognitive, affective, and psychomotor character- istics. These initial evaluations are necessary and important in establishing classroom order, routines, and structure (Cohen, 1972; First & Mezzell, 1980; Henry, 1971; Jackson, 1990; Waller, 1967).

Teachers will seek answers to a variety of questions about their students. Will they get along? Will they be cooperative? Are they academically ready for this grade or subject? What intellectual and emotional strengths and weaknesses do they have? What will interest them? How long are they likely to stay focused on tasks? What is the best way to organize the classroom to promote learning? Usually by the second or third week of school, teachers will have collected and evaluated information about their class that enables them to provide a viable social and academic class characterized by rules, routines, and common under- standings (Boostrom, 1991; Dreeben, 1967; Henry, 1971).

Teachers rely on many sources of information to learn about their students. These may include comments of prior teachers, special education teachers, or parents; comments in the teachers' room; official school records; the performance of prior siblings; formal and informal classroom observations; attitude inventory scores; and conversations with the students themselves. Teachers will also focus on what students say, do, and write. While the student characteristics that teachers focus on will vary by grade level, all strive to learn about and evaluate their students' characteristics early in the school year. The knowledge they acquire will form a set of perceptions and expectations that influence the manner in which they establish rules, plan for instruction, interact with students, carry out instruction, and interpret and judge student performance (McCaslin & Good, 1996).

A great deal of research suggests that teachers' expectations, defined as "the inferences that teachers make about the future behavior or academic achieve- ment of their students, based on what they know about these students now" (Good & Brophy, 1991, p.110) can have both positive and negative effects on teacher-student interactions and student outcomes (Beez, 1968; Brophy, 1983; Cooper & Good, 1983; Dusek, 1985; Eden & Shani 1982; Jones, 1986; Jussim, 1986; Kellaghan, Madaus & Airasian, 1982; Rosenthal & Jacobson, 1968; Schrank, 1968; Simon & Willcocks, 1981). The expectation effect, commonly referred to as the "self-fulfilling prophecy," was popularized by Robert Rosenthal and Lenore Jacobson (1968). The notion that false perceptions can lead to behavior that over time causes the initial expectation to come true can be especially damaging to students perceived to be low achieving. Furthermore, teachers' standards for academic success are often rooted in their own social or cultural background (Rist, 1977). The more congruent a student's background character-istics are with those of their teacher, the more likely the teacher will establish high expectations for that student. It is vitally important that teachers base their expectations on accurate perceptions of students while maintaining a high degree of awareness of how their own characteristics may influence classroom evaluations.

Much of the process of student and class evaluation is based on informal, observational, and idiosyncratic information. There are two major threats to its validity: stereotyping and logical errors. Stereotyping occurs when a teacher's beliefs or personal prejudices influence her/his evaluations (Steele, 1997). Judgments such as "girls are not good at science" and "students who come from that area are poorly prepared for learning" are stereotypes. Stereotyping becomes a particular concern when students with unique cultural, racial, language, or disability characteristics are being evaluated. Too often, such characteristics are erroneously judged and interpreted by teachers as student deficits rather than as student differences and assets (Delpit, 1995; Ladson-Billings, 1994). Logical errors occur when a teacher selects wrong or inappropriate evidence to evaluate a student's performance. For example, judging a student's ability in math by observing his/her attention in class or the neatness of his/her writing is a logical error.

The perspectives that teachers develop early in the school year can also create reliability problems. Informal, often fleeting, information gathered about students leads to subjective and idiosyncratic evaluation that later information might well change. Beginning-of-year perceptions are probably best regarded as hypotheses to be confirmed by additional observations or more formal information, which might be obtained from diagnostic tests or by having the student read aloud to judge his/her facility. The use of a variety of assessments will help teachers to confirm or reject initial perceptions. Among the strategies that teachers use are a variety of data sources to learn about students; not relying solely on informal evidence; observing a behavior or activity two or three times before associating a student with it; not prematurely judging students' needs and abilities (how students act in the first few days of school may not represent their typical performance); and observing student performance in structured activities such as spelling or math games.

EVALUATION IN PLANNING INSTRUCTION

The second area in which teachers employ evaluation is in planning instruction (Anderson et al., 2001). In this activity, four questions on which the instructional process is based are relevant. What are the important objectives that students should learn (the planning question)? How can I deliver instruction that leads to high levels of student learning and accommodates their individual needs, interests, and aptitudes (the teaching question)? How do I select or construct information that provides valid and reliable information about learning (the student achievement question)? How can I ensure that my objectives, instruction, and student assessment are aligned with each other (the alignment question)?

A substantial amount of a teacher's time is spent planning instructional activities. Teachers seek to develop a curriculum that will fit the readiness of students and the available instructional resources. Planning helps teachers in five ways. It reduces uncertainty by providing a sense of purpose and subject-matter focus. It provides an opportunity to review and become familiar with the material to be taught. It provides a way to get instruction started. It links daily instruction to more integrative topics or units. And lastly, planning instructional activities helps teachers assess and take into account students' readiness to learn the intended content.

Four sets of factors that influence teachers' instructional planning have been identified. First, knowledge of students' characteristics is essential. For example, teachers make judgments about what students are ready to learn; the skills they already have mastered; how well they work in groups; their preferred learning styles; disabilities in the classroom and how they are to be accommodated; the level of language and discourse used by the students; and how to accommodate students' individual and commonly held needs (Overton, 1996).

Teacher characteristics constitute a second set of factors that influence planning. Teachers' content knowledge, their beliefs about teaching and learning, instructional preferences, available technology, and physical limitations are all important. Teachers' choice of topics, the teaching methods they prefer, and the up-to-datedness of their content knowledge all intersect with student characteristics in planning decisions.

A third important factor in planning is the time available for instruction, which has to be balanced with other factors such as student readiness, coverage of a required curriculum, and teachers' instructional preferences. Every decision about what to teach and the emphasis it should be given is based on, or constrained by, instructional time.

Finally, the availability or lack of availability of instructional resources influences planning. Resources encompass a broad range of supports and materials which include teaching supplies, classroom aids and volunteers, up-to-date textbooks, computers, classroom space, collegial support, and the principal's support. The resources that are available determine not only the nature of instruction, but also learning outcomes. Richness of materials facilitates richness in instruction, while lack of materials limits instructional opportunities.

Having considered these four factors, the task of the teacher is to use the information in devising lesson plans. Typically, plans will be developed in the context of educational objectives that state intended student learning outcomes. The objectives describe desired student learning, not how objectives will be taught. In everyday activities, objectives provide a focus for what is important, for what has to be accomplished, as well as describing the kinds of content and process that students should learn (Alexander, Frankiewicz, & Williams, 1979; Ausubel, Novak, & Hanesian, 1978; Bloom, Madaus, & Hastings, 1981).

Objectives derive their importance from the fact that teaching is an intentional and normative act. It is intentional because teaching has a purpose. Teachers want students to learn something as a result of being taught. Teaching is also normative because what is taught is viewed as being worth learning. Regardless of how they are stated and what they are called, objectives are present in all teaching. Other common names for objectives are "learning targets," "educational objectives," "instructional objectives," "behavioral objectives," "pupil outcomes," "benchmarks," and "curriculum objectives." Objectives are usually the starting point in the instructional process since they identify the desired outcomes of instruction. Some have called the process of stating objectives a "backward approach" to planning since it starts by defining the end result of instruction (Wiggins & McTighe, 1998).

Most teachers' formal objectives are cognitive and emphasize intellectual activities such as memorizing, interpreting, applying, problem solving, reasoning, analyzing, and thinking critically. Virtually all the instruction and assessments that students are exposed to are intended to foster one or more of these cognitive processes. Examples of objectives keyed to various cognitive processes are: students can identify the correct punctuation marks in a writing assignment (knowledge); students can integrate the information from the science experiment into a general conclusion (synthesis); students can punctuate correctly in a writing task (application); students can translate French sentences into English (comprehension); and students can distinguish facts from opinions in eight newspaper editorials (analysis).

In addition to teacher developed objectives, there are two sources of class-room objectives, one based on teacher edition textbooks and the other on statewide standards. Teachers' textbooks and their accompanying aids provide a broad range of resources to help planning, delivery, assessment, and the evaluation of instruction and learning. However, because textbook authors can rarely tailor their objectives, materials, plans, and assessments to all textbook users, teachers' texts may not reflect the needs, readiness, and resources of particular teachers and classes. Thus, blindly following a teacher's textbook could undermine instruction and evaluation validity. It is up to the classroom teacher to ensure that objectives, instructional activities, and materials are well matched to the readiness and needs of their students. The simple task of selecting a textbook can have a considerable impact on the achievement of classroom instructional objectives. Three questions help guide an evaluation of the appropriateness of teachers' textbooks. Are the objectives and text materials clearly stated? Are they suitable for students in this particular classroom? Do they cover all the kinds of objectives and activities that these students should be exposed to? A negative answer to one or more of these questions will raise questions about the validity of instruction.

In addition to the objectives in textbooks, teachers in the United States have to take account of state and district-wide learning outcomes associated with standards-based education. Performance on state standards can have important consequences for students as well as for teachers and school administrators. State curriculum standards encourage teachers to emphasize instruction on the statewide standards, often creating a dilemma for them. Should they focus their planning on the standards or on outcomes that they consider more appropriate to their students' needs? Regardless of the form, nature, or source of objectives or standards, it is important that all teachers evaluate their appropriateness and feasibility when planning instruction.

Potential threats to the validity of instructional planning decisions include: failure to learn about student needs and abilities before planning; failure to include a range of instructional activities and strategies that fit students' needs; failure to recognize and plan for one's own knowledge and pedagogical limitations; and failure to take into account state curriculum standards or the school's curriculum specifications. Potential threats to reliability of planning instruction include: making planning decisions without checking the consistency and stability of information or initial perceptions that have not been confirmed by further observation.

EVALUATION DURING INSTRUCTION

While discussed separately here, it is important to bear in mind that planning and delivering instruction are integrally related. The instructional process constantly cycles from planning to delivery, to revision of planning, to delivery, and so on. The link between the two processes should be logical, ongoing, and natural. Both are necessary for successful teaching and evaluation.

However, a teacher's evaluation activities when stating objectives and planning instruction are very different from those when actually teaching. The most obvious difference is in the time at which evaluation occurs. Planning evaluations are developed during quiet time, when the teacher can reflect and try to identify appropriate objectives, content topics, and activities for instruction. Evaluations during instruction, on the other hand, take place on the firing line during teaching, and require quick decisions to keep instruction flowing smoothly. The fast pace at which evaluation occurs during instruction requires the teacher to understand the "language of the classroom" or to interpret informal student cues such as attention, facial expressions, and posture (Jackson, 1968). A more formal and important evaluation during instruction is questioning by both students and teacher.

Once instruction begins, teachers have a two-fold task: to teach the planned lesson and to constantly evaluate the progress of instruction, modifying it if necessary (Arends, 1997). To carry out these tasks, teachers "read" their students' minute-by-minute, sense their mood, and make decisions about how to maintain or alter instruction. They attend to student answers, detect their attention or confusion, choose who to call on to answer a question, judge individual and class participation, and watch for possible misbehavior. During these activities, they need to maintain a viable instructional pace and judge the quality of each answer. When students are divided into small groups, the number of events to observe, monitor, and regulate increase (Doyle, 1986).

During instruction, teachers seek information to help judge a variety of factors. These include the interest level of individual students and of the class as a whole; students' retention of previously learned content; apparent or potential behavior problems; the appropriateness of the instructional technique or activity employed; the most appropriate student to call on next to answer a question; the appropriateness of the answer a student provides; pace of instruction; the amount of time being spent on the lesson and its activities; the usefulness and consequences of students' questions; the smoothness of transition from one concept to another, and from one activity to another; the usefulness of examples used to explain concepts; the degree of comprehension on the part of individual students and of the class as a whole; and the desirability of starting or ending a particular activity (Airasian, 2001). Information gathered about these factors leads to decisions about other activities. For example, depending upon the appropriateness of the answer a student gives, the teacher may try to draw out a better answer from the student; seek another student to provide an answer; or ask the next logical question in the content sequence.

Three sources threaten the validity of teachers' classroom evaluations during instruction: lack of objectivity when observing and judging the quality of the instructional process; the limited range of indicators used to make decisions about instruction and student learning; and the difficulty of assessing and addressing students' individual differences. Being a participant in the instructional process can make it difficult for a teacher to be a dispassionate, detached observer about learning and instruction. Teachers have a stake in the success of their instruction and derive their primary rewards from it. They also have a strong personal and professional investment in the success of their work. Furthermore, they frequently gauge their instructional success on the basis of indicators that focus on the process of instruction rather than on student learning outcomes. While correct in focusing some attention on process factors, involvement and attention are only intermediate goals that hopefully, but not inevitably, result in student learning.

One of the difficulties in collecting reliable evidence about the instructional process stems from the fact that the teacher's opportunity to corroborate instructional observations and interpretations is limited. The more brief the opportunity to observe instruction, the less confidence a teacher can have in the reliability of observations. Thus, an important issue in assessing the reliability of instructional evaluations is the difficulty of obtaining an adequate sampling of student reactions and understandings, and especially their configuration over time.

One strategy to overcome this problem is to use questioning during instruction. Questioning students can serve to promote attention, encourage learning from peers, deepen understanding, provide reinforcement, control the pace and content of instruction, and yield diagnostic information. There are a number of types of questions that teachers can use, including open-ended ones (what is your reaction to the story?), diagnostic questions (what is the theme of this poem?), sequence questions (order these American presidents from earliest to latest), prediction questions (what do you think will happen to the red color when it is mixed with a green color?), and extension or follow-up questions (explain to me why you think that?). Questions can target lower-level skills requiring students to recall factual information, or they can involve higher-level skills when students are asked to predict, analyze, explain, or interpret. By questioning a number of students, teachers can improve the reliability and validity of their evaluations during instruction.

Strategies that can improve classroom questioning, minimize student anxiety, and inform student evaluation include: asking questions that are related to lesson objectives; avoiding overly vague questions; involving the entire class in the questioning process; being aware of patterns when calling on students; avoiding calling on the same students repeatedly; providing five seconds of "wait time" for students to form their responses; probing students who answer "yes" or "no" with follow-up questions asking "why?" or "can you give another example?"; bearing in mind that questioning is a social process in which students should be treated with encouragement and respect; and recognizing that good questioning also involves good listening and responding by the teacher (Morgan & Saxton, 1991).

EVALUATION OF ASSESSMENTS AND TESTS

In considering the evaluation of assessments and tests, a teacher asks: How do I construct or select strategies that will provide valid and reliable information about students' learning? Summative evaluations focus on teacher decisions that the school bureaucracy requires: grading, grouping students, recommending student placements of varied kinds, and referring students to special education services. They occur less frequently than formative evaluations (which are integrated into the instructional process and are designed to facilitate learning) and are based mainly on teacher-made tests and assessments, although commercial standardized tests and statewide assessments are also commonly used.

The teacher's main focus in assessing learning is to provide a fair opportunity for students to demonstrate what they have learned. Good classroom assessments and tests possess three main characteristics: students are tested or assessed on content they were taught; the exercises or questions in the test or assessment include a representative sample of stated objectives; and the test and assessment items, questions, exercises, directions, and scoring procedures are clear, unambiguous, and appropriate. If these conditions are met, the information teachers gather will provide a reliable and valid basis for evaluating students' achievements (AFT/NCME/NEA, 1990; Joint Advisory Committee, 1993).

To select appropriate assessments and tests, teachers must make a number of decisions. For example, what instructional topics should be assessed? What type or types of assessments should be used? Should a paper-and-pencil test be given and, if so, what kinds of test items should be used? Should observations, essays, portfolios, group projects, checklists, or rubrics be used? Regardless of the method used, the decision will be made after the teacher has identified the topics and processes that are to be assessed. Unless a teacher has reflected on the test or assessment to be administered and on the instruction it will cover, she or he cannot provide the instructional focus students need to prepare for the assessment. Teachers can enhance validity and student performance by providing a review (but they should not teach the test), and by ensuring that students understand item formats and what will be expected of them in the test or assessment.

If there is not a good match between objectives, instruction, and assessment, students' performance will provide a poor and invalid indication of their learning. Furthermore, assessments that do not align with objectives and instruction will have little positive influence in motivating and focusing student study. If students find little relationship between what they are taught and what they are tested on, they will undervalue the teacher's instruction.

When tests are used to evaluate student achievement, the items should be clearly presented. The following five guidelines will help to ensure this (Ahmann & Glock, 1963; Bloom, Madaus, & Hastings, 1981; Ebel, 1965; Gronlund, 1998). First, vocabulary that students do not understand and sentence structures that are ambiguous and confusing should be avoided. If the wording or sentence structure of items is confusing, students will not have an opportunity to demonstrate their learning, thus decreasing assessment validity. Second, questions should be short and to the point so that students can quickly focus on what is being asked. Third, items should have only one correct answer. With the exception of essay questions, most paper-and-pencil test items are designed to have students select or supply a best answer. Fourth, information about the nature of the desired answers should be provided. While the failure to properly focus the work of students is common to all types of test items, it is most often a concern in essay items. Although students will have freedom to structure their own responses, essay questions should require them to demonstrate mastery of key ideas, principles, or concepts and should provide students with guidance on the form, length, and other characteristics of the desired answer. Finally, clues to correct answers should not be provided. Unlike the other four guidelines, this one is concerned with instances in which teachers unknowingly provide clues to test items because of grammatical construction or implausible options.

The range of strategies that classroom teachers use in assessment is substantial and no single tool or technique can provide all the information needed to describe the richness of students' learning (Airasian, 2001; Arter, 1999). Common teacher-controlled formal classroom assessment types include the following:

• *Traditional paper and pencil tests* which can include (i) Selection items which require students to choose the best answer from among several options. Multiple-choice, true or false, and matching are frequently used formats for selection items. (ii) Supply items, which require students to write in or supply the answer, and include short answer, sentence completion, and essays. (iii) Interpretive exercises, which can be used to assess higher-level skills. Students are presented with material such as a map, political cartoon, poem, chart, graph, or data table, and are required to answer questions by analyzing or interpreting it. This item type can be formatted so that answer choices are provided (selection item) or students write in their responses (supply item).

• *Performance assessments* in which students carry out an activity or create a work product to demonstrate their learning, and include activities such as projects, simulations, lab experiments, music performances, and presentations. This type of assessment may be called "authentic" since students are showing what they can do in real situations (Wiggins, 1992). Teachers usually develop checklists, rating scales, or descriptive rubrics for scoring.

• *Portfolios assessments* are a unique type of performance assessment. Portfolios involve a systematic collection of selected student work compiled over a significant period of time such as a month, the school year, or throughout an instructional unit. Typically, portfolios involve strategies that require students to interpret and reflect on their work (in writing assignments, journal entries, artwork, book reviews, rough and final drafts), thus demonstrating their growth and development toward curriculum goals. Both performance and portfolio assessments are considered as "alternatives" to the traditional form of classroom assessment, the paper and pencil test.

• *Narrative assessments* are based on formal teacher observations of specific learning behaviors, and can involve measuring the ability of students to read out loud or present an oral report to the class. Like portfolios, they are also examples of performance assessments.

The availability of these data collection procedures allows classroom teachers to choose among a variety of approaches in obtaining information about student learning. Choice of procedure will depend on its purpose. Evaluation in establishing classroom equilibrium relies heavily on informal student observation. Evaluation during instruction relies on questioning of students. And evaluation of assessments and testing relies on a variety of formal, paper-and-pencil approaches (Taylor & Nolen, 1996; Tombari & Borich, 1999).

All these assessment procedures are controlled by the classroom teacher, who decides who to assess, when to assess, what to assess, how to assess, how to score, and how to use results. They are the fundamental ingredients of the classroom teaching, learning, and evaluation process. However, teachers do not control all classroom assessments. Two important types of assessment that are not controlled by teachers, but which are important, are commercial standardized tests and, in the U.S., state assessments.

Commercial standardized achievement tests, such as the *Iowa Tests of Basic Skills* (2000) and *Terra Nova* (1997), and state assessments are administered in classrooms relatively infrequently compared to teachers' own classroom assessments. Commercial standardized achievement tests are commonly used to compare the performance of students to national norms; to provide developmental information about student achievement over time; and to identify areas of student strengths and weaknesses. State assessments are mandated by state legislatures or boards of education and are used to assess students' performance, based on a set of state-mandated learning standards, to determine whether an individual student or school as a whole has achieved state standards of acceptable performance. Reports of state test results typically yield rankings of schools and districts, thus allowing for public comparisons.

Even if commercial standardized tests and state assessments are technically strong, with well-written items, and statistically sophisticated scoring, it is appropriate for an individual teacher to raise the issue of whether they provide valid evaluations of his/her students. Four factors influence their validity: the appropriateness of the alignment of objectives or standards and test items; the alignment of the content of the test with what is taught in the classroom; the conditions under which tests are administered; and the interpretation and use of test results.

Standardized tests and state assessments can have a strong impact on classroom practices. The lack of teacher control and the fact that they permit comparisons across schools and school districts make them important for teachers and school administrators. The public visibility that often accompanies results can put pressure on teachers to align their classroom tests or assessments to mirror the content and format of standardized tests and especially of state assessments (Canner et al., 1991; Mehrens, 1998; Smith & Rottenberg, 1991). This pressure can cause tension between teacher-based instruction and assessment and externally based assessment. It is often true that more attention will be paid to tests or assessments to which important consequences are attached than to ones to which such consequences are not attached.

EVALUATION FOR JUDGING AND GRADING LEARNING

Obtaining information based on tests, assessments, and other forms of classroom information is not an end in itself. The end is a judgment of the quality of teaching and learning in the classroom. To make such a judgment, the teacher has to answer the question: What is this information saying about the class or a student's performance?

It is important to note the difference between *scoring* and *grading* students' performances. Scoring involves summarizing performance, as when a teacher counts the number of multiple-choice items on a test which a student answered correctly. Grading, on the other hand, involves a judgment of the worth or quality of student performance. For example, when a teacher determines that a student's test performance merits an A, or should be placed in the second level of a five-level rubric scale, she/he has evaluated the student. Clearly, this is a sensitive process. Students learn very early in school that grades serve as sanctions for academic achievement (Dreeben, 1967), and can affect their perceptions of self-esteem and personal worth (Henry, 1957). Consequently, it is essential that teachers strive to ensure that their scoring and grading processes are fair, valid, and accurate.

Scoring selection-type items, as well as most short-answer items, is straight-forward: the teacher counts the number of items that the student has answered correctly in a test or assessment. Scoring essay items is more complicated. Items can be lengthy and complex, and account may be taken of style, neatness, handwriting, and grammar, as well as content. Strategies to improve the scoring of essay questions include defining the characteristics of an essay before administration; determining and indicating to students how handwriting, spelling, sentence structure, and organization will be judged; scoring students' work anonymously, if possible; scoring all students' answers to the first essay before scoring any student's second essay to provide consistency in scoring; and rescoring some essays at random to judge the reliability of scoring.

Grades are represented in a variety of forms, such as letters (A, A-, B+ ...), categories (excellent, good, fair, poor), numbers (100-90, 89-80, 79-70 ...), and checklists (e.g., in math, the student can count in order, recognizes numbers to 10, writes numbers clearly). The most common grading system used in schools involves letter grades (Polloway et al., 1994), which are used to provide information about student performance to students themselves, to their parents, to counselors, and to other teachers (Brookhart, 1999).

Classroom grading is dependent on teacher judgments, since teachers are typically the constructors and dispensers of grades. In most schools, teachers have wide latitude in the way they grade their students. Different teachers can have quite different grading strategies. Whatever a teacher's classroom grading system, three key questions should be asked: Against what standard will students' performance be compared? What student characteristics or performances should be included in the grade? And how should different characteristics or performances be weighted in the grades?

All grading is based on a comparison (Frisbie & Waltman, 1992). The two most common classroom grading standards are based on a comparison of a student's performance with the performance of other students (norm-referenced grading) and on a comparison of a student's performance with a set of predetermined standards of "good" or "poor" performance (criterion-referenced grading) (Brookhart, 1999; Friedman & Frisbie, 1993). Grading may also involve a comparison of a student's performance with a judgment of the student's ability, or a judgment of a student's improvement over a period of time.

Having made a decision about the grading comparison to be used, teachers face a series of other decisions to complete the process. They must decide the student performances (tests, projects, homework, etc.) that will be considered in the grading and then assign weights to each type of performances. Will tests count more than quizzes? Will projects count more than a test? And will homework count?

The quality of assessment information is influenced by three factors: (i) the conditions under which information is collected, including the opportunity students are afforded to show their typical or best behavior; (ii) the quality of the instruments used, which is affected by such factors as clarity of test items or performance criteria and the appropriateness of the language level of items; and (iii) the objectivity of the information, which could, for example be affected by biased scoring.

Five general cautions which relate to all types of evaluation, merit consideration when teachers are evaluating students. First, classroom evaluation information describes students' learned behaviors and their present status. For a variety of reasons (cultural, societal, economic, familial, etc.), some students learn more, retain more, and have more opportunities to learn than others. Whatever the cause of these learning differences, it is important to recognize that the information classroom evaluations provide describes only how students currently perform, not how they will perform in the future. Second, evaluation information provides an estimate, not an exact indication, of performance. There are always sources of error in students' performances and assessment procedures. Third, the results of a single assessment do not provide a sufficient basis on which to make important decisions about students that might affect their lives and opportunities. A by-product of relying on the results of a single assessment is a tendency to ignore additional information about students that might contribute to improving the validity of important decisions. Fourth, the tendency to form global and convenient labels such as "poor learner," "self-confident," or "hard worker," on the basis of a single student performance should be avoided. Finally, since evaluations only describe and judge student performance, they should not be interpreted as providing an explanation of performance. It rarely is possible to determine with certainty why a student performed as he or she did. Thus, the search for "explanations" of performance must go beyond the immediate evaluation information.

CONCLUSION

The discussion of classroom evaluation in this chapter addressed several aspects of teaching. Evaluation is an integral part of maintaining the social climate of the classroom, planning for instruction, implementing instruction, developing quality measurement tools, and judging or grading academic learning. Underpinning each of these specific parts of the educational process are three fundamental concerns.

First, there is growing diversity among students in most school populations. The number who manifest special needs and disabilities and who do not speak English as their first language is increasing in most classrooms. The diversity that this situation gives rise to increases the tension between goals and priorities that instruction and evaluation should emphasize. The goal of balancing quality and equity is commonly embraced but rarely attained. How should educational resources be allocated, in equal proportions to all students or in greater proportions to the most needy? The reality of student diversity has increased the complexity of classroom operations, making it more difficult to provide appropriate instruction, assessment, and evaluation to all students. At issue is how a teacher is to meet the needs of diverse student groups while simultaneously meeting the "one size fits all" demands of many classroom and most U.S. statewide evaluations.

Second, while there are many concerns about applying sanctions to students on the basis of their performance in standard-based assessments, the use of teacher and principal sanctions based on student performance should also be a matter of concern. In this case, the issue is the validity of decisions made on the basis of the results of student assessments. While an evaluation can indicate which students do well or poorly on the topics evaluated, using the results to evaluate teachers or administrators is another step which numerous intervening factors relating to students and instructional resources can invalidate. If evaluations are constructed for the main purpose of assessing student achievement, caution should be exercised in using them for other purposes. When used for multiple purposes, the validity of each purpose should be determined independently.

Finally, successful classroom evaluation relies heavily on the quality of instruction that was provided. While stating objectives and developing or selecting assessments are important aspects of classroom evaluation, the links among objectives/standards, instruction, and assessments are varied and complex. Defining objectives and standards and selecting and constructing assessments are largely "technologies" for which there are well-developed procedures. Planning, and even more so the delivery of instruction, are more arts than technology, especially when it comes to teaching higher-level knowledge and skills. Knowing how to state an objective does not mean that we know how to teach it to all students. Success in teaching means being able to teach a variety of students with a variety of characteristics in a variety of ways.

REFERENCES

Ahmann, J.S., & Glock, M.D. (1963). *Evaluating pupil growth*. Boston: Allyn & Bacon.

Airasian, P. (2001). *Classroom assessment. Concepts and applications* (4th ed.) New York, McGraw-Hill.

Alexander, L., Frankiewicz, R., & Williams, R. (1979). Facilitation of learning and retention or oral instruction using advanced and post organizers. *Journal of Educational Psychology*, **71**(5), 701–707.

American Federation of Teachers, National Council on Measurement in Education, and National Education Association. (1990). *Standards for teacher competence in educational assessment of students*. Washington, DC: The National Council on Measurement in Education.

Anderson, L.W., Krathwohl, D.R., Airasian, P.W., Cruikshank, K.A., Mayer, P.R., Raths, J., & Wittrock, M.C. (2001). *A taxonomy for learning, teaching, and assessing: A revision of Bloom's taxonomy of educational objectives*. New York: Longman.

Arends, R.I. (1997). *Classroom instruction and management*. New York, McGraw-Hill.

Arter, J. (1999). Teaching about performance assessment. *Educational Measurement: Issues and Practice*, **18**(2), 30–44.

Ausubel, D., Novak, J., & Hanesian, H. (1978). *Educational psychology: A cognitive view*. New York: Holt.

Beez, W. (1968). Influence of biased psychological reports on teacher behavior and pupil performance. *Proceedings of the 76th Annual Convention of the American Psychological Association*, **3**, 605–606.

Bloom, B., Madaus, G.F., & Hastings, J.T. (1981). *Evaluation to improve learning*. New York: McGraw-Hill.

Boostrom, R. (1991). The value and function of classroom rules. *Curriculum Inquiry*, **21**, 194–216.

Brophy, J. (1983). Research on the self-fulfilling prophecy and teacher expectations. *Journal of Educational Psychology*, **75**, 631–661.

Brookhart, S.M. (1999). Teaching about communicating assessment results and grading. *Educational Measurement: Issues and Practice*, **18**(1), 5–13.

Canner, J., Fisher, T., Fremer, J., Haladyna, T., Hall, J., Mehrens, W., Perlman, C., Roeber, E., & Sandifer, P. (1991). *Regaining trust: Enhancing the credibility of school testing programs. A report from The National Council on Measurement in Education Task Force*. Washington, DC: National Council on Measurement in Education.

Cohen, E.G. (1972). Sociology and the classroom: Setting the conditions for teaching-student interaction. *Review of Educational Research*, **42**, 441–452.

Cooper, H.M., & Good, T. L. (1983). *Pygmalion grows up: Studies in the expectation communication process*. New York: Longman.

Delpit, L. (1995). *Other people's children: Cultural conflict in the classroom*. New York: New Press.

Doyle, W. (1986). Classroom organization and management. In M.C. Wittrock. (Ed.) *Handbook of research on teaching* (pp. 392–431). New York: Macmillan.

Dreeben, R. (1967). The contribution of schooling to the learning of norms. *Harvard Educational Review*, **37**, 211–237.

Dusek, J.B. (Ed.). (1985). *Teacher expectancies*. Hillsdale, NJ: Erlbaum.

Ebel, R.L. (1965). *Measuring educational achievement*. Englewood Cliffs, NJ: Prentice-Hall.

Eden, D., & Shani, A. (1982). Pygmalion goes to bootcamp: Expectancy, leadership, and trainee performance. *Journal of Applied Psychology*, **67**, 194–199.

First, J., & Mezzel, M.H. (1980). *Everybody's business: A book about school discipline*. Columbia, SC: Southeastern Public Education Program, American Friends Service Committee.

Frisbie, D.A., & Waltman, K.K. (1992). An NCME instructional module on developing a personal grading plan. *Educational Measurement: Issues and Practice*, **11**(3), 35–42.

Friedman, S.J., & Frisbie, D.A. (1993). *The validity of report cards as indicators of student performance*. Paper presented at the annual meeting of the National Council on Measurement in Education, Atlanta.

Good, T.L., & Brophy, J.E. (1991). *Looking in classrooms* (5th ed.). New York: Harper Collins.

Gronlund, N.E. (1998). *Assessment of student achievement*. Boston, MA: Allyn & Bacon.

Henry, J. (1957). Attitude organization in elementary school classrooms. *American Journal of Orthopsychiatry*, **27**, 117–123.

Henry, J. (1971). *Essays on education. New York*; Penguin.

Iowa Tests of Basic Skills. (2000). Itasca, IL: Riverside Publishing, Houghton Mifflin.

Jackson, P.W. (1968). *Life in classrooms*. New York: Holt, Rinehart, & Winston.

Jackson, P.W. (1990). *Life in classrooms*. New York: Teachers College Press.

Jones, E. (1986). Interpreting interpersonal behavior: The effects of expectancies. *Science*, **234**, 41–46.

Jussim, L. (1986). Teacher expectancies: Self-fulfilling prophecies, perceptual biases, and accuracy. *Journal of Personality and Social Psychology*, **57**, 469–480.

Joint Advisory Committee. (1993). *Principles for fair students' assessment practices for education in Canada*. Edmonton, Alberta: University of Alberta.

Kellaghan, T., Madaus, G.F., & Airasian, P.W. (1982). *The effects of standardized testing*. Boston: Kluwer-Nijhoff.

Ladson-Billings, G. (1994). *The dreamkeepers: Successful teachers of African American children*. San Francisco: Jossey Bass.

McCaslin, M., & Good, T. (1996). *Listening to students*. New York: Harper Collins.

Mehrens, W.A. (1998). Consequences of assessment: What is the evidence? *Education Policy Analysis Archives*, **13**(6). Retrieved from http://epaa.asu.edu/epaav6n13.html

Merrow, J. (2001). Undermining standards. *Phi Delta Kappan*, **82**(9), 652–659.

Morgan, N., & Saxton, J. (1991). *Teaching, questioning, and learning*. New York: Routledge.

Overton, T. (1996). *Assessment in special education: An applied approach*. Englewood Cliffs, NJ: Merrill.

Polloway, E.A., Epstein, M.H., Bursuck, W.D., Roderique, R.W., McConeghy, J.L., & Jayanthi, M. (1994). Classroom grading: A national survey of policies. *Remedial and Special Education*, **15**, 162–170.

Rist, R.C. (1977). On understanding the process of schooling: The contribution of labeling theory. In J. Karabel, & A.H. Halsey (Eds.), *Power and ideology in education*. New York: Oxford University Press.

Rosenthal, R. & Jacobson, L. (1968). *Pygmalion in the classroom: Teacher expectations and pupils' intellectual development*. New York: Holt.

Schrank, W. (1968). The labeling effect of ability grouping. *Journal of Educational Research*, **62**, 51–52.

Simon, B., & Willcocks, J. (Eds.) (1981) *Research and practice in the primary classroom*. London: Routledge & Kegan Paul.

Smith, M.L., & Rottenberg, C. (1991). Unintended consequences of external testing in elementary schools. *Educational Measurement: Issues and Practice*, **10**(4), 7–11.

Steele, C.M. (1997). A threat in the air: How stereotypes shape intellectual identity and performance. *American Psychologist*, **52**, 613–629.

Taylor, C., & Nolen, S., (1996). A contextualized approach to teaching students about assessment. *Educational Psychologist*, **37**, 77–88.

Terra Nova. (1997). Monterey, CA: CTB/McGraw Hill.

Tombari, M., & Borich, G. (1999). *Authentic assessment in the classroom*. Upper Saddle River, NJ: Prentice Hall.

Waller, W. (1967). *The sociology of teaching*. New York: Wiley.

Wiggins, G. (1992). Creating tests worth taking. *Educational Leadership*, **44**(8), 26–33.

Wiggins, G., & McTighe, J. (1998). *Understanding by design*. Alexandria, VA: Association for Supervision and Curriculum Development.

26
Alternative Assessment

CAROLINE GIPPS

Kingston University, UK

GORDON STOBART

Institute of Education, University of London, UK

> "When I use a word" Humpty Dumpty said ... "it means just what I choose it to mean" ... "The question is," said Alice, "whether you can make words mean so many different things." "The question is," said Humpty Dumpty, "which is to be master – that's all." (Lewis Carroll, *Alice Through the Looking Glass*)

Seeking an agreed definition of "alternative assessment" has a Lewis Carroll feel to it. It is an umbrella term which shelters any alternatives to standardized multiple-choice testing (Oosterhof, 1996; Salvia & Ysseldyke, 1998); alternative, usually Information Technology (IT)-based, ways of testing (Bennett 1998; Klein & Hamilton, 1999); and, an alternative approach which makes assessment an integral part of the teaching and learning process (Shepard, 2000) and in which the focus is more directly on "performance" (Kane, Crooks, & Cohen, 1999).

Exercising our right to be master of the term, we shall use it essentially in relation to the last of these, that is, assessment which is seen as an integral part of teaching, and is designed to assess performance. The emphasis is on a "close similarity between the type of performance that is actually observed and the type of performance that is of interest" (Kane et al., 1999, p. 7). Within this approach sit a number of further categories which, following Shepard and Bleim (1995), we will treat as equivalent: "We use the terms *performance assessments*, *authentic assessments* and *direct assessments* interchangeably, the idea being to judge what students can do in terms of the actual tasks and end performances that are the goals of instruction" (p. 25). While this approach may not satisfy all (see Wiggins, 1989), it provides us with a broad base from which to work.

We argue that this approach reflects a paradigm shift from psychometric and measurement models to a model in which assessment is an integral part of the learning process ("assessment *for* learning") (Stobart & Gipps, 1997) and so is not restricted to summative purposes (Shepard, 2000). Of course psychometric

International Handbook of Educational Evaluation, 549–576
T. Kellaghan, D.L. Stufflebeam (eds.)
© *2003 Dordrecht: Kluwer Academic Publishers. Printed in Great Britain.*

tests can be used to support learning, but our concern is with assessments that are an essential part of the teaching/learning process. In this view, a close relationship between the assessment task and the goals of instruction is considered central to assessment. It also views learning as a process in which the learner actively constructs meaning and whose participation in the assessment process reflects an appreciation of the standard of performance required and the need for self-monitoring in learning (Sadler, 1989).

The chapter begins with a review of some of the assumptions underlying alternative assessment. The approach is located within the paradigm of educational assessment which is contrasted with the dominant psychometric model. Some of the key features of educational assessment are discussed: underlying constructivist views of learning, the use of tools and assistance in the assessment process, and the use of processes such as self-evaluation and feedback to enhance learning. These are developed at some length because we believe that they illustrate our assertion that *alternative assessment is not simply the use of alternative forms of assessment but is also an alternative use of assessment as part of the learning process*. This leads on to a brief treatment of the forms that alternative assessments may take, with particular reference to performance and portfolio assessments. We then look at the uses to which alternative assessments are being put. Originally, their primary use was as a means of reforming curriculum and instruction (Pellegrino, Baxter, & Glaser, 1999). They are widely used at classroom level where there is robust support for validity (Frederikson & Collins, 1989; Linn, Baker & Dunbar, 1991; Moss, 1992; Newmann, 1990). We tackle the more problematic area of use in large-scale high-stakes systems where the issue of reliability is central. Following that, the use of types of alternative assessment at state and national level is described, drawing on examples from the U.S.A., Australia, and the United Kingdom. We conclude by discussing the role of alternative assessment in systems in which accountability is one of the key functions of assessment and propose ways forward.

ASSESSMENT PARADIGMS AND APPROACHES

Assessment has traditionally been seen as something done to learners in order to grade/certificate, select, and report on them. Within the paradigm of psychometrics this is treated as an essentially quantitative activity. Tests based on psychometric theory have as a prime requirement measurement properties amenable to statistical analysis; reliability and norm-referencing are the prime concerns. This has profound implications for the style of task assessed, the limited ways in which tasks can be explained to students, and a lack of interaction with the tester. A critique of the traditional psychometric approach can be found in Gipps (1994a). For the purposes of this chapter key issues are that, in the psychometric model, the focus on reliability requires the standardization of administration and tasks as well as of scoring, while scoring is based mainly on norm-referencing.

Glaser (1963) championed criterion-referenced testing, heralding a move away from norm referencing. He made the point that the preoccupation of psychometrics with norms and norm-referenced testing stemmed from the focus of test theory on aptitude, selection, and prediction. An individual's performance was reported in relation to that of his/her peers, so that performance was seen in relative, rather than in absolute terms. Since students cannot control the performance of other students they cannot control their own grades.

In contrast, educational assessment deals with the individual's achievement relative to him or herself rather than to others; seeks to test for competence rather than for intelligence; takes place in relatively uncontrolled conditions and so does not produce well-behaved data; looks for best rather than typical performances; is most effective when rules and regulations characteristic of standardized testing are relaxed; and embodies a constructive outlook on assessment, where the aim is to help rather than sentence the individual (Wood, 1986).

The term competence refers to the product of education, training, or other experience, rather than an inborn or natural characteristic such as intelligence. We could more comfortably now use the term "achievement." Wood (1986) argues that a powerful reason why educational measurement should not be based on psychometric theory is that "achievement data arise as a direct result of instruction and are therefore crucially affected by teaching and teachers" (p.190). Aptitude and intelligence, by contrast, are traits which are unaffected by such factors. Achievement data are therefore "dirty" compared with aptitude data and should not/cannot be analysed using models which do not allow for some sort of teaching effect.

Goldstein (1994) also argues that we need to stop seeing testing as a static activity which has no effect on the student. On the contrary, the student is participating in a learning procedure while being tested, and his or her state will be altered at the end of it. For example, successfully completing early items in a test might boost confidence and result in a higher overall performance than failing, or being unable to complete, early items. Thus we need a more interactive model of assessment which does not assume that an individual's ability to respond to items remains constant during the test. The more "authentic" the assessment becomes, the more important it is to question the assumption that nothing happens to the student during the process of assessment.

The last 20 years have seen significant developments in this type of assessment. The resulting open-ended, realistic assessment tasks, collections of pieces of student work (done under more or less controlled conditions), in-depth projects, and informal assessment in the classroom with regular feedback to the student, are all "alternative" assessments designed to support the learning process, although they can be used to grade, select, and report. These approaches rely on human judgment of complex performance in marking. They often involve discussion between teacher and students about the task and about the assessment criteria or expected performance, and thus fall outside the traditional notion of the external examination/assessment. Furthermore, assessment in this view is something done *with* the student rather than *to* the student. The distinction can be summed up as "assessment *for* learning" as opposed to "assessment *of* learning" (Stobart & Gipps, 1997).

The key differences between traditional and alternative approaches to assessment are based in the conceptions of learning that underlie them, and in the perceived relationship between learning and assessment. What we believe about learning will affect our approach to assessment. Thus, statistical models used in early psychometrics were based on beliefs about fixed "innate ability" (Gould, 1996); multiple-choice standardized tests were readily adopted by behaviorist views of "knowledge in pieces" (Mislevy, 1993). Alternative approaches to assessment, on the other hand, based on (broadly) cognitive and constructivist models of learning (Shepard, 2000) require some considerable rethinking of how we assess (Gipps, 1999; Moss, 1996).

Along with new conceptions of learning, the drive to develop alternative models of assessment received support from the fact that traditional types of test (multiple-choice standardized tests in the U.S. and formal written examinations in the U.K.) have had unintended and negative effects on teaching and on the curriculum (Kellaghan, Madaus, & Raczek, 1996; Linn, 2000; Madaus, 1988). The stultifying effect of public examinations on the secondary school system in England has been pointed out by school inspectors (HMI, 1979, 1988) and was a major consideration in the shift towards the new examination at age 16 (General Certificate of Secondary Education) with its increased emphasis on a broader range of skills, a lessening of emphasis on the timed examination, and an opening up of the examination to a broader section of the age cohort. The limiting and damaging effect of standardized multiple-choice tests in the U.S.A. has also been well documented and analysed (e.g., Linn, 2000; Resnick & Resnick, 1992). "Under intense political pressure, test scores are likely to go up without a corresponding improvement in student learning. In fact, distortions in what and how students are taught may actually decrease students' conceptual understanding" (Shepard, 2000, p.13).

Because of the distorting effects of traditional types of assessment, particularly when used for high stakes and accountability purposes (Kellaghan et al., 1996; Madaus, 1988), attempts have been made to develop alternative accountability assessments, which aim to provide good quality information about students' performance without distorting good teaching practice and learning. However, Shepard (2000) again warns that recent experience in the U.S. shows that all assessment can be corrupted, undermining the belief that teaching to good tests would be an improvement on teaching "low-level basic skills curricula." Another problem in their development is that, of course, fairness demands that large-scale external accountability assessments are standardized in terms of content, administration, and timing. This means that it is particularly important to develop other forms of assessment to support learning that can be used alongside accountability assessment. There is, of course, a role for traditional examinations and standardized tests in assessment policy, but we need to look at the purpose of each assessment program (and the likely impact of testing), and then choose an assessment type that fits.

CONCEPTUAL FRAMEWORK AND ASSESSMENT IMPLICATIONS

In this section we consider some of the theoretical underpinnings of the educational assessment paradigm and how these generate alternative practices in the way teachers approach assessment. We use Shepard's framework and then review some practical implications: the use of "tools and assistance" within assessment and the role of processes such as self-evaluation and feedback in assessment *for* learning.

Shepard (2000) has developed a conceptual framework for new views of assessment based on cognitive and constructivist theories of learning. She summarizes the "new" view of learning in the following principles: (i) intellectual abilities are socially and culturally developed; (ii) learners construct knowledge and understandings within a social context; (iii) new learning is shaped by prior knowledge and cultural perspectives; (iv) intelligent thought involves "meta-cognition" or self-monitoring of learning and thinking; (v) deep understanding is principled and supports transfer; (vi) cognitive performance depends on dispositions and personal identity. Based on this framework, the following characteristics of classroom assessment can be identified. Classroom assessment (i) involves challenging tasks to elicit higher order thinking; (ii) addresses learning processes as well as learning outcomes; is an on-going process, integrated with instruction; (iii) is used formatively in support of student learning; (iv) makes expectations visible to students; (v) involves students actively in evaluating their own work; (vi) is used to evaluate teaching as well as student learning. These principles for classroom assessment also underpin the alternative assessment approach.

If in norm-referenced assessment students come to see themselves in terms of average or below average, rather than as having mastered certain aspects of mathematics or writing, this can be profoundly unhelpful for educational purposes (Crooks, 1988; Kluger, & DeNisi, 1996). Educational assessment is based on the understanding, developed from learning theory and the work of educators such as Bruner (1966) and Feuerstein (1979), that all children can learn, given the right input and motivation; and that achievement is not fixed, but is amenable to change through teaching. Educational assessment, therefore, is enabling in concept, and has a key role helping the individual to develop and to further his or her learning. This leads us, too, to the concept of looking for high or best performance in assessment rather than "standardized" performance. Looking for best performance by using assessments which elicit elaborated performance, or tests at the upper rather than lower thresholds of performance, has a good psychological pedigree, resonating with Vygotsky's (1978) *zone of proximal development*. In this process, assessor and student collaborate to produce the *best* performance of which the student is capable, given help from an adult, rather than withholding such help to produce *typical* performance, which is what happens in examinations. Such collaboration is done in teaching, and can be done in assessment.

THE USE OF TOOLS AND ASSISTANCE IN ALTERNATIVE ASSESSMENT

An important aspect of encouraging best performance is the use of tools and assistance in the assessment process. Vygotsky (1978) pointed to the importance of tools and aids in human action and hence also in learning. The use and internalization/appropriation of external supports is a key element in his account of the development of mental functions. However, assessment in the traditional examination and the psychometric model denies the student the use of external tools, thus reducing its usefulness and ecological validity. If we follow Vygotsky's ideas, we would develop assessment which allows the use of auxiliary tools (including adult support) to produce best rather than typical performance. Since such assessment is interactive it may be termed dynamic assessment. As Lunt (1994) explains:

> Dynamic assessment procedures ... involve a dynamic interactional exploration of a learner's learning and thinking process and aim to investigate a learner's strategies for learning and ways in which these may be extended or enhanced. Since it offers individuals an opportunity to learn, dynamic assessment has the potential to show important information about individual strategies and processes of learning and, therefore, to offer potentially useful suggestions about teaching. (p. 152)

However, even in dynamic assessment, help is at some point withheld, and an evaluation of unassisted performance made. As Newman, Griffin, and Cole (1989) put it:

> Dynamic assessment, then, shares a feature in common with the traditional testing method of assessment in that it requires putting the child "on her own." Support has to be removed until the child begins to falter. One difference between the two approaches lies in the fact that dynamic assessment achieves a finer-grained idea of the child's level of "independent ability." (p. 79)

An example of an interactive assessment approach that elicited best performance is to be found in the National Assessment program in England. In its early stages, the program required students to be assessed across the full range of the National Curriculum using external tests and teachers' own assessments. The tests were originally called Standard Assessment Tasks (SATs) and the teachers' assessments were called Teacher Assessment (TA). The SATs used in 1991 and 1992 involved performance, which was assessed in classroom-based, externally set, but teacher-assessed activities and tasks. For example, at age seven, reading was assessed by having the child read aloud a short passage from a children's book chosen from a list of popular titles. At age 14, there were extended investigative projects in mathematics and science, and assessments based on classroom work in English. What these tasks had in common across both ages, in addition to the performance element, was administration in the classroom, rather than a formal examination; interaction between teacher and student with ample opportunity to explain the task; and, at age seven, a reduced emphasis on written response.

An important point emerged from evaluation studies, at both age 7 and 14 (Gipps, 1992; SEAC, 1991). The SAT, with its emphasis on active, multi-mode assessment and detailed interaction between teacher and student, appeared to offer a good opportunity for children, particularly those from minority groups and those with special needs, to demonstrate what they knew and could do. In other words, they elicited best performance. The key aspects of the assessment seemed to involve: a range of activities, offering a wide opportunity to perform; match to classroom practice; extended interaction between student and teacher to explain the task; a normal classroom setting which therefore was not unduly threatening; and a range of response modes other than written.

The emphasis on non-standardized administration and classroom setting however, limited the reliability of the assessments. Considerable variation was found in administration, not only across teachers, but also between administrations by the same teacher (Gipps, 1994b). This finding reflects the inevitable tension between eliciting best performance, which may involve different treatment for different students, and reliability (and fairness) through standardization, in which all students are treated alike. Unfortunately, as well as giving rise to concern about reliability, the SATs were considered to be unacceptably time-consuming for national accountability assessment. This is a theme to which we return later. On the other hand, they were very useful tools for teacher's classroom based and formative assessment and for developing teachers' skills in these.

Interaction between student and assessor, such as in clinical interviews or in think-aloud protocols, is a way of providing assistance, as well as gaining insight into students' understanding, and is a key feature of dynamic assessment.

> Individual interviews [also] make it possible to conduct "dynamic assessments" that test, (and thereby extend) what a student can do with adult support. In these interactions a teacher-clinician is not merely collecting data but is gathering information and acting on it at the same time, thus completely blurring the boundaries between assessment and instruction. Clinical interviews, like a good teacher, require that teachers be knowledgeable about underlying developmental continua. (Shepard, 2000, p. 32)

As the work on the English SATs for 7-year-olds showed, interviews with small groups of students (though time-consuming and demanding) were highly effective in developing teachers' knowledge and understanding of both in-depth assessment and the children's learning in the subject areas (Gipps, Brown, McCallum, & McAlister, 1995).

There are some useful examples of the dynamic use of diagnostic assessments in the assessment of young children. A variety of approaches involving both observation and interview are used in the assessment of reading (Raban, 1983). Informal reading inventories have been developed which help teachers to assess the skills that students have mastered. These inventories can include checklists to assess attitudes to reading, checklists of examples to assess phonic skills (e.g., knowledge of initial and final letters), lists of books read by the student, activities to assess comprehension, and "miscue" techniques for analysing reading aloud. To assess comprehension, teachers will often ask questions after the student has read aloud about the content of the story, or about what may happen next, while the "running record" (Clay, 1985) uses a notation system to record miscues during reading aloud. Miscue analysis is essentially a formalized structure for assessment while hearing children read, a device which primary schools tradi- tionally use in the teaching of reading. When miscue analysis is used, reading aloud develops from a practice activity to a more diagnostic one. The teacher has a list of the most common errors children make, with a set of probable causes. By noticing and recording in a systematic way the child's errors and analysing the possible causes, teachers can correct misunderstandings, help the child develop appropriate strategies and reinforce skills. In other words miscue analysis is essentially an informal diagnostic assessment.

Building on these approaches in England, the Primary Language Record was developed in the late 1980s by teachers and researchers. This is a detailed recording and observation document which is filled in at several points during the school year to provide information that can inform teaching. Thus, it is designed as a formative assessment rather than as an administrative record. The assessment includes, indeed begins with, the parent's comments about the child's speech, writing, and reading activities. There is also a section for recording the child's view of him/herself as a reader, writer, and language user. A "conference" between teacher and child encourages the child to begin the process of self- assessment, something which is a key feature of profiles and records of achieve- ment. The reading assessment is about as different from a standardized reading test as it is possible to be: it is based on teacher assessment and it requires predominantly a written account of the child's interest in reading, enjoyment, strategies, difficulties, etc. This was quite a forward-looking approach to alternative assessment, involving as it did discussion between teacher and student, collection of samples of work, self-assessment, etc.

PROCESSES IN ALTERNATIVE ASSESSMENT

As well as considering the use of tools and assistance in alternative assessment, we need to consider the processes which contribute to this approach. We shall discuss self-evaluation and feedback since these lead us to an essential recon- sideration of the teacher-learner assessment relationship. The key assumption is that the learner is an active participant in the assessment process. Rather than assessment criteria and standards being the exclusive "guild knowledge" of the teacher (Sadler, 1989), the assumption is that they are shared with the learners who progressively take more control over their learning.

Self-Evaluation

Developing self-evaluation or self-assessment skills is important to help learners enhance their metacognitive skills. Metacognition is a general term which refers to a second-order form of thinking: thinking about thinking. It includes a variety of self-awareness processes to help plan, monitor, orchestrate, and control one's own learning. To do this, learners use particular strategies which hinge on self-questioning to make the purpose of learning clear, searching for connections and conflicts with what is already known, and judging whether understanding of material is sufficient for the task. An essential aspect of metacognition is that students appraise and regulate their own learning by self-assessment or self-evaluation. If students are to become self-monitoring and self-regulating learners (Broadfoot, 1996; Wittrock & Baker, 1991; Wolf, Bixby, Glenn, & Gardner, 1991), they will need sustained experience in ways of questioning and of improving the quality of their work, as well as supported experience in self-assessment, which includes understanding the standards expected of them and the criteria on which they will be assessed (Black & Wiliam, 1998; Sadler, 1989). Sadler (1998) also points out that:

> Ultimately the intention of most educational systems is to help students not only grow in knowledge and expertise, but also to become progressively independent of the teacher for lifelong learning. Hence if teacher-supplied feedback is to give way to self-assessment and self-monitoring, some of what the teacher brings to the assessment act must itself become part of the curriculum for the student, not an accidental or inconsequential adjunct to it. (p. 82).

Teachers commonly bring with them to the assessment setting an elaborate and extensive knowledge base, dispositions towards teaching as an activity, and sophisticated assessment skills. This expertise, particularly the criteria, appropriate standards, and how to make evaluative judgments, should be shared with students. Feedback can assist in this.

Feedback

Feedback from teacher to student is the process that embeds assessment in the teaching and learning cycle (Black & Wiliam, 1998; Crooks, 1988; Gipps, McCallum, & Hargreaves, 2000). It is a key aspect of assessment for learning and of formative assessment in particular. Formative assessment is the process of appraising, judging, or evaluating students' work or performance, and using this to shape and improve their competence. Sadler's (1989) detailed discussion of the nature of qualitative assessment gives feedback a crucial role in learning; he identifies the way in which it should be used by teachers to unpack the notion of excellence, so that students are able to acquire understanding of standards for themselves to help them become self-evaluating.

Research by Tunstall and Gipps (1996) to describe and classify feedback from teachers to young pupils suggests that it can be categorized as evaluative or descriptive. Evaluative feedback is judgmental, with implicit or explicit use of norms. Descriptive feedback is task-related, and makes specific reference to the child's actual achievement or competence. Two types of descriptive feedback were identified. One, *"specifying attainment and improvement,"* adopts a mastery-oriented approach. It involves teachers' acknowledgement of specific achievements, the use of models by teachers for work and behavior, diagnosis using specific criteria, and correcting or checking procedures. The other, which is labelled *"constructing achievement and the way forward,"* involves teachers' use of both sharp and "fuzzy" criteria, teacher-child joint assessment of work, discussion of the way forward, and the use of strategies for self-regulation of learning.

Teachers using the *"specifying"* forms of feedback are providing clarity but essentially retaining control of the pedagogical act. When teachers use the *"constructing"* forms of feedback, on the other hand, they are helping learners to develop self-evaluation and self-monitoring skills. In other words, they are sharing responsibility for assessment and learning with the students. Where the teacher and student are discussing or *"constructing"* achievement or improvement mutually, the student's role is integral to the feedback process itself. The student is being encouraged and supported in making a self-assessment or self-evaluation by reflecting on his or her performance in relation to the standard expected (and indicated by the teacher), and by thinking about how performance can improve. This end of the feedback spectrum therefore involves the use of metacognitive strategies, whereby students monitor or regulate their own learning. They are now supported by the teacher, but not dependent on her, in deciding on the value of a performance and how it could improve (Gipps et al., 2000). Teachers' use of this type of feedback shifts the emphasis to the students' own role in learning, using approaches which pass control to the student. The teacher becomes more "facilitator" than "provider" or "judge": teacher *with* the student, rather than *to* the student is the focus.

This research on feedback clearly indicated that teachers were developing children's self-evaluation skills even at ages 6 and 7. Although it may seem unlikely that children as young as this can engage in such sophisticated learning activity, it may actually be easier at this stage when students have had only limited exposure to the (traditional) didactic relationship.

The relationship between teachers and learner is a key issue in the school setting; teachers are experts and students are novices or apprentices. The relationship between them is crucial to the learning process, and can be constructed in a number of ways. In traditional assessment, it is hierarchical. The teacher sets and defines the task and determines how performance should be evaluated; the student's role is to be the object of this activity and, through the completion of tasks and tests, to be graded. However, there are other ways of seeing the relationship. In forms of assessment such as negotiated assessment in profiling and self-assessment, the student has a role in discussing and negotiating the terms and outcomes of the assessment. The hierarchical nature of the relationship between expert and apprentice is diminished by allotting the learner a more active role in which she or he is afforded responsibility and involvement in the assessment activity (Perrenoud, 1991; Taylor, Fraser, & Fisher, 1997; Torrance & Pryor, 1998). However, for many teachers and indeed for some students, developing a more equal or open relationship is not easy. The traditional hierarchical teacher-student relationship is deeply ingrained in many cultures. In an early evaluation of Records of Achievement in the U.K., a profiling, portfolio, scheme which involved student self-assessment and negotiation of target setting, Broadfoot, James, McMeeking, Nuttal, and Stierer (1988) found that secondary-school students viewed self-assessment as difficult, partly because they were not used to it, and partly because the assessment criteria were unclear. Students' perceptions of teacher expectations, their views on what was socially acceptable, and their anxiety not to lose face affected their self-evaluation. Furthermore, there were differences in relation to gender and ethnic group in approach to self-assessment and "negotiation" with teachers. Boys were more likely to challenge a teacher's assessment and to have a keen sense of the audience for the final record, while girls tended to enter into a discussion and to negotiate more fully.

So, it would appear that if student self-assessment is to be empowering, considerable development will be required of teachers, as well as preparation of students. Teachers will need to take a back seat rather than driving and controlling the process, and not only make the new ground rules clear to students, but also to persuade them that their evaluation is valued. For much younger students, although the ground rules need to be clear, there will be less need to modify students' experience and understanding of their traditional role vis-à-vis the teacher.

There is a lesson for alternative assessment here: Changing well-established practice will take time, for students as well as for teachers. Indeed, students can be quite traditional. If they are used to particular classroom practices (e.g., the teacher telling them how good/bad a piece of work is, what they should do to improve it, the use of multiple-choice items), they may well resist the change to other approaches. In a study of the use of alternative assessment in California, Herman, Klein, and Wakai (1997) found that while students could see that open-ended tasks were more interesting and challenging, and they had to (and did) try harder on them than on multiple-choice tests, they did not necessarily like this. The students understood that they had to adopt different thinking and answering strategies in open-ended items, but they found multiple-choice items easier to understand, believed that they were better at them, and (perhaps not surprisingly) preferred them.

A similar, changed relationship, which results from particular views of learning and assessment, is inherent in the model of the classroom as a learning community. In Bruner's (1996) view we should see the classroom as a community:

> of mutual learners, with the teacher orchestrating the proceedings. Note that, contrary to traditional critics, such sub-communities do not reduce the teacher's role nor his or her "authority." Rather, the teacher takes on the additional functions of encouraging others to share it. (pp. 21–22)

The teacher's role, rather than being diminished by sharing responsibility for assessment with the student, is augmented.

FORMS OF ALTERNATIVE ASSESSMENT

We have already provided examples of some of the forms that alternative assessment may take, for example, the "dynamic" use of diagnostic reading tasks and the self-assessment encouraged in records of achievement. In this section we review some of the forms more commonly identified with alternative assessment: performance assessments and portfolios. At the heart of these alternative forms is the recognition that a wider range of strategies is needed to assess a broader body of cognitive aspects than mere subject-matter acquisition and retention. Glaser (1990) considers some of these forms: portfolios of accomplishments; situations which elicit problem-solving behavior which can be observed and analysed; and dynamic tests that assess responsiveness of students to various kinds of instruction (see Feuerstein, 1979; Vygotsky, 1978).

Glaser's point is that assessment must offer "executable advice" to both students and teachers. To do this, the assessments must themselves be useful and must focus on the student's ability to use the knowledge and skills learnt. Knowledge must be assessed in terms of its constructive use for further action.

Performance Assessment

The aim of performance assessments is to model the real learning activities that we wish students to engage with (e.g., oral and written communication skills, problem solving activities) rather than to fragment them, as happens in multiple-choice tests (Kane et al., 1999; Linn et al., 1991; Shepard & Bleim, 1995). In the United States, performance assessment may include portfolio assessment and what in Britain is called classroom assessment or teacher assessment (teachers' assessment of students' performance).

We have not sought to distinguish performance assessment from authentic assessment. We treat authentic assessment as performance assessment carried out in an authentic context (i.e., it is produced in the classroom as part of normal work, rather than as a specific task for assessment). While not all performance assessments are authentic, it is difficult to imagine an authentic assessment that would not also be a performance assessment; thus performance assessment incorporates authentic assessment. Meyer (1992) suggests that in using the term "authentic assessment" the respects in which the assessment is authentic should be specified: the stimulus, task complexity, locus of control, motivation, spontaneity, resources, conditions, criteria, standards, and consequences.

Educational measurement specialists were writing about performance assessment as early as the 1950s (Stiggins & Bridgeford, 1982), and an evaluation of this early work led to a working definition:

> Performance assessment is defined as a systematic attempt to measure a learner's ability to use previously acquired knowledge in solving novel problems or completing specific tasks. In performance assessment, real life or simulated assessment exercises are used to elicit original responses which are directly observed and rated by a qualified judge. (p. 1)

Today, there is general agreement that "performance measurement calls for examinees to demonstrate their capabilities directly, by creating some product or engaging in some activity" (Haertel, 1992), and that there is heavy reliance on observation and/or professional judgment in the evaluation of the response (Mehrens, 1992).

Early developments of performance assessments in the United States were directed towards the reform of curriculum and instruction, rather than accountability. The assessments differed from traditional tests in a number of ways.

> First, the development process was informed by multiple perspectives, including cognitive psychologists, teachers, and subject-matter and measurement specialists. Second, the tasks generally consisted of open-ended prompts or exercises requiring students to write explanations, carry out a set of procedures, design investigations, or otherwise reason with targeted subject matter. Third, innovative multilevel scoring criteria or rubrics that gave consideration to procedures, strategies, and quality of response were favored over right/wrong scoring. Not surprisingly, given the state of the art, psychometric properties, particularly reliability, were of primary concern, as were practical considerations such as the time and cost of administration and scoring. (Pellegrino et al., 1999, p. 321)

In this work concern was expressed about generalizability of performance across tasks and about the cost and practicalities of designing, scoring, and administering the new forms of assessment. Further, the developments had minimal impact on instruction, and tasks did not necessarily measure higher level cognitive skills as had been anticipated. While the latter weakness was the result of inadequate technical and theoretical development, the limited impact was due to the large-scale nature of the testing which meant that the assessment activity was separated from instructional opportunity. However, experience in the United Kingdom, particularly in the case of science in the primary school, is that if large-scale testing is associated with high stakes and a mandated curriculum, then teachers do change their practice (Stobart & Gipps, 1997).

The next move in alternative assessment in the U.S. was to develop assessment that is integrated with classroom practice. The hallmark of this development was

> a focus on knowledge-rich domains, an emphasis on the development of conceptual understanding in a domain, and a view that assessment development should stem from an analysis of the various ways in which students conceptualize or explain situations or events. That is, an understanding of knowledge development in the domain serves as the guide for developing instruction and assessment. The assessment, in turn, provides feedback on instruction by calling attention to levels of student understanding at various times and in various contexts. Explicit attention to the iterative nature of teaching, learning, and assessment is the hallmark of the approaches ... (Pellegrino et al., 1999, p. 326)

It is crucial in these classroom-based formative assessment strategies that student understandings be carefully probed and analysed to facilitate student-specific adjustments to the "learning environment," thus influencing their learning trajectory.

Pellegrino et al. (1999) also describe assessment which is built into extended problem-based and project-based learning in mathematics and science. The SMART (Scientific and Mathematical Arenas for Refining Thinking) model provides opportunities for formative assessment and includes an emphasis on self-assessment to help students and teachers develop the ability to monitor their own understanding (Brown, Bransford, Ferrara, & Campione, 1983; Stiggins, 1994). The model involves the explicit design of multiple cycles of problem solving, self-assessment, and revision in an overall problem-based learning environment.

The range of problem-based projects is made up of activity modules. Within each module, selection, feedback, and revision make use of the SMART Website, which supports three high-level functions. First, it provides individualized feedback to students and serves as a formative evaluation tool. The feedback not only suggests aspects of students' work that are in need of revision, but also classroom resources that students can use to help them revise. The feedback does not tell students the "right answer," but rather it sets a course for independent inquiry by the student. The second function of the SMART Website is to collect, organize, and display the data collected from multiple distributed classrooms ("SMART Lab"). Displays allow the teacher and his or her class to discuss a variety of solution strategies. The third section of the SMART Website consists of explanations by student-actors ("Kids Online"). The explanations are text based with audio narration, and, by design, include errors. Students are asked to critically evaluate the explanations and provide feedback to the student-actor. The errors seed thinking and discussion on concepts that are frequently misconceived by students. At the same time, students are learning important critical evaluation skills (Pellegrino et al., 1999).

Evaluation findings indicate that students who use these resources and tools learn more than students who have gone through the same instructional sequence for the same amount of time without the benefit of the tools or of formative assessment. What is more, their performance in other project-based learning activity is enhanced. As the earlier section on self-evaluation and feedback makes clear this enhanced outcome would indeed be anticipated by the literature on metacognition and formative assessment.

Portfolios

At one level, portfolios may be regarded simply as collections of pieces of student work which are kept as a record. However, these collections can also be used as a basis for assessment, and so portfolios are often described as a method of assessment.

> A portfolio used for assessment and learning purposes involves documentation of achievements, self-evaluation, process artefacts and analyses of learning experiences. It is therefore significantly more than a collection of assignments. (Klenowski, 2000, p. 219)

Using collections of student work for assessment allows a wide range of approaches to marking, from traditional marks and grades assigned by teachers, through detailed written comments by teachers (with no grades), teacher-student discussion, and negotiation of the assessment to student self-evaluation. As with other forms of alternative assessment, the proponents of portfolio assessment present a rationale based on the enhancement of learning. First, assessment that celebrates achievement on an ipsative or criterion-referenced basis builds students' confidence and ultimately enhances their performance, which may be contrasted with the situation in which assessment draws attention to failure through the use of grades and marks, particularly when norm-referenced. Second, learning is enhanced if students understand clearly what they are trying to achieve, and are provided with personal and substantive feedback in trying to reach their target. Third, collecting, sorting, and annotating evidence to demonstrate achievement in the form of a portfolio of work is a valuable aid in developing the skills of self-evaluation, as well as for communicating standards in a relatively unambiguous and accessible way (Broadfoot, 1998). If portfolio assessment is to achieve the goal of enhancing learning, a number of principles need to be incorporated. These are: portfolio assessment involves a new perspective on learning in which the student is actively engaged in the learning process; it is a developmental process and the portfolio demonstrates growth; self-evaluation is an integral part of the process; the student must collect, select, and reflect on work; and the teacher's role as a facilitator is vital (Klenowski, 2000).

Conscious of the importance of portfolio assessment for supporting learning, its developers recommend the following procedures and practices:

- An increased use of evidence in the form of portfolios for formative purposes, to stimulate student reflection, to enhance summative communication, and as a base for setting standards;
- An increased emphasis on comprehensive descriptive recording rather than the use of grade and marks;
- An increased emphasis on teacher assessment in recognition that only the teacher can access students' performance on some of the most significant competencies;
- A growing involvement of students themselves in the preparation of portfolios in recognition of the power of assessment to inhibit or enhance student motivation. (Wolf & Koretz, 1998, p. 303.)

THE USE OF ALTERNATIVE ASSESSMENT

The account so far has focused largely on the use of alternative assessment to improve the quality of students' learning. We now address the issues raised when alternative assessments are incorporated into large-scale assessment systems, where they are used for accountability purposes.

Before considering the validity of alternative assessments, we will summarize current thinking on validity, which incorporates "reliability" and "equity." While recognizing that alternative assessments are subject to the same basic considerations as more conventional assessments (Messick, 1994), we take the view that there is a legitimate debate about whether increased validity in terms of "authenticity" (Newmann, 1990), "cognitive complexity" (Linn et al., 1991) or "directness" (Frederickson & Collins, 1989) can provide a challenge to the narrowness of standard applications of validity and reliability (Moss, 1992). We are confident that this challenge is effective when the uses and consequences of alternative assessment relate to the improvement of learning in the classroom. However, when used in large-scale, particularly high-stakes programs, the consequences of assessment differ, and are more problematic. In the same way that alternative assessments may have particular strengths, they may also have particular weaknesses in terms of generalizability (Kane et al., 1999).[1]

Current thinking treats validity as an integrated concept, organized around a broader view of construct validity (Shepard, 1993) and regards it is a property of test scores rather than of the test itself. As early as 1985, the American *Standards for Educational and Psychological Testing* were explicit about this: "validity always refers to the degree to which ... evidence supports the inferences that are made from the scores" (AERA, APA, NCME, 1985, p. 9). This unitary approach to validity also subsumes considerations about reliability which has traditionally been treated as a separate construct. Confidence in inferences must include confidence in the results themselves which inconsistencies in administration, marking, or grading will undermine.

More recent debate has focused on whether the concept of validity should also include the consequences of an assessment. Messick's (1989) view was that it should.

> For a fully unified view of validity, it must also be recognized that the appropriateness, meaningfulness, and usefulness of score-based inferences depend as well on the social consequences of the testing. Therefore, social values and social consequences cannot be ignored in considerations of validity. (p. 19)

While there is support for this position in both America (Linn, 1997; Shepard, 1997) and in England (Gipps, 1994a; Wiliam, 1993), it has been challenged by those who regard it as "a step too far." Critics such as Popham (1997) and Mehrens (1997) argue that while the impact of test use should be evaluated, this should be kept separate from validity arguments. "The attempt to make the social consequences of test use an aspect of validity introduces unnecessary confusion into what is meant by measurement validity" (Popham, 1997, p. 13). Part of Popham's concern is that the test developer would be responsible for what others do with test results. His claim that this approach will "deflect us from the clarity we need when judging tests *and* the consequences of test use" (Popham, 1997, p. 9) merits attention. What is important here is the emphasis on uses and consequences.

The Validity of Alternative Assessment

Messick (1994) has raised the issue of whether performance assessments should "adhere to general validity standards addressing content, substantive, structural, external, generalizability and consequential aspects of construct validity" (p. 13). His position is that they should. "These general validity criteria can be specialized for apt application to performance assessments, if need be, but none should be ignored" (p. 22). However, alternative assessment gives rise to a variety of problems that cannot be easily accommodated within conventional interpretations of validity and reliability. For example, students may be permitted "substantial latitude in interpreting, responding to, and perhaps designing tasks"; further, "alternative assessments result in fewer independent responses, each of which is complex, reflecting integration of multiple skills and knowledge; and they require expert judgment for evaluation" (Moss, 1992, p. 230). The dilemma is how much these "specialized" criteria can be used to offset limitations in terms of conventional requirements of reliability.

Moss (1994) has suggested that "by considering hermeneutic alternatives for serving the important epistemological and ethical purposes that reliability serves, we expand the range of viable high-stakes assessment practices to include those that honor the purposes that students bring to their work and the contextualized judgements of teachers" (p. 5). She draws telling examples from higher education to demonstrate alternative approaches: how we confer higher degrees, grant tenure, and make decisions about publishing articles. This approach is in line with Mishler's (1990) call to reformulate validation "as the social discourse through which trustworthiness is established," thus allowing us to see conventional approaches to reliability as particular ways of warranting validity claims, "rather than as universal, abstract guarantors of truth" (p. 420).

The importance of this line of argument lies in its challenge to narrow views of reliability which constrain what can be assessed and, therefore, what will be taught (Resnick & Resnick, 1992). Wolf et al., (1991) sum up this approach by suggesting that we need "to revise our notions of high-agreement reliability as a cardinal symptom of a useful and viable approach to scoring student performance" and "seek other sorts of evidence that responsible judgment is unfolding" (p. 63). Wiliam (1992) has proposed the concepts of *disclosure* ("the extent to which an assessment produces evidence of attainment from an individual in the area being assessed") and *fidelity* ("the extent to which evidence of attainment that has been disclosed is recorded faithfully") as an alternative way of thinking about the reliability of assessment of performance (p. 13).

Advocates of alternative assessment make other "specialized" claims which reflect the stronger validity argument that the directness of the relationship between assessment and the goals of instruction implies. For example, there is the appeal to "directness" and "systemic validity" by Fredericksen & Collins (1989), to "authenticity" by Newmann (1990), and to "cognitive complexity" by Linn et al. (1991).

The dilemma is whether such strengths can compensate for weakness in relation to other aspects of validity. Kane et al. (1999) make the case that any validity argument has to focus on the weakest link, as this is where validity will break down. For example, in multiple-choice tests, a key weakness is that of extrapolation from results to interpretation – a link that is often neglected (Feldt & Brennan, 1989). Kane et al., (1999) argue that for "performance assessment, this rule of thumb argues for giving special attention to the generalizability of the results over raters, tasks, occasions, and so forth" (p. 15).

Put more simply, alternative assessments are particularly vulnerable to reliability problems relating to sampling, standardization, and scoring. The concern with sampling is that because high-fidelity tasks are often time-consuming, assessment will be based on a restricted number of performances. The consequence is that "generalization from the small sample of high-fidelity performances to a broadly defined universe of generalization may be quite undependable" (Kane et al., 1999, p. 11) – Messick's "construct under-representation." Concern with sampling error associated with a small number of tasks has been repeatedly raised (Brennan & Johnson, 1995; Mehrens, 1992; Swanson, Norman, & Linn, 1995). Shavelson, Baxter, and Pine (1992) concluded that "task-sampling variability is considerable. In order to estimate a student's achievements a substantial number of tasks may be needed" (p. 26). Shavelson, Baxter, and Gao (1993) estimated that between 10 and 23 tasks would be needed to achieve acceptable levels of reliability. Kane et al. (1999) provide some ideas on how this might be done, for example by requiring students to complete, for assessment purposes, only one part of a lengthy task.

It has been our experience in national assessment in England that marker reliability is what most concerns policymakers, particularly if the marker is the student's teacher. Interestingly, the unreliability related to raters' scoring of performance assessments is seen by technical experts as less of a problem than Task × Person interaction (Shavelson et al., 1992). This is in part because rater reliability is susceptible to rapid improvement where care is taken with the scoring system and raters are well-trained (Baker, 1992; Dunbar, Koretz, & Hoover, 1991; Shavelson et al., 1993). Improvement can be achieved by standardizing tasks and procedures (asking all students to take the same tasks under similar conditions) and by providing detailed scoring rubrics (Swanson et al., 1995). The dilemma is that increased standardization – and reliability – will be accompanied by "a shrinking of the universe of generalization relative to the target domain" (Kane et al., 1999, p. 12). The issue is how to strengthen scoring without weakening the sampling of the target domain.

Another approach to enhancing scorer reliability is moderation, which is used widely in national examination systems in which teachers' assessments of students contribute to the final grade (Broadfoot, 1994; Harlen, 1994; Pitman & Allen, 2000). Moderation comes in a number of forms, ranging from work with teachers prior to final assessment to increase consensus on marking standards (Gipps, 1994c) to statistical adjustment of marks by means of a reference test. In the United Kingdom, moderation often involves external moderators reviewing a sample of work from each school and deciding whether the marks need to be adjusted.

Equity is an important consideration in any type or form of assessment, and one of the advantages attributed to alternative approaches to assessment is that they can help redress inequities and biases in assessment (Garcia & Pearson, 1991). According to Wolf et al. (1991) "there is a considerable hope that new modes of assessment will provide one means for exposing the abilities of less traditionally skilled students by giving a place to world knowledge, social processes, and a great variety of excellence" (p. 60). Neill (1995) argues that performance assessment and evaluation of culturally sensitive classroom-based learning have the potential to foster multicultural inclusion and facilitate enhanced learning. Others are more cautious, pointing out the alternative assessment on its own will not resolve issues of equity. Consideration will still have to be given to students' opportunity to learn (Linn, 1993), the knowledge and language demands of tasks (Baker & O'Neill, 1995), and the criteria for scoring (Linn et al., 1991). Furthermore, the more informal and open-ended assessment becomes, the greater will be the reliance on the judgment of the teacher/assessor. Neither will alternative forms of assessment, of themselves, alter power relationships and cultural dominance in the classroom. However, what we can say is that a broadening of approaches to assessment will offer students alternative opportunities to demonstrate achievement if they are disadvantaged by any particular form of assessment. Linn (1993) makes the point that "multiple indicators are essential so that those who are disadvantaged on one assessment have an opportunity to offer alternative evidence of their expertise" (p. 44). The best defence against inequitable assessment is openness (Gipps & Murphy, 1994). Openness about design, constructs, and scoring, will reveal the values and biases of the test design process, offer an opportunity for debate about cultural and social influences, and open the relationship between assessor and learner.

In summary, strong validity claims may be made for alternative assessment when uses and consequences are linked to classroom instruction and student learning. When the purpose shifts to certification and accountability in large-scale systems, the arguments are harder to sustain. While there are ways of increasing the reliability of alternative assessments, the need to increase standardization may begin to undermine the fidelity of the tasks. Our involvement in national programs in England, where forms of alternative assessment have been used, has taught us that arguments on validity rarely win the day, since policymakers, who often see the primary purpose of an assessment system as one of managerial accountability, operate with conventional views of reliability (assessment must be "externally marked" with a single grade/mark outcome, and "scientific" levels of accuracy are expected). We now turn to some examples of alternative assessment in practice that exemplify these pressures and concerns.

ALTERNATIVE ASSESSMENT IN LARGE-SCALE ASSESSMENT SYSTEMS

Large-scale testing seeks to provide a relatively simple and reliable summary of what a student has learned in a particular subject or skill. Performance assessment by contrast is time-consuming, tends to provide detailed multidimensional information about a particular skill or area (and, because of the time factor, depth may be exchanged for breath); scoring is generally complex and usually involves the classroom teacher. Standardization of the performance is not possible (or even desired) and, as a consequence, reliability in the traditional sense is not high. All these features, which render performance assessment valuable for assessment to support learning, become problematic when it is to be used for accountability purposes (Frechtling, 1991).

We have selected three examples of the use of alternative assessments in large-scale assessment programs. The first is the use of portfolio assessment in Kentucky and Vermont, two well-documented and salutary experiments. The second, in England, incorporates portfolio assessment and coursework. The third is a "good news story" from the state of Queensland in Australia, which, for over 30 years, has relied on teacher assessment of student coursework as the primary means of assessment.

In the U.S.A., a number of states use portfolios locally and/or experimentally (notably California), while two states (Kentucky and Vermont) have used portfolio assessment on a large scale in the core subjects (Stecher, 1998). The national assessment program (National Assessment of Educational Progress) has also experimented with them. In a review of the American experience, Stecher concentrates on the two main state developments, which:

> share some common features. Assessment portfolios contain the diverse products of students' learning experiences, including written material (both drafts and final versions), pictures, graphs, computer programs, and other outcomes of student work. Portfolios are usually cumulative. They contain work completed over a period of weeks or months. Portfolios are embedded in instruction, i.e. entries are drawn from on-going schoolwork. As a result, portfolios are not standardized. Since assignments differ across teachers, so do collections of students' work. Moreover, within a single class students will choose different pieces to include in their portfolios. Portfolios also have a reflective component – either implicit in students' choices of work or explicit in a letter to the reviewer explaining the selection of materials. Finally, there is an external framework for scoring the portfolios that contain different contents. (p. 337)

Stecher concludes that the research on the introduction of portfolio assessment offers support for some of the positive claims about the effect of such assessment on teachers' attitudes and beliefs, and changes in curriculum and instruction.

In the Kentucky and Vermont portfolio schemes, results were used for accountability purposes and, thus, marker reliability became a focus, as well as how the results related to other test measures (Koretz, 1998). In Kentucky, in particular, there was a high-stakes accountability purpose introduced even in the pilot stages, with teachers' salaries being affected by the results (Callahan, 1997). When the assessments in both Vermont and Kentucky showed considerable unreliability (Koretz, 1998), policymakers began to move towards more conventional, and reliable, testing. Hill (2000), an insider on the Kentucky scheme, grimly concludes:

> most of the initial innovations in Kentucky's assessment system were abandoned. After seven years, the assessment system had deteriorated into a series of external, on-demand tests that were largely multiple-choice with some open responses questions thrown in. Worse, the idea that assessment should derive first from the information the teacher had already had been lost, and the notion that external tests should be telling teachers what to do and how to do it had gained support. (p. 4)

The evidence for reliability and generalizability from the state-wide portfolio programs (Koretz, 1998) suggests that this approach is generally not suitable for accountability assessment in the U.S.A. Anderson and Bachor (1998) echo this view on the basis of their experience in Canada, and see the portfolio as much more likely to be used for assessment at classroom level than at provincial level for accountability.

This is not the end of the story, however. There is good evidence that teachers have the capacity to contribute to high stakes assessment. In Germany, where teachers enjoy high professional status, there is virtually no external assessment in the school system (Broadfoot, 1994). In England, also, performance assessment plays an accepted part in high stakes assessment in three public examinations: the General Certificate of Secondary Education (GCSE), a subject specific examination taken by 16-year olds at the end of compulsory schooling, in which students typically take an examination in seven to nine subjects; the General Certificate of Education Advanced Level (GCE A-level), normally taken by 18-year olds in two or three subjects, and the basis of most university admissions; and the Vocational Certificate of Education Advanced Level (VCE A-level). Each incorporates, to varying degrees, an element of teacher assessment of students. Coursework may take the form of a project (e.g., a historical investigation, a geography field trip, a mathematics task), a portfolio of work (English, all VCEs), an oral examination (modern languages), or a performance (in drama, music, physical education). The weighting of the component will vary in terms of "fitness-for-purpose" though the maximum contribution to a student's overall grade has been politically determined, in the case of the GCSE by a surprise announcement by the then Prime Minister, John Major, of a ceiling of 25 percent (Stobart & Gipps, 1997), which has subsequently been relaxed. Typically marks for coursework in GCE A-levels contribute around 20–30 percent, and VCE A-levels nearer 70 percent. The point is that these performance assessments are an accepted part of the assessment culture. Concerns about reliability have been addressed by increased standardization of tasks and by providing exemplification and training to teachers. Coursework is seen as both motivating and providing a more valid assessment within a subject; for example, GCSE English includes the assessment by teachers of students' speaking and listening, as well as their reading and writing. Furthermore, there is a well-established system of moderation and checking in the GCSE and the GCE, though not yet in the VCE.

An even greater commitment to performance assessment is demonstrated in the Australian state of Queensland, which abolished examinations over 30 years ago and replaced them with criteria-based subject achievement assessments by teachers. The system involves extensive moderation by over 400 district review panels, composed mainly of teachers. These panels review samples of work across subjects and schools and provide advice to schools (Pitman & Allen, 2000). The process is seen as an effective form of professional development in assessment. The only external assessment is the Queensland Core Skills Test (cognitive skills based on the "common curriculum elements") which is taken by 17-year-olds. This, together with teacher assessment, provides the basis for entry to tertiary education.

It seems, therefore, that it is possible to use alternative assessment in large-scale programs, even for certification purposes, in some educational and cultural contexts. It is interesting to speculate on what the social and cultural conditions are that make these approaches possible. The professional status of the teacher and confidence in the school system (as in Germany) are no doubt important factors. An emphasis on accountability and selection is likely to deter such developments, as are legal challenges to the fairness of teachers' assessments. The role and power of test agencies may also play a part (Madaus & Raczek, 1996).

CONCLUSION

Alternative assessment differs from traditional assessment in many ways. It is not simply that the tasks are different and require the student to produce a response; it embodies a different concept of assessment (as an essential part of the learning process), new understandings of learning itself, and a different relationship between student and teacher/assessor. Alternative assessment does indeed come from, and require, a different way of thinking about assessment.

A number of approaches to alternative assessment were outlined in this chapter, examples were provided, and technical difficulties when such assessment is used in large-scale accountability programs discussed. More detailed accounts of technical issues can be found elsewhere (Baker, O'Neil & Linn, 1991; Pellegrino et al., 1999). Major challenges face test developers and classroom assessment researchers in developing alternative forms of assessment. The focus shifts from assessing of discrete, de-contextualized items in standardized conditions to the assessing of important constructs, and looking to elicit higher-order skills in real-life contexts. These must involve the student as a more active participant in his/her own learning, and its evaluation. While the approaches will make greater demands on student and teacher/assessor, they have the potential to support good curriculum and instructional approaches, as well as high quality learning.

ENDNOTE

[1] These, and other authors, prefer the term generalizability to reliability. This reflects concern with the use of findings. However generalizability is determined by the reliability of an assessment; unreliable measures limit it (Salvia & Ysseldyke, 1998).

REFERENCES

AERA, APA, NCME (American Educational Research Association, American Psychological Association, National Council on Measurement in Education). (1985). *Standards for educational and psychological testing*. Washington, DC: Authors.

Anderson, J.O., & Bachor, D.G. (1998). A Canadian perspective on portfolio use in student assessment. *Assessment in Education*, **5**, 353–380.

Baker, E. (1992). *The role of domain specifications in improving the technical quality of performance assessment*. Los Angeles: CRESST, University of California at Los Angeles.

Baker, E., & O'Neil, H. (1995). Diversity, assessment, and equity in educational reform. In M. Nettles & A. Nettles (Eds.), *Equity and excellence in educational testing and assessment* (pp. 69–87). Boston: Kluwer Academic.

Baker, E., O'Neil, H., & Linn R. (1991). *Policy and validity prospects for performance-based assessment*. Paper presented at annual meeting of the American Psychological Association, San Francisco.

Bennett, R. (1998). *Reinventing assessment*. Princeton, NJ: Educational Testing Service.

Black, P., & Wiliam, D. (1998). Assessment and classroom learning. *Assessment in Education*, **5**, 7–74.

Brennan, R.L., & Johnson, E.G. (1995). Generalizability of performance assessments. *Educational Measurement: Issues and Practice*, **14**(4), 25–27.

Broadfoot, P. (1994). Approaches to quality assurance and control in six countries. In W. Harlen (Ed.), *Enhancing quality in assessment* (pp. 26–52). London: Chapman.

Broadfoot, P. (1996). *Education, assessment and society. A sociological analysis*. Buckingham, England: Open University Press.

Broadfoot, P. (1998). Records of achievement and the learning society: A tale of two discourses. *Assessment in education*, **5**, 447–477.

Broadfoot, P., James, M., McMeeking, S., Nuttall, D., & Stierer, S. (1988). *Records of achievement: Report of the national evaluation of pilot schemes (PRAISE)*. London: Her Majesty's Stationery Office.

Brown, A.L., Bransford, J.D., Ferrara, R., & Campione, J. (1983). Learning, remembering and understanding. In P.H. Mussen (Series Ed.), J.H. Flavell, & E.M. Markman (Vol. Eds.), *Handbook of child psychology: Volume 3. Cognitive development* (4th ed., pp. 77–166). New York: Wiley.

Bruner, J.S. (1966). *Toward a theory of instruction*. Cambridge, MA: Harvard University Press.

Bruner, J. (1996). *The culture of education*. Cambridge, MA: Harvard University Press.

Callahan, S. (1997). Tests worth taking? Using portfolios for accountability in Kentucky. *Research into the Teaching of English*, **31**, 295–330.

Clay, M.M. (1985). *The early detection of reading difficulties* (3rd ed.). Auckland, NZ: Heinemann.

Crooks, T.J. (1988). The impact of classroom evaluation practices on students. *Review of Educational Research*, **58**, 438–481.

Dunbar, S.B., Koretz, D., & Hoover, H.D. (1991). Quality control in the development and use of performance assessments. *Applied Measurement in Education*, **4**, 289–304.

Feldt, L.S., & Brennan, R.L. (1989). Reliability. In R.L. Linn (Ed.), *Educational measurement* (3rd ed., pp. 105–146). New York: American Council on Education/Macmillan.

Feuerstein, R. (1979). *The dynamic assessment of retarded performers: The learning assessment device, theory, instruments and techniques*. Baltimore, MD: University Park Press.

Frechtling, J. (1991). Performance assessment: Moonstruck or the real thing? *Educational Measurement: Issues and Practice*, **10**(4), 23–25.

Fredericksen, J.R., & Collins, A. (1989). A systems approach to educational testing. *Educational Researcher*, **18**(9), 27–32.

Garcia, G., & Pearson, P. (1991). The role of assessment in a diverse society. In E. Herbert (Ed.), *Literacy for a diverse society* (pp. 253–278). New York: Teachers College Press.

Gipps, C. (1992). Equal opportunities and the SATs for seven year olds. *Curriculum Journal*, **3**, 171–183.

Gipps, C. (1994a). *Beyond testing: Towards a theory of educational assessment*. London: Falmer.

Gipps, C. (1994b). Developments in educational assessment or what makes a good test? *Assessment in Education*, **1**, 283–291.

Gipps, C.V. (1994c). *Quality assurance in teacher assessment*. In W. Harlen (Ed.) *Enhancing quality in assessment*. London: Paul Chapman.

Gipps, C. (1999). Socio-cultural aspects of assessment. *Review of Research in Education*, **24**, 355–392.

Gipps, C., Brown, M., McCallum, B., & McAlister, S. (1995). *Intuition or evidence? Teachers and national assessment of seven year olds*. Buckingham, England: Open University Press.

Gipps, C., McCallum, B., & Hargreaves, E. (2000). *What makes a good primary school teacher? Expert classroom strategies*. London: Routledge Falmer.

Gipps, C., & Murphy, P. (1994). *A fair test? Assessment, achievement and equity*. Buckingham, England: Open University Press.

Glaser, R. (1963). Instructional technology and the measurement of learning outcomes: Some questions. *American Psychologist*, **18**, 519–521.

Glaser, R. (1990). Toward new models for assessment. *International Journal of Educational Research*, **14**, 475–483.

Goldstein, H. (1994). Recontextualising mental measurement. *Educational Measurement: Issues and Practice*, **13**(1), 16–19, 43.

Gould, S.J. (1996). *The mismeasure of man*. New York: Norton.

Haertel, E. (1992). Performance measurement. In M. Alkin (Ed.), *Encyclopaedia of educational research* (6th ed., pp. 984–989). London: Macmillan.

Harlen, W. (1994). Issues and approaches to quality assurance and quality control in assessment. In W. Harlen, (Ed.) *Enhancing quality in assessment* (pp. 11–25). London: Paul Chapman.

Herman, J., Klein, D., & Wakai, S. (1997). American students' perspectives on alternative assessment: Do they know it's different? *Assessment in Education*, **4**, 339–352.

Hill, R. (2000). *A success story from Kentucky*. Paper presented at 30th Annual Conference on Large-Scale Assessment, Snowbird, Utah.

HMI (Her Majesty's Inspectorate). (1979). *Aspects of secondary education in England*. London: Author.

HMI. (1988). *The introduction of the GCSE in schools 1986–1988*. London: Author.

Kane, M.T. (1992). An argument-based approach to validity. *Psychological Bulletin*, **112**, 527–535.

Kellaghan, T., Madaus, G.F., & Raczek, A. (1996). *The use of external examinations to improve student motivation*. Washington, DC: American Educational Research Association.

Klein, S.P., & Hamilton, L. (1999). *Large-scale testing*. Santa Monica, CA: RAND Education.

Klenowski, V. (2000). Portfolios: Promoting teaching. *Assessment in Education*, **7**, 215–234.

Kluger, A.V., & DeNisi, A. (1996). The effects of feedback interventions on performance: A historical review, a meta-analysis, and a preliminary feedback intervention theory. *Psychological Bulletin*, **119**, 252–284.

Koretz, D. (1998). Large-scale portfolio assessments in the US: Evidence pertaining to the quality of measurement. *Assessment in Education*, **5**, 309–334.

Linn, R.L. (1993). Educational assessment: Expanded expectations and challenges. *Educational Evaluation and Policy Analysis*, **15**, 1–16.

Linn, R.L. (1997). Evaluating the validity of assessments: The consequences of use. *Educational Measurement: Issues and Practice*, **16**(2), 14–16.

Linn, R.L. (2000) Assessment and accountability. *Educational Researcher*, **29**(2), 4–16.

Linn, R.L., Baker, E.L., & Dunbar, S.B (1991). Complex performance assessment: Expectations and validation criteria. *Educational Researcher*, **20**(8), 15–21.

Lunt, I. (1994). The practice of assessment. In H. Daniels (Ed.), *Charting the agenda: Educational activity after Vygotsky* (pp. 145–170). New York: Routledge.

Madaus, G.F. (1988). The influence of testing on the curriculum. In L. Tanner (Ed.), *Critical issues in curriculum. Eighty-seventh Yearbook of the National Society for the Study of Education, Part 1* (pp. 83–121). Chicago: University of Chicago Press.

Madaus, G.F., & Raczek, A.E. (1996). The extent and growth of educational testing in the United States: 1956–1994. In H. Goldstein, & T. Lewis (Eds.), *Assessment: Problems, developments and statistical issues* (pp. 145–165). New York: Wiley.

Mehrens, W.A. (1992). Using performance assessment for accountability purposes. *Educational Measurement: Issues and Practice*, **11**(1), 3–9, 20.

Mehrens, W.A. (1997). The consequences of consequential validity. *Educational Measurement: Issues and Practice*, **16**(2), 16–18.

Messick, S. (1989). Validity. In R.L. Linn (Ed.), *Educational measurement* (3rd ed., pp. 13–103). New York: American Council on Education.

Messick, S. (1994). The interplay of evidence and consequences in the validation of performance assessments. *Educational Researcher*, **23**(2), 13–23.

Meyer, C.A. (1992). What's the difference between *authentic* and *performance* assessment? *Educational Leadership*, **49**(8), 38–41.

Mishler, E.G. (1990). Validation in inquiry-guided research: The role of exemplars in narrative studies. *Harvard Educational Review*, **60**, 415–442.

Mislevy, R.J. (1993). Foundations of a new test theory. In N. Frederickson, R.J. Mislevy, & I.I. Bejar (Eds.), *Test theory for a new generation of tests* (pp. 19–39). Hillsdale, NJ: Erlbaum.

Moss, P.A. (1992). Shifting conceptions of validity in educational measurement: Implications for performance assessment. *Review of Educational Research*, **62**, 229–258.

Moss, P.A. (1994). Can there be validity without reliability? *Educational Researcher*, **23**(2), 5–12.

Moss, P.A. (1996). Enlarging the dialogue in educational measurement: Voices from interpretive research traditions. *Educational Researcher*, **25**(1), 20–28.

Neill, M. (1995). Some prerequisites for the establishment of equitable, inclusive multicultural assessment systems. In M. Nettles, & A. Nettles (Eds.), *Equity and excellence in educational testing and assessment* (pp. 115–157). Boston: Kluwer Academic.

Newman, D., Griffin, P., & Cole, M. (1989). *The construction zone: Working for cognitive change in school*. Cambridge, England: Cambridge University Press.

Newmann, F.M. (1990). Higher order thinking in social studies: A rationale for the assessment of classroom thoughtfulness. *Journal of Curriculum Studies*, **22**, 41–56.

Oosterhof, A. (1996). *Developing and using classroom assessments*. Englewood Cliffs, NJ: Prentice Hall.

Pellegrino, J.W., Baxter, G.P., & Glaser, R. (1999). Addressing the "two disciplines" problem: Linking theories of cognition and learning with assessment and instructional practice. *Review of Research in Education*, **24**, 307–346.

Perrenoud, P. (1991). Towards a pragmatic approach to formative evaluation. In P. Weston (Ed.), *Assessment of pupils' achievement: Motivation and school success* (pp. 77–101). Amsterdam: Swets & Zeitlinger.

Pitman, J., & Allen, R. (2000). *Achieving quality in assessment practices: Challenges and strategies for the new millennium*. Paper presented at 26th Conference of the International Association for Educational Assessment, Jerusalem.

Popham, W.J. (1997). Consequential validity: Right concern – wrong concept. *Educational Measurement: Issues and Practice*, **16**(2), 9–13.

Raban, B. (1983). *Guides to assessment in education: Reading*. London: Macmillan.

Resnick, L., & Resnick, D. (1992). Assessing the thinking curriculum: New tools for education reform. In B. Gifford & M. O'Connor (Eds.), *Changing assessments: Alternative views of aptitude, achievement and instruction* (pp. 37–75). Boston: Kluwer Academic.

Sadler, R. (1989). Formative assessment and the design of instructional systems. *Instructional Science*, **18**, 119–144.

Sadler, R. (1998). Formative assessment: Revisiting the territory. *Assessment in Education*, **5**, 77–84.

Salvia, J., & Ysseldyke, J.E. (1998). *Assessment* (7th ed.). Boston: Houghton Mifflin.

SEAC (School Examinations and Assessment Council). (1991). *National curriculum assessment at Key Stage 3: A review of the 1991 pilots with implications for 1992.* London: Author.

Shavelson, R.J., Baxter, G.P., & Gao, X. (1993). Sampling variability of performance assessments. *Journal of Educational Measurement*, **30**, 215–232.

Shavelson, R.J., Baxter, G.P., & Pine, J. (1992). Performance assessments: Political rhetoric and measurement reality. *Educational Researcher*, **21**(4), 22–27.

Shepard, L.A. (1993). Evaluating test validity. *Review of Research in Education*, **19**, 405–450.

Shepard, L.A. (1997). The centrality of test use and consequences for test validity. *Educational Measurement: Issues and Practice*, **16**(2), 5–8, 13.

Shepard, L.A. (2000). The role of classroom assessment in teaching and learning. In V. Richardson (Ed.), *Handbook of research on teaching* (4th ed., pp. 1066–1101). Washington, DC: American Educational Research Association.

Shepard, L.A., & Bleim, C.L. (1995). Parents' thinking about standardized tests and performance assessments. *Educational Researcher*, **24**(8), 25–32.

Stecher, B. (1998). The local benefits and burdens of large-scale portfolio assessment. *Assessment in Education*, **5**, 335–352.

Stiggins, R. (1994). *Student-centered classroom assessment*. New York: Merrill.

Stiggins, R., & Bridgeford, N. (1982). *The role of performance assessment in day to day classroom assessment and evaluation*. Paper presented at annual meeting of the National Council for Measurement in Education, New York.

Stobart, G., & Gipps, C. (1997). *Assessment: A teacher's guide to the issues*. London: Hodder & Stoughton.

Swanson, D., Norman, G., & Linn, R.L. (1995). Performance-based assessment: Lessons from the health professions. *Educational Researcher*, **24**(5), 5–11, 35.

Taylor, P., Fraser, B., & Fisher, D. (1997). Monitoring constructivist classroom learning environments. *International Journal of Educational Research*, **27**, 293–301.

Torrance, H., & Pryor, J. (1998). *Investigating formative assessment: Teaching, learning and assessment in the classroom*. Buckingham, England: Open University Press.

Tunstall, P., & Gipps, C. (1996). Teacher feedback to young children in formative assessment: A typology. *British Educational Research Journal*, **22**, 389–404.

Vygotsky, L. (1978). *Mind in society*. Cambridge, MA: Harvard University Press.

Wiggins, G. (1989). A true test: Toward more authentic and equitable assessment. *Phi Delta Kappan*, **72**, 700–713.

Wiliam, D. (1992). Some technical issues in assessment: A user's guide. *British Journal of Curriculum Assessment*, **2**(3), 11–20.

Wiliam, D. (1993). Validity, dependability and reliability in national curriculum assessment. *Curriculum Journal*, **4**, 335–350.

Wittrock, M.C., & Baker, E.L. (1991). *Testing and cognition*. Englewood Cliffs, NJ: Prentice Hall.

Wolf, A., & Koretz, D. (1998). Editorial. *Assessment in Education*, **5**, 301–307.

Wolf, D., Bixby, J., Glenn, J., & Gardner, H. (1991). To use their minds well: Investigating new forms of student assessment. *Review of Research in Education*, **17**, 31–74.

Wood, R. (1986). The agenda for educational measurement. In D.L. Nuttall (Ed.), *Assessing educational achievement* (pp. 185–203). London: Falmer.

27
External (Public) Examinations

THOMAS KELLAGHAN

Educational Research Centre, St. Patrick's College, Dublin, Ireland

GEORGE MADAUS

Boston College, MA, USA

In many countries, "external" examinations (sometimes called "public" or "national") occupy a central role in the assessment of individual students. Because of the wide variation in practice that they exhibit, however, it is difficult to define the examinations in a way that will include all to which the term is applied. Some examinations, though generally regarded as external or public, are not entirely external to the schools from which examinees come, while others are not public if that term is taken to mean that they are administered by a state authority, though they may be public in the sense that they are open to all.

Rather than attempting to reach a formal definition of external examinations, we will describe characteristics of the examinations, after which a brief description of their development will be presented. A discussion of major issues associated with examinations follows: validity, reliability, comparability of performances on examinations taken in different subjects or on different occasions, criterion-referencing, and equity. Finally, disadvantages attributed to public examinations and efforts to combine elements of school-based assessment with external examining are described.

Most of the chapter addresses issues relating to external examinations in Europe, Africa, and Asia. However, some consideration will also be given to recently introduced state-mandated tests in the United States since they resemble external examinations in other countries in a number of ways.

CHARACTERISTICS OF EXTERNAL EXAMINATIONS

Examinations to which the term external is applied possess a number of characteristics (see Eckstein & Noah, 1993; Keeves, 1994). First, they are set and/or controlled by an agency external to the schools from which candidates come. Second, the administering authority is usually a national or state

International Handbook of Educational Evaluation, 577–600
T. Kellaghan, D.L. Stufflebeam (eds.)
© 2003 Dordrecht: Kluwer Academic Publishers. Printed in Great Britain.

government or agency or, if it does not actually administer the examinations, it will have an overseeing function. Third, the examinations are based on prescribed syllabi in curriculum (or subject) areas (languages, mathematics, sciences, history, geography, etc). In line with a tradition in which the study of classical texts was the main feature of syllabi, the main emphasis tends to be on content rather than on skills. Fourth, examinations involve the application of a common test, in which examinees do not have access to books or other material, are separated from the classroom situation, and usually are administered to many students at the same time. There is a heavy emphasis on written tasks involving essay, supply, or selection items, though other forms of assessment may be included.

Fifth, most examinations serve a number of functions. The primary function is usually stated to be certification of examinees' achievements at the end of a period of study. Candidates are awarded a certificate or diploma that describes their performance on each subject in the examination, in letter grades (e.g., A, B, C, D, E), numbers (e.g., 1, 2, 3, 4, 5), percentages, or a proficiency statement (e.g., pass/fail). Usually grades are arrived at by simply summing marks allocated to sections of questions and across questions and components (or papers) if the examination has more than one component (or paper). The certificate or diploma, in addition to testifying to an examinee's performance in the examination may also confer rights, such as the right to be considered for (if not actually admitted to) some sector of the social, professional, or educational world. For example, in the past, possession of a school-leaving examination (e.g., the German *Abitur* or the French *Baccalaureat*) granted access to a university. In many countries, the selection of students for further education has become the main function of external examinations, though in some, the selection examination (e.g., the *concours* in France) is separate from the certification examination. In other cases, individual universities may hold their own examinations to select students (e.g., in Japan; see Amano, 1990). Examinations may also serve a motivational function. This may be the major function when no decision is based on performance (e.g., midway through secondary schooling), but the examination is thought useful to direct students in their study or to motivate them to work. When important consequences are attached to performance, however, we might expect the examination to have a stronger motivational influence. In addition to these functions, an examination may also be considered a way of controlling what goes on in schools, helping to ensure that similar content is taught, and contributing to uniformity of standards in teaching and in achievement. These can be important considerations where private schools represent a considerable proportion of schools, or where there is strong local control of schools.

Sixth, public examinations are voluntary (while their counterparts in assessments in the United States are not) in the sense that it is up to individual students to decide whether or not to take an examination. However, if a student wishes to proceed to third-level education, he/she will have no option but to take the examination if decisions about entry are based on examination performance.

Finally, the tradition of external examinations has been to make public the content of examinations and their results. This was so even before examinations were presented to candidates in written form. For example, after the oral examination of candidates at Dublin University during the first half of the 19th century, individuals who had been present wrote up and circulated the questions that had been asked. These questions were then used by students who were preparing for similar examinations in the future, establishing the tradition of having examinations determine curricula (Foden, 1989). In a number of countries (Germany, Ireland, New Zealand), in addition to making examination papers available, answer scripts are returned to students to allow them to evaluate the way their responses were scored.

While these general characteristics can be identified, there are many ways in which external examinations across the world differ (Madaus & Kellaghan, 1991; West, Edge, & Stokes, 1999; World Bank, 2002). First, there are differences at the stage at which examinations are held. Examinations are most common at the end of secondary schooling (and it is these examinations which are the main focus of this chapter). However, many countries also have examinations at lower levels – around the end of compulsory schooling (when students are about 16 years of age) and, in developing countries, because of a shortage of space to accommodate students in secondary schools, at the end of primary schooling. Second, there is variation between countries in the number of bodies involved in the administration of examinations. There may be a single examination authority for a country, often a government ministry of education; or, in a federal system, each state may have its own authority (e.g., Germany); or examinations may be administered by public or private examination boards (e.g., the United Kingdom); or administration may be localized (e.g., in regional *academies* in France).

A third way in which examinations differ is in the extent to which they are totally external to the school from which examinees come (and in which case the examinee will be unknown to the examiner) or in the extent to which they incorporate an element of school-based evaluation. School-leaving examinations are totally or almost totally external in only a few European countries (France, Ireland). At the other extreme, an "external" examination may be set by and/or marked by teachers within a school, with some form of external moderation. Between these extremes, a student's final grade will be a combination of marks on an external examination and marks for school work (which may be based on the student's performance over a period of time).

Fourth, there is variation in the number of subjects in which an examinee takes an external examination. At the end of secondary school, this ranges from a low of two in Italy, through three in Germany and the United Kingdom, to more than six in France, Ireland, and the Netherlands. Fifth, examinations vary in their formats and in the number of components that make up an examination in an individual subject. While essay-type questions have been predominant in many systems, short-answer constructed responses and objective (multiple-choice) items also feature. Many examinations also include "performance" tasks, in which oral, aural, and practical competencies are assessed. Finally, there is variation in the extent to which examinees are allowed a choice in examinations. Candidates may choose the subjects in which they wish to be examined. There may also be choice in the components or questions in the examination in any particular subject. Most allow some choice (though they might also include some common tasks), but the range of options from which a choice may be made, in for example a language test, is very large in some systems (e.g., the United Kingdom) and non-existent in others (e.g., France).

THE DEVELOPMENT OF EXTERNAL EXAMINATIONS

It is generally accepted that written competitive group examinations originated in China (Du Bois, 1970; Eckstein & Noah, 1993; Mathews, 1985; Morris, 1961). A regular performance examination has been traced back to the time of the Western Zhou Dynasty (1027–711 BC). Later, during the Han Dynasty (206 BC–220 AD) examinations included oral and written tests (Han & Yang, 2001). At varying times, district, prefectural, and provincial examinations were held to select individuals for positions in the civil service and the military, as well as to admit students to government schools in which they prepared for the civil service examinations. Features of examinations during the Ch'ing Dynasty in the 19th century can be readily identified with conditions under which examinations are held today (Miyazaki, 1976). The examinations were administered in a spacious hall or shed cut off from communication with the outside; candidates sat alone at their desks; answers were written in a book of folded plain white paper; and only the candidate's number appeared on the paper. A number of features of Chinese examinations, however, have not survived. Candidates are no longer required to write through the day until dark, nor are readers who graded papers prevented from leaving the hall until their work is complete. And candidates who write identical answers are no longer regarded as "recopying" model answers [see Madaus (1988) for examples of "recopying" in more recent examinations].

News had been coming through from China from missionaries and travellers since the 16th century about the Chinese examination system. The Jesuits incorporated written examinations into their schools, though these, of course, were not external (Eckstein & Noah, 1993). The *Ratio Studiorum* (1586) describes how a student was required to achieve an adequate standard on a written composition in Latin and in an oral examination on the grammar, syntax, and style of the composition (Madaus & O'Dwyer, 1999). It is surprising that examinations do not seem to have been held for admission to a medieval university or for licensing following study (Rashdall, 1936). However, there is evidence that at a later stage of study theses were presented in writing, and then disputed orally (Perreiah, 1984).

Large-scale group written examinations were first used in Europe in the 18th century for selection to the civil service, as had been the case in China. Germany (Prussia) led the way in 1748, and the practice was adopted in France (in 1793) following the revolution. Through the 19th century, written qualifying examinations were introduced in Britain for selection to the civil service and to the professions (e.g., apothecaries, solicitors) inspired by Benthamite principles of maximizing aptitude, minimizing expense, and controlling nepotism and patronage (Foden, 1989; Madaus & Kellaghan, 1991; Montgomery, 1965; Roach, 1971).

At the school level, universities played an important role in the 19th century in the introduction of group written examinations The *Abitur*, following its introduction in German schools (in 1788), soon became a qualification examination. In France, higher educational institutions administered the *Baccalaureat* examination which had been established by Napoleon (in 1808), and used it for making admission decisions. In the United Kingdom, several universities established procedures for examining local secondary school students (e.g., Cambridge, Dublin, London, Oxford), and strengthened their control of the examinations during the second half of the 19th century (Brereton, 1944; Madaus & Kellaghan, 1991; Montgomery, 1965, 1978; Roach, 1971; Wilmott & Nuttall, 1975; Wiseman, 1961).

In the United States, Horace Mann, faced with the impossibility of "committee men" conducting oral examinations for "over 7,000 children," introduced written essay examinations to the Boston Public Schools in 1845. In addition to facilitating the examination of large numbers of students, Mann recognized that the examinations allowed the examiner to pose an identical set of questions to students, under similar conditions, in a limited time frame, producing "comparable" scores, though he did not seem to hit on the idea embodied in Chinese practice of administering the same papers to everyone simultaneously (Madaus & O'Dwyer, 1999; Morris, 1961). Somewhat later, under the influence of British practice, the Civil Service Act of 1883 in the United States established competitive examinations to select personnel for government service. The examinations, however, were abandoned when Congress failed to make appropriations to continue them (Du Bois, 1970).

Today, external (public) examinations are a key feature of the educational systems of most countries in Europe, Africa, Asia, and the Caribbean (Bray, Clarke, & Stephens, 1986; Bray & Steward, 1998; EURYDICE, 1999; Kellaghan, 1992; Kellaghan & Greaney, 1992; Madaus & Kellaghan, 1991; West, Edge, & Stokes, 1999; World Bank, 2002). While they have not in the past featured in education systems in countries in the former Soviet Union or in eastern Europe, that situation is changing, and many countries are now establishing an external examination system, usually to assess students at the end of secondary schooling. External examinations have not been a feature of American education either, with the exception of the Regents' examination in New York state which, since the 1860s, has offered syllabuses and a system of examinations to students wishing to obtain a Regents' diploma. All secondary school students in the state are now required to take the examination for graduation.

Advocates of a "national" examination system in the 1980s and 1990s claimed that the fact that the U.S. was one of the few industrialized countries in the world that did not have common national examinations was a key reason why students performed poorly in international comparisons. They argued that a national examination system would provide teachers with clear and meaningful standards, and would motivate students to work if real consequences were attached to performance (Madaus & Kellaghan, 1991). While a national system has not been established, 49 states have introduced state-wide assessments, the results of which may be used for a variety of decisions about students, schools, school systems, and teachers (Shore, Pedulla, & Clarke, 2001). The examinations, which are called assessments or tests, however, differ in many respects from traditional external examinations in other countries.

First, the tests are mandated by local authorities (e.g., large school systems), state departments of education, state legislatures and, under the No Child Left Behind Act of 2001 (Reauthorization of the 1965 Elementary and Secondary Education Act), the United States Congress (U.S. Department of Education, 2002). However, they are almost always developed, administered, and scored by testing companies under contract to the authorizing agency. Second, while the tests are geared to state curriculum frameworks or standards, the emphasis at the elementary grades is on skills rather than on content. Third, the tests have a large multiple-choice component in addition to a small number of supply-type short-answer or essay questions. Fourth, while the main function of testing is to support standards-based reform, in practice the decisions based on performance are wider than is generally the case in public examinations, and include the awarding or withholding of a high school diploma, retention of a student in a grade, and holding teachers, schools, or school districts accountable.

Fifth, student performance is generally reported in the form of "performance categories" or standards (e.g., "advanced," "proficient," "basic or needs improvement," and "unsatisfactory or fail") which are arrived at through the use of a number of standard-setting methods (see Hambleton, 2001; Horn, Ramos, Blumer, & Madaus, 2000; Kane, 2001; Raymond & Reid, 2001). Scores (and standards) are linked from one year to another through the use of item response theory (IRT) technology (see Hambleton, Swaminathan, & Rogers, 1991; Mislevy, 1992). Sixth, while in many countries entrance to third-level institutions is based on performance on a public examination, in the United States, the tradition of using aptitude (SAT 1) and achievement (SAT 2) tests administered by the College Entrance Examination Board (CEEB) continues. Results of these, or of American College Testing Program Tests (ACT), are used in conjunction with class rank, class grades, and other factors in making admission decisions. Seventh, test authorities in the United States follow the tradition of public examinations in releasing test items each year. However, 10 to 20 percent of items may be withheld for year-to-year linking.

Eighth, testing in the United States differs from practice elsewhere in the range of grades in which assessments are carried out. The No Child Left Behind law provides for testing in a much wider range (grades 3 through 8) than is the case in public examination systems elsewhere. Ninth, all students are required to take tests, while public examinations in other countries are voluntary. Finally, while in many public examinations at the secondary school level, students can choose from a large range of subjects, and the items they wish to respond to in an examination, in most places in the United States, such choice is not available, and all students take examinations in the same subjects (e.g., English, mathematics, science, history).

VALIDITY

Content Validity

The claim to validity of external public examinations rests primarily on their content. Syllabi will provide more or less detailed guidance regarding content to be covered, and skills and knowledge to be acquired, and validity will be a function of the extent (based on professional judgment) that a test or examination is relevant and representative of the content, knowledge, and skills. This notion of validity fits well with the function of an examination as certifying the knowledge and skills of students.

Sampling and representation are very important in considering content validity. Since the knowledge and skills specified in syllabi are generally very numerous, the only way an agency can assess how well a student has learned is to measure his/her performance on a selected sample of topics. How the student responds to the topics, however, is of interest only insofar as it enables the agency to infer how well the student has acquired the knowledge as a whole and mastered all prescribed skills (Madaus & Macnamara, 1970). This situation gives rise to two problems. One is that examinations often have a relatively small number of questions, making it difficult to achieve any great degree of curriculum coverage. And secondly, allowing students choice, in selecting subjects or components of subjects or in responding to questions, may mean that they avoid important sections of the curriculum. Furthermore, options may not be marked to the same standard. Both issues have implications for reliability, for comparability of student responses, and for the use of performance on examinations to select students for further education.

A further point relating to content validity is the extent to which the intentions of the curriculum are reflected, not just in the examination tasks, but in the achieved scores of students, when those scores are used to rank-order students, say for admission to third-level education. Examinations are made up of many components, each of which will be allocated a mark loading which will indicate the total number of marks available for the component on a scale of achievement common to the examination as a whole. These loadings indicate the *intended* weightings of components. Thus within a subject, a theory paper might be allocated 200 marks and a practical or oral paper or teachers' assessments of students might be allocated 100 marks, on the basis that the theory is considered to be twice as important as the other component, or at any rate to merit twice the marks. When the marks obtained by students have been aggregated, the overall rank of examinees is determined, in which the influence of the component on the rank order will be represented by its *achieved* weight. It might be assumed that the outcome will reflect the intended weighting. However, this may not be the case. Even when less marks are available for a particular component, adding them to the marks for another component can completely reverse the order of merit of the examinees on the components to which the greater number of marks were assigned if the dispersion of the marks for the components differs. If this happens, the validity of the examination will be reduced insofar as the weightings will not operate as specified. To address this situation, it is necessary to take into account the proportion of the variance of the total marks attributable to a component and the correlation of the component marks with the total score (see Delap, 1994).

Criterion-Related Validity

The degree of empirical relationship between test scores and criterion scores to assess criterion-related validity is usually expressed in terms of correlations or regressions. While content validity is usually viewed as a singular property of a test or examination, an examination or test could be assessed in the context of many criterion-related validities. This might involve comparing performance in a job with performance on a test that assessed the knowledge and skills required for the job. It is difficult to identify a criterion with which performance on a school-leaving examination might be compared, apart from performance in later education (considered below under predictive validity).

Construct Validity

There is a sense in which an investigation of any aspect of validity may contribute to an understanding of construct validity, since this facet embraces almost all forms of validity evidence. Any evidence that elaborates on the meaning of the measure, its nature, internal structure, or its relationship to other variables may be regarded as relevant (Messick, 1989).

In a study of the Irish Leaving Certificate Examination carried out over 30 years ago, Madaus and Macnamara (1970) analyzed the nature of the abilities which students displayed in the examination using Bloom's (1956) *Taxonomy of Educational Objectives*, which classifies intellectual skills hierarchically. The study may be regarded as an evaluation of construct validity, as it may be assumed that the levels of knowledge reflected in the taxonomy would be ones that would find the approval of curriculum designers. Its findings indicated that examinations focused on the lower levels of the taxonomy (knowledge) rather than on the higher levels of analysis, synthesis, or evaluation, placing, the authors say, "an impossible and senseless burden on students' memories" (p. 113).

In a recent study, the performance of students on a public examination in Ireland was related to their performance on the OECD Programme for

International Student Assessment (PISA) tests in English, Mathematics, and Science. The PISA tests, it is claimed, measure competencies that students will need in later life, rather than the outcomes of exposure to any particular curriculum. Certainly, they are not based on Irish curricula, and so cannot be used as criteria to evaluate concurrent validity. However, if they are valid measures of competencies needed for later life (and that is open to question), a consideration of students' performance on them vis à vis their performance on the examination is of interest since programs of study in Irish schools also have the general long-term objective of preparation for later life. The relationships between PISA and external examination performances in all three domains (English, Mathematics, and Science) were in fact moderately strong (correlations were either 0.73 or 0.74), suggesting that, despite differences in the context, content, and methods of the assessments, there was considerable overlap in the achievements measured (Shiel, Cosgrove, Sofroniou, & Kelly, 2001). The finding can also be regarded as supportive of the construct validity of the examinations.

Predictive Validity

There have been a number of studies of the predictive validity of external examinations. In general, performance on one external examination predicts performance on an external examination taken some years later (r=0.82) (Millar & Kelly, 1999). However, the strength of the relationship varies across curriculum areas.

Several studies indicate that external examinations predict performance in university studies better than scholastic aptitude tests (Choppin & Orr, 1976; O'Rourke, Martin, & Hurley, 1989; Powell, 1973). In passing, it may be noted that relationships between performance on external examinations and scholastic aptitude tests have been found to be modest, ranging from about 0.20 to about 0.50 for a number of subjects at varying levels in secondary school, and with varying time intervals between testing (Madaus, Kellaghan, & Rakow, 1975; Martin & O'Rourke, 1984). A further indication of the predictive validity of external examinations may be obtained by looking at the relationship between examination performance and completion rates in university. In a recent study, a clear relationship was observed between the scores required for admission to courses and course completion (Morgan, Flanagan, & Kellaghan, 2001).

Consequences of Test Use

Messick's (1989) definition of validity points to the need to take account of the potential and actual consequences of test use, something that has frequently been overlooked in the past. Positive consequences of the use of information derived from a public examination may be said to occur if the examination fulfils the functions for which it is designed (i.e., certification, selection, motivation, and the control of teaching and learning in schools). The most obvious of these is perhaps selection (e.g., the extent to which the examination provides information that can be used to make adequate and equitable decisions in selecting students for higher education), but consequences also relate to the other facets. These may not all be positive; there is evidence that examinations to which high stakes are attached can have negative, if unintended, effects on teaching, on students' cognitive development, and on their motivation to achieve (see Disadvantages of External Examinations below).

RELIABILITY

The issue of reliability arises from the fact that human performance (physical or mental) is variable. In the case of examinations or tests, quantification of the extent to which an examinee's performance is consistent or inconsistent constitutes the essence of reliability analysis (Feldt & Brennan, 1989). When performance on a public examination is used for selection, the main issue is replicability. Would the same subset of individuals be selected if they took the examination on another occasion (Cresswell, 1995)?

A number of factors contribute to unreliability (Feldt & Brennan, 1989; Wiliam, 1996). Some are common to all types of assessment, while some are more likely to arise in the case of free-response assessments. First, examinees will perform differently on different occasions. This could be due to variation in the examinee relating to health, motivation, concentration, lapse of memory, or carelessness. Some students may consistently perform poorly under examination conditions (e.g., an anxious student) thus introducing a systematic error into the examination process. However, this is not the kind of error addressed in reliability concerns, in which error is considered random, not systematic. Second, fluctuations in external conditions can affect an examinee's performance. These may be physical (e.g., the examination hall may be too hot) or they may be psychological (e.g., an examinee may have experienced a traumatic event recently, such as the death of a relative).

Third, variation in the specific tasks required of an examinee in the assessment may affect his or her performance. Since an examination consists of questions or tasks that represent only a sample from a larger domain, the specific tasks in an examination might unintentionally relate more closely to the information of one examinee than to the information of another. The situation might be reversed if a different sample of tasks had been included.

Fourth, different examiners will give different marks to the same piece of work, and indeed, the same examiner may give different marks to the work if marked on a different occasion. This is not a problem with objective closed-response tests. In the case of free-response examinations, however, examiner inconsistency can constitute a major source of error. It has two components. First, there is the *general bias* of an examiner, that is, a tendency to mark "hard" or "easy" relative to the "average" marker. The extent of this may be calculated if examination scripts have been randomly allocated to examiners by subtracting the average of a set of marks assigned by a particular examiner from the average mark awarded by the entire group of examiners to the same questions or papers. A second source of error arises from *random fluctuation* in an examiner's marking. This is separate from any bias that may exist and relates to the marking of all examiners, whether or not they exhibit bias.

Early studies of examination marker reliability revealed considerable disagreement between separate scorings of essays (Hartog & Rhodes, 1935; Stalnaker, 1951; Starch & Elliott, 1912, 1913). Disagreement was likely to be greater in an English essay where imagination and style might be important qualities to be assessed than in a science examination where content will be more important. Madaus and Macnamara (1970) addressed both the issue of the general bias of examiners (the extent to which different examiners agreed in the marks they awarded to the same answers) and the inconsistency of individual examiners (the extent to which two sets of marks awarded at different times by the same examiner to the same answers agreed). Their first finding was that across subjects, there was generally a 1 in 20 chance that marks would swing up or down by about 10 percent. In an extreme case, for example in the case of English, it could result in an examinee being awarded 50 percent by one examiner and 28 percent (a fail) by another. Second, some examiners were more harsh than others. Third, the unreliability associated with the marks assigned by a single examiner on two different occasions was scarcely lower than that associated with the marks of two different readers. The findings are not greatly dissimilar to the those of other studies (e.g., Good & Cresswell, 1988; Hewitt, 1967).

In the case of tasks used in state-mandated assessments in the United States, the reliability of classification decisions is an important but generally overlooked issue. While standard errors for total tests are provided, they are not provided for individual cut-score points.

The requirement for high reliability in examinations has had profound effects on assessment practice. Highly reliable assessments tend to be associated with standardized conditions of administration, the use of detailed marking schemes, marker standardization to ensure that criteria and standards are uniform, and multiple marking of scripts. The downside of these conditions is that limitations are imposed on the kind of knowledge, skills, and understanding that can be assessed (Cresswell, 1995). Alternative approaches in Britain to address this issue by having teachers assess students' work using non-standard tasks taken under non-standard conditions supervised by one who knows the students well have run into problems from the point of view of the selection function of examinations relating to bias, reliability, and comparability.

COMPARABILITY OF PERFORMANCES ON EXAMINATIONS

A persistent issue in external examinations relates to the comparability of the grades obtained by examinees in different subjects taken in the same examination, and of grades in examinations administered in different years in the same subject. One might assume that grades in different examinations would be of comparable standard and that, for example, obtaining an A or a C in English should be no easier or harder than obtaining the same grade in mathematics. The issue acquires a particular significance when the grades are treated as of equal value for selection for further education, and has been the subject of much research in the United States (see Mislevy, 1992) as well as in Britain where the administration of examinations in the same subject by separate examination boards adds to comparability problems. It is also an issue in Germany and Australia where examination systems vary by state. During the 1970s, a number of techniques to address the problem were developed in Britain, and were widely used in grading decisions (Cresswell, 1988; Goldstein, 1986; Newton, 1997; Nuttall, Backhouse & Willmott, 1974). There was little further research until the 1990s when Dearing's (1996) review of qualifications for 16- to 19-year olds claimed that certain subjects were "harder" than others.

One way of dealing with the issue is by norm-referencing. If, for example, the sole purpose of a test is to select (as in the *concours*), all that is required is that students be rank-ordered in terms of their performance, and that those who seem best prepared for further education are identified. Reflecting this approach, the "pass" mark in some systems is determined by the number of available places at the next highest level in the education system.

Apart from addressing the selection issue, a normal distribution may be imposed on scores, or grade boundaries may be determined on the basis of the proportions of students to be allocated to grades, rather than on their actual achievements, to achieve uniformity in grading across subjects. Thus, the top 10 percent of scores might be assigned an A grade, the next 20 percent a B grade, and so on. These percentages may be applied across all subjects, and from year to year.

A norm-referenced approach, however, is not without its problems. First, it takes the focus off the knowledge and skills that are being assessed at a time when there is great emphasis on standards-based reform in education and in attempting to specify the knowledge and skills that students should acquire. Secondly, it will not register changes in standards if they deteriorate which, for example, they do when the proportion of the population taking examinations increases. Thirdly, it pays no attention to the differential requirements of subjects. Some subjects may require greater student effort and time. Fourthly, it does not recognize that perhaps because of those demands, some subjects may be more highly selective than others. Finally, it will not prevent students from shopping around for subjects in which the probability of obtaining a higher grade might be high relative to other subjects. In effect, the use of norm-referencing "solves" the problem of possible differences between the difficulty level of examination subjects by ignoring it.

A number of studies of between-subject comparability, despite limitations in the procedures used, provide at the very least prima facie evidence that comparability problems exist in the grading of subjects. In *subject-pair analysis*, in which the mean grade of examinees, converted into numerical scores (e.g., $A = 100$; $B = 90$, etc.), is compared with the mean grade achieved by those examinees on a comparison subject (or group of comparison subjects), differences in the mean scores (mean grade difference) attributed to a difference in grading standards have been found (Nuttall et al., 1974). A problem with the procedure is that results may differ when analyses are conducted for subgroups in an examination cohort. For example, in a test of its sensitivity using examination results in England, mathematics and English were found to have been graded in a similar manner for male examinees, while for females, English appeared to be more leniently graded than mathematics (Newton, 1997). This would be a problem if a correction factor based on the overall mean difference were applied to students' grades in an examination.

A second approach to examine the comparability of grades in different subject areas is to have a sample of examinees take an independent *"moderator" test* of aptitude or of general achievement (e.g., a verbal reasoning test) in conjunction with the examination, and to use scores on the test to match up performances on individual examination subjects. The assumption underlying the approach, which would be very difficult to sustain, is that the additional measure represents a major factor underlying diverse achievements, and that the factor is equally appropriate for all achievements. A further problem if the measure is used to adjust scores on examinations is the assumption that it is aptitude (or general ability), rather than achievement in individual subjects, that merits reward.

A third approach to examining the comparability of grades uses a measure of a student's *overall performance on the examination*, which is interpreted as an indication of "general scholastic ability". For example, grades might be converted to numerical scores and an overall index obtained for each candidate by summing scores for his/her six best subjects. It would then be possible to estimate the overall "ability" of examinees taking a particular subject by computing, for example, the percentage of examinees taking a subject that exceeded the median score on the overall performance scale. Such analyses reveal substantial differences between the "general scholastic ability" of candidates taking different subjects (Kellaghan & Dwan, 1995). Again, there are difficulties with the use of this measure of general scholastic ability. First, subjects that contribute to the score, and the level at which they are taken, vary from candidate to candidate. Secondly, the trait that is represented in the score may vary in its relevance to individual subject areas. Thirdly, in the case of examinations which have different levels, the score is directly affected by the level at which an examination is taken.

Yet another approach uses an *added value measure* to assess the comparability of standards in different subject areas. In this approach, examinations are regarded as comparable in standards if examinees with the same achievement on an examination taken some years earlier receive grades that are similarly distributed in the examination (Fitz-Gibbon & Vincent, 1995; Millar & Kelly, 1999).

Some commentators regard the notion of comparability across subjects as meaningless, when one considers that courses on which examinations are based differ in difficulty, in the demands they make on students, and in their motivational effects. Furthermore, students opting for different subject areas differ in their characteristics (Cresswell, 1996; Goldstein, 1986; Newbould & Massey, 1979; Newton, 1997; Wiliam, 1996). In light of these considerations, it has been suggested that what is really important is whether or not grades are accorded the same value by certificate users. The issue then becomes one of maintaining public confidence in the use of an examination for selection purposes (Cresswell, 1995). However, given the fact that analyses of the kind described above point to differences in grading standards, and the additional fact that students are making decisions based on this perception regarding subject choice, public confidence may well run out.

CRITERION-REFERENCING

Criterion-referencing, and the related concept of domain-referencing, grew out of dissatisfaction with the use of norm-referenced tests in classrooms, which were perceived to be of limited value for instructional purposes. The issue is also relevant to other assessment uses, for example in public examinations and in the establishment of standards or levels of proficiency in national and international assessments.

Both criterion and domain-referenced scores have been used to place individuals above or below specific performance standards (e.g., "minimal competency," "mastery"). In the case of public examinations, such scores would be used to determine the grade awarded to an examinee. It would seem reasonable to assume that transparency and reliability would be improved if the criteria for standard setting or for determining grade boundaries could be specified, that is, if written statements were available which prescribed the absolute level of achievement required to justify the award of a particular grade (see Nedelsky, 1954).

There were numerous efforts in British public examinations in the 1980s to identify the qualities of candidates' work appropriate to different grade levels, and many descriptions of specific standard-setting grade criteria are available (see e.g., Christie & Forrest, 1981; Orr & Nuttall, 1983; SEC, 1985). However, serious difficulties were encountered in their application. For example, some examination performances that would have merited a grade using conventional procedures would not have merited the same grade using the grade-related criteria, though examiners agreed that they should. It seems that the criteria could not accommodate the multidimensional nature of achievement by, for example, specifying the weight that should be attached to different aspects of performance when judging an individual examinee's work. Neither could the application of concise sets of explicit written criteria replicate the holistic value judgments made by qualified judges (Cresswell, 1996).

The situation today would seem to be that it is worthwhile having general, but not specific, descriptions of the achievement worthy of a grade. This view recognizes the subjective nature of the judgments involved, which have been compared to those made in evaluation of a work of art. Acceptance of this view may be a cause for concern to some given the decisions that are based on results. However, while the judgments or decisions of examiners may not be amenable to empirical verification, though they may be supported by empirical data, this does not mean that they are capricious or unreliable in the sense that they are difficult to replicate. On the contrary, they can be considered the results of a rational process, which can be supported by reason (Cresswell, 1996, 2000; Goldstein & Cresswell, 1996). In this situation, the experience and skills of examiners is paramount, together with adequate procedures to review judgments and achieve consensus. To aid such consensus, statistical data on the performance of students in the examination, as well as performance in previous years, is usually considered. The procedure is similar to that employed in setting levels of proficiency in the United States (see Hambleton, 2001; Loomis & Bourque, 2001; Raymond & Reid, 2001).

EQUITY

The issue of equity, reflected in the fact that examinations are carried out under standard conditions and that examinee responses are scored anonymously, has always been a central concern, and indeed justification, for external (public) examinations. However, given the importance of examinations in determining life chances, it is inevitable that questions have arisen about possible bias in the procedure which may limit the chances of particular groups (boys, girls, ethnic groups, language groups, urban–rural candidates, public/private school candidates) (see Mathews, 1985). While differences in performance have frequently been associated with the socioeconomic status, location, ethnicity, and gender of examinees, it has proved extremely difficult to determine whether these are reflections of the "achievements" of the groups or are a function of the examining instrument.

A consistent finding in a number of countries is that method of measurement may contribute to gender differences. Males obtain higher scores on standardized multiple-choice tests, while females do better on essay-type examinations (Bolger & Kellaghan, 1990; Mathews, 1985; Stage, 1995). A number of possible explanations have been put forward for this finding: that variables unrelated to content (e.g., quality of writing, expectations of readers) may affect the score awarded by examiners to an essay test, and the greater tendency for males, compared to females, to guess in answering multiple-choice questions.

DISADVANTAGES OF EXTERNAL EXAMINATIONS

Several commentators see a role for external examinations in raising academic standards (e.g., Eisemon, 1990; Heyneman & Ransom, 1992; Ross & Maehlck, 1990; Somerset, 1996). They argue that if the quality and scope of examinations is satisfactory, they will provide acceptable guides for teaching, leading to an adjustment of instructional and learning processes which, in turn, will enhance the quality of students' achievements. It is believed that impact can be strengthened by providing feedback to schools on how their students performed in specific subject areas, and even on individual questions or items.

On the basis of empirical and anecdotal evidence, there can be little doubt that examinations to which high stakes are attached affect teaching and learning (Crooks, 1988; DeLuca, 1993; Frederiksen, 1984; Kellaghan & Greaney, 1992). The consequences, however, are not always as intended; neither are they always positive (Kellaghan & Greaney, 1992; Madaus, 1988; Madaus & Kellaghan, 1992). First, examinations tend to emphasize scholastic skills (particularly ones involving language and mathematics), often paying little attention to knowledge and skills that would be useful in the everyday life of students. Students (and teachers) will focus their curriculum efforts on these areas, often excluding areas (both cognitive and non-cognitive) that are not relevant to the examination. Teachers often refer to past examination papers in deciding what areas of the curriculum to study (and not to study) in a phenomenon known as "teaching to the test". In effect, the examinations come to define the curriculum. The negative impact of the examination will be more pronounced if the knowledge and skills required to do well relate for the most part to the recall or recognition of factual information, rather than the ability to synthesize information or apply principles to new situations. If this is the case, students will spend much of their time in rote memorization, routine drilling, and the accumulation of factual knowledge, which in turn may inhibit creativity, experimentation, and the development of higher order and transferable skills. Process, planning, and perseverance skills will be accorded little attention.

Secondly, the results of experiments and field studies on the effects of students' goals on their cognitive processes suggest that examinations or tests to which high stakes or sanctions are attached affect students' learning goals, learning strategies, involvement in learning tasks, and attitudes to learning, in particular attitudes towards improving their competence. These studies distinguish between *learning (or mastery) goals*, which reflect the concern of individuals to develop new skills and increase their competence, understanding, and mastery of something new, and *performance (or ego) goals*, which reflect individuals' concern to demonstrate their ability and to gain favorable judgments or avoid negative evaluations of their ability or competence. Different patterns of behavior, cognition, and affect have been found to be associated with pursuit of the two categories of goal. For example, learning-goal students are more likely to apply self-regulating effective learning and problem-solving strategies, while performance-goal students make more use of strategies that are superficial or short-term, such as memorizing and rehearsing. Further, students who pursue learning goals are more positive and exhibit a preference for challenging work and risk taking, while students with performance goals tend to avoid challenging tasks and risk taking, especially if their self-concept of ability is low (Ames, 1992; Ames & Archer, 1988; Grolnick & Ryan, 1987).

Most people would probably agree that it would be preferable if schools promoted the development of learning goals rather than of performance goals. This view is very much in line with current standards-based reform efforts, particularly in the United States, that specify challenging definitions of the proficiencies that students will need in the information-based economies of the 21st century: higher order thinking skills, problem-solving abilities, investigative and reasoning skills, improved means of communication, and a commitment to life-long learning. The problem in the case of high-stakes examinations is that they tend to foster performance goals rather than learning goals (Kellaghan, Madaus & Raczek, 1996).

A third negative factor associated with high stakes examinations arises in the case of motivation. There seems little doubt that if sanctions are attached to students' examination performance, then some students will work quite hard for the examinations. However, two issues arise. One relates to the type of motivation that is engendered. It can be argued that because examinations rely primarily on extrinsic motivation, they will not provide optimal conditions for developing or sustaining interest in learning (intrinsic motivation). The second issue relates to the extent to which examinations are successful in motivating *all* students. It would seem that many students, on the basis of their past record of achievement, will make the realistic judgment that they are not going to be numbered among the successful. When such a negative conclusion is reached, there is evidence that some students become alienated (Lewis, 1989; Willis, 1977), others respond by indifference to the examination process (Hargreaves, 1989), others by disappointment and anger (Edwards & Whitty, 1994) and, in extreme cases, by discord and open rebellion (Kariyawasam, 1993).

Fourthly, in trying to obtain high scores on an examination, students (and sometimes teachers and others) may resort to various forms of malpractice. This is a serious issue in many developing countries, where bribing or intimidating examiners, purchasing copies of examination papers before the examination, impersonation, copying, and collusion between examinees, exam superintendents, and examiners are common (Greaney & Kellaghan, 1996).

Finally, there is a danger that schools will concentrate their efforts on those most likely to succeed on the examinations. As a result, students who are not expected to do well may be retained in grade, or drop out of school (Clarke, Haney, & Madaus, 2000; Greaney & Kellaghan, 1996; Haney, 2000; Kellaghan & Greaney, 1992; Little, 1982; Madaus, 1988; Madaus & Kellaghan, 1992).

SCHOOL-BASED ASSESSMENT

Just as education systems that relied entirely on school-based assessment are adopting some form of external testing, so systems with external examinations have been considering how some elements of school-based assessment might be incorporated into their examining. This is partly because of the advantages that teachers' assessments of their own students are perceived to have, and partly because of the disadvantages associated with examinations that are completely external to the school.

School-based assessment recommends itself because it should improve validity since teachers can use a great variety of assessment approaches, spread over a long period of time in realistic settings, and assess a wide range of practical skills, including oral fluency, ability to plan and execute projects, and ability to work with other students, which are very difficult, some would say impossible, to assess adequately in an external examination. Even oral tests of language administered by an external examiner are recognized as being extremely artificial and as unlikely to assess accurately the level of an examinee's competence. Teachers would seem well placed to capture the multidimensional aspects of students' performance and to incorporate judgments about the processes through which students develop understanding, and in which account is taken of their ability to reflect on the quality of their work (Wolf, Bixby, Glen, & Gardner, 1991).

Despite obvious advantages, it is recognized that problems arise if school-based assessments are incorporated into an examination on which performance will have important consequences for a student's educational future. To address them, a number of procedures have been adopted. In the first, efforts are made before the assessment is carried out to standardize the process of assessment in schools (Harlen, 1994). These efforts, which are made in the interest of *quality assurance*, include teachers meeting with other teachers in a school and with teachers in other schools to discuss students' work and how it is assessed, as well as visits of moderators to schools to help identify variation in assessment practice and in the application of criteria.

An alternative system of moderation involves adjusting the outcomes of assessments after the assessments have been carried out (*quality control*). This may be done by having all students take a "reference test" (e.g., a verbal reasoning test or other general test of skills or abilities). A rank order is then created of students based on their performance on the test, and teachers' assessments of the students are adjusted to conform to this order. This procedure addresses the issue of systematic variation between teachers in the criteria which they use for the award of grades or marks, and puts all students on a common scale, and may be used to generate scores for individuals or to determine group parameters for the statistical moderation of school assessments (McCurry, 1995). However, it is based on the questionable assumption that the characteristic measured by the reference test is an appropriate one on which to order student performance in other areas of achievement. This form of moderation was once used in the United Kingdom and is still used elsewhere (e.g., South Australia).

While school-based assessment is well developed in some countries, efforts to have it contribute to grades in countries in which the external element in public examinations has been very strong have run into difficulties because of cost, malpractice (individual students obtaining external assistance), and the pressures it places on teachers and students. Furthermore, teacher assessments include many sources of error, including variation in the types of assessment tasks they use, differences in the interpretation and application of performance criteria or marking schemes, and the intrusion of irrelevant contextual information in making judgments. It has also been noted that students from high status backgrounds, because of the availability of greater resources and support, are likely to do better, and that females are also likely to be awarded higher grades. Other criticisms relate to an increase in teacher workload; doubt about whether all teachers have the assessment skills required for the task, and administrative problems (e.g., dealing with student absences and transfers) (Elley & Livingstone, 1972; Harlen, 1994; Kellaghan & Greaney, 1992; Pennycuick, 1990).

CONCLUSION

All education systems are faced with two major tasks. The first is the certification of the achievements of students, both to maintain standards and to provide evidence which individual students may need to use in the market place. The second is the selection of students for further education in a situation which prevails everywhere, in which the number of applicants, at least for certain courses, exceeds the number of available places. A variety of procedures have been developed to meet these purposes, which attempt to satisfy standards of fairness and comparability, while ensuring that the objectives represented in school curricula are adequately reflected. The procedures have taken examinations in two opposite directions. Concern with fairness and equity is represented in the use of assessment procedures in which common tasks are presented to all students, administration conditions are standardized, and the student is unknown to the examiner. Concern with adequate assessment of all aspects of the curricula to which students have been exposed, on the other hand, is represented in procedures in which the performance of students is assessed using non-standard tasks under non-standard conditions by a teacher who knows the students well.

Sensitivity to these contrasting conditions and the need to meet the purposes they represent are apparent, on the one hand, in the movement in education systems in which assessment has relied heavily on external terminal examinations to incorporate some aspects of assessment by students' own teachers into the grade a student is awarded in an examination, and on the other, by the adoption of external examinations in systems that have traditionally relied entirely on school-based assessment for student certification. While these movements represent a convergence in practice between education systems, a more radical approach than one that combines existing practices may be required if assessment practices are to contribute to meeting the challenges facing education in the future, in particular fostering the development in students of the knowledge and skills required in contemporary knowledge-based economies. These involve a broader view of achievement than has traditionally been represented in most assessment procedures. Curricula in secondary and tertiary institutions are already responding to the needs of the changing workplace, as well as to the need to accommodate students who, as participation in secondary and higher education increases, are becoming more diverse in their abilities and interests. Unless radical steps to adjust assessment procedures are also taken, there is danger that these efforts will be inhibited.

While external public examinations have been in operation in some European countries for as long as two centuries, the United States is a newcomer to the scene. Although ostensibly inspired by practice elsewhere, the manner in which testing programs are being implemented in American states suggests that they are based on a very superficial knowledge on the nature, variety, and history of public examinations. American programs differ from practice in most European countries in their total reliance on evidence obtained from an external test; in the testing of elementary school students; in the narrow range of curriculum areas assessed; in lack of choice (either to take a test or in the test taken); and in the wide range of consequences attached to test performance for students, teachers, and schools. It would seem that the reformers were intent on adding a new set of problems to the many problems associated with public examinations in Europe and elsewhere.

Perhaps the lesson to be drawn from the American experience by education systems that are introducing or contemplating the introduction of new forms of assessment is the need to consider the range of options available, and indeed to look beyond well-established options, and then to assess carefully the advantages and disadvantages associated with each, before deciding on the form of assessment that best fits their educational traditions and expectations. It would indeed be ironic at a time when higher standards of achievement, such as deep conceptual understanding, an interest in and commitment to learning, a valuing of education, and student confidence in their capacities and attributes, are being proposed for *all* students, if the means adopted to meet these objectives inhibited, rather than facilitated, their attainment.

REFERENCES

Amano, I. (1990). *Education and examination in modern Japan* (W.K. Cummings & F. Cummings, Trans). Tokyo: University of Tokyo.

Ames, C. (1992). Classrooms: Goals, structures, and student motivation. *Journal of Educational Psychology*, **84**, 261–271.

Ames, C., & Archer, J. (1988). Achievement goals in the classroom: Students' learning strategies and motivation processes. *Journal of Educational Psychology*, **80**, 260–267.

Bloom, B.S. (Ed.). (1956). *Taxonomy of educational objectives. Handbook 1. Cognitive domain*. London: Longmans Green.

Bolger, N., & Kellaghan, T. (1990). Method of measurement and gender differences in scholastic achievement. *Journal of Educational Measurement*, **27**, 165–174.

Bray, M., Clarke, P.B., & Stephens, D. (1986). *Education and society in Africa*. London: Edward Arnold.

Bray, M., & Steward, L. (1998). *Examination systems in small states. Comparative perspectives on policies, models and operations*. London: Commonwealth Secretariat.

Brereton, J.L. (1944). *The case for examinations. An account of their place in education with some proposals for their reform*. Cambridge: University Press.

Choppin, B., & Orr, L. (1976). *Aptitude testing at eighteen-plus*. Windsor, Berks: National Foundation for Educational Research.

Christie, T., & Forrest, G.M. (1981). *Defining public examination standards*. London: Schools Council.

Clarke, M., Haney, W., & Madaus, G.F. (2000). High stakes testing and high school completion. *National Board of Educational Testing and Public Policy Statements (Boston College)*, **1**(3), 1–11.

Cresswell, M.J. (1988). Combining grades from different assessments: How reliable is the result? *Educational Review*, **40**, 361–383.

Cresswell, M.J. (1995). Technical and educational implications of using public examinations for selection to higher education. In T. Kellaghan (Ed.), *Admission to higher education: Issues and practice* (pp. 38–48). Princeton, NJ: International Association for Educational Assessment/Dublin: Educational Research Centre.

Cresswell, M. (1996). Defining, setting and maintaining standards in curriculum-embedded examinations: Judgemental and statistical approaches. In H. Goldstein & T. Lewis (Eds), *Assessment: Problems, developments and statistical issues* (pp. 57–84). Chichester: Wiley.

Cresswell, M. (2000). The role of public examinations in defining and monitoring standards. In H. Goldstein & A. Heath (Eds), *Educational standards* (pp. 69–104). Oxford: Oxford University Press.

Crooks, T.J. (1988). The impact of classroom evaluation procedures on students. *Review of Educational Research*, **58**, 438–481.

Dearing, R. (1996). *Review of qualifications for 16–19 year olds*. London: School Curriculum and Assessment Authority.

Delap, M.R. (1994). The interpretation of achieved weights of examination components. *Statistician*, **43**, 505–511.

DeLuca, C. (1993). *The impact of examination systems on curriculum development. An international study*. Dalkeith, Scotland: Scottish Examinations Board.

DuBois, P.H. (1970). *A history of psychological testing*. Boston: Allyn & Bacon.

Eckstein, M.A., & Noah, H.J. (1993). *Secondary school examinations. International perspectives on policies and practice*. New Haven CN: Yale University Press.

Edwards, T., & Whitty, G. (1994). Education: Opportunity, equality and efficiency. In A. Glyn & D. Milibrand (Eds), *Paying for inequality* (pp. 44–64). London: Rivers Oram Press.

Eisemon, T.O. (1990). Examination policies to strengthen primary schooling in African countries. *International Journal of Educational Development*, **10**, 69–82.

Elley, W.B., & Livingstone, I.D. (1972). *External examinations and internal assessments. Alternative plans for reform*. Wellington, New Zealand: New Zealand Council for Educational Research.

EURYDICE. (1999). *European glossary on education. Vol. I. Examinations, qualifications and titles*. Brussels: Author.

Feldt, L.S., & Brennan, R.L. (1989). Reliability. In R.L. Linn (Ed.), *Educational measurement* (3rd ed.; pp. 105–146). New York: American Council on Education/Macmillan.

Fitz-Gibbon, C.T., & Vincent, L. (1995). *Candidates' performance in public examinations in mathematics and science*. London: School Curriculum and Assessment Authority.

Foden, F. (1989). *The examiner. James Booth and the origins of common examinations*. Leeds: School of Continuing Education, University of Leeds.

Frederiksen, N. (1984). The real test bias: Influence of testing on teaching and learning. *American Psychologist*, **39**, 193–202.

Goldstein, H. (1986). Models for equating test scores and for studying the comparability of public examinations. In D.L. Nuttall (Ed.), *Assessing educational achievement* (pp. 168–184). London: Falmer.

Goldstein H., & Cresswell, M.J. (1996). The comparability of different subjects in public examinations: A theoretical and practical critique. *Oxford Review of Education*, **22**, 435–442.

Good, F.J., & Cresswell, M.J. (1988). *Grading the GCSE*. London: Secondary Schools Examination Council.

Greaney, V., & Kellaghan, T. (1996). The integrity of public examinations in developing countries. In H. Goldstein & T. Lewis (Eds), *Assessment: Problems, developments and statistical issues* (pp. 167–181). Chichester: Wiley.

Grolnick, W.S., & Ryan, R.M. (1987). Autonomy in children's learning: An experimental and individual difference investigation. *Journal of Personality and Social Psychology*, **52**, 890–898.

Hambleton, R.K. (2001). Setting performance standards on educational assessments and criteria for evaluating the process. In G.J. Cizek (Ed.), *Setting performance standards. Concepts, methods and perspectives* (pp. 89–116). Mahwah, N.J.: Lawrence Erlbaum.

Hambleton, R.K., Swaminathan, H., & Rogers, H. (1991). *Fundamentals of item response theory*. Newbury Park CA: Sage.

Han Min, & Yang Xiuwen. (2001). Educational assessment in China: Lessons from history and future prospects. *Assessment in Education*, **8**, 5–10.

Haney, W. (2000). The myth of the Texas miracle in education. *Education Policy Analysis Archives*, **8**(41). Retrieved from http://epaa.asu.edu/epaa/.

Hargreaves, A. (1989). The crisis of motivation in assessment. In A. Hargreaves & D. Reynolds (Eds), *Educational policies: Controversies and critiques* (pp. 41–63). New York: Falmer.

Harlen, W. (Ed.) (1994). *Enhancing quality in assessment*. London: Chapman.

Hartog, P., & Rhodes, E.C. (1935). *An examination of examinations*. London: Macmillan.

Hewitt, E. (1967). *Reliability of GCE O-level examinations in English language*. Manchester: Joint Matriculation Board.

Heyneman, S.P., & Ransom, A.W. (1992). Using examinations and testing to improve educational quality. In M.A. Eckstein & H.J. Noah (Eds), *Examinations: Comparative and international studies* (pp. 105–120). Oxford: Pergamon.

Horn, C., Ramos, M., Blumer, I., & Madaus, G.F. (2000). Cut scores: Results may vary. *National Board on Educational Testing and Public Policy Monographs (Boston College)*, **1**(1), 1–31.

Kane, M.T. (2001). So much remains the same: Conception and status of validation in setting standards. In G.C. Cizek (Ed.), *Setting performance standards. Concepts, methods, and perspectives* (pp. 53–88). Mahwah, NJ: Lawrence Erlbaum.

Kariyawasam, T. (1993). *Learning, selection and monitoring: Resolving the roles of assessment in Sri Lanka*. Paper presented at Conference on Learning, Selection and Monitoring: Resolving the Roles of Assessment, Institute of Education, University of London.

Keeves, J.P. (1994). *National examinations: Design, procedures and reporting*. Paris: International Institute for Educational Planning.

Kellaghan, T. (1992). Examination systems in Africa: Between internationalization and indigenization. In M.A. Eckstein & H.J. Noah (Eds), *Examinations: Comparative and international studies* (pp. 95–104). Oxford: Pergamon.

Kellaghan, T., & Dwan, B. (1995). *The 1994 Leaving Certificate Examination: A review of results*. Dublin: National Council for Curriculum and Assessment.

Kellaghan, T., & Greaney, V. (1992). *Using examinations to improve education. A study in fourteen African countries*. Washington, DC: World Bank.

Kellaghan, T., Madaus, G.F., & Raczek, A. (1996). *The use of external examinations to improve student motivation*. Washington, DC: American Educational Research Association.

Lewis, M. (1989). *Differentiation-polarization in an Irish post-primary school*. Unpublished master's thesis, University College Dublin.

Little, A. (1982). The role of examinations in the promotion of "the Paper Qualification Syndrome." In International Labour Office. Jobs and Skills Programme for Africa (Ed.), *Paper qualifications syndrome (PQS) and unemployment of school leavers. A comparative sub-regional study* (pp. 176–195). Addis Ababa: International Labour Office.

Loomis, S.C., & Bourque, M.L. (2001). From tradition to innovation: Standard setting on the National Assessment of Educational Progress. In G.J. Cizek (Ed.), *Setting performance standards. Concepts, methods, and perspectives* (pp. 175–217). Mahwah, NJ: Lawrence Erlbaum.

Madaus, G.F. (1988). The influence of testing on the curriculum. In L.N. Tanner (Ed.), *Critical issues in curriculum* (pp. 83–121). Eighty-seventh Yearbook of the National Society for the Study of Education, Part 1. Chicago: University of Chicago Press.

Madaus, G.F., & Kellaghan, T. (1991). Student examination systems in the European Community: Lessons for the United States. In G. Kulm & S.M. Malcolm (Eds), *Science assessment in the service of reform* (pp. 189–232). Washington, DC: American Association for the Advancement of Science.

Madaus, G.F., & Kellaghan, T. (1992). Curriculum evaluation and assessment. In P.W. Jackson (Ed.), *Handbook of research on curriculum* (pp. 119–154). New York: Macmillan.

Madaus, G.F., Kellaghan, T., & Rakow, E.A. (1975). *A study of the sensitivity of measures of school effectiveness*. Report submitted to the Carnegie Corporation, New York. Dublin: Educational Research Centre/Chestnut Hill, MA: School of Education, Boston College.

Madaus, G.F., & Macnamara, J. (1970). *Public examinations. A study of the Irish Leaving Certificate*. Dublin: Educational Research Centre.

Madaus, G.F., & O'Dwyer, L.M. (1999). A short history of performance assessment. *Phi Delta Kappan*, **80**, 688–695.

Martin, M., & O'Rourke, B. (1984). The validity of the DAT as a measure of scholastic aptitude in Irish post-primary schools. *Irish Journal of Education*, **18**, 3–22.

Mathews, J.C. (1985). *Examinations. A commentary*. Boston: Allen & Unwin.

McCurry, D. (1995). Common curriculum elements within a scaling test for tertiary entrance in Australia. In T. Kellaghan (Ed.), *Admission to higher education: Issues and practice* (pp. 253–360). Princeton, NJ: International Association for Educational Assessment/Dublin: Educational Research Centre.

Messick, S. (1989). Validity. In R.L. Linn (Ed.), *Educational measurement* (3rd ed.; pp. 13–103). New York: American Council on Education/Macmillan.

Millar, D., & Kelly, D. (1999). *From Junior to Leaving Certificate. A longitudinal study of 1994 Junior Certificate candidates who took the Leaving Certificate Examination in 1997*. Dublin: National Council for Curriculum and Assessment.

Mislevy, R.J. (1992). *Linking educational assessments: Concepts, issues, methods, and prospects*. Princeton, NJ: Educational Testing Service.

Miyazaki, I. (1976). *China's examination hell. The civil service examinations of Imperial China* (C. Schirokauer, Trans.). New York: Weatherhill.

Montgomery, R. (1965). *Examinations. An account of their evolution as administrative devices in England*. London: Longmans Green.

Montgomery, R. (1978). *A new examination of examinations*. London: Routledge & Kegan Paul.

Morgan, M., Flanagan, R., & Kellaghan, T. (2001). *A study of non-completion in undergraduate university courses*. Dublin: Higher Education Authority.

Morris, N. (1961). An historian's view of examinations. In S. Wiseman (Ed.), *Examinations and English education* (pp. 1–43). Manchester: Manchester University Press.

Nedelsky, L. (1954). Absolute grading standards for objective tests. *Educational and Psychological Measurement*, **14**, 3–19.

Newbould, C.A., & Massey, A.J. (1979). *Comparability using a common element*. Occasional Publication 7. Cambridge: Oxford Delegacy of Local Examinations, University of Cambridge Local Examinations Syndicate, Oxford and Cambridge Schools Examinations Board.

Newton, P.E. (1997). Measuring comparability of standards between subjects: Why our statistical techniques do not make the grade. *British Educational Research Journal*, **23**, 433–449.

Nuttall, D.L., Backhouse, J.K., & Willmott, A.S. (1974). Comparability of standards between subjects. *Schools Council Examinations Bulletin 29*. London: Evans/Methuen Educational.

O'Rourke, B., Martin, M., & Hurley, J.J. (1989). The Scholastic Aptitude Test as a predictor of third level academic performance. *Irish Journal of Education*, **23**, 22–39.

Orr, L., & Nuttall, D.L. (1983). *Determining standards in the proposed single system of examinations at 16+*. London: Schools Council.

Pennycuick, D. (1990). The introduction of continuous assessment systems at secondary level in developing countries. In P. Broadfoot, R. Murphy & H. Torrance (Eds), *Changing educational assessment. International perspectives and trends* (pp. 106–118). London: Routledge.

Perreiah, A.R. (1984). Logic examinations in Padua *circa* 1400. *History of Education*, **13**, 85–103.

Powell, J. L. (1973). *Selection for university in Scotland*. London: University of London Press.

Rashdall, H. (1936). *The universities of Europe in the middle ages* (Ed. F.M. Powicke & A.B. Emden) (3 vols). Oxford: Oxford University Press.

Raymond, M.R., & Reid, J.B. (2001). Who made that a judge? Selecting and training participants for standard setting. In G.J. Cizek (Ed.), *Setting performance standards. Concepts, methods, and perspectives* (pp. 119–157). Mahwah, NJ: Lawrence Erlbaum.

Roach, J. (1971). *Public examinations in England 1850–1900*. Cambridge: Cambridge University Press.

Ross, K.N., & Maehlck, L. (Eds). (1990). *Planning the quality of education. The collection and use of data for informed decision making*. Oxford: Pergamon/Paris: UNESCO.

SEC (Secondary Examinations Council). (1985). *Reports of the Grade-Related Criteria Working Parties*. London: Author.

Shiel, G., Cosgrove, J., Sofroniou, N., & Kelly, A. (2001). *Ready for life? The literacy achievements of Irish 15-year olds in an international context*. Dublin: Educational Research Centre.

Shore, A., Pedulla, J., & Clarke, M. (2001). *The building blocks of state testing programs*. Chestnut Hill, MA: National Board on Educational Testing and Public Policy, Boston College.

Somerset, A. (1996). Examinations and educational quality. In A. Little & A. Wolf (Eds.), *Assessment in transition. Learning, monitoring and selection in international perspective* (pp. 263–284). Oxford: Pergamon.

Stage, C. (1995). Gender differences on admission instruments for higher education. In T. Kellaghan (Ed.), *Admission to higher education: Issues and practice* (pp. 105–114). Princeton, NJ: International Association for Educational Assessment/Dublin: Educational Research Centre.

Stalnaker, J.M. (1951). The essay type of examination. In E.F. Lindquist (Ed.), *Educational measurement* (pp. 495–530). Washington, DC: American Council on Education.

Starch, D., & Elliott, E.C. (1912). Reliability of grading high school work in English. *School Review*, **20**, 442–457.

Starch, D., & Elliott, E.C. (1913). Reliability of grading work in mathematics. *School Review*, **21**, 254–259.

U.S. Department of Education. (2002). *No Child Left Behind Act of 2001: Reauthorization of the Elementary and Secondary Education Act*. Retrieved from http://www.ed.gov/offices/OESE/esea/

West, A., Edge, A., & Stokes, E. (1999). *Secondary education across Europe: Curricula and school examination systems*. London: Centre for Educational Research, London School of Economics and Political Science.

Wiliam, D. (1996). Standards in examinations: A matter of trust? *Curriculum Journal*, **7**, 293–306.

Willis, P. (1977). *Learning to labor. How working class kids get working class jobs*. New York: Columbia University Press.

Wilmott, A.S., & Nuttall, D.L. (1975). *The reliability of examinations at 16+*. London: Macmillan.

Wiseman, S. (Ed) (1961). *Examinations and English education*. Manchester: Manchester University Press.

Wolf, D., Bixby, J., Glen, J., & Gardner, H. (1991). To use their minds well: Investigating new forms of student assessment. *Review of Research in Education*, **17**, 31–74.

World Bank. (2002). *Toolkit on public examination systems in developing countries*. Retrieved from http://www.worldbank.org/exams.

Section 7

Personnel Evaluation

Introduction

DANIEL L. STUFFLEBEAM

The Evaluation Center, Western Michigan University, MI, USA

Handbooks and encyclopedias on evaluation typically focus on student, project, program, and policy evaluations and exclude the area of personnel evaluation. This is unfortunate, because the performance of personnel is one of the most fundamental determinants of quality in any human enterprise. This is especially evident in education, where the performances of principals, support specialists, and, in particular, teachers heavily influence what students learn, how well they learn it, and how well they grow up to be productive, fulfilled members of society. The role of teachers is especially crucial to schools' successes, as recent research has demonstrated (Sanders & Horn, 1998; Tymms, 1994, 1995; Webster, 1995). For example, based on analysis of data from the Tennessee Value-Added Assessment System database, Sanders and Horn (1998) concluded that teacher effectiveness explained student academic growth better than race, socio-economic level, class size, and classroom heterogeneity.

This section addresses the need for more and deeper exchange on the issues in educational personnel evaluation. The authors of the three chapters discuss personnel evaluation in relation to teachers, support personnel, and principals. All three chapters speak of the unique challenges associated with evaluating personnel, and hold in common an emphasis on using evaluation to assure that students are served by competent personnel. All point to the need for further development of the educational personnel evaluation enterprise.

TEACHER EVALUATION

Pearlman and Tannenbaum (two eminent researchers at the Educational Testing Service) ground their discussion in the optimistic note that teacher evaluation, when well done, can contribute to teachers' professional development and enhance professional practice. However, the theme of their chapter is that while some progress has been made, the teacher evaluation field is far from delivering what is needed.

The authors closely examine the relationships between teacher education, teacher quality, teacher certification/licensure, teaching standards, learning

International Handbook of Educational Evaluation, 603–608
T. Kellaghan, D.L. Stufflebeam (eds.)
© *2003 Dordrecht: Kluwer Academic Publishers. Printed in Great Britain.*

standards, student achievement, student testing, and legislated policy. They discuss the validity, reliability, political, and feasibility challenges in linking these things in a meaningful way. They cite research that confirms that teacher education impacts on teacher quality, which, in turn, impacts on student achievement. However, they also point out that "connecting teacher performance to student achievement and high stakes decisions and employment and compensation is fraught with difficulty and potential legal complications." Especially, they note that licensure test scores cannot predict the quality of teaching.

In the view of Pearlman and Tannenbaum, standardized tests are often grossly inappropriate and thus misapplied in teacher accountability schemes, noting especially that the most widely used multiple-choice measures of student achievement are not designed to measure complex cognitive skills or deep levels of subject matter understanding. They point out that this type of testing is often misaligned with teaching and learning standards that stress construction of knowledge and higher-order learning.

In assessing the current state of teacher evaluation theory and practice, Pearlman and Tannenbaum concentrate on actual (rather than theorized) practices of teacher assessment. These are mainly focused on evaluating new teachers during their induction processes, but also include the portfolio/assessment center evaluations employed by the National Board of Professional Teaching Standards to provide their imprimatur to outstanding, experienced teachers. The authors note that recent licensure, induction, and certification assessment programs reflect an improved link between the examinee's teaching task and the goal of the measurement. Thus, there is increased capacity to ground personnel decisions on relevant evidence. The chapter includes a comprehensive review of relevant publications in these areas.

The authors see clearer links now between student learning standards and teacher preparation standards than Dwyer and Stufflebeam reported in 1996. However, Pearlmann and Tannenbaum lament that states often undermine these links by hiring teachers that do not meet pertinent standards and, for example, assign teachers to subjects they are not prepared to teach. They say that the evaluation development community can do little more than produce better concepts and methods pertaining to licensure, certification, advancement, and pay, unless they develop capacity to influence authority and power groups to properly apply the concepts and methods.

Basically, Pearlman and Tannenbaum disregard conceptual developments in school-based teacher evaluation, that are reflected mainly in the literature, but little in practice. They conclude that there have been no noteworthy advances in how teachers are evaluated in schools and classrooms for over a decade.

EVALUATION OF SCHOOL PRINCIPALS

Glasman and Heck focus on the crucial function of evaluating the performance of school leaders, which they note has been poor in the past. Despite their misgivings about past practices, they say that the fundamental stages of principal evaluation are agreed upon, sound, and should proceed in three areas: base-line employment evaluation, fine-tuning evaluation, and secondary employment evaluation.

They state that recent changes in schools and the principalship have led to a need for new and different models for evaluating principals, noting that the changing role of the principal has been brought about by the devolution of responsibility and authority from a central office to the local school for directing and controlling schools. Under site-based management approaches, schools have been given more authority to determine curriculum, to hire and fire personnel, to allocate resources, etc. They have also been assigned greater responsibility for effecting and being accountable for student learning and other school functions. More than ever, principals are seen to be accountable to a broad group of stakeholders (e.g., parents, community, district administrators, teachers, staff, and school councils).

A problem that arises in district/central office supervisors and school board members fulfilling their role as evaluators of principals is that typically they are not adequately trained in personnel evaluation. To address this issue, Glasman and Heck recommend that administrative training programs should include a course in formative personnel evaluation and that advanced courses (e.g., inservice training) could focus on summative evaluation, which would attend to issues of accountability, equity, and efficiency. (While such training would strengthen administrators' command of evaluation, there is also a clear need to train the other persons who evaluate school principals, especially members of school councils.)

In the face of poor models and tools for assessing principals' performances, Glasman and Heck call for an improved principal evaluation approach, in which a principal evaluation's purposes, objects, criteria, and evaluator qualifications would be clarified. They point out that the *purposes* of an evaluation may be formative (e.g., professional development) or summative (e.g., preparation, certification, and selection of principals; granting tenure or promotion; reassignment or dismissal; fixing accountability for student outcomes). Its *objects* are defined as the aspects of the principal's work or role that are to be assessed (e.g., leadership, attitudes, behavior, decision making, competence, performance, effectiveness), with evaluative *criteria* providing a further breakdown of the objects (e.g., goal achievement, with an emphasis on efficiency and effectiveness, and taking into account what the school's stakeholders expect of the principal). Finally, they call for a careful determination of the *authorized evaluator(s)*, who might include the school district's superintendent, teachers, parents, peers, and/or members of the school's council.

Clearly, these authors see principal evaluation as a primitive area of practice in need of redefinition and great improvement. They point to the need for sound research and development, and have provided some useful ideas about how needed improvement can be pursued.

SUPPORT PERSONNEL EVALUATION

Stronge in his chapter emphasizes the importance of evaluating educators who work with students or faculty in a support capacity. These include counselors, psychologists, social workers, work-study supervisors, library-media specialists, computer specialists, content specialists, speech therapists, gifted/talented resource specialists, and nurses.

He states that historically, education has neglected to evaluate such specialists in terms that are relevant to their assignments and, compared to teacher evaluation, the evaluation of educational specialists has a "less developed support system of guidelines, training, and technical support." With increasing pressure for accountability, he notes that "performance evaluation has been extended more systematically to include all professional employees." Thus, he calls for an "evaluation process which recognizes and rewards the varied and diverse contributions of educational specialists" and provides them with direction for improvement.

Stronge notes that evaluating such specialists is unique and requires new, relevant models. These should be grounded in valid job descriptions; take account of the specialists' highly specialized training, functions, and associated theoretical orientations; and especially assess the non-instructional nature of much of their work.

Noting that observation – the primary method for evaluating teachers – has limited value in evaluating support specialists, Stronge suggests other methods, which include surveying client groups, collecting and assessing job artifacts, and documenting the specialist's contributions and impacts on student success.

Strong's proposals in the chapter and in his previous publications have a functional orientation. They are aimed especially at helping administrators/ supervisors to clarify specialist roles and evaluate performance against role requirements. Stronge proposes an evaluation model, with the following steps: identify system needs; develop roles and responsibilities for the job; set standards for job performance; document job performance; evaluate performance; and improve/maintain professional service.

SOME OBSERVATIONS ABOUT THIS SECTION

When one considers all three chapters on educational personnel evaluation, it seems that teacher evaluation is presented as the most straightforward and systematic but that an alternative technology is needed to evaluate specialists or principals. However, when one considers what is left unsaid as well as said in the teacher evaluation chapter, it seems clear that much research and development is needed there as well, especially in the evaluation of teachers in classrooms for both formative and summative purposes.

All three chapters comment on the push toward greater accountability. Clearly, teachers are heavily impacted by the emphasis on accountability based on student outcomes. However, the call for greater accountability affects all school personnel. It must not be forgotten also that accountability demands can greatly impact on students, since accountability not infrequently drives what is taught and determines which students are given most attention. The practice of accountability raises the stakes for everyone; as a consequence, it is crucially important that personnel evaluation practices be reasonable, accurate, and fair. All three chapters note the importance of formative evaluation, something that can easily be overlooked as the public and legislators focus their attention on summative evaluation, results, and accountability. It is perhaps ironic that the advancements in teacher evaluation cited by Pearlman and Tannenbaum are clearly more summative than formative.

The chapters vary in their consideration of the role of professional standards for guiding and assessing personnel evaluations. Stronge points to the importance of meeting the Joint Committee (1988) *Personnel Evaluation Standards* in evaluating educational specialists, stating that "In order for evaluation to be valid and valued for any educator, these issues [raised in *The Personnel Evaluation Standards*] must be adequately addressed." Glasman and Heck also discuss *The Personnel Evaluation Standards* in the context of schools using them as a part of a general approach to standards-based education. Pearlman and Tannenbaum do not consider the *Standards*, though clearly relevant to the problems they identify in high stakes evaluations of teachers. Obviously, teacher evaluation systems need to do a better job of meeting requirements for propriety, utility, feasibility, and accuracy, and it must be accepted that personnel evaluations can do harm (e.g., through misguided, corrupted high stakes testing), as well as good. It is critically important that personnel evaluation systems be regularly subjected to systematic metaevaluation, and that such metaevaluations be keyed to appropriate professional standards for judging personnel.

A reasonable conclusion to this overview of the state of educational personnel evaluation might be that the glass is half full. Given that the three chapters tend to focus on the shortcomings of current practice, their observations might be regarded as providing an agenda for research, development, and improvement in the educational personnel evaluation arena. Thinking about and the practice of educational personnel evaluation have improved over time. The field now has professional standards that define what is required in sound evaluation (Joint Committee, 1988), and some progress has been made, both in theory and practice, toward satisfying the conditions of propriety, utility, feasibility, and accuracy. There have been important advances in teacher evaluation, in recognizing that the teacher is the school's most influential asset in effecting sound student learning, in developing rigorous approaches to evaluating teacher induction and to certifying outstanding teaching competence, and in proposing new models for evaluating teacher performance in the classroom. In the area of support personnel, Stronge has brought to awareness the need to clarify roles for, and systematically evaluate, educational specialists, and has proposed a clear process for proceeding with such evaluations. The area of principal evaluation continues to be weak, and clearly needs much more attention.

REFERENCES

Dwyer, C.A., & Stufflebeam, D.L. (1996). Teacher evaluation. In D.C. Berliner & R.C. Calfee (Eds.), *Handbook of educational psychology* (pp. 765–786). New York: Simon & Schuster Macmillan.

Joint Committee on Standards for Educational Evaluation. (1988). *The personnel evaluation standards*. Newbury Park, CA: Sage.

Sanders, W.L., & Horn, S.P. (1998). Research findings from the Tennessee Value-Added Assessment System (TVAAS) database: Implications for educational evaluation and research. *Journal of Personnel Evaluation in Education*, **12**, 247–256.

Tymms, P. (1994, July). *Evaluating the long term impact of schools*. Paper presented at the National Evaluation Institute of the Center for Research on Educational Accountability and Teacher Evaluation (CREATE), Gatlinburg, TN.

Tymms, P. (1995). *Setting up a national "value added" system for primary education in England: Problems and possibilities*. Paper presented at the National Evaluation Institute of the Center for Research on Educational Accountability and Teacher Evaluation (CREATE), Kalamazoo, MI.

Webster, W.J. (1995). The connection between personnel evaluation and school evaluation. *Studies in Educational Evaluation*, **21**, 227–254.

28
Teacher Evaluation Practices in the Accountability Era

MARI PEARLMAN

Educational Testing Service, NJ, USA

RICHARD TANNENBAUM

Educational Testing Service, NJ, USA

In 1996, when Dwyer and Stufflebeam last surveyed teacher evaluation practices and philosophies, they made the following assertion:

> Teacher evaluation is a highly controversial area, with myriad stakeholders and a wealth of technical, psychological, political, ethical, and educational complexities. Teacher evaluation is relevant to every segment of the educational system, and society at large has an intense interest in how it is carried out and what its impact on education and on individuals' lives will be. Thus, the criticisms of theory and practice are strongly held, and how (or whether) these criticisms are resolved has direct implications for the quality of American schooling. (Dwyer & Stufflebeam, 1996, p. 768)

They then reported on a broad range of issues and challenges raised by the nexus of the burgeoning reform movement in education, the dynamic and complicated nature of teaching as a profession, and the technical standards for high quality personnel evaluation of any kind. As their introductory matrix of "Types of Evaluations and Decisions Involved in Preparation, Licensing, Employment, and Professionalization of Teachers" makes clear (see Appendix A), there was little consensus about what practices worked best in ensuring the overall quality of the education workforce. In addition, that teacher evaluation practices were deficient and inadequate was presented as a fact; the remainder of their survey in one way or another dealt with various aspects of improvement in these practices.

Years have passed, and nothing has occurred that would undermine the assertions in the quotation above. There are, however, two significant areas of change, in the public policy arena and in assessment methodologies, that could have profound effects on teacher evaluation practices in the next decade. The single most important shift in the public policy arena since Dwyer and Stufflebeam's survey is the emergence of a tidal wave of support for what is

International Handbook of Educational Evaluation, 609–642
T. Kellaghan, D.L. Stufflebeam (eds.)
© *2003 Dordrecht: Kluwer Academic Publishers. Printed in Great Britain.*

loosely called "teacher accountability." What this seems to mean in effect is a growing insistence on measurement of teacher quality and teacher performance in terms of student achievement, which is all too often poorly defined, crudely measured, and unconnected to what educators regard as significant learning. While there have been numerous explorations of varied approaches to teacher evaluation that could lead to increased sophistication, validity, or utility of teacher evaluation practices in schools by school personnel over the past decade, none of these has resulted in widespread application of new understandings of evaluation practice for teachers.

Because there is still little consensus about acceptable ways to meet the very substantial challenges posed by links between measures of student achievement and consequent conclusions about teacher effectiveness, the fact that this issue dominates current discourse about teacher evaluation is very significant, and somewhat alarming. This is not a new effort or a new issue, but the heated insistence on its power as the single most important criterion for establishing a teacher's effectiveness is new (Millman, 1997, pp. 6–7). Simply put, most efforts to connect student achievement to individual teacher performance have foundered in the past on these weaknesses:

• The measurement does not take into account teaching context as a performance variable
• The measurement is unreliable, in part because it does not include time as a variable – both the teacher's time with a cohort of students; and some model or models of sufficient time to see learning effects in students.
• The measures used to reflect student achievement are not congruent with best practice and philosophy of instruction in modern education.

Several notable efforts to address these deficiencies have been launched in the past decade; we discuss those below.

The second area of change has been in the area of teacher assessment. Here there is both good news and bad news. Teacher testing is now more than ever a high stakes enterprise. The most striking example of the potential stringency of teacher testing practices is provided by the experience of teachers in Massachusetts, which introduced a new teacher licensing testing program in 1998, the Massachusetts Educator Certification Tests (MECT). At its first administration in April 1998, only 41 percent of all test takers met the passing standard established by the state on all three parts of the test: reading literacy, writing literacy, and subject matter knowledge (Haney et al., 1999). There have been and continue to be numerous analyses of the technical and policy implications of the development, implementation, and continuing use of the MECT (Haney, et al., 1999; Ludlow, 2001; Melnick & Pullin, 1999; Melnick & Pullin, 2000; Luna, Solsken, & Kutz, 2000), but the essential point of the very public suffering of Massachusetts educators is how congruent this testing initiative and the responses to its results are with the rhetoric of "teacher accountability." All of the furor over the Massachusetts approach to teacher testing emphasizes in one way or another the critical validity concerns that the Massachusetts approach to evaluation raises for all stakeholders in the educational reform arena.

The Massachusetts teacher testing program began as a legislative and policy initiative that was intended to ensure the quality of teachers entering Massachusetts's education workforce. On the face of it, Massachusetts was merely implementing a quality assurance step in the licensing process for new teachers, something states do, and have both a right and responsibility to do, on a regular basis. It was both the very high stakes imposed on this new step in the licensing process and the methods policy makers used to impose this step that exploded Massachusetts teacher testing into headlines all over the U.S. (Sterling, 1998). All aspects of validation of the constructs that underlie testing teachers at the beginning of their careers – the technical standards the measurement profession believes that all test makers are obliged to meet – appeared to be negotiable and subject to policymakers', not test makers', quality standards. As Haney et al. make clear, all aspects of the development – from the contractor chosen, the time allotted to test development (six months), the policy decisions regarding consequences communicated to candidates and then rescinded and replaced, the methods for setting passing score standards, and the technical information provided by the test maker – were fraught with errors and violations of professional measurement standards (Haney et al., pp. 1–4). Furthermore, a critical and potentially divisive issue was enjoined by the Massachusetts controversy: who has the authority to set the standard for teachers' knowledge and skill? What is the proper balance of power among policymakers, legislators, teacher educators, teacher candidates, and the general public whose children are the reason for all of this concern (Brabeck, 1999)?

If licensure testing for beginning teachers appears to be fraught with controversy, the good news in teacher evaluation is that several of the assessment and evaluation ventures mentioned as promising but unproven by Dwyer and Stufflebeam have been developed and elaborated and are now more than promises. There has been effective application of theoretical knowledge to aspects of teacher evaluation, with some actual practical results. Some essential foundations for a degree of consensus about what teachers should know (one part of the assessment and evaluation challenge) and be able to do (the other – and far more vexing – part of the challenge) have been laid. Some actual decisions and actions that affect teachers' and students' interconnected lives are being taken as a result of this growing consensus. And there are innovative new assessments being designed and used to evaluate teachers in many locations.

HIGHLIGHTS OF THE LITERATURE

In the past decade considerable theoretical and empirical work has been accomplished in three areas: what student testing can and should do as a part of the instructional system; what teachers should know and be able to do and how to incorporate those values and standards into the preparation program for beginning teachers; and the links between teacher performance and student achievement. In addition, innovative evaluation strategies for both beginning and in-service teachers have been implemented in several states in the U.S. Many of these evaluation strategies combine assessment of teachers' performance with development and enhancement of teaching skills.

Beginning with what is known about current practice in student testing is an increasingly important part of any consideration of teacher evaluation practices, given the current political and policy climate. How teachers are prepared for their professional work and how they should be prepared to do that work well is the foundation for any evaluation system for professional performance. Clearly, with the emphasis on links between teacher performance and student achievement, how teachers are prepared for their instructional and motivational roles is essential. And the growing body of evidence about links between teacher performance and student achievement must be an influential element in evaluation of teachers' work and support for their ongoing learning to improve that work.

Student Testing

The most recent evaluative commentary on the use of student tests for the purpose of high stakes accountability decisions is incoming American Educational Research Association (AERA) President (2002) Robert Linn's 2000 survey of 50 years of student testing in the U.S. education system, and the effects of that testing (Linn, 2000). Linn concludes:

> I am led to conclude that in most cases the instruments and technology have not been up to the demands that have been placed on them by high-stakes accountability. Assessment systems that are useful monitors lose much of their dependability and credibility for that purpose when high stakes are attached to them. The unintended negative effects of the high-stakes accountability uses often outweigh the intended positive effects. (Linn, 2000, p. 14)

Given the current policy climate, this is a sobering and cautionary conclusion, coming as it does from such a major figure in the measurement community, and one known for his evenhanded and judicious treatment of measurement issues. It is clear that the most widely used current measures of student achievement, primarily standardized norm-referenced multiple choice tests developed and sold off-the-shelf by commercial test publishers, are useful for many educational purposes, but not valid for school accountability. Indeed, they may be positively misleading at the school level, and certainly a distortion of teaching effectiveness at the individual teacher level (Madaus & O'Dwyer, 1999; Barton, 1999). Concerns about the increased dependence on high-stakes testing has prompted a number of carefully worded technical cautions from important policy bodies as well in the past two to three years (Heubert & Hauser, 1999; Feuer et al., 1999; Elmore & Rothman, 1999; AERA, 2000). While it is possible to imagine a program of student testing that aligns the assessments used to the standards for learning and to the curriculum actually taught, and that employs multiple methods and occasions to evaluate student learning, the investment such a program would demand would increase the cost of student assessment significantly. Furthermore, involving teachers in the conceptual development and interpretation of assessment measures that would be instructionally useful, particularly when those measures may have a direct effect on the teachers' performance evaluation and livelihood, is no closer to the realities of assessment practice than it has ever been, which is to say that it is, in general, simply not part of the practice of school districts in the U.S.

Teacher Quality and Effectiveness

The emphasis on teacher quality has gained considerable momentum from the body of empirical evidence substantiating the linkage between teacher competence and student achievement. The "value-added" research, typified by the work of Sanders et al. (Sanders & Rivers, 1996; Wright, Horn, & Sanders, 1997; Sanders & Horn, 1998), reinforces the assumption that the teacher is the most significant factor impacting student achievement. Sanders' work in this area is the best known and, increasingly, most influential among policymakers. In the measurement community, however, independent analyses of Sanders' data and methods have just begun (Koretz, 2001; Kupermintz, Shepard, & Linn, 2001; Hamilton, Klein, & McCaffrey, 2001: Stecher & Arkes, 2001).

The "value added" research typified by Sanders et al. clearly points to the importance of teacher quality in one kind of student achievement, standardized multiple choice testing. What is not clear from such research, however, is an understanding of the factors that necessarily contribute to teacher quality.

Teacher Preparation

The question of "What are the qualifications of a good teacher?" has been addressed by Linda Darling-Hammond (1999). Darling-Hammond conducted an extensive review of state policies and institutional practices related to factors presumed to contribute to teacher quality. Such factors included teachers' subject matter knowledge, knowledge of teaching and learning, teaching experience, and certification status. Prominent among her findings was a consistent and significant positive relationship between the proportion of well qualified teachers in a state and student achievement on National Assessment of Educational Progress (NAEP) reading and mathematics assessments, even when controlling for students' characteristics such as language background, poverty, and minority status. A well-qualified teacher was defined as being state certified and holding a college degree with a major in the field being taught.

What emerges from Hammond's research is an appreciation for the impact that teacher education has on teacher quality, and, subsequently and presumably, student achievement. Appropriately prepared teachers are necessary for students to achieve. This is a particularly significant finding given the education labor market dynamics currently in force in the U.S. While schools and departments of education at U.S. universities are preparing more than enough undergraduates and graduates to fill the available jobs (Feistritzer, 1998), those students are either not entering the teaching profession or not willing to work in geographical locations that have teaching jobs available. Over the next decade, approximately two million teaching positions will need to be filled as the current cadre of teachers retires. As *Education Week's Quality Counts 2000* makes clear (Olson, 2000a, 2000b), unless state policies regarding teacher licensure and evaluation are radically revised, many of those positions will be filled with teachers whose subject matter knowledge and professional teacher education is at best unknown, as states grant emergency licenses and waive requirements so that there will be an adult in every classroom in the role of teacher. Thus, a widening gap between research findings regarding effective teaching and actual hiring practices is emerging.

Evaluation of Practicing Teachers: Using Student Achievement Data

While the evaluation of teachers is certainly not a new phenomenon, the context of evaluation has changed. Traditionally, teacher evaluation focused primary on what Danielson and McGreal (2000) label "inputs." Inputs refer to what teachers do, the tasks they perform. That is, the philosophy guiding this evaluative model is that teachers should be doing, behaving, interacting, demonstrating, and reinforcing those teaching and learning practices and attitudes valued by the educational system in which they are teaching. Assuming the presence of such factors as clearly defined and communicated values (evaluation criteria), well-trained evaluators, and a supportive professional climate, such an evaluation orientation contributes to teachers' professional development and enhances professional practice. The obvious merit of such systems is that they can provide constructive formative feedback to teachers. Typically absent from such teacher traditional evaluation systems are student achievement measures; that is, indicators of student achievement do not generally factor into the teachers' performance evaluation.

More recently, however, teacher evaluation systems have shifted attention to student achievement measures. The philosophy guiding these systems is that it matters less what teachers do if their actions do not lead to student achievement; student success is what matters most (Danielson & McGreal, 2000). H.D. Schalock (1998) summarizes the prevailing sentiment this way, "Put simply, if the purpose of teaching is to nurture learning, then both teachers and schools should be judged for their effectiveness on the basis of what and how much students learn"

(p. 240). This movement towards student outcomes as the benchmark of teacher quality has gained momentum from the often publicized lack of perceived academic competitiveness of students in this country compared to students in other industrialized nations (see, for example, Manzo, 1997; Sommerfeld, 1996; Walberg & Paik, 1997) and the mounting empirical evidence that teachers are the most significant factor in student achievement (see, for example, Greenwald, Hedges, & Laine, 1996; Sanders & Rivers, 1996; Wright, Horn, & Sanders, 1997). Teachers and, by extension, schools are being evaluated on the outcomes of their students. Teacher and school effectiveness are measured by the progress that students make in terms of their learning and achievement; "outputs" matter most (Danielson & McGreal, 2000). The use of student achievement as a gauge of teaching effectiveness is reasonable and appropriate; and some would argue that student learning is the most important criterion by which to evaluate teachers (Popham, 1997). As we report above, however, the measures by which student learning is currently assessed are far from adequate in most cases to the task of yielding trustworthy information by which teacher effectiveness can be gauged.

For the most part, Danielson and McGreal report, student achievement has been measured by standardized, multiple-choice assessments. Multiple choice assessments are neither inherently valid nor invalid. Validity is not a property of a test, but of the inferences and consequences tied to the scores of the test (Messick, 1990). Validity arguments should be framed around the question, "What does the testing practice claim to do?" (Shepard, 1993, p. 408). Widely used multiple choice-based tests developed by commercial publishers for the K-12 market primarily measure factual knowledge and procedural knowledge. In most cases they do not nor do they claim to measure complex cognitive skills or deep levels of subject matter understanding. Independent reviewers of accountability programs relying mainly on the use of standardized, multiple-choice tests, such as the Dallas Valued-Added Accountability System, are quick to underscore the misalignment of such testing with current teaching and learning standards stressing, for example, construction of knowledge and higher-order learning (Sykes, 1997). At the present time there are very few teacher evaluation systems that actually employ student achievement data as a part of the performance appraisal process. According to the Education Commission of the State (ECS), "Although no state has yet gone so far as to hold individual teachers accountable for the performance of their students, several states have implemented direct, performance-based assessments of teacher effectiveness" (Allen, 1999, p.1) That is, the data are being gathered and evaluated, though not yet employed as appraisal measures. The states currently gathering and analyzing such data are Tennessee, Texas, Minnesota, and Colorado. However, these states contrast dramatically in their methods of using these data. Furthermore, this is a fast-moving target, and changes in states' requirements for and uses of data are rapid; the ECS website is a valuable source of up-to-date policy information from states (Education Commission of the States, 2001).

OBSERVATIONS ON THE CURRENT LANDSCAPE
OF TEACHER EVALUATION

Teacher evaluation today is no less controversial than it was in 1992, but the stakes are much higher. An ever-increasing number of politicians, from the President of the United States to senators and representatives, to governors and state legislators, have made educational accountability a war cry. And by accountability, politicians most particularly mean teacher accountability for student learning. Demanding it, figuring out how to measure it and what a high "it" looks like, and then attaching rewards to it is the pattern of key political initiatives in many states.

This particular interpretation of accountability emerges from a national focus on education reform that has increasingly occupied center stage over the past decade. What followed the statement of purpose and commitment that marked President Clinton's 1996 National Education Summit (Achieve, 1997) was a notable surge of attention in states to both content and performance standards for students, and accompanying standards-based testing initiatives to help instantiate these standards for learning throughout the education system (U.S. Department of Education, 1999; National Research Council, 1999; Council of Chief State School Officers, 1998; Baker & Linn, 1997; Massell, Kirst, & Hoppe, 1997). This has, in turn, led to links between student learning standards and standards for teacher preparation (Cohen & Spillane, 1993; Smith & O'Day, 1997; National Association of State Directors of Teacher Education and Certification, 2000).

Talking tough about teacher quality appears to be a requirement for all state and national political figures, and the federal government has done more than talk. In Title II of the Higher Education Reauthorization Act of 1998 (Public Law 105–244), the Teacher Quality Enhancement Act, the Congress entered the fray, creating a law that specified that all states must report the passing rates of teacher education students on state-required teacher licensing tests, and that all institutions achieve a 70 percent passing rate in order to qualify for continued federal student loan subsidies to all of their students, not just students in the school or department of education. This requirement has led to complicated new reporting methods that require coordination and collaboration among testing organizations, state regulatory agencies, and teacher education institutions. It has also led to charges, primarily from institutions of higher education (Interstate New Teacher Assessment and Support Consortium [INTASC], 1999; American Association of Colleges for Teacher Education, 2000; Teacher Education Accreditation Council, 2000) that the information reported will be a distortion of the realities of teacher preparation and that the effort is punitive rather than supportive. The measure demonstrates, however, the seriousness of the movement to require empirical evidence that speaks to teacher evaluation.

There is more student testing today than ever before, though there are very few signs that such testing is any more effective or informative than it was 10 or 20 years ago, as the remarks by Robert Linn discussed above make clear. Nor are there signs that such testing is any more closely connected to learning than it ever was. There is, however, both more talk and more action on the use of tests for very high stakes: promotion to the next grade, high school graduation, access to special programs (see ECS, 2001; Olson, 2001). And student testing for high stakes inevitably focuses attention on teacher effectiveness and its measurement.

There has been an exponential increase in the number of standards documents, both for student learning and for teacher knowledge and performance. Both state student standards and national standards for teachers (INTASC, 1992; National Board for Professional Teaching Standards [NBPTS], 2002; National Council for Accreditation of Teacher Education [NCATE], 1997) have more or less thoroughly articulated the content standards in both professional and subject matter knowledge. What is harder to articulate are the performance standards, or the answer(s) to the question, "How much of all of this is enough for a particular purpose?" The growing acceptance of standards documents that define the content of teaching as a profession, convergence among the standards documents, in both language and content, and the powerful effects of a common vocabulary that can define "knowing enough" and "doing enough" as a teacher mean that it is now possible to achieve some consensus on a definition of effective teaching. The INTASC, NBPTS, and NCATE standards – for beginning teachers, for advanced and accomplished teachers, and for accreditation of teacher education institutions – form the basis of the "three-legged stool" cited as the essential foundation for the reform of teacher preparation and develop- ment in the report of the National Commission on Teaching and America's Future (National Commission on Teaching and America's Future [NCTAF], 1996). Citing the extensive and painstaking consensus methodology that all three organizations have used to create and validate these standards, the National Research Council (NRC) report on teacher licensure also uses these sets of standards as the basis for the working definition of teacher quality (NRC, 2001).

There has been remarkable progress as well in sophisticated methodologies for assessing teachers, from entry level to advanced practice. And there are signs from these methodologies that "testing" is coming much closer to its rightful place, as part of something larger and more important, "learning."

Links between student achievement and teacher effectiveness, and measurement or assessment methodologies to track such links, are increasingly connected to pay in the rhetoric of "teacher accountability" for performance teacher evaluation systems. Under discussion in several states, these evaluation systems integrate teacher development with monetary rewards for achieving new levels of professional achievement (see Blair, 2001, p. 1).

The Political Landscape

The first decade of the 21st century opens with education reform as arguably the most critical political issue facing states and the federal government. Increasingly insistent calls for teacher accountability and documented increases in student achievement; arguments over vouchers and charter schools; the growing shortages of qualified and fully licensed teachers in mathematics, science, and special education; the nationwide crisis in securing qualified school principals for the available open positions; and the continuing difficulty in staffing schools in high-poverty urban and rural areas with qualified educators are all contentious issues that dominate both politics and the media in unprecedented measure at the start of the new century. And all of this attention makes the issue of teacher evaluation much more complex than ever before. Teacher evaluation, a key component in any accountability system, is both more important and more beleaguered than ever as a result of the rising pressure to "fix education" from federal, state, and local officials and constituents. It remains to be seen whether or not states and local districts will be able to muster the resources and the will to implement what has been learned about teacher performance and assessment of both teacher and student achievement in the past decade. What has not changed – and, from a measurement perspective, is not likely to change – is that sound and valid assessment of complex behavior requires time and sustained resource allocation. As Linn's article (Linn, 2000) makes clear, support for this kind of assessment has not been a hallmark of K-12 education policy in the U.S. to date.

In addition, there is much more insistence on the necessary connection between teacher performance evaluation and student achievement, but no more clarity about how such a connection can be credibly and validly made. Neither educators nor politicians and parents disagree that student learning is a key outcome of effective teaching. The problem is what constitutes valid evidence of the outcome. Today parents and legislators insist in ever-louder voices that such evidence must be primarily gains in student achievement, which they see as a criterion for student learning. Educators and researchers are much less convinced of the clarity and credibility of such evidence, given the variability of school contexts and the almost innumerable influences on student achievement (Berk, 1988; Brandt, 1989; Frederiksen, 1984; Haas, Haladyna, & Nolen, 1990; Haladyna, 1992; Haertel 1986; Haertel & Calfee, 1983; Linn, 1987; Madaus, 1988; Messick, 1987; Shepard, 1989)

This disagreement, now more acute than ever before, has direct consequences for teacher evaluation methods. Historically, the perspective of educators – that the only way to include student achievement in teacher evaluation is to talk about the "likelihood" of student achievement, given certain teacher variables like content knowledge and pedagogical skill – has dominated teacher evaluation practices. That is likely to be forcibly changed in the next decade.

The Standards Movement & Student Testing

That a teacher's performance and students' achievement are inextricably linked is intuitively compelling as an argument for making how students perform on some array of assessments an important part of a teacher's performance evaluation. Exactly how to attribute any student's achievement in any particular year to the current teacher, how to control for variables far outside a teacher's control but profoundly important in affecting students' achievement, and creating and using really sound and valid assessments are some of the challenges in gathering the evidence to support the argument. And these challenges have proved sufficiently daunting that links between teachers' work in the classroom and students' scores on assessments have never really been systematically achieved in the U.S. The pressure to forge such links is immense at this time, and it is critical to the health and vitality of the education workforce that the link be credible and valid. A foundational validity issue is, of course, the quality and integrity of the methods states and districts have developed or adopted to measure student achievement. The teaching workforce has long disdained standardized national tests, the most commonly used assessments in school districts across the U.S. to represent student achievement, arguing persuasively that actual local and state curricula – and thus instruction – are not adequately aligned (or aligned at all) with the content of these tests. Furthermore, education reformers have almost universally excoriated these tests for two decades as reductive and not representative of the skills and abilities students really need to develop for the new millennium.[1]

The sweeping popularity across the U.S. of standards that articulate what students should know and be able to do, and the link between this articulation and an assessment strategy that would yield information about the status of student learning in relation to those standards, is thus, a critical part of the new landscape for teacher evaluation. *Education Week's Quality Counts 2000*, which focuses on teacher quality and states' efforts to assure that quality, summarizes the current state of state student standards and testing across the U.S. They report that by 2000, 49 states (all but Iowa) have adopted student standards in at least some subjects; 48 states administer statewide testing programs and 37 of them say they incorporate "performance tasks" in their assessments. Forty-one states assert that their student assessments have been matched to their standards in at least one subject.

All of this sounds quite promising, but the picture – at least from the perspective of holding teachers accountable in their performance evaluations for student achievement as reflected on these tests – is less than rosy. It turns out, for example, that states get counted as "aligned to standards" and as having "more sophisticated measurements" if they test against their standards at any grade level (not all levels tested) and if they include any kinds of questions other than multiple choice in their tests (Edwards, 2000, p. 84). Only 10 states use assessment evidence gathered outside the confines of the standardized test – evidence like writing or project portfolios or extended response questions in subjects other than English. Furthermore, only 10 states administer any standardized tests aligned with student standards at the elementary level (Jerald, 2000, p. 63; Edwards, 2000, p. 74).

This absence of alignment between tests and standards at the elementary level is not particularly good news for teacher evaluation, since fully half of the education workforce in the U.S. consists of elementary teachers. Furthermore, a critical part of the validity evidence for the link between student tests and teacher performance needs to be teachers' knowledge and awareness of the testing methodologies and test content, and the interface between those methodologies and that content and the curriculum that guides their instructional practices. Little information about such efforts to inform and guide teachers in instruction is available from states.

The Standards Movement & Teachers

Widely accepted standards for what teachers should know and be able to do – essentially a definition of effective teaching – is one of the important accomplishments in teacher evaluation over the past decade. The recognition that meaningful teacher evaluation systems must begin with evaluation of teacher preparation institutions is part of that accomplishment. The standards developed by the Council of Chief State School Officer's Interstate New Teachers Assessment and Support Consortium (INTASC) for beginning teachers and the National Board for Professional Teaching Standards for experienced and accomplished teachers have gained broad acceptance across the U.S. This acceptance crosses political and ideological lines, for the most part – virtually every notable education policy and reform organization, along with both national teacher organizations and virtually all discipline-specific membership organizations have supported these sets of standards and participated actively in their development and promulgation.

The thrust of the NCATE 2000 reform was to change the focus of accreditation from "inputs" to "outputs" or results. Performance-based accreditation, as expressed in the NCATE 2000 standards for schools and departments (NCATE 2000 Unit Standards) requires that institutions demonstrate the *results* of what they do. These results need not be standardized test scores, though some of those are also considered acceptable evidence. They include, however, documentation of the kinds of work students are required to complete; documentation of assessment methodologies and practices; documentation of student learning and instructional supports for that learning. As a culminating record, documentation of the proportion of students who pass licensing tests that are required by the state in which the institution is located is also required. The convergence of these accreditation requirements with the Federal Title II reporting requirements is noteworthy, as it lends credibility to the use of test scores as a means of program evaluation.

The publication in 1996 of the report of the National Commission on Teaching and America's Future (NCTAF), *What Matters Most: Teaching for America's Future* (NCTAF, 1996), solidified the influence of these standards and the organizations that championed them. Chaired by leading education reform spokesperson Linda Darling-Hammond, NCTAF articulated an approach to state policies for teacher evaluation and quality assurance that integrates the preparation, initial assessment, ongoing professional development, and advanced certification of teachers. Each of these stages in a professional educator's career would be supported by standards-based evaluations, in the Commission's schema. The report's metaphor of the "three-legged stool" on which a quality teaching work-force rests has become well known as an expression of this vision: the INTASC standards generate an approach to preservice teacher preparation and the initial induction period of a teacher's career; the NCATE 2000 performance-based accreditation standards and requirements generate an approach to formative and summative assessment of preservice teachers and their institutions; and the NBPTS standards generate, by implication, a professional development and career plan for teaching professionals that culminates in the NBPTS certification assessment (described in detail below). Each of these "legs" is to be supported by sophisticated assessment methodologies that yield a complex array of informa-tion about what a teacher at any stage of his or her career knows and is able to do.

The Worm in the Apple: Standards and Regulatory Action

One of the most important challenges to effective reform of teacher evaluation has always been the separation of the academy, which controls teacher prepara-tion, and the state regulatory apparatus, which controls access to professional practice in schools. The INTASC standards, the NCATE standards, the NBPTS standards, and the NCTAF report are all reform efforts dominated by the academy and practitioners, not the regulatory apparatus of state education bureaucracies. The latter establishes a different kind of "standard" for teachers, one that is expressed by requirements and rules for a teaching license. This attention to licensure standards affects the vast majority of teachers only in the first 3 to 5 years of their teaching careers. Few resources have been allocated for ongoing evaluation and development of career teachers after their initial entry into the profession. Even the regulation of entry into the profession is confused and complicated by differing standards from state to state. The recent National Research Council report on teacher licensure testing analyzes the current licensure regulations and their possible effects on the education workforce (NRC, 2001).

In the next decade, real progress in implementing meaningful teacher evaluation systems in U.S. schools, both for beginning teachers and for experienced teachers, will depend on the integration of education policy visions like that expressed in the NCTAF report with state regulatory functions. Currently, the two are far apart and in many cases opposed. One consistent difficulty is that state regulatory agencies are legitimately concerned about the cost of various assessments to prospective teachers, and the administrative feasibility of more performance-based assessments. Thus, even when sophisticated assessments exist, they are often not required because the state is loathe to require teacher candidates to pay the substantially higher fees for licensing tests that these would entail. Yet it is these more sophisticated kinds of assessments that promise a clearer picture of a teacher's knowledge and skill *as it is applied in the classroom*. If the definition of teacher quality, and consequential decisions about who can and should teach, depend on the connection between student achievement and teacher performance, the widespread use of more sophisticated assessment methodologies clearly has important implications for education reform.

Quality Counts 2000 reports that states continue to play "an elaborate shell game" (Edwards, 2000, p. 8) with teacher licensing. States set standards, often rigorous standards, for demonstrations of sufficient skill and knowledge to be licensed. For example, 39 states require all licensed teachers to pass a basic skills test (reading, mathematics, and writing), 29 require secondary teachers to pass subject-specific tests in their prospective teaching fields, and 39 require prospective secondary teachers to have a major, minor, or equivalent course credits for a subject-specific license. This means that a number of states require all three hurdles to be cleared before granting a license. In addition, most states require that the teacher's preparation institution recommend the candidate for the license. In every state but New Jersey, however, the state has the power to waive all of these requirements "either by granting licenses to individuals who have not met them or by permitting districts to hire such people" (Edwards, 2000, p. 8). And, perhaps most discouraging, *Quality Counts 2000* reports that only about 25 of the 50 states even have accessible records of "the numbers and percentages of teachers who hold various waivers" (Jerald & Boser, 2000, p. 44). Thus, reliance on rigorous state testing and preparation requirements to assure the quality of the education workforce is likely to lead to disappointment.

In 2000, 36 of the 39 states that require teachers to pass a basic skills test waived that requirement and permitted a teacher to enter a classroom as teacher of record without passing the test – and in 16 states, this waiver can be renewed indefinitely, so long as the hiring school district asserts its inability to find a qualified applicant (Edwards, 2000, p. 8). Of the 29 states that require secondary teachers to pass subject matter exams – most often only multiple choice tests, even though more sophisticated tests are available – only New Jersey denies a license and therefore a job to candidates who have not passed the tests. Eleven of these 29 states allow such candidates to remain in the job indefinitely, and all 29 but New Jersey waive the coursework completion requirement for secondary teachers if the hiring district claims that it cannot find a more qualified applicant for the position (Edwards, 2000, p. 8).

The situation for teacher evaluation – especially a system that would link student achievement to teacher performance – is further undermined by two almost universal hiring practices across states. First, states assign teachers to teach subjects in which they have little or no preparation. Eleven states do not even require permission for such assignment of a teacher for part of the school day. Twenty-two states have the power to penalize schools for overusing such assignment practices, but there is little or no enforcement effort; only Florida and Texas require that parents be notified if the teacher assigned to their children's classroom is not fully qualified. And the out-of-field teaching assignment is far more prevalent in high poverty urban or rural school districts, for whom filling the job with anyone at all is (NCES) an ongoing challenge (Olson, 2000a, p .14). The National Center for Education Statistics reports that in 1993–94, 47 percent of the teachers in schools with high proportions of low-income students did not have a college major or minor in the subjects they were assigned to teach (NCES, 1997). This situation is worsening as shortages of teachers who are interested in jobs in difficult-to-staff schools grows (see Hartocollis, 2000).

Second, almost all states have failed to allocate resources devoted to efforts to build a teaching force with strong content knowledge for middle school students. Despite the clear evidence that achievement at the high school level depends on solid preparation from sixth through eighth grade, only 17 states require secondary level licenses of middle school teachers, with all of the attendant content requirements. Of these, however, only nine require these teachers to pass content examinations as well. Seven more require subject-specific coursework in addition to an elementary license. Every other state requires middle school teachers to hold only an elementary generalist license in order to teach any subject in middle school. Only New Jersey and Colorado require that all middle school teachers have a college major in the subject they wish to teach (Jerald & Boser, 2000, p. 44).

Given the uneven state of regulation of teacher quality, even at the most basic level of licensing, connecting teacher performance to student achievement and to high stakes decisions about employment and compensation for individual teachers is fraught with difficulty and potential legal complications. Furthermore, though increasingly complex assessments are available (some of these are described in the next section), states have been slow to adopt an integrated assessment strategy that would build a high-quality teaching workforce by locating assessment in the much larger context of learning. If states create regulations only to ignore them because of the difficulties in filling open teaching positions, then state-sponsored implementation of sanctions for what is defined, on the basis of student achievement standards, as substandard teaching performance is legally indefensible.

TEACHER EVALUATION AND ACCOUNTABILITY: CURRENT PRACTICE

Concurrent with the increased emphasis on teacher quality and teacher education has been the proliferation of discussion and debate regarding teacher evaluation. There is an emergent new focus of interest and funding from legislatures in evaluation processes that are linked to teacher professional development. This new emphasis is particularly apparent in the growth of programs for the induction period – usually defined as the first two years of a new teacher's career. There is also increased attention in states to performance-based assessments for teachers that would lead to a career ladder in which compensation is based on skills and performance, not seniority. These links are motivated by the realities of the labor market for teachers (and principals) in the U.S. A very large proportion of the current cadre of teachers began teaching in the 1960s and will reach retirement within the next five years. There is already a shortage of teachers in certain subject matter fields like mathematics, the sciences, and exceptional needs. Rural and inner city schools are chronically understaffed. It has become increasingly difficult for school districts to recruit enough graduates who have completed a teacher preparation program to fill all available jobs (Bradley, 1999). All of these factors have focused attention on improvement of the quality of a teacher's working life and on creating possibilities for growth and advancement within a career as an educator. Thus increased interest in evaluation of teachers for accountability purposes is closely allied with the formative use of evaluation for recruitment, retention, and reward.

California's CFASST program for beginning teachers, for example, which offers beginning teachers a structured program of formative evaluation with individual mentors during the first two years of teaching appears to have cut attrition rates among new teachers by as much as 40 percent in certain school districts (Briggs et al., 2001). Cincinnati is implementing a program of teacher evaluation that is tied to a career ladder based on performance rather than the traditional time on the job and number of credits earned. (Cincinnati Federation of Teachers & Cincinnati Public Schools, 2000) Iowa, responding to its own analysis of the teacher labor market in the region, its difficulty attracting Iowa teacher preparation program graduates to in-state teaching jobs, and its concerns about the disparities in achievement between its rural and urban students, has begun work on a restructuring of teacher compensation that would evaluate teachers at several points in their careers and base salary increases on achievement of increased skills (Blair, 2001, p. 1). In all of these programs, teacher professional development and learning is an integral part of the evaluation structure.

Licensure Testing for Beginning Teachers

The first stage in teacher evaluation remains licensure testing, which is subject to the same professional and technical regulations as all licensure testing regardless of the scope or sphere of practice in a job or profession. There has been much debate in the past three years over the type, quality, and scope of licensure tests for teachers, prompted in many cases by the Massachusetts teacher testing controversy. The perceived importance of efforts to improve teacher quality, evidenced by the Teacher Quality Enhancement Act (Title II) discussed above, led the U.S. Department of Education to request that the National Academy of Sciences establish a panel of experts, called the Committee on Assessment and Teacher Quality, early in 1999. The committee's work and the structure of its final report provide a useful framework for a discussion of current practice in initial licensure testing for teachers.

According to the committee's final report, it "was asked to examine the appropriateness and technical quality of teacher licensure tests currently in use, the merits of using licensure test results to hold states and institutions of higher education accountable for the quality of teacher preparation and licensure, and alternatives for developing and assessing beginning teacher competence" (NRC, 2001, Executive Summary, pp. 2–3).

The NRC report on licensure testing explores five major areas: the appropriateness and technical soundness of current measures of beginning teacher competence; the methods and consequences of decisions made about candidates based on licensure tests; a technical evaluation of current licensure tests; the use of teacher licensure tests to hold states and institutions of higher education accountable for the quality of teacher preparation and licensure; and the value of innovative measures of beginning teacher competency in helping to improve teacher quality (NRC, 2001). The analyses and explorations in the full report are informative and important, but the conclusions the Committee reached are not startling. While the committee found that the current licensure tests they examined were, in general, technically sound and appropriately developed for their purpose, they asserted that "even a set of well-designed tests cannot measure all of the prerequisites of competent beginning teaching. Current paper-and-pencil tests provide only some of the information needed to evaluate the competencies of teacher candidates" (NRC, 2001, Executive Summary, p. 5). They recommended that states and regulatory bodies making decisions based on licensure tests follow best-practice guidelines concerning standard setting and examine the impact of their decisions not only on the competence of the licensed pool of teachers, but on the diversity of the teacher work force, on teacher education programs, and on the supply of new teachers (NRC, 2001, Executive Summary, p. 8). On the issue of the technical quality of licensure tests currently in use, the committee's conclusions were guarded, primarily because they were able to examine only licensure tests developed and delivered by one of the two major developers of such tests, Educational Testing Service. The committee report says in this regard,

> Solid technical characteristics and fairness are key to effective use of tests. The work of measurement specialists, test users, and policy makers suggests criteria for judging the appropriateness and technical quality of initial teacher licensure tests. The committee drew on these to develop criteria it believes users should aspire to in developing and evaluating initial teacher licensure tests. The committee used these evaluation criteria to evaluate a sample of five widely used tests produced by ETS. The tests the committee reviewed met most of its criteria for technical quality, although there were some areas for improvement. The committee also attempted to review a sample of NES tests. Despite concerted and repeated efforts, the committee was unable to obtain sufficient information on the technical characteristics of tests produced by NES and thus could draw no conclusions about their technical quality. (NRC, 2001, Executive Summary, p. 9)

On the controversial issue of using licensure test scores to hold states and institutions of higher education accountable for the quality of teacher preparation, the committee recommended that the federal government "should not use passing rates on initial teacher licensing tests as the sole basis for comparing states and teacher education programs or for withholding funds, imposing other sanctions, or rewarding teacher education programs" (NRC, 2001, Executive Summary, p. 15). Because this directly criticizes the federal Title II Teacher Quality Improvement provisions, this recommendation is likely to be among the most debated in the report. Finally, and not surprisingly, the committee recommended investigation of new methods and systems of evaluation of beginning teacher competencies (NRC, 2001, Executive Summary, p. 16). Several of these innovative assessment methods are discussed below. One critical element in teacher licensure, and its potential role in teacher quality improvement, that the NRC does not discuss is the role of regulatory agencies in states, which have the responsibility for setting the licensure requirements. More performance-based measures exist for beginning teachers; they are not being used by states because the regulations do not require them.

One issue in the debate over teacher licensure tests as a means to improve teacher quality has been both how rigorous these tests need to be and how "knowledge" for teachers should be defined and described (NRC, 2001). On the question of rigor, one side of the debate is represented by The Education Trust's 1999 report on teacher tests entitled *Not Good Enough* (Mitchell & Barth, 1999). The authors of that report contend that the teacher licensure tests they examined are far too easy and that they do not represent what they call "college-level understanding" of content (p. 3). The underlying assumption in this argument is that all teachers need to demonstrate a command of discipline-specific knowledge that is commensurate with academic tasks appropriate for college majors in a discipline, as such tasks are defined by the authors of the report (p. 17). The other side of the debate is represented operationally by the actual content of the ETS licensure tests the NRC Committee on Assessment and Teacher Quality examined. If the AERA/NCME/APA Joint Technical Standards for test development are used to guide the determination of the test specifications and content of test forms, then a long chain of evidence leads to the actual test forms. This begins, in the case of ETS licensure test development, with a careful cross analysis of relevant national and state standards, moves through a job analysis and test specification draft, and culminates in test items that are assembled into a form that is further validated by individual panels in states that are considering adoption of the test as a licensing instrument (NRC, 2001, Executive Summary, pp. 6–7). Since these are the same tests decried as far too easy by the proponents of more rigor, it is clear that the practitioner and job based approach required by professional standards is currently far separated from the approach of the proponents for "higher standards."

Another issue has been the call for predictive validity evidence for these licensing tests. That is, there is mounting demand for a licensure test whose scores can predict who will be an effective, or at least adequate, teacher (Dunkin, 1997; Schaeffer, 1996; Pearlman, 1999). The licensing tests state regulatory agencies have been willing to require are typically limited to tests of knowledge – basic skills, professional knowledge (pedagogy, developmental psychology, etc.), and content knowledge. Test scores are required prior to the test taker's occupation of a job. What a prospective teacher will do with this knowledge is unknown on the basis of this kind of test. Only a direct measure of the kinds of skills and knowledge *as they are used in the work of teaching* could afford any predictive validity, and that only after stringent analysis of the connections between what is tested and what the job requires. Thus, demands for predictive validity for current licensing tests seem unreasonable. The inherent difference between "job-related" knowledge and knowledge that, if held, would predict performance in a complex domain of professional judgment and behavior like teaching has been largely ignored in this debate, as has the virtually universal absence of such evidence for licensure tests across other jobs and professions. It is an accepted assumption that teachers must know the content they will have to teach and also know some principles of pedagogy, and most states require evidence of that knowledge in licensure tests for teachers. Similarly, the legal profession believes that lawyers must know some basic principles of the law and its interpretation over the centuries, and the bar examinations, both the Multi-State Bar Examination and state-specific bar examinations reflect that assumption. The medical profession believes that doctors must know about human anatomy, blood chemistry, and the like, and the medical licensure examination reflects that belief. What is not known or asserted in any of these cases, however, is how the newly licensed teacher, lawyer, or doctor will perform in the actual job he or she is licensed to do after reaching the passing standard on the licensing test. Licensure testing is implicitly said by the measurement profession to be necessary but not sufficient evidence of competence to practice.

Teacher licensure testing represents a complex and often chaotic picture for those interested in quality assurance for the national teacher workforce. Regulating professional licenses in the U.S. is a right reserved for state governments or their designated regulatory arms. This means, for teacher licensure, that there are 50 sets of rules, requirements, and regulations and a broad canvas for individualized and often idiosyncratic licensure testing practices. When many of these regulations were enacted, teachers tended to take jobs in the same states in which they were trained for the profession. Thus, regulation of the quality of the "pipeline" was largely a local concern, and state-specific regulations for licensing could be said, at least in theory, to represent a considered weighing of the usefulness of an independent criterion (the test) in addition to the trustworthiness of the preparation institutions' recommendations of graduates for licensure.

The situation over the past 10 years has changed dramatically. Teachers have become more mobile, states – and districts within state – compete for beginning teachers, and there is a critical shortage of teachers in certain fields and certain geographical areas (Edwards, 2000). Tests that offer some uniform and independent view of a beginning teacher's knowledge have thus grown more important as an indicator of one critical job-related criterion.

Sophisticated Tools for Teacher Assessment

The NRC Report on Assessment and Teacher Quality (NRC, 2001) ends with the following recommendation concerning what it calls "innovative measures of beginning teacher competence":

> Research and development of broad-based indicators of teacher com-
> petence, not limited to test-based evidence, should be undertaken; indicators
> should include assessments of teaching performance in the classroom, of
> candidates' ability to work effectively with students with diverse learning
> needs and cultural backgrounds and in a variety of settings, and of compe-
> tencies that more directly relate to student learning.
>
> When initial licensure tests are used, they should be part of a coherent
> developmental system of preparation, assessment, and support that reflects
> the many features of teacher competence. (NRC, 2001, Chapter 9, p. 16)

There have been notable advances in teacher assessment methodology during the past ten years which further these recommendations. In all of these innovative assessments two underlying beliefs are modeled: effective teaching can be recognized and evaluated, and the underlying knowledge and skills that make for effective teaching can be modeled and learned. Furthermore, the assessments embody a belief in the importance of opportunities to learn what the assessment will evaluate, and the belief that the assessment process itself must be embedded in learning.

The INTASC consortium's work on model assessments, the redesign of the PRAXIS™ series professional and pedagogical knowledge assessments for licensure, California's support for induction programs like CFASST, Ohio's com-bination of formative and summative performance assessments for licensure of beginning teachers in the Ohio Formative Induction Results in Stronger Teaching (FIRST) program, the use by several states of Educational Testing Service's standards-based induction portfolio, and the Connecticut BEST teacher licensing system have all been applications of innovative assessment methodologies for beginning teachers (Connecticut State Department of Education (CT DOE), 1996a, 1996b, 1998; Ohio Department of Education, 2001; INTASC, 1992, 2002; California Commission on Teacher Credentialing & The California Department of Education, 1999; Olebe, 1999). All of them have focused on simulated or direct measurement of actual teaching practice. In addition, the most elaborate of all innovations in the assessment of teaching, the National Board for Professional Teaching Standards certification assessments for experienced teachers, has demonstrated that very elaborate performance assessment methodologies can be operationalized at large volumes. All of these are now to some extent established and tested methodologies.

What characterizes all of these efforts is an assessment design strategy that insists on much tighter links between the task given to the examinee and the goal of the measurement. If the central validity question in all assessment is how much one can trust an inference based on a test score, then attention to the nature and quality of the evidence gathered in the course of the assessment process, and clear and explicit links between that evidence and what is purportedly being measured are critical. Evidence-centered design strategies have been discussed or at least written about in the research literature for more than a decade, as cognitive scientists and psychometricians have discussed ways to apply increasingly sophisticated theories of learning and performance to assessment, and to much more closely couple assessment and learning (see Glaser, Lesgold, & Lajoie, 1987; Mislevy, 1987, 1994, 2000; Mislevy et al., 1999). It is only in the past five years, however, that some serious attempts to change the way assessments are conceptualized and then used in operational settings have taken place.

Innovations in Teacher Tests

The first example of evidence-centered assessments for licensure and certification of educators that demonstrate the application of these theoretical principles to real testing situations, is INTASC's design for a simulation-based performance assessment of a beginning teacher's professional and pedagogical knowledge. Called the *Test for Teaching Knowledge*, the prototypes for this assessment were designed and field-tested on behalf of INTASC by Educational Testing Service from 1998–2000. The domain of the assessment is established in the INTASC *Model Standards for Beginning Teacher Licensing and Development* (INTASC, 1992, Council of Chief State School Officers, 1998). The assessment itself is four hours long and consists entirely of constructed response questions. Most of the questions are connected to cases, or detailed descriptions of actual teaching situations, and they ask test takers to evaluate what they have read in the case and respond based on their own professional knowledge and pedagogical experience (presumed to be in student teaching). The measurement assumption that underlies the test design is that tasks based on simulations of actual teaching practice will yield more credible and trustworthy evidence of a beginning teacher's ability to *use* his or her academic and very limited practical knowledge than do more conventional tests of knowledge (ETS, 2000).

A second example is Educational Testing Service's redesign of the Praxis™ series of licensure tests. There are two notable aspects of this redesign effort in addition to the reorientation of domains of content knowledge for test specifications, in light of the proliferation of content standards. First, the intent of the INTASC *Test for Teaching Knowledge* design – to influence licensing practice in many states – has been at least partially fulfilled. ETS's own *Principles of Learning & Teaching*, a test of a beginning teacher's professional and pedagogical knowledge, is being redeveloped with the INTASC standards as the explicit domain of assessment, and simulation-based (case-based) constructed response questions as the dominant task model. This assessment is widely used and increasingly popular among states as they seek to license teachers based not only on content knowledge in a subject field but also on professional teaching knowledge.

NATIONAL BOARD FOR PROFESSIONAL TEACHING STANDARDS

The most dramatic accomplishment in teacher evaluation in the past decade is represented by the achievements of the National Board for Professional Teaching Standards (NBPTS). Mentioned in Dwyer and Stufflebeam as a promising but unproven notion in 1996, this program has grown exponentially since the first candidates received certification results in 1994.[2] National Board Certification is now routinely mentioned as the hallmark of teacher excellence in policy and political discourse about teacher quality. Both from a public policy and from a measurement perspective the National Board Certification process represents a leap forward in teacher evaluation in the U.S.

Little has been published to date about the NBPTS assessment program from 1996 forward. Most writers on the NBPTS assessments have based their analyses and predictions on the early prototypes of the assessments that were field tested prior to 1996. Shinkfield and Stufflebeam's 1995 analysis of the NBPTS assessment model serves as a useful summary of early commentary on this ambitious assessment (Shinkfield & Stufflebeam, 1995, pp. 390–391). Because virtually no empirical data were available for anyone to review, most attention was directed at the NBPTS's statements of aspiration and procedures regarding consensus-building in the education community, creation of standards that could define effective practice, and technical scrutiny of all assessments and data associated with them, which were praised even as they were viewed with some skepticism. Far more worrisome to Shinkfield and Stufflebeam were the NBPTS's assessment methods. They state categorically, for example, that "the validity of outcomes is highly suspect, as there is not a thorough, well-planned, and well-executed observation of candidates by credible evaluators" (Shinkfield & Stufflebeam, 1995, p. 390). At the time of that writing, there seemed to be no viable alternative to live observation as a methodology for evaluating teaching authentically and directly. Indeed, until approximately 1994, the NBPTS itself regarded live observation as the only possible methodology for the kind of assessment they desired. It was the NBPTS's own research into the feasibility *and validity* of this methodology that led to a different medium for observation of instruction – videotape – in the assessment model finally adopted (see Land & Herman, 1994). Shinkfield and Stufflebeam echo many other observers in their additional concerns regarding scoring, which they believe to be very difficult to operationalize in a reliable and valid manner. They also express some concern about quality control and consistency across all assessments. Finally, they record the concern that the assessment may prove too expensive to be sustainable.[3]

In the discussion that follows, these observations are addressed, and an account of the current status of the assessment program is given. The success and phenomenal growth of the assessment program – in 1996, the Board offered six different assessments to approximately 600 candidates; in 2001 it offered 19 different assessments to approximately 14,000 candidates – has flouted conventional wisdom about public policy support for really innovative and resource-intensive assessment, as well as about assessment design and operational feasibility. The cost, size, and methodology of the assessments; nature of the scoring apparatus and its results, and magnitude of the validation and quality assurance documentation process – all of these were unprecedented in education in the U.S. before the NBPTS assessment program. In 2001, the fee for the assessment was $2,300 per candidate, validating at least one of Shinkfield and Stufflebeam's concerns. This makes National Board Certification one of the most expensive certification assessments used in any profession in the United States, including medicine and finance, both much more high-paying professions. One of the National Board's accomplishments has been its persuasive argument that states and the federal education budget should support this certification effort, since it is a key to real reform of teaching and, thus, increased student achievement. Over 95 percent of all National Board Certification candidates have fee subsidies, in whole or in part. At present, there are federally funded and state-administered fee subsidy programs in 40 states and 200 local districts. Financial rewards for successful candidates are awarded in 29 states and more than 140 school districts.[4]

Portfolio-based assessment has been written about extensively in the past decade, and it is often mentioned as the best assessment methodology to capture learning over time, complex understandings, self-analysis and reflection, and the like. It has been particularly praised as a methodology for formative assessment of teachers. (Blake & Bachman, 1995; Lomask & Pecheone, 1995; Supovitz & Brennan, 1997; LeMahieu, Gitomer, & Eresh, 1995; Stecher, 1998; Curry, 2000; Hewitt, 2001; Valencia & Au, 1997). Portfolio assessment has not been successfully operationalized on a large scale, however. The costs, the psychometric challenges, and the formidable feasibility issues have relegated portfolio use in most education settings to individual classrooms for low stakes.

The NBPTS program now represents the most elaborate high-stakes portfolio assessment in use in education in the U.S. today. The NBPTS assessment design engages some of the persistent problems that have bedeviled measures of teaching performance and complex performance assessment methodologies in general. In Samuel Messick's 1994 article on the validation issues that attend performance assessments, he defines both issues and criteria in the ongoing validation of complex performance assessments (Messick, 1994). In this analysis, he builds on the earlier work of Linn, Baker, and Dunbar (1991) and Frederiksen and Collins (1989) on validation criteria for performance assessment. Linn, Baker, and Dunbar included content quality and coverage, cognitive complexity, meaningfulness, cost and efficiency, transfer and generalizability, fairness, and consequences as validity criteria; Frederiksen and Collins suggest directness, scope, reliability, and transparency.

As principle conceptualizers and developers of these assessments, the authors believe that some analysis of salient features of this assessment program can demonstrate that Messick's validity criteria – which subsume those proposed by Linn, Baker, and Dunbar and Frederiksen and Collins – can be met. Indeed, the development and implementation history of the NBPTS assessments indicates that Messick's criteria for validation can be seen as guiding principles for the design and delivery of complex performance assessments. Messick's overarching assertion is that the validity standards and criteria for performance assessments are really no different from those that apply to more conventional assessments, an array of standards and criteria he explicated at length in his 1989 chapter in Linn's *Educational Measurement* (Messick, 1989). The criteria for evaluation of *any* assessments are both evidential and consequential. Proponents of performance assessment have long touted the positive consequences of complex performance assessment; Messick expresses concern that such supposed positive consequential validation might eclipse the equally important issues of evidential validity. As Messick makes clear, the issue for performance assessment is what constitutes credible evidence.

The NBPTS assessment program is built on a foundation of careful and methodical attention to definition of the purposes for the assessment, and the constructs of interest given that purpose. In the NBPTS assessment program, task design, the overall architecture of the collection of tasks that makes up an entire certification assessment, the integration of development of the evidence structure created by the tasks with development of the evaluation structure necessary to provide scores, and continuing attention to operational feasibility and implementation *as validity issues* have quite deliberately engaged the problems of construct underrepresentation and construct irrelevant variance. Included in the evidence-centered design approach taken by Educational Testing Service on behalf of the National Board is conscious attention to issues of fairness, equal opportunity to perform, cost and efficiency, cognitive complexity, breadth and depth of content coverage, and reliability and generalizability. The consequences of the certification decision – for those who are successful and those who are not – has been an issue systematically scrutinized by the National Board from the outset.

The NBPTS certification assessment consists of two parts, a teacher-made portfolio that assembles evidence from classroom practice and professional and collegial work outside the classroom according to standardized directions and a written, timed, secure "assessment center" that is focused primarily on content and pedagogical content knowledge and is delivered via computer. There are ten separately scored components with the portfolio components weighted more heavily than the assessment center components in the final weighted total score. The NBPTS Board of Directors set a passing score in 1996 of 275 on a scale that ranges from 75 to 425. The total weighted score scale is identical to the scale used to score individual parts of the assessment (NBPTS, 2000, p. 55–56).

National Board assessments are built following the guidelines of evidence-centered design, where, for example, the constructs to be measured are explicitly articulated at the outset, as are the kinds and nature of the score inferences to be rendered. These explicit parameters then guide and shape the nature and structure of the assessment, including the sources and types of evidence that will support those inferences. In this approach to assessment design, the assessment tasks and scoring rubrics are developed concurrently to better ensure a tight mapping between what is valued by the assessment tasks and what is valued by the scoring system. This principled approach to development extends to the rigorous training received by assessors before they engage in live, consequential scoring, which includes bias-reduction training – targeted to reduce construct irrelevant variance from entering into an assessor's judgment – extensive scoring practice and feedback opportunities, and the continual monitoring of assessor calibration during the scoring process. These and other structural properties of the assessments themselves (see Wolfe & Gitomer, 2000) have yielded reliability estimates that rival those of more traditional, less complex assessments.

While it is apparent that some of the distress articulated in earlier research regarding the reliability of complex performance assessment such as those offered by the National Board may have been soothed, the question of validity remained open. The critical validity question is just this: Do National Board certified teachers differ from non-certified teachers on agreed upon dimensions of quality teaching practice? The construct validity of National Board assessments was recently addressed by Bond, Smith, Baker, and Hattie (2000).

In that study, National Board certified teachers were compared to teachers not achieving certification on 13 dimensions of quality teaching practice and two dimensions of student learning. In total, evidence of quality teaching practice was collected from 65 teachers in two certificates areas, Early Adolescence/ English Language Arts and Middle Childhood/Generalist. Instructional objectives and lesson plans were collected, interviews of teachers and students were conducted, and classroom observations were conducted. All data collection was conducted without knowledge of a teacher's certification status. The results indicated that certified teachers performed differently from non-certified teachers on 11 of 13 dimensions. Certified teachers, for example, demonstrated greater flexibility in their pedagogical content knowledge, were able to improvise and alter their instruction appropriately, provided more developmentally appropriate learning activities for their students, had a greater understanding of the reasons for student success and student failure, and exhibited a distinct passion for teaching. The students of National Board Certified teachers also appeared to have a deeper and richer understanding of the instructional concepts compared to the students of non-certified teachers. Collectively, these results provide initial support for the validity of score inferences from National Board assessments.

CONCLUSION

Teacher evaluation remains and is likely to continue to be a pressing issue in education and educational reform. Undoubtedly, the teacher will occupy the central focus of concerns regarding student achievement, and causal links between teacher performance and student performance will persist, technical measurement concerns about the soundness of such attributions notwithstanding. Decisions about, how, and when the process and outcomes of teacher evaluation inform decisions pertaining to licensure, certification, advancement, and pay – variously, issues of teacher accountability – largely reside in the domain of policy formation and acceptance. Yet, such policy decisions no doubt may benefit from the lessons learned and advances witnessed in teacher assessment models and method-ologies in the past decade – scalable approaches that have successfully increased measurement fidelity by, proximity to the assessment of actual teaching practice – while maintaining high levels of technical quality, public acceptance, and operational feasibility.

ENDNOTES

[1] See the whole September/October 2000 issue of Journal of Teacher Education (Cochran-Smith, 2000). It is an attack on testing of students and teachers.
[2] Consider, for example, that in 1996 there were approximately 700 first-time candidates, and by 2000 that number rose to nearly 7,000; approximately 14,000 candidates will participate in 2001.
[3] The detailed knowledge of the development and implementation of this assessment program evinced in this section is based on the authors' direct and ongoing roles in the development and operational delivery of this assessment program on behalf of the NBPTS
[4] See the NBPTS website (http://www.nbpts.org) for a continuously updated list of all financial incentives and support offerings for NBPTS candidates in the 50 states.

REFERENCES

Achieve. (1997). *A review of the 1996 National Education Summit*. Washington, DC: Author. (ERIC Document Reproduction Service No. ED407705)

Allen, M. (1999, May). Student results and teacher accountability, *ECS Policy Brief*. Retrieved from http://www.ecs.org/clearinghouse/12/28/1228.htm

American Association of Colleges for Teacher Education. (2000). *Counterpoint Article: USA Today January 31, 2000: "We Need Time to Do the Job Right."* Retrieved from http://www.aacte.org/governmental_relations/time_do_job_right.htm

American Educational Research Association. (2000). *AERA position statement concerning high-stakes testing in preK-12 education*. Retrieved from http://www.aera.net/about/policy/stakes.htm

Baker, E.L., & Linn, R.L. (1997). *Emerging educational standards of performance in the united states.* (CSE Technical Report 437). Los Angeles: University of California, National Center for Research on Evaluation, Standards, and Student Testing.

Barton, P. (1999). *Too much testing of the wrong kind: Too little of the right kind in K-12 education*. Retrieved from http://www.ets.org/research/pic/204928tmt.pdf

Berk, R.A. (1988). Fifty reasons why student achievement gain does not mean teacher effectiveness. *Journal of Personnel Evaluation in Education*, 1(4), 345–364.

Blair, J. (2001, May 16). Iowa approves performance pay for its teachers. *Education Week*, 20(36), 1, 24, 25.

Blake, J., & Bachman, J. (1995, October). A portfolio-based assessment model for teachers: Encouraging professional growth. *NASSP Bulletin*, 79, 37–47.

Bond, L., Smith, T., Baker, W.K., & Hattie, J.A. (2000, September). *The certification system of the National Board for Professional Teaching Standards: A construct and consequential validity study*. (Center for Educational Research and Evaluation, The University of North Carolina at Greensboro). Washington, DC: National Board for Professional Teaching Standards.

Brabeck, M.M. (1999). Between Scyllan and Charybdis: Teacher education's odyssey. *Journal of Teacher Education*, **50**, 346–351.

Bradley, A. (1999, March 10). States' uneven teacher supply complicates staffing of schools. *Education Week*, **18**(26), 1, 10–11.

Brandt, R. (1989). On misuse of testing: A conversation with George Madaus. *Educational Leadership*, **46**(7), 26–30.

Briggs, D., Elliott, J., Kuwahara, Y., Rayyes, N., & Tushnet, N. (2001, March). *The effect of BTSA on employment retention rates or participating teachers*. (WestEd Task 2A Report). San Francisco: WestEd.

California Commission on Teacher Credentialing and the California Department of Education. (1999). *The CFASST Process*. [Brochure]. Sacramento, CA: Author.

Cincinnati Federation of Teachers and Cincinnati Public Schools. (2000). *Teacher evaluation system*. Cincinatti, Ohio: Author.

Cochran-Smith, M. (Ed.). (2000). *Journal of Teacher Education*, **51**(4).

Cohen, D.K., & Spillane, J.P. (1993). Policy and practice: The relations between governance and instruction. In S.H. Fuhrman (Ed.), *Designing coherent education policy: Improving the system* (pp. 35–95). San Francisco: Jossey-Bass Publishers.

Connecticut State Department of Education. (1996a). *The Beginning Educator Support and Training Program (BEST)*. [Brochure]. Hartford, CT: Author.

Connecticut State Department of Education. (1996b). *A guide to the BEST program for beginning teachers and mentors*. [Brochure]. Hartford, CT: Author.

Connecticut State Department of Education. (1998). *Handbook for the development of an English language arts teaching portfolio*. [Brochure]. Hartford, CT: Author.

Council of Chief State School Officers. (1998). *Key state education policies on K-12 education: Standards, graduation, assessment, teacher licensure, time and attendance: A 50-state report*. Washington, DC: Author.

Curry, S. (2000). Portfolio-based teacher assessment. *Trust for educational leadership*, **29**, 34–38.

Danielson, C., & McGreal, T.L. (2000). *Teacher evaluation to enhance professional practice*. Alexandria, VA: Association for Supervision and Curriculum Development.

Darling Hammond, L. (1999). *Teacher quality and student achievement: A review of state policy evidence*. (Tech. Rep. No. 99-1). University of Washington, Center for the Study of Teaching Policy.

Dunkin, Michael J. (1997). Assessing teachers' effectiveness. *Issues in Educational Research*, **7**, 37–51.

Dwyer, C.A., & Stufflebeam, D.S. (1996). Evaluation for effective teaching. In D. Berliner & R. Calfee (Eds.), *Handbook of research in educational psychology*. New York: Macmillan.

The Education Commission of the States. (2001). *A closer look: State policy trends in three key areas of the Bush Education Plan – Testing, accountability, and school choice*. Retrieved from http://www.ecs.org/clearinghouse/24/19/2419.htm

Educational Testing Service. (2000). *Candidate information bulletin: Test for teaching knowledge*. Princeton, NJ: Author.

Edwards, V.B. (2000, January 13). Quality Counts 2000 [Special issue]. *Education Week*, **19**(18).

Elmore, R.F., & Rothman, R. (Eds). (1999). *Testing, teaching, and learning: A guide for states and school districts*. Washington, DC: National Academy Press.

Feistritzer, E.C. (1998, January 28). The truth behind the "teacher shortage." *The Wall Street Journal*, p. A18.

Feuer, M.J., Holland, P.W., Green, B.F., Bertenthal, M.W., & Hemphill, F.C. (Eds). (1999). *Uncommon Measures: Equivalence and Linkage Among Educational Tests*. Washington, DC: National Academy Press.

Frederiksen, N. (1984). The real test bias: Influences of testing on teaching and learning. *American Psychologist*, **39**, 193–202.

Frederiksen, J.R. & Collins, A. (1989). A systems approach to educational testing. *Educational Researcher*, **18**(9), 27–32.

Glaser, R., Lesgold, A., & Lajoie, S.P. (1987). Toward a cognitive theory for the measurement of achievement. In R. Ronning, J. Glover, J.C. Conoley, & J.C. Witt (Eds.), *The influence of cognitive psychology on testing, Buros/Nebraska symposium on measurement*, *3* (pp. 41–85). Hillsdale, NJ: Lawrence Erlbaum Associates.

Greenwald, R., Hedges, L.V., & Laine, R.D. (1996). The effect of school resources on student achievement. *Review of Educational*, **66**, 361–396.

Haertel, E. (1986). The valid use of student performance measures for teacher evaluation. *Educational Evaluation and Policy Analysis*, **8**(1), 45–60.

Haertel, E., & Calfee, R. (1983). School achievement: Thinking about what to test. *Journal of Educational Measurement*, **20**(2), 119–132.

Haladyna, T. (1992) Test score pollution: Implications for limited English proficient students. In *Proceedings of the Second National Research Symposium on limited English proficient student issues: Focus on evaluation and measurement, 2,* (pp. 135–163). Washington, DC: U.S. Department of Education, Office of Bilingual Education and Minority Language Affairs.

Hamilton, L., Klein, S., & McCaffrey, D. (2001, April). Exploring claims about student achievement using statewide tests. In Daniel Koretz (Organizer/Moderator), *New work on the evaluation of high-stakes testing programs*. Symposium conducted at the National Council on Measurement in Education's Annual Meeting, Seattle, WA.

Haney, W., Fowler, C., Wheelock, A, Bebell, D., & Malec, N. (1999). Less truth than error?: An independent study of the Massachusetts Teacher Tests. *Education Policy Analysis Archives*, **7**(4). Retrieved from http://epaa.asu.edu/epaa/v7n4/

Hartocollis, A. (2000, September 2). Hiring of teachers is more than a matter of decree. *The New York Times*, p. B1.

Hass, N.S., Haladyna, T.M., & Nolen, S.B. (1990). *Standardized testing in Arizona: Interviews and written comments from teachers and administrators*. (Technical Report 89-3). Phoenix, AZ: Arizona State University West.

Heubert, J.P., & Hauser, R.M. (Eds.). (1999). *High stakes: Testing for tracking, promotion, and graduation*. Washington, DC: National Academy Press.

Hewitt, G. (2001). The writing portfolio: Assessment starts with a. *Clearing House*, **74**, 187–191.

Interstate New Teacher Assessment and Support Consortium. (1992). *Model standards for beginning teacher licensing and development: A resource for state dialogue*. Washington, DC: Council for Chief State School Officers.

Interstate New Teacher Assessment and Support Consortium. (1999). INTASC tackles challenges of new title II reporting requirements. *INTASC in Focus*, **2**(1), 1–6.

Interstate New Teacher Assessment and Support Consortium. (2002). Retrieved from http://www.ccsso.org/intasc.html.

Jerald, C.D. (2000, January 13). The state of states. *Education Week*, **19**(18), 62–65.

Jerald, C.D., & Boser, U. (2000, January 13). Setting policies for new teachers. *Education Week*, **19**(18), 44–45, 47.

Koretz, D. (2001, April). Toward a framework for evaluating gains on high–stakes tests. In Daniel Koretz (Organizer/Moderator), *New work on the evaluation of high-stakes testing programs*. Symposium conducted at the National Council on Measurement in Education's Annual Meeting, Seattle, WA.

Kupermintz, H., Shepard, L., & Linn, R. (2001, April). Teacher effects as a measure of teacher effectiveness: Construct validity considerations in TVAAS (Tennessee Value Added Assessment System). In Daniel Koretz (Organizer/Moderator), *New work on the evaluation of high-stakes testing programs*. Symposium conducted at the National Council on Measurement in Education's Annual Meeting, Seattle, WA.

Land, R., & Herman, J. (1994). *Report on preliminary observation scheme*. Greensboro, NC: National Board for Professional Teaching Standards, Technical Analysis Group, Center for Educational Research and Evaluation, University of North Carolina-Greensboro.

LeMahieu, P.G., Gitomer, D.H., & Eresh, J. (1995). Portfolios in large-scale assessment: Difficult but not impossible. *Educational Measurement: Issues and Practice*, **14**, 11–16, 25–28.

Linn, R.L. (1987) Accountability: The comparison of educational systems and the quality of test results. *Educational Policy*, 1, 181–198.

Linn, R.L. (2000). Assessments and accountability. *Educational Researcher*, **29**, 4–16.

Linn, R.L., & Herman, J.L. (1997). *A policymaker's guide to standards-led assessment*. (ERIC Document ED 408 680). Denver, CO: Education Commission of the States.

Linn, R.E., Baker, E.L. & Dunbar, S B. (1991). Complex, performance-based assessment: Expectations and validation criteria. *Educational Researcher*, **20**(8), 15–21.

Lomask, M.S., & Pecheone, R.L. (1995). Assessing new science teachers. *Educational Leadership*, **52**, 62–66.

Ludlow, L.H. (2001, February). Teacher test accountability: From Alabama to Massachusetts. *Educational Policy Analysis Archive*. Retrieved from http://epaa.asu.edu/epaa/v9n6.html

Luna, C., Solsken, J., & Kutz, E. (2000). Defining literacy: Lessons from high-stakes teacher testing. *Journal of Teacher Education, 51*(4), 276–288.

Madaus, G.F. (1988). The influence of testing on curriculum. In L.N. Tanner (Ed.) *Critical issues in curriculum. Eighty-seventh yearbook of the National Society for the Study of Education*, 83–121. Chicago: University of Chicago Press.

Madaus, G.E., & O'Dwyer, L.M. (1999). A short history of performance assessment: Lessons learned. *Phi Delta Kappa, 80*, 688–695.

Manzo, K.K. (1997). U.S. falls short in a 4-nation study of math tests. *Education Week*. Retrieved from http://www.edweek.org/ew/newstory.cfm?slug=35aft.h16

Massell, D., Kirst, M.W., & Hoppe, M. (1997). *Persistence and change: Standards-based reform in nine states*. CPRE Research Report Mo. RR-037. Philadelphia: University of Pennsylvania, Consortium for Policy Research in Education.

Melnick, S., & Pullin, D. (1999). *Teacher education & testing in Massachusetts: The issues, the facts, and conclusions for institutions of higher education*. Boston: Association of Independent Colleges and Universities of Massachusetts.

Melnick, S.L., & Pullin, D. (2000). Can you take dictation? Prescribing teacher quality through testing. *Journal of Teacher Education, 51*(4), 262–275.

Messick, S. (1987). Assessment in the schools: Purposes and consequences (Research Report RR-87-51). Princeton, NJ: Educational Testing Service. Also appears as a chapter in P. W. Jackson (Ed.) (1988) Educational change: Perspectives on Research and Practice. Berkeley, CA: McCutchan.

Messick, S. (1989). Validity. In R.L. Linn (Ed.) *Educational measurement* (3rd ed.), 13–103). Washington, DC: American Council on Education.

Messick, S. (1990). *Validity of test interpretation and use* (Rep. No. 90-11). Princeton, NJ: Educational Testing Service.

Messick, S. (1994). The interplay of evidence and consequences in the validation of performance assessments. *Educational Researcher, 23*(2), 13–23.

Millman, J. (Ed.), (1997). *Grading teachers, grading schools. Is student achievement a valid evaluation measure?* Thousand Oaks, CA: Corwin Press, Inc.

Millman, J., & Sykes, G. (1992). *The assessment of teaching based on evidence of student learning: An analysis.* Research monograph prepared for the National Board for Professional Teaching Standards, Washington, DC

Mislevy, R.J. (1987). Recent developments in item response theory with implications for teacher certification. In E.F. Rothkopf (Ed.), *Review of Research in Education, 14* (pp. 239–275). Washington, DC: American Educational Research Association.

Mislevy, R.J. (1994). Evidence and inference in educational assessment. *Psychometrika, 59*, 439–483.

Mislevy, R.J. (2000). *Validity of interpretations and reporting results – Evidence and inference in assessment* (U.S. Department of Education, Office of Educational Research and Improvement Award # R305B60002). Los Angeles, CA: National Center for Research on Evaluation, Standards, and Student Testing (CRESST); Center for the Study of Evaluation (CSE); and Graduate School of Education & Information Studies at University of California, Los Angeles.

Mislevy, R.J., Steinberg, L.S., Breyer, F.J., Almond, R.G., & Johnson, L. (1999). *Making sense of data from complex assessment* (Educational Research and Development Centers Programs, PR/Award Number R305B60002). Princeton, NJ: Educational Testing Service, The Chauncey Group International, and Dental Interactive Simulations Corporation.

Mitchell, R., & Barth, P. (1999). Not good enough: A content analysis of teacher licensing Examinations. *Thinking K-16, 3*(1).

National Association of State Directors of Teacher Education and Certification. (2000). T. Andrews, & L. Andrews (Eds.), *The NASDTEC manual on the preparation and certification of educational personnel* (5th ed.). Dubuque, IA: Kendall/Hunt Publishing Company.

National Board for Professional Teaching Standards. (2000). *Assessments Analysis Report: 1999–2000 Administration*. Southfield, MI: Author.

National Board for Professional Teaching Standards. (2002). *Standards and Certificate Overviews*. Retrieved from www.nbpts.org

National Center for Education Statistics. (1997). *NAEP 1996 mathematics report card for the nation and the states: Findings from the national assessment of educational progress*. Washington, DC: Author.

National Center for Education Statistics. (2000). *Reference and reporting guide for preparing state and institutional reports on the quality of teacher preparation: Title II, higher education act* (NCES 2000-89). Washington, DC: Author.

National Commission on Teaching and America's Future. (1996). *What matters most: Teaching for America's future*. New York: Author.

National Council for Accreditation of Teacher Education. (1997). *Technology and the new professional teacher: Preparing for the 21st century classroom*. Washington, DC: Author.

National Council for Accreditation of Teacher Education. (2001). *Professional standards for the accreditation of schools, colleges, and departments of education*. Washington, DC: Author.

National Research Council. (1999). M. Singer & J. Tuomi (Eds). *Selecting Instructional Materials: A Guide for K-12 Science*. Washington, DC: National Academy Press.

National Research Council. (2001). K.J. Mitchell, D.Z. Robinson, & K.T. Knowles (Eds.), *Testing teacher candidates: The role of licensure tests in improving teacher quality*. Washington, DC: National Academy Press.

Ohio Department of Education. (2001). *Ohio FIRST*. Retrieved from http://www.ode.state.oh.us/Teaching-Profession/Teacher/Certification_Licensure/ohio1

Olebe, M. (1999). California Formative Assessment and Support System for Teachers (CFASST): Investing in teachers' professional development. *Teaching and Change*, **6**(3), 258–271.

Olson, L. (2000a, January 13). Finding and keeping competent teachers. *Education Week*, **19**(18), 12–16, 18.

Olson, L. (2000b, January 13). Taking a different road to teaching. *Education Week*, **19**(18), p. 35.

Olson, L. (2001, January 24). States adjust high-stakes testing plans. *Education Week*, **20**(19), 1,18,19.

Pearlman, M. (1999). *K-12 math and science education – Testing and licensing teachers*. Testimony of Educational Testing Service before the House Science ?Committee, August 4. Princeton, NJ: Educational Testing Service.

Popham, W.J. (1997). What's wrong – and what's right – with rubrics. *Educational Leadership*, **55**(2), 72–75.

Sanders, W.L., & Horn, S.P. (1998). Research findings from the Tennessee Value-Added Assessment System (TVASS) database: Implications for educational evaluation and research. *Journal of Personnel Evaluation in Education*, **12**, 247–256.

Sanders, W.L., & Rivers, J.C. (1996). *Cumulative and residual effects of teachers on future student academic achievement*. (Research Progress Report). Knoxville, TN: University of Tennessee Value-Added Research and Assessment Center.

Schaeffer, B. (1996). Standardized tests and teacher competence. Retrieved from www.fairtest.org/empl/ttcomp.htm

Schalock, H.D. (1998). Student progress in learning: Teacher responsibility, accountability, and reality. *Journal of Personnel Evaluation in Education*, **12**, 237–246.

Shepard, L.A. (1989). Why we need better assessments. *Educational Leadership*, **46**(7), 4–9.

Shepard, L. (1993). Evaluating test validity. In L. Darling-Hammond (Ed.), *Review of research in education* (pp. 405–450). Washington, DC: American Educational Research Association.

Shinkfield, A.J., & Stufflebeam, D. (1995). *Teacher evaluation: Guide to effective practice*. Boston: Kluwer Academic Publishers.

Smith, M., & O'Day, J. (1997). Systemic school reform. In S. Fuhrman & B. Malen (Eds.), *The politics of curriculum and testing*. New York: Falmer Press.

Sommerfeld, M. (1996, March 27). High-level science exams in 5 nations studied. *Education Week*. Retrieved from http://www.edweek.org/ew/newstory.cfm?slug=27aft.h15

Stecher, B. (1998). The local benefits and burdens of large-scale portfolio assessment. *Assessment in Education: Principles, Policy & Practice*, **5**, 335–352.

Stecher, B., & Arkes, J. (2001, April). Rewarding schools based on gains: It's all in how you throw the dice. In Daniel Koretz (Organizer/Moderator), *New work on the evaluation of high-stakes testing programs*. Symposium conducted at the National Council on Measurement in Education's Annual Meeting, Seattle, WA.

Sterling, Whitney. (1998, December 9). What is the Massachusetts teacher exam really testing? *Education Week*, **19**(15), p. 37.

Supovitz, J.A., & Brennan, R.T. (1997). Mirror, mirror on the wall, which is the fairest test of all? An examination of the equitability of portfolio assessment relative to standardized tests. *Harvard Educational Review*, **67**, 472–506.

Sykes, G. (1997). The Dallas value-added accountability system. In J. Millman (Ed.), *Grading teachers, grading school: Is student achievement a valid evaluation measure?* (pp. 110–119). Thousands Oaks, CA: Corwin Press.

Teacher Education Accreditation Council. (2000). *Prospectus for a new system of teacher education accreditation.* Retrieved from http://www.teac.org

U.S. Department of Education (1999). *The condition of education, 1999.* Washington, DC: U.S. Government Printing Office.

Valencia, S.W., & Au, K.H. (1997). Portfolios across educational contexts: Issues of evaluation, teacher development, and system validity. *Educational Assessment*, **4**, 1–35.

Walberg, H.J., & Paik, S.J. (1997). Assessment requires incentives to add value: A review of the Tennessee Value-Added Assessment System. In J. Millman (Ed.), *Grading teachers, grading school: Is student achievement a valid evaluation measure?* (pp. 169–178). Thousands Oaks, CA: Corwin Press.

Wolfe, E.W. & Gitomer, D.H. (2000). The influence of changes in assessment design on the psychometric quality of scores. *Applied Measurement in Education*, **14**(1), 91–107.

Wright, S.P., Horn, S.P., & Sanders W.L. (1997). Teacher and classroom context effects on student achievement: Implications for teacher evaluation. *Journal of Personnel Evaluation in Education*, **11**, 57–67.

APPENDIX A

Types of Evaluations and Decisions Involved in Preparation, Licensing, Employment, and Professionalization of Teachers

Stages in the career of a Teacher

Activities in Each Career Stage	Preparation		Licensing		Practice		Professionalization	
Stage	Evaluations	Decisions	Evaluations	Decisions	Evaluations	Decisions	Evaluations	Decisions
Entry	• Evaluations of supply & demand • Evaluations of recruitment programs • Assessment of applications	• Ranking & funding training programs • Redesign of the programs • Selections of students	• Review of credentials	• Approval to enter the certifications process	• Evaluation of staffing needs • Evaluation of recruitment program • Evaluation of applicants	• Job definitions, job search • Program redesign • Selection of staff members	• Examination of staff needs and institutional needs • Assessment of needs & achievements of teachers • Assessment of basic qualifications for national certification	• Continuing education opportunities • Approval of study leaves & special grants • Participation in a national certification program
Participation	• Intake evaluations • Evaluations of students' mastery of course requirements • Cumulative progress reviews	• Planning student programs • Grades • Counseling • Remediation • Counseling • Revising student programs • Termination	• Induction evaluation during a probationary year • Licensing	• Provisional state license • Partial qualification for a license	• Comparison of job requirements & teacher competencies • Performance review • Investigation of charges	• Assignment • End of probation • Promotion • Tenure • Merit pay • Staff development • Honors • Rulings on grievances	• Intake evaluations • Examination of competence	• Designing individual education programs • National certification

cont'd...

cont'd...

Stages in the career of a Teacher

Activities in Each Career Stage	Preparation		Licensing		Practice		Professionalization	
Stage	Evaluations	Decisions	Evaluations	Decisions	Evaluations	Decisions	Evaluations	Decisions
Exit	• Final evaluation of students' fulfilment of graduation requirements • Exit interviews • Follow-up survey	• Graduation • Program review & improvement • Program review & improvement	• Review of success in teaching for a designated period	• Permanent or long-term license	• Comparison of resources, staff needs, & staff seniority • Performance review	• Reduction in force • Termination or sanctions	• Participant achievement in continuing education • Examination of competence & aptitude	• Qualification for future leaves • New assignments

29
Principal Evaluation in the United States

NAFTALY S. GLASMAN

University of California at Santa Barbara, CA, USA

RONALD H. HECK

University of Hawaii at Manoa, HI, USA

THE CONTEXT

Evaluation is an administrative function in education (Glasman, 1979; Razik & Swanson, 1995; Stufflebeam & Webster, 1988). It is one of several that include decision making, problem solving, and instructional supervision. The evaluation of school principals is a personnel administrative function (Seyfarth, 1991). It is also one of several others such as the selection and induction of school principals and other personnel, compensation, staff development, and reassignment (Van Zwoll, 1964). Personnel administration as a whole figures prominently in education because education is a labor-intensive industry (Webb, Greer, Montello, & Norton, 1987). While the institutional nature of schools has often resisted change (Tyack & Cuban, 1995), over the past several decades, the role of personnel evaluation has become central to policymakers' efforts aimed at promoting academic improvement and long-term school effectiveness. Consequently, the evaluation of school principals has become increasingly prominent in personnel administration because principals are pivotal in schools and because the evaluation of principals reveals where schools are and where they are going (Glasman & Nevo, 1988).

The intersection of evaluation and the school principalship is a relatively new domain of academic inquiry (Duke & Stiggins, 1985; Ginsberg & Berry, 1990; Glasman & Heck, 1992; Glasman & Nevo, 1988). Despite current interest in appraising the principal's performance, the empirical study of principal evaluation has been slow to develop, has not experienced a high degree of systematization, and has not been guided by firmly established theoretical foundations (Glasman & Heck, 1992). In response to the current state of the art in the evaluation of the principal, the purposes of this chapter are to: (1) examine the increasing importance of principal evaluation in light of changing conditions in education;

International Handbook of Educational Evaluation, 643–670
T. Kellaghan, D.L. Stufflebeam (eds.)
© 2003 Dordrecht: Kluwer Academic Publishers. Printed in Great Britain.

(2) describe conceptual frameworks and methods of developing a prescriptive structure for principal appraisal systems; (3) provide some examples of such systems that are in use currently; and (4) comment on issues likely to impact on the development of principal appraisal systems in the future.

Images of the school principal have evolved over time (Glasman & Heck, 1992; Hallinger & Heck, 1996; Leithwood & Duke, 1999). Early American school "principal teachers" shared responsibility with lay leaders in developing the curriculum. As the school expanded, so did the role. Added duties for principal teachers included keeping the school enrollment and attendance records, preparing reports, and supervising the work of teachers (Glasman & Nevo, 1988). These latter functions were performed with minimal lay participation. By the second half of the 19th century, school principals had been gradually relieved of teaching duties so they could devote more attention to the school's organization and management. No systematic data are available about early principal evaluation. Perhaps compliance with prevailing education values was one evaluation criterion. Expected exemplary behaviors were possibly others.

By the end of the century, school administration had become more professionalized, as training and licensing became more specific (Glasman & Nevo, 1988). The 20th century brought some additional changes. Efficiency-focused evaluation criteria emerged in the society and in the schools during the municipal reform early in the century (Callahan, 1962). Accounting procedures related to the outcomes of production were of major importance in organizations. Principals of this era attended more and more to increasing the efficiency of the management of their schools.

In the 1950s and 1960s, concerns for equality of educational opportunities intensified. Intensification of federal and state legislation and court decisions had significant implications at the local school level. Schools and school principals took on new tasks which required the establishment and coordination of a network of agencies and individuals (Ubben & Hughes, 1997). Research on effective schools during the 1970s and 1980s accentuated the school principal's leadership role in producing student achievement indirectly (Glasman & Nevo, 1988; Hallinger & Heck, 1996), focusing on such activities as developing vision and school purpose, setting goals, communicating expectations for academic performance, "gatekeeping" with parents and other community interests, providing support, allocating resources, and monitoring the work activities at the school. As a result of the evolving role, at least six different conceptualizations have been used over the past several decades to describe aspects of the principal's leadership (Leithwood & Duke, 1999). At the same time, the evaluation of principals became much more complex because of the multiplicity of evaluation criteria (Smrekar & Mawhinney, 1999).

More recently, accountability has emerged as a dominant and influential social value (Lessinger, 1971). In schools, demands for accountability focused on student accomplishment, independent review, and public support. The quality, fairness, and acceptability of educational accountability generated intense public debates (Glasman, 1983) over the quality of the curriculum, the length of the school year, graduation requirements for students, the preparation and certification of educational personnel, and evaluation processes at the state, district, and school levels (Hess, 1991; Wirt & Kirst, 1989).

In several states, evaluating school principals was a response to legal, political, and market accountability demands. From the mid 1970s to the late 1980s the number of states that mandated formal evaluation of principals increased dramatically from 9 to 40 (Snyder & Ebmeier, 1992). The increased demands for school accountability gradually resulted in changes in the principal's work and authority. School reforms during this period emphasized ways to redistribute power from central offices to the local school (e.g., shared decision making, charter schools) as a means of creating greater accountability. Several goals drove this change including the belief that decentralization would lead to greater educational efficiency, would empower local stakeholders, and would shift the responsibility for poor outcomes away from the school district as a whole to the individual site (Glasman & Heck, 1992). The expectation was that school leadership could facilitate increased school effectiveness and student academic improvement (Hallinger & Heck, 1999).

The changing political context surrounding education brought about numerous new issues associated with the criteria of evaluating principals. Preliminary attempts to evaluate principals formally focused on developing evaluation systems that defined and measured essential principal competencies in performing the job (Ellett, 1978; Gale & McCleary, 1972; Walters, 1980). There was little agreement, however, about which competencies should be required for various evaluation purposes (e.g., preparation, certification, routine performance appraisal). Where previously the principal had been viewed as a middle manager in the educational hierarchy who implements the demands of the central office, structural reforms that focused on shifting greater decision-making authority and responsibility highlighted the principal's role in working with various groups to facilitate school improvement.

In perhaps the most far-reaching redistribution of power from administrators to local stakeholders (e.g., parents, community interests), in the late 1980s Chicago principals were granted greater authority for running the school, but their continuance as school leaders was related to their ability to establish consensus about the school's educational program, foster high expectations for school goals, and implement educational changes that would lead to improved outcomes (Glasman & Heck, 1992; Hess, 1991). Instead of enjoying lifetime administrative tenure, principals became primarily accountable to a local school site council whose support they needed to maintain to have their contracts renewed. Site councils were mandated broad responsibilities including assessment of the principal with performance-based criteria, hiring of staff, approval of the school improvement plan, and advisory power over policies and programs that affect students and instruction (Hess, 1991; Wong & Rollow, 1990). Over the past decade, some other districts have begun to adopt this approach by tying the evaluation of principal performance to the school's academic outcomes (e.g., Education Week, 1995; Richard, 2000).

Currently, other types of environmental forces (e.g., globalization, privatization, choice) continue to reshape the principal's work and expand the boundaries of the school (Leithwood & Duke, 1999). Under this new set of expectations, the specific nature of the principal's work within any particular school may be quite varied and not easily standardized for purposes of evaluation (Ginsberg & Thompson, 1992). As a result, for some districts principal evaluation has gradually moved from determining individual competencies and products (Duke & Stiggins, 1985; Glasman, 1979) to also examining the processes in which the principal engages to reach decisions about school goals, budget allocations, and program implementation (Smylie & Crowson, 1993).

Compared with their role as middle manager of the previous era, principals in decentralized governance systems (e.g., site-based management) assume greater responsibility for the development of the school's goals, its strategic plan, its implementation, and its demonstrated results. Principals also assume greater responsibility for the school's budget and for evaluating the school's staff (Hess, 1991). They may be expected to assume a larger role in getting new curriculum designed and implemented within their schools (Smylie & Crowson, 1993). They may also be expected to work with a wide variety of social service agencies (Smylie & Hart, 1999). Ironically, however, principals are also accountable to a broader range of stakeholders (e.g., parents and community members, teachers and staff, district administrators) for the results of their efforts. This tension between increased responsibility for results and less control (e.g., over decision making) results in a range of approaches that have been adopted toward principal evaluation.

CONCEPTUAL FRAMEWORKS

Unfortunately, little empirical research exists on actual principal evaluation practices, so little is known about the purposes, nature, and quality of the procedures used (Duke & Stiggins, 1985; Ginsberg & Thompson, 1992; Glasman & Heck, 1996). At least three conceptual frameworks have been offered in recent years for the purpose of examining the practice of principal evaluation: role-based, standard-based, and outcome-based evaluation (Heck & Glasman, 1993). These frameworks determine the criteria that will be used in the evaluation.

Role-Based Evaluation

Role-based evaluation of principals is anchored in formally articulated responsibilities and tasks (e.g., job description) as well as in contextual expectations (Hart, 1992). The tasks imply the responsibilities that go with the role of a middle manager. The expectations imply the building and maintaining of cohesive social relationships within the school and between the school and community. Each principal is considered to have a unique school context. The key evaluation criterion becomes the extent to which the principal complies with the school community's expectations. Such compliance has been labeled a set of "right" behaviors (Duke & Iwanicki, 1992). They include analyzing the needs of the school and community and implementing strategies that correspond to the chosen goals.

In recent years, several structural reforms (charter schooling, decentralization, school choice) have developed with a profound effect on the role of the school principal (Glasman & Heck, 1992). As shown in the Chicago example, shared leadership, for example, features parents and teachers who are empowered to participate in school-wide decisions (Smylie & Crowson, 1993). The principal's role has become a first among equals in the management of the school. In addition to being an "instructional" leader, these structural changes free the principal to adopt new roles such as a "transformational" leader who is concerned with establishing a vision for the school (Leithwood & Duke, 1999) and a "moral" leader whose role includes the maintenance of ethical behaviors in the school and advocacy for students (Dillard, 1995; Sergiovani, 1990). In fact, Leithwood and Duke also suggest at least three other conceptualizations of principal leadership that have drawn considerable attention recently. Participative leadership stresses group decision-making processes, such as those mandated in Chicago. Managerial/strategic leadership emphasizes the functions, tasks, or behaviors of the principal that when carried out competently will facilitate the work of others in the school. Contingent leadership involves how leaders respond to and solve the unique organizational circumstances and problems that they face.

As the role of the principal becomes more complex, role-based evaluation becomes more challenging. The formal tasks and the social expectations blend within the role in very specific patterns for each principal. Despite this increased complexity, Smylie and Crowson (1993) and Goertz and Duffy (2000) argue that role-based evaluation is still central in educational evaluation. They call for expanding the evaluation criteria to include all those which are pertinent to the multiple tasks and expectations.

From this standpoint, any of the six leadership conceptualizations identified by Leithwood and Duke (1999) could constitute the focus of role-based evaluation but, of course, each might have different evaluation purposes, objects that are evaluated, and criteria which are associated with judging the principal's performance or effectiveness. While there is obvious overlap within these conceptualizations, an evaluation of the principal's instructional leadership could center on efforts to define the school's academic goals, implement changes to strengthen the instructional program, and strengthen the norms of the academic climate in the school. Evaluating the principal's transformational leadership might focus on how the principal helps build a school vision, establishes school goals, works to establish high expectations for performance, provides support, and fosters school participation in decision making. Evaluating the principal's management/strategic leadership could assess efforts to provide financial and material resources, distribute the resources so they are most useful, accommodate

policies and initiatives undertaken by the district, buffer staff by reducing inter-
ruptions to their classroom instruction, attend to students, and mediate conflicts.
The evaluation of the principal's contingent leadership might focus on how
principals interpret problems, set goals, anticipate constraints, use their personal
values and principles, develop solution processes, and implement those
processes.

Standard-Based Evaluation

A contrasting perspective on evaluation is embedded in a standard-based
approach. Educational reformers have adopted standard setting as a prominent
improvement strategy in the 1990s for students, educational professionals, and
schools (Sykes, 1999). Standard-based evaluation includes delineating the
information requirements through the interaction with decision-making
audiences, obtaining the needed information through a formal data collection
process, and communicating the information to decision makers in a clear and
concise format. Standard-based evaluation of the school principal is grounded in
the criteria used to judge the individual's knowledge, skills, and attitudes as these
are exhibited in the on-going work. It often stems from a job description of the
principal's duties (Stufflebeam & Nevo, 1993).

A well-known set of pertinent educational evaluation standards was prepared
by the Joint Committee (1988). The standards were defined as "principles agreed
upon by representatives of professional organizations whose members engage in
the professional practice of evaluation" (p. 12). The standards are intended to
guide professional practice, hold the professionals accountable, and provide
goals for upgrading the profession's services (Stufflebeam & Nevo, 1993). They
are intended to provide a comprehensive basis for assessing and improving
principal evaluation systems (e.g., the design, implementation, and potential
impact on the educational system). The Joint Committee conceived of four sets
of standards: propriety, utility, feasibility, and accuracy.

Propriety standards are aimed at ensuring that the rights of personnel (in this
case, school principals) are protected. These include service orientation, formal
evaluation guidelines, conflict of interest, access to personnel evaluation reports,
and interaction with evaluators. Utility standards guide the evaluation so that it
becomes as informative as possible. The intention is that the information will be
timely and influential. These include constructive orientation, defined uses,
evaluator credibility, functional reporting, and follow-up procedures. Feasibility
standards focus on conducting evaluations in institutional settings which possess
limited resources and are influenced by a variety of external forces. The standards
in this set are practical procedures, political viability, and fiscal viability.
Accuracy standards concern the dependability of the information. Standards in
this group are defined role, work environment, documentation of procedures,
valid measurement, reliable measurement, systematic data control, bias control,
and monitoring systems.

Standard-based evaluation is intended to evaluate the approaches used including the procedures, instruments, and evaluation systems themselves within different agencies that supervise principals' career paths (e.g., university preparation programs, state education departments, districts). Evaluation standards are intended to diagnose strengths and weaknesses and provide guidance for improving the systems. While there is little empirical work on this perspective in the literature (Glasman & Heck, 1996), in one empirical study of the utilization of the standards in principal evaluation systems, Glasman and Martens (1993) found that different districts emphasize different evaluation standards in their systems for evaluating school principals. On the average, as a group, utility standards had the highest priority (i.e., the goal being that the evaluation be informative, timely, and influential). In contrast, accuracy standards (e.g., reliability and validity of the data collected) had the lowest priority. When asked what the standards actually meant to them, most district officials in charge of principal evaluation and the principals themselves saw them as evaluation "philosophies" or "values." This may be the clue as to how broadly standard-based evaluation criteria may be defined.

Outcome-Based Evaluation

The third framework is outcome-based evaluation of school principals. This approach focuses on the effectiveness of principals. Criteria which are used to judge effectiveness within this perspective relate to results including parent satisfaction, student dropout rate, and, most prominently, student achievement. Actually, as defined previously, the effectiveness of the school principal has only recently become an integral part of principal evaluation (Goertz & Duffy, 2000). Earlier, the effectiveness of the school as a whole was of interest, with the principal identified as one variable among many that contributed (e.g., Brookover & Lezotte, 1977). Ultimately, effectiveness became personalized: the principal and the teaching staff. Strong demands for educational accountability were the cause. Illustrating this shift in thinking about accountability, currently in 19 states, school personnel must write or revise a school improvement plan when they are identified as low performing under some set of criteria. Moreover, in 10 states legislation exists allowing for replacement of the principal or teachers in continually low-performing schools (Jerald & Boser, 1999).

Over the past two decades, the literature on school improvement has emphasized a variety of ways in which principals may affect school improvement (Hallinger & Heck, 1999). Despite these identified linkages, however, no clear blueprint for school improvement has emerged, that is, information that school leaders can actually utilize to create academic improvement. While some argue that assessment should focus primarily on principals' interactions because of the uncertainty of the role in producing outcomes (e.g., Duke & Iwanicki, 1992; Hart, 1992), Ginsberg and Thompson (1992) suggest that principal evaluation should focus squarely on results of the principal's efforts, rather than on the specifics of how he or she gets there.

Outcome-based evaluation of principals has assumed both a direct (explicit) and an indirect (implicit) linkage between principals and levels of student achievement (Adams & Kirst, 1999). Snyder and Ebmeier (1992) for example, emphasized the indirect approach. They studied the linkage between actions taken by principals and what they labeled as "intermediate effects" or "organizational processes" (instruction, teachers' work, satisfaction). Their assumption was that principals have some control over these "outcomes" and, thus, these outcomes may constitute evaluation criteria (Rallis & Goldring, 1993).

Those outcomes over which principals have partial responsibility and may, thus, serve as "ethical" outcome evaluation criteria have constituted insufficient responses to demands for accountability in several states (Goertz & Duffy, 2000; Heck & Glasman, 1993). More explicit criteria have been appearing slowly. One example includes actions taken by principals to improve student outcomes directly (Glasman, 1992). Such actions include examining test scores, identifying learning problems, mobilizing the staff to plan and implement instructional interventions, and examining test scores again. These actions can then be related to results of school-initiated efforts to address student outcomes.

The future of outcome-based evaluation of principals is unknown. It may be just a temporary phenomenon in a constantly changing political arena. It may also imply more rhetoric than actual practice (e.g., see Davis, 1998), but it could also be a very useful vehicle to improve educational practice. Although the stakes are high, including sanctions or reward for performance, there has been little empirical study documenting actual processes and results of outcome-based principal evaluation.

A PRESCRIPTIVE STRUCTURE

Although the field of principal evaluation has been labeled as fuzzy (Heck & Marcoulides, 1992), our understanding of this role and its responsibilities is more advanced than it was only two decades ago (Hallinger & Heck, 1996; Murphy, 1988). In this section of the chapter, we outline a prescriptive structure for principal evaluation. Major components of this structure include the evaluation purposes, the objects being evaluated, evaluation criteria, and the authority and qualification to evaluate. Principals' actions constitute specific objects of evaluation and may be observed in an effort to assess the effectiveness of their performance.

In designing principal evaluation systems within any of the conceptual frameworks that we have outlined, we must view the pertinent action in regard to some specific evaluation purpose and collect the right data about principal actions with respect to this evaluation purpose (Glasman, 1992). The type of data collected and the manner in which it is reported back to principals will thus vary. Moreover, the entire set of relationships including evaluation purposes, objects, criteria, and method is embedded within two important contexts which themselves overlap somewhat (Glasman & Glasman, 1990). One is the political context within which policies are made at the state, district, and building levels. The other is the evaluation context which has been politicized at the federal, state, and local levels (Heck & Glasman, 1993). These contexts help determine the conceptual frameworks that underlie the approach taken toward principal evaluation.

Evaluation Objectives

A first concern in the design of a principal evaluation system is the identification of the objectives, or purposes, of the evaluation. With growing attention to accountability in recent decades, personnel evaluation has become one strategy utilized in efforts to improve schools. Personnel evaluation can have a variety of objectives. For the evaluation of educators in general, Stufflebeam and Nevo (1993) offered a classification of four stages in the career of an educator to which evaluation objectives may correspond. These stages include preparation, licensing, practice, and professionalization (pp. 27–28).

For the evaluation of administrators, the objectives for each stage have often been poorly articulated (Glasman & Heck, 1992). This has constituted a constraint in the development of meaningful administrator appraisal systems. In their review of the literature on principal evaluation, Ginsberg and Berry (1990) found a wide range of reported practices, but with little empirical support demonstrating the relationship of each practice to its effectiveness in meeting its evaluation objective.

The evaluation process itself consists of both description and judgment (Glasman & Nevo, 1988). In actual practice, it is apparent that establishing purposes of evaluation leads back to value positions policymakers have about those purposes (Glasman & Martens, 1993; Williams & Pantili, 1992). These value positions must be acknowledged in the process of developing a conceptual framework to guide the evaluation (i.e., role-based, standard-based, outcome-based). At least three general types of evaluation purposes can be defined. These include those purposes that are more formative in nature (e.g., improvement oriented), more summative in nature (e.g., certification, selection, dismissal), or that are designed to hold someone accountable (e.g., for outcomes). These particular evaluation objectives can differ across educational contexts and nations.

Some formative evaluations are conducted on a routine basis. The purpose is often to help the person improve what she or he is doing or promote the individual's professional growth. This could include participating in certain types of professional development activities. While the routine evaluation of principals has not received sufficient attention from researchers (Blase, 1987), the evidence that does exist on principal evaluation suggests that most principal appraisal is directed toward professional development (Brown & Irby, 1998; Clayton-Jones et al., 1993). In one preliminary study in Australia, Clayton-Jones and colleagues found that principals perceived positive benefits of evaluation aimed at the purpose of professional development. It is unclear from existing research, however, how participation in these types of professional-development programs might impact on the school administrator's effectiveness within certain dimensions of the role.

There are several summative evaluation objectives. One set in this category includes preparation, certification, and selection of principals (Sirotnik & Durden, 1996; Williams & Pantili, 1992). Typically, states monitor administrative preparation through requiring a prescribed set of courses, intern experiences, and an advanced academic degree (e.g., master's) as part of the initial process of evaluating the applicant's eligibility to receive a credential or license. At present, there is little consistency in requirements for entry. Hence, the specific process varies somewhat from state to state (e.g., screening, educational requirements, specific course work). By 1993, 45 states required at least a master's degree (or equivalent courses) for a principal's license (Tryneski, 1993). As a result of state mandates, many preparation programs for administrators have begun to revise their course requirements, program selection criteria, and assessment instruments in an effort to upgrade their standards for licensing administrators (McCarthy, 1999).

Another evaluation purpose is the determination of the extent to which the principals fulfills, or implements, particular evaluation routines. One example might be the evaluation of teachers and other staff on a yearly basis. Another example might be the extent to which the principal abides by particular evaluation mandates that are passed (but are not necessarily routine). For example, legislation could be passed that requires principals to prepare and submit a budget to a site counsel, to create a school improvement plan (as in Chicago), or to attend to special education procedures. The purpose of the evaluation, then, would be to ascertain that the principal complies.

Another set of summative evaluation purposes is associated with granting tenure or promotion, or focusing on reassignment and dismissal (Davis, 1998). Evaluation of school principals has also been linked to salary adjustments and personal rewards for school performance (e.g., Clayton-Jones et al., 1993; *Education Week*, 1995). More recently, formal evaluation practices have also resulted in the removal of school principals (Richard, 2000).

A final type of evaluation objective concerns principals' and teachers' accountability for student outcomes. This is a relatively new evaluation purpose as far as administrators are concerned. Accountability for outcomes is not a basic task or function of the role, as it might be more directly for teachers but, rather, is an impact or consequence. Currently, much educational evaluation, and personnel evaluation more specifically, is outcomes focused. This represents a new type of evaluation, as it does not necessarily depend upon direct observation or self-assessments about what the principal is doing on the job.

One caution is that while the effect of the principal's leadership in school effectiveness and school improvement has been established empirically, evaluators must also consider the impact of the school's context on principal leadership and its potential impact on the evaluation of school administrators (Hart, 1992). This is especially apparent in districts that emphasize decentralized decision making through site-based management and greater public responsibility for and control in hiring and evaluating school administrators. The context may muddy the waters surrounding the delimitation of the type and parameters of evaluation that should be utilized to monitor principal performance for the specific purpose, as principals do not have complete control of the school's inputs (e.g., student composition, resources). In one empirical study on the impact of context on administrative performance, Heck (1995) determined that the organizational context exercised a measurable effect on how the performance of the new administrator was rated in several different domains – that is, the school context affected how well administrators performed the tasks associated with their role.

Davis (1998) examined superintendents' perspectives on the involuntary departure of principals – that is, reasons why they lost their jobs. Principals' lack of interpersonal relationships was the primary reason superintendents gave for dismissing principals. Other reasons included their failure to perform various duties (e.g., not meeting expectations for student achievement, not providing a safe campus environment, resistance to change). The study does not specifically mention the evaluation process used in these decisions. With respect to our discussion of outcome-based evaluation, however, it is interesting that while policymakers are moving in the direction of applying political pressures on superintendents to remove principals who fail to perform in the role, superintendents report using these types of performance criteria less than the interpersonal domain.

Policymakers interested in outcomes-based evaluation must keep in mind the extent to which administrators can (and should) be held accountable for the overall effectiveness of their schools. Personnel decisions made by boards of education, superintendents, or lay-controlled site councils about the performances of educators with respect to school outcomes should only be made after a careful consideration of research concerning the how the school's context and its processes impact on its academic outcomes.

Evaluation Objects

Evaluation objects help evaluators determine what type of information should be collected and how that information should be analyzed. Clear object identification helps keep the evaluation focused and serves to resolve value conflicts among stakeholders and others likely to be affected by the evaluation (Glasman & Nevo, 1988). Major categories of evaluation objects include personnel, programs, and student learning. With respect to the evaluation of principals, more specifically, evaluation objects concern what it is exactly about the principal's work or role that is being evaluated (Heck & Glasman, 1993).

It is apparent that leadership is a major component of the role. As we have noted, Leithwood and Duke (1999) recently identified several different classifications of leadership that have been used in research on the principal's role (e.g., instructional, transformational, participative, contingent, managerial). These conceptualizations provide hints as to what could be evaluated. The objects chosen might be different under each type of leadership evaluated. Identifying clearly articulated evaluation objects may be more difficult in evaluating principals, however, because of the complexity of the role.

In choosing potential evaluation objects, one useful step is to determine who is accountable for what and to whom. As we have suggested, this issue involves determining responsibility and control. All dimensions of the work of principals for which they are responsible constitute potential evaluation objects. As to control, however, only objects should be evaluated over which the principal exercises guiding power. No evaluation object should be chosen over which the principal has no control or little responsibility.

To illustrate this idea in more detail, in evaluating a principal's instructional leadership, accountability for student learning is shared by teachers and administrators, the students, their parents, governmental agencies that provide support, and the general public (Gorton & Snowden, 1993). It can be somewhat difficult to identify objects that are associated with the principal's role more directly. Examples might be the principal's skills and efforts in visiting classrooms (e.g., monitoring teachers' lesson design, delivery, and evaluation) or aligning the curriculum with district standards and benchmarks.

Similarly, when thinking about the principal's transformational leadership role, the principal may be responsible for helping to define and articulate the school's goals and educational objectives, the commitment of its staff toward attaining those goals, its programs and plans to reach its objectives, and its progress in reaching those objectives (Ginsberg & Thompson, 1992; Gorton & Snowden, 1993). In terms of managerial/strategic leadership, some of the principal's responsibilities might include assignment of teachers to classes, supervision and evaluation of teachers and staff, administrative procedures and resources needed to achieve school objectives, and student discipline. Contingent leadership responsibilities might have objects related to problem solving (e.g., problem identification, use student achievement data to determine areas of instructional need, cognitive processes used to construct solutions).

As Glasman and Heck (1992) summarize this part of the evaluation process, possible evaluation objects therefore could include a wide array of principals' attitudes, behavior, cognitive processes (e.g., the ability to solve instructional problems or make appropriate decisions), competence (e.g., skills), performance (on-the-job behavior), and effectiveness (results-oriented activities such as improvement in outcomes, achievement of benchmarks). Delimiting the objects becomes an important part in ensuring the validity (and generalizability) of the evaluation results. The more specific the evaluation object, the more there is a need to include a large number of objects in the evaluation because highly specific objects "cover" only a small portion of what is being evaluated. In contrast, the broader the object, the more ambiguous it becomes. More information is needed about the degree of specificity of the evaluation objects that districts use in their principal assessment practices, as well as that which is desirable in creating effective principal evaluation systems.

It is important to emphasize that the evaluation objects should link to what it is about the principal's work that is being assessed and the overall evaluation purposes. For example, the principal could be evaluated in isolation in terms of his or her managerial skills and effectiveness (e.g., communication, decision making, instructional supervision). In contrast, the principal could be assessed with respect to the entire staff in terms of his or her ability to contribute to school improvement (e.g., goal setting, planning and implementing a school-improvement program, evaluating the results of the staff efforts). The principal could also be evaluated with respect to the school in terms of its inputs, processes, and outcomes.

Concerning this latter type of evaluation, as we have suggested, more recently some districts are tying principal evaluation to levels of student outcomes (e.g., Education Week, 1995; Sack, 2000). In this case, the performance of the principal may not even be directly assessed, with the assumption being that the outcome is the product of the performance. Current evaluation practices have generally been inadequate for this particular purpose for which decision makers would like to collect information about the principal. Several states now have been granted legislative authority to remove the principal of a failing school (White, 1999). Because of the complexity of relationships involved in producing student outcomes, it is hard to determine exactly what data should be collected and how that data should be analyzed to determine the extent to which personnel should be accountable for outcomes and improvement (Heck, 2000). Since few states or districts make any attempt to adjust outcomes by student composition or other types of educational indicators, at this time it is probably best to proceed with caution when using this type of evaluation object.

Evaluation Criteria

Once evaluation purposes and objects are determined, evaluation criteria are needed in order to judge the quality of the performance. Criteria concern how the merit of the evaluation object will be assessed. Judging the merit of evaluation objects is one of the most difficult tasks in educational evaluation (Glasman & Nevo, 1988). Debates concerning the most appropriate types of criteria have existed since the study of the field of principal evaluation emerged (Ginsberg & Thompson, 1992).

One approach is that evaluation should attempt to determine whether goals have been achieved (e.g., Provus, 1971; Tyler, 1950). It depends, however, on what is meant by "goal achievement." Some goals may be trivial, while other stated objectives may not be worth achieving. The achievement of "important" goals is one possible way to deal with evaluation criteria (Glasman & Nevo, 1988). At one time, evaluators looked at this as the effectiveness versus efficiency argument. Effectiveness is concerned with the extent to which a goal is attained (accountability), whereas efficiency is concerned with how much one gets with how many resources. Currently, accountability and effectiveness appear to be dominating.

A second approach concerns meeting standards that are set. This could involve developing some type of criteria-based standards derived from the performance that is desired on given tasks or functions of the role. More specifically, an example might be a role-based approach that emphasizes the managerial conceptualization of principal leadership. In this approach, standards could be set by experts or other relevant groups about the important aspects of the job. For example, the National Association of Secondary School Principals and the National Association of Elementary School Principals established the National Commission for the Principalship for preparing and licensing principals. They argued that most principal licensing requirements were irrelevant to current demands and that preparation should reflect the day-to-day realities of operating schools (National Commission for the Principalship, 1990). The National Commission identified 21 functional domains and attempted to delineate the knowledge and skill base for principals in each domain (Thompson, 1993).

The approach is not without problems, however. There has been considerable debate over what should be the core knowledge and skills required for school leaders. While the National Commission on the Principalship laid out functional domains, some have questioned the wisdom of attempting to develop a knowledge and skill base at all (Bartell, 1994; Donmoyer, 1995). Given the varied nature of the principal's work, the problems of specificity of tasks and the situational nature of the job (Ginsberg & Thompson, 1992; Glasman & Heck, 1992; Hart, 1992), it is difficult to specify what domains, tasks, and behaviors principals should pursue beyond very broad areas such as decision making, teacher supervision, facilities management, and school improvement. Because organizations such as schools are socially constructed, participants must share in the defining and solving of problems. The evaluation criteria for each principal may be closely related to the problems of each specific school. Because of the complexity of interrelationships among the school's context, its learning-related processes, and student outcomes, it is likely that the assessment of the performance of one principal would be quite different from that of the performance of another principal. It is also difficult to specify how "good" someone should be in each of these defined domains (i.e., what level of skill one should possess).

Whatever evaluation criteria are chosen should meet the evaluation standards described in the Joint Committee on Standards for Educational Evaluation (1988) publication on the evaluation of teachers and other educational personnel. As we have suggested, these include standards addressing utility, propriety, feasibility, and accuracy. Glasman and Martens (1993) found documentation of activities related to principal performance to be relatively informal and lacking in detail. Perceived weaknesses included an absence of formal observation formats, a lack of written comments and conferencing following each observation or other data collection method, and few formative reports during the evaluation process. Principals perceived as problematic the lack of formal training for evaluators, little time and emphasis on evaluation process development, and poor psychometric qualities of the measurements taken. Principals perceived that utility evaluation standards had the top priority, possibly because they are intended to make evaluation informative, timely, and influential.

As Ginsberg and Thompson (1992) argue, principal evaluation criteria may not necessarily be based on a preset standardized set of goals for all principals. Criteria could also be developed for principal accountability for school outcomes. As we have suggested, a number of states have passed legislation that allows the state to move to replace principals and staff in schools that are identified as low producing over time. In these states, this legislation tends to move the authority for evaluation away from districts and to the state level. Because of the variety of influences on student achievement, however, it is unclear exactly to what extent principals should be held accountable for outcomes. This makes the delineation of criteria and associated evaluation standards more difficult to determine.

Significant questions remain with regard to principal evaluation criteria in light of the fact that this type of evaluation typically requires more sophisticated analyses to determine, for example, how much educational value schools contribute to student learning (Heck, 2000). The types of criteria could include how well the school has done (i.e., the level of school performance in terms of raw scores), how much the school has added (i.e., educational value added by the school over and above student composition effects), or how well does the school compare to other schools (i.e., how well has it met a standard set of criteria like graduation rates, percent of students who achieve a particular standard).

Authority and Qualifications to Evaluate

Before one deals with evaluation methodology, one needs to ask who is to be involved in the appraisal of principals. In the past, most systems have been hierarchical (Fletcher & McInerney, 1995; Newman, 1985). This means that principals are evaluated by superiors (assistant superintendents or superintendents). Other evaluators have also been proposed (Garrett & Flanigan, 1991). For example, Blase (1987) and Ballou and Podgursky (1995) argue that teacher feedback would be an important part of the process. Garrett and Flanigan suggest that information from parents could also be utilized in the evaluation. These groups traditionally have not had the authority to evaluate educational professionals. Duke and Stiggins (1985) and Brown, Irby, and Neumeyer (1998) suggest that principal peer evaluation would be desirable.

Others have contended that self-assessment be a part of the process (Brown, Irby, & Neumeyer, 1998). For example, the use of portfolios has gained popularity in the 1990s in programs to prepare administrators for licensing (Barnett, 1995). The portfolios include materials documenting what the individual has learned over a period of time – ability to apply learning concepts to completing complex tasks, personal reflections, letters of support from others with whom the trainee has worked (McCarthy, 1999). The strength of this method is that the principal is the one who knows what he or she did. On the other hand, this assessment is subjective.

The choice of evaluator has both political (authority to evaluate) and technical (knowledge and skills) implications for how the evaluation is to be conducted. It can also affect the types of information that will be collected (Clayton-Jones et al., 1993). Earlier work about the authority to evaluate educational personnel derived from the definition of authority as "legislated power to act" (Gorton & Snowdon, 1993). With specific regard to authority to evaluate, then, the assumption used is that she or he who has the legislated power to act (e.g., guide, give instructions) has the legislated power to evaluate that person whose work s/he supervises (Dornbush, 1975). If the authorized evaluator is the sole data source for the evaluation of personnel, then the evaluator also has the legislated power to choose the criteria for evaluation.

In the domain of principal evaluation, there are several data sources, however. This is so because of the complexity of the role of the principal and the multiple interaction the role incumbent has with other people who could serve as evaluation data sources. The choice of these sources is up to the authorized evaluator. Typically, the evaluator chooses sources which qualify as relevant data sources, that is, individuals who are exposed to actions and behaviors of the principal and who have clearly articulated criteria which they can use to describe what they see and hear and over which they can render judgment about the worth of their data (Glasman, Killait, & Gmelch, 1974). These sources also need to understand the unique set of the principal's job expectations and the context within which s/he works (Glasman & Nevo, 1988; Hoy & Miskel, 1982).

METHODOLOGY

Types of Information

Many kinds of information can be collected regarding each object that is being evaluated (Glasman & Nevo, 1988). Because of the complexity of assessing the principal's role (e.g., cognitive processes, actions, effects), evaluation should reflect critical perspectives on the role, be flexible enough to allow for variation in how the role is perceived, multidimensional to adequately cover central aspects or purposes of the evaluation, and include multiple information sources (e.g., different types of evaluators, different methods of data collection). Inconsistences in evaluation can develop because of differences in the principal's work across school levels and specific school sites and the nature of evaluation decoupled from context.

As we have suggested, one issue to be considered is the types of purposes on which to focus – role-based aspects such as the principal's skills and tasks (e.g., communication, monitoring instruction, disciplining students), processes in which the principal engages (e.g., school planning decisions, resolving instructional problems, planning staff development), or outcomes (e.g., implementation of programs, effects of programs). Stufflebeam's (1972) CIPP (context, input, process, product) evaluation approach, for example, suggests focusing on four sets of information pertaining to each evaluation object: the goals of the object; its design; its implementation; and its outcomes. From this standpoint, the evaluation of the principal might include information collected about his or her goals in terms of improving the school, the quality of the improvement plan, the extent to which the plan is carried out, and its results.

A second issue is what type of information to collect about the principal's tasks, skills and behavior. One type of information is that which is collected directly about the principal's performance (e.g., ratings, observations, interviews, checklists of tasks completed). Regarding principal ratings, a major concern in the literature on principal evaluation has been the development of valid and reliable instruments to assess principal effectiveness (Pitner & Hocevar, 1987). There have been criticisms raised about the instruments used to collect data about principal performance (Heck & Marcoulides, 1992). Often, instruments used to examine administrative job performance are constructed in a manner that makes it difficult to measure actual job performance (Marcoulides, 1988). A supervisor is most often asked to judge as "below average," "average," or "above average," generally without operational definitions of these terms or on what observations the judgments should be based. Early attempts typically used ratings concerned with competencies (Ellett, 1978; Gale & McCleary, 1972; Walters, 1980). Typically, they are not directed at professional growth (Fontana, 1994).

Another type of information collected that has been used as part of the principal evaluation process is data about the school (e.g., its processes and outcomes). In this type of evaluation, the data collection tends to be more indirect, in that it focuses on the results of efforts, as opposed to the efforts themselves. The data could include student achievement information, dropout rates, patterns of course taking, and discipline. Some of this type of information is collected as part of states' "report card" or educational indicators systems (Heck, 2000). This approach can help ascertain how much educational value is added (e.g., improvement). It can also enhance comparisons among schools in terms of how well schools have reached performance standards. There are few consistencies in the type information that is collected and the use of this information currently for principal evaluation.

Evaluators

There are other issues involved with who is providing the information used in the evaluation. Some empirical work exists on the quality of assessments using various evaluators. In one examination of teacher ratings of their principal, Marcoulides and Heck (1992) determined that teacher ratings were subject to considerable error (almost half of the observed variance in the leadership effectiveness score was due to combined teacher error components). They concluded that the number of teachers providing information about the principal's performance is extremely important in obtaining reliable estimates. There may be other rating biases due to ethnicity, gender, or experience. For example, Ballou and Podgrusky (1995) determined that teachers rated principals of the same ethnicity and gender higher. In another exploratory study of others' assessments of principal leadership, Heck (2000) found considerable consistency among parent, student, and staff ratings.

Another evaluator is the principal him or herself. An obvious strength of this approach is that principals are close to the source regarding evaluation objects. A weakness is that the information is more subjective. In one study of self-assessment versus teacher assessment of the principal's leadership effectiveness, Heck and Marcoulides (1996) determined that principals rated their own performance systematically higher across several dimensions of the role, as compared to their teachers' assessments. Marcoulides and Heck (1993) also identified inconsistencies in how assistant principals rated their leadership skills in several domains versus how their supervising principals rated their assistant principals' leadership skills. No systematic rating bias emerged in this latter study, however, across the two sets of evaluators.

About the General Method

Despite the existence of the various problems associated with principal evaluation methodologies, the fundamental stages of the evaluation process generally are agreed upon (Stufflebeam & Webster, 1988). First, the choice of an evaluation purpose is made. Then, the evaluation objects (evaluands in the evaluation jargon) are determined in the direction "from the general to the most specific." Once the specific objects are determined, choices of data sources are made as well as choices of data collection procedures. Analyses of the data and data reporting follow.

With regard to principal evaluation, several basic issues have been raised and dealt with, some successfully, and some are still being debated. For example, as we have noted, the rating scales which are used in some questionnaires are insufficiently descriptive. The rating is too abstract as a result. Other instruments may not meet various evaluation standards (e.g., accuracy). The "growth contracting" which has emerged with outcome-based evaluation left not totally resolved as to whose responsibility it is to define the levels of possible outcomes (Glasman & Heck, 1996). For the future, such contracting may include self-evaluation in the main, which will focus on areas for improvement, plans for improvement, and long-range personal goals.

Finally, a proposed use of ad hoc committees (e.g., site councils) for principal evaluation is only emerging in selected districts. The outstanding issues here are ways of keeping the evaluation confidential, the ways to agree on evaluation criteria, the ways to respond to demands for open disclosure of the evaluation process, the ways to increase validity, and the ways to decrease the time spent on the evaluation.

Evaluation Consequences

When the fundamental consequences of evaluation are followed, the evaluation product can be easily used by decision makers (Alkin, Daillak, & White, 1970; Patton, 1978). In principal evaluation, the decision makers are those individuals who have legislative power over the principal (e.g., district superintendent, assistant superintendent, site council). The use of the evaluation results is guided by the purpose for which the evaluation is done. A few possibilities include hiring versus not hiring, reassigning versus not reassigning, taking certain kinds of actions to promote improvement versus taking other actions, and rewarding the principal on the basis of student achievement outcomes versus not rewarding (Razik & Swanson, 1995).

Clearly, there must be a correspondence between the evaluation objective and results and the audience with whom the results are shared. At times, it is appropriate to share the results with no one. At other times, it is important to share with others not only the results of the evaluation, but also the actions taken as a result of the evaluation (Glasman, 1995).

EVALUATION SYSTEMS IN CURRENT USE

In this section, we provide five examples of principal evaluation systems that are currently in use in different parts of the United States. These examples are by no means inclusive of all evaluation systems in use. They represent, however, different evaluation approaches. Table 1 summarizes these five evaluation systems in some detail.

Three of the five are formative systems. One is role-based. Another is also role-based, but is in the process of adding standard-based elements as well. These are based mainly on performance of duties and job responsibilities. The elements do not appear to be tied to the meeting of specific goals.

The third is standard-based. In comparison, the other two of the five evaluation systems are more summative and accountability centered. One employs a standards–outcomes approach in combination. The other is outcome-based. These latter two systems have been recently reconfigured with a stronger emphasis on outcomes as part of the evaluation objects. These include elements of standard setting for principals, in terms of identifying goals and working toward the achievement of those goals. The assessment appears to be increasingly tied to meeting these goals. These have stronger sanctions for failure to meet goals (e.g., removal of the principal) than the formative systems.

Table 1 suggests that principal evaluation purposes clearly determine which objects are chosen for evaluation. For example, school districts which restrict their purpose to that of improvement seem to choose evaluation objects such as the principals' execution of formally assigned responsibilities. Districts which are in need of making summative decisions seem to focus the evaluation on

Table 1. Evaluation Practices in Selected School Districts

District	1	2	3	4	5
Size	Midsized	Very large	Midsized	Large	Very large
Location	Rural	System	Suburban	Urban	Urban
Evaluation Purposes	1. Improve leadership 2. Assess competence	1. Improve leadership 2. Communicate expectations	1. Improve leadership 2. Meet performance standards	1. Reassign 2. Place on probation 3. Remove	1. Remove 2. Provide incentives
Evaluation Objects	1. Decision making behaviors 2. Interpersonal relations 3. Supervision of students and learning environment 4. Managing school plant 5. Monitoring student progress	1. Management of all assigned responsibilities 2. Unifying staff 3. Commitment to school improvement	1. Instructional leadership 2. School management 3. Focus on achievement 4. School–parent relations	1. Leadership in developing curricular frameworks 2. Attracting and retaining good teachers 3. Student achievement scores	1. Student achievement scores 2. Efforts to enhance student achievement scores
Evaluator	Superordinate	Superordinate	Superordinate	Superordinate	Superordinate
Evaluation Methodology Decisions	Made by evaluator	Made by evaluator	Made by a committee headed by the evaluator	Made by the evaluator on the basis of recommendations made by an external and, later, an internal committee	Included in contract agreements by the school board and the administrator association
Evaluation Consequences	1. Evaluatee–evaluator discussions and follow-up 2. Rating	1. Evaluatee–evaluator discussions and follow-up 2. Rating	1. Evaluatee–evaluator discussions and follow-up 2. Rating 3. Sharing results with school board	1. Reassignment 2. Placement on probation 3. Removal	1. Removal 2. Providing incentives 3. Loss of tenure as administrators
Overall Evaluation Approach	Role-based	Role-based with increased inclusion of standards	Standard-based	A standard-outcome combination	Outcome-based

principals' efforts associated with overcoming deficiencies found in the school (e.g., curriculum, teachers, student achievement).

The evaluation methodologies follow suit. In the formative principal evaluation systems included in Table 1, the principals' superordinate alone makes the design choices, with only minimum information consultations. In the outcome-based systems, years are needed to study the relevant design parameters and their acceptability by all relevant stakeholders. While the final design choices are made here, too, by the principal's superordinate (e.g., superintendents, boards of education), the input s/he receives is formal and known to the public.

FURTHER THOUGHTS

So far, this chapter has addressed the increased significance of principal evaluation as a function of changing conditions of education. We also provided a conceptual framework for viewing principal evaluation systems and a variety of related considerations found in the literature pertaining to school principals as evaluatees. A brief outline of selected evaluation systems in current use then followed. We now close this chapter with further thoughts about principal evaluation practice, training and research.

Practice

Logic suggests that improvement in the quality of principal evaluation practices should include at least three evaluation subsystems:

(1) a base-line employment evaluation (related to a hiring purpose);
(2) a fine-tuning evaluation (related to an improvement purpose);
(3) a secondary employment evaluation (related to a summative purpose such as reassignment).

The base-line employment evaluation might include:

(a) data gathered and judgments made in the process of making the employment decision;
(b) organizational expectations regarding vision and task;
(c) indicators of the extent to which the expectations will be met.

The fine-tuning evaluation might include:

(a) data gathered in relation to organizational expectations;
(b) judgments about needed adjustments and ways of monitoring their implementation.

The secondary employment evaluation might include:

(a) judgments about the principal's suitability to handle a crisis or a change in superordinate personnel;
(b) judgments about benefits and costs of making a subsequent summative decision.

The extent to which school districts need to, and/or wish to, follow this logic is unknown at this time. One could contend that improvement of training (pre-service and inservice) of both evaluators and evaluatees in this case may lead to improvement of principal evaluation itself.

Training

Evaluation fundamentals (e.g., assessment, testing) are not taught in most administrative training programs although they are offered in almost all schools and colleges of education. A bit of "program" or "teacher" evaluation is offered in some preliminary administrative training programs and "principal" evaluation is taught in some advanced programs, but without the fundamentals (Glasman, 1997). In large school districts which have research and evaluation units, principals may attend workshops in which they learn to diagnose student achievement test scores in order to help them guide future instruction. But principal evaluators seldom acquire sufficient knowledge needed to evaluate principals adequately.

So principal evaluators, typically former principals themselves, are probably reluctant to engage in evaluation for which they know they lack competence. Neither are they sufficiently competent to enter the debate about whether or not principals should be evaluated in the context of the evaluation of the entire school or as a separate evaluation object (Goertz & Duffy, 2000). If they express an opinion in favor of the former, they would not be certain which incentive to give to some schools or how to "punish" others. If they favor the latter approach, they would not know how to correct for the fact that principals typically have no direct control over student learning (Dornbush, 1975), rendering outcome-based evaluation, for example, totally unfair and even unethical (Darling-Hammond, 1994).

In preliminary administrative training programs, a course could be required in formative personnel evaluation.

Beginning with evaluation purposes (Joint Committee, 1988), the course could briefly cover evaluation objects associated with teacher evaluation (see Pearlman and Tannenbaum, this volume) as well as those associated with principal evalua-tion (Glasman & Heck, 1992; Heck & Glasman, 1993). Students might also examine documents and practices in nearby school districts. The rest of the course could be devoted to fundamentals of personnel evaluation methodology, including the nature of data needed, data sources, data collection procedures, data reporting and data analysis. Evaluation consequences could be taught in connection with teacher supervision and principal evaluation followup (Glasman & Marten, 1993).

Advanced administrator training programs could capitalize on what has been learned in preliminary preparation programs, in principal on-the-job experience and in inservice training in personnel evaluation. Advanced courses could perhaps focus on summative evaluation approaches because the principals' superordinate-evaluators need to consider accountability, equity and efficiency in their evaluation criteria. If, in the future, district decentralization plans allow for increased autonomy and if school principals increasingly work within such organizational contexts, then training for "team leadership" in such schools and for "collective personnel evaluation" should be included in these advanced training programs (Nevo, 1998).

Research

Many questions in the area of principal evaluation remain unanswered. Since principals, by definition, must engage in educational politics, the process of principal evaluation is embedded in two surrounding contexts – an evaluation context and a political context. We have only rudimentary descriptive evidence about actual principal evaluation systems in use.

We know little about specific methodological designs and implementation processes. We can certainly learn about each one of the evaluation systems by conceptualizing each as a case in itself. We can also survey a sample of them with the recognition that we gather only documentation and opinions rather than primary facts. In pursuing the path of studying methodologies, we need to make choices about how far we wish to understand a given evaluation system versus how strongly we wish to be able to offer generalizations from our findings. One example might concern the correspondence between the evaluators used, their individual ratings of the principal's skills, and the overall evaluation purposes. Accounting for the sources of variation in observed performance can be a difficult task (Marcoulides & Heck, 1992).

A second area of research may focus on the politics of principal evaluation. We know that in some cases the evaluation purposes are not made public. Unintended ones are. We know of cases in which a crisis atmosphere is induced and a call for evaluation of principals is made (Glasman & Glasman, 1990). We know of subjective choices of unbalanced data sources. We know of using data out of context. These are only a few examples of the use of "political" evaluations. However, we lack systematic data about these instances. If we pursue this line of research, we may contribute to the debate about the extent to which some kinds of principal evaluations are, in fact, and should be, in fact, a political value (Glasman, 1986). Entering the debate assumes a recognition that principal evaluation is not a pure professional education practice and that its study is not a pure scholarly educational endeavor.

REFERENCES

Adams, J.E., & Kirst, M.W. (1999). New demands and concepts for educational accountability: Striving for results in an era of excellence. In J. Murphy & K. Seashore-Lewis (Eds.), *Handbook of research on educational administration* (2nd ed.) (pp. 463–490). San Francisco: Jossey-Bass.

Alkin, M.C., Daillak, R., & White, P. (1979). *Using evaluation*. Newbury Park, CA: Sage.

Ballou, D., & Podgursky, M. (1995). What makes a good principal: How teachers assess the performance of principals. *Economics of Education Review*, **14**(3), 243–252.

Barnett, B. (1995). Portfolio use in educational leadership programs: From theory to practice. *Innovative Higher Education*, **19**, 197–206.

Bartell, C. (1994, April). *Preparing future administrators: Stakeholder perceptions*. Paper presented at the annual meeting of the American Educational Research Association, New Orleans, LA.

Blase, J. (1987). Dimensions of effective school leadership: The teacher's perspective. *American Educational Research Journal*, **24**(4), 589–610.

Brookover, W., & Lezotte, L. (1977). *Changes in school characteristics coincident with changes in student achievement* (Occasional Paper #17). East Lansing, MI: University Institute for Research on Teaching.

Brown, G., & Irby, B. (1998). Seven policy considerations for principal approval. *School Administrator*, **55**(4), 10–11.

Brown, G., Irby, B., & Neumeyer, C. (1998). Taking the lead: One district's approach to principal evaluation. *NASSP Bulletin*, **82**(602), 18–25.

Callahan, R.E. (1962). *Education and the cult of efficiency*. Chicago: University of Chicago.

Clayton-Jones, L., McMahon, J., Rodwell, K., Skehan, J., Bourke, S., & Holbrook, A. (1993). Appraisal of school principals in an Australian department of education. *Peabody Journal of Education*, **68**(2), 110–131.

Darling-Hammond, L. (1994). Performance-based assessment and educational equity. *Harvard Educational Review*, **64**(1), 5–29.

Davis, S. (1998). Superintendents' perspectives on the involuntary departure of public school principals: The most frequent reasons why principals lose their jobs. *Educational Administration Quarterly*, **34**(1), 58–90.

Dillard, C. (1995). Leading with her life: An African American feminist (re)interpretation of leadership for an urban high school principal. *Educational Administration Quarterly*, **31**(4), 539–563.

Donmoyer, R. (1995, April). *The very idea of a knowledge base*. Paper presented at the annual meeting of the American Educational Research Association, San Francisco.

Dornbush, S. (1975). *Evaluation and the exercise of authority*. San Francisco, CA: Jossey-Bass.

Duke, D., & Iwanicki, E. (1992). Principal assessment and the notion of "fit." *Peabody Journal of Education*, **68**(1), 25–36.

Duke, D., & Stiggins, R. (1985). Evaluating the performance of principals: A descriptive study. *Educational Administration Quarterly*, **21**(4), 71–98.

Education Week. (January 25, 1995). *Cincinnati links administrators' pay, performance*, 1,6.

Ellett, C. (1978). Understanding and using the Georgia principal assessment system (GPAS). *CCBC Notebook*, **7**(2), 2–14.

Fletcher, T., & McInerney, W. (1995). Principal performance assessment and principal evaluation. *ERS Spectrum*, **13**(4), 16–21.

Fontana, J. (1994). Principal assessment: A staff developer's idea for a complete overhaul. *NASSP Bulletin*, **78**(565), 91–99.

Gale, L., & McCleary, L. (1972). Competencies of the secondary school principal: A needs assessment study. RIEOCT73.

Garrett, R., & Flanigan, J. (1991). Principal evaluation: A definitive process. *Journal of School Leadership*, **1**(1), 74–86.

Ginsberg, R., & Berry, B. (1990). The folklore of principal evaluation. *Journal of Personnel Evaluation in Education*, **3**(3), 205–230.

Ginsberg, R., & Thompson, T. (1992). Dilemmas and solutions regarding principal evaluation. *Peabody Journal of Education*, **68**(1), 58–74.

Glasman, N.S. (1979). A perspective on evaluation as an administrative function. *Educational Evaluation and Policy Analysis*, **1**(5), 33–44.

Glasman, N.S. (1983). Increased centrality of evaluation and the school principal. *Administrator's Notebook*, **30**(7), 1–4.

Glasman, N.S. (1986). *Evaluation-based leadership*. New York: SUNY.

Glasman, N.S. (1992). Toward assessing the test score-related actions of principals. *Peabody Journal of Education*, **68**(1), 108–123.

Glasman, N.S. (1995). Generating information for the evaluation of school principals' engagement in problem solving. *Studies in Educational Evaluation*, **21**, 401–410.

Glasman, N.S. (1997). (Ed.) New ways of training for school leadership. *Peabody Journal of Education*, **2**(2).

Glasman, N.S., & Glasman, L. (1990). Evaluation: Catalyst for or response to change. In S.B. Bacharach (Ed.), *Education reform* (pp. 392–399). Boston: Allyn & Bacon.

Glasman, N.S., & Heck, R. (1992). The changing leadership role of the principal: Implications for principal assessment. *Peabody Journal of Education*, **68**(1), 5–24.

Glasman, N.S., & Heck, R.H. (1996). Role-based evaluation of principals: Developing an appraisal system. In K. Leithwood, J. Chapman, D. Corson, P. Hallinger, & A. Hart (Eds.), *International handbook of educational leadership and administration* (pp. 369–394). London: Kluwer Academic Publishers.

Glasman, N.S., Killait, B.R., & Gmelch, W. (1975). *Evaluation of instructors in higher education*. Santa Barbara, CA: Regents of the University of California.

Glasman, N.S., & Marten, P.A. (1993). Personnel evaluation standards: The use of principal assessment systems. *Peabody Journal of Education*, **68**(2), 47–63.

Glasman, N.S., & Nevo, D. (1988). *Evaluation in decision making*. Boston, MA: Kluwer.

Goertz, M., & Duffy, M. (2000, April). *Variations on a theme: What is performance-based accountability?* Paper presented at the annual meeting of the American Educational Research Association, New Orleans, LA.

Gorton, R.A., & Snowden, R.E. (1993). *School leadership and administration*. Madison, WI: Brown & Benchmark.

Hallinger, P., & Heck, R. (1996). Reassessing the principal's role in school effectiveness: A review of the empirical research, 1980–1995. *Educational Administration Quarterly*, **32**(4), 5–44.

Hallinger, P., & Heck, R. (1999). Can leadership enhance school effectiveness? In T. Bush et al., (Eds.) *Educational management: Redefining theory, policy, and practice* (pp. 178–190). London: Paul Chapman Publishing.

Hart, A. (1992). The social and organizational influence of principals: Evaluating principals in context. *Peabody Journal of Education*, **68**(1), 37–57.

Heck, R. (1995). Organizational and professional socialization: Its impact on the performance of new administrators. *The Urban Review*, **27**(1), 31–49.

Heck, R. (2000). Examining the impact of school quality on school outcomes and improvement: A value-added approach. *Educational Administration Quarterly*, **36**(4), 513–552.

Heck, R., & Glasman, N.S. (1993). Merging evaluation and administration. *Peabody Journal of Education*, **68**(2), 132–142.

Heck, R., & Marcoulides, G. (1992). Principal assessment: Conceptual problem, methodological problem, or both? *Peabody Journal of Education*, **68**(1), 124–144.

Heck, R., & Marcoulides (1996). The assessment of principal performance: A multilevel Evaluation Approach. *Journal of Personnel Evaluation in Education*, **10**, 11–28.

Hess, C. (1991) *School restructuring, Chicago style*. Newbury Park, CA: Corwin Press.

Hoy, W., & Miskel, C. (1982). *Educational administration: Theory, research, and practice* (2nd ed.). New York: Random House.

Hoyt, D.P. (1982). Evaluating administrators. In R.F. Wilson (Ed.), Designing academic profession barriers. *New directions in higher education, No. 37*, **10**(1), 89–100.

Jerald, C., & Boser, U. (Jan. 11, 1999). Taking stock. *Education Week*, **28**(17), 81–97.

Joint Committee on Standards for Educational Evaluation. (1988). *The personnel evaluation standards*. Newbery Park, CA: Sage.

Leithwood, K., & Duke, D. (1999). A century's quest to understand school leadership. In J. Murphy & K. Seashore-Lewis (Eds.), *Handbook of research on educational administration* (2nd ed.) (pp. 45–72). San Francisco: Jossey-Bass.

Lessinger, L.M. (1971). The powerful notion of accountability in education. In L. Bowder (Ed.), *Emerging patterns of administrative accountability* (pp. 62–73). Berkeley, CA: McCatelan.

Marcoulides, G. (1988). From hands-on measurement to job performance: The issue of dependability. *The Journal of Business and Society*, **2**(1), 132–143.

Marcoulides, G., & Heck, R. (1992). Assessing instructional leadership with "g" theory. *International Journal of Educational Management*, **6**(3), 4–13.

Marcoulides, G., & Heck, R. (1993). Examining administrative leadership behavior: A comparison of principals and vice principals. *Journal of Personnel Evaluation in Education*, **7**, 81–94.

McCarthy, M. (1999). The evolution of leadership preparation programs. In J. Murphy & K. Seashore-Lewis (Eds.), *Handbook of research on educational administration* (2nd Edition) (pp. 119–140). San Francisco: Jossey-Bass.

Murphy, J. (1988). Methodological, measurement, and conceptual problems in the study of instructional leadership. *Educational Evaluation and Policy Analysis*, **11**(2), 117–134.

National Commission for the Principalship (1990). *Principals for our changing schools: Preparation and certification*. Fairfax, VA: National Policy Board for Educational Administration.

Newman (1985). Staff appraisal in the South Midlands and the South West. *Educational Management and Administration*, **14**, 197–202.

Patton, (1978). *Utilization focused evaluation*. Newbury Park, CA: Sage.

Pitner, N., & Hocevar, D. (1987). An empirical comparison of two-factor versus multifactor theories of principal leadership: Implications for the evaluation of school principals. *Journal of Personnel Evaluation in Education*, **1**(1), 93–109.

Provus, M. (1971). *Discrepancy evaluation*. Berkeley, CA: McCutchan.

Rallis, S.F., & Goldring, E.B. (1993). Beyond the individual assessment of principals: School-based accountability in dynamic schools. *Peabody Journal of Education*, **68**(2), 3–23.

Razik, T.A., & Swanson, A.D. (1995). *Fundamental concepts of educational leadership and management*. Englewood Cliffs, NJ: Merrill.

Richard, A. (Feb. 2, 2000). Principals approve new contract in New York City. *Education Week*, **29**(21), 5.

Sack, J. (May 2, 2000). Del. ties school job reviews to student tests. *Education Week*, **19**(34), 24, 27.

Sergiovani, T. (1990). *Value-added leadership: How to get extraordinary performance in schools*. New York: Harcourt Brace Jovanovich, Publishers.

Seyfarth, J.T. (1991). *Personnel management for effective schools*. Boston, MA: Allyn & Bacon.

Sirotnik, K., & Durden, P. (1996). The validity of administrator performance assessment systems: The ADI as a case-in-point. *Educational Administration Quarterly*, **32**(4), 539–564.

Smrekar, C.E., & Mawhinney, H.B. (1999). Integrated services: Challenges and linking schools, families, and communities. In J. Murphy & K. Seashore-Lewis (Eds.), *Handbook of research on educational administration* (2nd ed.) (pp. 443–463). San Francisco: Jossey-Bass.

Smylie, M., & Crowson, R. (1993). Principal assessment under restructured governance. *Peabody Journal of Education*, **68**(2), 64–84.

Smylie, M., & Hart, A. (1999). School leadership for teacher learning and change: A human and social capital development perspective. In J. Murphy & K. Seashore-Lewis (Eds.), *Handbook of research on educational administration* (2nd ed.) (pp. 421–442). San Francisco: Jossey-Bass.

Snyder, J., & Ebmeier, H. (1992). Empirical linkages among principal behaviors and intermediate outcomes: Implications for principal evaluation. *Peabody Journal of Education*, **68**(1), 75–107.

Stufflebeam, D. (1972). The relevance of the CIPP evaluation model for educational accountability. *SRIS Quarterly*, **5**, 3–6.

Stufflebeam, D., & Nevo, D. (1993). Principal evaluation: New directions for improvement. *Peabody Journal of Education*, **68**(2), 24–46.

Stufflebeam, D., & Webster, W.J. (1988). Evaluation as an administrative function. In N.J. Boyan (Ed.), *Handbook of research on educational administration* (pp. 569–602). New York: Longman.

Sykes, G. (1999). The "new professionalism" in education: An appraisal. In J. Murphy & K. Seashore-Lewis (Eds.), *Handbook of research on educational administration* (2nd ed.) (pp. 227–250). San Francisco: Jossey-Bass.

Thomson, S. (Ed.), (1993). *Principals for our changing schools: The knowledge and skill base*. Fairfax, VA: National Policy Board for Educational Administration.

Tryneski, J. (1993). *Requirements for certification of teachers, counselors, librarians, and administrators for elementary and secondary schools 1993–4*. Chicago: University of Chicago Press.

Tyack, D., & Cuban, L. (1995). *Tinkering toward utopia: A century of public school reform*. Cambridge, MA: Harvard University Press.

Tyler, R. (1950). *Basic principles of curriculum and instruction*. Chicago: University of Chicago Press.

Ubben, G., & Hughes, L. (1997). *The principal*. Boston, MA: Ally & Bacon.

Van Zwoll, J.A. (1964). *School personnel administration*. New York: Appleton-Century-Crafts.

Walters, D. (1980). The measurement of principal competencies. *Phi Delta Kappan*, **61**(6), 423–425.

Webb, L.D., Greer, J.T., Montello, P.A., & Norton, M.S. (1987). *Personnel administration in education*. Columbus, OH: Merrill.

White, K. (Jan. 11, 1999). Keeping the doors wide open. *Education Week*, **38**(17), 12–13.

Williams, J., & Pantili, L. (1992). A meta-analytic model of principal assessment. *Journal of School Leadership*, **2**(3), 256–279.

Wirt, F., & Kirst, M. (1989). *Schools in conflict* (2nd ed.). Berkeley, CA: McCutchan.

Wong, K., & Rollow, S. (1990). A case study of the recent Chicago school reform. *Administrator's Notebook*, **34**(5-6), 1–4.

30
Evaluating Educational Specialists

JAMES H. STRONGE

College of William and Mary, VA, USA

INTRODUCTION

How do you evaluate the array of professional support staff in today's schools who are neither administrators nor teachers? Counselors, school psychologists, librarians/media specialists, school nurses, and other professional support personnel represent a growing and invaluable group of educators who fulfill an array of duties and responsibilities which are fundamental to the support of students, teachers, and, indeed, the entire educational enterprise (Stronge, 1994; Stronge & Tucker, 1995a). "As American schools in recent decades have labored to include and educate *all* children, the role of these specialists has expanded to serve these students' many and diverse needs" (Stronge & Tucker, 1995a, p. 123). Despite their growing importance in contemporary schooling, evaluation of educational specialists has been relatively rare, uneven, and inadequate (Gorton & Ohlemacher, 1987; Helm, 1995, Lamb & Johnson, 1989; Norton & Perlin, 1989; Stronge & Helm, 1991; Stronge, Helm, & Tucker, 1995; Tucker, Bray, & Howard, 1988).

Strategic plans, mission statements, and school improvement efforts are important documents for defining current priorities and future goals but they are not sufficient alone. There must be quality people to implement those plans and programs, make improvements, and work toward fulfilling the school's mission. No school or program is better than the people who deliver its services. And related to the delivery of quality services, both programs and the people responsible for implementing them must be assessed on a regular basis to maintain and improve performance. Evaluation, therefore, can be a catalyst for school improvement and effectiveness (Stronge & Tucker, 1995b).

As with teachers and administrators, the basic need for educational specialists in a quality personnel evaluation system is for a fair and effective evaluation based on performance and designed to encourage improvement in both the employee being evaluated and the school (Stronge, 1997). The purpose of this chapter is to explore key elements for constructing and implementing quality evaluations for all educational specialists. Specifically, the chapter addresses the following questions:

International Handbook of Educational Evaluation, 671–694
T. Kellaghan, D.L. Stufflebeam (eds.)
© 2003 Dordrecht: Kluwer Academic Publishers. Printed in Great Britain.

1. Who are educational specialists?
2. What is the history of evaluation of educational specialists?
3. What is the status of educational specialists' evaluation?
4. What is unique about the evaluation of educational specialists?
5. How should educational specialists' performance be documented?
6. How can educational specialists be evaluated?
7. What is the connection between educational specialist evaluation and the Personnel Evaluation Standards (Joint Committee, 1988)?

WHO ARE EDUCATIONAL SPECIALISTS?

Educational specialists include non-teaching, non-administrative professionals who provide a myriad of support services to students, teachers, and parents. This expansive definition is intended to include educators who are either licensed or certificated in their respective fields; however, it does not include individuals who provide auxiliary-type support services to the school district (e.g., clerk-of-the-works, architect, purchasing agent). Moreover, while the work of non-certificated, non-licensed staff positions (e.g., custodian, food service worker, secretary) is vitally important to schools, these positions are not addressed in the educational specialist definition of this chapter.

Depending on the size and organization of a school system, educational specialists may work in a single school, multiple schools, or the central office (Stronge, Helm, & Tucker, 1995). Although not exhaustive, the following list includes many of the typical educational specialist positions found in school settings:

- *Pupil services personnel* – counselors, school psychologists, social workers, school nurses
- *Instructional support services personnel* – deans, work-study supervisors, library-media specialists, instructional computer specialists
- *Academic/curriculum development services personnel* – directors, coordinators, content specialists, gifted and talented resource specialists
- *Special education personnel* – self-contained classroom teachers, resource-consulting teachers, speech therapists, occupational therapists, physical therapists

A common thread that runs through the job expectations of these varied educational specialist positions is that they include "those educators who work with students or faculty in a support capacity" (Helm, 1995, p. 105). In essence, these individuals are playing a fundamental role in fulfilling the school's mission.

Over the last two decades, as schools have become responsible for providing and coordinating a wider array of educational and related services, the number and types of specialized support staff has increased dramatically. In a typical elementary school, 30–45 percent of the professional school staff who walk through the schoolhouse door each day likely are educational specialists of one variety or another (Stronge & Tucker, 1995b).[1]

WHAT IS THE HISTORY OF EVALUATION OF EDUCATIONAL SPECIALISTS?

"As the most visible professional within the school environment, the classroom teacher has been evaluated for as along as we have had schools" (Stronge, & Tucker, 1995a, p. 123). As Shinkfield and Stufflebeam (1995) noted, "Socrates' pupils undoubtedly had opinions about his teaching skills in the 5th century BC" (p. 9). While formal evaluation of teachers may not have occurred on a systematic and large-scale basis until the turn of the 20th century, there is a deep and growing base of knowledge regarding the ways and means of effectively evaluating teaching (see, for example, texts such as Millman & Darling-Hammond, 1990; Peterson, 1995; Shinkfield & Stufflebeam, 1995; Stronge, 1997). Unfortunately, research and knowledge of best practice related to the evaluation of educational specialists lags far behind that of teachers (Stronge & Tucker, 1995a). To illustrate this point, a search of journal articles and manuscripts indexed in the Educational Resources Information Clearinghouse (ERIC) revealed the following frequency counts (shown in Table 1) during the selected time periods.

Research from disciplines such as counseling, school psychology, and library science repeatedly cites the use of inappropriate evaluation criteria and instruments with educational specialists in the schools and the lack of valid, conceptually sound evaluation procedures (Kruger, 1987; Norton & Perlin, 1989; Turner & Coleman, 1986; Vincelette & Pfister, 1984). This is in sharp contrast to the "wide consensus on the general goals of evaluation and areas of competence for teachers" (Sclan, 1994, p. 25). Only in recent years have the major job responsibilities for educational specialists begun to be defined by various state education agencies and national organizations representing the respective professional groups.

A number of studies have documented the inappropriate or inadequate evaluation of educational specialists. Helm (1995) noted that in two educational specialist positions for which there exists a significant body of literature and extensive evaluative activity (the school counselor and the school library-media specialist), "we still find inappropriate evaluation a common complaint" (p. 106).

In a study of counseling practices in the state of Nevada, Loesch-Griffin, Spielvogel, and Ostler (1989) found that 63 percent of the counselors were evaluated using an instrument not specifically designed for school counselors. Similarly, Gorton and Ohlemacher (1987) found that approximately 38 percent of secondary school counselors in Wisconsin were evaluated with a teacher evaluation form with most of the criteria either inappropriate or inapplicable to the evaluation of counselors. Only 17 percent of the counselors were evaluated on the basis of explicit, written criteria specific to their professional roles.

Table 1.   Frequency of Selected Uses of the Descriptor, "Evaluation," in ERIC

ERIC Search Descriptors	1966–1989	1990–1999
Teacher Evaluation	4,441	2,816
Counselor Evaluation	327	136
Media Specialist Evaluation	29	12
School Psychologist Evaluation	99	41

Regarding library media specialists, Scott and Klasek (1980) found in a study of 80 northern Illinois high schools that almost 98 percent of the criteria on the evaluation forms were the same criteria used for classroom teachers. Coleman and Turner (1985) found only marginal improvement in their national study, in which "slightly more than one-third of the state education agencies either mandated or recommended procedures or forms for evaluating school library media specialists" (cited in Helm, 1995, p. 106).

WHAT IS THE STATUS OF EDUCATIONAL SPECIALISTS' EVALUATION?[2]

In an effort to obtain more accurate information regarding requirements for the evaluation of all school personnel, including educational specialists, a national survey of the 50 state education agencies was conducted in 1993 as a replication of a 1988 study. Respondents for each state education agency were asked to (a) identify the source of state-level legal mandates regarding the evaluation of school personnel and (b) indicate the level of technical support provided by the state education agency in the implementation of the legal mandates for teachers as compared to educational specialists. Forty-two of the 50 surveys were received from state education agencies, resulting in a response rate of 84 percent, which is considered statistically adequate (Borg & Gall, 1989) to draw conclusions about national trends.

Analysis of the surveys revealed a differentiated response to the evaluation of teachers as compared to educational specialists. The specialists had a less developed support system of guidelines, training, and technical support. Additionally, the states as a whole tended to omit guidelines for the evaluation of educational specialists far more often than they did for teachers. Relatively few states provided technical support or formal training for evaluation of either group – teachers or professional support personnel. In all cases, substantially less attention was focused on the evaluation of educational specialists.

State Guidelines

As shown in Table 2, more than half (55 percent) of the responding states provided guidelines to local educational agencies regarding teacher evaluation in comparison to 38 percent or less that provided guidelines for the evaluation of selected educational specialist positions. The evaluation of counselors received the most attention of all the educational specialists (38 percent), while the fewest number of states provided evaluation guidelines for school social workers (17 percent) and school nurses (12 percent).

Formal Training

A similar pattern of state involvement can be noted in Table 2 for state-sponsored formal training in personnel evaluation. Thirty-six percent of the responding states provided formal training to local educational agencies in the evaluation of teachers while 24 percent or less provided training in the evaluation of educational specialists. Library/media specialists (24 percent) received the most attention followed by counselors (21 percent). The least amount of support was provided for school social workers (14 percent), school psychologists (14 percent), and school nurses (12 percent). The level of state-supported guidance and formal training are contrasted in Figure 1.

Technical Assistance

As might be expected, the level of technical assistance offered by state education agencies for the various educational specialist positions was consistent with the level of support for formal training and guidelines. Technical assistance for teachers was provided in 50 percent of the states compared to 38 percent which provided assistance in the evaluation of educational specialists. Table 3 contains

Table 2.   Guidelines and Formal Training for Personnel Evaluation (N = 42)

Professional Group	Guidelines	Formal Training
Teachers	23 (55%)	15 (36%)
Counselors	16 (38%)	9 (21%)
School Psychologists	10 (24%)	6 (14%)
School Social Workers	7 (17%)	6 (14%)
School Nurses	5 (12%)	5 (12%)
Librarians/Media Specialists	11 (26%)	10 (24%)
Program/Project Directors	8 (19%)	7 (17%)
Coordinators of Curriculum/Instruction	9 (21%)	8 (19%)
Content/Curriculum Specialists	9 (21%)	8 (19%)

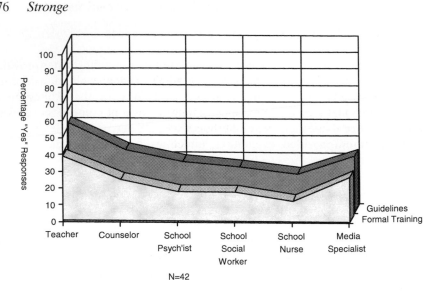

Figure 1:   A National Survey of Guidelines Versus Formal Training for Educational Specialists

Table 3.   Technical Assistance Provided by States for Personnel Evaluation (N = 42)

Professional Group	Yes	No
Teachers	21 (50%)	21 (50%)
Education Specialists	16 (38%)	26 (62%)

the relative numbers of states offering technical assistance. Overall, the discrepancy in technical assistance between teachers and educational specialists is less marked than with formal training, but in many states the available technical assistance was of a generic nature and not specialized to reflect the specific needs of educational specialists.

WHAT IS UNIQUE ABOUT THE EVALUATION OF EDUCATIONAL SPECIALISTS?

The need for an effective and comprehensive evaluation based on performance and designed to encourage improvement in both the school and the employee is basic, regardless of the specific position (Stronge, 1997; Tucker, Bray, & Howard, 1988). Implementation of a comprehensive evaluation system for educational specialists, however, can be unique and likely will require special attention if the evaluations are to be valid and contribute to the overall effectiveness of the school or educational program (Stronge, 1993). A number of factors, including the following, help explain why evaluating many educational specialists is unique:

- specialized theoretical orientations and highly specialized practices and training required in many of the positions;
- lack of well-defined job descriptions for many professional support personnel;
- non-instructional nature of much of their work;
- erosion of traditional unity of command in education.

Specialized Orientation and Training

The training and orientation of many educational specialist disciplines (e.g., occupational therapist, social worker, school psychologist, nurse) is substantially different from that of teachers. Moreover, their professional backgrounds often are unfamiliar territory for building principals – the primary evaluators for school-based educational professionals – and, without a common base of understanding regarding professional expectations, evaluation can be challenging for both parties.

Lack of Well-Defined Job Descriptions

As noted earlier, inappropriate or nonexistent evaluation criteria too frequently have been commonplace for many educational specialists (American School Counselor Association, 1990; Gorton & Ohlemacher, 1987; Kruger, 1987; Lamb & Johnson, 1989). This, in part, has been due to the lack of well-defined roles within schools for these specialists. Although general program goals may be defined, specific duties for educational specialists tend to be more ad hoc depending on the circumstances of the particular school. The result is that some counselors, for example, find themselves responsible for discipline, attendance, and a variety of miscellaneous tasks that are unrelated to their professional training (Stronge, Helm, & Tucker, 1995).

Non-Instructional Nature of Work

The diversity of duties performed by educational specialists places a premium on developing better understanding of their unique roles and responsibilities within the educational enterprise if we are to create more meaningful evaluations of their work. In addition to teaching, many educational specialists also are responsible for functions such as those delineated in Table 4.

Many educational specialists actually do not devote significant time to actual instruction. Nonetheless, all of their major job domains are focused on improving or sustaining quality performance among the primary target audience – the

Table 4.   Common Job Domains for Educational Specialists

Common Job Domains for Educational Specialists	Descriptions
• Planning/Preparation	Designing activities that change the program or its implementation
• Administrative/Management	Organizing, directing, or coordinating programs that include responsibility for budgeting, staffing, reporting, and other similar activities
• Assessment/Evaluation	Gathering and interpreting data from individuals, groups, or programs to evaluate needs/performance
• Instruction/Direct Intervention Services	Delivering services to improve skills/functional abilities or inform receipients
• Consultation	Collaborating with school personnel and/or parents to assist with and coordinate the delivery of services to students
• Liaison/Coordination	Coordinating information and program delivery within the school and between the school and its major constituents
• Staff Development	Facilitating the staff's achievement of desired professional goals
• Professional Responsibilities	Developing and improving individual competence and skill and delivering services consistent with professional standards

students. Given the diverse nature of their jobs, however, a pure classroom instructional model of evaluation which samples a restricted set of job duties simply does not satisfy their evaluative needs.

Erosion of Unity of Command

American education has a long history of control based on the classical administrative principle of unity of command. Adopted from the work of Henri Fayol (cited in Gulick & Urwick, 1937) and others, unitary command structures in schools has meant that every employee has had one immediate supervisor and that formal communications and evaluations within the organization have occurred within the linear chain of command (e.g. superintendent to principal to teacher). This principle is codified in virtually all schools in the form of the organization chart, resulting in a simplified, bureaucratic decision structure (Stronge, 1993).

Unity of command has eroded in recent years in favor of more complex and collaborative evaluation processes, especially as it relates to educational specialists.

These itinerant personnel, while part of a school's staff, are shared with other schools. They are here today and gone tomorrow and, under such an amorphous work schedule, fall outside the normal control loop of the school. Problems related to this change in organizational structure are especially acute when it comes to evaluation. Who is responsible for monitoring performance and conducting the evaluation? Is it the principal in School A or School B? Or is it both? Or is evaluation now charged to someone entirely outside both schools, such as the special education director or school nurse supervisor? Under any one of these … evaluative scenarios, one point is clear: evaluating many educational specialists is especially complex. (Stronge, Helm, & Tucker, 1995, p. 18)

HOW SHOULD EDUCATIONAL SPECIALISTS' PERFORMANCE BE DOCUMENTED?[3]

Given the multiplicity of duties performed by educational specialists, their specialized training, multiple supervisors, and the confidential nature of some aspects of their work, evaluation techniques need to be adapted to the unique characteristics of these positions. As one example of a modification in traditional teacher evaluation methodologies, there is a need for using multiple data source in educational specialists' evaluation.

The most common method for evaluating classroom teachers, in recent decades, has been a clinical supervision model consisting of a pre-conference, observation, and post-conference. In fact, as noted in a study conducted by the Educational Research Service (1988), 99.8 percent of American public school administrators used direct classroom observation as the primary data collection technique. However, primary reliance on formal observations in evaluation poses significant problems (e.g., artificiality, small sample of performance) for teacher evaluation (Medley, Coker, & Soar, 1984; Scriven, 1981), and its value is even more limited for evaluating many educational specialists. Issues of confidentiality actually preclude observation in some cases (e.g., for a school psychologist in a confidential session) and, thus, require creative use of multiple data sources to provide an accurate measure of job performance. In addition to observation, documentation of performance should include:

- input from client groups (i.e., informal or formal surveys from parents, students, classroom teachers, or other collaborating peers);
- collection and assessment of job artifacts (portfolios, dossiers, copies of pertinent correspondence, relevant news clippings, etc.); and
- documentation of performance of the educational specialist's impact on student success.

Observation

As previously mentioned, observation does not hold the same potential for acquiring useful information about the job performance of educational specialists that it does for documenting teachers' classroom performance. Specialists such as librarians/media specialists, nurses, counselors, school psychologists, and others spend much of their time engaged in activities that would either be:

1. tedious to observe (e.g., a nurse performing record-keeping functions or a curriculum specialist planning for a curriculum meeting or in-service program); or
2. in violation of the professionally and legally required confidentiality that must be maintained (e.g., a counselor working with a student having personal problems or a social worker discussing a student's home situation with the student).

In spite of the inherent and substantial limitations of observation for evaluating educational specialists, however, it can play a meaningful role in the data collection process if used appropriately.

Performance observation can be classified as systematic or incidental. In *systematic observation*, the supervisor conducts a semi-structured, planned observation of an employee who is presenting a formal program to staff, students, or some other client group. The potential of this type of systematic observation is relatively limited, but specific situations may be conducive to its use. *Incidental observation* is less direct and structured than systematic observation. It might include observation, for example, of a specialist participating in faculty meetings or committee meetings. In this kind of observation, the evaluator would be alert for evidence of constructive contributions such as articulate expression of ideas, ability to relate to other staff in the meeting, and so forth. An important factor for evaluators to remember when compiling incidental observation data is that they must always focus on specific, factual descriptions of performance. Also, it is important to obtain a representative sampling of performance observations (Stronge & Helm, 1991, pp. 175–177).

Client Surveys

Surveying and interviewing – both formally and informally – those with whom an educational specialist works about their perceptions of that employee's effectiveness constitutes an important source of documentation. This is particularly true in view of the fact that data collection through traditional observational channels is limited. A more complete picture of an employee's performance can be obtained by surveying a representative sampling from the various constituencies with whom the specialist works. The following example may help illustrate the use of 360-degree evaluation (Manatt, 2000; Manatt & Benway, 1998; Manatt & Kemis, 1997).

A librarian/media specialist's work can impact the teaching staff, the students in the school, and the library/media aides (adult or student) who assist the individual in his or her job. Therefore, it would be appropriate to survey the teaching staff with special attention to those who use the library and media equipment most heavily in connection with their classes. Surveys of teachers could elicit perceptions about the library/media specialist's effectiveness in meeting their needs, ability to keep equipment in working order, and so forth. Students might be surveyed to determine their use of the library, their experiences in receiving help when needed, and their perceptions of the responsiveness of the library staff to their questions. Above all, however, the questions should be designed with the employee's specific job responsibilities in mind and with recognition that these data merely constitute one source of evaluative information (Stronge & Helm, 1991, pp. 180–182).

Portfolios and Job Artifacts

Another important source for obtaining documentation of a person's job performance is frequently overlooked in many educational systems: the collection of written records and documents produced by the employee as a part of his or her job responsibilities. These written materials are sometimes referred to as portfolios (see, for example, Wheeler, 1993; Wolf, Lichtenstein, & Stevenson, 1997) or dossiers (Peterson, 1995).

The term *portfolio* in the context of personnel evaluation is by no means universally defined. Wolf (1996) described one form that portfolios have taken as "scrapbooks" – a version that has proven to be neither practical nor useful. A more productive definition of portfolios for the purposes of evaluation is a collection of materials by and about an employee that is limited in scope, yet whose specific contents remain the choice of the individual (Dietz, 1995; Gareis, 1999; Hurst, Wilson, & Cramer, 1998; Peterson, 1995; Wolf, 1996). This approach to artifact collection and review can be a more revealing process in terms of performance evaluation (Gareis, 1999).

Much of the portfolio data collected to provide insight into an educator's performance can and should be collected by the employee. Thus, the portfolio collection and review process becomes a type of structured self-assessment, especially when reflection *about* performance, written by the specialist, is included in the portfolio. An example of this self-reflective side to portfolios would be the inclusion of a narrative summary highlighting major accomplishments and areas for continued growth.

Moreover, a supervisor with responsibility for evaluating a specialist's performance will find it useful to file pertinent artifacts as they cross his or her desk. This doesn't necessarily entail significant additional record keeping for either the evaluatee or the evaluator, but rather the collection and later analysis of materials pertinent to fulfilling specific job responsibilities. Some examples of portfolio entries include:

- logs of meetings, conferences, activities, and students served;
- written products such as brochures, handouts, monographs, reports produced by the educator;

- pictures of displays or performances (e.g., snapshots of media center displays or videos of presentations);
- copies of solicited or unsolicited commendatory letters or memos regarding the educator's performance.

Measures of Student Success

School accountability as a fundamental aspect of contemporary education is reflected in states and local communities across America and, indeed, the world. Parents, policymakers, and educators alike have examined the state-of-the-art of public schools and are calling for – even demanding – improvement. Calls for school reform are taking a variety of forms, with one of the most prominent being higher teacher and educator standards and improved student performance (Stronge & Tucker, 2000).

Given the central role that teachers and other educational professionals have always played in successful schools, connecting teacher performance and student performance is a natural extension of the educational reform agenda (see, for example, Mendro, 1998; Sanders & Horn, 1998). "The purpose of teaching is learning, and the purpose of schooling is to ensure that each new generation of students accumulates the knowledge and skills needed to meet the social, political, and economic demands of adulthood" (McConney, Schalock, & Schalock, 1997, p. 162). Although the use of student success measures is technically and politically challenging, their use should be considered and appropriate measures incorporated into the evaluation process for educational specialists.

For many educational specialist positions, direct measures of student performance can be directly documented. Just as with classroom teachers, a value-added – or gain score – approach (Wright, Horn, & Sanders, 1997; Stronge & Tucker, 2000; Webster & Mendro, 1997) can be employed for selected educational specialists to document their influence on student success. For example, the improvement in students' language development as it relates to the services provided by a speech therapist, or the academic improvement by students with disabilities on selected aspects of Individual Educational Plans as it relates to the instruction delivered by a special education resource-consulting teacher, can be readily documented.

For other educational specialists, the connection between student success and the specialist's role is more tenuous and far more difficult to document. For example, a school nurse delivers health screening and selected medical services that are fundamentally important to the school and to the health and safety of its students. Nonetheless, attempting to directly link the school nurse's health-related services to student academic success would be a virtual impossibility. Nonetheless, the challenge in connecting the educational specialist's performance to student performance doesn't negate the value of the specialist's work, nor should it excuse the specialist from appropriate accountability measures. Rather, the impact of the specialist's performance needs to be judged on relevant measures. For example, the nurse's success in screening for selected health problems and then following through with appropriate medical referrals can be readily documented. For another example, performance of a high school guidance counselor who is charged with the responsibility of assisting students with academic advising and transition to college could be based, at least partially, on students' awareness of available scholarships and the counselor's assistance in applying for and securing the scholarships.

In all instances where student success (regardless of the measures of student performance that might be assessed) is linked to employee success, it is essential to ascertain a direct link between the employee's and students' performance. It is insufficient to merely identify how an educational specialist might indirectly influence a student's performance on a given performance measure. For example, while graduation rates and SAT scores most certainly are linked to school factors, connecting these measures to any one employee, in almost all cases, simply is not possible. If employee success is to be meaningfully linked to student success, then it is imperative that a causal link be clearly established.

To summarize, the use of multiple sources of data to document educational specialists' performance offers numerous advantages (Helm, 1995). In particular, multiple data sources are essential to a fair and valid evaluation. Integrating multiple data sources to document performance provides for a process of triangulation, blending low inference and high inference data as well as objective and subjective data, all of which contribute to a richly textured and far more complete portrait of the specialist's performance.

HOW CAN EDUCATIONAL SPECIALISTS BE EVALUATED?[4]

As with any type of meaningful evaluation, personnel evaluation must provide a sound conceptual framework upon which to build. Moreover, it is important to consider the unique contributions made by each educational specialist position to the accomplishment of the school's mission if the personnel evaluation system is to be effective. The Goals and Roles evaluation model (Stronge, 1997, 1988, 1995; Stronge & Helm, 1990, 1991, 1992)[5] is one that offers a practical, research-based model. It is designed generically for use with a variety of positions and it may serve well as the basis for an evaluation system not only for educational specialists but also for teachers and administrators (Stronge, 1997).

The Goals and Roles evaluation model reflects two phases with six distinct steps in the evaluation process:

Development Phase
1. Identify system needs;
2. Develop roles and responsibilities for the job;
3. Set standards for job performance;

Implementation Phase
4.   Document job performance;
5.   Evaluate performance;
6.   Improve/Maintain professional service.

The following provides a brief description of each step as represented in Figure 2.

Development Phase

Step 1: Identify System Needs

Each school has specific needs that relate to its mission and that are met through the collective performance of all personnel (e.g., principals, classroom teachers, resource specialists, counselors). A systematic examination of the needs of the school's constituents will help clarify its mission and purpose. Goals should be developed within the context of the greater community and in consideration of relevant variables such as financial and personnel resources. School or district-wide goals often are found in a mission statement, a set of educational goals, a multi-year school plan, or a strategic plan.

   Once school goals have been established, attention should turn to the matter of translating those goals into operational terms. One logical way of accomplishing this task is to consider all programs (e.g., math curriculum, guidance-counseling services, athletic program) in light of whether they contribute to the accomplishment of the school's goals, and, then, to relate program objectives to position expectations (Stronge & Tucker, 1995a). In essence, a domino effect is initiated in this line of planning and evaluation:

   ⇒ school goals dictate which programs are relevant to the school's mission;
      ⇒ program objectives dictate what positions are needed in order to fulfill those objectives; and finally,
         ⇒ individual positions are implemented (and, ultimately, evaluated) in light of the duties and responsibilities dictated by the program objectives.

Determining the needs of the organization is a prerequisite for all remaining steps if the evaluation process is to be relevant to the school's mission and, ultimately, responsive to public demands for accountability (Castetter, 1981; Connellan, 1978; Goodale, 1992; Patton, 1986; Stufflebeam et al., 1971). Moreover, it is important to recognize the primary needs of any educational organization are based on the needs of its students. Making certain, to the greatest degree possible, that students are safe and secure, healthy, and have the fullest opportunities to develop their academic potential *is* the mission of the school. Simply put, the collective activities and efforts of our schools don't count unless they positively impact the lives of students.

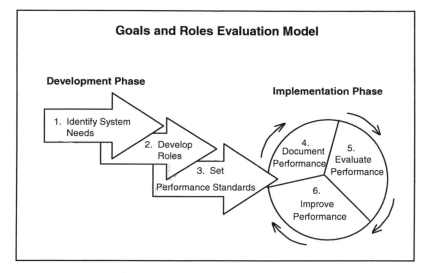

Figure 2:   Goals and Roles Evaluation Model

Step 2: Identify Job Responsibilities

Accurate and appropriate descriptions of the educational specialist's roles and responsibilities can be developed only from clear statements of school or district goals and philosophies. Once school goals are determined, then it is only sensible to relate program expectations to position expectations. Typical major job domains for educational specialists might include planning, management, assessment, direct services, professionalism, and others. These job domains can serve as a framework for the categorization of more specific responsibilities (or "duties") (Olsen & Bennett, 1980; Redfern, 1980; Scriven, 1988).

Because job performance must reflect behavior in order to be evaluated, an important addition to the definition of the specialist's role and responsibilities is a set of sample performance indicators. While professional responsibilities are intended to capture the essence of the job, it is difficult, if not impossible, to document the fulfillment of professional responsibilities without some measurable indication of their accomplishment. Thus, to give meaning to the educational specialist's responsibilities, it is recommended to select a *sampling* of performance indicators that are both measurable and indicative of the job (Bolton, 1980; Redfern, 1980; Valentine, 1992). Figure 3 uses a school counselor example to illustrate how steps 1 and 2 can be integrated in the Goals and Roles evaluation model.

School Counselor	
System Goal The school district will address the needs of the whole child to ensure academic success. **Area of Responsibility** Intervention/Direct Services (I)	
Duties	**Performance Indicators**
Duty I-1: Provides individual and group counseling services to meet the developmental, preventive, and remedial needs of students.	1. Provides effective services in assisting the student to cope with family, interpersonal, and educational issues. 2. Trains students to use effective techniques for conflict resolution/ management.
Duty I-2: Provides follow-up activities to monitor student progress	1. Communicates effectively with parents and teachers. 2. Provides prompt and specific feedback to students and staff in a constructive manner.

Figure 3:   Sample Duties and Performance Indicators for School Counselors

Step 3: Set Performance Standards

Setting standards involves determining a level of acceptable performance as well as performance that exceeds or fails to meet the acceptable standard. Although operational definitions for standards may vary from organization to organization, they must be standard and consistently implemented within the school or school district in order to ensure fairness and legal defensibility. This step is important in any goals-oriented personnel evaluation system (Joint Committee, 1988; Manatt, 1988; Scriven, 1988; Stufflebeam et al., 1971).

Implementation Phase

Step 4: Document Job Performance

Documentation is the process of recording sufficient information about the employee's performance to support ongoing evaluation and to justify any personnel decisions based on the evaluation. The basic question is: How will the educational specialist's performance of the roles and responsibilities of the job be demonstrated? The use of multiple data sources can include observation, client surveys, collection and analysis of artifacts, and student success measures. The strengths and limitations of each of these data gathering techniques are discussed in detail earlier in the chapter.

Step 5: Evaluate Performance

Evaluation is the process of comparing an individual employee's documented job performance with the previously established roles and responsibilities and acceptable performance standards. While this step clearly entails an end-of-cycle summative evaluation, evaluating performance also must include periodic formative feedback. By providing feedback throughout the evaluation cycle, the employee is supported in his or her ongoing efforts to fulfill performance expectations and is able to identify areas of performance that need attention. Additionally, an opportunity for adequate notice is provided through periodic formative feedback, leading to a fair summative evaluation in which there should be no surprises.

Summative evaluation provides an opportunity to determine individual merit based on performance. Further, the evaluation affords the basis for judging worth, first, by viewing evaluation performance in light of the school's goals and, second, by maintaining compatibility between individual performance and school goals. In an ongoing, systematic evaluation process, identifying system needs and relating those needs to performance ensures that the evaluation is concerned with both the merit (internal value) and worth (external value) of performance (Bridges, 1990; Frels & Horton, 1994; Medley, Coker, & Soar, 1984; Scriven, 1995; Valentine, 1992).

Step 6: Improve/Maintain Professional Service

With an emphasis in the evaluation process on both improvement (i.e., formative) and accountability (i.e., summative) purposes, Step 6 brings the Goals and Roles evaluation process full circle. Formative aspects of evaluation, intended to provide recognition for noteworthy performance, along with immediate and intermediate feedback for performance improvement and correction where needed, should be ongoing throughout the evaluation process and are implicit in this model. Nonetheless, it is beneficial to provide an explicit step for improving or maintaining professional service as the culmination of the evaluation cycle and as an entrée into the following cycle.

This step suggests the importance of professional development with a balance between the interests of the employee and the interests of the school in a continuous improvement cycle (Little, 1993). After all, the most fundamental purpose of an evaluation is to *improve* both the individual's and institution's performance (Hunter, 1988; Iwanicki, 1990; McGreal, 1988; Stufflebeam, 1983).

WHAT IS THE CONNECTION BETWEEN EDUCATIONAL SPECIALIST EVALUATION AND THE PERSONNEL EVALUATION STANDARDS?[6]

Although there may be unique aspects to the nature and needs of educational specialists' work, they have in common with all educational personnel the need for fair, job-relevant, and meaningful evaluations. Unfortunately, as with teachers and administrators, educational specialists have suffered from numerous systemic problems with the state-of-the-art of personnel evaluation. The Joint Committee on Standards for Educational Evaluation (1988) asserted that personnel evaluation has been ineffectively conducted in educational organizations, despite the centrality of the process. They specifically identified the following personnel evaluation practices as commonly *not* being satisfied:

* screen out unqualified persons from certification and selection processes;
* provide constructive feedback to individual educators;
* recognize and help reinforce outstanding service;
* provide direction for staff development programs;
* provide evidence that will withstand professional and judicial scrutiny;
* provide evidence efficiently and at reasonable cost;
* aid institutions in terminating incompetent or unproductive personnel;
* unify, rather than divide, teachers, educational specialists, and administrators in their collective efforts to educate students (pp. 6–7).

In order for evaluation to be valid and valued for any educator, these issues must be adequately addressed. A brief discussion of how the four basic attributes of sound evaluation can be incorporated in educational specialist evaluation follows.

Propriety Standards

Propriety Standards "require that evaluations be conducted legally, ethically, and with due regard for the welfare of evaluatees and clients of the evaluations" (Joint Committee, 1988, p. 21). In compliance with the five Propriety Standards (Service Orientation, Formal Evaluation Guidelines, Conflict of Interest, Access to Personnel Evaluation Reports, Interactions with Evaluatees), the evaluation of educational specialists should seek to create a personnel evaluation system that directly supports the primary principle – that schools exist to serve students. The educator evaluation exists within a legal context and with a strong goal orientation. In addition, the Propriety Standards' aim "at protecting the rights of persons affected by an evaluation" (Joint Committee, 1988, p. 11) and are addressed through substantive and procedural sensitivity to the unique needs of educational specialists (Stronge & Helm, 1991, p. 68).

Utility Standards

"Utility Standards are intended to guide evaluations so that they will be informative, timely, and influential" (Joint Committee, 1988, p. 45) as reflected in Constructive Orientation, Defined Uses of the Evaluation, Evaluator Credibility, Functional Reporting, and Follow-up and Impact. As with teachers and other educators, educational specialists' evaluation should provide an informative and timely evaluation service delivery through an emphasis on formal and informal communication. Additionally, the evaluation should inform decision makers regarding goal accomplishment. Although providing evaluative feedback to individuals, the collective evaluations of all employees should relate individual performance to the overarching organizational goals (Stronge & Helm, 1991, pp. 68–69).

Feasibility Standards

The Feasibility Standards require that evaluation systems be "as easy to implement as possible, efficient in their use of time and resources, adequately funded, and viable from a number of other standpoints" (Joint Committee, 1988, p. 71). These standards include Practical Procedures, Political Viability, and Fiscal Viability. The utility of any personnel evaluation system can be found in its ability to be simultaneously effective for its intended purposes and efficient in its use of resources. Thus, a constructive evaluation system will be applicable specifically to educational specialists and, yet, be aware of the role of evaluation within the educational organization (Stronge & Helm, 1991, p. 69).

Accuracy Standards

Accuracy Standards require that obtained information "be technically accurate and that conclusions be linked logically to the data" (Joint Committee, 1988, p. 83). The eight standards as they relate to the educational specialists' evaluation are summarized in Table 5.

CONCLUSIONS

Despite the fact that evaluation in education has a history as long as public schooling, its use has been restricted largely to teachers and, to a lesser degree, administrators. In recent years, primarily in response to a push for public accountability, performance evaluation has been extended more systematically to include all professional employees. As schools become responsible for providing and coordinating a wider range of services, specialized support staff are beginning to constitute a larger proportion of a school staff and play a more

Table 5.   Accuracy Standards Applied to Educational Specialist Evaluation

Accuracy Standards	Application to Educational Specialist Evaluation
A1 Defined Role	Educational specialist evaluation should be based on clearly defined job responsibilities
A2 Work Environment	Evaluation is an open system in which contextual issues must be considered in the evaluation.
A3 Documentation of Procedures	The use of multiple data sources in educational specialists' evaluation should be emphasized.
A4 Valid Measurement	A fundamental requirement for any good evaluation is that it be valid for is intended audience, in this instance, educational specialists.
A5 Reliable Measurement	Valid evaluation cannot occur in the absence of consistency; therefore, specialists' evaluation must provide a methodology that encourages procedural standardization and consistent performance evaluations.
A6 Systematic Data Control	Systematic and accurate analysis of data is considered fundamental for a fair evaluation system.
A7 Bias Control	*Fairness in both evaluation processes and outcomes can be enhanced by using trained evaluators who are knowledgeable about the roles and reponsibilities of educational specialists.*
A8 Monitoring Evaluation Systems	By monitoring the application of the educational specialists' evaluation system, it can be refined throughout each evaluation cycle.

central role in fulfilling the school's mission. Many school systems are beginning to recognize the need to maximize services and expertise offered by these professionals. To do so requires an evaluation process which recognizes and rewards the varied and diverse contributions of educational specialists.

Ultimately, evaluation is nothing more than a process for determining how an individual, program, or school is performing its assigned functions in relation to a given set of circumstances. When evaluation is viewed as more than this process (i.e., evaluation as an end within itself), it gets in the way of progress and, thus, becomes irrelevant. "When evaluation is treated as less than it deserves (i.e., superficial, inadequate evaluator training, invalid evaluation systems, flawed implementation designs), the school, its employees, and the public at large are deprived of opportunities for improvement and the benefits that accountability afford. All of us, whatever our relationship to the educational enterprise, deserve high quality evaluation" (Stronge, 1997 p. 18).

ENDNOTES

[1] Percentages are based on the number of people who provide support services, including special education personnel, and not full-time equivalents. In a similar analysis of a high school, it was found that 20–25 percent of the staff members provided support services.

² This section is adapted from Stronge and Tucker 1995a.
³ This section is adapted from Stronge and Helm (1991).
⁴ This section is adapted from Stronge (1997) and Stronge, Helm, and Tucker (1995).
⁵ Initial work on the model was in the context of evaluation for educational specialists (e.g., school counselor, school psychologist) described as "professional support personnel." The model is intended to provide an evaluation paradigm that can be adapted to each individual and institution. Permission is granted for use in this text.
⁶ This section is adapted from Stronge and Helm, 1991.

REFERENCES

American School Counselor Association. (1990). The school counselor and their evaluation. In *Position statements of the American School Counselor Association*. Alexandria, VA: American School Counselor Association.

Bolton, D.L. (1980). *Evaluating administrative personnel in school systems*. New York: Teachers College Press.

Borg, W.R., & Gall, M.D. (1989). *Educational research: An introduction*. New York: Longman.

Bridges, E.M. (1990). Evaluation for tenure and dismissal. In J. Millman & L. Darling-Hammond (Eds.), *The new handbook of teacher evaluation: Assessing elementary and secondary school teachers* (pp. 147–157). Newbury Park, CA: Sage Publications.

Castetter, W.B. (1981). *The personnel function in educational administration* (3rd edition.). New York: Macmillan.

Coleman, J., Jr., & Turner, P. (1986). Teacher evaluation: What's in it for us? *School Library Journal*, 32(10), 42.

Connellan, T.K. (1978). *How to improve human performance: Behaviorism in business and industry*. New York: Harper & Row.

Dietz, M.E. (1995). Using portfolios as a framework for professional development. *Journal of Staff Development*, 16(2), 40–43.

Educational Research Service. (1988). *Teacher evaluation: Practices and procedures*. Arlington, VA: Author.

Frels, K., & Horton, J.L. (1994). *A documentation system for teacher improvement and termination*. Topeka, KS: National Organization on Legal Problems in Education.

Gareis, C.R. (1999). Teacher portfolios: Do they enhance teacher evaluation? (located in CREATE News section). *Journal of Personnel Evaluation in Education*, 13, 96–99.

Goodale, J.G. (1992). Improving performance appraisal. *Business Quarterly*, 5(2), 65–70.

Gorton, R., & Ohlemacher, R. (1987). Counselor evaluation: A new priority for the principal's agenda. *NASSP Bulletin*, 71(496), 120–124.

Gulick, L. & Urwick, L. (Eds.). (1937). *Papers on the science of administration*. New York: Institute of Public Administration, Columbia University.

Helm, V.M. (1995). Evaluating professional support personnel: A conceptual framework. *Journal of Personnel Evaluation in Education*, 9(2), 105–122.

Hunter, M. (1988). Create rather than await your fate in teacher evaluation. In S.J. Stanley & W.J. Popham (Eds.), *Teacher evaluation: Six prescriptions for success* (pp. 32–54). Alexandria, VA: Association for Supervision and Curriculum Development.

Hurst, Wilson, Cramer. (1998). Professional teaching portfolios: Tools for reflecting, growth, and advancement. *Phi Delta Kappan*, 79, 578–582.

Iwanicki, E.F. (1990). Teacher evaluation for school improvement. In J. Millman & L. Darling-Hammond (Eds.), *The new handbook for teacher evaluation*. Newbury Park, CA: Sage Publication.

Joint Committee on Standards for Educational Evaluation. (1988). *The personnel evaluation standards: How to assess systems of evaluating educators*. Newbury Park, CA: Sage Publications.

Kruger, L.J. (1987, March). *A functional approach to performance appraisal of school psychologists*. Paper presented at the Annual Meeting of the National Association of School Psychologists, New Orleans, LA.

Lamb, A., & Johnson, L. (1989). An opportunity, not an albatross. *The Book Report*, 8(3), 11–24.

Little, J.W. (1993). Teachers professional development in a climate of educational reform. *Educational Evaluation and Policy Analysis*, **15**, 129–151.

Loesch-Griffin, D.A., Spielvogel, S., & Ostler, T. (1989). *Report on guidance and counseling personnel and programs in Nevada*. Reno, NV: University of Nevada, College of Education. (ERIC Document Reproduction Service No. ED 317 340).

Manatt, R.P. (1988). Teacher performance evaluation: A total systems approach. In S.J. Stanley, & W.J. Popham (Eds.), *Teacher evaluation: Six prescriptions for success* (pp. 79–108). Alexandria, VA: Association for Supervision and Curriculum Development.

Manatt, R.P. (2000). Feedback at 360 degrees. *The School Administrator*, **9**(57), 10–11.

Manatt, R.P., & Benway, M. (1998). Teacher and administrator performance: Benefits of 360-degree feedback. *ERS Spectrum: Journal of Research and Information*, **16**(2), 18–23.

Manatt, R.P., & Kemis, M. (1997). 360 degree feedback: A new approach to evaluation. *Principal*, **77**(1), 24, 26–27.

McConney, A.A., Schalock, M.D., & Schalock, H.D. (1997). Indicators of student learning in teacher evaluation. In J.H. Stronge (Ed.), *Evaluating teaching: A guide to current thinking and best practice* (pp. 162–192). Thousand Oaks, CA: Corwin Press, Inc.

McGreal, T.L. (1988). Evaluation for enhancing instruction: Linking teacher evaluation and staff development. In S.J. Stanley & W.J. Popham (Eds.), *Teacher evaluation: Six prescriptions for success* (pp. 1–29). Alexandria, VA: Association for Supervision and Curriculum Development.

Medley, D.M., Coker, H., & Soar, R.S. (1984). *Measurement-based evaluation of teacher performance*. New York: Longman.

Mendro, R.L. (1998). Student achievement and school and teacher accountability. *Journal of Personnel Evaluation in Education*, **12**, 257–267.

Millman, J. & Darling-Hammond, L. (1990). *The new handbook of teacher evaluation: Assessing elementary and secondary school teachers*. Newbury Park, CA: Corwin Press, Inc.

Norton, M., & Perlin, R. (1989). Here's what to look for when evaluating school psychologists. *Executive Educator*, **11**(8), 24–25.

Olsen, L.D., & Bennett, A.C. (1980). Performance appraisal: Management technique as social process? In D. S. Beach (Ed.), *Managing people at work: Readings in personnel* (3rd ed.). New York: Macmillan.

Patton, M.Q. (1986). *Utilization focused evaluation* (2nd ed.). Newbury Park, CA: Sage Publications.

Peterson, K.D. (1995). *Teacher evaluation: A comprehensive guide to new directions and practices*. Thousand Oaks, CA: Corwin Press.

Redfern, G.B. (1980). *Evaluating teachers and administrators: A performance objectives approach*. Boulder, CO: Westview.

Sanders, W.L., & Horn, S.P. (1998). Research findings from the Tennessee Value-Added Assessment System (TVAAS) database: Implications for education evaluation and research. *Journal of Personnel in Education*, **12**, 247–256.

Sclan, E.M. (1994, July). *Performance evaluation for experienced teachers: An overview of state policies*. Presented at the annual conference of the National Evaluation Institute, Gatlinburg, TN.

Scott, J., & Klasek, C. (1980). Evaluating certified school media personnel: A useful evaluation instrument. *Educational Technololgy*, **20**(5), 53–55.

Scriven, M.S. (1981). Summative teacher evaluation. In J. Millman (Ed.), *Handbook of teacher evaluation* (pp. 244–271). Beverly Hills, CA: Sage Publications.

Scriven, M.S. (1988). Duties-based teacher evaluation. *Journal of Personnel Evaluation in Education*, **1**, 319–334.

Scriven, M. (1995). A unified theory approach to teacher evaluation. *Studies in Educational Evaluation*, **21**, 111–129.

Shinkfield, A.J., & Stufflebeam, D. (1995). *Teacher evaluation: Guide to effective practice*. Boston: Kluwer Academic Publishers.

Stronge, J.H. (1988). *Evaluation of ancillary school personnel training model* (Illinois Administrators' Academy). Springfield, IL: Illinois State Board of Education.

Stronge, J.H. (1993). Evaluating teachers and support personnel. In B.S. Billingsley (Ed.), *Program leadership for serving students with disabilities* (pp. 445–479). Richmond, VA: Virginia Department of Education.

Stronge, J.H. (1994). How do you evaluate everyone who isn't a teacher: A practical evaluation model for professional support personnel. *The School Administrator*, **11**(51), 18–23.

Stronge, J.H. (1995). Balancing individual and institutional goals in educational personnel evaluation: A conceptual framework. *Studies in Educational Evaluation, 21*, 131–151.

Stronge, J.H. (1997). Improving schools through teacher evaluation. In J.H. Stronge (Ed.), *Evaluating teaching: A guide to current thinking and best practice* (pp. 1–23). Thousand Oaks, CA: Corwin Press, Inc.

Stronge, J.H., & Helm, V.M. (1990). Evaluating educational support personnel: A conceptual and legal framework. *Journal of Personnel Evaluation in Education, 4*, 145–156.

Stronge, J.H., & Helm, V.M. (1991). *Evaluating professional support personnel in education.* Newbury Park, CA: Sage Publications.

Stronge, J.H., & Helm, V.M. (1992). A performance evaluation system for professional support personnel. *Educational Evaluation and Policy Analysis, 14*, 175–180.

Stronge, J.H., Helm, V.M., & Tucker, P.D. (1995). *Evaluation Handbook for Professional Support Personnel.* Kalamazoo: Center for Research on Educational Accountability and Teacher Evaluation, Western Michigan University.

Stronge, J.H., & Tucker, P.D. (1995a). Performance evaluation of professional support personnel: A survey of the states. *Journal of Personnel Evaluation in Education, 9*, 123–138.

Stronge, J.H., & Tucker, P.D. (1995b). The principal's role in evaluating professional support personnel. *NASSP Practitioner, 21*(3), 1–4.

Stronge, J.H., & Tucker, P.D. (2000). *Teacher evaluation and student achievement.* Washington, DC: National Education Association.

Stufflebeam, D.L. (1983). The CIPP model for program evaluation. In G. Madaus, M.S. Scriven, & D.L. Stufflebeam (Eds.), *Evaluation models: Viewpoints on educational and human services in evaluation* (pp. 117–141). Boston: Kluwer-Nijhoff.

Stufflebeam, D.L., Foley, W., Gephart, W., Guba, E.G., Hammond, R., Merriman, H., & Provus, M. (Phi Delta Kappa National Study Committee on Evaluation). (1971). *Educational evaluation and decision making.* Itasca, IL: F.E. Peacock.

Tucker, N.A., Bray, S.W., & Howard, K.C. (1988). *Using a client-centered approach in the principal's evaluation of counselors.* Paper presented at the annual meeting of the Assessment Conference. (ERIC Document Reproduction Service No. ED 309 341)

Turner, P.M., & Coleman, J.G., Jr. (1986, January). *State education agencies and the evaluation of school library media specialists: A report.* Paper presented at the Annual Meeting of the Association for Educational Communications and Technology, Las Vegas, NV.

Valentine, J.W. (1992). *Principles and practices for effective teacher evaluation.* Boston, MA: Allyn and Bacon.

Vincelette, J.P., & Pfister, F.C. (1984). Improving performance appraisal in libraries. *Library and Information Science Research, An International Journal, 6*, 191–203.

Webster, W.J., & Mendro, R.L. (1997). The Dallas value-aded acountability system. In J. Millman (Ed.), *Grading teachers, grading schools: Is student achievement a valid evaluation measure?* (pp. 81–99). Thousand Oaks, CA: Corwin Press.

Wheeler, P.H. (1993). *Using portfolios to assess teacher performance* (EREAPA Publication Series No. 93–7). (ERIC Document Reproduction Service No. ED 364 967) (TEMP Abstract No. 11231).

Wolf, K. (1996). Developing an effective teaching portfolio. *Educational Leadership, 53*(6), 34–37.

Wolf, K., Lichtenstein, G., & Stevenson, C. (1997). Portfolios in teacher evaluation. In J.H. Stronge (Ed.), *Evaluating teaching: A guide to current thinking and best practice* (pp. 193–214). Thousand Oaks, CA: Corwin Press, Inc.

Wright, S.P., Horn, S.P., & Sanders, W.L. (1997). Teacher and classroom context effects on student achievement: Implications for teacher evaluation. *Journal of Personnel Evaluation in Education, 11*, 57–67.

Section 8

Program/Project Evaluation

Introduction

JAMES R. SANDERS, Section Editor
The Evaluation Center, Western Michigan University, MI, USA

In her chapter, Dr Jean King defined program evaluation and project evaluation in the following way:

> Programs are typically long-term ongoing activities representing coordinated efforts planned to achieve major educational goals (e.g., a school district's language arts program) .... Educational projects, by contrast, are short-term activities with specific objectives and allocated resources (e.g., professional development training for a school faculty) (Nevo, 1995, p. 119) .... the process of evaluating educational programs and projects, however, [is the same and need not be separated].

This is the definition that will be used in this section. Evaluation is defined as a systematic process of determining the merit or worth of an object (Joint Committee, 1994): in this, case programs or projects.

Program and project evaluations can be viewed alternatively as a recently developed methodology and practice or one that dates back to the beginnings of recorded history. By other names, program and project evaluations have been with us for thousands of years as new ways of doing things are tried and then accepted or rejected. Examples abound in every international context. The biggest challenge of this section is where in time and geography to begin.

Four international settings where educational program and project evaluation experiences have developed were selected for this section. Three are "Western" settings while the fourth, in developing countries, offers a provocative contrast.

The four authors of the chapters in this section chose different starting points. Dr Gila Garaway described unique characteristics of program and project evaluations in developing countries. In her chapter, she used illustrative cases to build the reader's understanding of contextual differences between educational evaluations conducted in the West and those conducted in Third World countries. She contrasted them in educational systems and context, sociopolitical and cultural contexts, players and their roles, evaluation impact, and ethical considerations in evaluation. Having made these contrasts, Garaway proceeded to lay out a view of future development of educational evaluation in developing countries. The foremost issue is the extent to which program evaluation in

697

International Handbook of Educational Evaluation, 697–700
T. Kellaghan, D.L. Stufflebeam (eds.)
© *2003 Dordrecht: Kluwer Academic Publishers. Printed in Great Britain.*

developing countries is shaped by non-Western realities in those countries. New evaluation models, methods, and standards are not developed overnight. Yet, a strong argument can be made for the need to develop new ways of practicing program evaluation in developing countries. There is also the issue of evaluation cost and its influence on what gets evaluated, who does it, who can pay for it, and ultimately the impact of the evaluation on local programs. Needs in developing countries also include locally trained evaluators, new methods to address local realities, relevant and timely information and access to it at the local level, and common understandings about the purposes, roles, procedures, and underlying values of program evaluation.

Dr Jean King traced the development of program and project evaluation in the United States, beginning with roots in experimental research design, testing, and accreditation. The great leap in the development of program and project evaluation in the United States, however, took place in the late 1950s and the 1960s, spurred on by government mandates for evaluating funded education programs and projects. This rapid growth slowed noticeably after 1980 with much of the federal role in stimulating program evaluation switching to the states. Processes such as testing and accreditation have been institutionalized in U.S. schools. The future development of program and project evaluation in the United States will be affected by the rapid growth of technology and information processing, by the development of an evaluation profession with professional organizations that provide networks of support for evaluators, and by the concept of organizational learning that expands the role of program evaluation in schools to supporting change.

Dr Alice Dignard described developments in Canada that address the two most common purposes of program and project evaluation: accountability and program improvement. Each of Canada's 10 provinces and 3 territories is responsible for its own education system. Consequently, the organization of education and the use of evaluation in education differs across geopolitical boundaries. Dr Dignard used examples to illustrate the kind of development taking place in educational program evaluation in Canada during the 1990s. For instance, the government in the province of Québec created a commission responsible for, among other responsibilities, evaluation of the quality of educational programs in Québec colleges. Public reports with recommendations are aimed at program improvement. The Québec legislature also affected evaluation practices by developing a policy on university funding based on accountability measures. Another evaluation initiative was developed in Manitoba with the financial support of a Canadian charitable foundation. The Manitoba School Improvement Program uses program evaluation as a means of stimulating significant school improvement. The Canadian experience illustrates the important roles of government and private foundations in developing program evaluation practices in schools and colleges. Evaluation is taking on an important role in education in Canada, although the specifics differ across provinces.

Dr John Owen discussed the supply and demand for project and program evaluation in Australia. Evidence of both reveals an important role that government is playing in requesting evaluations while evaluators are coming out of many disciplines and professions, including education. Dr Owen used program evaluations to illustrate three approaches to program evaluations that are developing in Australia: (1) evaluations of innovations that acknowledge the complexity of educational change; (2) development of accountability frameworks; and (3) development of an evaluation culture within educational organizations. Important implications of these developments for evaluation practice in education in Australia include more involvement of evaluators in policy development and in organizational development.

Looking across these four chapters, some threads become apparent. Program and project evaluation is a human activity that is as old as mankind. It is used to make choices and decisions. It motivates change. It is used to develop understanding. It is used to justify investments of resources. In many ways program and project evaluation has been and will continue to be embedded in human cognition and behavior.

Formal program and project evaluation, characterized by systematic, public processes open to examination and revision (if warranted) and aimed toward assessing the value of some object, goes beyond opinion justified by intuition, anecdotes, or casually collected pieces of evidence. When important decisions affect large numbers of students or investments of large amounts of educational resources or result in significant changes that affect the well being of society, formal program and project evaluations are expected and justified.

Formal program and project evaluation does not follow one set of procedures, however. Depending on the stage of inquiry, the cultural context in which evaluation is conducted, the central value questions that frame the evaluation, the availability or accessibility of vital information, the resources available for evaluation, and the diversity of perspectives of the program or project, evaluations are shaped accordingly. It is fair to say that every program or project evaluation is unique in many ways and consequently that the practice of evaluation is complex.

Evaluation communities throughout the world must be concerned about the quality of their evaluations. With so many decisions affecting evaluation practice, on what basis can one judge program or project evaluation designs or finished projects? In the United States and Canada, a group of professional associations have collaborated in defining The Program Evaluation Standards (Joint Committee, 1994). These standards are intended to communicate shared learning about sound evaluation practice from program and project evaluators and from consumers of program and project evaluations in education. As the field of evaluation evolves, these standards will be revised to reflect this evolution. Evaluation communities throughout the world should consider defining their standards in order to communicate their expectations for sound program and project evaluation. Each chapter in this section provides a beginning discussion of what constitutes good evaluation practice in a particular sociopolitical context. This is a start to global analyses of the differences and commonalities of program and project evaluation methodologies that best fit the realities of different cultures.

Needs for future developments in program and project evaluation have been identified. They include the following:

1. Capacity building for localized evaluation practitioners;
2. New evaluation methods that address the realities of the local context;
3. Information made available when it is needed and to whom it should inform;
4. Better awareness and expectations for the roles that evaluators and evaluations play in local contexts;
5. Better use of technology to enhance the effectiveness of program and project evaluations, including the development of institutional memory and the ability to be analytical about educational programs;
6. Continuing to build professional networks of support for program evaluators;
7. Resources to continue to stimulate program evaluation at all levels of societies;
8. Involvement of program evaluators in policy development;
9. Involvement of program evaluators in organizational development.

Drs Garaway, King, Dignard, and Owen have provided an important agenda for the development of program and project evaluation throughout the world. Each agenda item can be considered to be a significant project by itself. It is incumbent upon the evaluation communities found locally, nationally, regionally, and globally to take these challenges seriously and to continue the evolution of program and project evaluation.

REFERENCE

Joint Committee on Standards for Educational Evaluation. (1994). *The program evaluation standards: How to assess evaluations of educational programs*. Thousand Oaks, CA: Sage.

31
Evaluating Educational Programs and Projects in The Third World

GILA GARAWAY

Moriah Africa, Israel

Educational evaluation in "third world" or developing nations is by no means a new phenomenon. It can, however, be quite different than that found in the "west" and thus warrants a separate view. The portrait and discussion that follow are general strokes. The aim is not to provide a definitive statement of what program evaluation looks like in third world countries, but rather to open a door onto some of the realities that are different than those in the west by providing samplings of what it looks like, how it's different, and then some thoughts about its future.

WHAT DOES IT LOOK LIKE?

Sample #1

It is a rural area in any one of a large number of developing nations. The evaluator has come from the city to look at the implementation of the latest initiative to improve rural education. Sitting on a bench in front of the small crumbling structure, she is surrounded by the children who have arrived today. Some sit around her on the bench, touching her books and asking her simple questions. Others play here and there in the bare, dirt yard surrounding the school. Although the teacher has not come yet, the children seem unperturbed. After what seems like an endless wait, the evaluator looks at her watch and wonders if it is worth waiting longer. It has been a very long walk down dirt tracks to get here. She did not send word ahead that she was coming, as she wanted to capture the program "as it is." She asks the children if they know where the teacher is. No, they say, they don't. He often does not come. The children do not seem in any hurry to leave. Thin, they too have walked a long way to get here.

Soon she leaves and heads to her next destination, a school closer to the main road. Here she finds teachers and several small dark buildings packed with students. School is in progress and as she approaches she sees that the children

701

International Handbook of Educational Evaluation, 701–720
T. Kellaghan, D.L. Stufflebeam (eds.)
© 2003 Dordrecht: Kluwer Academic Publishers. Printed in Great Britain.

are sitting relatively quietly and attentively, crammed one next to the other on the small benches that fill the rooms. Quite a few hold small slates and tattered primers. As soon as they notice her arrival, everyone wants to stop in order to greet this new friend properly. It is not often that they have guests. They are sorry they did not know she was coming or they would have prepared in some way. Clearly, all are pleased she has come and are eager to please. After many warm smiles and greetings around, the evaluator takes a place in the back of one of the rooms, by which to try to get an objective view of activity. Later she will test the children with the testing instruments she has brought with her. Designed by the foreign evaluation consultant hired by the foreign donor, they are meant to test the children's achievement, the central measure of the success or failure of the program.

Back in the city, the 'evaluation' has pre-empted almost all other program activity. The foreign consultant has just arrived in country to oversee the data gathering. Given budget constraints, he has only a short time period allotted to spend in-country and thus an in-depth look at things will not be possible. To add to that, there have been a number of unexpected problems and delays and so they will only be able to do about half of what was planned. Fortunately, the education ministry has an evaluation department with a number of trained evaluators. This has been a great help to the foreign consultant. In addition to the tests, participatory techniques and activities have been incorporated and implemented where possible.

The small evaluation team covering the rural area closest to the city has just returned from a day of testing. As the team sits to share findings, the discussion turns to focus group interviews. The feedback from each team member is the same. Generally the local authority figure was present and led the discussion. "Everyone agreed and everything was positive … no, the women present really had nothing to say." The consultant questions this uniformity of response from the team but the answers seem to skirt the issue. He has a growing feeling that the evaluation design is missing the mark. The discussion changes and takes on a fairly technical dimension related to validity and reliability. This is a complicated issue in this setting and the outside evaluator knows he will have to bridge it in the writing of his report. Efforts have been made to address the issue with some brief training in test administration given to locals and with instruments modified for local use, although this was complicated given the multilingual nature of the overall educational setting. At this point, for the consultant the important point is being able to convey concrete quantitative information to the multi-lateral donor so that it can in turn account to its support base.

Sample #2

It is an urban setting in a secondary city of a developing nation. The evaluator hired by the international NGO (non-governmental organization, in this case an international relief and development agency) has just completed an evaluation of a large integrated child-headed household program which contained elements of health, education, and self-help activities framed in an overall objective of community capacity building. The donor providing funds for this program (a western government) has stipulated a one-year maximum time frame for implementation of activities in any particular area with phase-out expected to find local authority fully carrying on with the program.

Two separate focus group sessions are arranged – one with the local education authorities where the program just finished and one with the NGO program staff, the majority of whom are nationals. In the session with the local education authorities, the goal is to determine to what degree the program has stimulated local ownership and responsibility for ongoing implementation of the program. The meeting is called for 9:00 and by 10:30 all have arrived. Each has come with a plan for how activity will continue and each is eager to share. There is a sense of great expectancy in the air. Not fully aware of the risks involved, the evaluator decides to lay aside her earlier planned format and let the session take its own shape, a series of presentations made by each of the authorities present. As the session unfolds, it becomes increasingly clear to the evaluator that the locals do not understand her role or position in the organization as each of the presentations ends with a rough budget and a request for ongoing funding. Although she prefaced the beginning of the session with an explanation of the purposes of the session (to gather information about the success/sustainability of the program) and her relationship to the organization (outside consultant), and although all present are aware that the program's funding was for one year only with the overall objective being hand-over and local maintenance, it is clear they have not understood or have not wanted to understand. She realizes she must reclarify her position to avoid further misunderstanding regarding her ability to get them funds. The response however is unanimous and clear – surely she must have voice and power within the organization to advocate for them or they would not have sent her as their emissary. Can't she see that they cannot continue without continued outside support? It is now that she fully recognizes the pitfall: Her presence has bred expectations. And unmet expectations can lead to disappointment and quite possibly rejection of gains made during the life of the program. Instantly she realizes she will need to redirect the focus while at the same time promoting the continued presentation of ideas.

In the session with the NGO staff she is prepared. They too have come with requests: for better working conditions, better salaries, and more equipment. While this feedback is valid and will form part of her report to her client, the NGO home office, it is not what she had intended for the session. Instead she had hoped that staff would focus more directly on program components. She thus steers the discussion in that direction and to her relief the staff enter into a meaningful discussion related to perceptions of process and why (or why not) certain steps are adhered to. Staff are animated and many are taking notes. She leaves hopeful that the discussion might catalyze positive changes in the coming round of implementation activity in other parts of the country.

Sample #3

It is a provincial center in a central African nation. A "participatory" evaluation of a training program is underway. Although the main structure and approach of the evaluation has been designed by an outside consultant it is still considered participatory because many of the questions and areas of investigation were compiled from suggestions made collectively by program staff and program beneficiaries.

One of the components of the evaluation is interviews with local political authority, an attempt to adhere to social custom as well as to gain local perspectives on the strengths and weaknesses of the program. As the data gathering period comes to closure, the evaluator receives a call from someone in the ministry of education questioning what the evaluator told a particular provincial authority. Evidently the evaluator had solicited ideas and suggestions from the provincial authority who in turn understood it to mean that they would be implemented as changes in the program. The evaluator explains to the educational ministry that he had only been giving the provincial authority suggestive voice not deliberative voice. The response is that for the provincial authority there is no difference, in his position everything is deliberative voice.

HOW IS IT DIFFERENT?

Differences can be viewed from a number of perspectives. I have selected five, as they reflect many of the issues involved: educational systems and structures, socio-political and cultural elements, players and their roles, evaluation's impact and ethical considerations.

Educational Systems, Structures, and the Context in which They Are Found

From the perspective of systems, structures and contexts, funding, staffing, facilities, and conflicts are just a few of the elements contributing to the contrasts. In most third world countries, an ongoing problem is funding. With low GNPs and possibly shrinking foreign assistance, limited funds must be stretched to cover the massive requirements of running a country: transport, industry, agriculture, health, communication, internal and external security, to name but a few. Invariably, education tends to get left with little in her bag. This translates into a number of different realities: (1) a large portion of educational programming is supported by outside (non-national governmental) sources; (2) monies intended for some specific educational activity may get funneled to other necessary activities; (3) there are great disparities between schools. With limited funds earmarked for education, the bulk of monies tends to go toward supporting urban schools in order to provide at least one sector with minimally adequate resources. This reality in combination with weak rural local economies leaves rural areas with little on which to build and run their schools. In many rural areas of the world, the classroom is simply a spot under a tree. Those fortunate enough to have a building may have more than 100 students crammed into each class. Most often these classrooms are bare other than for the benches and a faded blackboard up front. Paper, pencils, or other material resources that in the west are considered absolutely minimum essentials may quite possibly be absent. When a program (and its evaluation) is a regional or nationwide one, which is often the case, all of this means vastly different conditions under which the program is being implemented. The lack of any kind of standard greatly constrains the comparison of program implementation across sites and greatly challenges the designers of evaluation in their attempts to fairly represent a whole picture.

Skilled personnel is another area of challenge in the functioning of educational systems. Most developing countries suffer a severe shortage. Even on the highest level, ministries of education often lack sufficiently trained staff to help steer them through the quagmire of complexities that surround building an educational system equipped to meet the challenges of modern society. Further, with inadequate financial means, ministries of education are often critically strapped to provide teachers with even a bare minimum salary. If someone has gained a secondary education, what would be the purpose of staying in a rural area if there is a better paying job in town? This often leaves rural authorities with a very small pool of teachers to draw from, many of them barely educated themselves. Another problem is absence. In addition to high absenteeism and dropout rate amongst students, there is the phenomenon of teacher absenteeism. Teachers too have activities of daily living and errands to do. With no transport but by foot, taking care of personal business or obligatory attendance at community meetings means a day off work. If the teachers are not consistently present, parents often find little worth in sending their children off each day when they could be put to much better use taking care of younger siblings, doing chores around the house or working in the fields. For many mothers who already carry a heavy workload, sending girls off poses especial hardships.

Staffing challenges also have a direct impact on evaluation and evaluation-related activities. Governments often work very hard to attract large donor funding. Donors in turn look very closely at the potential recipient's capacity to make effective use of funds. Because of perceived or real gaps, donors often provide funds with provisos that outside non-national program expertise will be brought in for both the design and the evaluation of the program. For governments and donors, identifying, training, and then payrolling national evaluation staff is often a low priority. This means that evaluations are primarily conducted by outsiders, in the fullest sense of the word. It also means that design and output have a higher likelihood of missing the mark in terms of relevance or appropriateness to the context.

Facilities or access to them offer additional challenges. Lack of roads or means of transport other than by foot means children are required to walk long distances to get to and from school, which may or may not be an equipped structure, as described above. For an evaluator, it also means that access to schools is limited and difficult requiring huge expenditures of time. This factor alone is a major constrainer in conducting a thorough evaluation of an educational program. As Bhola (1998) shares with respect to his evaluation of a nationwide literacy program in Namibia, visits to the six educational regions meant elephants, buffalo, and journeying on unmarked trails and across flooded plains.

In addition to drought, flood, and famine, many of the world's developing nations have suffered and continue to suffer ongoing cycles of civil strife and/or war. While the impact of drought, flood, and famine might be more clearly understood, the insidious impact of war is less so. Wars, particularly the simmering ongoing conflicts found in many places around the globe, have had a devastating impact on massive numbers of children. Wars are powerfully destabilizing psychologically, not to mention physically. In terms of education they often mean damaged or poorly maintained structures and disruptions in day-to-day functioning. Added to this, changes in governments often mean changes in ministries of education, rendering many educational systems with little or no continuity.

How do you factor these elements into an evaluation? Although it may be clear to all that the contextual factors are having a significant impact on a program's delivery, how can the evaluator really understand or get at all of the dynamics impacting on a program? If he or she is an outsider, insider understandings are absent and key elements may be altogether missed. If a local, he or she may be so much a part of the fabric as to not even see the individual threads.

Socio-Political and Cultural Issues

The concept of hierarchical distance – the degree of verticality – goes a long way in helping to describe some of the differences between western socio-political relationships and those found in many developing nations. Bollinger and Hofstede (1987) maintain that in high verticality societies, wealth and power tend to be concentrated in the hands of an elite, the society tends to be static and politically centralized, and subordinates consider their superiors to be better than themselves, having a right to privilege. There is minimal attention to the future because life will go on regardless. Contrasted to this is the more horizontal society in which planning for the future is deemed necessary for survival, the political system is decentralized, wealth is widely distributed and people are deemed more or less equal. Bollinger and Hofstede maintain that high verticality prevails in warmer climates, where the survival of the group is less dependent on saving, future planning, and technological advancements. While this thesis on things may be debatable, the point is that countries around the world have vastly different social, political, and cultural systems, and that differences are not just a function of isolated discrete manners and customs but rather of systems that penetrate behavior at all levels.

In a treatise on African culture, Etounga-Manguelle (2000) maintains that in spite of differences between nations, tribes, and ethnic groups across Africa, there is a common ground of shared values, attitudes and institutions. He notes several: subordination of the individual by the community, a resistance to changes in social standing, and thought processes that avoid skepticism, skepticism being a mental endeavor tied to individualism. In addition, there is a high level of acceptance of uncertainty about the future. Given the very high value placed on sociability, social cohesion, and consensus, differences in opinion, thought, or viewpoint are often masked or rejected in both a conscious and subconscious move to avoid conflict and promote conviviality. This is contrasted to societies where individualism reigns and conquering the future is related to aggressiveness, anxiety, and institutions oriented to change. Western thought and evaluation, as concept and practice quite nicely fall into the last category.

Few of us are aware of the degree to which cultural values pervade all aspects of our practice. A brief look at our operational definitions provides just part of the picture. In the West, poverty is equated with lack of material wealth. When needing to determine the impact of poverty on a program we thus might look at family income or condition of the family dwelling rather than at the locally defined measure, distance from the community water tap, or we might be inclined to give a higher value to the little hut in the midst of a lush looking garden than the dusty tent in the midst of barren ground even though by local definition it is the pastoralist tent dweller who has "wealth" because only the "poor" work the ground. Our biases can also be seen in our choice of approach. Because of the multiplicity and complexity of intervening variables in a developing nation context, the evaluator usually feels a greater need to involve a variety of people in his or her attempt to get at truth. Added to this is often a desire to "help change things," to promote the development which seems so needed. Participatory approaches and their proliferation are a natural response to this. This seems good and is in fact often an indication that we are attempting to realize the principles of fairness outlined in the Guiding Principles for Evaluators (AEA, 1995). What we fail to realize however is that the way we design and implement our participatory approach may be rooted in our own cultural view of things; that is, "fairness" is an issue of voice; time is to be maximized, "extraneous" social banter minimized; getting it all "out on the table" is the most efficient and effective way to begin processes of learning and change; women should have an equal representation. Quite clearly, the more participatory type approaches assume a democratic frame, or are an attempt to create one.

And what about our definition? Evaluation as defined by many in the field is all about judgment, and judgment speaks criticism. And criticism, as any evaluator knows, breeds defensiveness and wall building; it hinders learning. In many developing nations, where people are not used to open criticism at all because of social and cultural constraints to anything which might appear to be stirring up conflict, this wall building is magnified. In fact "dialogue" as critical communication may not only be avoided but resisted and frowned upon. Rather consensus building is the expected and acceptable norm. Hence the failure of many focus group interviews to produce the interactions that the evaluator wants and expects.

In much of the developing world the concept of evaluation is little understood. Evaluations are generally called for by foreign development agencies to meet their donor needs, be it information for decision making or information to satisfy their donor population's demand for accountability – did you succeed in doing what you said you were going to do? While these aims are fully justified, the information gained usually leaves with the evaluation, leaving those locally involved in the evaluation with little understanding of its purposes or conclusions. In cases where more participatory approaches have been implemented, social interaction patterns employed may have generated negative reactions and a resistance to any form of western evaluative activity, with control and "social transformation" perceived as its primary focus.

In many ways, this same statement about lack of understanding of evaluation could be made about developed countries, where the stated (or unstated) role and purposes of evaluation may be as varied as the evaluation approaches themselves. Within the variation however are common threads, perhaps common understandings. Many if not most (Cronbach et al., 1980; House, 1993; Worthen, 1990;) would support the statement that evaluation is essentially political activity. With an eye on issues of ethics, justice, and cultural fairness, House (1993) points to evaluation's authority, it's role as a strong and significant force in the process of social change, and points to the responsibility of the evaluator to conduct professional fair democratic practice. Clearly, in the West evaluation is a growing source of social authority in societies with increasingly fragmented social structures.

What then does this mean for program evaluation in developing countries where social systems and structures may be far more intact and functioning and where people may be far less willing to concede any authority to evaluation? Surely the evaluator is still accountable and responsible for ethical, professional practice. But what do we assume in the design and conduct of practice? In terms of design are we assuming certain social structures, roles, and modes of interaction? Do we include women and children in inappropriate ways? Do we pattern our discourse along critical dimensions or do we seek to understand and implement local patterns? And if we respect local patterns and give voice according to local custom, are we aware of the implications in terms of subsequent expectations? Have we accounted for the power of social obligation? In terms of conduct, do we extend ourselves to step outside our own limited perception of the way things should be? In one study done in an African nation, the rural dwellers could not quite understand why this stranger had come to ask questions and stir things up. Was he just a troublemaker? Didn't he know that it is the leaders who know? It is they who are responsible to know and provide for us. Is this outsider trying to undermine that? Does our design or approach relate to the way things are?

Players and Their Roles

How is the client, the evaluator, or the stakeholder different in developing nation evaluation? In terms of the client, in developed nations most educational programs (and thus their evaluations) are funded by national or state government entities. In contrast in developing nations the program donors are very often foreign international development agencies, external non-national sources like UNESCO, World Bank, an NGO or others with social and political cultures, agendas and perspectives quite different than those of the program population. Large donors often have very little, if any, exposure to the program and its context and thus are far more dependent on an evaluator/evaluation to be their eyes and ears in the field.

In terms of the evaluator, in developing nations, there is both far more freedom for creativity and a far greater responsibility to hold oneself accountable to professional practice given the distance from a context with defined expectations of practice. This is significant given that the individual evaluator's ultimate power and authority is usually far greater than in the west. There are several reasons for this. In the west, if a program gets a poor report, it may be revised or discarded; the education system, however, continues to function. In contrast, in countries where there is heavy dependence on outside resources to support or provide significant amendments to national educational system budgets, a poor report can potentially have dramatic and far-reaching consequences on maintenance of the educational system itself. Combined with this reality is the power of a single evaluation. In the west, a large program will very possibly include several evaluation studies; in developing nations, it will be at best one. Thus the report made by even a single evaluation has the power to significantly affect future funding.

With respect to foreign evaluators, the greater disparities and differences between the donor population, the evaluator, and the program population mean that there is a greater need to establish common understandings and to examine the assumptions underlying not only evaluation practice but also those under-lying educational practice in that context. What is the big picture, extending even beyond the program? Who are the educational service providers, beyond those assumed? What are the roles of the education ministry? What are the assumptions underpinning educational action? Although such inquiry may be critically important in a particular setting, it carries with it real costs in terms of time, effort and resources.

With respect to national evaluators, differences can be found in the realm of the socio-cultural pressures under which they may be operating. They may be subject to strong cultural mores that demand loyalties that can both interfere with objectivity as well as a full presentation of findings.

Stakeholder differences include teachers with limited understanding of the concept of program evaluation, its role and purposes; students and their families with no understanding of the concept evaluation, particularly so in less democratic societies where there is a tremendous dependency on "leaders." In addition to these factors are the issues of gender and class and their interplay with a program. This latter issue in particular can pose a dilemma in the identification of participants for specific evaluative activity.

Local authority structures can be another area of difference. While there may be a clearly defined and set up educational system with its own set of authority and power brokers, there often are parallel but less apparent traditional authority structures that may be the important ones with which to reckon. This may be the area chief or community elders. Showing deference to local authority and custom requires care and sensitivity however, as misunderstandings can easily be created with respect to control of the evaluation and/or the program. This is important in all aspects of the evaluation, from data gathering to dissemination of information.

Evaluation Impact

Impact made by an evaluation can be viewed from two perspectives: impact made by the evaluation process during the conduct of the evaluation and impact related to post-evaluation use of findings. In terms of impact made by process, there is on one hand the unintentional impact related to inappropriate implementation of process and the sometimes negative response to western critical social interaction patterns, which can leave program implementers less enthusiastic about the western model program at hand. On the other hand are large numbers of appropriately implemented participatory processes that have resulted in learning and tremendous program improvement. Among other things this may be due to a greater receptiveness to participatory approaches, a function of a far higher value placed on collective activity than in the west where an individualist mindset prevails.

In terms of impact related to post-evaluation utilization of findings, there are the issues of ability to use and of systematic use. With respect to ability to use, there is first of all the problem of findings leaving the country of program implementation; this is matched by the other problem mentioned above, language of the evaluation report. Language of the report is more than an issue of English, French, Tamil, or Nepali. It is as much the level of language, use of terms, technicality, and clarity of presentation. Any or all of these can pose real barriers to local access to meaningful or useful information. While the observations may be valid, over technicality can be overwhelming and lengthy narrative reports can leave the reader without a clear definitive picture of anything. With respect to systematic use, though evaluation findings and recommendation may not be readily usable by nationals, they are often used by development agencies to make changes. A common problem, however, is that the changes are usually non-systematic – disconnected changes are made and subsequent programs and their evaluations focus only on the latest program with little systematic evaluation of overall sets of changes and their impact. This is a function both of a lack of continuity in donor base – new programs being supported by new donors with new agendas and little interaction between donor – as well as a lack of use of available evaluation document resources (World Bank, UNESCO, etc).

Ethical Considerations

In his piece on ethical issues in international evaluations, Bamberger (1999) refers to the Joint Committee on Educational Evaluation's Program Evaluation Standards (Joint Committee, 1994) and the American Evaluation Association's Guiding Principles for Evaluators (AEA, 1995) as a jumping off point for his discussion and identifies issues of particular importance in the international arena. One of the questions he raises, plus several others, are discussed here: To what extent should local custom be observed? To what extent is the evaluator accountable to the program population? And whose concerns take precedence, those of the donor or those of the program population? While none of these questions have simple answers, an attempt to address them brings to light a number of ethical issues specific to evaluation in developing nations.

To What Extent Should Local Custom Be Observed?

With reference to the Guiding Principles, we see that a central ethical issue in conducting evaluation relates to the need to respect differences in culture. It has been said that evaluators frequently fail to do so, either intentionally or unintentionally. Yet often we are faced with dilemmas, the dilemmas most often arising when one or more of the Guiding Principles come into conflict. A common dilemma revolves around how and when to give voice to women, children, and vulnerable groups. We want to honor the principle of meeting the needs of different stakeholders particularly when the stakeholders are women and children with serious needs. Yet to do so may mean disregarding and disrespecting local customs and consequently causing the opposite effect than that hoped for. An irate husband may severely beat his wife for simply attending a meeting where participatory voice is promoted. Or a village headman seeking to be responsible in his position of maintaining social order may throw bureaucratic obstacles in the way of program functioning, leaving children or the vulnerable without the services intended. As Bamberger points outs, a western unidimensional focus on gender or apparent vulnerability may fail to recognize and factor in deeper and more complex issues of ethnicity, class, and social structures. Another issue is approach. To what degree should process be defined by local social custom? Close adherence to local custom often requires greatly increased expenditures of time to attend to social protocol and its definitions of people to visit and expected time period spent at each visit. The big question for the evaluator is where to draw the line? How much is warranted and valid? This can be an especially difficult dilemma given on one hand the costs to the donor in terms of evaluator time and to the local in terms of his time and money to provide for the evaluator hospitably, and on the other hand, the potential negative effect on the program if he/she fails to observe local social etiquette.

To What Extent is the Evaluator Accountable to the Program Population?

With reference again to the Program Evaluation Standards and Guiding Principles for Evaluators, a number of areas of accountability are suggested and addressed here.

Accountable to conduct professional practice:
Clearly evaluators are accountable to conduct professional practice but professional practice can be interpreted to mean sensitive and culturally inappropriate invasion of program population privacy. Or it may mean lengthy interviews or group meetings with teachers, parents, or other program beneficiaries that require they walk long distances. Evaluators have an infinitely higher status than the program population and so the program population will unquestioningly do whatever is asked of them. Professionalism then must be defined as including a definitive assessment of all factors involved when designing steps for action.

Accountable to meet the needs of stakeholders:
The need to know and the need to have a say in directing actions affecting one's life are two central needs discussed in the literature. The latter has a fairly clear political dimension and raises the sensitive question if it is indeed the evaluator who is to wield (or attempt to wield) that type of authority in that particular context. This is in contrast to western thought where support of "right to know" and broad inclusion of stakeholders can be considered to be neutrality and only a stand for a particular position to be advocacy (Datta, 1999). With respect to the former, perhaps the need to know (be informed) must be preceded by the need to learn (be trained). While it can be said that learning is a feature of all evaluations, we must explicitly ask, do those learning have an adequate knowledge base to absorb or benefit from the information provided? Are the methods we are using promoting or hindering learning? And who is learning? Are all those that need to learn the ones learning? For more than a decade, the Organization for Economic Cooperation and Development (OECD) and others have been discussing the need to place a priority on increasing the evaluation and policy analysis capacity of developing nations, indicating both the need to train and for nationals to gain an expanded knowledge base on which to build understandings related to evaluation process and product.

Accountable to inform the evaluation population of evaluation's purposes and planned approaches for gathering information:
Professional evaluation surely has an ethical responsibility to ensure that all affected groups understand the potential risks and benefits that can result from

an evaluation. The question here relates to *informing*. Is merely informing the population adequate? In practice, terms of reference or scope of work are usually worked out ahead of time with the donor/client leaving no room for design and selection of locally appropriate approaches in partnership with local bodies. Beyond the more obvious risks and benefits involved in evaluation related to the possible conclusions and recommendations that will be drawn are those related to the impact of the evaluation process itself. Perhaps it might be better to say that we are accountable both to inform the population of *donor* needs and purposes and also to involve that population in the process of identifying local information needs/purposes and appropriate approaches given the particular purposes or sets of purposes of all parties.

Accountable to disseminate findings:
The questions in developing countries are what findings, how much, to whom, and by whom? Information (and more specifically the delivery of information) means power and thus decisions related to the dissemination of same often cannot or should not be made independently by the evaluator. It is thus of particular importance that understandings related to information dissemination be reached between the evaluator, donor, and program population at the outset. In cases where the evaluator has full latitude, he or she must ask what does local custom demand? Is information expected to be given by the evaluator or the village elders? If by the elders, by what mechanism can the evaluator ensure that the information gets disseminated? Again, this raises the issue of another aspect of information dissemination: the report itself – its definitiveness, readability, and understandability.

Whose Concerns Take Precedence, those of the Donor or those
of the Program Participants?

A familiar response to "it's the donor who's paying," goes something like, "but isn't everyone else too?" Stakeholder or participatory approaches, discussions of ethics, and establishment of the Guiding Principles are each just a part of the expression of the profession's concern over participant rights. It is in fact in the third world that participatory approaches have found their greatest expression (Feuerstein, 1986; Garaway, 1995; Narayan-Parker, 1991; Rebien, 1996), where the separation in every sense of the word between the donor and recipient seems greatest and where perceptions are most wide spread that the donor (be it a multilateral agency like World Bank, UN or others) is the bad guy and the recipient the victim. The tendency or temptation to support the underdog is strong. In contrast to this however are findings like those of Morris (1999) who reports that empirical research on ethics in evaluation shows concern over differential attention to stakeholders. Donors in fact may have well-founded accountability concerns. Given poor performance records there are often tremendous external pressures on donors to find out why. In the face of the temptation to advocate, the evaluator's responsibility must be to remain as an open channel of communication about concerns on all sides and as a facilitator endeavoring to create a clear picture and balance.

WHAT IS ITS FUTURE?

What then is the future of educational program evaluation in the developing world? What are the issues and how can it be shaped and directed to best serve the needs of both clients and stakeholders? What follows is a summary look at some of the issues and needs discussed here followed by a look at some suggestions for the future with respect to definition, aims, purposes, and practice.

Summary Look at Some of the Issues and Needs Presented

Looking at the issues raised above there is first and foremost the fundamental issue of the form and roles of program evaluation and its alignment with non-western realities. Who defines it and how is it perceived? Is it a welcome newcomer on the block of social authority? What and where is the value of evaluation and where and how can it interweave and become a more beneficial element in the educational arena? There is also the issue of the costs of evaluation – limited resources for payrolling trained local evaluation staff or for conducting locally generated studies on one hand, and the high costs of foreign consultant evaluation to foreign donors on the other hand. And in both cases, there is a need for evaluations to pay for themselves in terms of real savings to donors, improvements in programs, and/or positive impact. There are also the issues of lack of information or inaccessible information and lack of knowledge and understanding related to evaluation. These issues in turn speak of the following needs: locally equipped practitioners, effective and efficient practice (a positive cost/benefit relationship), relevant and timely information and access to same, relevant and appropriate practice, common understandings with respect to aims, purposes and process, and finally common understandings with respect to values underpinning it all.

Direction for the Future: Definition, Aims, Purposes, and Practice

Definition

Several definitions have bearing on developing nation evaluation. One is of conventional aid evaluation (OECD, 1992), which defines evaluation activity as the objective assessment of a project, the analysis of effects, the calculation of comparative advantages, and establishment of causal relationships between inputs and outputs.

Another is that of World Vision, "the facilitation of informed judgments about the merit and worth of something based on verifiable evidence" (Cookingham, 1992, p. 21). A third is that of Brunner and Guzman (1989), "an educational process through which social groups produce action oriented knowledge about their reality, clarify and articulate their norms and values, and reach a consensus about further action" (p. 11). The first implies evaluator control, quantitative measurement, experimental research, judgment, and a heavy focus on accountability concerns. The second implies facilitation, quantitative measurement, experimental research, judgment, and a focus on shared process concerns. The third implies facilitation, qualitative measurement, discovery, and a focus on learning and growth concerns.

In terms of operational definition for program evaluation, Lapan (in print) outlines the logic of evaluation in four steps: (1) establishing criteria of merit; (2) constructing standards; (3) measuring performance and comparing it to standards; and (4) synthesizing and integrating the performance data into conclusions of merit and worth.

Clear and concise, the four steps could be applied in any of the three definitions given above, with clarification and articulation of norms and values, as expressed by Brunner and Guzman, falling into "establishing criteria of merit." The question remains however, is this adequate or is there some fundamental element or perspective missing in practice and concept?

Science is all about observation and discovery. It flows from our desire to know about our surroundings – things, people, places, events. We observe and we draw conclusions. Research is disciplined inquiry. The notion of research came from our desire to certify or be more certain about the conclusions we are drawing from our observations.

Experimental research stands as the centerpiece of traditionally implemented forms of research. It asks questions about cause and effect. Did A have an impact on B? Did taking this medicine result in the remission of that disease? Evaluation, program evaluation in particular, is a more recently developed and practiced form of research. It asks questions about a variety of things. In addition to questions about cause and effect, it may ask, did program X produce the desired results? What were the benefits derived from Y program? Were the objectives of Z program achieved? The answers to these questions in turn are expected to help us answer the ultimate question, does X, Y, or Z program have merit or worth? In a nutshell, we can say experimental research undertakes rather defined activity that will, it assumes, determine with some measure of certainty if A causes B. Program evaluation research undertakes rather diverse activity that will, it hopes, determine with some measure of plausibility if program X, Y, or Z has merit and worth.

The problem, however, is that the determination of merit and worth is intricately interwoven into the realm of values and values vary. Variation can be especially critical in developing nations where the values held by the society implementing a program may be quite different foundationally than the values underpinning both the educational program and its evaluation. This is not to imply that implementing western model programs in a developing nation setting is necessarily inappropriate or inadequate. It is to say, however, that given the complex of value issues, the design and evaluation of programs must reckon with the local context, its values and their impact on a program.

Aims

There are a number of questions that can be asked here which suggest possible directions: Is social authority an appropriate or acceptable role of evaluation? Is judgment the construct within which evaluation is to be defined and confined? Is the ultimate underlying aim of practice only the determination of merit and worth or is it both the determination and discovery of same?

Looking at the last question, in strictly semantic terms *determination* of merit and worth implies measurement, judgment, and rather close-ended conclusions. *Discovery* of merit and worth implies measurement, an exploration for and of value, and open-ended learning. Measurement is an acknowledgement of accountability concerns and the need for scientific authority. Discovery is an acknowledgement of the need to learn as well as of colors that might be out of the range that I am accustomed to seeing – I may see only the leg of the elephant, but that does not mean that the leg is all there is. It also does not mean that the reality of the elephant is necessarily constructed by you or me.

The exploration for and definition of underlying aims must be a joint process conducted in-country by those directly involved in evaluation for that context.

Purposes

A number of purposes have been put forth for program evaluation:

1. Contribute to decisions about program installation;
2. Contribute to decisions about program continuation;
3. Contribute to decisions about program modification;
4. Obtain evidence to rally support;
5. Obtain evidence to rally opposition;
6. Contribute to the understanding of basic psychological, social and other processes;
7. Promote improvement;
8. Promote social change;
9. Promote learning (implying a training function and information dissemination).

The first six purposes can be considered to be information accumulation and delivery and can be viewed as the development of a clear concise picture of the way things are in order to provide for, among other things, corrected vision, the making of decisions, and justification; it can also be a means of providing new views and suggested perspectives on how things might be.

Promoting improvement is less clear cut. If we speak of improvement as being one of evaluation's purposes, then we must ask ourselves how efficient is it at doing so? As conventional process, there is no built-in mechanism that can ensure utilization of findings and recommendations that will in turn (we hope) promote improvement. Given its lack of control over post-evaluation utilization of findings, evaluation as practice and process can only directly address the issue of improvement to the degree it of itself as *process* impacts improvement. This is a major point of consideration in developing nations given the lack of access to findings and recommendations by those on the micro/local level on one hand, and the higher donor accountability concerns on the macro level on the other hand.

In evaluating programs, four common criteria are relevance, effectiveness, efficiency, and impact: To what degree is the program relevant, effective, efficient, and making an impact? From a metaevaluation perspective, we can use these same points to examine our evaluation practice: Is the evaluation *process* relevant, effective, efficient, and making an impact? We can even go one step further and ask, how can the evaluation process itself fulfill these criteria and at the same time *promote* these qualities in the evaluand? By asking these questions and then designing accordingly, we not only expand improvement as a purpose for evaluation, we also render evaluation as a proactive rather than reactive component in the system.

Social change as a purpose has been discussed here and has been implied as a purpose inherent in all evaluation activity. The questions here are who has determined the need for change and who has defined it and who is driving the process? And are these articulated in our evaluations?

Learning/training encompasses both information delivery, discussed above, and improvement purposes. With respect to learning and information delivery, Crespo, Soares, and de Mello de Souza (2000) in their discussion of the growing role of evaluation in Brazil's educational system note the increasing role of incoming information in the administration of educational programs. Given the information explosion in the past decade with computers and internet access, this is not surprising. However this underlines the gap between developed and developing nations in information access. In developing nations where access to computers, and thus information, is limited, evaluation process may have a more specific role and responsibility in addressing the issue of information access and delivery. This could mean among other things closer attention to the way information is compiled and presented, with the gathering and compilation process promoting use, and with definitive information presented in a concise, organized, and clearly understandable way.

With respect to training and improvement, there is both program improvement (discussed above) and individual improvement. With respect to individual improvement, an example suggests some possible direction. In one African country, a number of different evaluation studies were conducted over a period of some years. In the first study to be conducted, a local translation helper who showed great interest in learning was included as a colleague in the evaluation process. An informal hands-on training/learning process thus began that proved beneficial to both the outside evaluation "facilitator" and the local, and continued over several years through subsequent evaluation studies, with the local playing an increasingly greater role in defining practice. In the process, the "trainee" gained invaluable understandings about development and program design as well as about disciplined inquiry, and subsequently became not only a skilled evaluator but also a skilled educator and program designer, capable of defining locally meaningful and effective practice. The outside evaluation facilitator in turn gained invaluable insights and understandings about assumptions under-pinning practice, the need to examine these, and the beauty of evaluation when it is more closely aligned to local realities.

Practice

What might practice look like? If one were to follow on the suggestions given above, there is *measurement* (as much as possible using multiple methods) in order to convey key and timely information, and *discovery of merit and worth*, with a focus on values exploration, in order to promote learning, growth and improvement. Further, there is practice that can stand the tests of "relevance," "effectiveness," "efficiency," and "impact."

In terms of *relevance*, practice could be the development of common understandings gained via an examination of assumptions and creation of a common language for evaluation. As a value-tied endeavor, it demands explication and at least some examination of who, where, and what we are, and with respect to evaluation, what it is, what it's for, how it's done, who's doing it, and then, given all those understandings, how the process and product can fulfill defined purposes. This implies the need for both insider and outsider perspectives, along the lines of "dialogue" evaluation as suggested by Nevo (2000).

In terms of *effectiveness*, practice could be appropriate and understandable language, in process and presentation. In addition, it could be trained and mentored local practitioners, definitions of effectiveness and culturally appro-priate discourse patterns, identification of strengths – social, cultural, and political – and building bridges to them. Further it could be clearly understood and appropriate approaches that support rather than detract from program purposes and that promote the thorough gathering of adequate, accurate, relevant information. Some possible approaches include the systems approach put forth by Bhola (1997) where the educational program is seen as part of a greater system made up of many subsystems. In this approach, the evaluation process includes a definition and examination of the evaluand's system components, and the evaluation report becomes a "situated discourse," the rendition of the evaluation findings being framed within a presentation of the system as a whole. Or approach could involve use of a model conducive to cross-cultural study (Garaway, 1996), in which case there is development of a big picture which is methodically and systematically looked at over time and program to provide an extended time-frame picture of an educational entity and its health.

In terms of *efficiency*, practice can be more than providing needed information in a timely and easily accessible format to donors and other decision makers. Efficiency can be practice that makes the most of the time spent, addressing the needs of both the participants and the donors. It can be practice that brings about a range of benefits that help outweigh costs. It can be a tool for learning, an embedded part of existing systems and structures, with the evaluation designed not only to gather information but also to help address learning needs and form bridges to new understandings. If the local need is for increased skill capacity to be able to deliver educational services, then evaluation could be designed as a deliberative part of the curricular process (i.e. definition of aims → design → planning → implementation → evaluation → and back to aims), thus allowing participants an opportunity to expand their base of skills in the process of gathering information.

As *impact*, practice could be addressing local needs for adequate knowledge to process evaluation information, and further, presenting information in locally meaningful, useable ways. Further, it could be practice designed specifically to support rather than detract from program purposes. In terms of client or decision making processes, it could be practice that maintains elements of scientific authority in the gathering of data rather than discarding the more "objective" measures as meaningless. It could also be systematicity: following on previous studies and taking the time in the beginning of a study to refer to existing bodies of knowledge. In terms of "process" impact – the impact of the process of an evaluation on the program being evaluated (impact being enhancement, improvement and learning) – it could be an evaluation process that engenders a greater understanding of program elements. It could be a process intertwined with program in ways that improve delivery of educational services. And finally, it could be a process that of itself brings about a paradigm shift related to evaluation: evaluation process becoming equated with endeavor that promotes learning rather than with endeavor that measures it.

Given the very real educational needs in many developing nations, the constraints to educational delivery, and the multiple costs of conducting evaluations, ever greater efforts should be put into aligning evaluation with the overall needs of a particular educational setting. It is both responsibility and opportunity. As responsibility, it is to design and conduct our activity according to mutually agreed upon standards and common understandings. It is also to create a fair representative picture of the entity being studied that will benefit and meet the needs of both the donor population and the program population. As opportunity it is a chance to expand the expression and understanding of our practice to meet the challenges and realities of a myriad of settings. The potential is tremendous for expressions of professional practice as richly varied as the world's nations themselves, a rich global heritage.

REFERENCES

American Evaluation Association Task Force on Guiding Principles for Evaluators. (1995). Guiding principles for evaluators. *New Directions for Program Evaluation*, **66**, 19–26.

Bamberger, M. (1999). Ethical issues in conducting evaluation in international settings. In J.L. Fitzpatrick, & M. Morris (Eds.) Current & emerging ethical challenges in evaluation. *New Directions for Program Evaluation*, **82**, 89–99.

Bhola, H.S. (1997). Systems thinking, literacy practice: Planning a literacy campaign in Egypt. *Entrepreneurship, innovation and change*, **6**(1), 21–35.

Bhola, H.S. (1998). Program evaluation for program renewal: A study of the National Literacy Program in Namibia (NLPN). *Studies in Educational Evaluation*, **24**(4), 303–330.

Bollinger, D., & Hofstede, G. (1987). *Les differences culturelles dans le managements*. Paris: Les Editions Organisation.

Brunner, L., & Guzman, A. (1989). Participatory evaluation: A tool to assess projects and empower people. In R.F. Conner, & M. Hendricks (Eds.), International innovations in evaluation methodology. *New Directions for Program Evaluation*, **42**, 9–18.

Cookingham, F. (1992), Defining evaluation. *Together* **3**, 21.

Crespo, M., Soares, J.F., & de Mello e Souza, A. (2000). The Brazilian national evaluation system of basic education: Context, process and impact. *Studies in Education Evaluation*, **26**(2), 105–125.

Cronbach, L.J., et al. (1980). *Toward reform of program evaluation*. San Francisco: Josey-Bass.

Datta, L. (1999). The ethics of evaluation neutrality and advocacy. In J.L. Fitzpatrick, & M. Morris (Eds.), Current & emerging ethical challenges in evaluation. *New Directions for Program Evaluation*, **8**, 77–89.

Etounga-Manguelle, D. (2000). Does Africa need a cultural adjustment program? In L.E. Harrison, & S.P. Huntington (Eds.), *Culture matters: How values shape human progress* (pp. 65–77). Huntington, NY: Basic Books.

Feuerstein, M.T. (1986). *Partners in evaluation: Evaluating development and community programmes with participants*. London: Macmillan.

Garaway, G. (1995). Participatory evaluation. *Studies in educational evaluation*, **21**, 85–102.

Garaway, G. (1996). The case-study model: An organizational strategy for cross-cultural evaluation. *Evaluation*, **2**(2), 201–212.

Giddens, A. (1987). *Social theory and modern sociology*. Cambridge: Polity.

House, E.R. (1993). *Professional evaluation*. Newbury Park, CA: Sage.

Joint Committee on Standards for Educational Evaluation. (1994). *The program evaluation standards: How to assess evaluations of educational programs*. Thousand Oaks, CA: Sage.

Lapan, S.D. (in press), Evaluation research. In K.B. deMarrais, & S.D. Lapan (Eds.), *Approaches to research in education and the social sciences*. Mahwah, NJ: Lawrence Erlbaum.

Morris, M. (1999). Research on evaluation ethics: What have we learned and why is it Important. In J.L. Fitzpatrick & M. Morris (Eds.) Current & emerging ethical challenges in evaluation. *New Directions for Evaluation*, **82**, 89–99.

Narayan-Parker, D. (1991). *Participatory evaluation: Tools for managing change in water/sanitation*. New York: PROWESS/UNDP/IBRD/UNICEF/WHO.

Nevo, D. (2000, June). *School evaluation: Internal or external?* Paper presented at the International Seminar on School Evaluation, Seoul, Republic of Korea.

OECD. (1992). *Development assistance manual: DAC principles for effective aid*. Paris: OECD.

Rebien, C. (1996). Participatory evaluation of development assistance: Dealing with power and facilitative learning, *Evaluation*, **2**(2), 151–172.

Worthen, B.R. (1990). Program evaluation. In H.J. Walberg & G.D. Haertel (Eds.), *International encyclopedia of educational evaluation* (pp. 42–46). Oxford: Pergamon.

32
Evaluating Educational Programs and Projects in the USA

JEAN A. KING

University of Minnesota, MN, USA

The past forty years have witnessed a dramatic increase in the amount and variety of educational evaluation in the USA. Program and project evaluations in this country come in many shapes and sizes, as the following examples suggest:

- Near the end of a three-year project funded by a foundation grant that developed a critical thinking curriculum for gifted students, a building principal contacts an external evaluator to conduct a study of project outcomes.
- A federal grants administrator in a large urban school district collaborates with the district's evaluation unit to compile mandated federal program data and prepare routine reports that are sent to the state department and ultimately to Washington, DC.
- A superintendent calls a program director into her office and orders an evaluation of an expensive and controversial new program.
- An evaluation consultant has a continuing contract with an education agency to study innovative programs as they develop, often traveling to sites in a number of states.

National events triggered a rise in program evaluation from the late 1950s to the late 1970s, due in large part to the creation of federally funded education programs that mandated evaluation. Since 1980, a focus on accountability and standardized testing to measure student achievement has reduced the emphasis on program evaluation in many educational settings, despite the fact that the evaluation function is exercised to some degree in most American school districts. This chapter will discuss the evolution of American educational evaluation, its current practice, and likely future.

In beginning, it may be helpful to distinguish between educational programs and projects. Their difference lies in the scope of activities and the resources committed to them (Payne, 1994). Programs are typically long-term, "ongoing activities representing coordinated efforts planned to achieve major educational goals," for example, a district's integrated language arts program or a university's

International Handbook of Educational Evaluation, 721–732
T. Kellaghan, D.L. Stufflebeam (eds.)
© *2003 Dordrecht: Kluwer Academic Publishers. Printed in Great Britain.*

chemical engineering degree program. Educational projects, by contrast, are "short-term activities with specific objectives and allocated resources" (Nevo, 1995, p. 119), for example, a project to provide a semester's worth of multi-cultural training to a school faculty or a foundation-funded project to integrate technology into a college's classrooms. Although expected outcomes might differ, the process of evaluating educational programs and projects, however, is identical, and therefore this chapter will not distinguish between them.

THE HISTORY OF PROGRAM/PROJECT EVALUATION IN THE USA

Evaluation texts identify numerous antecedents to current practice in educational program and project evaluation – for example, ancient Chinese civil service examinations, 19th century royal commissions in Great Britain, Horace Mann's mid-19th century reports on student learning in Massachusetts schools, and Joseph Rice's turn of the 20th century exposés of ineffective spelling instruction (Cronbach et al., 1980; Worthen, Sanders, & Fitzpatrick, 1997). Broadly speaking, educational evaluation in the USA had its roots in two distinct activities – school accreditation and standardized testing – that are discussed in other sections of this handbook (see Section 6 on Student Evaluation, as well as Chapters 35 and 41).

School accreditation marked an early form of educational evaluation. Since the end of the 19th century when "schoolmen" organized regional accreditation organizations (e.g., the North Central Association) in order to create compliance models for quality schools, "school evaluation has been an integral part of the U.S.'s system of voluntary accreditation of schools" (Gallegos, 1994, p. 41). In recent years, accreditation and other school-wide improvement efforts have broadened their perspectives, moving from mere bean counting (e.g., the number of books in the library, teachers' credentials) to direct measurement of the outcomes of effective schools (e.g., student achievement on standardized measures, improved student attitudes). The earlier accreditation models have evolved to school improvement models, i.e., "towards models that focus on both performance (outcomes) and diagnostic information and data (improvement)" (Gallegos, p. 43). When coupled with site-based management/decision making, such models may hold the potential to effect continuous improvement in educational programs.

Like school accreditation, the use of standardized tests to assess student achievement has been a mainstay of educational evaluation practice for eighty years. The growth and expansion of the accountability movement in the past two decades has affirmed a central role for such tests, including the use of per-formance assessments at the classroom and district level – a fairly recent addition to the commonly used student assessment toolkit. In addition to accreditation, for the first half of the 20th century educational evaluation was in large part indistinguishable from testing and measurement. While other social scientists in the 1930s advocated "the use of rigorous research methods to assess social programs" (Rossi, Freeman, & Lipsy, 1999, p. 10), educational researchers sought improved ways of assessing student achievement in schools (Norris, 1990).

A notable example is the oft-cited Eight Year Study that brought Ralph Tyler, the man who can rightly be called the father of educational evaluation in this country, to national prominence. Starting in 1932, the Progressive Education Association secured sizeable grants (almost $700,000) to conduct a longitudinal study of approximately 3,600 students in matched pairs as they moved through 30 high schools – half experimental progressive schools and half traditional high schools – then on to colleges across the nation (Kleibard, 1995, p. 183). Tyler's evaluation innovation was to make a connection between educational outcomes and educators' intentions prior to instruction; as he and a colleague put it, "An educational program is appraised by finding out how far the objectives of the program are actually being realized" (Smith & Tyler, 1942, cited in Kleibard, 1995, p. 188). This approach – linking program objectives to outcome measures – was "to organize the tasks and goals of evaluation in a framework that was to be the dominant paradigm for almost half a century" (Baker & Niemi, 1996, p. 927). Wolf (1990) credits Tyler's approach with fostering the notion of evaluation as an integral part of the educational process. Stufflebeam and Webster (1988), however, blame the "ritualistic application" of this approach for just the opposite, i.e., for "suggesting that evaluation is applied only at the end of a project" (p. 570). They also contend that the objectives-based approach narrowed evaluation only "to those concerns evident in specified objectives" and encouraged people to "define success in terms of objectives without also evaluating the objectives" (p. 570)

In the area of social programs, "program evaluation research" – the application of social science research methods to study program effectiveness – was widespread by the end of the 1950s (Rossi et al., 1999, p. 11). In the education arena, by contrast, the quarter century from 1940 to 1965 saw a consolidation of earlier developments in program and project evaluation – improving standardized testing and teacher-made classroom tests, accreditation, and school surveys in the 1940s and the expanded use of behavioral objectives and published taxonomies of educational objectives (cognitive and affective) in the 1950s and early 1960s (Worthen et al., 1997, p. 30; see Bloom, Engelhart, Furst, Hill, & Krathwohl, 1956; and Krathwohl, Bloom, & Masia, 1964).

However, events in Washington, DC in the middle 1960s jump-started a new thrust in educational evaluation, leading to an unprecedented era of development, both practical and theoretical. Talmage (1982) points out that the fourth edition of the *Encyclopedia of Educational Research*, published in 1969, contained no entry for evaluation research (or program evaluation); yet by the end of the 1970s, numerous journals and yearbooks, new scholarly associations, and more than a 1,000 percent increase in the budget of the Office of Planning, Budgeting, and Evaluation of the U.S. Office of Education documented tremendous growth in the field (p. 593). Sharp (1981) estimated that $100 million in federal funds were spent to hire "extramural performers" to conduct educational evaluations in 1977 alone (p. 223).

The impetus for increased evaluation activity stemmed both from federal accountability mandates and from a dramatic increase in federal funding for such work. "These funds were earmarked for two distinctly different purposes at two slightly overlapping points in time: massive curriculum development efforts preceding social intervention programs" (Talmage, 1982, p. 593). In response to the Russian launch of Sputnik in 1957, the National Defense Education Act (NDEA) led to the development of the federally supported "alphabet soup curricula" of the late 1950s and early 1960s (e.g., those developed by the Biological Sciences Curriculum Study [BSCS], the Physical Sciences Study Committee [PSSC], and the Chemical Education Material Study [CHEM Study]). The nationwide implementation of these curricula created demands for large-scale evaluation efforts to demonstrate that they actually improved American students' achievement in science and mathematics. NDEA program evaluations "revealed the conceptual and methodological impoverishment of evaluation in that era" (Worthen et al., 1997, p. 30). The results of the curricular horse races between old and new curricula suggested that students learned whatever the curriculum they studied taught them; there were no universal winners or losers (Walker & Schaffarzick, 1974).

President Lyndon Johnson's War on Poverty and Great Society programs marked a second area that spurred the development of program and project evaluation. In federal offices, the mandatory implementation – at least on paper – of the Planning, Programming, and Budgeting System (PPBS) that Secretary Robert McNamara introduced to the Department of Defense under President John F. Kennedy initiated an approach to systematic evaluation over time (Cronbach et al., 1980, pp. 30–31). It was a legislative action, however, that yielded more dramatic outcomes. Worthen, Sanders, and Fitzpatrick (1997) write, "The one event that is most responsible for the emergence of contemporary program evaluation is the passage of the Elementary and Secondary Education Act (ESEA) of 1965" (p. 32). Prior to this act, only two federal programs had congressionally mandated evaluation components. By insisting that the ESEA include mandatory evaluation that would track the results of federal funding, Senator Robert F. Kennedy created an instant market for program evaluators, coupled with extensive funding to support their practice (McLaughlin, 1975).

"Through a coordinated program of federal grants and contracts supporting key university groups [during the 1960s], hotbeds of educational evaluative activity were created throughout the country .... Predictably, academics used what they knew as the basis for their strategies" (Baker & Niemi, 1996, p. 928), i.e., traditional research designs and methods. Unfortunately, "the educational community was ill-prepared to undertake such a massive amount of evaluation work" (Wolf, 1990, p. 10), and "evaluators of curriculum development efforts and those engaged in evaluation of social intervention programs soon recognized the limitations of their respective research traditions in addressing pertinent evaluation questions" (Talmage, 1982, p. 593). Cook and Shadish (1986, cited in Alkin & House, 1992) summarize the lessons learned during this stage of the field's development:

Late in the 1960s and early in the 1970s evaluation assumed the task of discovering which programs ... worked best. Most evaluators thought that social science theory would point to the clear causes of social problems and to interventions for overcoming them, that these interventions would be implemented and evaluated in ways that provided unambiguous answers, that these findings would be greeted enthusiastically by managers and policymakers, and that the problems would be solved or significantly improved. They were disappointed on all counts. (p. 463)

From the perspective of the intended users – the Congress and educators at all levels – "viewed collectively, these evaluations were of little use" (Worthen et al., 1997, p. 33). From the perspective of educational evaluation, this broad social change – the increased role of federal and state government in education with accompanying evaluation requirements – dramatically increased and helped to institutionalize the practice of educational evaluation in school districts across the United States. As Nevo (1994) notes, "local school districts became the focal point for the commitment to evaluation in the complex relationship among the various levels of the American educational system" (p. 89).

Ronald Reagan's election as President was important to the history of program evaluation in this country because, following his move to the White House, the burgeoning evaluation practice connected with increased federal funding of public education slowed dramatically. However, earlier research conducted in the late 1970s – research on program evaluation funded by the National Institute of Education (e.g., Lyon, Doscher, McGranahan, & Williams, 1978; Kennedy, Apling, & Neumann, 1980) and the deliberations of the Program Evaluation Committee of the National Research Council (National Academy of Sciences) that resulted in a report (Raizen & Rossi, 1981) – documented the status of educational evaluation shortly before Reagan took office. King, Thompson, and Pechman (1982) summarize the outcomes of three nationwide surveys of the evaluation units of large city school districts (Lyon et al., 1978; Rose & Birdseye, 1982; Webster & Stufflebeam, 1978): district personnel supported by local funds – not external consultants – conducted the evaluations; "evaluation" in these district contexts meant testing programs; and there was little emphasis on instructional or program improvement. At the local level, in large and small districts alike, federal program evaluations were largely compliance-driven (Holley, 1981) and funded with program grant funds (Reisner, 1981).

Holley (1981) described the work of a local district evaluator. In many districts, especially those that were not large or urban, "public school evaluation is an all-consuming role. An evaluator works 12 months, with summer bringing heaviest work load; because resources are often inadequate, the workday and workweek are far longer than those of the average worker" (p. 261). People given the work of evaluation might have "neither training nor experience in evaluation methodology, measurement, or statistical analysis" (p. 258), and "enormous variation both from state to state and from district to district" was the norm (p. 246).

As noted previously, the rapid expansion of program evaluation slowed dramatically after 1980. The fiscal conservatism Reagan directed at social programs shifted the field's focus to matters financial – to "assessing the expenditures of social programs in comparison to their benefits and to demonstrating fiscal accountability and effective management" (Rossi et al., 1999, p. 18; see also House, 1993). Much of the responsibility for evaluation simultaneously shifted to the states, many of which did "not have the capabilities or the will to undertake the rigorous evaluation needed" (Rossi et al., 1999, p. 19). Webster (1987) summarized the effect of these shifts:

> The golden age of evaluation, from a funding standpoint, is over. The level of formative and summative program evaluation in the nation's public schools has declined precipitously. The testing function remains as a major consumer of resources and a major barometer by which school districts are judged (appropriately or inappropriately) …. What has happened is that the data for program improvement emphasis of the late sixties and seventies has been largely replaced by the accountability movement of the eighties. (p. 49)

More than a decade after the publication of Webster's article, this educational accountability movement has not only remained, but intensified. President George W. Bush's proposed national testing program for public school students in the USA is a highly visible reminder of the centrality of testing to educational evaluation in the first decade of the 21st century.

EDUCATIONAL PROGRAM EVALUATION PRACTICE IN THE USA

Program evaluations in the USA can focus on different types of objects. Baker and Niemi (1996) identify two types of programs that are most commonly evaluated: innovative programs and complex, large-scale programs. "The most commonly evaluated programs are stand-alone, innovative programs," they write. "Thousands of evaluations of specific interventions have been conducted, probably accounting for the lion's share of evaluation efforts undertaken in the past 20 years [mid 1970s-mid 1990s]" (Baker & Niemi, 1996, p. 933). The reasons for evaluating these innovative programs and projects are typically externally motivated, often as a condition of funding, and deal simultaneously with formative and summative evaluation. Because they are innovative – outside of traditional practice – these programs and their evaluations "do not threaten the educational status quo directly, nor do they immediately impinge on mainstream educational practice" (Baker & Niemi, 1996, p. 934). Either internal or external evaluators may conduct such studies, examples of which include the innovative curriculum projects of the 1960s (e.g., BSCS biology, which continues its evolution), many federally funded Title III innovations, local implementations of the Drug Abuse

Resistance Education (DARE) program, and projects funded by the Fund for the Improvement of Post-Secondary Education (FIPSE).

The second type of evaluation object identified by Baker and Niemi (1996) is the complex, large-scale program like Headstart or Title I – programs that have multiple sites, often across the country.[1] Given the multiple actors engaged in such programs, these evaluations take on a complexity that unavoidably challenges those involved, evaluators and politicians alike:

> Evaluations of large-scale programs almost always have to serve a combina-
> tion of needs: to account for the use of public funds, to examine whether
> the intervention is operating as intended, to shore up or perhaps undermine
> political and public support, and to determine at the point of reconsideration
> or reauthorization whether the programs have been successful enough to
> continue. Such evaluations are often thought to be negative political acts
> (Baker & Niemi, 1996, p. 934).

External evaluators or teams of evaluators typically conduct such studies in order to emphasize the objectivity of the evaluation process.

In addition to innovative programs and large-scale, complex programs, there is a third target for program evaluation: ongoing curricula or existing programs. Internal evaluators often conduct these evaluations, and the concept of developmental evaluation (Patton, 1997) is helpful in framing studies of programs that are neither large-scale nor innovative. Examples include curriculum self-studies – for example, examining a K-12 district social studies scope and sequence or focusing on the course offerings of a single department – and evaluations of standing programs, for example, a teacher education program, the middle school implementation in a district, or an undergraduate advising program.

Regardless of the program or project identified for study, evaluators in the United States – formative and summative, internal and external – use a variety of approaches and methods at the local, state, and federal levels. Evaluation approaches, which are linked closely to purpose, have evolved over time to create a wide variety of options, moving from the dominance of the accreditation and Tylerian goal-oriented versions discussed earlier. To compile an exhaustive listing of these approaches is beyond the scope of this chapter (see Worthen et al., 1997). Indeed, King (1999) notes that there are easily over two dozen adjectives that can be attached to the word *evaluation* to identify different writers' approaches (e.g., goal-free, discrepancy, free-range, democratic-deliberative, and so on). There are, however, several commonly used approaches that have been influential in the field and exemplify its diversity:

- Educational evaluators used formal experiments and quasi-experiments to study the effects of large federal programs in the 1960s, and the experimental paradigm remains the backbone of studies designed to demonstrate causation.
- The notion that evaluators should provide information directly to decision makers marked an important development in the field in the late 1960s

(Stufflebeam, 1971). The CIPP model, for example, identified four areas of potential study: context, input, process, and product. More than twenty years later, the Center for Research on Educational Accountability and Teacher Evaluation (CREATE) used these as the basis for four core recommendations for "achieving sound educational evaluation of U.S. education" (Stufflebeam, 1994; see also Chapter 2).

• In the consumer-oriented approach to evaluation, programs or projects are evaluated using set criteria and standards, just as products are in a *Consumer Reports* study. One way to do this is by using a Key Evaluation Checklist (Scriven, 1991).

• Michael Quinn Patton's utilization-focused evaluation encourages evaluators to frame studies around " intended use of data by intended users," targeting specific individuals throughout the evaluation in an effort to increase the likelihood of use (Patton, 1997; see also Chapter 11).

• Responsive evaluation emerged in the early 1970s and emphasized responding to the concerns and issues of program or project stakeholders, rather than attending solely to "preordinate" design issues (Stake, 1975; see also Chapter 3). Over the years, this notion of responsiveness has evolved to include the active involvement of program staff and participants in participatory forms of evaluation, including fourth generation evaluation (Guba & Lincoln, 1989) and empowerment evaluation (Fetterman, 1994).

• Theory-driven evaluation (Chen, 1990; Chen & Rossi, 1983) bases studies on the theory underlying programs, enabling evaluators to address both informal and formal theories in developing program descriptions and studying effects.

In light of the numerous approaches extant in the field, Baker and Niemi (1996) document the "striking range of conceptual schemes that have been turned to the purpose of sorting and comparing evaluation models" – they describe seven such efforts – but label the existing typologies "somewhat limited in their practical applications" (p. 931).

The absence of an overarching typology or a single integrative approach potentially creates both flexibility and frustration for evaluators and their clients. On the one hand, the wide diversity of approaches suggests that a well-versed and skilled evaluator can custom tailor an appropriate approach to virtually any evaluation context. On the other hand, this diversity may prove challenging to novice evaluators and confusing to evaluation clients as they seek to commission a useful study. Although Michael Scriven has framed the "transdiscipline" of evaluation (Scriven, 1994), the absence of a generally accepted, unified framework is a notable challenge in the field's theoretical development.

The implications for practice are, fortunately, less daunting. As Stufflebeam (1994) notes, "the importance of the different viewpoints on educational evaluation is not in their distinctiveness but in what particular concepts, strategies, and procedures they can contribute collectively to the planning, execution, reporting, and use of sound evaluation" (p. 5). Baker and Niemi (1996) provide a pragmatic question for evaluators choosing among competing approaches: "What is likely to be the most effective approach to serve particular purposes in a particular context?" (p. 932). What is clearly evident is the importance of evaluators being well-grounded in the full range of available approaches, which may be a challenge given the lack of systematic training and credentialing of program evaluators in the USA.

Regardless of the approach selected, program and project evaluators use a variety of data collection methods as they conduct studies. From an early reliance on quantitative data, evaluators over the past two decades have broadened their methodological perspective so that qualitative data are now commonplace and mixed methods are widely accepted in practice (Greene, Caricelli, & Graham, 1989). Evaluators use a variety of procedures for collecting data, including the following: tests and psychological scales; surveys; individual or group interviews, focus group interviews, and polls; observations and site visits; unobtrusive measures; content analysis of existing documents and data; and less common procedures such as the Delphi technique or the Q-sort.

WHITHER PROGRAM AND PROJECT EVALUATION IN THE USA?

The first years of the new millennium find district-based educational program and project evaluation in the USA on the horns of a dilemma. On the one hand, evaluation processes of a sort have been institutionalized in schools across the nation where a limited version of evaluation related to standardized testing programs is steady work due to increasing numbers of data-driven accountability mandates, both internal and external. Despite a decline in federally supported evaluation for the past two decades, "the function of evaluation appears to have been institutionalized in enough agencies that the career opportunities for evaluators once again look promising" (Worthen et al., 1997, p. 43). The rapid development of technology (e.g., management information systems, inexpensive personal computers, the Internet, and hand-held devices) has enabled districts to compile, communicate, and use data in ways that were unimaginable even ten years ago. Externally funded innovations and federal programs continue to require evaluation, and evaluation is surely alive and well and living in district evaluation units, often staffed (at least in larger districts) by trained professionals with expertise in evaluation, measurement, and statistics. Professional organizations with an evaluation focus provide networks of support for these individuals.

On the other hand, given their standardized testing and accountability focus, these evaluation units risk serving a "signal function," providing compliance indicators to people both inside and outside the district (King & Pechman, 1984; Stufflebeam & Welch, 1986) rather than generating information directly relevant to improving instructional programs and practices. Program evaluation activities distinct from norm referenced and/or standards-based testing programs may find little support in the ongoing competition for district funds, a striking parallel to the situation of large city school evaluation units twenty years ago (Lyon et al.,

1978; King, 2002). Current efforts in "value added" teacher evaluation, for example – seeking to identify the specific learning outcomes attributable to individual teachers – may provide excellent information to administrators, but prove less useful to teachers seeking to improve their practice (Mendro & Bembry, 2000). School-based evaluation and accreditation efforts may offer some hope by involving school communities in collecting and analyzing relevant data, but, as Baker and Niemi (1996) note, "the ability to provide the time and resources necessary for true local engagement in evaluation may be limited in the short term by both will and economics" (p. 938). Sanders (2000) speaks to the need for school districts to find the resources and the will to conduct program evaluations in this environment.

This is not to say, however, that program and project evaluation is likely to fade from the evaluation landscape in the USA. Triggered by events at the national level, the emergence of evaluation as a profession has created an ongoing role for evaluation in the development of educational programs and projects in a number of settings, funded in a variety of ways. The concept of organizational learning – building evaluation capacity within organizations over time (Preskill & Torres, 1999; King, 2000) – further expands evaluation's role and potential for supporting change and may well mark the integration of program and project evaluation into the ongoing work of educational organizations.

ENDNOTE

[1] Such large-scale program evaluations are often part of educational policy studies conducted to help policymakers determine their course of action. While policy evaluation may differ from program evaluation in its scope, it clearly shares conceptual and methodological similarities.

REFERENCES

Alkin, M.C., & House, E.R. (1992). Evaluation of programs. In M.C. Alkin (Ed.), *Encyclopedia of educational research* (6th ed.) (Vol. 2, pp. 462–467). New York: Macmillan Publishing Co.

Baker, E.L., & Niemi, D. (1996). School and program evaluation. In D.C. Berliner & R.C. Calfee (Eds.), *The handbook of educational psychology* (pp. 926–942). New York: Macmillan.

Bloom, B.S., Engelhart, M.D., Furst, E.J., Hill, W.H., & Krathwohl, D.R. (1956). *Taxonomy of educational objectives: Handbook I. Cognitive domain*. New York: David McKay.

Chen, H. (1990). *Theory-driven evaluation*. Newbury Park, CA: Sage.

Chen, H., & Rossi, P.H. (1983). Evaluating with sense: The theory-driven approach. *Evaluation Review*, **7**, 283–302.

Cronbach, L.J., Ambron, S.R., Dornbusch, S.M., Hess, R.D., Hornik, R.C., Phillips, D.C., Walker, D.F., & Weiner, S.S. (1980). *Toward reform of program evaluation*. San Francisco: Jossey-Bass Publishers.

Fetterman, D.M. (1994). Empowerment evaluation. *Evaluation Practice*, **15**, 1–15.

Gallegos, A. (1994). Meta-evaluation of school evaluation models. *Studies in Educational Evaluation*, **20**, 41–54.

Greene, J.C., Caricelli, V.J., & Graham, W.F. (1989). Toward a conceptual framework for mixed-method evaluation designs. *Educational Evaluation and Policy Analysis*, **11**, 255–274.

Guba, E.G., & Lincoln, Y.S. (1989). *Fourth generation evaluation*. Thousand Oaks, CA: Sage.

Holley, F.M. (1981). How the evaluation system works: The state and local levels. In Raizen, S.A., & Rossi, P.H. (Eds.), *Program evaluation in education: When? how? to what ends?* (pp. 246–274). Washington, DC: National Academy Press.

House, E.R. (1993). *Professional evaluation: Social impact and political consequences*. Newbury Park, CA: Sage Publications.

Kennedy, M.M., Apling, R., & Neumann, W.F. (1980). *The role of evaluation and test information in public schools*. Cambridge, MA: The Huron Institute.

King, J.A. (1999, June). *Making evaluations useful*. Paper presented at the annual meeting of the American Cancer Society's Collaborative Evaluation Fellows Program, Atlanta, GA.

King, J.A. (2000, November). *Building evaluation capacity in Lake Wobegone ISD: How many Minnesotans does it take to use data?* Paper presented at the annual meeting of the American Evaluation Association, Honolulu, HI.

King, J.A. (2002, Spring). Building evaluation capacity in a school district. In Compton, D.W., Baizerman, M., & Stockdill, S.H. (Eds.), *The art, craft, and science of evaluation capacity building. New Directions in Evaluation*, **93**, 63–80.

King, J.A., & Pechman, E.M. (1984). Pinning a wave to the shore: Conceptualizing school evaluation use. *Educational Evaluation and Policy Analysis*, **6**(3), 241–251.

King, J.A., Thompson, B., & Pechman, E.M. (1982). *Improving evaluation use in local schools*. (Final report of NIE Grant G-80-0082). New Orleans, LA: New Orleans Public Schools. (ERIC Document Reproduction Service No. ED 214 998).

Kleibard, H.M. (1995). *The struggle for the American curriculum, 1893–1958* (2nd ed.). New York: Routledge.

Krathwohl, D.R., Bloom, B.S., & Masia, B.B. (1964). *Taxonomy of educational objectives: Handbook II. Affective domain*. New York: David McKay.

Lyon, C.D., Doscher, L., McGranahan, P., & Williams, R. (1978). *Evaluation and school districts*. Los Angeles: Center for the Study of Evaluation.

McLaughlin, M.W. (1975). *Evaluation and reform: The Elementary and Secondary Education Act of 1965*. Cambridge, MA: Ballinger.

Mendro, R., & Bembry, K. (2000, April). *School evaluation: A change in perspective*. Paper presented at the annual meeting of the American Educational Research Association. New Orleans, LA.

Nevo, D. (1994). Combining internal and external evaluation: A case for school-based evaluation. *Studies in Educational Evaluation*, **20**, 87–98.

Nevo, D. (1995). *School-based evaluation: A dialogue for school improvement*. New York: Elsevier Science Inc.

Norris, N. (1990). *Understanding educational evaluation*. New York: St. Martin's Press.

Patton, M.Q. (1997). *Utilization-focused evaluation* (3rd ed.). Thousand Oaks, CA: Sage Publications.

Payne, D.A. (1994). *Designing educational project and program evaluation: A practical overview based on research and experience*. Norwell, MA: Kluwer Academic Publishers.

Preskill, H., & Torres, R.T. (1999). *Evaluative inquiry for learning in organizations*. Thousand Oaks, CA: Sage Publications.

Raizen, S.A., & Rossi, P.H. (Eds.). (1981). *Program evaluation in education: When? how? to what ends?* Washington, DC: National Academy Press.

Reisner, E.R. (1981). Federal evaluation activities in education: An overview. In Raizen, S.A., & Rossi, P.H. (Eds.), *Program evaluation in education: When? how? to what ends?* (Appendix A, pp. 195–216). Washington, DC: National Academy Press.

Rose, J.S., & Birdseye, A.T. (1982, April). *A study of research and evaluation offices and office functions in the public schools*. Paper presented at the annual meeting of the American Educational Research Association, New York, NY.

Rossi, P.H., Freeman, H.E., & Lipsey, M.W. (1999). *Evaluation: A systematic approach* (6th ed.). Thousand Oaks, CA: Sage Publications.

Sanders, J.R. (2000, April). *Strengthening evaluation use in public education*. Paper presented at the annual meeting of the American Educational Research Association, New Orleans, LA.

Scriven, M. (1991). *Evaluation thesaurus* (4th ed.). Newbury Park, CA: Sage.

Scriven, M. (1994). Evaluation as a discipline. *Studies in Educational Evaluation*, **20**, 147–166.

Sharp, L.M. (1981). Performers of federally funded evaluation studies. In Raizen, S.A., & Rossi, P.H. (Eds.), *Program evaluation in education: When? how? to what ends?* (Appendix B, pp. 217–245). Washington, DC: National Academy Press.

Stake, R.E. (1975). *Evaluating the arts in education: A responsive approach*. Columbus, OH: Merrill.

Stufflebeam, D.L. (1971). The relevance of the CIPP evaluation model for educational accountability. *Journal of Research and Development in Education*, **5**, 19–25.

Stufflebeam, D.L. (1994). Introduction: Recommendations for improving evaluations in the U.S. public schools. *Studies in Educational Evaluation*, **20**, 3–21.

Stufflebeam, D.L., & Webster, W.J. (1988). Evaluation as an administrative function. In N.J. Boyan (Ed.), *Handbook of research on educational administration* (pp. 569–601). New York: Longman.

Stufflebeam, D.L., & Welch, W.L. (1986). Review of research on program evaluation in United States school districts. *Educational Administration Quarterly*, **22**, 150–170.

Talmage, H. (1982). Evaluation of programs. In H.E. Mitzel (Ed.), *Encyclopedia of educational research* (5th ed.) (pp. 592–611). New York: The Free Press.

Walker, D.F., & Schaffarzick, J. (1974). Comparing curricula. *Review of Educational Research*, **44**, 83–111.

Webster, W.J. (1987). The practice of evaluation in the public schools. In T.C. Dunham (Ed.), *The practice of evaluation: Proceedings of the Minnesota Evaluation Conference*. Minneapolis, MN: Minnesota Research and Evaluation Center.

Webster, W.J., & Stufflebeam, D.L. (1978, April). *The state of theory and practice in educational evaluation in large urban school districts.* Paper presented at the annual meeting of the American Educational Research Association, Toronto, Ontario.

Wolf, R.M. (1990). *Evaluation in education: Foundations of competency assessment and program review.* New York: Praeger Publishers.

Worthen, B.R., Sanders, J.R., & Fitzpatrick, J.L. (1997). *Program evaluation: Alternative approaches and practical guidelines* (2nd ed.). New York: Longman.

33
Evaluating Educational Programs and Projects in Canada

ALICE DIGNARD

Ministère des Ressources naturelles, Quebec, Canada

Like other countries, Canada cannot escape from the worldwide movement toward increased accountability of public services including the education system. All education institutions – public or private, large or small, elementary-level up to university-level instruction – aim at producing the highest quality learning experience for every Canadian. Furthermore, they must demonstrate that they are executing their educational mission effectively in a more and more competitive climate. How did we get here?

Let's recap some historical facts. Dennisson and Gallagher (1986) stated that "the decade of the 1960's was truly a 'golden age' for public education in Canada" (p. 11). The public demand for more advanced education, the need to adapt to changes in technologies, and the need to meet the demands of the labour market and industry coincided with the financial capability of governments in Canada to respond favourably to these demands. It resulted in the introduction of new concepts of accessibility to higher or postsecondary education and the establishment of new institutions and new curriculum, including the technical and vocational training. According to these authors the term accountability was not frequently used:

> The emphasis at that time was on expanding access to post-secondary education as the improvement of accessibility was a dominant goal of virtually all colleges, technical institutions, and universities [...]. Colleges were implicitly accountable for making it possible for more students to obtain more kinds of post-secondary education. And they did the job well: more than 300,000 full-time students now attend Canada's colleges. (Dennisson & Gallagher, 1986, p. 252)

Then, in the early 1980s, came the financial problems facing all governments. Education was definitely in competition with other public priorities. The reductions in government grants both at the federal and provincial levels required more responsibilities to meet the challenge of ensuring the highest

International Handbook of Educational Evaluation, 733–750
T. Kellaghan, D.L. Stufflebeam (eds.)
© 2003 Dordrecht: Kluwer Academic Publishers. Printed in Great Britain.

quality in education, to demonstrate that resources are not wasted, and to adapt to the changing needs of learners and of society. Parents and consumers were also asking for solid evidence of graduate employability.

Furthermore, many commissions, parliamentary committees, and advisory panels around the country recommended – in the context of deregulation and decentralization of governments' responsibilities to the lower level – processes that allow the assessment of performance in education institutions. The search for quality in education, the task of continuous improvement, and the demonstration of the value and quality of the programs or the schools are the main targets of effective evaluation.

Everyone is for quality and improvement, but now let us see how good intentions have been translated into action. This chapter will give an overview of some evaluation bodies, processes, and projects that have been put in place to permit the implementation of educational programs evaluation in Canada. This also means that it will not be possible to cover everything coast-to-coast. Through a variety of concrete examples, mainly from higher level education, I will try to show that there is an increasing concern for the implementation of a lasting evaluation culture. But before anything else, the first part of this chapter will introduce the reader to the educational system in Canada.

THE EDUCATIONAL SYSTEM IN CANADA

Canada has 10 provinces and 3 territories,[1] with a population of more than 30 million (national census: summer 1996). The Canadian Constitution grants the provinces full jurisdiction with respect to education. Therefore education is the responsibility of each one of them. Developed under historical and cultural heritage, the educational system varies from province to province. On the whole, most provinces and territories provide pre-elementary programs (one year of pre-school programs or kindergarten to five year olds), six to eight years of elementary school, four or five years of secondary education (high school), and three or four years at the university undergraduate level. The secondary level offers a great variety of vocational programs (job training) as well as academic. In brief, schooling is generally required from age 6 or 7 to age 16, and once secondary school has been successfully completed – that is to say after 12 years of schooling – students may go directly to university or to the network of technical colleges.

Québec is an exception: It's the only province with a college education level, which falls between the 11 years of compulsory schooling (primary and secondary education) and university and provides both technical and pre-university education. These public general and vocational colleges are also called *cégeps* (from the French *collège d'enseignement général et professionnel*). The pre-university studies last for 2 years and constitute a route to university. The technical studies last for 3 years and are a preparation for the labour market. Meeting all the specific conditions, some of the technical sector graduates may also be allowed to attend university (Commission d'évaluation de l'enseignement collegial [CEEC], 1997, p. 3).

According to the Canadian Education Statistics Council, in 1993–94 "there were a total of 16,233 public and private educational institutions in Canada [...]. Of these, 12,441 offered elementary instruction; 3,509, secondary education; 206, college-level education; and 77, university-level instruction" (Canadian Education Statistics Council, 1996, p. 14). From year to year, the number of colleges and universities is quite stable, but the number of elementary and secondary institutions can vary from one jurisdiction to another.

CREATING NEW EVALUATION BODIES

The next step is to introduce some of the evaluation bodies that can provide various values and practices that contribute to the establishment of education evaluation in Canada. These structures can be at a national or provincial level and involve high school education and higher education. In this second part, two agencies working at a provincial level are described. These agencies, put in place in the 1990's, have obtained substantial results.

Overview of Two Provincial Bodies

Commission d'Évaluation de l'Enseignement Collégial (Québec, 1993)

In the summer of 1993, the National Assembly of Québec set up the Commission d'évaluation de l'enseignement collegial – College Education Evaluation Commission (CEEC). This happened in the context of the reform called *College Education Renewal*, which sought to provide all Quebecers with "access to a high-caliber, top-quality college education that enables them to attain the highest possible skills standards" (Ministère de l'enseignement supérieur et de la science, 1993, p. 13). In fact, this *Renewal* caused an increase in the colleges' academic responsibilities which was counterbalanced by more rigorous mechanisms for external evaluation, the CEEC for instance.

In the process of creating the Commission, an autonomous body, the Government simultaneously abolished the Colleges Council and the Universities Council. This evaluation body consists of three commissioners,[2] one of whom is the chairperson. For the financial year 2000–2001, the CEEC had a budget of $1.9 million and 28 permanent employees, 16 of them professional analysts or evaluators.

The Commission's mandate includes evaluating the quality of the implementation of the educational programs provided in Québec colleges, and it also involves evaluating the institutional policies adopted by the colleges on evaluation of student achievement and on program evaluation. To do this, the legislation attributes three main powers to the Commission: the power to verify, the power to make recommendation to the colleges and to the Minister, and a declaratory power. More precisely it can:

- evaluate how some or all institutions implement any college program of studies it designates;
- develop evaluation criteria and instruments and ensure their dissemination; form advisory committees and determine their powers, duties, and operating rules; retain the services of experts;
- conduct an evaluation whenever it deems expedient and according to the procedures it establishes;
- recommend that the educational institution take measures to enhance the quality of its evaluation policies, programs, or program implementation. These measures can also concern the organization, operation and academic management of the institution;
- make recommendations to the Minister on any matter relating to programs of studies and evaluation policies, including any governmental or ministerial policy affecting college management of programs of studies and evaluation;
- recommend that the Minister authorize an educational institution to award the Diploma of College Studies;
- make public its evaluation report in whatever manner it deems appropriate;
- authorize individuals to visit any educational institution being evaluated and gather whatever information they require.[3] (CEEC, 1994, pp. 5–6)

The Commission enjoys considerable autonomy in its work. Its mission focuses on developing the quality of college education and, in this perspective, one of its main enterprises is to evaluate the implementation of programs established by the Minister of Education, as well as those established by the 146 public and private college educational institutions.

To carry out its mission as rigorously as possible, the Commission uses techniques and procedures that are widely used in higher education evaluation agencies in Canada, the United States, and Europe. The evaluation model is based on a self-evaluation process conducted by the colleges with the help of a guide provided by the Commission. The evaluation approach chosen enables colleges and their academic staff to be directly involved in the process of evaluation. Self-evaluation also gives colleges the opportunity to take into account their culture, their structures, and the context in which the program is implemented.

Furthermore, the Commission attaches great importance to teachers' involvement in the process. They can be members of an advisory body at the Commission, or members of a self-evaluation committee at their college, they can voice their opinions on program strengths and weaknesses, they can sit as experts in their fields of study on a CEEC's visiting committee to an institution, and more recently they can even work at the Commission to acquire the technical expertise to perform evaluation when they return to their college. For this last purpose, the Commission keeps a few remunerated positions for teachers who are loaned by their colleges, generally for a term of two years. There is a sincere belief in the idea that the teachers and executive staff are a deciding factor in the improvement of a program. With the assistance of the Commission, the colleges are in fact developing their own evaluation expertise.

Each evaluation process essentially includes the following steps:

- formation of an advisory body by the Commission and the production of a specific guide for the program under scrutiny;
- self-evaluation of the program by the institution and preparation of the self-evaluation report to be transmitted to the Commission;
- analysis of this report and visit to the institution by Commission with a committee of experts from appropriate working fields and academic experts from colleges and universities;
- drafting of the Commission's preliminary report; college reactions and discussions on the report;
- producing the final public report, which is sent to the institution and the Minister of Education – the final report may contain suggestions for improvements as well as recommendations and this report is also available on the Commission's Internet site;
- follow-up measures.

More precisely, the judgement given by the Commission on a program takes generally one of these three forms; the Commission recognizes the quality of the program, the program presents some strengths and weaknesses, or the program is problematic. For possible improvements, the Commission will refer an issue to the college using recommendations, suggestions, and comments. In approximately 95 percent evaluation reports produced, there is one or more recommendations. One year after the release of the final report, the college has to make a follow-up report to explain to the Commission what measures were put in place to meet all of its recommendations. When the analysis of the follow-up is satisfactory, a summary of the actions that have been carried out is added to the final report already on the Commission's Internet site.[4] Most of the time, this part is taken seriously by the colleges, and many of them also indicate what measures they took to meet all the suggestions and other comments found in the evaluation report.

The Commission will also gather data on graduation rates, course success rates, perseverance in the program, etc. Most of these data are collected by the department of Education. However, the college's organizational culture; its location, the number and the kind of educational programs it offers; and the composition of its student body, including their average mark obtained in high school, are some of the factors that differentiate one college from another and are taken into account. With the adoption by each college of an institutional policy on program evaluation came the establishment, by each college, of a functional information system for the programs. This gives the colleges the opportunity to develop their own indicators suitable for their particular situation and characteristics. With a qualitative and formative approach, the Commission's aim is to help to improve the quality of education. There is no grading or ranking of institutions.

Since its creation, the Commission has conducted six major evaluations: *Technical Education Programs in Early Childhood Education (1994–1996)*, *Computer Sciences Programs (1994–1996)*, *Social Sciences Program (1995–1997)*, *Business Administration Technology and Cooperation Sectors Programs (1996–1999)*, *Programs Leading to an Attestation of College Studies* (AEC)[5] *in the Private and Non Subsidized Institutions (1997–1999)*, and the *General Education Component of Programs of Studies (1997–2001)*. Each evaluation was done simultaneously in all colleges offering the program.

In the fall of 2000, the Commission was engaged in the evaluation of the *Implementation of the Institutional Policy on Program Evaluation* (IPPE) in all the colleges that offer programs leading to the Diploma of College Studies (DEC). This time the Commission required that each college designate a program to be evaluated. More precisely, the program was chosen according to their own priority and needs. This evaluation is also the first to be carried out in the absence of specific guidelines provided by the Commission. The responsibilities and the self-evaluation process, and procedure are described in the college's program evaluation policy. This also means that the Commission recognizes that there are different ways to establish mechanisms leading to effective evaluation. Therefore, the purpose of this project, still active in 2001, is to prove that the self-evaluation was done in accordance with the college's policy and to demonstrate its efficacy.

More than 600 evaluation reports to the colleges have been produced under these processes. To ensure openness, transparency, and real public access to the results, the Commission has decided to disclose the entire contents of its evaluation's reports on its own Web site.[4] On this site you can also find all its publications. As we can see, the Commission's autonomy is also apparent in the way it releases the results of its evaluations to the public. This was made possible because the legislation provided provisions where the Commission was obligated to send a copy of its evaluation report to every educational institution concerned and to the Minister. The Act specifies also that "the report shall be made public by the Commission in the manner it considers appropriate" (Gouvernement du Québec, 1993, chapter 26).

In addition, an institutional evaluation was launched in June 2000. This new process has three objectives:

(1) on the one hand, it will help the colleges fulfill even more fully their educational mission;
(2) on the other hand, it will testify to the efforts the colleges invest in reaching their objectives and to the results they obtain;
(3) finally, in the medium term, it will use the institutional evaluation to justify its decision to recommend that the college be authorized to grant the Diploma of College Studies (CEEC, 2000, p. 1).

As mentioned previously, this project was undertaken because the legislation establishing the Commission stipulates that it "may recommend to the educational institution [...] measures concerning the organization, operation and academic management of the institution" (Gouvernement du Québec, 1993, article 17). Furthermore, the Commission can "recommend to the Minister that an educational institution be authorized to award the Diploma of College Studies" (Gouvernement du Québec, 1993, article 17). For the moment, this sanction is an exclusive right of the Minister. After developing its own culture of evaluation and through self-evaluation of a certain number of programs, the Commission believes that it's now time to introduce "a continuous and concerted process of analysis and appreciation of the carrying out of the educational mission of an institution": institutional evaluation (CEEC, 2000, p. 3). The Commission has released guidelines outlining this process.

The Commission, through an interactive process, has covered a lot of ground and throughout the last seven years has implemented program evaluation in the *cégep* system based on these main features:

- The program evaluation process relies on the participation of people who are involved in local implementation of the program to be evaluated (teachers, management, support staff). It is clear to the Commission that the teachers are central to pedagogical activities and they have a key role to play in any evaluation process.
- The Commission uses the following six criteria to evaluate a program: the program's relevance; the program's coherence; the value of teaching methods and student supervision including appropriate support; the appropriateness of human, material and financial resources according to education needs; the program's effectiveness; and the quality of program management.
- The Commission uses its power of recommendation to identify ways of improving the quality of the programs.
- The program evaluation reports on each college are put on the Commission's Web site; this gives a public access to the results.
- The follow-up is taken seriously; the college has a year to implement the Commission's recommendations and to send in a follow-up report.
- With the adoption of an *Institutional Policy on Program Evaluation* (IPPE), each college has to put in place not only an evaluation process but also an information system to monitor their programs. Qualitative and quantitative indicators have been developed by the colleges and efforts are being made to incorporate a variety of assessment information, including periodic follow-ups with graduates, and to incorporate data from the province and other sources. The colleges are in the process of developing more comprehensive systems.
- From an organizational perspective, the institutional evaluation will commit the colleges to a process of continuous improvement. This new process will not reduce the importance of program evaluation.

It is clear that the colleges in the province of Québec have more responsibilities toward making college education a success. Working within budgetary restraints, they are finding new ways to fulfill their primary role and the search for quality in education is an endless movement.

Manitoba School Improvement Program Inc. (Manitoba, 1991)

Established in 1991, the Manitoba School Improvement Program Inc. (MSIP) is another example of a project that is supporting, in this case, secondary school initiatives for more effective education. Approximately 30 secondary schools have received grants to support their improvement efforts including evaluation projects. For the MSIP, evaluation is a key aspect of the process, following Fetterman's view on empowerment evaluation. This approach uses "evaluation concepts, techniques, and findings to foster improvement and self-determination" (Lee, 1999, p. 157, quoted Fetterman, 1996, p. 4). Fetterman also says that "evaluators serve as coaches or facilitators to help others conduct a self-evaluation" (Fetterman, 1996, p. 11).

The MSIP, a quite unique organization in Canada, is in fact financially supported by the Walter and Duncan Gordon Foundation, a Canadian charitable foundation. In 1997 it became a "non-profit, non-governmental organization, independent organization" (Lee, 1999, p. 157). MSIP is dedicated to supporting youth, and especially at-risk students, through the improvement of public secondary schools in Manitoba, the province the Foundation selected as its testing ground. MSIP's approach to evaluation began with a participatory approach and then moved into an empowerment model of evaluation. MSIP strongly believes "that having the teachers who are the 'owners and the doers' of their own evaluation processes is indeed a powerful tool in stimulating and sustaining significant school improvement" (Lee, 1999, p. 159). From the beginning in 1991 to 1999, the Foundation has invested more than $5 million to support innovative secondary school projects. In addition, MSIP schools receive professional support for skill development, including support for program evaluation.

The MSIP infrastructure includes a full-time program coordinator, a part-time evaluation consultant, and an advisory committee that provides advice to school communities. More recently, other consultants and volunteers have also joined in the project. This agency can provide external help to school personnel for program evaluation. Such help would include consultative and technical support to understand the importance of evaluation (evaluation workshops, consultative assistance) and to teach school personnel how to collect data and use them for planning, decision making, and problem solving. Various ways are used to collect information: surveys, focus groups, interviews, reflection meetings, visits to other schools, and learning from each other. The MSIP participatory approach involves stakeholders: teachers, school staff, and students. From Lee's perspective (1999), the MSIP evaluation consultant, "teachers in some schools have taken extensive ownership of the evaluation process, something for which, historically, they have not had responsibility." She adds, "this has truly empowered teachers to be key players in transforming their schools" (Lee, 1999, p. 156). The next step was to involve students as researchers or evaluators. The MSIP has had experiences with students in half a dozen schools. "One of MSIP's goals is to further assist in the development of student empowerment through evaluation project" (Lee, 1999, p. 173).

For example, a group of 18 students at three high schools in the district of the Seven Oaks School Division and their three teachers participated in a follow-up study of former high school students. This project was a part of the requirements to complete their Language and Transactional English course. With the assistance of the MSIP evaluation consultant, a series of questions, including the students' suggestions, was designed to be used in telephone interviews. In one month the students had conducted 410 telephone interviews out of a potential population of about 1300 former students in the two years chosen for the study. This sample represented approximately 30 percent of the total population. The students worked in teams to interpret their school's data and prepared several presentations which they gave at the district high school conference, at their school's staff meeting, at a meeting of the school board, as well as in their own classrooms to their peers. Finally, the students wrote research reports, and their schools were able to use their findings in their school planning and evaluation process.

This sort of research project, done by 12th grade students or any students ending their program, is not only a great model for curricular activity or a comprehensive assessment that could constitute a summative conclusion to their studies, but it is also an example of how MSIP has in recent years encouraged significant people in the school community to become involved in the processes of inquiry and data collection. Furthermore,

> Student voice in this case had the opportunity to be credible and information-based. The process pushes thinking about the potential of evaluation as a tool for empowerment. [...] the potential that evaluation can become a tool for learning and a tool for change. (Bryant, Lee, & Zimmerman, 1997, p. 3)

Over time, schools built their own internal capacity in the area of evaluation and were becoming continuously improving organizations. But how well did they succeed? In 1997, an overall evaluation of the Manitoba School Improvement Program was undertaking by Earl and Lee. They measured individual school success using various forms of evidences. To do so, they constructed four individual indexes of success or impact to measure the extent to which MSIP Schools achieved their *projects goals*, influenced *student learning*, influenced *student engagement* and established *school improvement process* (Earl & Lee, 1999, p. iv). For example, student learning was estimated using indicators such as grades/ marks, graduation rates, credits, retention rates, and quality of student work.

Using all the factors included in their evaluation model, the authors did classify schools by success score on a range of overall scores from 4 through 16. Each of four indexes had a scale of 1 to 4, with 4 being the highest score. Seven schools got a score of 11 or above (16-point scale); 10 schools got a score of 8 to 10; 4 schools got a score below 8; and one school had insufficient data. Earl and Lee made three general observations:

- First, success is not easy, but possible. Many schools made progress on all four dimensions – 17 schools if one takes scores of 8 and above; some schools went quite far.
- Second, success is not linear or static. The 10 schools in the second category, for example, could go one way or the other in the future [...] time is a factor. Depending on new developments some schools will push forward, others may lose ground[...].
- Third, this is a collective effort, not 22 isolated initiatives [...]. Plans are underway for MSIP to go on for many years. The Foundation has committed resources through the year 2000, as MSIP, now a locally based entity, is working to establish a basic infrastructure to continue to work beyond the year 2000. The commitment to keep going, based on the experiences over the past seven years, is one of the strongest indicators of the worth of the program. (Earl & Lee, 1999, p. v)

The most original finding is the "urgency-energy-agency-more energy pattern of success" discovered by Earl and Lee in the most successful schools. They explain the urgency by the fact that many teachers in secondary schools in Canada and elsewhere have a great sense of urgency about the future of many students in their classrooms. Something has to be done to engage them in learning and teachers can find new ways to help kids learn. But Earl and Lee speculate that "this potential energy is fragile. Without any opportunity to act on it, it can easily turn into despair and cynicism. The MSIP provided the stimulus to take action and to persevere" (Earl & Lee, 1999, p. v). As we can see, external involvement from an agency and internal collaboration can bring the opportunity to get started and to focus action on the effectiveness of teaching and learning.

ESTABLISHING POLICIES

In this section we will see how the new *Québec Policy on University Funding* associated with accountability measures will also have a positive impact on the need for effective educational evaluation. A variety of similar projects were also put in place by other provinces.

Québec Policy on University Funding (Québec, 2000)

In the 1990s, when the federal transfer cuts came with budget restraint at the provincial level, provinces across Canada began to re-evaluate their university system and to examine their funding. Through several consultations, discussion papers, reports, policies, and strategic plans, a trend has developed towards creating new frameworks for change with a clear view toward making institutions more efficient. One of the research analyses done in 1996 by the Legislative Research Service from the Ontario Legislative Library drew a picture of the post-secondary education reforms that were taking place in the provinces of Canada. The conclusion of this paper revealed some constant themes:

> responsiveness to the labour-market needs of the students, cost and accessibility, transition among secondary, college and university education, efficiency and accountability appear as issues in all the provinces that are examining their systems [Nova Scotia, Newfoundland, Québec, Manitoba, Saskatchewan, Alberta, and British Columbia]. Other common elements among provinces are: the establishment of committees, task forces or elaborate studies; slow, consensus-based implementation of many of the resulting recommendations; and rationalization of the number of colleges and universities, or of programs in the system. (Drummond, 1996, p. 7)

From this perspective, it is interesting to examine some aspects of a concrete result like the new funding mechanism associated with accountability measures of the Québec Policy on University Funding.

On December 1, 2000, the Minister of State for Education and Youth launched the Québec Policy on University Funding. After cutbacks in public funding, the Government of Québec has announced a reinvestment of $1 billion in education over a three-year period and universities will have access to an additional $323 million annually starting in the 2002–2003 academic year. Most of this amount ($230 million) will be used to provide general funding for the 18 universities, and around $90 million will be allocated to priority needs. This recurrent amount represents for the universities an unprecedented increase of 25 percent. In return, the State expects the universities to use the funding efficiently and to account for how they manage it. The policy was the subject of a vast consultation with the institutions, teachers, sessional lecturers, professionals, technical and support staff and the students.

On one hand, this policy introduces a new formula for distributing financial resources based on a more equitable and transparent method. On the other hand, the policy sets directions and priorities for government action. Furthermore, this project presents several criteria useful for carrying out programs and institutional evaluation. These criteria focus primarily on the relevance and effectiveness of programs and appropriateness of resources, but also on the efficiency of management by universities including their accountability and their results. The following directions are certainly related to evaluation:

- modernization of basic equipment and infrastructures (libraries, studios, scientific and laboratory equipment, information technologies, etc.) to ensure that they meet teaching needs;
- optimal management of program offerings;
- an increase in the number of students in master's and, especially, doctoral, programs;
- greater interaction between the universities and the various stakeholders;
- the adoption of strategies to help graduates enter the workforce;
- the optimal use of available resources, efficient management by universities, and accountability of universities to society and the public authorities for the management of public funds they receive, for the main orientations of their development and the results they achieve;
- in-depth reviews of the universities' short programs in relation to those offered by college-level institutions, in order to ensure complementarity, consistency with the specific missions of universities and colleges, as well as an economical use of resources within the education system.[6] (Ministère de l'Éducation, 2000, p. 9)

According to the policy, available data on graduation rates in short programs (other than degree programs) and other information such as the types of programs and the student status and profiles will be important to analyse. Afterwards, the department of Education (Ministère de l'Éducation du Québec) "would like to work with universities to establish a streamlined mechanism to certify the quality and relevance of such programs for funding purposes [...] and to monitor graduation rates (graduate follow-up surveys)." This project will be carried out from 2000–2001 to the 2002–2003 university year.

Furthermore, this reinvestment plan is conditional upon the signing, in 2000–2001, of a performance contract between the Minister and each university. This public contract stipulates the commitment made by the institution to use the new funding for projects that will improve the quality of teaching and supervision and excellence in research as well. Specific funding will be set aside to provide universities with financial support for projects that will ensure optimal management of their program offerings. To be eligible, projects must involve the rationalization of program offerings, the pooling of resources, and partnerships with college-level institutions and other activities that will ensure optimal management of the programs.

In the fall of 2000, some universities said they were almost ready to sign their performance contract. The contract submitted to the Minister by the Sherbrooke University calls into question the viability of a dozen of their study programs (l'Université de Sherbrooke, 2000). Facing a decrease in the student enrolment in some programs, the Rector said that the institution is now ready to do the painful analysis that could result in giving up some programs. In the majority of the programs that are being analysed, they saw their student enrolment decreasing, in some cases up to 50 percent in five years. Furthermore, they were hoping that the agreement would give more power to their academic deans so they can increase the workload of professors whose research involvement is obviously low. This institution is committing itself to put in place a "management-evaluation system" for the achievement of its teaching staff. At the moment this performance evaluation is used for the senior managers, a teacher's promotion, or a contract renewal. This will require some negotiations with the union. (Chouinard, 2000, pp. 1, 8).

It is clear that the performance contract was developed around the priorities of the Minister: the work of the professors, the target success rates, and the rationalization of the programs. The result is important because the ratification of this contract will give access to a part of the budget to be granted to the university.

No one can deny that the purpose of the *Québec Policy on University Funding* is not only funding but also to improve the effectiveness of the system. New measures are put in place to enforce accountability. Québec's higher education is funded in large part by the State. It is then normal that the government take a closer look at the way universities perform even if they enjoy a great deal of autonomy. For these institutions, this policy is a clear message to evaluate their programs and to demonstrate their value for students, parents, employers and society. This project is also a good example of an accountability strategy that will increase the need and usefulness of effective educational programs evaluation. The link between assessment and accountability is necessary to improve the quality of education.

DISCUSSION

The public and the governments are asking for evidence that educational institutions are providing the highest quality learning experience for every student and value for their money. From the 1990s, there has been a variety of responses to the growing demands for public accountability in Canada. This chapter presented three different answers: (1) the establishment of a governmental agency: the *College Education Evaluation Commission* (CEEC, Québec, 1993); (2) the establishment of a non-governmental agency: the *Manitoba School Improvement Program Inc.* (MSIP, Manitoba, 1991); (3) the establishment of a new policy funding for educational institutions: the *Québec Policy on University Funding* (Québec, 2000). As we can see in our three examples, educational evaluation has various purposes. The characteristics of the different processes are presented in Table 1.

In different places and times, the responses to the demands for public accountability were adapted to the historical, social, cultural and economic contexts where they took root. High schools in Manitoba and *cégeps* and universities in Québec have different background.

For example, the interest in Québec for evaluation, at the college education level, took a more concrete form in 1978 with the creation of the College Council including its own evaluation Commission. After ten years, a study concluded that

Table 1.   Characteristics of the different processes presented

	(1) CEEC (Québec)	(2) MSIP (Manitoba)	(3) Funding Policy (Québec)
Purposes	• compulsory/state regulation (ACT) • accountability for the institution performance, effectiveness and results	• voluntary/self-regulation • self-improvement	• related to funding/external control • accountability to inform, to explain and to justify its decisions and choices, to prove efficient management and results (performance contract)
Approaches	• formative and learning • participatory/self-evaluation • use expert academic peers (college and university) and experts from working fields • internal and external procedures (CEEC)	• formative and learning • participatory to empowerment evaluation • use assistance and support of external evaluator • internal procedures	• universities were allowed considerable freedom to run their own affairs • tension between autonomy and accountability • internal and external procedures
Objects	• focus on quality of programs and their improvement; efficiency of institutional policies; student's success and student's achievement; educational mission	• focus on student learning and student's success	• focus on rationalization of the program offerings; relevance and effectiveness of programs; appropriateness of resources to meet teaching needs
Results	• access to the results and public statement	• results are communicated to the stakeholders	• access to some results

evaluation gained an increasing importance mostly in the field of student learning evaluation (Conseil supérieur de l'éducation, 1999, p. 35). As I said before, in the context of the reform called *College Education Renewal* came the creation of the College Evaluation Commission (CEEC) in replacement of the College Council and the Universities Council. Since then, each college has not only the obligation to adopt an institutional program evaluation policy but also, to apply this policy and to evaluate its programs. The CEEC exists only at the college education level in Québec's public and private institutions. It is quite obvious that without an act setting up the Commission, the evaluation in the colleges would not have been so strongly put in place. We also have to remember that the *cégeps* network was set up in 1967 and it coincided with the vast movement setting up teachers' unions (Corriveau, 1991, p. 12). In the field of education, each province has its own story leading to a more or less important place for evaluation.

MSIP did demonstrate that institutions could themselves be responsible for insuring quality in learning and in teaching. To achieve this, the schools' staff needed external help and time. The resources and assistance provided by MSIP did support creating their own locally based data and indicators with the appropriate tools (survey, focus groups, etc.); getting the data to circulate around the school community for discussion and analysis; improving the school staff evaluation skills with an emphasis on formative evaluation rather than on accountability and control; involving teachers, parents, students and community in the processes; and putting in place schools improvement activities with a focus on student learning and achievement.

The CEEC and MSIP experiences underline that there is more than one way to get improvements in education. Furthermore, the institutions are moving in a complex system at different speeds, some slower others faster. This is quite normal since the situation varies from one institution to another. At the university level we are witnessing an increase in the demand for more visible and external evaluation. Close examination of the *Québec Policy on University Funding* project revealed that one university was already anticipating major changes, such as a reduction in the number of programs, keeping the effective ones.

In this situation, generalization can be difficult but it is possible to bring out some consensus:

- *Decentralization and accountability movement*: At all levels of education, every institution has a responsibility for maintaining and improving the quality of education, its basic mission.
- *External pressures*: There are a whole range of external pressures (budget restraint; educational reform; administrative reform requiring accountability for results and transparency through strategic plan, performance plan, success plan or annual report; publications bringing out academic performance indicators[7]) on institutions to demonstrate the value and quality of their programs and to improve their results including students' success and achievement. Key stakeholders (public, governments, parents, students, employers, boards, professional corporations, research organizations; and others) are asking for results and for more obvious facts measuring performance in education and the overall impact of quality improvements efforts.
- *Internal pressures*: There are also internal pressures to improve quality of teaching and learning from the teachers and management staff who are more and more concerned with the future of their students.
- *External input*: The different processes presented in this chapter emphasize the need for some kind of external input to start a self-improvement process including evaluation activities.

CONCLUSION

Action does not always lead directly to a traditional evaluation process but to different mechanisms, where performance, accountability, transparency, responsibilities, continuous improvement, outcomes and stakeholders information are the main focus. The evaluation issue is more about establishing an effective performance management process in each school, college or university. Furthermore, this movement, which is gaining ground everywhere in Canada, does include evaluation activities based on facts: developing a local information system, collecting data, producing performance indicators, evaluating student performance, monitoring satisfaction of the stakeholders, and producing and releasing a report on the performance of an educational institution. These activities are taking place in an organizational culture that encourages improvement efforts. At the moment, the implementation of evaluation varies from one province to another but also from one education level to another and from one institution to another.

Local institutions must find ways to take charge of their own performance. In this view, Koffi, Laurin and Moreau (2000) stressed a new management model for the educational institutions entering in the 21st century. Their model is based on concrete strategies such as school-focused management; collegial work as a school team; teacher and management staff empowerment; team decision making; teacher professionalism, partnership, self-leadership, and super-leadership of the school executive; and accountability in carrying out their educational mission.

At last, we have to recognize the need for continual evaluation of all Canadian educational institutions to maintain a competitive position in the world. I sincerely believe that its success will only be possible with appropriate resources, training, tools, support, and incitement to carry out evaluation activities.

ENDNOTES

[1] Alberta, British Columbia, Manitoba, New Brunswick, Newfoundland and Labrador, Nova Scotia, Ontario, Prince Edward Island, Québec, Saskatchewan, Nunavut, Northwest Territories, and Yukon.

[2] The three commissioners are appointed by the Government for a five-year term, which may be renewed once. In fact, their term was renewed in September 1998.

[3] This part was largely extracted from sections 13 and 19 of the Act constituting the Commission.

[4] http://www.ceec.gouv.qc.ca

[5] Regular education, both pre-university education (2 years) and technical education (3 years), is provided for the vast majority of college students; this leads to the Diploma of College Studies (DEC, from the French *Diplôme d'études collégiales*). Under continuing education, colleges offer technical programs leading to an Attestation of College Studies (AEC, from the French *Attestation d'études collégiales*). These programs are provided for people who have interrupted their studies for more than one academic year or left the labour market and who wish to resume studying either part-time or on an intensive basis.

[6] Note: only 7 out of 15 directions are mentioned in this text.

[7] For instance, the Fraser Institute, an independent Canadian economic and social research and educational organization, publishes Annual Report Cards on three provinces' Secondary Schools

(or High Schools): British Columbia's (since 1998), Alberta's (since 1999), Québec's (since 2000 with the Montreal Economic Institute) and Ontario's (since 2001). The role of these reports is to collect objective indicators of school performance, compare the performance and improvement of individual schools, and produce an overall rating out of 10. The schools are ranked according to their performance. The Fraser Institute Report Cards are planned for all ten Canadian provinces by 2002. For more information visit their Web site at http://www.fraserinstitute.ca

REFERENCES

Bryant, C., Lee, L.E., & Zimmerman, M. (1997). *Who is the evaluator anyway? How the Manitoba School Improvement Program has used participatory evaluation to help improve schools*. Paper presented at the Canadian Evaluation Society Conference, Ottawa, Canada.

Canadian Education Statistics Council. (1996). *Education indicators in Canada, Pan-Canadian Education Indicators Program*. Toronto, Canada: Author.

Chouinard, M.-A. (2000). Grande remise en question à l'Université de Sherbrooke. Le «contrat de performance» pourrait signifier la disparition d'une douzaine de programmes. (2000, October 26), *Le Devoir*, pp. 1 & 8.

Commission d'Évaluation de l'Enseignement Collégial. (2000). *The institutional evaluation guide*. Québec: Gouvernement du Québec.

Commission d'Évaluation de l'Enseignement Collégial. (1997). *Evaluating programs of study in Québec, case study: Technical education programs in early childhood education at the Cégep de Saint-Jérôme*. Québec: Gouvernement du Québec.

Commission d'Évaluation de l'Enseignement Collégial. (1994). *The Commission d'évaluation de l'enseignement collégial: Its Mission and directions*. Québec: Gouvernement du Québec.

Conseil Supérieur de l'Éducation. (1999). *L'évaluation institutionnelle en éducation: Une dynamique propice au développement, Rapport annuel 1998–1999 sur l'état et les besoins de l'éducation*. Sainte-Foy: Gouvernement du Québec.

Corriveau, L. (1991). *Les Cégeps question d'avenir*. Québec: Institut québécois de recherche sur la culture.

Dennison, J.D., & Gallagher, P. (1986). *Canada's community colleges: A critical analysis*. Vancouver, Canada: University of British Columbia Press.

Drummond, A. (1996). *Post-secondary education reforms in other provinces*. Toronto: Government of Ontario. Retrieved from Ontario Legislative Library Web site: http://www.ontla.on.ca/library/repository/mon/1000/10262792.htm

Earl, L.M., & Lee, L.E. (1998). *Evaluation of the Manitoba School Improvement Program*. Toronto: Walter and Duncan Gordon Foundation. Retrieved from http://www.gordonfn.ca/resfiles/MSIP-evaluation.pdf

Fetterman, D.M. (1996). Empowerment evaluation: An introduction to theory and practice. In D.M. Fetterman, S.J. Kaftarian, & A. Wandersman (Eds.), *Empowerment evaluation: Knowledge and tools for self-assessment and accountability* (pp. 3–46). Thousand Oaks, CA: Sage.

Gouvernement du Québec. (1993). *An act respecting the Commission d'évaluation de l'enseignement collégial and amending certain legislative provisions*.

Koffi, V., Laurin, P., & Moreau, A., (2000). *Quand l'école se prend en main*. Sainte-Foy, Québec, Canada: Presses de l'Université du Québec.

Lee, L.E. (1999). Building capacity for school improvement through evaluation: Experiences of the Manitoba School Improvement Program Inc. *The Canadian Journal of Program Evaluation*, pp. 155–178.

Ministère de l'Éducation. (2000). *Québec policy on university funding*. Québec: Gouvernement du Québec. Retrieved December 5, 2000 from: http://www.meq.gouv.qc.ca/reforme/pol_financ/index.htm

Ministère de l'Enseignement Supérieur et de la Science. (1993). *Colleges for the 21st century*. Québec: Gouvernement du Québec.

Université de Sherbrooke. (2000). *Constat et contrat de performance. Une proposition de l'Université de Sherbrooke au ministre de l'Éducation du Québec, monsieur François Legault*. Retrieved December 6, 2000 from Sherbrooke University website: http://www.usherb.ca

34
Evaluating Educational Programs and Projects in Australia[1]

JOHN M. OWEN

The University of Melbourne, Centre for Program Evaluation, Victoria, Australia

INTRODUCTION

This chapter focuses on the evaluation of educational programs in Australia. At the outset it should be said that there is a strong interest in evaluation across the country and that there is an emerging body of evaluation practice. While some of this practice could be regarded as less than the highest quality, there is a sufficient corpus of action which qualifies an entry into a handbook devoted to a discussion of contemporary developments in evaluation work.

What are some of the indicators of a thriving evaluation milieu in Australia? Many readers will know that Australians who have evaluation interests have established extensive contacts with their counterparts around the world. For example, Australia has been well represented at the annual meetings of the American and European evaluation societies over the past decade.

From these and other formal contacts, for example, visits of overseas evaluators to organisations in Australia, meaningful ongoing linkages have been made between Australian evaluators and colleagues in other countries. The fruitfulness of these contacts is manifest in the increasing influence of Australians in thinking about evaluation issues, as seen in the production of books and journals, and by the number of papers given by Australians at the overseas evaluation meetings mentioned in the previous paragraph.

Internally, there has been a heightened interest in evaluation within Australia (and New Zealand) over the past decade. This interest crosses discipline or area boundaries, such as health, welfare, and education. One can understand this is terms of demand and supply.

Demand Side

On the demand side, there has been a genuine interest by government and the helping professions in evaluation work. One indication is the large number of

International Handbook of Educational Evaluation, 751–768
T. Kellaghan, D.L. Stufflebeam (eds.)
© *2003 Dordrecht: Kluwer Academic Publishers. Printed in Great Britain.*

advertisements for evaluation studies in the national press. Another is the number of requests from agencies for evaluation assistance. I estimate that the Centre for Program Evaluation (CPE) gets at least five inquiries each week from agencies wanting us to respond to an evaluation brief or to meet with them to discuss their evaluation needs.

While the interest in evaluation has been driven somewhat by mandate, I am aware of many instances of agencies voluntarily allocating resources for evaluation. I see the following as key impetuses for evaluation work. These are the need for information to:

- set up the same or similar programs in other locations;
- provide evidence which can be used for external accountability purposes;
- modify programs and arrangements within an agency to improve the general quality of organisational implementation and provision to those who use the services of the agency.

I come back to these as they apply to educational settings later in the chapter.

Taking a broader view, it is possible to link the degree of evaluation work and the nature of this work to the prevailing political climate. As a democratic country, there is a strong commitment to openness and access to information, and in recent times, an increasing propensity to the use of what might be called "systematic enquiry" in decision making (Lindblom & Cohen, 1979). This is manifest in trends such as the use of evidenced-based practice in the medical and nursing professions and an increased interest in the role of research in the development of social and educational policy (Holbrook et al., 1999). It is also interesting to note that support for evaluation has also varied across states and over time with the preferences of various Commonwealth and State government openness to evidence over ideology.

Supply Side

A major manifestation of the interest in doing evaluations has been the development of the Australasian Evaluation Society (AES), which had membership of over 700 persons as of December 2000. AES has served to "professionalise" evaluation in that it has provided an avenue for practitioners to disseminate their work, provided guidelines on standards of practice, and promoted an annual conference and associated events each year. The cross-disciplinary nature of the membership is notable. If one classifies university staff as educators in addition to those working in schools and educational systems, educators would form a sizeable but not major proportion of the participants at the conference each year. The plurality of membership and their interests is reflected in the identity of keynote speakers. For example, the AES conference held in Perth in 1999 had three keynote speakers, one of whom had interests in crime prevention, another in performance auditing, and the third in education. What this and other trends reveal is that evaluation in Australia is cross-disciplinary in nature and multifaceted.

One can observe parallels between the development and demography of Australasian and European evaluation societies. Both tend to be influenced by practitioners: by encouragement for new evaluators to make their mark and by a view of evaluation as an approach to enquiry which can support decision making at all phases of program development. This can be contrasted to the situation in the United States. In the U.S., the evaluation profession has been heavily influenced by academics, where there is an emphasis on determination of program outcomes using well tried social science methodology; and by annual meetings which are dominated by a small group of well known evaluators (Rossi & Freeman, 1989).

EDUCATIONAL PROGRAMS AND EVALUATION

To address the brief of this chapter, I had to make some key decisions about emphasis. Given my earlier statement, that there was a strong body of evaluation practice in Australia, how could I go about representing what has been achieved?

One option would be to describe the entire range of recent educational evaluation activities in as much detail as possible. But a systematic database of educational evaluation in Australia over the past five years does not exist.

There is no doubt that such a description would have benefits, as such a compilation would be useful to those on both the demand and supply side of evaluation practice. But the compilation of a directory of practice in educational evaluation would be a daunting task. The compilation would need to identify evaluation in sectors such as early learning and kindergartens, primary and secondary schooling, and university education. In addition, one can add in the technical and further education sector and the adult learning sector, each of which has burgeoned over the past decade or so.

What to do? I decided that, in the light of the lack of readily available systematic information to describe the population of evaluation practice, I would be selective. I decided to use my own informal knowledge of evaluation practice in Australia to describe and examine a small number of initiatives which should be of interest to evaluators worldwide.

I will call these initiatives *evaluation perspectives*. These perspectives stand out on the evaluation landscape for one reason or another. They can be regarded as initiatives which have been noticed as signalling new developments in evaluation in Australia over recent times. They should not necessarily be regarded as good practice, although I believe that there are elements of desirability in each of them. A more apt description would be that they represent examples of new ground being broken, signalling an element of risk in program provision, and a belief that the boundaries of evaluation practice can be expanded through trying new ways of doing things.

I will now discuss three perspectives in turn.

Perspective 1. Evaluation of Educational Innovations which Acknowledge the Complexity of Educational Change

In Australia, studies of educational policy innovation are frequently commissioned.[2] Policymakers and managers of programs and other interested parties wish to know whether their program "works." Managers have a right to be defensive about negative findings about programs for which they are responsible. But I have found that educational administrators in Australia tend to take on board constructive criticisms that have the potential to improve program provision. Most evaluations with this purpose rely on the involvement and experience of a trained external evaluator.

There is an increasing understanding among evaluators that one of the first tasks is to work with decision makers to make explicit the key feature of the program being evaluated. That is, the program logic needs to be explored. The need for the development of the program logic has been dealt with over time through the contributions of key theorists such as Joe Wholey and Midge Smith. Australian evaluators have made major contributions to thinking about how best to develop program logic in organisational settings (Funnell, 1997). Assisting program managers to develop program logic has become an important process in its own right, without necessarily leading to a subsequent impact evaluation (Rogers et al., 2000). However, within this perspective, the development of the logic usually facilitates discussion about what aspects of the program need to or can be tracked as the program is implemented.

Within this perspective, the key to the development of logic is to recognise that the educational innovation is systemic in nature, that it is supported across an educational system by a central authority which has championed its take up by a population of individual users (e.g in schools).

There is now a well grounded theory base which has the potential to give systemic change efforts in education some internal coherency through linking policy development at the system (e.g., state education department) level with the practice-based approach of individual schools within the system.

This research shows that broad requirements for systemic change are based on several elements. The first concerns the importance of aligning components of the process so that they are consistent and supportive of each other and form a coherent policy (Elmore, 1996). A second requirement is based on the recognition that innovation requires some degree of external pressure to provide motivation and support for implementation efforts. A third element is to move the locus of responsibility for establishing and maintaining an innovation from central control to provide greater autonomy for schools in the management of the innovation process. Finally, there needs to be a process by which individual schools provide gross accountability information to the system for what has been achieved (Knapp, 1997). The model suggests that if these elements are in place, the innovation is likely to become sustained across a school system (Harvey, 2000).

These research findings provide the basis for the program logic. Evaluators can use this logic as the basis for systematic analyses of the impact of major educational innovations.

Examples of this Perspective

Evaluation of Turning the Tide in Schools (TTIS)
TTIS represented a major initiative to support the development of drug education in schools by the Department of Education, Employment and Training (DEET) in the State of Victoria, Australia. Following a major government-initiated enquiry into drugs in the community, over AUD $14 million was earmarked for the development and implementation of this strategy in the period 1995 to 1999. The TTIS was based on the notion of harm minimisation, and recognition that many school-aged students would encounter drugs in their every day life. Adoption by school of a harm-minimisation approach meant a major change in direction in those schools which had previously adopted a policy of zero tolerance of drugs.

The TTIS strategy in practice closely reflected the change principles described above. Centralised support was manifest in the development of an articulated policy, the availability of teaching materials, and the employment of experienced consultants to support schools and teachers.

All schools were expected to set up an internal team led by a senior member of staff to plan a school level strategy which responded to the needs of the school, and was consistent with the TTIS policy. This plan was called the Individual School Drug Education Strategy (ISDES). The consultants were also entrusted with "signing off" on the quality of the plan on behalf of DEET.

In 1998, DEET commissioned an external evaluation of TTIS. The major stakeholders were policymakers who had supported and developed the TTIS framework. The major policy decision related to the future of the TTIS, specifically whether there was a need for further or ongoing support to schools.

The first step in the evaluation was the explication of the TTIS program logic, which appears in Figure 1 and reflects the change theory discussed above. This was the basis for:

- the creation of a common understanding between policy clients and the evaluators of the way the program was supposed to operate;
- developing a range of data collection methods, foremost of which was a survey which sought data from schools on the success of each aspect of the program logic;
- formulating ways in which the findings would be disseminated.

The evaluation found that implementation was generally successful with the exception of the family/community links component (see Figure 1). While it was too early to be definite about outcomes, there were indications that the TTIS had major influences on the thinking of students about drug issues where the school had developed an integrated approach to harm minimisation (McLeod, 1999). The report also alerted policymakers to the need for additional support for many schools to ensure that widespread implementation would be achieved. DEET has committed additional resources to maintain consultants to achieve this objective.

An unanticipated outcome was to examine the existing theory to find an element or elements which could benefit from further investigation. In this case, it was found that there had been little research on the notion of school-level sustainability of innovations. Further evaluation is being undertaken to check the sustainability of the program of TTIS in selected schools with a view to contributing to the knowledge base on educational change (Harvey, 2000).

The Frontline Management Initiative (FMI)

FMI is a training program developed by the Australian National Training Authority, the major national education body which is concerned with vocational education. FMI is designed to provide professional development for middle level managers in a range of industries. Features of this innovation are individual training plans for participants, on the job learning, recognition of prior learning, use of accredited training providers to structure the training, and a system of national recognition of achievement across industries.

FMI has been adopted by a range of industries as a means of skilling middle management. Evaluations of the impact of FMI are being undertaken across the country. Within the context of this perspective and the relevant research, the impact of FMI within one organisation is of major interest. A major government agency, the Department of Natural Resources and the Environment, has begun to implement FMI across a number of dispersed sites. An evaluation of the impact of this initiative has been commissioned in conjunction with its implementation, to be undertaken by myself and colleagues at the Centre for Program Evaluation. As with the previous example, the evaluation commenced by making the program logic explicit and using it to design an ongoing study of its impact. The evaluation will conclude toward the end of 2001.

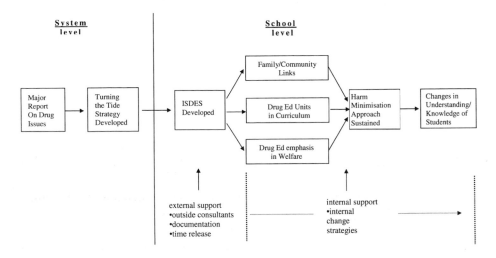

Figure 1:   Turning the Tide in Schools: Program Logic

Perspective 2. Development of an Accountability Framework Across a School System

As the title implies, the focus here is on the use of evaluation for accountability purposes. In general terms accountability is predicated on the assumption that government and citizens have the right to know whether programs funded from the public purse are making a difference. As I have said elsewhere,

> In times of economic stringency particularly, the public has a right to know that money spent in the public arena has been translated into effective social or educational interventions …. For a given program stakeholders have a right to expect that programs, where possible, meet their intended goals and do not lead to negative side effects. Parents at a local school are rightly interested in whether the literacy approach taken by the school in meeting the needs of the children. (Owen & Rogers, 1999, p. 263).

A notable development in this area has been the increased emphasis on performance auditing in democratic societies. Government auditing offices have become key arms of political decision making. In evaluation terms we are seeing closer links between performance auditing and outcomes focussed evaluation practices (Leeuw, 1996). Performance auditors have a strong presence in most professional evaluation societies, particularly in Europe (Pollitt & Suuma, 1996).

The TTIS example illustrated that policy interventions can be the object of systematic evaluation (the evaluand). In evaluations which fit within Perspective #2, the object of the evaluation is usually not a policy but an organisation or agency. In educational terms this means that the unit of analysis would be a university or a school.

An issue is, How does government set up a system of educational provision within which accountability mechanisms can be meaningful to those with a legitimate interest in the findings?

Example of this Perspective

The School Accountability Framework
In 1992, a recently elected conservative government set up a major program of structural, curriculum, and accountability reform which was designed to change the ways schools operated in the State of Victoria. While there was a wide range of reasons for this, a major impetus was a report by the Victorian Commission of Audit in 1992, which reported that there was virtually no systematic data on the performance of the government school system in the state. It recommended to the government that the state education department should arrange for periodic, independent reviews of school performance against a wide variety of benchmarks and other indicators.

There is not space to trace the detail of ways in which this framework evolved over a period of eight years. However, it is important to describe key features because the experiment with accountability in Victoria has been of great interest to educators in Australia and overseas. These features are outlined with reference to Figure 2.

Beginning in 1992, all government schools were required to be involved in the following:

(1) The development of a planning document, known as the school charter. This was a plan for the next three years of the work of the school. The charter was designed to enable schools to identify long-term goals and implementation strategies. While the original charters concentrated on school priorities, those developed later in the 1990s were also required to incorporate government policy directions and priorities, for example a statewide focus on literacy.

It is important to note that four areas that had to be given attention in the school charter were educational programs, school environment, financial management, and human resource management. The list reflected the interest of government in school management issues. This was perceived by many teachers as taking the emphasis away from the schools' core business of teaching and learning.

The charter document was used as the "first order" accountability strategy by the department of education. It was signed by the president of the school council, and the principal, and countersigned by the Director of Schools.

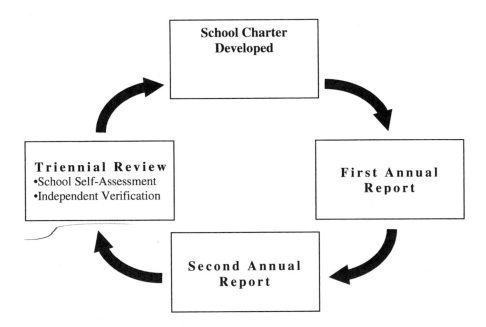

Figure 2:   The Accountability Framework

The charter involved significant work by staff, in particular by the principal. In addition to the planning side of the charter, the school was also asked to develop methods by which the plan could be monitored. While some assistance was available in the form of guidelines and instruments, this evaluation task was an additional one for schools not accustomed to the collection and use of systematic data.

(2) School annual reports. These were designed to be interim evaluative reports for the school community and the Department of Education. They often featured major school and student achievements, and commented on progress towards the achievement of charter objectives. Schools also included scores on a set of common performance indicators, some of which were provided from a central source (the Office of Review), which reflected government priorities, e.g., student literacy achievement.

(3) Triennial school reviews. The review process had two stages: (i) school self-assessment conducted within guidelines developed by the Office of Review and (ii) external verification conducted by an independent external review team or an individual. In some cases, university faculty have been involved in the external verification. The original aim of the independent review was to verify that the school's self assessment represented a fair statement of the school's achievements over the three-year period. In this sense the reviewer played the role of an external inspector on behalf of the central authority. However, as the framework has matured, there has been an increased emphasis in the review process on formative improvement focussed input from reviewers.

The process has been modified during the years since its inception. This can be understood with reference to competing needs for information at different times. There is some evidence to support a claim that the original reason for the development of the accountability processes was to enable the Department of Education to account to the State Treasury for the expenditure on school education. In order to obtain this information, school-level data had to be aggregated to provide a system-level picture. It is widely held that the development of the original school charter arrangements and the measures which were to be collected were driven more by the information needs of the central educational authority than by the information needs of individual schools. This was reinforced by the education department introducing student tests of basis skills to put alongside information which had to be obtained from schools. By the end of the 1990s the Department of Education was able to show trends on statewide indicators that the achievement of students was on the increase.

Once the imperative to set up gross statewide indicators had been achieved, the Office of Review gave more of its attention to ways in which data collected centrally and by individual schools could be used for individual school improvement.

By 1999, the triennial school review had taken on a much more formative perspective. This had been brought about by a combination of factors, including the sympathy of most external reviewers towards the information needs of the schools and the provision of indicator information that was meaningful to principals and school review panel members. This included information which allowed them to compare the performance of the school with "like schools" – those with similar student populations on socio-economic grounds (incorrectly labelled benchmarks in the Office of Review literature).

There has not to this date been a systematic metaevaluation of the Accountability Framework. However, there is some anecdotal information available from colleagues who have been close to the action. An interesting reflection is that, by and large, there were concerns with the relevance and quality of much of the data and its interpretation assembled by schools as part of their charter monitoring (an example is the use of parent opinion surveys). Yet, there has been widespread satisfaction in the latter years of the Framework with the availability of comparative data provided by the government and the feedback and consultancy processes in which external evaluators play a leading role. One explanation for this is that schools see systematic data as important if they confirm or explain knowledge of a more tacit nature which the schools accumulate through more informal methods. This knowledge is also used to make alterations to the new charter which formalised the school plan for the subsequent three year period.

However, 1999 also brought in a change of government in Victoria and the almost inevitable formal review of educational provision. In regard to the Accountability Framework just described, the review made the following statement:

"Several initiatives are now in place that might strengthen the focus of school planning on continuous improvement while retaining core elements of accountability. These initiatives include:

• the Learning Improvement Fund, announced recently by the Minister, which allocates school improvement funding to schools. Funds are provided to address student learning issues ... following the school's triennial review;
• the development of support materials for schools to evaluate the effectiveness of their *core procedures* [italics added]. The first three sets of these materials relate to social outcomes of schooling, student welfare processes, and approaches to teaching. They are designed to facilitate school program evaluation and to assist schools to align their behaviour with the educational values espoused in their charters;
• the provision of benchmark data annually to all schools to enable them to establish appropriate points of comparison in assessing their own standards.

While these activities are valuable in their own right, there is a need for the Department to develop and articulate a coherent policy framework which establishes a commitment to school improvement and identifies the strategies the Department intends to adopt to support schools in their improvement efforts. This is reflected in the issues raised in both the focus groups and submissions to the review in the general area of school improvement. These included:

- workload issues related to the preparation of annual reports and triennial review self assessments;
- a general tension between the school's responsibility for program evaluation and the accountability requirements of the Department;
- a view that the Department needs to support schools in improvement and especially in narrowing the gap in achievement between schools;
- a concern that the measures of school performance used in the accountability framework are too narrow and do not include the wide range of things schools achieve outside the purely cognitive domain;
- a view that the timeframes and structures associated with school charters and triennial reviews lack the flexibility necessary to cater for a range of school performance (Government of Victoria, 2000, pp. 58–59)".

This report encapsulates much of the misgivings about the Accountability Framework which had been put in place by the previous administration. The Office of Review has been reorganised and renamed the Accountability and Development Division. A challenge for them will be to retain some of the established procedures from the previous Framework while at the same time providing resources and guidelines for the development and evaluation of outcomes which are less managerial and more in tune with the core work of schools.

Perspective 3. Creating an Evaluation Culture within Educational Organisations

In most western countries we have witnessed an increase in organisational-level involvement in evaluation. At the basis of this support are some fundamental beliefs about the control of providers over program development and delivery. Some time ago, Ronald Havelock recognised these beliefs in the Problem Solving model of change (Havelock, 1971). The model describes an organisational setting where those responsible for a given problem have the ability and inclination to deal with that problem. If outsiders are involved they are involved on the terms set by providers, that is outsiders are not there to hand down knowledge. The model is thus predicated on the adequacy of local expertise to deal with local problems and to recognise the need for outside assistance when it is needed. In such a scenario, there is an assumption that external knowledge, and in particular accumulated research-based knowledge, is of lesser relevance than "local" knowledge. Thus, external policies and directives do not play a major role in shaping program delivery and associated evaluative procedures. The evaluator is employed to provide input and in some cases support the agenda of the local practitioners.

The Problem Solving model is the basis for a cluster of evaluation approaches which I have drawn together and labeled Interactive Evaluation (Owen & Rogers,

1999, p. 222). In Interactive Evaluation, participants play a major part in setting goals and in program delivery, and evaluation efforts are influenced strongly by those who are "close to the action." Consistent with this is a view that each program initiative is "new"; that is, it can be regarded as an innovation from the perspective of those involved in its delivery.

Programs which are consistent with this view attempt to address problems that have not been subject to program intervention before and/or employ program structures or processes that are unique, at least from the point of view of the program staff.

Typically, program objectives and delivery are evolving rather than preordinate, sometimes not fully explicit and thus open to debate. Those directly involved might expect to come to a steady state in terms of general direction over a period of time, but continue to reserve the right to use new or alternative strategies to achieve program goals, that is, there is ongoing adaptation and responsiveness.

Program delivery can be idiosyncratic and there is little, if any, regard for consistency of treatment, uniform implementation or outcomes. In some areas, there is government support for this approach to problem solving, based at least partly on an ideological position that there should be local control over decisions that affect the local community.

The Problem Solving perspective is also consistent with the more recent literature on developing a culture of learning within organisations (Preskill & Torres, 1996) and the broader need for continuous relevant knowledge for decision making in social, political and economic spheres of endeavour (Sowell, 1996). This has led to a burgeoning interest in integrating evaluation into the day-to-day processes of organisations that adopt a commitment to systematic examination of what they do and how they might become more effective and efficient (Rowe & Jacobs, 1996). We see an increasing need for trained evaluators to provide timely information for organisational decision making at all levels, formal and informal leaders to those working on the "shop floor" (Owen & Lambert, 1998).

Interactive Evaluation is thus concerned with:

- the provision of systematic evaluation findings through which local providers can make decisions about the future direction of their programs;
- assistance in planning and carrying out self evaluations;
- focussing evaluation on program change and improvement, in most cases on a continuous basis;
- a perspective that evaluation can be an end in itself, as a means of empowering providers and participants.

So, ideally, a trained evaluator provides a direct service to program providers based on her expertise, working in close contact, and providing a range of inputs and advice. The evaluator may be asked to observe what is happening, to help participants make judgements about the success or otherwise of a given strategy or program initiative, with a view for future planning. In some approaches the evaluator can be thought of as an extension of the program team, helping to make decisions about program direction. In addition to collecting and analysing information, the evaluator might assist decision makers in setting directions and, in some cases, actually assisting with change and improvement strategies.

Evaluations based on this perspective have been a strong feature of the educational landscape in Australia over the last two decades. Some education authorities have actively encouraged action research among schools.

Examples of this Perspective

The National Professional Development Program

The Commonwealth Government has supported the National Professional Development Program (NPDP), which encouraged partnerships between schools and universities. Objectives of this national program were to:

- develop schools as learning communities in which research, rethinking and renewal are regarded as essential work practices;
- provide participating schools with access to academic associates for advice and expertise on current research and theory relating to the area of concern for the school.

Schools were provided with small amounts of money, about AUD $5000, and encouraged to:

- engage in participative management structures in the workplace;
- engage in a program of research and action directed towards examining and changing work organisation practices in order to provide a working environment and a collaborative culture in which the competence of teachers might be enhanced and the learning outcomes for all students improved;
- collaborate with colleagues from an associated university in the development of research and action plans (Yeatman & Sachs, 1995, p. 18).

An evaluation of this program showed that extensive improvements were achieved by cooperative efforts that has often been more than could reasonably be expected from the participants.

School Based Research and Reform

A similar initiative, the School Based Research and Reform program was supported by the South Australian Department of Education and Training and Employment. The central aims of the program were to:

- improve the organisational and educational practices at the school level;
- share the outcomes of this research and evaluation so as to influence principles and practices within the organisation and share its future directions;
- evaluate the extent to which these practices have been successful (Mader, 1998).

Initially 20 schools were funded to undertake a range of innovations, after success in a competitive tender process. Principals were informed that the topics the Department would support were those designed to influence learning outcomes for students and which were consistent with previously identified strategic directions. Typically schools received AUD $6,000 to support their evaluation efforts, which could buy the expertise of external evaluators and time release for teachers. Some of the issues schools investigated included:

- A School Wide Approach to Reducing Bullying;
- Middle Schooling and Social Justice;
- Developing Oral Language through Play.

Individual Internal School Evaluation
The role of external evaluators in school level evaluation and change efforts has been mentioned above. During 1998, the Centre for Program Evaluation (CPE) undertook an evaluation of the use of technology at a private independent school for girls in Melbourne. The problem here was that school had been unable to develop a curriculum policy which incorporated the use of technology and in particular, notebook computers, which all students had been asked to purchase at not inconsiderable expense.

In terms of the involvement of practitioners in decisions about evaluation, it is important to note that the stimulus for the evaluation came from heads of subject departments who were concerned about the ineffective use of notebook computers in the school. Subsequently, the school principal had approached the CPE to provide evaluation expertise for the study.

Working intensively with the school management, including the principal, the following set of questions were developed as a basis for the evaluation:

- What is the level and nature of existing use of notebooks?
- What are the opinions of staff and other key persons, regarding the effectiveness of this usage up to now?
- In what ways could the effective educational usage of notebooks be increased?
- How can the school and its administration support the effective usage of notebooks?

Over a period of four months, CPE staff worked intensively in the school. The approach taken was to provide feedback about the conduct of the evaluation to staff and management; for the latter, this involved regular face-to-face meetings. In addition the CPE staff assisted the principal to disseminate information to parents.

Key "products" of the evaluation, which was completed in mid-September 1998, were:

- the clarification of what was meant by a Computer Enhanced Curriculum (CEC). This provided a policy position to be achieved and key findings about the nature of the future curriculum in the school;

- the development of a typology of notebook computer use;
- reports which went to management and staff. These were written specifically with these audiences in mind. For example the report to management addressed issues related to the future financing of the use of technology in schools, and implications for structural reorganisation of the curriculum to incorporate computer use;
- an end of evaluation conference of staff, at which the implications of the findings were discussed, and where "existing good practice" was presented by teachers;
- development of plans by which the position could be achieved, that is strategies to improve the use of notebooks and technology in the future and, in particular the next school year (Livingston et al., 1998).

It is clear from these examples that evaluation within this perspective is responsive to the decision needs of the school, and driven by the school agenda. The programs under review are unique to the school, not only in content but also in style. There are also implications for evaluation in that each evaluation design needs to be developed individually. This behoves those engaged in school level evaluation to have a range of skills which meet different situations. This applies not only to data management skills but also to those associated with social interaction.

DISCUSSION

What can we learn from these perspectives in terms of their potential influence on educational evaluation in Australia and around the world?

Perspective 1 sees evaluation in terms of the determination of systemic impact of an innovation. The success of evaluation work within this perspective relies on the evaluator having a detailed knowledge of educational change theory. Ideally, this theory should be available to developers when they are preparing educational policy. This is most likely to happen if the evaluation is planned at the same time the policy is being developed. However, even if this is not the case, evaluators can base post hoc evaluations of the relevant theory, as a basis for pointing out any shortcomings of a given program or innovation. There is also an opportunity for evaluators to act as educators to inform policy makers about theory with a view to improving their general conceptual understanding about innovation impact.

In the Australian context, I believe that there is an emerging trend to undertake impact educational evaluations using these guidelines.

Perspective 2 sees evaluation in terms of setting up monitoring systems and using the findings of these systems to make decisions about programs and organisations. The evaluator must have expertise in translating organisational goals into meaningful performance information, both qualitative and quantitative indicators. Those engaged in evaluations of this kind must understand the limitations of indicators in the synthesis of information and the development of conclusions about the state or condition of a given organisation at a given time.

In the Australian context, I believe that educational evaluations based on good practice within this perspective are difficult to find, either because they have not been widely attempted or have not been published.

Perspective 3 sees evaluation as an activity which complements local decision making and program delivery. The evaluator must have a grasp of organisational change principles and group dynamics in addition to more conventional evaluation skills, and be prepared to work with the agenda set by the organisation. In the Australian context, I believe that there is a significant set of evaluators who have worked within this perspective and that there will be a continuing increase in the need for evaluation consultants to work in this way.

While the perspectives are in themselves an indication of the diversity of evaluation practice in Australia, it is useful to now examine what is common across them. In all cases, the program under review and the context are interlinked. As evaluators, we would not do justice to providing a full understanding of any of these situations if the task was merely perceived as evaluating a single entity. In Perspective 1, the fate of the Turning the Tide was dependent on school- and system-level effects and the interaction between them. In Perspective 2, an important issue was the competing needs of the schools and the central authority for information about the effects of the school charter policy. In Perspective 3, the objective of small scale in-school programs were also designed to have a whole school impact. The interactions described here represent the need for systems level thinking. Put simply, in social and educational settings, there is an interlinkage of programs and organisational arrangements. If one makes a change in one part of an organisational system, other parts are also affected by that change.

Neophyte evaluators have often been advised to become familiar with the evaluand or program under review as part of the evaluation process. It follows from the previous paragraph that evaluators need to do more than this. An essential requisite for a well-founded evaluation is to become familiar, not only with the program, but with a broader framework which includes the organisational setting or the educational system within which the program is nested. At the planning and negotiation phase of an evaluation, this knowledge can be invaluable in determining the direction of the evaluation study and the key issues which focus the data collection and analysis.

Finally, an issue which suggests itself is whether evaluators can or wish to work across a range of evaluation situations. The perspectives presented here indicated the variety of evaluation practice which one can expect to encounter in Australia and elsewhere. There is also an associated issue of preference. An evaluator may be at home working closely with providers but feel uncomfortable working in evaluations with a strongly managerial orientation. There are arguments for plurality of practice and specialisation. What is important, however, is that prospective evaluators in training programs have an opportunity to appreciate the range of potential evaluation practice, and make informed choices of the area or areas in which they decide to work.

ENDNOTES

[1] The editors of this handbook asked me to examine the evaluation of educational programs and projects within the Australian context. I note that other writers have made this distinction, see for example (Shadish, Cook, & Leviton, 1991). The implication is that there is a hierarchy of interventions, with projects seen as the "on the ground" manifestation of the program. There is also the implication that providers have little influence on the design of the program. This is generally not the case in Australia where there is more of a tradition of local program design and direct funding of local action. A more appropriate distinction in the Australian context is between "big P" and "little p" programs. "Big P" programs are typically those provided by federal and state governments, while "little p" programs are managed by agencies directly responsible for their implementation. For simplicity I use the generic term "program" in the text to refer to both levels of program development and provision.

[2] An innovation, for the purposes of this discussion is a policy or program that is regarded as new by those who develop it and/or in the eyes of the potential users of the entity (Rogers, 1995).

REFERENCES

Elmore, R. (1996). Getting to scale with successful educational practices. In S. Furhman, & J. O'Day (Eds.), *Rewards and reforms: Creating educational incentives that work* (pp. 249–329). San Francisco: Jossey Bass.

Funnell, S. (1997). Program logic: An adaptable tool for designing and evaluating programs. *Evaluation News and Comment*, **6**(1), 5–17.

Government of Victoria. (2000). *The next generation: Report of the Ministerial Working Party.* Accountability and Development Division, Department of Education, Employment and Training, November 2000.

Harvey, G. (2000). *Sustaining a policy innovation: The case of turning the tide in schools drug education initiative.* Unpublished doctor of education thesis proposal, Melbourne, Australia, Centre for Program Evaluation.

Havelock, R.G. (1971). *Planning for innovation through dissemination and utilization of knowledge.* Ann Arbor MI: Center for Research on Utilization on Scientific Knowledge.

Holbrook, A., et al. (1999). *Mapping educational research and its impact on Australian schools.* Camberwell, Victoria: Australian Council for Educational Research.

Knapp, M.S. (1997). Between systemic reforms and the mathematics and science classroom: The dynamics of innovation, implementation and professional learning. *Review of Educational Research,* **67**(2), 227–266.

Leeuw, F.L. (1996). Auditing and evaluation: Bridging a gap, worlds to meet? In C. Wisler (Ed.). Evaluation and Auditing: Prospects for Convergence. *New Directions for Evaluation,* **71**, 51–60.

Lindblom, C.E., & Cohen, D.K. (1979). *Usable knowledge.* Newhaven and London: Yale University Press.

Livingston, J.J., Owen, J.M., & Andrew, P.F. (1998). *The computer enhanced curriculum: Use of notebook computers in the middle school curriculum.* Melbourne, Victoria: Centre for Program Evaluation, The University of Melbourne.

Mader, P. (1998). School based research and reform. *Proceedings of the Annual Conference of the Australasian Evaluation Society,* **2**, 714–731.

McLeod, J. (1999). *Turning the tide in schools.* (Report to the Department of Education, Employment and Training, Melbourne, Vic, November, 1999). Melbourne, Victoria: McLeod Nelson & Associates.

Owen, J.M., & Lambert, F.C. (1998). Evaluation and the information needs of organisational leaders. *American Journal of Evaluation,* **19**(3), 355–365.

Owen, J.M., & Rogers, P. (1999). *Program evaluation: Forms and approaches.* (2nd ed.). London: Sage.

Pollitt, C., & Suuma, H. (1996). Performance audit and evaluation: Similar tools, different relationships? In C. Wisler (Ed.). Evaluation and Auditing: Prospects for Convergence. *New Directions in Program Evaluation,* **71**, 29–50.

Preskill, H., & Torres, R.T. (1996, November). *From evaluation to evaluative enquiry for organisational learning.* Paper presented at the annual meeting of the American Evaluation Association, Atlanta, GA.

Rogers, E.M. (1995). *Diffusion of innovations.* (4th ed.). New York: The Free Press.

Rogers, P., Hacsi, T.A., Petrosino, A., & Huebner, T.A. (Eds.). (2000). Program theory in evaluation: Challenges and opportunities. *New Directions for Evaluation,* **87**.

Rossi, P.H., & Freeman, H.E. (1989). *Evaluation, A systematic approach.* Newbury Park, CA; Sage.

Rowe, W., & Jacobs, N. (1996). *Principles and practices of organisationally integrated evaluation.* Unpublished paper.

Shadish, W.R., Cook, T.D., & Leviton, L.C. (1991). *Foundations of Program Evaluation.* Newbury Park: Sage.

Sowell, T. (1996). *Knowledge and decisions.* New York: Basic Books.

Yeatman, A., & Sachs, J. (1995). *Making the links: A formative evaluation of the first year of the Innovative Links Project between univerisities and schools for teacher professional development.* Murdoch University, School of Education.

Section 9

Old and New Challenges for Evaluation in Schools

Introduction

GARY MIRON, Section Editor

The Evaluation Center, Western Michigan University, MI, USA

Education systems and schools have changed considerably in recent years. There has been a shift from steering schools by planning inputs and monitoring processes to steering through the measurement of outcomes. Connected to this have been trends toward decentralization, increasing autonomy for schools, increasing reliance on market mechanisms to determine funding levels, and the creation or expansion of school choice. These changes can also be seen across a large number of countries.

Side by side with the changes, the demands and needs for evaluation in schools have also changed. These include (i) increasing pressure on schools to demonstrate success and to market themselves; (ii) increasing demands for evaluative information from parents (consumers) and policymakers; and (iii) increasing demands on school leaders to demonstrate effectiveness as measured by standardized tests.

This section of the handbook contains a collection of chapters that address old and new challenges for evaluation in schools. Broadly defined, the challenges include institutionalizing the practice of evaluation in schools; developing evaluation practices to address new demands for accountability and to serve the information needs of consumers; and evaluating new aspects of schools, such as the implementation of technology and the use of new technologies in instruction.

INSTITUTIONALIZING EVALUATION IN SCHOOLS

A problem of long standing for schools that has not gone away is the institutionalization or mainstreaming of the practice of evaluation. While some school leaders have come to appreciate, and benefit from, evaluation, few have been able to incorporate it into the daily practice of schools, while those who have succeeded have struggled to sustain its use and application. Evaluators and practitioners alike remain doubtful that we will be able to institutionalize evaluation practices in a satisfactory manner in schools.[1] This skepticism, however, does not mean that efforts to achieve it have subsided. Two academics who together have spent nearly a half century wrestling with this issue are Daniel Stufflebeam and James Sanders. Both have contributed chapters to this section of the handbook.

International Handbook of Educational Evaluation, 771–774
T. Kellaghan, D.L. Stufflebeam (eds.)
© 2003 Dordrecht: Kluwer Academic Publishers. Printed in Great Britain.

Daniel Stufflebeam describes the requirements of a sound and fully functional evaluation system in a school. His integration of the literature on learning organizations and metaevaluation informs his idealized model for systematically adopting, installing, operating, and assessing a school evaluation system which should be designed to address the evaluation of students, personnel, and programs. Stufflebeam also identifies concrete steps that can be taken to institutionalize evaluation and provides an overview of strategies for acquiring the leadership, expertise, and assistance needed to succeed in this endeavor.

The following chapter by James Sanders and Jane Davidson offers more of a hands-on approach. It contains an extensive overview of examples of school evaluation practices, as well as presenting a general model to guide the development and implementation of evaluation. The model was adapted from one developed earlier by Stufflebeam, and incorporates the program evaluation standards and reflects the components of the CIPP model. The authors argue that the model is eclectic and can be applied in the context of a range of other evaluation approaches commonly used today.

The first two chapters contain useful tools to guide educators whose task it is to incorporate evaluation into the mainstream of their work. The tools include models of, and lists of logical steps in implementation, as well as lists of questions to consider and possible indicators. While the Stufflebeam paper is more theoretical, it contains insightful tables that logically present the areas and levels of evaluation in schools. The Sanders and Davidson chapter provides links to a wide range of Web-based evaluation tools.

RESPONDING TO NEW DEMANDS FOR ACCOUNTABILITY AND SERVING THE INFORMATION NEEDS OF CONSUMERS

Changes in education have made it more important that evaluations should focus on outcomes and serve the emerging information needs of consumers as well as of practitioners and policymakers. For example, increasing school autonomy, school choice, and demands for accountability have spurred the need for easily accessible information about school performance. This information is important for policymakers and school administrators that steer the schools and for parents who want easily accessible and comparable information about schools to make informed decisions on where to enroll their child(ren).

In the third chapter in the section, Robert Johnson examines the development and uses of school report cards, or school profiles, as he refers to them, and draws on his earlier work with Richard Jaeger and Barbara Gorney to provide a complete and thorough review of what is known about them.

Indicators of school performance, both quantitative (such as student attendance rates, pupil-teacher ratio, and grade-level achievement scores) and qualitative (such as information about school and community partnerships and awards received by the school) are examined. Other important topics covered include potential stakeholder audiences for school-level profiles, changes and trends in profiles over time, advice in the selection of indicators for profiles, guidance in the formatting and presentation of data, as well as selection of comparison groups and dissemination of the information profiles provide. Examples of school profiles from a variety of countries are provided in the chapter.

EVALUATING NEW ASPECTS OF SCHOOLS: THE IMPLEMENTATION AND USE OF NEW TECHNOLOGIES

In the last 15 years there has been enormous public and private investment in technology for primary and secondary schools. Early studies have focused on quantifying the available equipment by school or classroom, while later studies have attempted to link the technology with changes in instructional practices and learning processes that could be measured through observed behavior, changed attitudes, and improved student performance.

The last chapter in the section, prepared by Catherine Awsumb Nelson, Jennifer Post, and William Bickel, examines one of the new challenge areas for school evaluation – the evaluation of technology programs. The authors argue that it is necessary to develop human capital in order to successfully institutionalize technology in the culture and practices of schools, and propose an evaluation framework in which the growth of school-level ownership of technology over time is assessed as a series of three interrelated learning curves: maintaining the technology infrastructure; building teacher technology skills; and integrating technology into teaching and learning. Through the development of building-level human capital, schools gradually move up each learning curve and (ideally) from one learning curve to the next, increasing their ownership of the technology and the extent to which it is integrated into the core educational processes of teaching and learning.

The authors found that to use the learning curves as an evaluation framework, it was necessary to further specify that movement on each curve proceed along three dimensions: depth (quality of technology use); breadth (quantity and variety of technology use); and sustainability (infrastructure to support technology experiences over time). For each dimension of the three learning curves, the evaluation generated a set of factors related to successful technology implementation and eventual institutionalization in school learning environments.

To illustrate the successful application of the model, the authors described a multi-year evaluation of school technology implementation in a large urban district in the U.S. The two-part framework for evaluating implementation presented in the chapter has a number of demonstrated and potential uses for educators and policymakers interested in understanding and enhancing the potential for technology to become institutionalized in schools.

OBSTACLES TO INSTITUTIONALIZING EVALUATION IN SCHOOLS

Schools are involved in evaluation activities whether they wish to or not. In fact, many school leaders and educators are largely unaware of the extensive evaluation that goes on at their school because it is often done by persons outside the school and it serves the needs of external stakeholders rather than those of school staff. For example, most externally funded programs are likely to be evaluated. Likewise, schools are often the focus of state or district level evaluations, as well as of studies conducted by universities or private sector organizations, but may not receive results of the studies. In order to institutionalize evaluation, and to serve their information needs, school staff will need to become more actively engaged in evaluating their school, and school leaders will need to coordinate and adapt the various evaluation activities already taking place that involve their school. Schools will also need to find ways to overcome the most commonly cited obstacles to institutionalizing evaluation such as a lack of human and financial resources and the fact that evaluation is low on lists of priorities.

Recent reforms that emphasize greater accountability are placing increased emphasis on evaluation in schools, yet these reforms also introduce new obstacles such as the increasing involvement of private groups and a tendency to narrowly evaluate schools based on student performance alone. While leaders in the field will continue to think about ways to overcome the many obstacles that inhibit the use of evaluation in schools, any long-term solution will be likely to require a number of changes that involve preservice and inservice education of educators, the provision of technical assistance, and specific mandates that are supported by adequate funding and steered with a balance of "carrots and sticks."

ENDNOTE

[1] At the 2000 annual meeting of the American Evaluation Association, I chaired a session entitled "Institutionalization of Evaluation in Schools." The presenters identified obstacles to the institutionalization of evaluation, and none appeared optimistic about succeeding in this endeavor. At the close of the session, I asked the large audience a direct question: "How many believe that in 5 or 10 years we will still be wrestling with how to incorporate evaluation into the mainstream of work activities in schools?" Three-quarters answered in the affirmative.

35
Institutionalizing Evaluation in Schools[1]

DANIEL L. STUFFLEBEAM

The Evaluation Center, Western Michigan University, MI, USA

Evaluation, which is the systematic process of assessing the merit and/or worth of a program or other object, is essential to the success of any school or other social enterprise. A functional school evaluation system assesses all important aspects of the school, provides direction for improvement, maintains accountability records, and enhances understanding of teaching, learning, and other school processes. The focus of this chapter is on how schools can institutionalize a sound system of evaluation. Institutionalization of school-based evaluation is a complex, goal-directed process that includes conceptualizing, organizing, funding, staffing, installing, operating, using, assessing, and sustaining systematic evaluation of a school's operations. The chapter is directed to persons and groups dedicated to improving a current evaluation system or installing a new one. These include school councils, principals, teachers, and those university, government, and service personnel engaged in helping schools increase their effectiveness.

Advice in the chapter is conveyed in "Type I" and "Type II" models. A Type I Model is defined as a representation of the requirements of a sound and fully functional evaluation system, a Type II Model as an idealized process for institutionalizing such a system. The example of a Type I Model that is presented is the CIPP Model (Stufflebeam, 2000), which is widely used throughout the U.S. and in many other countries. CIPP is an acronym that denotes four main types of evaluation: Context to assess needs, problems, and opportunities; Inputs to assess planned means of addressing targeted needs; Process to assess implementation of plans; and Products to assess intended and unintended outcomes.

Work in developing learning organizations (Fullan, 1991; Kline & Saunders, 1998; Senge, 1990; Senge, Kleiner, Roberts, Ross, & Smith, 1994) is worth considering in efforts to install evaluation systems in individual schools. However, Senge's five proposed disciplines of a learning organization (personal mastery, shared vision, mental models, team learning, and systems thinking) need to be extended to include a sixth and most fundamental discipline: evaluation. Furthermore, since in Bloom's (1956) *Taxonomy of Educational Objectives*, evaluation was accorded the highest level in the learning process, the process for institutionalizing evaluation in a school must include evaluation of the evaluation system, or what evaluators call *metaevaluation* (Stufflebeam, 2001).

International Handbook of Educational Evaluation, 775–806
T. Kellaghan, D.L. Stufflebeam (eds.)
© 2003 Dordrecht: Kluwer Academic Publishers. Printed in Great Britain.

The chapter is divided into three parts. The first lays out a Type I model for a school evaluation system. In part two, the literature on learning organizations and metaevaluation is used to suggest a Type II model for systematically adopting, installing, operating, and assessing a school evaluation system. The final part considers how schools can acquire the leadership, expertise, and assistance needed to successfully institutionalize evaluation.

A TYPE I MODEL FOR EFFECTIVE SCHOOL EVALUATION

The Type I Model is presented in response to 11 questions that school personnel need to ask when determining how best to conceptualize evaluation. Responses to the questions in the chapter are not intended as *the* answers for any person, group, or particular school, but rather as examples for consideration when a "Type I" concept of evaluation is being defined.

1. Why Should School Professionals Conduct Evaluations, and What Important Differences Do They Make Anyway?

This question poses an issue that every educator needs to settle firmly in order to proceed confidently with evaluations and convince others that the evaluations are worth doing. All schools have problems, and evaluation is needed to delineate and help solve them. Furthermore, evaluation is inevitable, since grading homework and other student products is part and parcel of the teaching process. Moreover, schools are learning organizations and should therefore promulgate a process that helps their staff continually study, assess, and improve services. School personnel need to constantly improve their understanding of the needs of their students and how much they are learning. Current practices should not be considered fixed but instead subject to innovation and improvement. School staff should value mistakes for what they can teach, should share lessons learned with colleagues, and should archive the lessons for later use by new generations of school personnel. They should conduct holistic assessments to assure that the school's various components are interacting functionally to produce the best possible educational outcomes. Clearly, a school's professionals need evaluation in order to increase their understanding of their students and school services; strengthen the services accordingly; function as a coherent, improving system; identify intended and unintended outcomes; and earn reputations as highly successful, responsible professionals.

2. What Parts of a School Should be Evaluated?

The general response to this question is that school personnel should evaluate all important aspects of the school and constantly seek to improve them individually and collectively. The most important objects for school evaluation are students, personnel, and programs. This response sets priorities rather than discounting the importance of evaluating buildings, grounds, vehicles, equipment, bus routes, policies, and other objects. As appropriate, all important aspects of the school should be evaluated. However, a three-part system of student, personnel, and program evaluation is a good place to begin. The school's most important clients are the students. Its most important resources are its teachers, administrators, and other personnel. And it makes its most important contributions by delivering effective programs. Thus, all three parts of this crucial triad should be subjected to evaluation.

Student evaluation involves assessing the needs, efforts, and achievements of each student. These evaluations should be carried out to help plan and guide instruction and other school services, to give feedback to students and their parents or guardians, and to document students' accomplishments.

Personnel evaluations include assessments of job candidates, clarification of staff members' duties, assessments of their competence, and determination of performance strengths and weaknesses. These evaluations are vital in selecting, assigning, developing, supervising, rewarding, and retaining or dismissing school staff. An effective personnel evaluation system addresses all these aspects of a professional's involvement with the school.

Program evaluations cover all of the instructional and other goal-directed services offered to students, in, for example, math, science, and language programs, and recreation, health, food, and transportation services. Curricular program evaluations examine the fit of instructional offerings to assessed student needs, the quality of materials, the coverage of content, the appropriateness and comprehensiveness of offerings for the full range of students' abilities and special needs, the offerings' cost-effectiveness compared with other available approaches, the vertical and horizontal coherence of programs, and their individual and collective effectiveness.

Noncurricular program evaluations include assessments of such endeavors as counseling, home visitation, health services, professional development, and school breakfasts. In general, evaluations of noncurricular programs and services look at many of the concerns that are studied in curricular programs (e.g., comparative costs and effects of options and responsiveness to students' assessed needs). They may also look at safety, maintenance requirements, efficiency, and other such general matters. Program evaluations are important for assessing new, special projects and ongoing programs and services. Sanders, Horn, Thomas, Tuckett, and Yang (1995) provided a useful manual for assessing the full range of school programs, facilities, and services.

3. At What Levels Should School Evaluation be Conducted?

It is crucial to evaluate at all school levels. Basically, these are the students, classroom, and school as a whole. From the perspectives of students and parents, student-level evaluation is an essential means of highlighting and effectively addressing each student's special needs. At the classroom level, the teacher needs to look not only at the needs and progress of individuals, but also of the full group of students and pertinent subgroups. This is necessary to plan instruction that is both efficient and effective and to assess the impacts of both individualized and group instructional approaches. Evaluation across the entire school is especially important in assessing the extent to which the school's different parts are effectively integrated and mutually reinforcing. For example, instruction at each grade level should effectively and efficiently build on instruction in the previous grade and prepare the student for the next grade level's offerings. A systems concept should govern the evaluation process, so that the school's parts fit well together and reinforce each other and so that the overall achievements are greater than the sum of achievements of the school's individual parts.

4. What Main Questions Should be Addressed?

According to the CIPP Model (Stufflebeam, 2000), there are four types of evaluation questions. Each may be presented in proactive and retrospective forms so that evaluations are appropriately applied both to guide a school's efforts and to assess them after the fact.

- What assessed needs should be, or should have been, addressed? (*context*)
- By what means can targeted needs best be addressed, or were the plans for services appropriately responsive to assessed needs and better than other available courses of action? (*inputs*)
- To what extent is the planned service being implemented appropriately, or to what extent was it well executed? (*process*)
- What results are being or were produced, and how good and important are they? (*products*)

These questions denote generic categories of questions. It will be necessary for each school person or group to derive more specific questions depending on circumstances. Questions should be selected to comprehensively assess an object's merit and worth and to address issues that require someone's timely and substantive response to improve and/or be accountable for services. The four questions provide a general framework in which to identify the more specific questions.

Table 1 provides examples of questions that often need to be addressed in evaluating context, inputs, processes, and products in schools. In reviewing this table, keep in mind that the questions at the student level are those the teacher might ask in assessing student-level needs, plans, progress, and achievements. The questions at the teacher level are those that might be asked by the principal, a peer group of teachers, an inspector, or the teacher. The questions at the program level might be addressed by the school council, an outside sponsor, a government official, or the school staff as a whole. The proactive questions are

Table 1.   Sample Questions to Guide Evaluations of Students, Personnel, and Programs

Objects of Evaluation	Four Types of Evaluation			
	Context	*Inputs*	*Process*	*Products*
Students Proactive:	• What are the students' entering levels of proficiency? • What are their special, course-related needs, individually and collectively? • Considering the assessed needs and school standards, what learning objectives should each student achieve?	• What instructional approaches did previous teachers use successfully with these students, individually and collectively? • What steps can be taken to secure support and involvement of these students' parents/guardians?	• To what extent is the sequence of learning activities proving to be appropriate for these students? • Are the students doing their part to learn all they can during the year? • To what extent are parents doing all they can and should do to support their child's education?	• To what extent are the students achieving intermediate learning objectives? • To what extent are the students making progress toward fulfilling the school's expected outcomes? • To what extent are the students developing positive attitudes toward learning?
Retroactive	• To what extent did each student receive instruction that was targeted to her or his assessed needs? • To what extent did the total group of students receive instruction at levels consistent with the school's standards?	• To what extent did the students or their parents agree that the instructional schedules and procedures had been planned in consideration of the students' assessed needs and the school's standards?	• To what extent was the instructional plan implemented for each student? • To what extent did instructional plans prove workable and effective?	• To what extent were students' assessed needs for this course met, individually and collectively? • To what extent are the students individually and collectively ready to enter the next level of schooling?
Personnel Proactive:	• What are this teacher's assigned duties? • What assessed needs of the incoming students should this teacher address or arrange to have others address? • What school instructional standards should this teacher meet?	• Is this teacher carrying out an effective planning process for meeting students' assessed needs and fulfilling other assigned duties? • Is the teacher appropriately providing for students with special needs?	• Is the teacher succeeding in motivating all the students to learn? • Is the teacher effectively engaging all the students in the learning process? • Is the teacher effectively engaging the parents in their child's learning process?	• To what extent is the teacher succeeding in meeting the assessed needs of all the students? • To what extent are students' attitudes to learning positive or negative as a result of the course?

Continues on next page

Table 1.   Continued

	Four Types of Evaluation			
Objects of Evaluation	*Context*	*Inputs*	*Process*	*Products*
	• What goals and priorities should guide this teacher's work in the coming semester/year	• Does the teacher's instructional plan appropriately provide for assessing student progress? • Is the teacher adequately prepared to teach the course content to the full range of students?	• Is the plan of instruction being followed, and is it working? • Is the teacher communicating effectively with all the students? • Are classroom activities being managed effectively? • Is the teacher effectively assessing and responding to each student's progress?	
Retroactive	• To what extent did the teacher study the students' educational needs and set goals and priorities accordingly? • To what extent did the teacher address all her or his assigned duties? • To what extent did the teacher address the school's instructional standards?	• Did the teacher develop and and work from sound instructional plans? • Did the teacher make appropriate provisions for serving the students with special needs? • Did the teacher take appropriate steps to fully prepared to teach the course's content?	• Did the teacher faithfully carry out her or his instructional plans or revise them as needed? • Did the teacher succeed in getting students to engage in their part of the learning process? • Did the teacher engage in efforts to involve parents, and were those efforts successful? • Was the class well managed? • Did the teacher effectively assess and respond to each student's progress?	• To what extent did all students make reasonable learning gains, given their assessed needs and the school's instructional standards? • To what extent did all students finish the course with a positive attitude toward school and a love of learning?
Programs Proactive:	• How is the program related to meeting the school's standards? • To what extent is the program targeted? • What are the assessed needs of the targeted students?	• Is the program plan sufficiently responsive to assessed student needs and school standards? • Is the program plan better than alternatives being implemented in other schools?	• Is the program being carried out according to the plan? • Does the plan need to be modified? • Is there a need to further train staff to carry out the program?	• To what extent are student needs being met? • To what extent are the school's student outcome standards being met?

Continues on next page

Table 1. Continued

Objects of Evaluation	Four Types of Evaluation			
	Context	*Inputs*	*Process*	*Products*
	• What program goals would be responsive to students' assessed needs and consonant with the school's standards? • To what extent are program goals in need of revision?	• Is the program plan understood and accepted by those who will have to carry it out? • Does the program plan include a defensible complement of content and a reasonable sequence across the grades? • Is the plan workable and affordable? • Does the plan provide sufficiently for assessment of process and product?		
Retroactive	• Were program objectives and priorities based on assessed needs of the students to be served? • Were program objectives and priorities consonant with the school's student outcome standards? • Were program objectives appropriately revised as more was learned about the students?	• Was the strategy for this program fully responsive to program goals, assessed students needs, and school standards? • Was the strategy for this program fully functional, affordable, acceptable to the staff, and workable? • Was the strategy for this program better than alternatives being used by other schools? • Did the program plan include an adequate evaluation design?	• Was the program adequately implemented? • Was the plan appropriately improved? • Were staff adequately trained to carry out the program? • Did all the staff fulfill their responsibilities?	• To what extent were all the students' targeted needs met? • To what extent were the school's program outcome standards fulfilled? • To what extent were the program outcomes worth the investment of time and resources? • To what extent was the program free of negative side effects?

oriented to getting the evaluation input needed to plan and carry out services successfully. The retroactive questions are focused on responding after the fact to audiences that want to know what services were offered, why, according to what plans, how well, and with what effects.

5. What Purposes Should Guide School Evaluation?

The four main purposes of a school evaluation are improvement, accountability, understanding, and dissemination. The first purpose is ongoing improvement of the school and its particular services, all the way down to the teaching provided to individual students. Complementing this purpose is the imperative that the school and its participants supply information for accountability at all levels of the school. Evaluations should also be cumulative, and over time they should help school staff and constituents gain better insights and understanding of the school's functioning. The evaluation system should also supply evidence of use to outsiders who are interested in the school's offerings and might want to transport, adapt, and apply them elsewhere; hence, the fourth purpose of dissemination.

6. Who Should Conduct Evaluations in the School?

The general answer to this question is that all the school's professionals and policymakers should conduct the evaluations needed to fulfill their responsibilities. Teachers regularly have to obtain evidence on the needs, efforts, and achievements of their students and should, periodically, examine the effectiveness of their teaching methods. Principals/headmasters need to evaluate how well each teacher is performing and, with their faculties, how the school as a whole is functioning. School councils must evaluate principals, school policies, resource requirements, and the appropriateness of resource allocations. These examples confirm that evaluation is both a collective and individual responsibility of all those persons charged with making the school work for the benefit of the students and community.

In certain cases it will be important to engage independent evaluators. Examples include district evaluation offices in countries that have school districts, intermediate educational service centers, state or national government offices of evaluation, evaluation companies, and university-based evaluation centers. These specialized organizations can add objectivity, technical competence, and credibility to school evaluations.

7. When Should Evaluations be Conducted?

Ideally, evaluation will be integrated into all the school's processes and will be an ongoing activity. Insofar as possible, teachers should embed evaluative questions and feedback into their teaching materials and daily instructional processes. Developing curriculum-embedded evaluation should be a primary objective of all schools that aspire to be effective learning organizations. Evaluations that are command performances and only yield results weeks or months following data collection may be necessary to support the purposes of public accountability and understanding in a research sense, but are of limited utility in guiding and improving instruction for particular students and groups of students. For that purpose, evaluations should be scheduled to provide timely and relevant feedback to users, in consideration of their agenda of decisions and other functions that require evaluative input.

During the year, the principal should evaluate or engage others to evaluate designated teachers' performances and provide feedback for improvement. When feasible, each year all teachers should be provided with feedback they can use to strengthen performance. But each teacher need not be formally evaluated every year. It is best to limit the formal evaluations to those teachers who most need attention, to those who obviously have problems, or to those who are being considered for tenure and/or promotion. Following this idea, the evaluations can be targeted where and when they will do the most good and conducted with rigor as opposed to being conducted as a superficial ritual involving all teachers every year.

At least once, and preferably twice a year, the principal and the total school staff and/or logical groupings of staff should be engaged in evaluating selected programs and planning for improvement. As in the case of teacher evaluations, not every program should be evaluated every year. Rather, the staff should target programs of particular concern and over time should periodically evaluate all the programs with the central goal of program improvement. Program staffs periodically should compare their programs with others that might be adopted or that might be developed locally. While innovation and creativity are to be encouraged and supported, evaluations should be planned and conducted in concert with the innovative activities. Evaluations should be conducted when plans for new programs are submitted to screen those that are worthy of execution or tryout from those that predictably would fail, be dysfunctional, and/or waste resources.

In the school council's evaluation of the principal, it can be useful to have a phased process across the year. For example, in a first quarter (it might be either summer or autumn) the principal and council could examine student achievement results from the previous year and clarify school priorities for the current school year. In the second quarter, they could examine the school's plans for achieving the new priorities and define the performance criteria for which the principal will be held accountable. In the third quarter, the council and principal could meet to review and discuss the principal's progress in leading the school to carry out the year's plans of action. Finally, in the fourth quarter, they could examine school and student outcomes, and the council could compile and present its evaluation of the principal's service and accomplishments. As appropriate, during this fourth quarter the council might also prescribe an improvement plan for the principal. Most important, the principal and council should use the year's principal evaluation results to plan for improvements in the coming year. This example shows how evaluation can be integrated into a school's functions. The point of the illustrative process for evaluating the principal is not just to issue judgments of her or his performance, but to do so in consideration of the school's ongoing planning, review, and improvement process.

8. What Audiences Should School Evaluations Serve?

School evaluations should not be carried out in the abstract, or as a ritual, but should serve the functional information needs of particular persons or groups. Key audiences include parents, students, teachers, the principal, the school council, government agencies, funding organizations, and others as appropriate. Sometimes the evaluator and audience are the same, such as when the teacher gathers evaluative information on the effectiveness of teaching procedures as a basis for planning future instruction. In other cases, the audience is distinct from the evaluator, such as when the teacher provides student report cards for review by the student and parents/guardians. In general, the school staff should identify the full range of audiences for evaluation findings, project and periodically update their information needs, and design and schedule evaluations to meet the information needs. Ideally, evaluations during the year will be guided by a basic annual evaluation plan developed at the year's beginning.

9. What Evaluative Criteria Should be Employed?

The specific criteria for given evaluations depend on the particular audiences, objects of the evaluation, etc. These should be carefully determined in the planning process. To assist in this process, the school's personnel may find it useful to consider eight classes of generic criteria: basic societal values, especially equity and excellence; criteria inherent in the definition of evaluation, particularly merit and worth; criteria associated with context, inputs, process, and products; defined institutional values and goals; areas of student progress, including intellectual, social, emotional, vocational, physical, aesthetic, and moral; pertinent technical standards, especially in the cases of the safety and durability of facilities, vehicles, and equipment; duties and qualifications of personnel; and more specific, idiosyncratic criteria.

10. What Evaluation Methods Should be Employed?

A general response to this question is that evaluations generally are conducted in four stages: (i) delineating the questions and other important focusing matters; (ii) obtaining the needed information; (iii) reporting the findings; and (iv) applying the lessons learned. The delineating stage is aimed at achieving clarity about such aspects as the object of the evaluation and the questions, criteria, and time line. The obtaining stage typically employs multiple methods of data collection, including both qualitative and quantitative approaches. It also involves verifying, coding, and storing information and the required analytic procedures, again both qualitative and quantitative. The providing stage concerns presentation of reports. The reporting process will employ a variety of media including printed reports, oral presentations, group discussions, and multimedia renderings. The particular modes of presentation should be chosen to get the message across to the different audiences in terms that address their interests and that they will accept and understand. The applying stage is concerned with using findings for pertinent purposes. As noted above, these can include improvement, accountability, understanding, and dissemination. This stage particularly sees the evaluator (who might be a teacher, principal, or evaluation specialist) working with audiences, in settings such as workshops, to help them understand and use evaluation findings in their decision processes.

11. What Are the Standards of Sound Evaluation?

In the United States and Canada, this question is answered by invoking the standards produced by the Joint Committee on Standards for Educational Evaluation. The Committee has produced standards for personnel evaluations (1988) and program evaluations (1994) and currently is developing standards for student evaluations. All the Joint Committee's standards are grounded in four basic requirements of a sound evaluation: utility, feasibility, propriety, and accuracy.

The utility standards require evaluators to address the evaluative questions of the right-to-know audiences with credible, timely, and relevant information and to assist audiences to correctly interpret and apply the findings. According to the feasibility standards, evaluations must employ workable procedures and be politically viable and cost-effective. The propriety standards require evaluators to meet pertinent ethical and legal requirements, including working from clear, formal agreements; upholding the human rights of persons affected by the evaluation; treating participants and evaluatees with respect; honestly reporting all the findings; and dealing appropriately with conflicts of interest. The accuracy standards direct evaluators to produce valid, reliable, and unbiased information – about the described object of the evaluation – and to interpret it defensibly within the relevant context (see Chapter 13 for an explication of the Joint Committee's standards.)

Experience has shown that the utility, feasibility, and accuracy standards are quite applicable across cultures. However, some cultures would not accept the American propriety standards that deal with such matters as freedom of information, conflicts of interest, human rights, and contracting. While American educators should meet the Joint Committee standards, school personnel in other countries can probably best consult these standards as a potentially useful reference. Ultimately, they should determine and apply evaluation standards that are appropriate in their cultures.

An Example Representation of the Type I Model for Evaluating Programs

Figure 1 provides a summary of the Type I evaluation model as it might be applied to program evaluations. This model is adapted from the original version (Stufflebeam, 1993), which was keyed to evaluations of school administrators. The general scheme of the Type I model, however, can be adapted for use in evaluating students, personnel, programs, and other school aspects. The model is grounded in a set of standards for evaluations requiring that they be useful, feasible, ethical, accurate, and that they include ongoing assessment, communication, and integration in school functions. The model for program evaluation

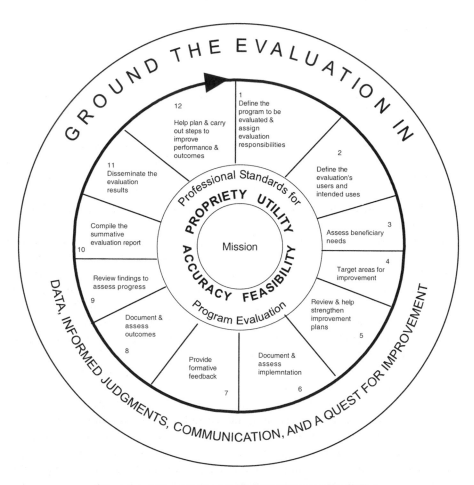

Figure 1:   A General (Type I) Model for Program Evaluation

is further based on the school's overall mission. The evaluation steps around the middle circle reflect the unique characteristics of program evaluation. While the steps are presented in a logical sequence, it must be emphasized that they will often be conducted interactively and not in the order given. The best order will be determined by the ongoing interactions of evaluator and users and will vary from situation to situation.

So far, this chapter has illustrated the questions and responses that a school's personnel individually and collaboratively might employ in developing their school evaluation systems. None of the above views should be uncritically adopted. Rather, interested readers should examine them, determine their own questions and responses about sound evaluation, devise their own evaluation models, internalize and apply them, and periodically evaluate and improve their evaluation approaches. The school's staff should devise separate models for evaluating students, personnel, and programs. They should then bind the models together as mutually reinforcing parts of the overall evaluation system. The most important bonding agents will be locally adopted standards for evaluation, the school's mission, and ongoing assessments of students' needs.

A TYPE II MODEL FOR INSTITUTIONALIZING A SOUND SYSTEM OF EVALUATION

Given a schoolwide commitment to install a sound evaluation system and develop a generalized notion of the types of required evaluation, a school's staff needs to undertake an effective process of installation. In order to be concrete and avoid generalized advice that fits no particular subset of schools, the following presentation addresses a particular class of schools believed to be at least not uncommon across the world.

The steps that are presented are designed to serve an elementary school with approximately 500 students, 1 principal, 20 teachers, 20 support staff (including teachers' aides, parent assistants, and specialists in such areas as bilingual education, health, speech and hearing, psychological testing, counseling, social work, special education, and evaluation and improvement), a community-based school council, and a government oversight authority. The unusual but desirable element added to what is typical in such schools is an evaluation and school improvement specialist among the 20 support staff. The U.S. and Canada Joint Committee standards for educational evaluations have been used as a proxy for the school's evaluation standards. Furthermore, attention is focused on schools that are committed either to improving their existing practices of student, personnel, and program evaluations, or to designing and installing new evaluation systems for one or more of these areas. By addressing the needs of this hypothetical class of schools and by working from a published set of evaluation standards, the discussion aims to provide actionable advice and general processes that are applicable to a wide range of schools. Twelve steps for installing evaluation are proposed.

1. Staff the Institutionalization Effort

At the outset, the school's principal should appropriately staff the institution-alization effort. Staffing should provide for both widespread participation and the needed evaluation expertise.

To begin, the principal should consider appointing a representative joint committee of about 15 members, who might include the principal, at least three teachers, two parents, two teacher's aides, two support staff, two sixth grade students, two representatives of the business community, and the school's evalu-ation and improvement specialist. The point is to include all perspectives that will be involved in conducting and using the evaluations. Except for the principal and evaluation/improvement specialist, it is probably wise to include at least two members from each category of committee members, both for comfort in numbers and to provide significant voice in the committee's decision making. Perhaps the most problematic aspect of this recommendation is the inclusion of two sixth grade students. However, their input can be invaluable in that they have had regular opportunities during more than five years in elementary school to observe and think about teaching and learning in their classrooms. However, their participation should be included only if it can be efficient and enhance rather than detract from their learning process in the school. If students are not included on the committee, their input might be gathered in other ways, such as in discussions by an evaluation improvement committee member with small groups of students. Whatever procedure is adopted, it is important to find some way to give students a voice in the evaluation improvement process, since they are the school's key stakeholders.

The principal should prepare, or engage someone else on the committee to prepare, a charge for the committee. This charge might be to devise general models for program, personnel, and student evaluation; to acquire the know-ledge necessary to develop the models; to review and examine the school's past evaluation experiences as one basis for model development; to develop a state-ment on how the school should interrelate the three evaluation models; to obtain assessments of the committee's composition and planned work from the school's other stakeholders; and to develop a budget for the committee's first year or two of projected work. Such a charge will be demanding and require that the com-mittee essentially be a standing body. It could be expected that, on average, each member would need to devote about eight hours a month to the evaluation improvement process. After the initial evaluation improvement process, the committee's membership should be updated. This could be on a three-year cycle. With the exception of the principal and evaluation/school improvement specialist, about a third of the membership should be replaced each year, with each member serving a three-year term. The evaluation/school improvement specialist will have a key role in helping the rest of the committee learn what they need to know about evaluation standards, models, procedures, and uses in schools. The principal and committee should also consider the possibility and appropriateness of obtaining additional assistance from outside evaluation experts.

2. Adopt Standards for Guiding and Judging Evaluations

For the projected evaluation system to work, it must be a shared and valued process and be integral to what the school does. Since evaluation is often an anxiety-provoking and sometimes a contentious process, its successful application requires development and maintenance of trust throughout the school, collaboration, and firm grounds for settling disputes. One of the strongest ways to address these needs is through adoption, internalization, and application of professional standards for evaluations.

When firmly established and employed, such standards provide criteria and direction for planning, judging, and applying evaluations in a fair, effective, and accountable manner. They also provide a shared vision about good evaluation that is central to an effective learning organization. By firmly learning and applying standards, school staffs will have an objective basis for deliberating and resolving issues in their work, assessing and improving evaluation operations, and making sure they yield valid and reliable assessments. In the Type I model part of the paper, the North American Joint Committee standards were advanced as an exemplar for schools to study as they decide what standards should undergird their evaluation work.

3. Use the Adopted Standards to Evaluate the School's Current Practices of Student, Personnel, and Program Evaluation

Having adopted a set of evaluation standards, the school's staff will be in a strong position to begin examining and improving or replacing current evaluation systems. The principal should engage the staff to reach agreement on whether to evaluate current evaluation approaches in the school and, if so, whether the evaluations should focus on students, personnel, and/or programs. The staff's recommendation should then be presented to the school council or other authority for approval as appropriate.

For each evaluation system that is to be examined (student, personnel, program), the evaluation improvement committee should compile the evaluation materials that are being used, such as sample guidelines, instruments, data sets, and reports. They should also characterize how the evaluation approach is intended to operate and how it actually operates. As this work proceeds, the principal should encourage each committee member to use the evaluation improvement experience to gain deeper insights into the school's new evaluation standards.

Once the relevant materials have been compiled and the needed characterizations have been made, the principal should assign members to task forces for each evaluation area to be examined. The task forces may be made up entirely of evaluation improvement committee members or include additional members from the school and/or community. The charge to each task force should be to assess the assigned evaluation model or approach presently in use against the school's new evaluation standards. If two or more task forces are involved, they should periodically be convened together to review each other's work. Together they should also look at how the school's existing models/approaches do or do not complement each other.

The committee should constantly aim to produce student, personnel, and program evaluation models that are compatible and that work together for the benefit of the school. The most important unifying agent is the school's set of evaluation standards. This assessment activity should result in reports on how well each evaluation system meets each of the school's evaluation standards (utility, feasibility, propriety, and accuracy). In this complex process of applying the school's evaluation standards to evaluate existing practices, it would be helpful to engage one or more outside evaluation experts to oversee and evaluate the effectiveness of the evaluation task forces' efforts.

4. Develop Improved or New Models for Evaluating Students, Personnel, and/or Programs

Once the diagnostic work of examining existing evaluation practices has been completed, the evaluation improvement committee should turn to the development of new or improved systems for evaluating students, personnel, and programs. As a first step, the committee should reach consensus on whether any or all of the school's existing evaluation approaches are acceptable as they are or are in need of revision or of replacement. If crucial standards such as evaluation use and valid measurement are not being met, then the systems should be revised and possibly replaced.

When new or improved models are needed, the principal should appoint task forces to proceed with the needed work. These would likely be the same task groups that evaluated the existing evaluation systems but could be reconstituted as appropriate. Each task force would be charged to use the school's evaluation standards and the evaluations of the existing evaluation systems to develop new or improved models of evaluation. The principal should also encourage each task force member to constantly consider how the task force's work in developing new models would apply in the member's specific area of responsibility. This will provide constant reality checks for the task force and also accelerate each member's preparation to apply the new models.

To launch the task forces' work, the principal should train or arrange for a consultant to train the task force members in the requirements of sound evaluation. This training should look at the formal requirements of sound operating models, review applicable models found in the literature, and revisit the school's evaluation standards.

The task forces then should deliberate, conceptualize the needed improvements or new models, and write them up. In this process, the task forces should meet periodically in plenary sessions to compare, contrast, and critique each other's progress. They should especially strive to ensure that the models will be complementary and mutually reinforcing. The model development process should culminate with a commissioned independent evaluation of each produced evaluation model. The external evaluation should examine the models, individually and collectively, for their soundness as working models, compatibility with each other and the school environment, and their compliance with the school's evaluation standards.

5. Summarize the New/Improved Models and Operating Guidelines in Draft Users' Manuals

Using the improved or new evaluation models and the external evaluations of these, the task forces should next develop manuals to guide school personnel in implementing the models. Each manual should be grounded in the school's standards; provide a mental model for thinking about and sequencing the steps in the particular evaluation approach; clearly outline responsibilities for carrying out the evaluation work; and provide sample tools, charts, etc. Tables 2, 3, and 4 contain sample outlines of evaluation manuals for students, personnel, and programs respectively.

Once manuals have been drafted, it is time to communicate the committee's progress to the entire school staff. In distributing the draft manuals, the committee should encourage the individual school staff members to study them in the context of how they can or cannot use them in their own evaluation work. In addition to the manuals, it can be helpful to set up a resource library of materials relevant to carrying out effective student, personnel, and program evaluations. The committee should also make sure that each school staff member has and is attending to a copy of the school's evaluation standards. Furthermore, the committee should provide orientation and training sessions focused on developing understanding of the draft evaluation manuals for all school staff members. Technical assistance should be made available to staff members who plan to conduct or participate in field tests of the manuals.

Follow-up group training should also be provided for school members who want to exchange information on their views of the new models. This can provide each member with a better understanding of the models. In these various group meetings on the new models, participants should closely examine how the different models fit together and how well they do or do not support the school's overall mission.

It is crucial that the new models themselves be evaluated – not just in the testing stage, but also in their future regular use. Thus, metaevaluation (provisions for periodically evaluating the evaluations) should be built into each evaluation manual.

6. Thoroughly Review and Test the New Evaluation Manuals

Following the efforts to acquaint the school's staff members with the draft evaluation manuals, it is next appropriate to thoroughly evaluate and improve each

Table 2.   A Sample Table of Contents for a Student Evaluation Manual

1. The School's Mission in Serving Students
2. Nature and Importance of Student Evaluation
3. Standards for Sound Student Evaluation
4. Areas of Student Growth and Development
5. Key Audiences for Student Evaluation Findings
6. Responsibilities for Student Evaluation
7. The School's General Approach to Student Evaluation
8. Schoolwide Evaluations of Students
9. Evaluation of Students in the Classroom
10. Resources to Support Student Evaluation
11. Focusing the Student Evaluation
12. Collecting, Storing, and Analyzing Student Evaluation Information
13. Reporting Evaluation Findings
14. Using Evaluation Findings
15. A Sample Calendar of Student Evaluation Activities
16. A Matrix of Example Student Evaluation Questions
17. Sample Data Collection Instruments
18. Sample Student Evaluation Reports
19. Provisions for Metaevaluation
20. Student Evaluation References

Table 3.   A Sample Table of Contents for a Personnel Evaluation Manual

1. The School's Mission in Serving Students
2. The School's Commitment to Support and Develop its Personnel
3. Nature and Importance of Personnel Evaluation
4. Standards for Sound Personnel Evaluation
5. The School's General Approach to Personnel Evaluation
6. Defined Users and Uses of Personnel Evaluation
7. Responsibilities for Personnel Evaluation
8. The School Member's Job Description
9. School Priority Areas for Improvement
10. Work Conditions and Possible Mitigating Circumstances
11. Current Accountabilities, Weights, and Performance Indicators
12. Staff Member's Plan for Meeting the Accountabilities
13. Midyear Self-Appraisal
14. Supervisor Appraisal
15. Peer Appraisal Form
16. Form for Summarizing Peer Appraisals
17. End-Of-Year Supervisor Appraisal
18. Growth Plan for Coming Year
19. Resources to Support Personnel Evaluation
20. A Sample Calendar of Student Evaluation Activities
21. A Matrix of Example Personnel Evaluation Questions
22. Provisions for Metaevaluation
23. Personnel Evaluation References

manual. The committee should engage all or most staff members in reviewing each manual and submitting a written critique, including strengths, weaknesses, and recommendations for each. The staff members should be asked to key their critiques to the school's evaluation standards and to indicate how well they think

Table 4.   A Sample Table of Contents for a Program Evaluation Manual

1. The School's Mission in Serving Students
2. The Nature of Programs and their Role in Fulfilling the School's Mission
3. Nature and Importance of Program Evaluation
4. Standards for Sound Program Evaluation
5. The School's General Approach to Program Evaluation
6. Defined Users and Uses of Program Evaluations
7. Responsibilities for Program Evaluations
8. School Priority Areas for Improvement
9. Needs Assessments
10. Evaluation of Program Plans
11. Evaluation of Program Implementation
12. Evaluation of Program Outcomes
13. Selection of Programs for Evaluation
14. Resources to Support Program Evaluation
15. Contracting for Outside Evaluation Services
16. The Annual Focus for Program Evaluations
17. A Matrix of Example Program Evaluation Questions
18. Provisions for Metaevaluation
19. Program Evaluation References

the approaches and operating manuals will function in their areas of responsibility. They also should be invited to note what added inservice training and support they will need to implement the new or revised approaches. They should especially be asked what additional materials are needed in each manual and what existing materials need to be clarified. It would be well for the committee to convene focus groups to assess the new manuals and systematically develop recommendations for strengthening them. Such groups could be productively engaged in estimating the time and resources required to implement the new evaluation approaches.

It is highly desirable that each evaluation manual be tested in actual evaluations in addition to the individual and group critiques. This, itself, could require a year or more; institutionalizing new evaluation approaches involves time-consuming, complex activity. The more the school can make the needed investment, the more likely it will succeed in producing a functional, valuable evaluation system that will work over time and help staff improve the school.

7. Revise the Evaluation Manuals Based on the Reviews and Field Tests

After completing the reviews and tests of the evaluation manuals, the evaluation improvement committee should revise them for use throughout the school. The committee should subsequently print and distribute copies of the finalized manuals to all school staff members. This should be followed by arranging for, scheduling, and publicizing the training and support to be provided to help all school staff effectively implement the evaluations. Shortly after distributing the manuals, the committee should hold discussions to help school staff begin preparing to implement the new evaluation approaches. It will be essential that the school council firm up a resource plan for implementing the new models. In the course of arranging for resources, the committee should evaluate the evaluation improvement effort to date for use by the school council and the entire school faculty.

8. Provide Resources and Time Necessary to Implement the School's New or Improved Evaluation Models

As the implementation stage gets under way, the school's leaders must match the rhetoric with action. They must provide school staff with the time and resources needed to do the evaluations. The principal should engage staff to make known their needs for help in carrying out the evaluations and in collaboration with the school council should allocate the needed time and resources in accordance with the needs and provisions in the evaluation manuals. As staff members run into challenges and difficulties in conducting the evaluations, the principal should encourage them and creatively support them to increase their repertoires for doing sound evaluation work. Early in the installation process it can be especially cost effective to engage external evaluation experts to support and train staff to meet their individual evaluation responsibilities and to help the principal and evaluation improvement committee coordinate student, personnel, and program evaluations. The first year of installation is a good time to institute the regular practice of annually evaluating and, as appropriate, strengthening the evaluation operations. It can be highly cost effective to annually engage one or more external evaluation experts to review and provide recommendations for strengthening the student, personnel, and program evaluation systems.

9. Annually Plan and Carry Out Student, Personnel, and Program Evaluations

Insofar as is possible, the evaluation improvement committee should work with all school staff members to integrate evaluation operations into regular classroom and school processes. Individual staff members should be encouraged to adapt the models to their individual circumstances. This will be especially true of teachers who need to take into account the needs of their particular students. They should also be asked to help evaluate and improve the models over time. Periodic metaevaluations should look closely at questions of compatibility and integration as well as positive impacts.

10. Apply the Evaluation Findings to Improve Administration, Teaching, and Learning throughout the School

Every evaluation should be keyed to a schoolwide view of how evaluation can help staff improve services at every level. Each evaluation plan should specify who will use the evaluation and how it will be used. If these matters cannot be clarified at the outset, then it is doubtful if the evaluation is worth doing. In providing evaluation training, school members should be taught not only to conduct evaluations, but also to make appropriate use of results. To promote use, the principal should encourage and support feedback workshops in which school staff members go over evaluation results and formulate pertinent improvement plans together. All evaluations should be planned and conducted in consideration of how the findings can be used to strengthen not just the part of the school being focused on, but the functioning of the total school. A constant aim should be to make the evaluations cost-effective for the entire school.

11. Administer a System of Recognitions and Rewards for Effective Evaluation Work

The evaluation improvement committee, principal, and school council should take every opportunity to encourage and reinforce effective evaluation work. One strategy is to administer a program of recognitions and rewards for especially effective evaluation work. School personnel might be involved in defining what level of contributions should be rewarded. In setting up the awards program, rewards should be used to motivate staff to conduct sound evaluations and to upgrade their evaluation skills. Reward recipients might subsequently be invited to conduct team learning sessions for other school staff members. As with all other aspects of the school's evaluation system, the awards program should be evaluated periodically to assure that it is fair, constructive, and effective for the school.

12. Commission External Evaluations as Needed

It is important to periodically supplement internal evaluations with external evaluations. This adds objectivity, credibility, technical expertise, and external perspectives. The principal should communicate with school personnel to determine the conditions under which external evaluations should be approved and supported. Together they also should clarify the expectations that external evaluators should meet. External evaluators should be asked to provide information that the individual school staff members can use to strengthen their services. When external evaluations are conducted, the school principal should ensure that the affected and interested school staff members are informed of results and helped to use them to improve school services. In the case of sizable external evaluations, the principal should consider employing an external metaevaluator to assess the merit and worth of the evaluation.

Institutionalization Themes

In addition to presenting the 12 institutionalization steps, six themes ran through the preceding discussion. In improving evaluation, school staffs need to develop a shared vision of what constitutes sound evaluation, develop working models that all school staff can adapt and internalize, foster the development of personal mastery of the needed evaluation skills by all school staff members, engage in collaboration and team learning, put all the evaluation concepts and operations in a systems concept, and subject the evaluation itself to evaluation.

Table 5 is a summary of the preceding discussion. It is designed to help school personnel systematically consider what steps they need to undertake to institutionalize a sound system of evaluation. The horizontal dimension of the matrix includes Senge's (1990) five disciplines of learning organizations plus the added discipline of evaluation. The vertical dimension lists 12 steps, defined above, to help schools install evaluation systems. The cells in the matrix contain key actions that a school's staff probably would find useful in the installation process. The contents of this matrix reflect a wide range of experience in helping schools and other organizations assess existing evaluation systems and develop new ones. It is suggested that school groups planning to improve their evaluation system closely study and consider carrying out the tasks depicted in Table 5.

ACQUIRING THE LEADERSHIP AND EVALUATION EXPERTISE NEEDED TO INSTITUTIONALIZE SOUND EVALUATION

The institutionalization process described above is not easy. It requires expertise, personnel time, resources and, above all, strong leadership. It is assumed that the school's principal will provide much of the needed evaluation-oriented leadership and that the school's evaluation and school improvement specialist will provide some of the needed specialized expertise. A broadly representative school evaluation improvement committee would be expected to devote the equivalent of about a day a month to implementing the planning and development process, with the principal and evaluation specialist devoting about a day a week to the enterprise. It is suggested that the school allocate funds to hire outside evaluation experts to support the institutionalization process and to provide external perspectives and that thereafter the school council allocate funds for ongoing support of the evaluation system.

This is a bare bones projection of the support needed to develop the school evaluation system. One implication of this overview is that school principals and other school personnel must develop a mindset for effective school evaluation and a functional level of proficiency in evaluation theory and methodology. National ministries of education and universities can find an important role to play here and should consider offering substantive, hands-on continuing education programs in evaluation, as well as technical support to principals and other educators.

An Ohio Project to Institutionalize Evaluation in Six School Districts

One example of such training and technical assistance occurred when The Ohio State University Evaluation Center conducted a semester-long evaluation seminar

Table 5. Using Disciplines of a Learning Organization to Institutionalize Evaluation

Institutionalization Steps	Shared Vision	Mental Models	Personal Mastery	Team Learning	Systems Thinking	Evaluation
			Six Disciplines of Learning Organizations			
1. *Staff* the institution-alization effort	Appoint a representative committee to lead the institutional-ization effort.	Charge the committee to reach consensus on proposed models for evaluating students, personnel, and programs.	Assign the school's evaluation specialist to help the committee gain sophistication in evaluation.	Engage the committee to jointly examine past student, personnel, and program evaluation experiences in the school and form goals for improving the evaluations.	Engage the committee to consider how the different evaluation systems can be better tied together and integrated into the regular work of the school.	Assess the committee's composition and agenda to assure that it will be credible and successful.
2. Adopt *Evaluation Standards*	Determine and adopt standards as school policies to guide and assess evaluations.	Plan steps to ingrain such standards concepts as utility, feasibility, propriety, and accuracy in all the school's evaluations.	Help each staff member assess his/her evaluation plans and reports against the standards.	Teach the standards to all school professionals.	Configure evaluations so that they are compatible with the system and yield useful findings.	Periodically examine the school's evaluations against the school's evaluation standards.
3. *Evaluate the school's current approaches* for evaluating students, personnel, and programs	Agree to evaluate the school's existing evaluation approaches against the school's new evaluation standards.	Compile pertinent artifacts of the school's current evaluation practices and characterize the existing models/ approaches for student, personnel and program evaluation.	Encourage each committee member to use this experience to gain deeper insights into and more proficiency in the school's new evaluation standards.	Form three task forces and engage them, respectively, to examine the school's existing models/ approaches for evaluating students, personnel, and programs.	Periodically engage the task forces to review one another's work and to look together at how the the school's existing models/approaches do or do not complement each other.	Engage one or more outside evaluation experts to oversee and evaluate the effectiveness of the evaluation task forces' efforts.

Continues on next page

Table 5.   Continued

Institutionalization Steps	Six Disciplines of Learning Organizations					
	Shared Vision	*Mental Models*	*Personal Mastery*	*Team Learning*	*Systems Thinking*	*Evaluation*
4. Develop *improved or new models* for evaluating students, personnel, and programs	Agree on whether new or improved models are needed for evaluating students, personnel, and programs.	Engage task forces to construct or improve models for evaluating students, personnel, and programs as appropriate.	Assign each task force member to constantly consider how the new model being developed would work in her or his sphere of responsibility.	Teach the requirements of sound evaluation models to each task force and engage them in reviewing pertinent evaluation models found in the literature.	Periodically convene the task force members to assess the compatibility of the models under development and their fit to the school's evaluation standards.	Engage one or more external evaluators to assess the soundness of the new or improved models, their compatibility, and their fit to the school's evaluation standards.
5. Summarize the new/improved models and operating guidelines in draft *users' manuals*	Develop school-wide users' manuals for student, personnel, and program evaluation.	Encourage and support each teacher and other professional staff members to adapt and internalize the school's new evaluation models.	Provide a resource library and technical assistance for school staff to use in upgrading their knowledge of evaluation. Train all the school's staff members in the new models for evaluating students, personnel, and programs.	Conduct in-service education so that school staff can share and obtain help in improving their own approaches to evaluation, including especially adaptation and use of the school's new or improved evaluation models.	Conceptualize the school's overall approach to evaluation in a general manual. Include school, class, and student levels; show their interconnections; and show how they all embrace a common set of evaluation standards.	Include metaevaluation in all school evaluation models and periodically evaluate the evaluation models and their implementation.
6. Thoroughly *review and test* the new evaluation manuals	Engage all the school's staff in critiquing the	Ask the staff to indicate how they think they could make	Ask the staff to indicate what in-service training and	Convene focus groups to assess the new models and develop	Analyze the time and resources required to	Formally field-test the new or improved models in selected

Continues on next page

Table 5. Continued

Institutionalization Steps	Six Disciplines of Learning Organizations					
	Shared Vision	*Mental Models*	*Personal Mastery*	*Team Learning*	*Systems Thinking*	*Evaluation*
	proposed evaluation models.	the models function in their areas of responsibility.	support they would need to implement the new/revised models.	recommendations for improvement.	implement the new models.	settings in the school.
7. *Revise the evaluation manuals* based on the reviews and field tests	Engage the evaluation improvement committee to make the needed revisions.	Update the users' manual for each evaluation model and disseminate the manuals.	Project the types of training and support to be provided to help all school staff effectively implement the new models.	Hold discussions to help school staff begin preparing to implement the new models.	Firm up a resource plan for implementing the new models.	Review the finalized models to identify any areas still to be addressed.
8. Provide the *resources and time* necessary to implement the school's new or improved evaluation models	Determine with staff a common understanding of what level of resources and time should and will be invested in evaluation.	Allocate time and purchase technical support to help school staff members develop and apply the needed conceptualizations of evaluation.	Provide time and resources for individual staff to use in developing their repertoire of evaluation procedures. Consider hiring an evaluation specialist to work with school staff and coordinate school-level evaluation.	Provide time and resources for needed team learning sessions.	Examine how evaluation can work toward a goal of being "cost free" by helping to increase efficiency and effectiveness.	Provide resources and time for annual metaevaluations.
9. Annually schedule and carry out a plan of *student, personnel, and program evaluations*	Key each evaluation system to the Evaluation Standards.	Annually adapt and improve the school's models for student, personnel, and program evaluations as appropriate.	Key each type of evaluation to strengthening both individual performance and overall school improvement.	Engage groups of staff to assess the different evaluation systems against the evaluation standards.	Ensure that the different evaluation systems are compatible and functionally appropriate for the school.	Periodically evaluate the different evaluation models and systems and the extent to which evaluation

Continues on next page

Table 5.   Continued

Six Disciplines of Learning Organizations

Institutionalization Steps	Shared Vision	Mental Models	Personal Mastery	Team Learning	Systems Thinking	Evaluation
						operations are adequately integrated into school operations.
10. *Apply the evaluation findings to* strengthen the school	Key every evaluation to a school-wide view of how evaluation is to help staff improve services at every level.	Specify in every evaluation plan who will use the evaluation and how they will use it.	Train school staff not only in the conduct of evaluation but in the use of results.	Conduct workshops in which groups of school staff go over evaluation findings and formulate pertinent recommendations for school improvement.	Always plan and conduct evaluations in consideration of how they can help school staff rethink and strengthen the school's functioning.	In evaluating evaluations, pay close attention to their impacts and functionality compared with their costs and disruptive qualities.
11. Administer a system of *recognitions and rewards* for effective evaluation work	Involve the school staff in defining what level of evaluation contributions should be rewarded.	Consider what exemplary aspects of the award-winning evaluations the school should encourage and use.	Use the rewards to motivate staff to conduct sound evaluations and upgrade their skills.	Engage award winners to conduct team learning sessions in evaluation.	Regularly work to strengthen the overall evaluation system.	Periodically evaluate the recognitions and awards program to assure that it is fair, constructive, and effective for the school.
12. Provide for obtaining *external evaluations* as needed	Reach a consensus about when external evaluations should be commissioned and what they should yield for the school.	Clarify the models of evaluation to be implemented by external evaluators.	Ensure that external evaluations provide information that individual staff members can use to strengthen their services.	Ensure that affected and interested school staff are schooled in the results of external evaluations.	Ensure that external evaluations are functionally related to helping the school improve its services and accountability to the public.	Provide for evaluating all external evaluations against the school's evaluation standards.

aimed at institutionalizing program evaluation in six U.S. school districts. The participants included six three-person teams, one for each school district. Each team included the district's lead administrator and evaluator and a university graduate student specializing in evaluation. The seminar group met weekly in three-hour sessions. At the outset, the group was schooled in three main topics: standards for judging evaluations, the CIPP Evaluation Model (as the Type I Model to be considered by each district), and a Type II Evaluation Installation Process (similar to that summarized in Table 5). In the next segment of the seminar, each team adapted the CIPP Model for use in the district and communicated the model to the school board and school district staff. In the last segment of the seminar, the teams devised a Type II strategy for installing the new program evaluation system and communicated the installation process to the school board and school staff. Following the seminar, the districts installed the new or improved program evaluation systems, with several of the districts hiring the graduate students who had participated in the seminar process. It seems that universities and ministries of education could adapt this process to help interested schools systematically learn evaluation and install new or improved systems of evaluation.

Ralph Tyler's Eight Year Study

One example of an extensive effort to help schools become evaluation-oriented learning organizations was the famous Eight Year Study in the United States (Tyler, Smith, & the Evaluation Staff, 1942). Between 1934 and 1942, an evaluation-talent-rich Evaluation Committee led by Ralph Tyler helped 30 schools clarify educational objectives, develop assessment techniques, measure and study students' progress, and use the findings for school improvement. The Evaluation Committee did not evaluate the schools. The philosophy of the Eight Year Study was that the responsibility for evaluating a school's program belonged to the school's staff and clients.

With the Evaluation Committee's expert assistance, participating schools devised and applied innovative means of assessing students' progress and obtained information to address the questions of a variety of audiences. The Evaluation Committee oriented and trained teachers and other school personnel in the conduct of evaluation and in the use and interpretation of results. The school staffs formulated objectives. The Evaluation Committee classified the objectives. The school and evaluation staffs then refined the objectives. The Evaluation Committee developed responsive assessment devices. The school staff applied the assessment tools and obtained information on student outcomes. The Evaluation Committee helped the schools record student outcomes, using a variety of quantitative and qualitative methods, and report them to students, parents, teachers, colleges, and the general public. These schools became richly deserving of the label of "the progressive schools" that was given to them.

The collaborative effort produced a number of important insights into effective, evaluation-guided schools. It was concluded that a comprehensive school evaluation program should serve a broad range of purposes: (i) grading students; (ii) grouping students; (iii) guiding students; (iv) reporting to parents on their students' achievements; (v) reporting to school councils and boards on the achievements of students, schools, and classrooms; (vi) validating the hypotheses under which a school operates; (vii) reinforcing teachers; and (viii) providing feedback for public relations. Over time, the collaborative project classified objectives under the following categories: (i) effective methods of thinking; (ii) work habits and study skills; (iii) social attitudes; (iv) interests; (v) appreciation of music, art, and literature; (vi) social sensitivity; (vii) personal-social adjustment; (viii) information; (ix) physical health; and (x) consistent philosophy of life. In spite of the wide differences among the 30 schools and a variety of curricular programs, the Evaluation Committee found general, content-free objectives that applied to all of the schools and courses. These encompassed higher order thinking skills, such as critical thinking, interpreting data, applying principles in new situations, and using proofs in arguments. The project found that the evaluation's audiences needed different kinds of information and that student performance data should be collected at the individual, class, school, and district levels. Thus, the project established the need for multiple measures and multidimensional scoring. The school staffs also found that evaluative feedback provided invaluable direction for continued inservice training. The hallmark of the project was collaboration: Universities and schools worked together to institutionalize relevant and systematic evaluation as a means of increasing effectiveness at all levels of the school.

Combining Internal Evaluation and External Evaluation of Schools in Israel

An effort to develop school-based evaluation was reported by David Nevo (1994), who described a project in Israel designed to combine internal evaluation and external evaluation in "a complementary rather than contradictory way." Nevo noted that Israel had a very narrow and weak tradition of school evaluation and that evaluations mainly had been based on superficial inspections and tests used for the selection and classification of students and comparison of schools, which was the subject of sharp criticism by school personnel. Due to dissatisfaction with external evaluations, some schools developed internal evaluation mechanisms. While the schools' personnel judged these mechanisms to be useful, outside audiences often found them not to be credible.

To address this dilemma, the Israeli Ministry of Education and some local and regional education authorities supported a new school evaluation project aimed at combining internal and external evaluation. The central office in the Ministry of Education or regional or local authorities helped volunteer schools develop school-based evaluation mechanisms.

This general arrangement parallels the two examples provided earlier in this section. One might characterize the arrangements as involving *responsible autonomy*, wherein schools have freedom to conduct evaluations in the ways that best serve their needs but must also be accountable to an outside group for addressing external audiences' questions and meeting the requirements of sound evaluation. According to Nevo, such school-based evaluations must provide both formative and summative evaluation. The additional important element here is that the external, administering group must provide training and technical support to help the schools conduct high quality evaluations.

The project was conducted in four stages. Nevo (1994) described the stages as follows:

> The *first* stage comprises regional inservice training workshops attended by principals and teachers from schools interested in developing internal school evaluation mechanisms. The workshops are conducted on a weekly or biweekly basis and provide 70 to 80 hours of basic training in program evaluation, testing, data collection procedures, and data analysis.
>
> At the *second stage* ... participating schools establish internal evaluation teams comprising three or four teachers who attended the training workshops. The decision to establish an internal evaluation team is usually made by a school towards the end of the first stage of the project. A school that has established an evaluation team chooses its first evaluation object (a school project, a program of instruction, or some domain ...) on which it will practice its internal evaluation capability with the technical assistance provided by an external tutor ... who works individually with the school on a weekly or biweekly basis.
>
> At the *third stage* the internal evaluation team is institutionalized ... The composition of the team changes periodically ...
>
> At the *fourth stage*, the school is ready for external evaluation ... (pp. 91–92)

Based on this project's early history, Nevo (1994) drew a number of conclusions. First, school people best understand the meaning of evaluation through the distinction between description and judgment. Second, students and their achievements should not be the only object of school evaluation. Third, outcomes or impacts should not be the only thing examined when evaluating a program, a project or any other evaluation object within the school. Fourth, school evaluation has to serve information needs for planning and improvement, as well as for certification and accountability. Fifth, there is no meaningful way to judge overall quality of a school (or a teacher, or a student or a program). Sixth, the internal evaluation needs can be best served by a team of teachers and other educators supported by appropriate training and external technical assistance. Seventh, it is necessary to mobilize alternative tools and methods of inquiry and to adapt them to the needs of the school and the capabilities of amateur evaluators. Eighth, learning-by-doing is still the best way to do evaluation. Ninth, internal evaluation is a prior condition to useful external evaluation. Finally, internal evaluators are more appropriate to serve formative evaluation, and external evaluators better serve summative evaluation (pp. 92–96).

Based on this study and his considerable experience with American education, Nevo questioned America's recent moves to stress external evaluation based on summative tests over what he sees as the additional essential ingredient of school-based, internal, formative evaluation. In support, he quoted the U.S. Department of Education (1991): "real education improvement happens school by school, the teachers, principals and parents in each school must be given the authority – and the responsibility – to make important decisions about how the school will operate" (p. 15). He also suggested that "We must stop using it (evaluation) as a source of coercion and intimidation, and start using it as a basis for a dialogue between the schools, their teachers and principals, and the rest of the educational system and the society at large" (Nevo, 1994, p. 97). Along with the Ohio State and Eight Year Study experiences, the Israeli project provides useful ideas for mounting collaborative projects to develop and institutionalize school-based evaluation.

CONCLUSION

Schooling is one of the most vital processes in any society. It should be done well, meet the needs of students, and constantly be improved. Every school should be an effective learning organization. Ongoing, defensible evaluation is essential to help schools identify strengths and weaknesses and obtain direction for school improvement, especially in areas of student learning, teaching and other personnel functions, and programs.

If evaluation is essential to effective schooling, it is also a monumental task. This chapter illustrates the extensive work needed to effectively conceptualize and institutionalize sound evaluation. Many schools could not succeed in conducting the needed planning and institutionalization processes by themselves. They need resources, technical support, external perspectives, and strong leadership. Ministries of education, universities, and educational resource centers exist to assist schools in these ways. The examples given in this chapter's final section demonstrate that such organizations can effectively help schools install sound and effective evaluation systems.

Readers should consider the ideas, models, and strategies discussed in the chapter as something like a set of empty boxes that they should fill in as they see best. The important point is to take steps to assure that their efforts to develop and sustain their schools as learning organizations be grounded in the development and use of sound evaluation systems. For it is only through the use of sound evaluation at all levels of the school that true learning can take place.

ENDNOTE

[1] This chapter is based on a paper, titled "Evaluation and Schools as Learning Organizations," presented at the III International Conference on School Management, University of Deusto, Bilbao, Spain, September 12–15, 2000.

REFERENCES

Bloom, B.S. (Ed.). (1956). *Taxonomy of educational objectives. Handbook I: The cognitive domain.* New York: David McKay.

Fullan, M. (1991). *The meaning of educational change.* New York: Teachers College Press.

Joint Committee on Standards for Educational Evaluation. (1988). *The personnel evaluation standards.* Newbury Park, CA: Sage.

Joint Committee on Standards for Educational Evaluation. (1994). *The program evaluation standards.* Thousand Oaks, CA: Sage.

Kline, P., & Saunders, B. (1998). *Ten steps to a learning organization* (2nd ed.). Arlington, VA: Great Ocean Publishers.

Nevo, D. (1994). Combining internal and external evaluation: A case for school-based evaluation. *Studies in Educational Evaluation,* **20**(1), 87–98.

Sanders, J., Horn, J., Thomas, R., Tuckett, M., & Yang, H. (1995). *A model for school evaluation.* Kalamazoo, MI: CREATE, The Evaluation Center, Western Michigan University.

Senge, P. (1990). *The fifth discipline: The art and practice of the learning organization.* New York: Doubleday.

Senge, P., Kleiner, A., Roberts, C., Ross, R., & Smith, B. (1994). *The fifth discipline: The art and practice of the learning organization.* New York: Doubleday.

Stufflebeam, D. (1993, September). Toward an adaptable new model for guiding evaluations of educational administrators. *CREATE Evaluation Perspectives,* **3**(3). Kalamazoo, MI: The Evaluation Center, Western Michigan University.

Stufflebeam, D.L. (2000). The CIPP model for evaluation. In D.L. Stufflebeam, G.F. Madaus, & T. Kellaghan (Eds.), *Evaluation models: Viewpoints on educational and human services evaluations* (2nd ed.) (pp. 279–317). Boston: Kluwer Academic.

Stufflebeam, D.L. (2001, Spring-Summer). The metaevaluation imperative. *American Journal of Evaluation,* **22**(2), 183–209.

Tyler, R., Smith, E., & the Evaluation Staff. (1942). Purposes and procedures of the evaluation staff. In E.R. Smith, & R.W. Tyler, *Appraising and recording student progress, III.* (Chapter 1) New York: Harper.

U.S. Department of Education. (1991). *America 2000: An education strategy.* Washington, DC: Author.

REFERENCES

36
A Model for School Evaluation[1]

JAMES R. SANDERS

The Evaluation Center, Western Michigan University, MI, USA

E. JANE DAVIDSON

The Evaluation Center, Western Michigan University, MI, USA

School evaluation can be defined as the systematic investigation of the quality of a school and how well it is serving the needs of its community, and it is one of the most important investments we can make in K-12 (kindergarten through high school) education. It is the way we learn of strengths and weaknesses, the way we get direction, and the way critical issues get identified and resolved. It addresses the needs of many parents who want to know how to choose a good school and the needs of teachers, school administrators, and school board members who want to know how to improve their schools. It also provides important information to local, state/province, and national leaders by informing their decisions. As an integral part of good management practice, it contributes to (i) identifying needs; (ii) establishing goals; (iii) clarifying goals; (iv) selecting strategies to achieve goals; (v) monitoring progress; and (vi) assessing outcomes and impact. It can be used for public relations and communications, as school report cards to the public (Jaeger, Gorney, Johnson, Putnam, & Williamson, 1994), as well as to give direction to planning or to select materials or programs for adoption. In light of contemporary proposals for site-based management, school choice, and school restructuring, evaluation at the school level is needed more today than ever before.

The size of the investment in the United States in federal, state, and local school district evaluations of schools, school accreditation, evaluations of the performance of teachers and others who work in schools, and in accountability reporting by schools is hard to estimate, but we know it is large just through enumeration of evaluation practices. There is also a long history of practice, which can be traced back to the mid-1800s, when Horace Mann submitted annual reports to the board of education in Massachusetts that identified educational concerns that were supported by empirical documentation, and when the Boston School Committee undertook the Boston Surveys.

International Handbook of Educational Evaluation, 807–826
T. Kellaghan, D.L. Stufflebeam (eds.)
© 2003 Dordrecht: Kluwer Academic Publishers. Printed in Great Britain.

There are many good practices of school evaluation around the world. The problem is not one of lacking good models. Rather, it is one of sorting through good practices and identifying the best of the models that exist and melding them into a coherent generalizable model. This is what we have attempted in this chapter.

Evaluation models vary widely in many respects, especially with regard to their focus, and to the level of detail they provide. The model presented in this chapter will certainly not fit all situations for school evaluation, nor does it provide comprehensive guidance for every step of the evaluation process. Rather, it is intended to provide a useful guide for designing and planning an evaluation, and for generating useful questions for investigation. It provides rather less guidance in the specific interpretation of the answers to those questions, or in the synthesis of multiple answers to draw overall conclusions about a school's performance. Because of the widely varying budgetary, time, and resource constraints faced by evaluators in different contexts, the model may need to be modified for use. More will be said about this later in the chapter.

Our purpose is to review the practice of school level evaluation in its many forms, to identify what are reported in the literature to be good practices and problematic practices, and to use what we have learned to develop a workable, generalized model. The model is intended for use by educators who are faced with a multitude of evaluation demands and options, who cannot be aware of all that is out there and what constitutes good practice.

The chapter comprises three main sections, which are supported with references to an online collection of detailed evaluation tools to help get an evaluation started. In the first, we describe what we have found in our review of school evaluation practices. In the second, a generalized model and process for school evaluation that allows evaluators to select their focus for evaluation from a menu of options is described. In the third and final section, we offer some concluding comments about the strengths and limitations of the model, its relation to other evaluation models and approaches, and some suggestions for model enhancement and opportunities for innovation. In the collection of school evaluation tools (available online at http://evaluation.wmich.edu/tools/), we provide direction in the critical first stage of evaluation – that of asking questions. The reader is then pointed toward resources that can be used to support efforts at refining the questions, getting answers, and using evaluation findings to make changes.

SCHOOL EVALUATION PRACTICES

Evaluation involves the identification of the characteristics of a good school (i.e., the criteria) and then working a judgment based on these criteria about how well it actually is performing. This involves two basic acts: gathering information so that conclusions and/or judgments will be informed and supportable, and using criteria to assess or judge the level or adequacy of school performance, or some aspect of it. These will result in a listing of strengths and weaknesses that can be used to guide future decisions, and/or a concise, overall assessment of school effectiveness.

School evaluation takes many different forms, some of which are known by different terms in different countries, and many of which are evolving in a way that blurs traditional distinctions. Four main (but overlapping) types of practice can be identified: self-study plus visitation-based evaluations; indicator-based evaluations; self- or district-initiated school evaluations; and ad hoc school evaluations initiated by local, state, or national organizations. The approaches reflect contemporary practice, and provide a starting point for improving school evaluation.

Self-Study plus Visitation-Based Evaluation

Self-study plus visitation-based evaluation includes both "accreditation" (used in the United States) and "inspection" systems with a self-study component. Accreditation is a process of self-study by school staff using published criteria, often followed by a site visit and report by an external accreditation team appointed by a regional or state association. The first regional accreditation association in the U.S. was the North Central Association, which was founded in 1898. The process is guided by the National Study of School Evaluation's (1987) *Evaluative Criteria* or state guides for public schools and similar guides for private schools.[2] These guides are supplemented by materials developed by regional and state accreditation associations that also administer the school accreditation process.

Similar systems combining the sequential use of self- and external visitation-based evaluation are used in various other countries in Europe and Australasia (Learmonth, 2000; Scheerens, Gonnie van Amelsvoort, & Donoughue, 1999; Tiana, in press). The latter systems use an inspection system, and so differ from accreditation. While inspection is a government-mandated system in which the visitation component is carried out by government-appointed inspectors, accreditation is a voluntary system run by education professionals. However, inspection-based systems are included in this section because they are increasingly moving toward an approach that combines the benefits of self-evaluation with the complementary perspective of an external review team (Scheerens et al., 1999; Tiana, in press). Even systems based almost exclusively on external evaluation are beginning to promulgate self-evaluation checklists, in addition to publishing lists of the evaluative criteria to be used (e.g., New Zealand Education Review Office, 2000a; OFSTED, 2000).

As stated in the *Evaluative Criteria* of the National Study of School Evaluation (1987), the *Criteria* profile the important characteristics of a quality school. "It offers a systematic process by which to assess the effectiveness of a school and to stimulate a school and community to establish a planned program of continuous growth so that its school may become progressively better" (p. v).

Accreditation and inspection-based approaches to school evaluation provide a guide for evaluating the school and community relationships, school philosophy and goals, curriculum subjects, auxiliary services, guidance services, learning media, school facilities, school staff and administration, student activities programs, other school programs, and school faculty members. Forms are provided and questions are asked about each aspect of the school. National Society for the Study of Education (NSSE) forms and questions have been used in the U.S. since 1940 and have been revised about every ten years since then. They have evolved into a well-refined set of good questions. In 1951 the Southern Association Cooperative Study in Elementary Education defined the standards that are still used today, with little change, for evaluating elementary schools. These standards were categorized as knowledge of the children to be taught, scope of the program, organization for learning, the teaching-learning process, resources, and personnel. What has been missing from most accreditation, however, is the study of student performance.

Indicator-Based School Evaluation

Indicator-based school evaluations began in the U.S. in the 1960s in response to public demands for school accountability. They have continued to the present, and now all U.S. states have some form of accountability program. This is a trend that is increasing globally, and many other examples can be found of states mandating the collection of a range of indicator data, such as school pass rates on national examinations and/or achievement tests. These are sometimes made public, as is the case with the so-called "league tables" published in England (Scheerens et al., 1999; Tiana, in press).

State-mandated evaluations of schools take various forms in the U.S. Some states rely solely on test score averages as an indicator of school quality, and this appears to also be the case in several other countries (Cahan & Elbaz, 2000; Tiana, in press). Some countries have developed fairly complex school reporting processes, such as multi-indicator profiles and "school report cards" (Johnson, 2000). Still others have developed "baseline assessment" systems, which are used either to measure the "value" added by schools (based on increases in key indicators), and/or to identify schools needing additional resources due to low initial baseline scores (Lindsay & Desforges, 1998; Wilkinson & Napuk, 1997).

Caution is required in using indicators of school quality to judge an individual school. Just because an indicator such as student-teacher ratio is correlated with effective teaching does not mean that it is essential for a given school to function well. A particular school may have large classes, but it might also employ effective classroom management techniques that more than compensate for this. Moreover, single tests of student performance fail to take into consideration contextual factors that affect student achievement, such as student characteristics and school finances. This does not mean that indicators are not useful; the descriptive information they provide can stimulate productive thinking and discussion about needs and direction for school improvement. Coupled with other information, indicators can play a useful function in school evaluation.

Brown (1990) described 40 state accountability models in the U.S. that are based on the indicators approach. She listed input indicators that included curriculum guides, revenues, teacher qualifications, and categorical funding. Process indicators included the use of non-administrators in school decision making, development of plans, and legal due process. Outcome indicators included test scores and performance reports. She reported, for example, that Utah school-level reports cover 18 items including test scores, fiscal information, attendance and dropout rates, course taking patterns in high schools, professional data on teachers, and demographic data on students. More recently, Johnson (2000) described the current use of school profiles and report cards. Indicators include student characteristics, school facilities, school finance, staffing and characteristics of teachers (race, education, pupil/teacher ratio, etc.), programmatic offerings, student services, school environment (e.g., after-school programs, school climate, PTA), student engagement (attendance, suspension, dropouts), school success (retention, PE, honors, math pass rate), high school success (post-graduation plans, graduation rate), and student achievement (reading, math, Scholastic Aptitude Test). Profiles are presented in narrative and/or tabular form, depending on the intended audience.

Very few of the indicators currently in use assess quality of instruction or of teachers. Neither do they indicate how the data can be used to improve low performing schools or sustain high performing ones. A recent international review suggests that there is increasing consensus among European school inspectorates that a broad range of indicators should be used, including measures of teaching quality such as structure, clarity, challenge, strategy, assessment, resource development, providing for differences, and efficiency (Deketelaere, 1999).

Self- or District-Initiated School Evaluation

Self- or district-initiated school evaluations were developed in the U.S. in the 1970s and continue to the present as supplements to state-mandated school evaluation and in response to local calls for accountability. More recently, school districts have developed evaluation models that can be used by school staff and state education agencies to guide school improvement. Several other countries (especially in northern Europe) have a very strong and/or increasing emphasis on local (rather than national-level) accountability, with the Netherlands being a notable example (Scheerens et al., 1999). There is also increasing emphasis in some parts of Europe on "bottom-up" (school-driven) rather than "top-down" (government-mandated) evaluation systems (Tiana, in press), and on the use of evaluation to help schools become 'learning organizations' that continually improve practices based on their own and others' experience (e.g., Leithwood, Aitken, & Jantzi, 2001).

Most countries practicing regular school evaluation tend to have a fairly uniform national system, with not a lot of local variation. However, in the United States, many school districts have developed their own approaches to evaluation, incorporating state reporting and accreditation into their model. These approaches vary according to the roles that evaluation is expected to play. In one approach, teams of educators – in this case student teachers, administrators, and university teachers/researchers – use an action research model (Elliot, 1991) to study school practices and to initiate change (Ackland, 1992). Relying on critical reflection (Weiss & Louden, 1989), Ackland focused on classroom teaching practices and learning patterns, guidance and counseling needs and practices, curriculum content, student motivation, and school policy. A lesson from this work was that teacher and administrator participation and ownership in the evaluation process is essential to bringing about change.

Cheng (1990) identified the organizational learning model (Argyris, 1982; Argyris & Schön, 1974, 1978;) as the one that may hold the most promise for schools. The model promotes continuous improvement and adaptation to the environment. The popularity of writings by Senge (1990) and Gray (1993) appear to support this approach, which has spawned several models (e.g., Leithwood et al., 2001). Climaco (1992) added that any school evaluation model must be simple and understandable, answer information needs of stakeholders, promote self-evaluation and reflection at the school level, and involve teachers and relevant others in its conception, planning, and monitoring. He proposed a model using indicators grouped by context, resources, functioning, and results. Sirotnik and Kimball (1999) proposed a set of 11 standards that accountability-based evaluation systems should meet. These included the use of multiple indicators, flexibility for application in different multicultural environments, and maintaining a balance between comparative evaluation (benchmarking against other schools) and context relevance.

Many U.S. school districts are using an indicators- or outcomes-based model for school evaluation, often using longitudinal data on selected indicators to describe progress and highlight needs for change (e.g., DeMoulin & Guyton, 1989). By using data on their own systems for comparisons, they are following a recommendation by Glass (1977) who advocated the use of local norms as a logical standard for school evaluation. School report cards or school profiles (Alberta Department of Education, 1991; Gaines & Cornett, 1992; Jaeger et al., 1993, 1994; Johnson, 2000) are a variation on the indicators theme used to produce public accountability reports. The content of school report cards, recommended in the research of Jaeger et al. should include information on the following: (i) standardized test performance; (ii) student engagement; (iii) school success; (iv) school environment; (v) school staffing and the characteristics of teachers; (vi) programmatic offerings; (vii) school facilities; (viii) student services; (ix) background characteristics of students; and (x) school finances.

Lafleur (1991) described a cyclical program review system that could be adopted by or adapted to fit most school districts of any size in the U.S. A model of this type has been developed by the Vicksburg (MI) Community Schools. Lafleur's model is noteworthy in that it is highly structured and simple, features that lead Blasczyk (1993) to argue that it is overly prescriptive. His position is that school personnel should build models together through a collective problem-solving process. "The act of building a model is an opportunity to learn new skills, is empowering, and transforms people into competent problem-solvers who believe they can transform institutions and practices. Needed is a kind of starter kit (or set of recipes which good cooks can add to)" (p. 11). The notion espoused in this approach of evaluation as the production of critical knowledge, by and for those who use it, is consistent with a view put forward by Sirotnik (1987).

Ad Hoc School Evaluation Approaches

Ad hoc school evaluations appeared in the 1970s in response to citizen needs for information about schools. Documents published by local boards of realtors about local schools, by citizens councils concerned with local schools, and by organizations such as the National School Public Relations Association (NSPRA) in the United States serve as guides for evaluating a school.

There are occasions when external groups or individuals organize to evaluate a school, an approach that adds the important perspective of citizens to school evaluation. Their motives may vary, but they often want an answer to the question, "How good is this school?" In the U.S., the NSPRA published a review of what the effective schools literature says about the characteristics of effective schools and describes schools that have these characteristics (Tiersman, 1981). They concluded that schools are only as effective as the people and ideas that shape them. The Northwest Regional Educational Laboratory (1990) also brought together a list of effective schooling practices based on the effective schools literature. Instruments such as the School Assessment Survey (Research for Better Schools, Inc., 1985), Connecticut School Effectiveness Questionnaire (Gauthier, 1983), the San Diego County Effective Schools Survey (San Diego County Office of Education, 1987), and The Effective School Battery (Gottfredson, 1991) all grew out of this literature. The criteria identified in these publications can be used to establish evaluation standards for different aspects of a school, but we must be careful not to apply these criteria blindly. The criteria are merely heuristics that suggest aspects of a school to study, and there will always be exceptional schools that fall short on one or more of them.

Some organizations have published criteria to guide citizens in evaluating schools. Again, these criteria can be used to establish standards for judging different aspects of a school. Noteworthy publications have been prepared by the Citizens Research Council of Michigan (1979), The National Committee for Citizens in Education (Thomas, 1982), and the New Zealand Educational Review Office (2000a, 2000b). The Appalachia Educational Laboratory has developed a school study guide for use by external evaluators. Their Profile of School Excellence (Pro/Se) can be used to generate a report to guide school improvement planning.

There is a wealth of information, approaches, ideas, and experiences with school evaluation, as the preceding review indicates. The challenge is to identify the dominant themes and strengths from the idiosyncratic and somewhat limited elements of current practices to improve school evaluation practice. Van Bruggen

(1998) noted the following broad international trends in the evaluation of schools and other institutions: (i) increased use of self-evaluation by schools (some mandated, some voluntary); (ii) increased prevalence of systems for comprehensive school inspection; (iii) greater realization of the importance of national (and perhaps international) consensus regarding quality indicators for stimulating a clear dialog about school quality and its improvement; (iv) a growing emphasis on accountability, including public reporting of self- and external evaluations, and action plans for improvement; (v) the realization that school evaluation should be frequent, ongoing, and linked to continuous improvement; and (vi) an understanding of the value added by both self- and external evaluation.

A MODEL FOR SCHOOL EVALUATION

On the basis of the preceding review of school evaluation approaches, a general 11-step process (see Figure 1) is proposed for school evaluation. Included with each step is a reference (in parentheses) to relevant evaluation standards (Joint Committee on Standards for Educational Evaluation, 1994). These standards define the touchstones that are needed to identify sound school evaluation processes and to improve our own evaluation processes.

The model is designed for use by school stakeholders (educators, citizen groups, school boards, school administrators, and other interested parties) who want to initiate school self-evaluation. The Evaluation Center developed a general model to guide program evaluations (see the model in the previous chapter as well as Stufflebeam [1994]), and this model has been adapted for a variety of purposes. Figure 1 is the adaptation for school evaluation.

The discussion of school evaluation in the remaining sections of this chapter covers each step in the model and highlights linkages with other contributions to the evaluation literature. These include checklist-based approaches (Scriven, 2000; Stufflebeam, 2001), utilization-focused evaluation (Patton, 1997), empowerment evaluation (Fetterman, Kaftarian, & Wandersman, 1996), action research (Argyris & Schon, 1978, 1996), responsive evaluation (Davis, 1998; Stake, 1976), and evaluative inquiry for organizational learning (Preskill & Torres, 1999).

1. Identify School Components to Be Evaluated

There are many aspects of a school that may fall under the heading of school evaluation. School evaluation is broader than program evaluation, personnel evaluation, and evaluation of student performance, and can include evaluation of school facilities, school finances, school climate, school policies, school record keeping. In an attempt to compile a menu of important aspects of a school that may be included in an evaluation, we have drawn entries from many different sources. The resulting menu is presented as Table 1.

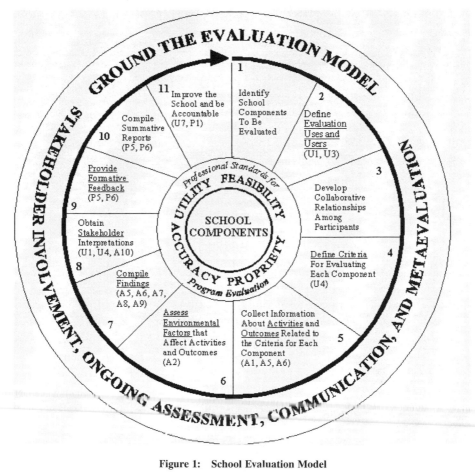

Figure 1: School Evaluation Model

School evaluation leaders may select the components they want to include in their school evaluation plan from the list in Table 1. If something in the menu is not relevant to a situation, it should not be included. If something important cannot be found in the menu, it should be added. However, only aspects of the school that are of immediate interest should be included. Often a scanning of Table 1 can serve to highlight the components most in need of review and change. Comprehensive lists of questions for all components set out in the table are available at http://evaluation.wmich.edu/tools/.

2. Define Evaluation Uses and Users

Among the first questions that school evaluation leaders should ask themselves are, "Who will use the evaluation findings?" and "How do they plan to use them?" Answers to these questions will clarify the purpose of the evaluation and identify

Table 1.   Aspects of a School That May be Included in a School Evaluation

School Context and Input	School Design	School Services	Student Outcomes

• School Climate
• Personnel
  Qualifications
	• School
	  Organization
	• School
		• Instruction
		• School Counseling Programs
		• School Record Keeping
		  Practices
		• Student Assessment
			• Cognitive Development
			• Social Development
			• Emotional Development
			• Physical Development
			• Aesthetic Development

• Parent
  Involvement
• School Safety
	Facilities
	• School
	  Curriculum
		• School Finance
		• Food Service
		• Custodial Service
		• Transportation Services
		• Extracurricular Activities
		• School Professional
		  Development Programs
			• Vocational Development
			• School Policy
			• Moral Development

the intended users of the information it will provide. Discussion with users – people or groups – will help to identify important questions that need to be addressed and the best ways to obtain information. The scope of an evaluation will be determined in part by the expectations of intended users, and the role that it will play in the school in part by those for whom it is intended. That role can be formative, giving direction to school improvement activities, or summative, involving accountability reporting to outside audiences.

3. Develop Collaborative Relationships Among Participants

One of the important lessons in school evaluation that is reported frequently is that school staff and other important audiences must be involved in planning and implementing the evaluation process. Unless there is some sense of "ownership," findings are not likely to lead to action. This is not to say that certain people or groups should dictate the evaluation process. It does say, however, that school participants need to see the importance and utility of the evaluation. Imposed or standard "off the shelf" evaluations often result in pro forma, unused evaluation information, a drain on scarce school resources.

It is important to identify those who need to know about the evaluation, who can provide assistance, the time and other commitments that will be required, and whether or not technical assistance will be required. Evaluation is a human activity and it is important to take time to nurture those relationships that will enable the process to work. People should be informed all along the way, and a structured time line that will help people see what is happening should be provided.

It helps to develop collaborative relationships among participants if the leaders of the evaluation process invite all who want to join them to become part of an evaluation steering team for the school. This team would coordinate activities and be responsible for reporting findings to those people or groups who need to know, when they need to know. Participants in the process should be able to see the value of the evaluation and to assume responsibility for contributing to its success. Often small group and individual discussions about the evaluation process will be needed to develop a common and constructive mind set toward the evaluation.

4. Define Criteria for Evaluating Each Component

Evaluation is a process of collecting information about objects and then applying criteria to what is known about them to arrive at evaluative conclusions. Criteria help determine whether something is good, adequate, or poor. If a curriculum is being evaluated, it is necessary to identify the attributes of a good curriculum at the beginning. The same can be said about teaching performance or any other component of a school. Of course, since several perspectives often exist about what is important, criteria from the point of view of different stakeholders or groups will need to be defined and applied. The important thing is to identify criteria at the beginning, and then to refine them as new ideas are introduced.

There are several sources of criteria. They come from professional and research literature on the objects being evaluated; from norms or generally accepted practices; from accreditation standards or other standards set by a professional group; from expectations established by a school board, a funding agency, or other important participants in education; from school policies, laws, and regulations; and from mission statements, goal statements, democratic ideals, known needs, comparable objects from outside the school, and other points of reference. The definition of criteria is not easy, and can be controversial. However, it is crucial that criteria be defined and shared explicitly in an open, participatory manner. An example of criteria used to evaluate the clarity of instruction, and relevant sources of information, is shown in Table 2. Many other specific resources are available online at http://evaluation.wmich.edu/tools/.

5. Collect Information About Activities and Outcomes Related to the Criteria Defined For Each Component of the School Being Evaluated

Collecting information is critical if judgments about each school component being evaluated are to be informed. Fact-free evaluations amount to little more than opinions. Information about any school component can be quantitative (numerical) or qualitative (narrative). For example, the criteria for evaluating a curriculum may include how much time is spent on each unit (quantitative) and the ways in which it contributes to some ultimate educational goal such as development of lifelong learning skills (qualitative). For each criterion in step 4 of the model, it is important to identify the information needed to make a

Table 2.   **Specific Criteria for Evaluating the Clarity of Instruction**

Questions	How to Answer the Questions	Resources
Does the teacher 1. review procedures, information, and/or directions before moving to new material? 2. give simple, concise directions and list them on the chalkboard when necessary? 3. rephrase questions, often repeat statements, and encourage students to ask questions? 4. use many examples to explain a point in a less abstract and confusing way? 5. pace the lesson to coincide with varying rates of learning? 6. establish smooth transitions from subject to subject and situation to situation? 7. expect students to learn and communicate this expectation? 8. plan – including short- and long-term goals, behavioral performance objectives, a description of methods, content, and evaluation system? 9. have organizational skills and attend to detail? 10. explain how the work is to be done?	Self-assessment, observation by by principal or peer	Use the checklist of observation, teacher self-assessment instrument, and survey items to teachers in *A Research-Based Self-Assessment System. Analysis and Action Series* (Reinhartz & Beach, 1983). Other useful items that can be used in surveys can be found in *Formulating Instrumentation for Student Assessment of Systematic Instruction* (Nelson, 1976).

judgment and how information (observe, ask, test, survey, compile records, scan documents) will be collected.

6. Assess Environmental Factors That Affect Activities and Outcomes

Parts of a school, and the school itself, do not work a vacuum. School district, state, and national policies, resources, and constraints can affect their performance. Likewise, politics, economic conditions, demographics, and cultural history can affect school programs and services. Therefore, it is worth looking at the institutional context of the school and the components of the school being evaluated. Are there environmental influences such as local politics, fiscal resources, human resources, material resources, the physical milieu, cultural influences, access or geographical conditions, or other factors that are affecting performance of the component (hindering *or* facilitating) or the level of outcomes? Assessing context is best done through group discussion. Some things may go unnoticed by one person but are picked up by another. Environmental influences can often be as powerful as the component itself and deserve attention in helping identify the "whys" of the outcomes.

7. Compile Findings

Information collected for a school evaluation can become overwhelming if not filed properly and summarized as it comes in. One of the best ways to file information is by criteria that are being used to evaluate the school (see step 4). Each criterion could have a separate file folder in which information about context (see step 6), activities and outcomes (see step 5) is deposited. When compiling information, it will be a matter of summarizing what has been found on each criterion. Organize and summarize what you are finding as you go along with the evaluation, rather than waiting until the end. A daily summary memo of findings would help.

8. Build Stakeholder Perspectives into Interpretations

It would be a mistake to expect information to speak for itself. One person's interpretations of the information provided by an evaluation may be that "all is fine and that no changes are needed," while another may find that "we are way off base and need to make some corrections." While one person may focus on one criterion as being the most critical, another may value other criteria.

There are two possible strategies for dealing with the issue of multiple stakeholder values, each of which has tradeoffs associated with it. One is for the evaluator to spend some time understanding the values and standards relevant to the evaluation, including multiple stakeholder perspectives, and to draw an informed overall conclusion about school performance based on that information. This allows a single evaluative conclusion based on multiple viewpoints, which has the advantage of that it removes the opportunity for stakeholders to use any ambiguity in the report as a leeway for political maneuvering. Its disadvantage is that it reduces the extent of stakeholder buy-in to the results, since they may feel less involved in the creation of an overall conclusion.

A second alternative for capturing this diversity of viewpoints is to ask key stakeholders to think about what the compiled information means to them in light of the criteria being used to judge the school. Where are its strengths and weaknesses? How should resources be apportioned to maintain strengths and address needs? What are their recommendations for the future, given what they now know? In a group meeting each key stakeholder could come prepared to provide her/his interpretation of the findings. As stakeholders speak, it should soon become evident where consensus and where disagreements exist. Further discussion or more information collection may be needed to get a clear sense of direction out of the evaluation. Clearly, this approach involves considerable time commitment on the part of the stakeholders, while still leaving open the possibility of failing to reach consensus. However, experience suggests that it is critical to include this step if buy-in to, and ownership of, school change is to be achieved.

Typical stakeholders that might be involved in steps 4 and 8 are teachers and school staff, parents, employers, and students. Others too may need to be involved in the interpretation of data and in making recommendations. Outside participants help to control for bias, enhance ownership and credibility, and avoid conflicts of interest.

9. Provide Formative Feedback

Formative evaluation is used internally by school personnel to improve what they are doing. A coordinator or steering team should provide evaluation feedback, both positive and negative, to those who can use it to improve the school at a time when it can best be used. Formative evaluation is most effective when it is continuous. It does not need to be in the form of formal reports. Practices can be informed and improved as relevant information becomes available. Hallway conversations, staff meetings, short memos, and brief presentations are all good ways to provide formative feedback.

10. Compile Summative Reports

Summative evaluation is used for public reporting and accountability. School evaluations are of interest to the community and may even be mandated by a local board of education, a state department of education, or a funding agency. It is the duty of the evaluation team to provide formal reports that are accurate, ethical, and useful for the particular purposes of the requesting audience. Reports should be interesting, to the point, and targeted toward specific audiences. The message should not be lost in a forest of details. The use of an external evaluation advisory panel to review the evaluation process and reports prior to their public release will serve to enhance their credibility, impartiality, and balance. This review process is called "metaevaluation," or evaluation of the evaluation (processes and products). *The Program Evaluation Standards* (Joint Committee, 1994) and *The Personnel Evaluation Standards* (Joint Committee, 1988) provide a framework for this work.

11. Improve the School and Be Accountable

Good evaluation does not stop with evaluation reports. There is a need to act on the reports. Individuals who were involved in an evaluation are often in a good position to help recipients use the results. For example, school evaluation leaders or a steering committee might plan follow-up meetings with recipients to help them understand and apply what has come out of the evaluation process. As the Standards note, evaluation is a poor investment of resources if it is not used.

By formalizing the process of school evaluation, a school staff can accomplish more than simply evaluating the school. Several benefits have been reported in the literature. First, stakeholders will be encouraged to work together on behalf of students, rather than in isolation. Second, a time schedule for the evaluation will facilitate getting it done. Third, evaluators will make better use of existing information and will be in a position to assess whether other routine but unused information really needs to be collected. Fourth, new ideas about change in a school will surface where they might ordinarily be mentioned but die an untimely death due to lack of follow-up. Fifth, information that teachers and others have collected through everyday experiences will be transmitted to others. Thus an evaluation can provide a forum for communicating important information and knowledge that might otherwise never be shared. Sixth, stakeholders will develop ownership in the school and its students. Seventh, "drift" in the school (i.e. gradual changes that occur unknowingly and without reasons) will be identified. Changes based on evaluation occur knowingly and with justification.

CONCLUSION

An examination of Figure 1 will serve to underline the centrality of the Standards to school evaluation. Thus, an evaluation that is sound will be useful, feasible, proper, and accurate. Furthermore, our review of school evaluation approaches shows that the best evaluation has four characteristics: stakeholder involvement, ongoing assessment, good communication, and metaevaluation.

We will now proceed to consider some of the strengths and limitations of the model, as well as its relation to many of the other types of evaluation models and approaches being used in the discipline of evaluation today. We also consider how the fusion of some cutting-edge ideas might provide opportunities for innovation in school evaluation.

The model presented in this chapter represents a step-by-step, relatively detailed guide for the evaluator designing and planning a school evaluation. A range of rich and detailed evaluation tools (available online at http://evaluation.wmich.edu/tools/) provides the evaluator with some very comprehensive sets of criteria, evaluation questions, and suggestions for information sources. These may be used in their entirety, or relevant sections may be excerpted for use in a more focused evaluation that concentrates on a limited set of issues.

Evaluators around the world work under time, budgetary, resource, and political constraints that vary widely. For this reason, it may be impossible, or even unwise, in the case of a particular evaluation project to attempt to encompass *all* the elements mentioned in the 11-step model. For example, time and budgetary constraints may mean that it is not feasible to obtain all stakeholder groups' interpretation of results. Furthermore, this could compromise evaluation credibility if the independence of the evaluation is important politically. Similar considerations will come into play for many of the other steps, which the evaluator should take into account when designing an evaluation.

One area in which the model provides minimal advice for the evaluator is in how exactly the answers to evaluation questions can be converted from descriptive information into explicit determinations of merit, especially when stakeholder consensus is either difficult or not appropriate to obtain. For example, should a dropout rate of 15 percent for an Australian high school in a working class area of Sydney be considered good, mediocre, or poor? The answer will necessarily include applying a combination of comparative and absolute standards that take into account the school's context, the real-life impact of the dropout rate, and a number of other factors. The limited scope of this chapter precluded the development of detailed algorithms and/or heuristics for this difficult merit determination step.

Another important evaluation step, and it is one that is critical in the interpretation of evaluation results and in the presentation of information to stakeholders, is the combination of multiple evaluative results into *either* a more concise summary of results (partial synthesis for profiling), *or* an overall conclusion about the school (full synthesis) (Davidson, 2001; Scriven, 1994). For example, consider the criteria for evaluating teacher-student relations, a subcomponent of school climate, listed in Table 3. To convert results into a comprehensible form for stakeholders (most of whom will not have the time, expertise, or inclination to interpret raw results themselves), several synthesis steps are required. First, data gathered from all four stakeholder groups (students, the principal, parents, and teachers) need to be condensed to provide a single answer to each evaluation question. Second, answers to all 12 questions need to be condensed, and the overall merit of teacher-student relations determined. Third, the results for teacher-student relations need to be somehow combined with those for the other nine subcomponents of school climate (security and maintenance, administration, student academic orientation, student behavioral values, guidance, student-peer relationships, parent and community-school relationships, instructional management, and student activities; see the Evaluation of School Climate tool at http://evaluation.wmich.edu/tools/) to determine how positive school climate is overall. This would be the option if the evaluator needed to present a profile of how well the school was doing on all 25 aspects listed in Table 1. For a full

Table 3.   Specific Criteria for Evaluating Teacher-Student Relations

Questions	How to Answer the Questions	Resources
Teacher-Student Relations:	Survey to students,	Available surveys are
1. Are students treated individually?	the principal,	*School Climate Survey*
2. Do teachers greet students in the hallway?	parents, and	(Kelley et al., 1986),
3. Are students willing to go to teachers with personal and academic problems?	teachers	*School Climate and Context Inventory*
4. Do teachers give students the grades they deserve?		(Wayson, 1981), School Climate Profile (in Howard
5. Do teachers in this school like their students?		et al., 1987). Information
6. Do teachers help students to be friendly and kind to each other?		on more instruments can be found in *School climate*
7. Are teachers patient when students have trouble learning?		*assessment instrument: A review* (Gottfredson &
8. Do teachers make extra efforts to help students?		Castenada, 1986).
9. Do teachers understand and meet the needs of each student?		
10. Do students receive praise more than they are scolded by their teachers?		
11. Are teachers fair to students?		
12. Do teachers explain carefully so that students can get their work done?		

synthesis, this information would need to be condensed one step further (by synthesizing the subevaluation for school climate with those of the other 24 dimensions) to provide an overall determination of school merit or worth.

The Relation of the Model to Other Evaluation Approaches

The 11 steps in the model (or a subset of them) may be applied to many of the types of school evaluation that are practiced around the world. For example, a school self-study project (which may be facilitated by an external evaluation consultant) could apply the steps just as easily as a fully external evaluation team, or even an individual school inspector using more of an expertise-oriented (or "connoisseur") approach.

The model may also be applied in the context of a considerable range of other evaluation approaches in use today, an application that has the potential to lead to some extremely fruitful innovations in the practice of evaluation, both in schools and elsewhere. One area of application might be program theory in participatory evaluation, which is becoming an important tool for allowing schools (and other organizations) to experiment with new ideas and learn about what works and why (Rogers, Hacsi, Petrosino, & Huebner, 2000). Although the expense of using program theory does not always outweigh the benefits, it has huge potential for engaging stakeholders in the evaluation process, helping them articulate their assumptions, and allowing not only organizational learning, but also organizational *un*learning, to occur.

With some adjustment to the nature of stakeholder input into evaluation design and the interpretation of results, many of the steps could also be applied to a fully consumer-oriented and/or goal-free evaluation (Scriven, 1974). In this case, the evaluator would gather extensive input from direct and indirect downstream impactees (e.g., students, parents, future employers), but would minimize the role of staff, teacher, and administrator agendas in the process.

The evaluation criteria, questions, and information sources listed in the 11-step model could also be blended with some of the ideas from the Balanced Scorecard approach to organizational improvement (Kaplan & Norton, 1992) and to augment the work being done in the development of school profiles and report cards (e.g., Johnson, 2000). Again when a comprehensive system for reporting on school merit/worth is combined with an inquiry-based approach (e.g., Preskill & Torres, 1999), the move to transform schools from the more mechanistic structures of yesteryear into the more organic, living and learning organisms that are starting to emerge in the new millennium is enhanced.

ENDNOTES

[1] This chapter is based on the book, *A Model for School Evaluation*, (Sanders, Horn, Thomas, Tuckett, & Yang, 1995). We wish to acknowledge the contributions of Jerry L. Horn, Rebecca

Thomas, D. Mark Tackett, and Huilang Yang to the book and to the evaluation tools which can be found at http://evaluation.wmich.edu/tools/

[2] Published by the National Catholic Educational Association (e.g., Self-Study Guide for Catholic High Schools) and the National Independent Private Schools Association, Accreditation Program.

REFERENCES

Ackland, J.W. (1992, April). *Collaborative school-based curriculum evaluation: A model in action*. Paper presented at the annual meeting of the American Educational Research Association, San Francisco, CA.

Alberta Department of Education. (1991). *Achieving the vision: 1991 report*. Edmonton, Alberta: Author.

Argyris, C. (1982). *Reading, learning and action: Individual and organizational*. San Francisco: Jossey-Bass.

Argyris, C., & Schön, D.A. (1974). *Theory in practice: Increasing professional effectiveness*. San Francisco: Jossey-Bass.

Argyris, C., & Schön, D.A. (1978). *Organizational learning*. Reading, MA: Addison-Wesley.

Argyris, C., & Schön, D.A. (1996). *Organizational learning II: Theory, method, and practice*. Reading, MA: Addison-Wesley.

Blasczyk, J. (1993). *The aphorisms about the relationships of self-study evaluation to school improvement*. Paper presented at the 1993 annual meeting of the American Evaluation Association, Dallas, TX.

Brown, P.R. (1990). *Accountability in education: Policy briefs, No. 14*. San Francisco, CA: Far West Laboratory. (ERIC Document Reproduction Service No. 326 949).

Cahan, S., & Elbaz, J.G. (2000). The measurement of school effectiveness. *Studies in Educational Evaluation*, **26**, 127–142.

Cheng, Y. (1990). Conception of school effectiveness and models of school evaluation: A dynamic perspective. *CUHK Education Journal*, **18**(1), 47–61.

Citizens Research Council of Michigan. (1979). *Evaluating the educational outcomes of your local schools: A manual for parents and citizens*. (Report No. 257). Lansing, MI: Author.

Climaco, C. (1992). Getting to know schools using performance indicators: Criteria, indicators and processes. *Educational Review*, **44**, 295–308.

Davidson, E.J. (2001). *The meta-learning organization: A model and methodology for evaluating organizational learning capacity. Dissertation Abstracts International*, **62**(05), 1882. (MMI No. 3015945).

Davis, R. (Ed.) (1998, May). *Proceedings of the Stake Symposium on Educational Evaluation*. Champaign: University of Illinois at Urbana-Champaign.

Deketelaere, A. (1999). *Indicators for good schools: Comparative analysis of the instruments for full inspection of primary and secondary schools in England, Flanders, the Nederlands and Scotland*. Report from a workshop given at the Standing International Conference of Central and General Inspectorates of Education (SICI), Bruges, Belgium-Flanders.

DeMoulin, D.F., & Guyton, J.W. (1989, November). *Attributes for measuring equity and excellence in district operation*. Paper presented at the annual meeting of the Southern Regional Council on Educational Administration, Columbia, SC.

Elliot, W.L. (1991). *RE-FOCUS program – redefine efforts: Focus on change under supervision*. (Report No. CS507609). Kansas City, MO: Hickman Mills Consolidated School District. (ERIC Document Reproduction Service No. ED 337 830).

Fetterman, D.M., Kaftarian, S.J., & Wandersman, A. (1996). *Empowerment evaluation: Knowledge and tools for self-assessment and accountability*. Thousand Oaks, CA: Sage.

Gaines, G.F., & Cornett, L.M. (1992). *School accountability reports: Lessons learned in SREB states*. Atlanta, GA: Southern Regional Education Board. (ERIC Document Reproduction Service No. ED 357 471).

Gauthier, W.J., Jr. (1983). *Instructionally effective schools: A model and a process* (Monograph No. 1). Hartford, CT: Connecticut State Department of Education. (ERIC Document Reproduction Service No. ED290216).

Glass, G.V. (1977). *Standards and criteria* (Occasional Paper #10). Kalamazoo, MI: The Evaluation Center, Western Michigan University. (Also available at http://www.wmich.edu/evalctr/pubs/ops/).

Gottfredson, G.D. (1991). *The effective school battery*. Odessa, FL: Psychological Assessment of Resources.

Gottfredson, G.D., & Castenada, ??. (1986). *School climate assessment instruments: A review*. (ERIC Document Reproduction Service No. ED 278702).

Gray, S.T. (1993). *A vision of evaluation*. A report of learnings from Independent Sector's work on evaluation. Washington, DC: Independent Sector.

Howard, E., Howell, B., & Brainard, E. (1987). *Handbook for conducting school climate improvement projects*. Bloomington, IN: Phi Delta Kappa Educational Foundation.

Jaeger, R.M., Gorney, B., Johnson, R., Putnam, S.E., & Williamson, G. (1994). *A consumer report on school report cards*. A Report of the Center for Educational Research and Evaluation. Greensboro: University of North Carolina.

Jaeger, R.M., Gorney, B., Johnson, R.L., Putnam, S.E., & Williamson, G. (1993). *Designing and developing effective school report cards: A research synthesis*. A research report. Greensboro: Center for Educational Research and Evaluation, University of North Carolina.

Johnson, R.L. (2000). Framing the issues in the development of school profiles. *Studies in Educational Evaluation*, **26**, 143–169.

Joint Committee on Standards for Educational Evaluation. (1988). *The personnel evaluation standards*. Newbury Park, CA: Sage.

Joint Committee on Standards for Educational Evaluation. (1994). *The program evaluation standards* (2nd ed.). Thousand Oaks, CA: Sage.

Kaplan, R.S., & Norton, D.P. (1992). The balanced scorecard: Measures that drive performance. *Harvard Business Review*, **70**(1), 71–79.

Kelley, E.A., Glover, J.A., Keefe, J.W., Halderson, C., Sorenson, C., & Speth, C. (1986). *School climate survey*. Resto, VA: The National Association of Secondary School Principals.

Lafleur, C. (1991). *Program review model*. Midhurst, Ontario: The Simcoe County Board of Education. (ERIC Document Reproduction Service No. 348 388).

Learmonth, J. (2000). *Inspection: What's in it for schools?* London: Routledge Falmer.

Leithwood, K., Aitken, R., & Jantzi, D. (2001). *Making schools smarter: A system for monitoring school and district progress* (2nd ed.). Thousand Oaks, CA: Corwin Press.

Lindsay, G., & Desforges, M. (1998). *Baseline assessment: Practice, problems and possibilities*. London: David Fulton.

National Study of School Evaluation. (1987). *Evaluative criteria*. Falls Church, VA: Author.

Nelson, D.E. (1976). *Fomulating instrumentation for student assessment of systematic instruction* (Report No. JC 760324). Texas City, TX: College of the Mainland. (ERIC Reproduction Service. No. ED 124 243).

New Zealand Education Review Office. (2000a). *Evaluation criteria*. Retrieved from http://www.ero.govt.nz/AcctRevInfo/ERO_BOOK_AS_HTML/ERO_CONTENTS_HTML/Contents.html.

New Zealand Education Review Office. (2000b). *Choosing a school for a five year old*. Retrieved from http://www.ero.govt.nz/Publications/pubs2000/choosingaschoolfive.htm.

Northwest Regional Educational Laboratory. (1990). *Effective schooling practices: A research synthesis*. Portland, OR: Author. (ERIC Document Reproduction Service No. ED 285 511).

OFSTED (Office for Standards in Education) (2000). *Handbook for inspecting secondary schools*. Her Majesty's Chief Inspector of Schools in England. Retrieved from http://www.official-documents.co.uk/document/ofsted/inspect/secondary/sec-00.htm.

Patton, M.Q. (1997). *Utilization-focused evaluation* (3rd ed.). Thousand Oaks, CA: Sage.

Preskill, H., & Torres, R.T. (1999). *Evaluative inquiry for learning in organizations*. Thousand Oaks, CA: Sage.

Reinhartz, J., & Beach, D.M. (1983). *Improving middle school instruction: A research-based self-assessment system. Analysis action series*. (Report No. OEG-7-9-780085-0131-010). New Orleans, LA: Xavier University of Louisiana. (ERIC Document Service No. ED 274 051).

Research for Better Schools, Inc. (1985). *School assessment survey. Information for school improvement. A technical manual*. Philadelphia, PA: Author.

Rogers, P.J., Hacsi, T.A., Petrosino, A., & Huebner, T.A. (Eds.) (2000). Program theory in evaluation: Challenges and opportunities. *New Directions for Evaluation*, **87**.

San Diego County Office of Education. (1987). *Effective schools survey*. San Diego: Author.

Sanders, J.R., Horn, J.L., Thomas, R.A., Tuckett, D.M., & Yang, H. (1995). *A model for school evaluation*. Kalamazoo: Center for Research on Educational Accountability and Teacher Evaluation (CREATE), The Evaluation Center, Western Michigan University.

Scheerens, J., Gonnie van Amelsvoort, H.W.C., & Donoughue, C. (1999). Aspects of the organizational and political context of school evaluation in four European countries. *Studies in Educational Evaluation*, **25**, 79–108.

Scriven, M. (1974). Prose and cons about goal-free evaluation. In W.J. Popham (Ed.), *Evaluation in education: Current applications* (pp. 34–42). Berkeley, CA: McCutchan Publishing.

Scriven, M. (1994). The final synthesis. *Evaluation Practice*, **15**, 367–382.

Scriven, M. (2000). *The logic and methodology of checklists*. Retrieved from http://www.wmich.edu/evalctr/checklists/.

Senge, P.M. (1990). *The fifth discipline*. New York: Doubleday Currency.

Sirotnik, K.A. (1987). The information side of evaluation for local school improvement. *International Journal of Educational Research*, **11**, 77–90.

Sirotnik, K.A., & Kimball, K. (1999). Standards for standards-based accountability systems. *Phi Delta Kappa*, **81**, 209–214.

Stake, R.E. (1976). A theoretical statement of responsive evaluation. *Studies in Educational Evaluation*, **2**, 19–22.

Stufflebeam, D.L. (1994). Evaluation of superintendent performance: Toward a general model. In A. McConney (Ed). *Toward a unified model: The foundations of educational personnel evaluation* (pp. 35–90). Kalamazoo: Center for Research on Educational Accountability and Teacher Evaluation (CREATE), The Evaluation Center, Western Michigan University.

Stufflebeam, D.L. (2001). *Guidelines for developing evaluation checklists: The Checklists development checklist (CDC)*. Retrieved from http://www.wmich.edu/evalctr/checklists/.

Thomas, M.D. (1982). *Your school: How well is it working? A citizens guide to school evaluation*. Columbia, MD: National Committee for Citizens in Education.

Tiana, A. (in press). *INAP – Innovative approaches in school evaluation*. Socrates Programme Project 14. Brussels: The European Commission.

Tiersman, C. (1981). *Good schools: What makes them work*. (Report No. EA 014276). Education USA, special report. Arlington, VA: National School Public Relations Association. (ERIC Document Reproduction Service No. ED 210797).

van Bruggen, J. (1998). *Evaluating and reporting educational performance and achievement: International trends, main themes and approaches*. London: The Standing International Conference of Inspectorates.

Wayson, W.W. (1981). *School climate and context inventory*. Paper presented at the Annual Meeting of the Mid-South Educational Research Association, Lexington, KY.

Weiss, J., & Louden, W. (1989). *Images of reflection*. Unpublished manuscript. Toronto, Canada: Ontario Institute for Studies in Education, University of Toronto.

Wilkinson, J.E., & Napuk, A. (1997). *Baseline assessment: A review of literature*. Glasgow: Department of Education, University of Glasgow.

37

The Development and Use of School Profiles

ROBERT L. JOHNSON

University of South Carolina, Department of Educational Psychology, SC, USA

School profiles, report cards, performance reports, and accountability reports are all common labels for reports used to inform the public about the status of schools. (In this chapter, "school profiles" is used in place of the litany of labels that are used across settings.) Contained in the school profiles are indicators of school performance, which include such quantitative information as student attendance rates, pupil/teacher ratio, and grade-level achievement scores. In some profiles, qualitative indicators about school performance provide information about school and community partnerships and awards received by the school. Potential audiences for school-level profiles include parents, real estate agents, principals, teachers, superintendents, and school board members. Although also potential consumers of school report card information, less than a third of the general public and about 50% of educators report having seen a school profile (Olson, 1999).[1]

Profiles may be printed and individually issued for each school, or they may be published in a compilation of schools in a district (Jaeger, Johnson, & Gorney, 1993). Educational agencies also have begun to publish profiles on the Internet. For example, a website in England provides school performance tables for individual schools associated with each local education authority (United Kingdom Department for Education and Employment, 2001). Also on the Web are lengthier evaluation reports, such as England's school inspection reports and New Zealand's accountability review reports (New Zealand Education Review Office, 2000). In the United States, 26 states published school report cards on the World Wide Web as of 1999 (Olson, 1999). One state has produced an interactive CD-ROM that allows stakeholders to examine performance trends for individual schools or districts over a 5-year period and download customized reports.

In a review of school profiles published from 1985 to 1992, Jaeger, Johnson, and Gorney (1993) reported that compiled reports typically allocated two pages to each school profile, and the individually issued profiles often were four to six pages in length. The most prevalent formats for reporting data were tabular and narrative. Tabular profiles organized indicator labels and statistics in tables and figures to report the status of schools. Narrative profiles accompanied tables and

International Handbook of Educational Evaluation, 827–842
T. Kellaghan, D.L. Stufflebeam (eds.)
© 2003 Dordrecht: Kluwer Academic Publishers. Printed in Great Britain.

figures with verbal summaries and provided qualitative indicators of school performance (e.g., recognition received by students and staff members).

Indicators used in school profiles can be grouped into four categories: context, resource, process, and outcome. *Context indicators*, such as the percentage of students who participate in free or reduced lunch, the percentage of students by ethnicity, and mobility rate, provide demographic information about the student body and community. *Resource indicators*, which may include per-pupil expenditure, rate of staff turnover, and teacher educational level, address the types of resources that are available to a school in the delivery of its services. *Process indicators* reflect factors, such as educational policies and practices, that the school can modify to impact on student learning; examples include the percentage of the school day dedicated to reading, average number of student hours in academic courses, attendance rate, and results of school climate surveys. *Outcome indicators* address desired educational results and typically include graduation and dropout rates, scores on norm-referenced tests or criterion-referenced tests, and percentage of students meeting state achievement standards. These categories will be used in this chapter to synthesize findings about indicators across studies of school profiles.

From 1985 to 1992, the indicators most frequently used in profiles published in the United States provided information about such context indicators as student enrollment by ethnicity and enrollment by special education status (Gorney, 1994). Resource indicators most often provided information about staff qualification in terms of the number of teachers with a master's degree and years of teaching experience. Process indicators addressed attendance and programs offered in the school, such as special education, bilingual, honors/academically gifted, and Title I classes. The most frequently used outcome indicators were norm-referenced test scores in reading and mathematics.

As with earlier profiles, a majority of profiles published in the late 1990s contained such context indicators as student characteristics (Olson, 1999). Similar to earlier profiles, approximately half of current profiles include the resource indicator of class size; however, in 1999 fewer than half of the states with school report cards included resource indicators related to teacher qualification. In 1999, profiles also often included the process indicator of attendance rates. As with previous profiles, a majority of report cards continued to include such outcome indicators as test scores; however, unlike earlier profiles, a majority of school report cards in 1999 included dropout rate and graduation rate. In accord with their accountability purpose, report cards started including an overall performance rating that assigns a letter grade to a school (e.g., A, B, or C) or labels the school (e.g., exemplary, acceptable, or unacceptable), but these were in a distinct minority as of 1999.

DEVELOPMENT OF SCHOOL PROFILES

In the development of school report cards an agency should establish a committee of parents, high school students, public leaders, teachers, administrators, research and evaluation staff, and other stakeholders to provide input about their needs as consumers of profile information. In the development of school report cards, these potential consumers should address the selection of indicators, methods for data summarization, and format of the profile.

Selection of Indicators

To select indicators, the profile development committee needs to consider the purpose of the profile, the definition of each indicator, and stakeholder informational needs. Furthermore, in the case of indicators that school teams may target for change in order to improve student outcomes, investigations should examine whether a stable relationship exists between the targeted input (i.e., context and resource) and process indicators and the desired educational outcomes.

Purpose of the Profile

School profiles are central to accountability (Center for Community Change, 2001; Olson, 1999; Rafferty, & Treff, 1994), in part, because taxpayers and parents assume that publication of test scores and graduation rates will motivate educators to work harder to improve school performance (Olson, 1999). Other purposes of school profiles include the following: providing information for site-based decision making (Lingen, Knack, & Belli, 1993; Mestinsek, 1993; Webster, 1995; Webster & Mendro, 1995); informing school-choice decisions (Rafferty & Treff, 1994); meeting state-mandated reporting requirements (Clements & Blank, 1997); screening schools for state-level recognition for accomplishments (Fetler, 1989); and providing information about the school's academic environment to college and university admissions officers (National Association of Secondary School Principals, 1992; Pelowski, 1994).

Establishing a clear purpose for the school profile is critical since the profile's purpose guides the selection of potential indicators for inclusion in the report. For example, a profile designed to inform school improvement efforts would report outcome indicators with process indicators. In this case, a profile might include achievement scores, graduation rates, and results from school climate surveys. The need for congruence between the identified purpose of the school profile and the selection of indicators is illustrated in the experience of one school system that produced profiles to inform the development of school improvement plans (Howell, 1995). Principals in the school district questioned the disproportionate number of demographic indicators included in the profiles, expressing the view that such indicators provided few insights into changes that should be considered in school improvement efforts.

When the purpose of the report card is to support stakeholders' judgments about school quality, it becomes a tenable prospect to support such judgments if a review process has identified educational outcomes that are valued by the stakeholders in that community. Education agencies are beginning to involve stakeholders, such as parents, business leaders, and school faculty, in the development of accountability systems and school profiles. In the Dallas school district, an Accountability Task Force composed of high-school students, parents, teachers, administrators, members of the business community, and representatives of employee organizations identified the valued outcomes of schooling and reviewed the methodology of the accountability system, the testing program, and the rules for school awards (Webster, 1995; Webster & Mendro, 1995).

Stakeholder involvement in California resulted in valued outcomes being expanded to include reducing incidents of violence in a school, reclassifying students with limited English proficiencies, and lowering dropout rates (Fetler, 1989). Omission of these valued outcomes may present an image of a successful school when in actuality a rise in dropout rates may result in a public perception of problems in school quality. The absence of profile information about desired outcomes would undermine the credibility of the school report card since the information would not be congruent with information used by stakeholders to form judgments about the status of schools.

When the primary purpose of a school profile is accountability, the selection of outcome information will focus on achievement information. Outcome indicators may be combined with context and resource indicators to allow equitable comparisons to be made between schools with similar challenges in meeting student needs. Furthermore, the achievement measures included in the profile must align with the expectations of the accountability legislation. If demonstrating progress based on the state curriculum is the emphasis of legislative reform, then criterion-referenced assessments that are aligned with state or local curricula are appropriate. When comparisons with national levels of achievement are of interest, then scores from standardized norm-referenced achievement tests should be reported.

A misalignment between reform intentions and outcome indicators is likely to result in inappropriate judgments about school effectiveness. Such would be the case for the implementation of a state curriculum and use of national norm-referenced tests as the sole student outcome in a profile. In these circumstances, the national achievement tests are likely to establish the instructional goals in a school, and these goals may, or may not, align with state and local curricula. As the goals associated with the state curricula and the goals assessed in the national test depart from alignment, the inferences made about school progress become questionable. Thus, the outcome measures reported in the profile should align with the profile purpose.

Clear Definition

Accuracy of stakeholders' decisions about the status of schools requires that each indicator has a specific, unambiguous definition. Comparability of data across schools, and across time, is contingent on the extent that an indicator is clearly defined. Stakeholders assume that the statistic accompanying the indicator is created in the same manner across schools. However, a study of indicators used by state departments of education in the United States found that comparison of graduation rates across governing bodies was not warranted because the authors found three different formulas used by states to calculate such rates (Clements & Blank, 1997). To establish common meanings for indicators, some education agencies have included a glossary of terms in compilations of profiles (Jaeger, Johnson, & Gorney, 1993; United Kingdom Department for Education and Employment, 2001).

The meaning of an indicator to stakeholders should be investigated in order to operationalize it in a form congruent with stakeholders' understanding (Kernan-Schloss, 1999). For example, when stakeholders express the need for information about safety in a school profile, the profile development committee should review potential methods for operationalizing the indicator to select a form congruent with stakeholders' understanding of the indicator. In the instance of a safety indicator, would information about disciplinary actions address stakeholder concerns? Or, does the public want survey data about how safe students feel in their schools?

Stakeholder Informational Needs

For school report cards to serve the decision making of stakeholders, the content should reflect consumer information needs. In Alberta, Canada, stakeholders (i.e., students, educators, administrators, support staff, parents, and the general public) selected indicators for review of the Grande Prairie School District's educational programs (Mestinsek, 1993). Stakeholders selected resource indicators relating to instruction (e.g., professional attributes, inservice, and substitute days) and funding (e.g., cost efficiency, and staffing) and process indicators relating to school climate (e.g., student morale, teacher morale, and attendance). Stakeholders selected such outcome indicators of student achievement as scores on provincial achievement tests, diploma exams, and retention rates.

Although stakeholder audiences may be treated as a generalized group, it may be more appropriate to determine informational needs of specific stakeholder groups (Nevo, 1974). Across studies of school profiles, parents consistently endorsed such resource indicators as class size (Kochan, Franklin, Crone, & Glascock, 1994; Olson, 1999) and teacher qualifications (Jaeger, Gorney, Johnson, Putnam, & Williamson, 1993; Kochan et al., 1994; Olson, 1999). Parents also endorsed process indicators such as attendance (Kochan et al., 1994; Olson, 1999) and types of program offered (e.g., special education courses and advanced courses for the gifted) (Jaeger, Gorney et al., 1993; Olson, 1999). In addition, parents consistently indicated a desire for information about the school environment, such as safety and percentage of students suspended/expelled (Jaeger, Gorney et al., 1993; Kochan et al., 1994; Olson, 1999).

Across studies, parents endorsed outcome indicators, such as student achievement (Jaeger, Gorney et al., 1993; Kochan et al., 1994; Lee & McGarth, 1991; Olson, 1999), graduation rates (Jaeger, Gorney et al., 1993; Olson 1999), and dropout rates (Kochan et al., 1994; Olson 1999). Parents questioned reliance on test scores alone to determine school performance. However, when interpreting school profiles, these same parents found student performance results important in rating school quality (Jaeger, Gorney et al., 1993; Olson, 1999).

School board members considered it important to include context indicators about student characteristics (Jaeger, Gorney et al., 1993) and such resource information as school facilities, school finance, and characteristics of teachers and staff. Board members indicated a preference for process indicators that provided information about the types of services available to students, a school's programmatic offerings, and school environment, as well as for indicators based on standardized testing information and school success information (e.g., graduation and promotion rates, number of 'A's awarded, and students' post-graduation plans).

School faculty endorsed the inclusion in school profiles of resource indicators such as teacher qualification and class size and the process indicator of attendance (Kochan et al., 1994; Olson, 1999). They also supported test scores as an outcome indicator (Kochan et al., 1994; Lee & McGarth, 1991; Olson, 1999), but at a lower rate than the general public (Lee & McGarth, 1991; Olson, 1999). Dropout rate was also endorsed by educators across studies (Kochan et al., 1994; Olson, 1999).

The previous paragraphs examined the indicators that various stakeholder groups endorsed; however, across studies some stakeholders questioned the reporting of some indicators. Parents considered gender and ethnicity data to be useless information when reviewing school profiles to judge the quality of schools (Jaeger, Gorney, et al., 1993), and expressed reservations about reporting student socioeconomic status (Franklin, 1995). Some stakeholders expressed the viewpoint that demographic information is possibly divisive or may prejudice stakeholder expectations for students in a school, whereas, others simply considered the information irrelevant (Olson, 1999).

Stable Relationship between Input Indicators and Outcomes

Before inclusion of input indicators in a school profile, members of the profile development committee should review the relationship between outcome indicators and input indicators. This step allows stakeholders to make an informed decision about the inclusion of an indicator due to its demonstrated relationship with student outcomes or, in instances where no statistical relationships exist, the inclusion of an indicator for the sake of the information itself.

The relationship between indicators is generally examined in terms of the amount of outcome variance that can be accounted for by resource, context, and process indicators. In a series of studies of district-level profiles, Bobbett and his colleagues found that input indicators included in school profiles did not account for 40 to 75 percent of the variance in student achievement outcomes. One contextual indicator consistently reported to demonstrate a relationship with achievement outcomes is that of socioeconomic status (SES). Specific SES indicators linked with student achievement include the percentage of students receiving free and reduced lunch (e.g., Bobbett, Achilles, & French, 1994; Bobbett, French, & Achilles, 1993; Bobbett, French, Achilles, & Bobbett, 1995b; Bobbett, French, Achilles, McNamara, & Trusty, 1992; Franklin, Glascock, & Freeman, 1997), the percentage of parents with a college education, median income of the community, and educational level of a county (Bobbett et al., 1994).

Resource indicators associated with achievement scores include teacher turnover (Bobbett et al., 1995a; Bobbett et al., 1995b; Franklin et al., 1997) and per-pupil expenditure in elementary and middle schools (Bobbett et al., 1993). Another resource indicator that demonstrated a consistent relationship with student outcomes was teachers' career-ladder status. In Tennessee, a career-ladder system for teacher advancement based on merit was implemented in the 1984–1985 school year. Bobbett et al. (1993) found that the percentage of teachers at the higher levels of the career ladder consistently contributed to the prediction of student achievement.

In school improvement efforts, decision making often focuses on changes in process in order to improve outcomes. In a review of school-effectiveness research, Oakes (1989) reported that previous studies had demonstrated relationships between outcome measures and organizational policies, such as time (i.e., the length of the school day or year), and curriculum emphases (i.e., courses taken in science and mathematics). Other promising process indicators included parent involvement, grouping or tracking practices, primacy of teaching, collegiality, and administrative leadership. Because these indicators have not been studied in the context of school profiles, it is possible that any relationship between them and student outcomes may disappear when investigated in the context of hundreds of schools.

Some indicators that have demonstrated an association with student achievement in studies of school profiles may be considered either outcome or process. For example, indicators of course offerings that have been shown to account for variance in achievement outcomes, such as the percentage of students in advanced placement programs and the percentage of students enrolled in foreign language (Bobbett et al., 1995a), may be more appropriately considered as measures of student outcomes than as predictors of student achievement. In other words, the percentage of students in advanced placement classes may be viewed as a proxy measure of student outcomes rather than a process variable that can be changed to improve achievement outcomes. The distinction is important because school improvement efforts directed at changing the conditions associated with a proxy measure (percentage of students in advanced placement classes) may misdirect resources that should be allocated for addressing underlying conditions (such as school climate) that may at the same time increase the percentage of students in advanced classes and improve achievement outcomes.

Other indicators that may similarly be conceptualized include attendance and dropout rates (Bobbett et al., 1994; Bobbett et al., 1993; Bobbett et al., 1992; Bobbett et al., 1995a; Bobbett et al., 1995b).

Although a strong relationship between outcome measures and process/resource indicators may exist under some circumstances, it may disappear under other conditions. The instability of indicators across school and grade levels has been documented (e.g., Bobbett et al., 1992; Bobbett et al., 1993, Bobbett et al., 1995a; Franklin et al., 1997). The amount of variance accounted for in student outcomes also differs by the achievement measures that are selected (Bobbett et al., 1992; Bobbett et al., 1995a). Furthermore, the statistical analyses used to explore the relationship between input indicators and outcome indicators influence conclusions about the relationship between indicators (Bobbett et al., 1993). Thus, there is a need to conduct analyses across conditions to clarify relationships between input indicators and outcome measures.

METHODS FOR DATA SUMMARIZATION

The selection of summary statistics, such as the percentage of students receiving scores in the bottom quartile of a norm-referenced achievement test or the mean normal curve equivalent (NCE) for all the students in a school, has implications for program decisions and should be congruent with stakeholder informational needs. Examples of summary statistics include percentile rank, normal curve equivalents, quartiles, local percentiles, raw scores (Gorney, 1994) and percentage passing (Linn, 2001). The types of comparisons reported in school profiles include comparisons within the school, such as the school's scores in previous years and scores by gender, ethnicity, and socioeconomic status (Gorney, 1994; Olson, 1999). External comparisons may be made with scores in the district, state, and in similar schools.

Selection of Summary Statistics

The selection of the statistic (e.g., percentage of students in bottom quartile, or mean NCE) for reporting outcomes has implications for school improvement decisions (Rafferty & Treff, 1994). In one example, it was noted that use of percentage passing to summarize test scores focused decision making and school resources on students who scored near the cut score. In their study of an inner school district, Rafferty and Treff reported that none of the students receiving Title I or gifted services contributed to district changes in percentage passing rates. The use of percentage passing ignores the gains of students below the cut score, as well as those instances where students above it fail to show progress. Thus, stakeholders must realize that the decision to use percentage passing as an indicator of school improvement may dilute school improvement efforts for students at either extreme of the achievement spectrum.

Mean scores incorporate the scores of all student populations; however, they may be unduly affected by changes in achievement among gifted or Title 1 populations (Rafferty & Treff, 1994). Decision making in school improvement planning may then focus primarily on one, or both, of these groups rather than the entire student population. It follows that selection of the summary statistic should be an informed choice made by stakeholders in congruence with their focus on school improvement efforts.

In terms of stakeholder preferences, when asked, "What do you think is more important: knowing how a child is doing against a set standard or knowing how a child is doing relative to other children?" parents and the general public were split (Olson, 1999). Approximately half of teachers wanted comparisons to be with other children and a third wanted comparisons with set standards. In fact, stakeholders generally expressed a desire for both types of comparison, but it is unclear whether they realized the potential implications for assessing with both standards-based and norm-referenced tests.

Forming Comparison Groups

School outcomes may be compared with those of the nation, the school district, or similar schools. However, reports that compare student outcomes for a school with all other schools ignore the natural grouping in schools and the consequences of students not beginning their school experience at the same educational level. In recognition of this situation, school outcomes have been compared with student achievement in similar schools in a large number of states.

The selection of indicators that will be used to form comparison groups (also referred to as grouping indicators) should meet two criteria: the indicators should be factors beyond the control of the schools, and research should indicate that there is a relationship between the grouping indicators and student outcomes (Salganik, 1994; Webster & Mendro, 1995; Willms, 1992). A grouping indicator that meets both criteria is socioeconomic status. Thus, equity would require that the achievement levels in schools be compared with achievement in schools of similar socioeconomic status.

Other context indicators used to form comparison groups include parent education, unit size (including urbanicity and population density), limited-English proficiency, and student mobility. Comparison groups also have taken into account parent occupation, ethnicity, mean teacher salary, percentage of female students, time watching television, number of books and magazines in the home, average daily membership change, funding formula, and first grade test scores. Assessment of student achievement levels at entry to a school, such as the readiness test formerly used in the South Carolina accountability model (Mandeville, 1994), is also considered necessary for forming fair comparison groups (Willms, 1992).

Approaches for grouping that take into account contextual information typically compare a school's performance with clusters of similar schools or compare
a school's performance with its predicted performance through use of regression
or mixed-effects models (Fetler, 1989; Salganik, 1994; Sanders, Saxton, & Horn,
1997; Webster & Mendro, 1995; Willms, 1992; Willms & Kerckhoff, 1995). An
advantage of comparing schools grouped on a clustering variable is that stakeholders will more readily understand the basis for the comparison. Regression
and mixed-effects models eliminate the need for grouping schools; however, the
more complex analyses are likely to impede stakeholder understanding of the
basis for the comparison.

While the rationale for forming comparison groups is to provide fair comparisons of student outcomes for schools operating with similar student populations
and resources, to some stakeholders the practice of adjusting outcomes according to the differential impact of student demographics may suggest that lower
expectations for some students are acceptable (Fetler, 1989; Linn, 2001; Olson,
1999). To avoid this implicit assumption, Fetler (1989) suggested that profiles
should provide trend data for the school and comparisons based on school
clusters and all schools. Linn (2001) concurs with the use of trend data; however,
he indicates that ranking schools based on comparisons with similar schools may
result in confusion. He provides an example of performance ranking for five
elementary schools in a district. When compared to all other schools, the performance ranking of one elementary school was the lowest in the district. However,
when compared to similar schools, the ranking of the school was the highest in
the district. Such a reversal in rankings may create doubt for stakeholders about
the credibility of the information. The situation is avoided if Linn's counsel is
taken and school improvement is used as the measure of school effectiveness,
rather than current performance, since improvement allows for different starting
points but similar expectations in terms of improvement for all.

Formatting School Profiles

As with the selection of indicators, the design of profiles should take into consideration audience preference in terms of format and data presentation. For
example, lengthy school profiles are considered problematic by stakeholders
(Olson, 1999). Participants in one study approved of the report cards published
for schools in New York until they realized that the report was about 12 pages in
length. Extremely short profiles, however, do not appear to be a requirement of
stakeholders: Jaeger, Gorney et al. (1993) reported that parents and school
board members preferred four-page rather than two-page profiles. In another
study, parents indicated a preference for report cards that are specific to school
level (i.e., elementary, middle, and high school) to avoid having empty tables,
such as student dropouts at the elementary level (Kochan et al., 1994).

Data Presentation

Presentation of data should consider consumer needs; however, research on the preferences of stakeholders in this area is not conclusive. One study found that school board members preferred tabular presentation of data over narrative and that parents also had a slight preference for tabular reports rather than narrative (Jaeger, Gorney et al., 1993). However, in a review of Louisiana school profiles, parents wanted more information presented in narrative (Kochan et al., 1994). To assist stakeholders in the interpretation of profile data, Rhode Island provided short narratives below tables and charts to explain "what you're looking at" and "what you're looking for" (Olson, 1999, p. 36). Parents have also indicated that the narrative in school profiles should be monitored for readability (Caldas & Mossavat, 1994; Kochan et al., 1994). To address these stakeholder needs, the Louisiana school profiles supplemented the tabular presentation of data with explanatory text that is written at an 8th grade reading level.

To facilitate interpretation of data, Louisiana parents suggested that data in tables be modified so that frequencies accompany percentages (Kochan et al., 1994). Stakeholders generally favor the inclusion of trend data for student outcomes (Jaeger, Gorney et al., 1993; Olson, 1999). Furthermore, school board members have indicated that pupil-teacher ratios and attendance rates should be compared with district information (Jaeger, Gorney et al., 1993). A desire for points of comparison was the focus of some comments in Delaware (Lee & McGarth, 1991) where respondents indicated that high school results should be compared with other schools in the state and nation.

Accuracy of Stakeholder Judgments

Accuracy of stakeholder interpretation was investigated by Jaeger, Gorney et al. (1993) by manipulating two format features of school profiles: length (two pages or four pages) and data presentation (tabular or narrative). The indicators in the reports were varied to create school profiles that reflected four levels of quality: "good" (e.g., schools with high test scores and attendance rates), "consistently mediocre" (e.g., schools with test scores and attendance rates that were between the "good" and "poor" schools), "inconsistently mediocre" (e.g., schools with low math test scores and high reading test scores), and "poor" (e.g., schools with low test scores and low attendance rates). Stakeholders were asked to judge the quality of the schools on the basis of these profiles.

Parents were most accurate with a four-page, narrative profile and least accurate with a two-page, narrative profile (Jaeger, Gorney et al., 1993). School board members were most accurate with the four-page profile; the results were inconsistent for the narrative and tabular formats. Superintendents were most accurate with the four-page, narrative profile and the two-page, tabular profiles, and least accurate with the four-page tabular profiles. In general, the longer profile, containing more information, appears to enhance the accuracy of decision making for stakeholder groups.

UTILIZATION OF SCHOOL PROFILES

School profiles have existed at least since 1969 when individual school report cards were published in a compilation entitled *The Columbus School Profile: A Report of the Columbus Public Schools to the Community* (Merriman, 1969). However, the fact that many of the profiles published in the late 1980s and early 1990s appeared in compilations raises doubt about their distribution to a broad audience and questions about their role in providing information about the schools to the general public. Use of profiles as accountability tools assumes that the reports will be distributed to stakeholder groups; that stakeholders will be prepared to use the information contained in the reports; and that profile use will be integrated into school policy and procedures.

Distribution of School Profiles

As mentioned earlier, education agencies have begun to publish school report cards on the World Wide Web. However, since parents may not be able to readily access such information, report cards should also be sent to students' homes (Center for Community Change, 2001). In some instances, the state or district is required to mail a school profile to all families of enrolled students. In addition, profiles should be made available to the public at community locations (e.g., library, or district office) (Kernan-Schloss, 1999). Another method for distribution and communication of profile information is for schools to share information with parents on school report card nights (Kernan-Schloss, 1999; Olson, 1999). Thus, schools must take an active role in identifying methods for getting the information in school profiles to stakeholders.

Preparation of Stakeholders for Use of Profiles

The effective use of report cards requires that stakeholders be able to interpret the information; however, it is likely that stakeholders will require training in order to understand the indicators and the implications of the information they provide. If administrators and teachers are to use profile information to plan for school improvement, and if they will be expected to assist parents in the interpretation of the information, then staff development will need to address these skills (Kernan-Schloss, 1999; Soholt & Kernan-Schloss, 1999). Training should not be reserved only for school employees; for example, some states offer workshops for news reporters (Olson, 1999).

If school profiles are conceptualized as a tool for parents to effect change (Center for Community Change, 2001), then education agencies will need to assist parents in understanding how such information can be used in school reform. The preparation of parents to use school profiles is required because parents have indicated that, although they would use the information to select schools, it would be unlikely that such information could be used to effect change (Olson, 1999). One method for assisting parents is offered by Ohio where suggestions are provided about how stakeholders can follow up on report card information and the type of questions they might ask their public schools (Olson, 1999).

Integration Into Policy and Procedure

Some policies for school profiles will be mandated by national, state, or provincial governing bodies; however, many issues in the publication, distribution, and utilization of profiles will be left to local school boards to set policy. Local boards may specify additional avenues for distribution of profiles to the public, they may identify areas for staff development, and they may elect to set policy about the use of profiles in planning school improvement (Soholt & Kernan-Schloss, 1999). If the profile is to be an accountability tool, schools should be required to write an action plan based on report card information (Brown, 1999).

In addition to incorporating profiles into school planning, education agencies will want to establish review cycles for the revision of profiles (Johnson, 2000). Stakeholder information needs are likely to change over time and can be identified and addressed in such a cycle. The inclusion of profiles in a review cycle also allows the education agency to assess the quality of indicators once the publication of profiles begins. Indicators identified as of little public interest, or that bear little relationship to school outcomes, can be re-evaluated by the review committee as profiles are revised.

CONCLUSION

Based on the state of the art in research on school profiles, the following issues appear relevant in the design and use of profiles. Educators and the public generally approve of the inclusion of achievement measures in profiles; however, stakeholders also express reservations about sole reliance on this type of indicator. Other outcome indicators endorsed by stakeholders include graduation and dropout rates. Stakeholders consistently express an interest in information that provides a broader base for making conclusions about school effectiveness. Across studies of school profiles, stakeholders indicate an interest in information about safety and teacher qualifications. Stakeholders also indicate that comparisons and trend data should be provided in profiles. Agencies in the process of developing or revising schools profiles should determine if the information needs of their stakeholders parallel those expressed in these studies.

The differing purposes of profiles, and the unique information requirements of stakeholders, may require tailoring profiles for different stakeholder audiences, such as parents and school board members. School profiles will also need to be tailored to each school level to allow inclusion of indicators relevant for each student population, such as dropout rates for high schools. To promote understanding of the information, publishers of profiles should consider accompanying data that are presented in tables with explanatory text, and percentages should be accompanied by frequencies. Length of profiles should be approximately four pages and the narrative written at the stakeholders' reading level.

Finally, education agencies will need to establish multiple avenues for the distribution of profiles. Effective use of profiles will require staff development for school personnel and opportunities for the general public to interpret profile information with teachers and administrators. Establishment of a review cycle for the revision of school profiles will allow education agencies to keep indicators current with stakeholders information needs and to study the relationship between indicators and student outcomes.

ENDNOTE

[1] Examples of school profiles are readily available from the Internet so readers who wish to see and study sample profiles can easily do so. The Center for Education Reform and the Heritage Foundation both maintain lists of links to school report cards across the United States: <http://www.edreform.com/ education_reform_resources/school_report_cards.htm> and <http://www.heritage.org/reportcards>. Standards & Poors, which traditionally reviews and evaluates corporations, has also developed school evaluation services. Currently they have developed rather unique school profiles for two states and hope to expand these services in the future: <http://www.ses.standardandpoors.com>. Profiles for schools in Ontario, Canada are available at <http://esip.edu.gov.on.ca/English>.

REFERENCES

Bobbett, G., Achilles, C., & French, R. (1994). *Can Arkansas school districts' report cards on schools be used by educators, community members, or administrators to make a positive impact on student outcome?* Paper presented at annual meeting of the Southern Regional Council on Educational Administration, Atlanta, GA.

Bobbett, G., French, R., & Achilles, C. (1993). The impact of community/school characteristics on student outcomes: An analysis of report cards on schools. Paper presented at annual meeting of the American Educational Research Association, Atlanta, GA.

Bobbett, G., French, R., Achilles, C., & Bobbett, N. (1995a). *An analysis of Nevada's report cards on high schools.* Paper presented at annual meeting of the Mid-South Educational Research Association, Biloxi, MS.

Bobbett, G., French, R., Achilles, C., & Bobbett, N. (1995b). *Texas' high school report cards on schools: What parents, educators, or policymakers can glean from them.* Paper presented at annual meeting of the Mid-South Educational Research Association, Biloxi, MS.

Bobbett, G., French, R., Achilles, C., McNamara, J., & Trusty, F. (1992). *What policymakers can learn from school report cards: Analysis of Tennessee's report cards on schools.* Paper presented at annual meeting of the American Educational Research Association, San Francisco, CA.

Brown, R. (1999). Creating school accountability reports. *School Administrator, 56*(10), 12–14, 16–17.

Caldas, S., & Mossavat, M. (1994). *A statewide program assessment survey of parents', teachers', and principals' perceptions of school report cards.* Paper presented at annual meeting of the American Educational Research Association, New Orleans, LA.

Center for Community Change. (2001). *Individual school report cards: Empowering parents and communities to hold schools accountable.* Washington, DC: Author.

Clements, B., & Blank, R. (1997). *What do we know about education in the states? Education indicators in SEA reports.* Paper presented at annual meeting of the American Educational Research Association, Chicago, IL.

Fetler, M. (1989). *Assessing educational performance: California's school quality indicator system.* Paper presented at annual meeting of the American Educational Research Association, San Francisco, CA.

Franklin, B. (1995). Improving Louisiana's school report cards: Public opinion. *AERA SIG: School Indicators and Report Cards Newsletter*, 1–3.

Franklin, B., Glascock, C., & Freeman, J. (1997). *Teacher retention as an indicator: Useful or not?* Paper presented at annual meeting of the American Educational Research Association, Chicago, IL.

Gorney, B. (1994). *An integrative analysis of the content and structure of school report cards: What school systems report to the public.* Paper presented at annual meeting of the American Educational Research Association, New Orleans, LA.

Howell, J. (1995). *Using profiles to improve schools.* Paper presented at annual meeting of the American Educational Research Association, San Francisco, CA.

Jaeger, R., Gorney, B., Johnson, R., Putnam, S., & Williamson, G. (1993). *Designing and developing effective school report cards: A research synthesis.* Kalamazoo: Center for Research on Educational Accountability and Teacher Evaluation (CREATE), The Evaluation Center, Western Michigan University.

Jaeger, R., Johnson, R., & Gorney, B. (1993). *The nation's schools report to the public: An analysis of school report cards.* Kalamazoo: Center for Research on Educational Accountability and Teacher Evaluation (CREATE), The Evaluation Center, Western Michigan University.

Johnson, R. (2000). Framing the issues in the development of school profiles. *Studies in Educational Evaluation*, **26**, 143–169.

Kernan-Schloss, A. (1999). School report cards: How to tell your district's story – and tell it well. *American School Board Journal*, **186**(5), 46–49.

Kochan, S., Franklin, B., Crone, L., & Glascock, C. (1994). *Improving Louisiana's school report cards with input from parents and school staff.* Paper presented at annual meeting of the American Educational Research Association, New Orleans, LA.

Lee, S., & McGrath, E. (1991). *High school profile impact study.* Dover, DE: Delaware Department of Public Instruction.

Lingen, G., Knack, P., & Belli, G. (1993). The development and use of school profiles based on opinion survey results. *Measurement and Evaluation in Counseling and Development*, **26**, 81–92.

Linn, R. (2001). *Reporting school quality in standards-based accountability systems.* (CRESST Policy Brief 3). Los Angeles, CA: Center for Research on Evaluation, Standards, and Student Testing, University of California.

Mandeville, G. (1994). The South Carolina experience with incentives. In T. Downes, & W. Testa (Eds.), *Midwest approaches to school reform: Proceedings of a conference held at the Federal Reserve Bank of Chicago* (pp. 69–91). Chicago: Federal Reserve Bank of Chicago.

Merriman, H. (1969). *The Columbus school profile: A report of the Columbus Public Schools to the community.* Columbus, OH: Columbus Public Schools.

Mestinsek, R. (1993). District and school profiles for quality education. *Alberta Journal of Educational Research*, **39**(2), 179–189.

National Association of Secondary School Principals Committee on School-College Relations. (1992). *Guidelines for designing a school profile.* Reston, VA: Author.

Nevo, D. (1974). Evaluation priorities of students, teachers, and principals (Doctoral dissertation, Ohio State University, 1974). *Dissertation Abstracts International*, **35**, 11A. (University Microfilms No. AAI7511402).

New Zealand Education Review Office (2000). *Accountability review process.* Retrieved from http://www.ero.govt.nz/AcctRevInfo/ARprocesscontents.htm.

Oakes, J. (1989). What educational indicators? The case for assessing school context. *Educational Evaluation and Policy Analysis*, **11**, 181–199.

Olson, L. (1999). Report cards for schools: No two states report exactly the same information. *Education Week*, **18**(17), pp. 27–28, 32–36.

Pelowski, B. (1994). Developing a school profile in an overseas setting. *International Schools Journal*, **27**, 15–17.

Rafferty, E., & Treff, A. (1994). School-by-school test score comparisons: Statistical issues and pitfalls. *ERS Spectrum*, **12**(2), 16–19.

Salganik, L. (1994). Apples and apples: Comparing performance indicators for places with similar demographic characteristics. *Educational Evaluation and Policy Analysis*, **16**, 125–141.

Sanders, W., Saxton, A., & Horn, S. (1997). The Tennessee Value-Added Assessment System: A quantitative outcomes-based approach to educational assessment. In J. Millman (Ed.), *Grading teachers, grading schools: Is student achievement a valid evaluation measure?* (pp. 137–162). Thousand Oaks, CA: Corwin Press.

Soholt, S., & Kernan-Schloss, A. (1999). School report cards: The board's policy role. *American School Board Journal*, **186**(5), 48.

United Kingdom. Department for Education and Employment. (2001). *School and college performance tables*. Retrieved from http://www.dfee.gov.uk/perform.shtml.

Webster, W. (1995). The connection between personnel evaluation and school evaluation. *Studies in Educational Evaluation*, **21**, 227–254.

Webster, W., & Mendro, R. (1995). Evaluation for improved school level decision-making and productivity. *Studies in Educational Evaluation*, **21**, 361–399.

Willms, J. (1992). *Monitoring school performance: A guide for educators*. Washington, DC: Falmer Press.

Willms, J., & Kerckhoff, A. (1995). The challenge of developing new educational indicators. *Educational Evaluation and Policy Analysis*, **17**, 113–131.

38
Evaluating the Institutionalization of Technology in Schools and Classrooms[1]

CATHERINE AWSUMB NELSON

Evaluation Consultant, Paw Paw, Michigan, USA

JENNIFER POST

Learning Research and Development Center, University of Pittsburgh, PA, USA

WILLIAM BICKEL

Learning Research and Development Center, University of Pittsburgh, PA, USA

Schools around the globe are scrambling to make sure that their students do not end up on the wrong side of the "digital divide." As technology assumes an increasingly central role in economic development, no nation can allow its next generation, or any segment of it, to be left behind. Under pressure from parents, politicians, and the public, schools have invested heavily in the most visible accoutrements of the "wired" or "high tech" school: hardware, software, and connectivity. Finding the resources to invest in technology has been one of the dominant concerns of schools over the last decade. As the installed base of technology in schools continues to grow, a second, and perhaps more educationally significant, digital divide looms. While equity in basic access to technology remains a problem within and between nations, an increasing gap is appearing even among those schools that are well equipped with basic technological tools. This second digital divide is the gap in the ability to use technology in educationally significant ways to achieve specific, meaningful learning goals. In this chapter, we propose a framework that evaluators and school personnel can use to assess capacity building and institutionalization efforts that increasingly have been identified as essential to the effective implementation and use of educational technology.

Scriven (1967) argued that evaluators must always be explicit about their evaluative criteria, that is, the standards of value they are using to judge the merit or worth of the program under study. Our framework for evaluating educational technology implementation focuses on the crucial issues of *human capital* (the extent to which a school's personnel have developed the knowledge, skills, and confidence to use the school's technology in educationally valuable ways), and *institutionalization* (the extent to which technology is self-sustaining and has

International Handbook of Educational Evaluation, 843–870
T. Kellaghan, D.L. Stufflebeam (eds.)
© *2003 Dordrecht: Kluwer Academic Publishers. Printed in Great Britain.*

become a core part of the school's culture and classroom practice, a taken-for-granted part of the way the school operates). Each element of the framework is oriented to assessing how well a given educational technology implementation meets the standards of building human capital and achieving institutionalization.

The chapter addresses the issue of whether or not technology has been successfully institutionalized in a school, that is, whether it has become a core part of the school's culture and classroom practice, as opposed to an add-on program distinct from the school's most important activities and goals. Based on our review of the literature and our evaluation work in the field of educational technology, we posit that the development of a school's human capital is the key to making its investments in the physical capital of technology pay off. Thus, the framework we present is structured around the learning curves that school personnel must climb, and the dimensions of development needed to climb each one, in order to successfully weave technology into the school's core and make it an important contributor to teaching and learning.

SCALE OF INVESTMENT IN TECHNOLOGY

The worldwide flood of public and private investment in technology for primary and secondary schools shows no signs of abating.[2] In the United States, for example, Meyer (1999) reported that "by 1994, 98 percent of American schools had one or more computers for instructional use ... in contrast to fewer than 20 percent in 1981" (p. 3). A 1999 *Education Week* survey noted that American schools currently have an average of one instructional computer for every 5.7 students (Smerdon et al., 2000, p. 5). Internationally, among the 12 developed countries participating in the 1998–99 Information Technology in Education Study, the student-to-computer ratio ranged from 11.1 to 157.1 at the primary level, 8.8 to 43.7 at the lower secondary level, and 8 to 34.1 at the upper secondary level (OECD, 2001, p. 260).

The growing investment in hardware and software that these statistics represent has been further bolstered by the more recent commitment in school systems to connect schools to the Internet. In 1994, only 35 percent of U.S. schools had access to the Internet (Coley, Cradler, & Engle, 1997). By 1999, 89 percent of schools and more than 50 percent of classrooms were connected (Jerald & Orlofsky, 1999). Internationally, the 1998–99 Information Technology in Education Study showed that in almost all participating countries more than 50 percent of schools were connected to the Internet at all levels of education, with many countries in the 70–90 percent range. Even more significantly, nearly every country had a goal approaching 100 percent of schools being connected to the Internet by 2001, with the notable exception of Japan, which appears to be taking a much more cautious approach to this investment (OECD, 2001, p. 260). Perhaps the most compelling statistics are those that show ratios of student to Internet-connected computers. According to Jerald and Orlofsky (1999), there were 19.7 students for every connected computer in United States schools in 1998. One year later, that ratio was 13.6 to 1. Clearly, schools around the world are investing heavily in both the sheer numbers of computers available for use and in the resources to which computers are connected.

While it is admittedly difficult to get accurate information on costs, it is estimated that the cost of technology in U.S. schools in 1994–1995 was about $3.2 billion or about $70 per pupil. One estimate is that the additional investment to provide "technology rich learning environments" would be in the neighborhood of $300 per student (Coley et al., 1997, p. 58). As U.S. public schools worked to build such environments, they spent an estimated $5.67 billion on technology in 1999–2000 (Weiner, 2000, citing Market Data Retrieval's annual survey), almost double in a single year the cost of the entire installed base just five years previously.

RATIONALES FOR EDUCATIONAL TECHNOLOGY INVESTMENT

Why the investment in technology? There are two broad justifications. The first rests with a vision of the workplace and the implications that this has for student preparation. The Organisation for Economic Co-operation and Development (OECD) speaks of the need for schools around the world to "prepare students for the information society" (OECD, 2001, p. 246). Similarly, a presidential advisory panel in the United States noted that "information technologies have had an enormous impact within America's offices, factories, and stores over the past several decades" (President's Committee of Advisors on Science and Technology, 1997 p, 4). The implication is clear: "to get the high paying job, a graduate of high school or college must be technologically literate" (Cuban, 2000, p. 42). The second broad rationale for investment in technology concerns anticipated efficiencies in the organizational and teaching/learning processes of educational institutions: "such technologies have the potential to transform our schools ... [providing the justification] for the immediate and widespread incorporation within all of our schools" (President's Committee, 1997, p. 4). The OECD argues that technology is "potentially a powerful catalyst for growth and efficiency" (2001, p. 246). The projected transformations take many forms, but essentially include support for "individual and group learning, instructional management, communication (among all players), and a wide range of administration functions" (Wenglinsky, 1998, p. 7). The International Society for Technology in Education (ISTE) characterized the "new learning environments" to be created with technology as "student-centered learning," "multipath progression," "collaborative work," "inquiry-based learning," "critical thinking," and "authentic, real world context" (ISTE, 1998). The desired outcome domains involve, among others, enhanced student learning (both in core curriculum subjects and in terms of technical applications), more powerful instructional processes, and increased organizational efficiencies. The vision of the promise of technology among its advocates is both comprehensive and shining, with use resulting "in the penetration of technology into every aspect of the school day, theoretically making conventional teaching techniques [among other things] obsolete" (Wenglinsky, 1998, p. 7).[3]

THE ROLE OF HUMAN CAPITAL IN TECHNOLOGY INVESTMENTS

Investments in technology during the 1990s tended to focus on hardware, software, and connectivity and the basic physical infrastructure that supports their use. This is beginning to change, as the "human capital" question receives more attention (OTA, 1995). This shift reflects a recognition (quite well understood in the private sector) that the machines alone are not sufficient to bring about improvements in an organization's core functions. For investments in the physical capital of technology to pay off, educators must be comfortable not only with the technical functioning of the tools at their disposal but also with appropriate strategies for applying them to educational tasks. Research suggests that current practices fall far short of what is desirable in this regard. Among 13 countries participating in the 1998–99 Information Technology in Education Study, between 70 and 90 percent of principals in all schools in each country reported having established goals for training all teachers in technology, but the percentage reporting that all teachers had actually received such training ranged only from 8 to 30 percent (OECD, 2001, 245). Cuban (1999) described the extent to which available technology is actually used in U.S. schools:

> Here's a puzzle for both cheerleaders and skeptics of using new technologies in the classroom. Out of every 10 teachers in this country, fewer than two are serious users of computers and other information technologies in their classrooms ... three to four are occasional users ... and the rest ... never use the machines at all. (p. 68)

Indeed, in a 1998 survey, only 20 percent of U.S. teachers felt "very well prepared" to integrate educational technology into their teaching (U.S. Department of Education, 1999). What is equally disturbing is the fact that too often when teachers are using technology the applications are relatively low level and traditional:

> The advent of computers and the Internet has not dramatically changed how teachers teach and how students learn. Computers have typically been used for ... drill and practice and computer education (as opposed to solve problems and conduct research) (Smerdon et al., 2000, p. 101).

Increased growth in the availability of machines (and growing personal use of technology on the part of teachers) has not been accompanied by a concomitant increase in the use of technology in the classroom, especially if one's target is use that facilitates new levels of learning and understanding (what Schofield [1995] has termed the "transformative potential" of the computer). What is clear is that research shows that helping teachers learn how to integrate technology into the curriculum is a critical factor for the successful implementation of technology applications in schools; and that most teachers have not had the education or training to use technology effectively in their teaching. (Coley et al., 1997, p. 5)

The lack of sound teacher pre- and inservice preparation for applying technology has been identified as a crucial barrier to more effective use of technology in schools (Bickel, Nelson, & Post, 2000a; Glennan & Melmed, 1996; Schofield, 1995; Smerdon et al., 2000). However, in the past few years there is some evidence that educational organizations are getting the "human capital building" message in the technology arena. Recent surveys indicate that school spending for staff development is modestly up 3 percent in 2000 compared to 1999 (Editorial Projects in Education, 2001, p. 52). However, for 1998–99, U.S. schools projected spending only $5.65 per student on teacher technology training, as compared to $88.19 per student on hardware, software, and connectivity, far from the 30 percent of their technology budgets the U.S. Department of Education recommends allocating to professional development (CEO Forum, 1999, p. 6). Research underscores the importance of key elements of human capital development such as adequate time, focused and timely assistance, broad institutional support, and a certain vision for the educational purposes of technology, as important in successful training and staff development efforts (Bickel, Nelson, & Post, 2000a; Nelson & Bickel, 1999; OTA, 1995; Schofield, 1995).

As investment in technology and professional development related to its implementation continue, the hard and still largely unanswered questions about its educational value are increasingly difficult to ignore. Thus, the evaluation of investments in human capital within technology initiatives is critical both for providing continuous, formative feedback to improve implementation, and to inform the field about unique factors that influence the institutionalization of technology in schools and classrooms. Evaluators need both a broad conceptual framework and knowledge of the factors that research has shown affect the successful investment in human capital to institutionalize technology use. While we have found no single model of evaluation specific to the institutionalization of technology via investments in human capital, we can draw on information gleaned from at least two distinct "pockets" in the literature base: characteristics of effective staff development (both generally and technology-specific) and frameworks for evaluating staff development. The contributions and limitations of each of these to the evaluation of human capital investments in technology are discussed in turn.

CHARACTERISTICS OF EFFECTIVE STAFF DEVELOPMENT

Much has been learned about the general characteristics of effective staff development (both overall and content-specific). The professional development literature provides both general and specific recommendations for creating and implementing professional development that may lead to improved instructional practices and enhanced student learning (Asayesh, 1993; Guskey, 1994; Guskey & Huberman, 1995; Joyce & Showers, 1980; Joyce, Showers, & Rolheiser-Bennett, 1987; Kennedy, 1999; Loucks-Horsley, Hewson, Love, & Stiles, 1998). Numerous organizations have attempted on the basis of such research to establish broad principles and characteristics of effective staff development (e.g., American Federation of Teachers, U.S. Department of Education, National Partnership for Excellence and Accountability in Teaching, National Staff Development Council, National Center for Research on Teacher Learning, and Northwest Regional Educational Laboratory). These characteristics are now being translated into state- and district-level standards for professional development. Research-based characteristics of effective staff development can aid evaluators in identifying factors within the school or district that should be examined to provide formative feedback. However, these are global staff development characteristics and are not situated within a conceptual or temporal framework. Evaluators must be aware of these principles of effective staff development but also can benefit from a broad conceptual framework so that key variables are not overlooked. Furthermore, these characteristics are not specific to a content area and must be "translated" into the context of technology professional development. Numerous researchers have conducted studies to identify the characteristics of effective technology staff development (e.g., Brand, 1997; Bray, 1999; Meyer, 1999; Norton & Gonzales, 1998).

Brand's (1997) review of the staff development and educational technology literature identified several characteristics of effective staff development specific to technology, which are presented in such a way that they provide program developers with key issues to consider as an initiative is developed and implemented. Key issues cited include provision of time, consideration of individual differences in teacher learning needs, provision of flexible staff development opportunities, provision of continued support, provision of opportunities to collaborate, provision of incentives, provision of on-going staff development, explicating the link between technology and educational objectives, communication of a clear administrative message, and provision of intellectual and professional stimulation. Missing from this list are indications of relationships between their presence or absence and key "milestones" along the path to successful technology institutionalization. Further, they are not tied to a larger framework for organizing and evaluating the development of human capital over time.

Bray (1999) presents 10 steps for installing effective technology staff development which include the creation of a staff development subcommittee, provision of examples of how technology can be used, utilization of a needs assessment instrument, development of individual learning plans, identification of technology leaders, creation of a list of on-site learning opportunities, circulation of the list of off-site learning opportunities, provision of time for grade-level or departmental meetings, exchange of success stories, and continuous planning and evaluation. As with Brand's characteristics, Bray's steps are most useful in considering how to develop a technology staff development program and may signal elements that evaluators should look for, but they do not provide a full-fledged framework for evaluators in technology staff development contexts.

Hasselbring et al.'s (2000) literature review lists and explains the major barriers to the integration of technology into curriculum. It addresses preservice teacher education, teacher licensure, staff development characteristics, administrative policies, and technological infrastructure. Specific barriers to and enablers of technology infusion that have been identified in the research base are described. Such barriers and enablers are extremely useful for program developers and policymakers but would be more useful for evaluators if they were situated within a larger conceptual framework of the phases in building human capital.

EXISTING FRAMEWORKS FOR EVALUATING STAFF DEVELOPMENT

In addition to the characteristics of effective technology staff development, comprehensive frameworks for evaluating staff development can provide a starting point for evaluators examining the development of human capital within a technology initiative. Guskey (2000) presents five levels of effectiveness criteria that have been used to evaluate professional development generally. The most basic and most often utilized criterion involves determining participants' reactions to the staff development experience (e.g., "Did the participants like the staff development session?"). The second level is the assessment of the teachers' gains in knowledge or skills as a result of the professional development experience (e.g., "What did the participants learn?"). The third level is the assessment of organizational support and change which involves an examination of the extent to which policies, procedures, and resource allocation facilitate the aims of the professional development. The fourth level of criteria is aimed at assessing the extent to which participants integrate the new knowledge or skills into instructional practice (e.g., "Are the participants using it in the classroom?"). Finally, the most significant but least prevalent criterion in evaluating staff development effectiveness involves measuring the impact of participants' changes in knowledge and skills on student learning (e.g., "How are the changes in teaching practice affecting what students know or are able to do?").

This model is extremely useful for evaluating the effects of human capital investments, but it does not address issues specific to technology staff development. It implies a temporal sequence in terms of the order in which change should occur (participants' initial reactions → participants' learning → organizational support → participants' use of knowledge or skills → student learning). However, this "temporal" sequence does not accurately represent what we have observed in technology initiatives. For example, the development and maintenance of the technical infrastructure can serve as a barrier to the development of teacher skills and use regardless of the quality of the staff development itself. Neither does the model provide specifics in terms of factors that may serve as barriers to or enablers of the institutionalization of technology at each of the levels. The approach is more geared toward assessing outcomes than to assessing processes or understanding when and under what conditions technology use is institutionalized in the school and classrooms. Thus, Guskey's model serves as a good starting point but does not provide the level of detail or the focus on implementation needed to evaluate investments in human capital for the purpose of institutionalizing technology use.

While the model encompasses the evaluation of professional development across context or content areas, we are interested in the provision of a conceptual framework specific to the development of human capital in technology. This framework should be structured to reflect research-based findings regarding the temporal sequence of development, be geared toward processes and implementation variables rather than outcomes, and focus on assessing institutionalization of technology. In the next section we describe the evaluation context in which we worked to develop such a framework.

CONTEXT AND METHODOLOGY FOR THE FRAMEWORK'S DEVELOPMENT

The framework we present in this paper was developed in the course of our work on a small-scale evaluation project taking place within the context of a comprehensive, district-wide technology integration effort in a large urban school district in the United States. District plans originally envisioned a $100 million technology enhancement effort. In the face of an ongoing deficit crisis in the district, the technology plan was downsized through several rounds of board negotiations, finally settling at about a quarter of its original size. The plan ultimately adopted focused almost exclusively on hardware and software, was targeted only to specific grade levels and subject areas, and was to be phased in over three years.

One of the most significant implications of the downsized plan was the elimination of training funds from core district funding of the plan. Grant funds from the state and a local foundation were used to support a much reduced training agenda. Rather than district-wide staff development, technology training was to be provided only to a team of six to eight teachers and administrators within each school who were then expected to disseminate their new skills to the rest of their school's faculty. The training initially focused largely on developing teachers' basic computer and software skills, with relatively little attention to how to integrate technology into the curriculum to help students reach learning objectives. The slimmed-down plan also delegated almost all responsibility for technical support to the school level. Schools were to designate "technical support teachers" to maintain and support both lab and classroom computers, although no explicit provisions were made at the district level to free up time for them to perform these functions.

Political and fiscal constraints left the district with a technology plan that no one would have deliberately designed, one that was focused entirely on hardware and software with no funds for training or support. As many others have recognized (e.g., Meyer, 1999; Norton & Gonzales, 1998; OTA, 1995), adequate hardware is necessary but hardly sufficient for the infusion of technology into instructional processes. But even orphan programs – with designs so unlovable no one would claim them – have a logic of their own. As evaluators it is important to spell out the theory of a program after it has been through the political mill as it will actually be enacted, not as it would be in some ideal world. In doing so, we of course recognize that the reality of program implementation can fall far short of sound program theory. By identifying up front the district's critical assumptions about how this pared-down plan was intended to produce improvements in student learning, we were in a stronger position to understand implementation.

The key implementation vehicle became the "school technology team," which included the principal, the librarian, classroom teachers from the grade levels and subject area targeted for technology integration (language arts), and one or two "technology support teachers" (classroom teachers who volunteered for the role because they had the skills or at the very least the interest to support others in the use of instructional technology). Using grant funds, the team from each school was provided with a baseline of training (totaling about 90 hours) designed to enable members to take the lead in disseminating and supporting technology use in their schools.

The study was structured by one overarching question: How did the district technology implementation (including staff development) affect teachers' capacities to apply technology to strengthen learning processes in classrooms? Our work in answering this question was informed by a human capital approach to investing in technology which underscores that it is how the technology is implemented and supported that conditions the classroom payoff. We had to track crucial intermediate variables between the intervention (providing small teams in each school with some basic computer skills training) and the desired outcome (integrating technology into classroom practice in meaningful ways). In practice, this meant that our evaluation questions centered on documenting how the program's basic change theory assumptions were actually being realized in the field:

- How was the training provided to each school's tech team being disseminated to the rest of the school?
- How and to what extent were the technology skills being learned by teachers being integrated into curriculum?
- How could the implementation of the program's key assumptions about the process of change be strengthened to shore up the connection between the training intervention and student learning effects?

The framework presented in this chapter was originally developed to structure our investigations. The study on which this paper draws was by no means a formal, comprehensive evaluation of the outcomes of the district's technology plan, or even of the direct, classroom outcomes of the much smaller training component. Rather, it took place in the context of a formative evaluation agenda. Our evaluation was designed to produce immediately useful feedback to program leadership and participants about barriers and best practices as they emerged in implementation, and insights to key funders about the value of supporting staff development in this area. Data collection activities consisted of the following:

- Observation and documentation of training sessions;
- Focus groups with two types of training participants (subject-area teachers and "technical support teachers") centering around expectations for in-school implementation;
- Surveys of principals in all participating schools;
- In the first year of program implementation, year-long implementation case studies of three schools (elementary, middle, and high). The design of these case studies included: structured interviews with the technical support teachers at intervals throughout the year; observations of team meetings; principal interviews; observations of several full-day samples of computer lab usage; and lesson profiles in which teachers were interviewed about their plans for a technology-based lesson, the lesson was observed, and the teacher was then debriefed.
- In the second year of program implementation, a year-long panel study of technology implementation in 10 schools, based on a series of individual and group interviews with a panel of teacher technology leaders (classroom teachers who were identified by district technology staff as having taken on leadership of technology implementation in their schools).

The evaluation framework presented in this chapter was developed and refined in the course of our two-year experience documenting and providing formative feedback to the instructional technology capacity-building effort in a large school district. Having found the framework to be a useful intellectual structure for analyzing data and reporting results, we then validated and further refined it based on our review of the literature on effective professional development for educational technology use. Because of district budgetary pressures, the framework was developed in a program context where there was an extreme imbalance between investment in the physical and human capital needed for successful educational technology implementation. Indeed, with the exception of private grant funds, institutionalization at the school level was left almost entirely to school-level initiative and resources, making this an extreme test case for evaluating the factors needed for school-level capacity building. While other educational technology implementation contexts may have a more deliberate human capital development component, we contend that the issues of human capital development highlighted by this framework will be salient in the evaluation of almost any educational technology intervention. Certainly the political, social, educational, and investment contexts of school technology use will vary widely among the international readers of this handbook, and we do not claim that every element of the framework is universally applicable to every school in every country.

However, we do argue that, as a set, they comprise a useful framework of factors for evaluators to attend to in assessing whether schools have the capacity to use their technology in educationally productive ways.

THE FRAMEWORK

Our review of the relevant literature and our evaluation work in this field suggest to us the need for evaluators to focus on the question of how human capital is developed in schools to support the investment in the physical capital of technology. As part of the district-wide but school-focused instructional technology implementation evaluation described above, we proposed and refined a conceptual framework showing how the growth of school-level ownership of technology over time can be assessed as progress on three interrelated learning curves (Bickel, Nelson, & Post, 2000b). In Figure 1 we attempt to show how the institutionalization of technology in a school's culture and practice can be understood as movement up the learning curves of three aspects of human capital relevant to successful instructional technology implementation: growing and maintaining technical infrastructure; building teacher technology skills; and achieving curriculum integration.

The curves show how as a school builds each of these aspects of human capital there is movement both over time (along the X axis) and in terms of increasing building-level ownership of the technology (along the Y axis). We also propose that the curves are sequential from left to right, with development on one laying the ground for movement on the next. A functioning technical infrastructure is a necessary precondition for the development of teachers' basic software skills,

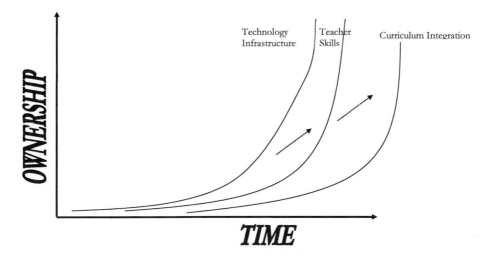

Figure 1:   Three learning curves for the development of human capital and the institutionalization of technology in a school

which in turn are required for the effective integration of technology into the curriculum, the necessary precursor to the ultimate goal of investments in instructional technology-enhanced student learning.

While we found this broad conceptual framework of the three learning curves extremely useful in structuring our evaluation work, organizing data collection, and communicating findings to evaluation clients, our experience showed that to maximize the utility of the learning curves as an evaluation framework we needed to further specify how schools move up the curves. Thus we added a second level to the framework, positing that movement on each of the three learning curves proceeds along three dimensions: depth (quality of technology use), breadth (quantity and variety of technology use), and sustainability (infrastructure to support technology experiences over time).

Our fieldwork indicated that for growth on a given learning curve to occur, all three dimensions had to be in place. Thus, even if technology is spread *broadly* across grades and curriculum areas and is *deeply* integrated with the design of instruction, technology integration cannot be said to be institutionalized in the school's curriculum if those experiences are not *sustainable* over time.

Our general framework consists of the three interrelated learning curves and the three dimensions of growth necessary to climb each. For each dimension the evaluation project described above also generated a set of factors related to successful technology implementation and eventual institutionalization in school learning environments as these were evidenced in our case context. We present these factors as examples, although by no means a complete set, of what educators and evaluators should be aware of when using this framework since they were found to be important in influencing the program under investigation. As others apply the framework, we fully expect that additional experiences will extend both the structure presented as well as elaborate on and modify specific factors.

The evaluation framework can be conceptualized as the intersections of each of the three learning curves with each of the three dimensions of growth. In this section of the chapter, we examine each intersection in turn, presenting examples of the factors that most affect the ability of schools to achieve growth towards that aspect of the institutionalization of technology in their school culture and classroom practice. Because the factors emerge from the specific context of one evaluation study they should not be construed as a comprehensive list that is automatically generalizable to every school and every situation. Indeed, we are certain that variables including school and district size, national goals for technology use, and levels and kinds of technology investments would influence the factors that shape a given school's technology implementation. However, given the central role of human capital development in the success of technology implementation in any context, we believe the factors presented will be suggestive of issues that most schools will face. We also note a high degree of overlap between the factors we identified in our evaluation work and those cited in other studies as crucial to successful educational technology implementation (Editorial Projects in Education, 1999, 2001; Ertmer, 1999; Meyer, 1999; OTA, 1995; Schofield, 1995). We thus present the factors that follow not as an absolute and definitive checklist for every school, but as a range of issues that evaluators and school personnel may find useful to probe (and as a springboard for identifying other factors specific to their context) as they seek to assess how well a given school is moving up the successive learning curves towards successful institutionalization of technology.[4]

LEARNING CURVE #1: MAINTAINING THE TECHNICAL INFRASTRUCTURE

Depth

The goal of developing depth in maintaining the technical infrastructure is for school-level personnel to become comfortable with increasingly sophisticated and complex issues in maintaining and upgrading their technology. From our study, factors related to developing this depth of expertise may include:

Comfort with Routine Glitches, Leading to Increased Autonomy

As school personnel gain experience and confidence that they can handle common problems such as a frozen screen or a jammed printer, they become more autonomous in managing the technology in their own classrooms. This comfort with basic technical problems is an important aspect of human capital development with regard to technology because it means that routine glitches during a technology-based lesson no longer bring instruction to a halt until "technical support" can be found. The more teachers can provide their own technical support, the higher the school climbs on this learning curve.

Breadth

The goal of developing breadth in maintaining the technical infrastructure is for *more* school-level personnel to become comfortable managing technical issues. Rather than seeing "technical support" as a specialized role or function, it becomes an aspect of every teacher's job. Three factors that may signal the development of this breadth have been identified.

Dissemination of Technical Expertise

School-wide training in managing technology is likely to be needed if this kind of expertise is to be broadly disseminated. Without explicit training, less technically inclined teachers may view technical support as "someone else's job," rather than something they need to be able to do in order to provide technology-based instruction. In addition to formal training, evaluators should look for support and reinforcement mechanisms such as printed "troubleshooting" materials and a "buddy system" matching technical novices with more technically savvy teachers that help schools to climb this learning curve.

Specialization of Roles

Broadening the base of school personnel with basic technical expertise allows for the complementary strategy of developing specialized roles. Although each teacher should have the capacity to manage the most common technical glitches that could interrupt instruction in the classroom, it is more efficient if people develop different kinds of specialized knowledge. When one person in the school becomes known as the person to go to with networking problems, another as an expert in designing Internet searches, and a third as a whiz in spreadsheets, everyone in the school knows who to go to with a particular issue, and no one person is overwhelmed with requests from help from colleagues.

Strategic Use of Student Expertise

Most teachers today are aware that there are students in their classroom whose knowledge of technology exceeds their own. While some teachers see student expertise as intimidating, it can be put to good use to fill the void in technical support that exists in many schools. Giving students who have an interest in technology formal roles as "technology assistants" or "lab monitors" not only keeps technology-based instruction flowing more smoothly, it can sometimes draw in previously disengaged students. Schools that are not afraid to give students these kinds of roles broaden their ability to manage their technical infrastructure.

Sustainability

The goal of developing sustainability in maintaining technical infrastructure is for school personnel to take ownership for maintaining the technology they need to deliver instruction, rather than looking to outside sources of support. Factors indicating that schools are developing this kind of sustainability over time include:

Standardized Platforms and Configurations

Having a hodge-podge of operating systems and hardware and software configurations across a district or within a school building impedes the ability of school personnel to move smoothly into new instructional environments and to work together in solving technical problems and sharing lesson ideas. By contrast, standard platforms and configurations allow useful information about both technical issues and instructional ideas to be disseminated and implemented more easily, making for a more sustainable and useful technical infrastructure.

Avoiding Over-Reliance on Individuals

Very few schools can count on the specialized corps of technical support personnel that keep computers running in the business world. Instead, teachers must take on many basic technical support tasks themselves, or see computers go unused. Schools where technical expertise stays heavily concentrated in just a few individuals put the sustainability of their technical infrastructure at risk. The few teachers known to be "techies" will be besieged by often urgent requests for help from their colleagues, leaving them with the choice of either leaving a fellow teacher stranded or cutting into their own teaching and planning time. These individuals are often zealous enthusiasts for the educational uses of technology and will make great personal sacrifices to support their school's infrastructure for a period of time, but they are highly vulnerable to burn-out.

Routinized Policies, Procedures, and Responsibilities

To maintain their technical infrastructure over the long haul, schools need to move away from a crisis mode in which ad hoc solutions are organized in response to particular problems and towards a predictable routine of preventative maintenance. For example, in many schools teachers and groups of students shuffle in and out of heavily used computer labs all day long, with no continuity of oversight to report and deal with technical problems. In schools that are developing the human capital to take ownership of their infrastructure, evaluators will likely see the development of systems such as lab monitors or problem tracking forms to identify and address problems before they derail the instruction of the next unsuspecting teacher to bring a class to the lab.

Supply Budget

Adequate supply budgets prevent hardware and software from sitting idle for lack of basic replenishable supplies such as printer ribbons and disks, and are thus a key component to look for in a sustainable school-level technology infrastructure.

Flexible Time

Technical glitches have the potential to cause a carefully designed lesson to break down, wasting the valuable time of teachers and students unless they can be remedied quickly. Indeed, the fear of such glitches is a major reason many teachers are wary of relying on technology for instructional delivery. Keeping learning going requires on-the-spot technical support, which requires flexible time from those who know how to solve the problems. Schools that are developing a sustainable technical infrastructure build flexible time for technical support into their schedule, either through establishing a formal technical support role with some time freed from teaching duties, or at least by ensuring that the planning periods of technically expert teachers are distributed so that one is always available to get their peers out of a jam.

Stable Funding

Almost every factor listed so far as something to look for in evaluating the sustainability of a school's ability to maintain its own technical infrastructure implies the need for time: time for training, time for troubleshooting, time freed from teaching to provide technical support. And time, of course, implies money. Although schools will probably never approach the ratio of spending on ongoing support versus spending on hardware and software that is typical in corporations, they cannot hope to rely entirely on improvisation to keep their infrastructure functioning. One estimate put the "total cost of ownership" (including upgrades, support, and training) to a school of a $2,000 personal computer at $1,944 per year (Fitzgerald, 1999). A realistic financial commitment to ongoing technical support is a zero factor in assessing the sustainability of a school's technical infrastructure.

LEARNING CURVE #2: BUILDING TEACHER TECHNOLOGY SKILLS

Depth

The goal of developing depth in building teacher technology skills is for teachers to learn how to use the available technology (hardware and software) well. This means teachers moving beyond being novices to becoming experts in the various applications and understanding their potential uses to accomplish tasks. Three factors are related to achieving depth in teacher technology skills.

Quality of Training

The extent to which technology training meets the needs of adult learners, provides adequate guidance, fosters higher-order thinking and application, and is sensitive to teachers' fears and concerns is important in setting the tone for technology use in the school and in establishing teachers' level of base knowledge. In particular, the extent to which the training helps teachers see connections between the technology and their professional and instructional obligations can be a good predictor of teachers' perspectives on the utility of the technology and thus the potential depth of their skill development. Familiarity with and application of the large and growing body of research that identifies and explains characteristics of effective professional development design and implementation is one indicator that schools are building the capacity to implement high quality technology training.

Follow-Up from Training

Opportunities for teachers to receive additional assistance, instruction, or clarification after the initial training can help reduce fears, answer questions, deepen teacher skill levels, and set the stage for teachers to begin utilizing their new technology skills. It seems particularly important for teachers to have the opportunity for some one-on-one interaction after the initial training to answer specific questions and receive guidance on their own "experimentation." We know from research that content covered in "one-shot workshops" is often left in a dusty corner of teachers' minds. Evaluators should look for the systematic provision of follow-up and reinforcement of training as an indicator of potential depth of skill development.

Incentives to Apply

School or district incentives to begin applying newly learned technology skills can provide the motivation for teachers to experiment with and ultimately apply the technology in desired ways. Evaluators should look for recognition or other rewards for teachers who expand their technology skills, which can provide impetus for teachers to continue deepening their knowledge and skills.

Breadth

The goal of developing breadth in building teacher technology skills is for the entire teaching staff to build and maintain their skills in technology (hardware and software). Rather than just a few "techies" having the knowledge and skills for expert-level use of applications, the entire teaching staff becomes capable of employing technology at an advanced level. At least two factors are related to developing this breadth.

Voluntary Training vs. Mandates

If technology skill development remains voluntary for teachers, it is likely that other strong incentives will be needed if technology skills are to spread broadly beyond the early adopters. Many technology teacher leaders we have worked with are adamant that mandates for training and its application are a necessary catalyst to develop breadth of teacher technology skills in the school. Without mandates, students of teachers who are resistant to technology, or are not lured by existing incentives, are at a disadvantage relative to other students in the school.

Flexibility and Appropriateness of Training and Materials

When schools institute a plan to build human capital in technology, staff members bring a broad range of prior experience, comfort, and skill with technology to the task. The extent to which the training and materials are sensitive to these differences can affect the breadth of teacher technology skills achieved. Furthermore, the staff at individual schools within a district may have a wide range of technology training needs. Attention to the appropriateness of training strategies and materials for the specific context of the school and staff is critical to institutionalizing technology among the entire staff.

Sustainability

The goal of developing sustainability in building teacher technology skills is for school personnel to take ownership of maintaining and expanding teachers' technology skills rather than relying on sporadic "workshops" provided by outside consultants. A number of factors indicate that schools are developing sustainability:

Plan for Dealing with Personnel Turnover

Although most preservice teacher education programs are investing tremendous resources in enhancing their curriculum to prepare new teachers to utilize technology, the content and quality are highly variable. Thus, schools must have in place a plan for ensuring that new teachers have the required skills.

Plan for Refresher and Update Training

Technology is changing rapidly and schools must develop a plan for keeping theirs up-to-date or risk the erosion of teachers' ability to use updated hardware and software. Continued professional development is necessary to sustain high quality technology preparation for students.

School-Wide Strategy for Dissemination, Follow-Up, and Use

The presence of a clear strategy to disseminate new technology to teaching staff can be a good indicator of the school's ability to sustain technology skill development over time. Such a strategy includes an ongoing commitment to both group and individual training and a plan for identifying new, useful technology and sharing it with staff. A clear plan for providing follow-up assistance to teachers as they practice the new technology is also important for ensuring that skills learned during a training session are not allowed to go unused. Schools that hope to sustain the development of teacher technology skills also establish opportunities for teachers to use technology skills in their daily professional practices. Having teachers create lesson plans in a word processing application, submit student grades electronically, and communicate with administrators and other staff using e-mail are just a few ways that daily operating procedures can serve to foster the sustainability of teacher technology skill building. Evaluators should look for the institutionalization of such opportunities for skill development and application, as opposed to an ad hoc approach.

Environment that is "Safe" for Experimentation

A school culture that values innovation and risk-taking, and accepts the corresponding failures and mistakes, is important in setting the stage for teachers to continue to challenge themselves, broaden and deepen their technology skills, and share their experiences with colleagues. It is crucial that the energy and enthusiasm around technology use be such that resistant teachers are both comfortable and motivated to "play" with the technology. Evaluators should look for a school environment that uses "mistakes" as learning opportunities and provides patient guidance to teachers learning new skills.

LEARNING CURVE #3: ACHIEVING CURRICULUM INTEGRATION

Depth

The goal of developing depth in curriculum integration is for technology to be used in ways that meaningfully advance learning objectives, not simply replicate or dress up traditional lessons. To assess depth of curriculum integration, evaluators should be looking for examples of what Schofield (1995) calls "transformative" learning, in which technology is used to give students access to experiences and perspectives that would otherwise be unavailable and to deepen their understanding. Several factors can influence the depth of curriculum integration achieved in a given school technology implementation.

Longer Instructional Periods

In many schools, an instructional period is less than an hour. Teachers know that this is often inadequate for engaging in tasks of any intellectual depth. Add in the logistical challenges and time demands (booting up, logging on, saving, printing, etc.) of a technology-based lesson and the length of the instructional period becomes a significant factor conditioning the potential for depth of curriculum integration.

Attention to How Technology Changes Classroom Dynamics

Studies of classroom technology implementation demonstrate that technology has the potential to transform the teaching and learning process in a number of ways, including enhancing student engagement, loosening boundaries in the traditional roles of teacher and student, and increasing the potential for work that is project-based, inquiry-oriented, collaborative, and/or learner-directed (Ertmer, 1999; Means & Olsen, 1995; Schofield, 1995). Teachers who are aware of this potential (through training, familiarity with the literature, or their own experimentation and discovery) are more likely to be able to capture this kind of depth in their own use of technology. Not only do teachers need to be aware of the likely changes, they also need to be given opportunities and guidance to develop the requisite knowledge and skills to use such instructional approaches effectively. Without such assistance, teachers are often fearful of "losing control" in a technology-infused classroom and will resist technology or utilize it in very traditional ways. In assessing the potential depth of curriculum integration, evaluators should look for the systematic development and application of such knowledge about classroom dynamics in the wired classroom.

Teacher–Student Ratio

The potential of technology to transform classroom dynamics increases the possibility of deepening student understanding, but the same features of individualization, collaboration, and role-blurring can present classroom management challenges. Evaluators should look for scheduling strategies that support teachers with a second pair of adult hands in the lab. Having another adult in the lab to provide technical and instructional support and help with classroom management issues greatly increases the confidence and ability of classroom teachers to engage their students in more complex learning tasks.

Curriculum-Specific Training

Although teachers need to become comfortable with basic computer skills in order to use technology instructionally, those skills should never be treated as ends in themselves. Training that focuses exclusively on skill development without attending to the specific context of teachers' work may increase teachers' use of technology for professional tasks (lesson planning, communication, student record management, preparation of lesson materials, etc.) while doing little to help them make the transition to curriculum integration and classroom use. This observation is borne out by American survey data that show that teachers who received curriculum-specific technology training were significantly more likely to use technology with their students than teachers who only received skills training (Editorial Projects in Education, 1999).

Mentoring

The availability of individualized, classroom-based coaching from an experienced peer is an effective strategy for helping many teachers make the transition from personal and professional use of technology to instructional use. This kind of customized assistance deepens integration by helping teachers make the necessary link between the functionality of their technology and the learning objectives of their curriculum. Evaluators should look for both the policy infrastructure that makes mentoring possible and a culture that supports it.

Instructional Accessibility of Hardware, Software, and Connectivity

Technology will be underutilized if equipment is not physically located where it is convenient for teachers and students to integrate it into the flow of teaching and learning. If equipment is physically separate or inaccessible, it will always be an add-on or special treat, not a tool that is routinely used to extend understanding. Evaluators should look for significant clusters of classroom-based computers and/or for computer labs that are easy for teachers to schedule their class into and convenient for teachers and students to move in and out of.

Existing Teacher Comfort Levels with Basic Skills

Only when teachers feel comfortable with their own ability to use hardware or software will they begin to see opportunities to use the technology as a tool to reach instructional objectives, and be willing to use it with students without fear of a lesson-derailing glitch. Evaluators should consider this is as a zero factor in assessing the potential for depth of curriculum integration; teachers who have not achieved a basic comfort level with the technology are unlikely to use it with students at all, much less use it in transformative ways.

Existing Student Skill Levels

In classrooms where students are unfamiliar with the keyboard and/or with basic on-screen navigation, most instructional time will be consumed with technical issues rather than engagement with content. Thus, for depth of integration to be possible, evaluators should look for technology implementations with a specific strategy for preparing students to participate in and take advantage of transformative uses of the technology.

Access to Concrete Lesson Ideas

Teachers who are just developing their own technology skills and sense for how to use them instructionally benefit from concrete models of how technology that is available in their classrooms can be applied to the curriculum they are expected to teach. Once they have gotten their feet wet with ready-made materials they will be more likely to innovate and deepen their use of technology. Although hundreds of thousands of technology-based lesson plans exist on the web, few teachers have the time or skills to sift through them and evaluate their quality and relevance to their particular curriculum. Evaluators should look for strategies and structures that facilitate the sharing of high-quality, relevant lesson ideas both from central education offices and among schools and classrooms.

Planning Time to Develop Lessons

To develop and refine lessons that take advantage of technology to deepen student understanding requires a significant investment of teacher time. In the absence of adequate planning time, teachers are likely to stick with the "tried and true," perhaps adding a superficial touch of technology but not fundamentally rethinking lesson design.

Link to Curriculum Standards

In many countries teachers are under increasing pressure to help their students reach defined curriculum standards. Such standards are often accompanied by testing and incentive systems that carry high stakes for schools, teachers, and students. At the same time, schools are making large investments in technology, accompanied by either formal mandates or less formal pressures for its use. Rarely, however, are the pushes for standards and technology use explicitly linked. Indeed, teachers may see the two as competing rather than complementary priorities. Evaluators should look for technology implementations that have an explicit link to standards, that is, mechanisms such as teacher technology training that is grounded in curriculum and "lesson banks" that show teachers that technology can be a tool for achieving standards, not a competing demand on instructional time.

Breadth

The goal of achieving breadth of curriculum integration is for more teachers (across grade levels and subject areas) to make technology part of their routine toolkit for helping students achieve learning objectives. As the access of a given student to technology too often depends on the training and inclination of the teachers they are assigned, breadth is a significant equity issue. At least three factors may condition the breadth or spread of a given technology implementation across a school and its curriculum.

Content-Rich Applications Aligned with Curriculum

Most schools will have teachers who will be early adopters, enthusiastically figuring out ways to use whatever technology is available to enhance the student learning experience. Such teachers have the skills and initiative to take content-free productivity software (word processors, spreadsheets, presentation packages, etc.) and use it to achieve instructional objectives. If classroom use is to be institutionalized beyond that core, however, more hesitant teachers need to see technology with built-in content that is clearly linked to their curriculum. The level of investment in software that is explicitly tied to the content of a school's curriculum, thus reducing the need for novice teachers to make the leap between technology and curriculum unaided, can help evaluators predict the spread of instructional use.

Student and Parent Demand

In many parts of the world, students are coming to school with an increasingly high baseline of technology skills. They are accustomed to accomplishing tasks with the computer and thus may raise the issue even when teachers are hesitant. Similarly, as parents become more and more computer literate and convinced of the importance of technology for their children's future, they may push technology-shy teachers into greater utilization of the school's computers. Assessing the demand of students and parents for instructional technology can help evaluators predict the spread of classroom computer use beyond those teachers who are early and enthusiastic adopters.

Instructional Champions

In many schools there will be one or more teachers who are so convinced of the importance of instructional technology for student learning that they serve as informal coaches to their peers, providing concrete ideas about specific products, websites, or lesson plans. Librarians can also be vital in playing this role in their schools. In the absence of someone at the school-level playing a formal role of instructional technology coach or coordinator, the existence of such "champions" who do it on their own time out of sheer enthusiasm can be an important predictor of the spread of curriculum integration.

Sustainability

The goal of sustainability in curriculum integration is for technology to become institutionalized as one of the tools that teachers throughout a school use to achieve their instructional objectives. Rather than being seen as a separate program or objective, technology is woven throughout the school's core curriculum. For this to occur, teachers need to develop both their technical skills and knowledge and their understanding of how that functionality can be used in instructional design. There are several factors that are related to a school's ability to achieve sustainable curriculum integration that evaluators should look for.

Development of Student Technology Use Standards and Evaluation Criteria

Standards and goals for students should make it clear that technology use is a vital element of the learning process. Ideally, these goals should be woven into content area standards rather than standing on their own, signaling to teachers and students alike the role of technology as a tool, not an end in itself.

Alignment of Teacher Evaluation System with Goals for Technology Integration

One of the most powerful ways that educational administration can signal a commitment to technology integration is to build goals for substantive, curriculum-embedded technology use into teacher evaluation systems. Such incentive systems would be strong evidence of a commitment to capacity building.

Instructional Support

Like all professionals using technology as a tool, teachers need support that helps them keep the computers up and running so they can do their jobs. In addition to technical support, however, teachers need support that is tied to the substance of the task at hand: using the technology to enhance student learning. This kind of individualized, classroom-based assistance can be characterized as "instructional support." The presence of informal and formal mechanisms for providing instructional support for teachers integrating technology is important evidence in an evaluation that a school is building the necessary human capital to institutionalize technology as part of the teaching and learning process. Valuable elements of instructional support that evaluators should look for include school-based capacities for: (i) working with teachers to think through their grade-level and subject area curriculum to identify opportunities for technology-infused lessons to reach curricular objectives; (ii) assisting teachers with Internet searching and the evaluation of curriculum-specific software to identify resources that are both relevant and of high quality; (iii) prompting teachers with creative ideas about how functions of commonly available productivity software (word processors, spreadsheets, etc.) can be used instructionally; (iv) assisting teachers in planning for the unique timing, classroom management, assessment and other instructional design issues that come up in running a lab-based lesson; (v) helping teachers set up the lesson (create templates, bookmark relevant websites, etc.); (vi) providing hands-on support ("a safety net") when the teacher is actually teaching the lesson.

Administrative Priorities

Building human capital for the sustainable integration of technology into the curriculum requires a commitment of time and resources. The use of technology in a school is unlikely to become systematic, widespread, or sustainable without a tangible commitment from administration at the school and higher levels. Evaluators should seek evidence of administrative priorities through the allocations given to technology in schedules and budgets, leadership through modeling technology use, and the creation of incentive systems that reward instructional technology use.

Cooperation Between District-Level Technology and Curriculum Staff

Because the administrative structure of education departments evolves over time and is rarely re-thought from the ground up, "technology" is often a separate department from "curriculum." These two fiefdoms are likely to have staff who vary in background and expertise, have little communication or coordination of activity, and articulate different, perhaps seemingly conflicting, priorities. However, if technology is to become integrated into teaching and learning, it is vital that schools get the message that it is not an end in itself but a tool to help students master the curriculum. Evaluators seeking evidence of sustainable technology integration should look for a deliberate effort to coordinate message, activities, and incentives regarding technology and the curriculum from the top of a system.

Network of Contacts Beyond School

When teachers need fresh inspiration for how to use technology to teach a given lesson, contacts with peers in other schools or experts in education departments or universities can make the difference between retreating to the familiar and continuing to climb the learning curve of curriculum integration.

Collaborative Planning Time/Opportunities to Observe and Share Lessons

As much as teachers need instructional support in their own classrooms from expert mentors, they also need opportunities to learn from peers who are working to climb the same learning curve of curriculum integration. Instructional technology use is much more likely to spread beyond isolated classrooms and become institutionalized in a school's approach to teaching and learning if teachers have structured opportunities to see what their peers are doing and learn from each others' successes and failures. Evaluators should look for systematic opportunities for peer-to-peer learning and dissemination.

Stable Funding

All of the above factors imply to some extent the commitment of time and other resources. For instructional technology use to become institutionalized in a school, these commitments need to become part of the base budget, not dependent on year-to-year or special program funding.

CONCLUSION

The two-part framework for evaluating educational technology implementation presented in this chapter has a number of demonstrated and potential uses for educators and policymakers interested in understanding and enhancing the potential for technology to become institutionalized in schools. We expect that evaluators will find the general framework of the three learning curves and three dimensions of growth to be the most useful aspect of the work as they go about conceptualizing their own evaluations in this field. The specific implementation variables we present as examples of the content of the framework will not all be relevant to every evaluation, but as a set should help evaluators think about the range and kinds of factors that will be significant in their particular contexts. The specific variables may be of more use to educators and policymakers planning and managing the implementation of school-level technology implementations, as a kind of checklist of factors that were found in another set of schools to influence the success of implementation.

We found this framework to be a useful tool not only for gathering, organizing, and analyzing implementation data but also for identifying and communicating best practices and potential pitfalls as implementation was unfolding. As a simple, consistent communication tool we could use when sharing data across sites and among different levels of the program, it enhanced the formative value of our work. Furthermore, we believe that the basic dimensions of the framework, as well as many of the specific variables within them, would be applicable to the planning, management, and evaluation of other educational technology programs. More broadly, we believe that this framework can serve as a useful starting point for planning and conducting other research in the crowded field of educational technology evaluation.

ENDNOTES

[1] This work was supported by the Heinz Endowments as part of the Evaluation Coordination Project based at the University of Pittsburgh's Learning Research and Development Center. The views expressed herein are those of the authors; no official endorsement of the sponsoring organization should be inferred.

[2] The concept of "technology" can encompass a wide range of elements. For the purpose of this discussion, we will use the term broadly, while recognizing that much of the debate and reporting is about computer and networked communication accessibility and applications.

[3] These authors recognize that the case for technology is not without its critics. It is beyond the purview of this paper to address the pros and cons of technology in education. For some interesting discussions of this issue see Cuban (2000) and Schofield (1995).

[4] In practice, evaluators will find that many of the factors cited here impact more than one learning curve and more than one dimension of growth. In general, we have located each factor in the cell we found it to influence most strongly. In a few cases, particularly powerful factors appear in more than one cell. In using this framework, evaluators should consider the importance of factors on multiple aspects of technology institutionalization.

REFERENCES

Asayesh, G. (1993). Staff development for improving student outcomes. *Journal of Staff Development*, **14**(3), 24–27.

Bickel, W.E., Nelson, C.A., & Post, J.E. (2000a). *Does training achieve traction? Evaluating mechanisms for sustainability from teacher technology training*. Paper presented at annual meeting of the American Evaluation Association, Honolulu, HI.

Bickel, W.E., Nelson, C.A., & Post, J.E. (2000b). *Briefing report: PPS technology professional development program*. Pittsburgh, PA: Learning Research and Development Center, University of Pittsburgh.

Brand, G.A. (1997). What research says: Training teachers for using technology. *Journal of Staff Development*, **19**(1).

Bray, B. (1999). *Ten steps to effective technology staff development*. Retrieved from the George Lucas Educational Foundation Web site: http://www.glef.org/.

CEO Forum. (1999). *Professional development: A link to better learning*. Washington, DC: Author.

Coley, R.J., Cradler, J., & Engle, P.K. (1997). *Computers and classrooms: The status of technology in US classrooms*. Princeton, NJ: ETS Policy Information Center.

Cuban, L. (1999). The technology puzzle. *Education Week*, **18**(43), 68, 47.

Cuban, L. (2000). Is spending money on technology worth it? *Education Week*, **19**(24), 42.

Editorial Projects in Education (1999). Technology counts '99: Building the digital curriculum. *Education Week*, **19**(4).

Editorial Projects in Education (2001). Technology counts 2001: The new divide. *Education Week*, **20**(5).

Ertmer, P.A. (1999). Addressing first and second order barriers to change: Strategies for technology integration. *Educational Technology Research and Development*, **47**(4), 47–61.

Fitzgerald, S. (1999). Technology's real costs: Protect your investment with total cost of ownership. *The School Technology Authority, September*. Retrieved from http://www.electronic-school.com/199909/0999sbot.html.

Glennan, T.K., & Melmed, A. (1996). *Fostering the use of educational technology: Elements of a national strategy*. Santa Monica, CA: RAND.

Guskey, T.R. (1994). Results-oriented professional development: In search of an optimal mix of effective practices. *Journal of Staff Development*, **15**(4), 42–50.

Guskey, T.R. (2000). *Evaluating professional development*. Thousand Oaks, CA: Corwin Press.

Guskey, T.R., & Huberman, M. (Eds.) (1995). *Professional development in education: New paradigms and practices*. New York: Teachers College Press.

Hasselbring, T., Smith, L., Williams Glaser, C., Barron, L., Risko, V., Snyder, C., Rakestraw, J., & Campbell, M. (2000). *Literature review: Technology to support teacher development*. Report prepared for NPEAT Project 2.1.4.

ISTE (International Society for Technology in Education). (1998). *National Educational Technology Standards for Students*. Eugene, OR: Author.

Jerald, C.D., & Orlofsky, G.F. (1999). Raising the bar on school technology. *Education Week*, **19**(4), 58–62.

Joyce, B., & Showers, B. (1980). Improving inservice training: The messages of research. *Educational Leadership*, **37**(5), 379–385.

Joyce, B, Showers, B., & Rolheiser-Bennett, C. (1987). Staff development and student learning: A synthesis of research on models of teaching. *Educational Leadership*, **45**(2), 11–23.

Kennedy, M.M. (1999). Form and substance in mathematics and science professional development. *NISE Brief*, **3**(2), 1–7.

Loucks-Horsley, S., Hewson, P.W., Love, N., & Stiles K.E. (1998). *Designing professional development for teachers of science and mathematics*. Thousand Oaks, CA: Corwin Press.

Means, B., & Olson, K. (1995). *Technology's role in educational reform: Findings from a national study of innovating schools*. Washington, DC: Office of Educational Research and Improvement, U.S. Department of Education.

Meyer, T.R. (1999). *A general framework for good technology integration in schools and criteria for the development of an effective evaluation model*. Paper presented at annual meeting of the American Evaluation Association, Orlando, FL.

Nelson, C.A., & Bickel, W.E. (1999). *Evaluating instructional technology implementation: A framework for assessing learning payoffs*. Paper presented at annual meeting of the American Evaluation Association, Orlando, FL.

Norton, P., & Gonzales, C. (1998). Regional educational technology assistance initiative – phase II: Evaluating a model for statewide professional development. *Journal of Research on Computing in Education*, **31**, 25–48.

OTA (Office of Technology Assessment). (1995). *Teachers and technology: Making the connections*. (S/N 052-003-61409-2). Washington, DC: U.S. Government Printing Office.

O.E.C.D. (Organisation for Economic Co-operation and Development). (2001). *Education at a glance: OECD indicators*. Paris: Author.

President's Committee of Advisors on Science and Technology. (1997). Report to the President on the use of technology to strengthen K-12 education in the United States. Washington, DC: Author.

Schofield, J. (1995). *Computers in the classroom*. Cambridge, MA: Cambridge University Press.

Scriven, M. (1967). The methodology of evaluation. In R.E. Stake (Ed.), *Curriculum evaluation* (pp. 39–83). Chicago: Rand McNally.

Smerdon, B., Cronen, S., Lanahan, L, Anderson, J., Iannotti, N., & Angles, J. (2000). *Teachers' tools for the 21st Century: A report on teachers' use of technology*. Washington, DC: National Center for Education Statistics, U.S. Department of Education.

U.S. Department of Education. (1999). *Teacher quality: A report on the preparation and qualifications of public school teachers*. Washington, DC: National Center for Education Statistics.

Weiner, R. (2000, November 22). More technology training for teachers. *New York Times*.

Wenglinsky, H. (1998). *Does it compute? The relationship between technology and student achievement in mathematics*. Princeton, NJ: ETS Policy Information Center.

Section 10

Local, National, and International Levels of System Evaluation

Introduction

THOMAS KELLAGHAN, Section Editor

Educational Research Centre, St. Patrick's College, Dublin

Evaluation in education has for the most part focused on assessment of the achievements of individual students. Students are assessed informally, day-in, day-out, in classrooms throughout the world as an integral part of the work of teachers, who use a variety of procedures to determine learning progress, to identify difficulties students may be experiencing, and to facilitate learning. Evaluation becomes more formal when students take tests or examinations, which may be administered by teachers or by external agencies, to provide evidence of achievement that may be used for certification or selection for further education.

In recent years, interest has grown in obtaining information about the achievements of a system of education as a whole (or a clearly defined part of it), in addition to information about the achievements of individual students. The information may be obtained for a nation or state in an exercise called a national or local statewide assessment (also sometimes called a system assessment, learning assessment, or assessment of learning outcomes), or it may involve obtaining comparative data for a number of states or nations (in an exercise called an international comparative study of achievement). In both cases, individual students complete assessment tasks, but usually only aggregated data are considered in analyses and reports. However, in some statewide and national assessments, data may also be used to make observations or decisions about individual schools, teachers, or even students.

In this introductory note to the section, some of the factors that have contributed to a growth in interest in providing data on the achievements of education systems are considered. This is followed by a description of national assessments (purposes, procedures, and uses) and of recent expansion in national assessment activity. International assessments are then briefly described before the chapters in the section are introduced.

DEVELOPMENT OF INTEREST IN ASSESSING SYSTEM ACHIEVEMENTS

While it has not been common practice, there have been occasions in the past when the performances of individual students have been aggregated to provide

International Handbook of Educational Evaluation, 873–882
T. Kellaghan, D.L. Stufflebeam (eds.)
© *2003 Dordrecht: Kluwer Academic Publishers. Printed in Great Britain.*

an indicator of the quality of the education system as a whole. Perhaps the most outstanding examples of this are the payment-by-results schemes which were introduced to the British Isles and to a number of other countries in the 19th century. In 1862, a scheme was inaugurated in the Revised Code of the Privy Council for England, and was later extended to Ireland, in which teachers' salaries were dependent in part on the results of annual examinations in reading, spelling, writing, and arithmetic conducted by school inspectors as an inducement to make teachers work harder. National percentages of success rates were calculated and published annually. Sir Patrick Keenan (1881), in an address to the National Association for the Promotion of Social Science, reviewed the scheme when it had been in operation in Ireland for ten years. In a comparison of the educational returns of 1870 with those of 1880, he identified an increase in the percentage of students "passing" in reading from 70.5 to 91.4, in writing from 57.7 to 93.8, and in arithmetic from 54.4 to 74.8. Keenan introduced an international dimension to the analysis by observing that the 1880 figures were better than those obtained in England with the exception of arithmetic, for which figures were similar in both countries. Even at this stage, however, the validity of the national findings was being questioned. The school inspectors who carried out the assessment pointed out that students could pass the reading test without actually being able to "read". In 1895, one of them reported that reading is "generally indistinct in articulation, the words are so falsely grouped and proper emphasis and pauses so much neglected, that it has become often an unintelligible jumble" (quoted in Coolahan, 1977, p. 15).

While these schemes were not unique, for the most part educational policy-makers and administrators tended to view educational quality in terms of inputs to the system (e.g., student participation rates, physical facilities, curriculum materials, books, and level of teacher education). The assumption seems to have been that if inputs are of high quality, so too will student learning.

That perception changed in the final decades of the 20th century when concern with the outcomes of education grew. Several factors, ranging from the interpretation of research evidence, to economics, to ideological positions regarding the function of schooling seem to underlie this shift in focus. For example, the failure of the Equal Educational Opportunity Survey (Coleman et al., 1966) to demonstrate a strong relationship between school resources and students' achievements was associated with a change in the definition of equality of opportunity from one based on school resources to one based on student achievements. The results of international comparative studies of achievement also served to focus attention on outcomes when they were interpreted in the United States as indicating that students were not being adequately prepared to compete in a globalized information-based economy (see National Commission on Excellence in Education, 1983).

Concern about the knowledge and skills that students were acquiring was not limited to the United States or to industrialized nations. It was also growing in developing countries, but for different reasons. It resulted in part from a realization that very little information was available on the effects of the very substantial investments that were being made in the provision of education, and the limited information that was available indicated that students with short educational careers benefited very little. There was a further concern that even the competencies acquired by students who stayed in the education system for a long time might fail to meet the needs of the economies of the 21st century. These concerns were reflected in the document adopted by the World Conference on Education for All in Jomtien, Thailand in March, 1990 when it stated that the provision of basic education for all was meaningful only if students actually acquired useful knowledge, reasoning ability, skills, and values. As a consequence, Article 4 of the *World Declaration on Education for All* (UNESCO, 1990) stated that the focus of basic education should be "on actual learning acquisition and outcome, rather than exclusively upon enrolment, continued participation in organized programs and completion of certification requirements" (p. 5). More recently, *The Dakar Framework for Action* (UNESCO, 2000), produced at the end of the ten-year follow-up to Jomtien, again highlighted the importance of learning outcomes. One of its agreed goals specified that "recognized and measurable learning outcomes are achieved by all, especially in literacy, numeracy and essential life skills" (p. 17).

Growth in interest in the outcomes of education at the system level may also be related to the development in many countries, industrialized and developing, of a corporist approach to administration and an associated rise in "managerialism". The approach draws heavily on ideas from the business world, such as strategic and operational planning, continuous improvement, the use of performance indicators, a focus on "deliverables" and results, quality assurance, a growth in incentive and accountability systems based on results (e.g., performance-related pay), and the concept of the citizen as consumer. The performance management movement, which had its roots in the 1930s, but grew in popularity in the late 1980s and in the 1990s, placed a heavy emphasis on obtaining data on the achievements of education systems. Performance would be defined in terms of results, performance targets would be set, the extent to which results were achieved would be determined using performance indicators, and decisions (including ones on resource allocation) would be based on performance information. The aim of the activities was to provide rapid and continuous feedback on a limited number of outcome measures considered to be of interest to politicians, policy makers, administrators, and stakeholders (Kellaghan & Madaus, 2000).

While national and international assessments would seem to fit well with the purposes of performance management, it is difficult to estimate the extent to which information derived from assessments is actually being used for such purposes as target setting or the allocation of resources. This is partly because such uses may not be publicly documented. However, some evidence of use is available. For example, in Great Britain, the white paper *Excellence in Schools* set as targets for 2002 that 80% of 11-year-olds would reach the standards expected of their age in English, and 75% would do so in mathematics (Great Britain, 1997). There are also several examples of the use of national assessment data to decide on resource allocation (e.g., France [Michel, 1995]; Uruguay [Benveniste, 2000]), as well as evidence of the use of the results of international studies in a managerial context, in particular to adjust school curricula (see Kellaghan, 1996).

NATIONAL ASSESSMENTS

At least the germs of contemporary procedures in national assessment using standardized tests can be found in a survey to measure reading standards carried out in England in 1948 with the purpose of obtaining data that would be relevant to suggestions that "backwardness" and "illiteracy" had increased during the second world war (see Kellaghan & Madaus, 1982).

More systematic and elaborate achievement monitoring procedures, as described by Torrance in this volume, were introduced in 1974 when the Assessment of Performance Unit (APU) was established. Its life, however, was relatively short, and the current system of assessment of the national curriculum was introduced in 1988. The American National Assessment of Educational Progress (NAEP), described by Jones in this volume, had been set up almost two decades earlier (in 1969). Other early entries to the national assessment scene were Ireland in 1972, France in 1979, and Chile in 1984.

Most countries in the industrialized world, with the notable exception of Germany, had established national assessment systems by 1990. During the 1990s, capacity to carry out assessment studies developed rapidly in developing countries, particularly in Africa and Latin America (Kellaghan & Greaney, 2001a). The activity for the most part seems attributable to the stress in the Declaration of the World Conference on Education for All (UNESCO, 1990) on the importance of knowing to what extent students were actually learning.

National assessments are all designed to describe the level of achievements, not of individual students, but of a whole education system, or a clearly defined part of it (e.g., fourth grade students or 11-year-olds) (Greaney & Kellaghan, 1996; Kellaghan, 1997; Kellaghan & Greaney, 2001b). The most commonly identified areas for assessment have been students' first language and mathematics, followed by science, a second language, art, music, and social studies. Assessments at primary school have been more common than at higher levels in the education system. In some countries, only one assessment has been carried out to date; in others, assessments are carried out on a regular basis.

All assessments seek answers to one or more of the following questions. (i) How well are students learning in the education system (with reference to general expectations, the aims of the curriculum, or preparation for life)? (ii) Is there evidence of particular strengths and weaknesses in students' knowledge and skills? (iii) Do particular subgroups in the population perform poorly? Are there, for example, disparities between the achievements of boys and girls, of students in urban and rural locations, of students from different language or ethnic groups, of students in different regions of the country? (iv) What factors are associated with student achievement? To what extent does achievement vary with characteristics of the learning environment (e.g., school resources, teacher preparation and competence, type of school) or with students' home and community circumstances? (v) Do student achievements change over time? (Kellaghan & Greaney, 2001b).

While all national assessment systems address these questions, there is considerable variation in the procedures that are used. First, an assessment may be based on a sample of schools/students, or all students at the relevant age/grade level in the education system may be assessed. Second, an assessment may be based on an analytic view of achievement and rely on tests administered under standardized conditions in a few sessions, or an assessment may be designed to be holistic and performance-based, to be integrated into everyday classroom practice, and to be administered over several days by teachers. Third, each student may take only a fraction of a large number of assessment tasks, allowing for extensive curriculum coverage without requiring students to spend a lot of time responding to tasks, or in keeping with a more holistic view of achievement, there may be no provision for systematically allocating different tasks to students. Finally, an assessment may be designed to provide teachers with exemplars of good assessment practices which, it is hoped, would influence their curriculum priorities and methods of assessment, and/or information about the performance of individual students, teachers, schools or districts. Most assessments, however, are not designed to impact directly on schools and teachers, though the information derived from them might be used to reach policy decisions that would eventually impact on them (Kellaghan & Greaney, 2001b).

A variety of approaches are implemented in some countries. In Chile, all students are assessed in Spanish and arithmetic, while a 10% sample is assessed in natural sciences, history, and geography (Himmel, 1996). An alternative combination operates in France. In one operation, samples of students are selected about every five years at the end of grades 7, 9, and 10 to provide information on achievements at the system level in relation to the national curriculum. In a separate operation, the total population of students take "diagnostic" assessments on the commencement of study in grades 3, 6, and 10 (Michel, 1995) to provide information on individual schools, and feedback is sent to schools, students, and students' parents. Although NAEP in the United States uses a sample of students, most states have now put in place programs assessing the learning of all students, and in which teachers and/or students are held accountable for learning outcomes (Shore, Pedulla, & Clarke, 2001). When assessments allow the identification of individual school districts, schools, teachers, and even students, they may be considered as surrogates for public examinations, and, not surprisingly, the development of this type of assessment has been most marked in countries which do not have a public examination system (the United States and Latin American countries).

A further important factor differentiating assessments is the use that is made of results. Some assessments may primarily represent a *symbolic activity*, an effort to imbue the policy-making process with the guise of scientific rationality

(Benveniste, 2000; Meyer & Rowan, 1978) or, in developing countries, to satisfy the requirements of donors supporting reforms. In these cases, the act of assessment would seem to be of greater consequence than its outcomes (Airasian, 1988).

Assessments may also be mechanisms of disciplinary power and control, procedures that are used to modify the actions of others (Foucault, 1977). Two procedures can be identified. In the first, which may be termed *diagnostic monitoring*, an attempt is made to identify problems and remediate learning deficiencies (Richards, 1988). Following identification, various resources (new programs, new educational materials, and inservice training for teachers) may be provided.

An alternative procedure, based on principles of microeconomics, may be termed *performance monitoring*; in this case, the focus is on organizational outcomes and the objective is to improve student achievement primarily through competition. Its basic rationale – that assessment procedures to which high stakes are attached have the ability to modify the behavior of administrators, teachers, and students – has a long pedigree, and its proponents would be comfortable in the presence of the ghosts of John Stuart Mill and Adam Smith. No specific action may be required beyond the publication of information about performance (e.g., in league tables). However, in some cases inducements for improved performance may be provided; for example, schools and/or teachers may receive money if students achieve a specified target (e.g., if 85% reach a satisfactory level of proficiency).

Whether a national assessment can be used for diagnostic or performance monitoring will depend on its design. If it is based on a sample of schools/students (e.g., the American NAEP), it can be used only for diagnostic purposes, and then only for diagnosis at the system level. Census-based national assessments, on the other hand, have the option of operating either a system of diagnostic monitoring or of performance monitoring. An example of the former is to be found in the national assessment in Uruguay (Benveniste, 2000), and of the latter in the national assessment in England and in many mandated state assessment programs in the United States.

INTERNATIONAL ASSESSMENTS

International comparative studies of achievement were developed by the International Association for the Evaluation of Educational Achievement (IEA) which was founded following a meeting of leading educationists at the UNESCO Institute for Education in Hamburg in 1958. The educationists, conscious of the lack of internationally valid "standards of achievement", proposed studies of measured outcomes of education systems and their determinants, which they anticipated would capitalize on the variability that existed across education systems, exploiting the conditions which "one big educational laboratory" of varying school structures and curricula provided, not only to describe existing conditions, but to suggest what might be educationally possible (Husén, 1973;

Husén & Postlethwaite, 1996). Thus, the studies were envisaged as having a research perspective (largely in the tradition of structural functionalism), as well as policy implications.

International assessments share many procedural features with national assessments, though they differ from them in a number of respects (Beaton, Postlethwaite, Ross, Spearritt, & Wolf, 1999; Goldstein, 1996; Greaney & Kellaghan, 1996; Kellaghan & Greaney, 2001b). As in national assessments, instruments are developed to assess students' knowledge and skills. However, instead of representing the curriculum of only one education system, the instruments have to be considered appropriate for use in all participating systems. The age or grade at which the instruments are to be administered has to be agreed, as have procedures for selecting schools/students to participate. A unique feature of these assessments is that they provide an indication of where students' achievements in a country stand relative to the achievements of students in other countries.

Participation in international assessments has been more a feature of industrialized than of less economically developed countries. Reasons for this may be limitations in finances, infrastructure, and human resources, as well as the realization that differences in the conditions of education systems render documentation of associated differences in achievement superfluous and possibly embarrassing (Kellaghan & Greaney, 2001a).

A number of problems arise in international assessments that do not arise in national assessments (see Beaton et al., 1999; Goldstein, 1996; Kellaghan & Grisay, 1995). One relates to the difficulty in designing an assessment procedure that will adequately measure the outcomes of a variety of curricula, given that education systems differ in their goals and in the emphasis and time they accord different topics in a curriculum. A second relates to the equivalence across countries of the populations and samples of students that are being compared. A problem also arises (and may arise in some national assessments) if it is necessary to translate assessment instruments into one or more languages. In practice, it is difficult to ensure that the ways questions are phrased and the cultural significance of content are equivalent in all language versions of an assessment task (see Blum, Goldstein, & Guérin-Pace, 2001).

It is perhaps for reasons such as these that the findings of international assessments appear to be less consistent than the findings of national assessments. For example, differences between the performances of Irish students in science have been observed when their results are compared on the International Assessment of Education Progress 2 (IAEP2) (Martin, Hickey, & Murchan, 1992), the Third International Mathematics and Science Study (TIMSS) (Martin, Mullis, Beaton, Gonzalez, Smith, & Kelly, 1997), and the Programme for International Student Assessment (PISA) (Shiel, Cosgrove, Sofroniou, & Kelly, 2001). In the first, performance was below average, in the second it was average, and in the third, above average. Similar disparities are found in the results of reading literacy studies. Two of the studies (the IEA Reading Literacy Survey [Martin & Morgan, 1994] and the International Adult Literacy Survey [OECD/Statistics Canada, 2000]) placed Irish participants towards the lower end of OECD countries, while

PISA (Shiel et al., 2001) placed them towards the upper end. Differences in performance are also in evidence in comparisons involving other countries (O'Leary, Kellaghan, Madaus, & Beaton, 2000). It seems unlikely that these findings reflect actual differences in "achievement"; more likely they are due to variation in the knowledge and processes assessed, response rates, or the criteria used in the definition of proficiency levels.

In considering international comparisons, Goldstein (1996) has identified further inherent weaknesses including problems in assumptions regarding the nature of achievement when results are reported in terms of single achievement scores (in, for example, "reading" or "mathematics"). Among the issues he has identified as in need of attention are: the scaling and interpretation of data; the relevance of items to each country's curriculum, and indeed why particular "common" items were chosen by test constructors in the first place; and the development of explanatory models (which would include information on students' prior achievements) as a basis for interpreting observed differences between countries. In identifying these issues, Goldstein reflects the views of the founding fathers of international studies regarding the role that the studies might play in advancing our understanding of the contribution of formal education to students' development. However, whether the considerable methodological work in the design and execution of studies proposed by Goldstein will receive support is another matter. Policy makers and managers, whose main interest in assessment results is likely to be for managerial purposes (e.g., defining performance in terms of results, setting performance targets, allocating resources) and diagnostic monitoring, rather than for "understanding", may be reluctant to provide the required resources.

PAPERS IN THE SECTION

In the first two papers in this section, descriptions are provided of two major national assessment systems: national assessment in the United States (Lyle Jones) and assessment of the national curriculum in England (Harry Torrance). Both papers describe the history of the assessments, and how they have changed since they were instituted, in the United States in 1969, and in England in 1988. The histories differ considerably. This is not surprising, given that the systems differed radically in their conception. In the United States, the focus was mainly on diagnostic monitoring and on tracking changes in educational achievement, while in England assessment was designed for performance monitoring. Apart from the fact that the systems were introduced to address different political priorities, differences in the educational contexts in which they were implemented also contributed to differences in the ways in which the systems evolved. However, there is also some evidence of convergence between practice in the two countries. Thus, the English system has moved towards the use of more standardized and less complex assessment procedures. On the other hand, while the American system continues to be based on samples of schools and provides data only for identifiable groups of students, not individual schools or students, recent legislation provides for the testing of all students in grades 3 through 8. Individual states have also developed their own standards and assessment programs, and results of the programs are being used to determine grade promotion and high school graduation for individual students.

In their chapter on the complex area of state and school district evaluation activity in the United States, William Webster, Ted Almaguer, and Tim Orsak consider some of the implications for public school evaluation units of the increase in state activity in assessment and accountability activities. They observe that public school evaluation units have not prospered during the 1990s, and that increase in state involvement may have led to a sacrifice in concepts such as validity and equity in evaluation in the interest of political expediency.

The final two papers in the section deal with international studies of educational achievement. Tjeerd Plomp, Sarah Howie, and Barry McGraw describe the purposes and functions of such studies and the organizations that carry them out. Central issues relating to the design of studies and methodological considerations occupy a considerable portion of the chapter. In the final chapter, William Schmidt and Richard Houang address the measurement of curriculum and its role in international studies which is considered as three-fold: as the object of an evaluation, as the criterion for it, and as the context in which an evaluation is interpreted.

REFERENCES

Airasian, P.W. (1988). Symbolic validation: The case of state-mandated, high-stakes testing. *Educational Evaluation and Policy Analysis*, **10**, 301–313.

Beaton, A.E., Postlethwaite, T.N., Ross, K.N., Spearritt, D., & Wolf, R.M. (1999). *The benefits and limitations of international educational achievement studies.* Paris: International Institute for Educational Planning/International Academy of Education.

Benveniste, L. (2000). Student assessment as a political construction: The case of Uruguay. *Education Policy Analysis Archives*, **8**(32). Retrieved from http://epaa.asu.edu/epaa/.

Blum, A., Goldstein, H., & Guérin-Pace, F. (2001). International Adult Literacy Survey (IALS): An analysis of international comparisons of adult literacy. *Assessment in Education*, **8**, 225–246.

Coleman, J.S., Campbell, E.Q., Hobson, C.J., McPartland, J., Mood, A.M., Weinfeld, F.D., & York, R.L. (1966). *Equality of educational opportunity.* Washington, DC: Office of Education, U.S. Department of Health, Education, and Welfare.

Coolahan, J. (1977). Three eras of English reading in Irish national schools. In V. Greaney (Ed.), *Studies in reading* (pp. 12–26). Dublin: Educational Company.

Foucault, M. (1977). *Discipline and punish. The birth of the prison* (A. Sheridan trans). New York: Viking.

Goldstein, H. (1996). International comparisons of student achievement. In A. Little, & A. Wolf (Eds), *Assessment in transition. Learning, monitoring and selection in international perspective* (pp. 58–87). Oxford: Pergamon.

Greaney, V., & Kellaghan, T. (1996). *Monitoring the learning outcomes of education systems.* Washington, DC: World Bank.

Great Britain. (1997). *Excellence in schools.* White paper on education. London: Her Majesty's Stationery Office.

Himmel, E. (1996). National assessment in Chile. In P. Murphy, V. Greaney, M.E. Lockheed, & C. Rojas (Eds), *National assessment. Testing the system* (pp. 111–128). Washington, DC: World Bank.

Husén, T. (1973). Foreword. In L.C. Comber & J.P. Keeves (Eds), *Science achievement in nineteen countries* (pp. 13–24). New York: Wiley.

Husén, T., & Postlethwaite, T.N. (1996). A brief history of the International Association for the Evaluation of Educational Achievement (IEA). *Assessment in Education*, **3**, 129–141.

Keenan, P. (1881). *Address on education to National Association for the Promotion of Social Science*. Dublin: Queen's Printing Office.

Kellaghan, T. (1996). IEA studies and educational policy. *Assessment in Education*, **3**, 143–160.

Kellaghan, T. (1997). Seguimiento de los resultados educativos nacionales. (Monitoring national educational performance.) In H.B. Alvarez, & M. Ruiz-Casares (Eds), *Evaluación y reforma educativa. Opciones de política* (Evaluation and educational reform. Policy options) (pp. 23–65). Washington, DC: U.S. Agency for International Development.

Kellaghan, T., & Greaney, V. (2001a). The globalisation of assessment in the 20th century. *Assessment in Education*, **8**, 87–102.

Kellaghan, T., & Greaney, V. (2001b). *Using assessment to improve the quality of education*. Paris: International Institute for Educational Planning.

Kellaghan, T., & Grisay, A. (1995). International comparisons of student achievement: Problems and prospects. In OECD, *Measuring what students learn. Mesurer les résultats scholaires* (pp. 41–61). Paris: Organisation for Economic Co-Operation and Development.

Kellaghan, T., & Madaus, G.F. (1982). Trends in educational standards in Great Britain and Ireland. In G.R. Austin & H. Garber (Eds), *The rise and fall of national test scores* (pp. 195–214). New York: Academic Press.

Kellaghan, T., & Madaus, G.F. (2000). Outcome evaluation. In D.L. Stufflebeam, G.F. Madaus, & T. Kellaghan (Eds), *Evaluation models. Viewpoints on educational and human services evaluation* (2nd ed., pp. 97–112). Boston: Kluwer Academic.

Martin, M.O., Hickey, B., & Murchan, D.P. (1992). The Second International Assessment of Educational Progress: Mathematics and science findings in Ireland. *Irish Journal of Education*, **26**, 5–146.

Martin, M.O., & Morgan, M. (1994). Reading literacy in Irish schools: A comparative analysis. *Irish Journal of Education*, **28**, 5–101.

Martin, M.O., Mullis, I.V.S., Beaton, A.E., Gonzalez, E.J., Smith T.A., & Kelly, D.L. (1997). *Science achievement in the primary school years. IEA's Third International Mathematics and Science Study (TIMSS)*. Chestnut Hill, MA: TIMSS International Study Center, Boston College.

Meyer, J., & Rowan, B. (1978). The structure of educational organizations. In M. Meyer (Ed.), *Environments and organizations* (pp. 78–109). San Francisco: Jossey-Bass.

Michel, A. (1995). France. In OECD, *Performance standards in education. In search of quality* (pp. 103–114). Paris: Organisation for Economic Co-Operation and Development.

National Commission on Excellence in Education. (1983). *A nation at risk. The imperative for educational reform*. Washington, DC: U.S. Government Printing Office.

OECD (Organisation for Economic Co-Operation and Development)/Statistics Canada. (2000). *Literacy in the information age. Final report of the International Adult Literacy Survey*. Paris: OECD/Ottawa: Statistics Canada.

O'Leary, M., Kellaghan, T., Madaus, G.F., & Beaton, A.E. (2000). Consistency of findings across international surveys of mathematics and science achievement: A comparison of IAEP2 and TIMSS. *Education Policy Analysis Archives*, **8**(43). Retrieved from http://epaa.asu.edu/epaa/.

Richards, C.E. (1988). A typology of educational monitoring systems. *Educational Evaluation and Policy Analysis*, **10**, 106–116.

Shiel, G., Cosgrove, J., Sofroniou, N., & Kelly, A. (2001). *Ready for life? The literacy achievements of Irish 15-year olds in an international context*. Dublin: Educational Research Centre.

Shore, A., Pedulla, J., & Clarke, M. (2001). *The building blocks of state testing programs*. Chestnut Hill, MA: National Board on Educational Testing and Public Policy, Boston College.

UNESCO. (1990). *World Declaration on Education for All. Meeting basic needs*. New York: Author.

UNESCO. (2000). *The Dakar Framework for Action. Education for All: Meeting our collective commitments*. Paris: Author.

39
National Assessment in the United States: The Evolution of a Nation's Report Card

LYLE V. JONES[1]

University of North Carolina at Chapel Hil, Department of Psychology, NC, USA

In many countries, education is a responsibility of government, but in the United States of America, it is among the functions of government for which both funding and policy is the responsibility of the 50 states of the union, and often of school districts within states. Given that context, it is especially interesting that the National Assessment of Educational Progress (NAEP), a federal project, was established, has survived, and has had considerable influence both nationally and in the states. In this chapter, evidence bearing upon these issues is presented. The chapter also serves as a history of the formation and the development of NAEP.

An Act of Congress in 1867 established a United States Department of Education "for the purpose of collecting such statistics and facts as shall show the condition and progress of education in the several states and territories, and of diffusing such information ... as shall aid the people of the United States." Almost a century later U.S. Commissioner of Education Francis Keppel recognized that statistics and facts such as those envisaged in the 1867 Act were being neither collected nor diffused. In 1963, he expressed the belief that something should be done, and asked Ralph Tyler to outline a remedy.

Tyler, a pioneer in educational evaluation, was at that time Director of the Center for Advanced Study in the Behavioral Sciences. He responded with a memorandum to Keppel, who encouraged the Carnegie Corporation of New York to sponsor two conferences to consider the matter. The Corporation's Board of Directors in 1964 allocated $100,000 to support an Exploratory Committee for the Assessment of Progress in Education (ECAPE). Tyler became chairman, and Stephen Whithey, on part-time leave from the University of Michigan, was appointed Staff Director. As discussed at length by Greenbaum (1977), the final design of the National Assessment (NAEP) essentially unchanged from Tyler's 1963 plan.

RALPH TYLER'S VISION OF NAEP

Two decades earlier, Tyler had codified his approach to educational assessment while he served from 1934 to 1942 at The Ohio State University as Research

International Handbook of Educational Evaluation, 883–904
T. Kellaghan, D.L. Stufflebeam (eds.)
© 2003 Dordrecht: Kluwer Academic Publishers. Printed in Great Britain.

Director of "the Eight-Year Study." That study was designed to evaluate the effectiveness of education at each of 30 participating high schools in the United States. As outlined by Tyler (1942), it was to serve several major purposes: (i) to indicate the need for improvements in the education program of each school; (ii) to validate the hypotheses upon which each school operated; (iii) to provide information basic to effective guidance of individual students; (iv) to give confidence to school staff, parents, and teachers that the educational program is effective; and (v) to provide a sound basis for public relations. Tyler (1942) also presented basic assumptions underlying the development of the evaluation project. Among his assumptions were: (i) education seeks to change the behavior patterns of students; (ii) the kinds of changes desired become the educational objectives of a program; (iii) the aim of evaluation is to discover the extent to which the objectives are realized; (iv) behavior patterns are complex and no single score or category or grade can adequately summarize any phase of a student's achievement; (v) evaluation should not be limited to paper-and-pencil tests but should entail other techniques appropriate for the behaviors being appraised; and (vi) the nature of the appraisal may be expected to influence the processes of teaching and learning.

A demanding task to be undertaken prior to any evaluation is the formulation of educational objectives. In the Eight-Year Study, the objectives for each school were developed by faculty members in the school. In the design for NAEP, the formulation of objectives entailed deliberation by a broad array of stakeholders, and required a consensus among parents and public citizens as well as teachers and educational specialists.

This, then, was Tyler's basis for the plan presented to ECAPE. To elaborate on these general guidelines and to translate them into concrete assessment procedures, Tyler in early 1965 selected a four-person Technical Advisory Committee (TAC) of Robert Abelson, Lee Cronbach, Lyle Jones, and John Tukey (Chairman). Both Cronbach, who had been Tyler's Ph.D. student, and Tukey, an eminent statistician at Princeton University, had attended the first Carnegie Corporation Conference and had actively supported Tyler in his presentations there. It was unlikely, then, that TAC would challenge Tyler's vision for the design of NAEP.

PLANNING FOR THE FIRST ASSESSMENT

As soon as it was constituted, TAC became the working arm for ECAPE, with active assistance from Tyler and Jack Merwin from the University of Minnesota, who had replaced Steven Whithey as Staff Director. An early decision was to design assessments for ages 9, 13, 17, and young adults in ten subject areas: art, citizenship, career and occupational development, literature, mathematics, music, reading, science, social studies, and writing. It was agreed that lay panels would establish learning objectives for each area based upon what citizens should know, rather only upon what schools were teaching. It also was specified that the tasks presented were to cover a wide range of difficulty to properly evaluate the performance of both deficient and advanced performers. The first-round national assessment would include citizenship, reading, and science.

Tyler earlier had met with potential contractors and, in March of 1965, TAC reviewed preliminary proposals from the American Institutes for Research (AIR), the Educational Testing Service (ETS), Measurement Research Corporation (MRC), the Psychological Corporation (Psych Corp), and Science Research Associates (SRA). Prime contractors were AIR for Citizenship, SRA for Reading, ETS for Science, the Research Triangle Institute (RTI) for sample design and exercise administration, and MRC for the printing of exercise materials and the scoring of responses. From 1965 to 1969, contractor personnel met frequently with TAC, which monitored their work.

Following the first grant from the Carnegie Corporation to ECAPE, the Ford Foundation and its Fund for the Advancement of Education granted $1.7 million to ECAPE between 1965 and 1969, and the Carnegie Corporation provided an additional $2.3 million. The first federal funding came in 1966 in the form of a $50,000 award from the Office of Education (OE) for a series of conferences on assessment.

The funding from Carnegie and Ford supported the formulation of assessment objectives, the development of exercises related to those objectives, and a variety of pilot studies and feasibility studies that had been called for by TAC. Based in part upon findings from these studies, TAC established several innovative guidelines for the assessment. Sampling frames were designed both for in-school and out-of-school assessments. Exercises were to be administered in schools in 50-minute sessions to small groups of children, and out of schools in longer sessions to individual 17- and 18-year-olds and young adults at ages 26 to 35. For in-school administrations, a booklet of common exercises would be presented to the group of respondents with a tape recording of a male voice reading aloud each question to be answered, and all respondents thus would proceed at the same pace through the exercise booklet. Different randomly selected groups typically would receive different exercise booklets, in a "matrix-sampling" design. Thus, for a given age level, there might be ten distinct exercise booklets, yielding performance results for ten times the number of exercises that were administered to any individual student. As an additional innovation, to discourage guessing and to reduce non-responses alternative answers to multiple-choice exercises always included "I don't know" as one possible answer.

Between 1965 and 1967, Tyler and ECAPE held many discussions at various sites with representatives of the educational establishment. Of special importance was the effort to encourage cooperation from the American Association of School Administrators (AASA). To conduct assessment tryouts, it would be necessary to gain access to students in selected schools, for which school-administrator approval was needed. In an attempt to satisfy some expressed concerns about possibly invidious comparisons, Tyler and ECAPE assured AASA that assessment results would not be reported for individual students, or for schools, districts, or states. (Despite the general recognition that state-by-state results would be useful, it became clear that AASA would not tolerate such a design.)

The AASA executive committee initially had recommended to its members that they refuse to participate in the project. In response to pressures from both within and outside AASA, the AASA Executive Committee later agreed that the issue could be studied further, and a joint AASA-ECAPE Committee was appointed for this purpose. At about the same time, in 1967, the National Education Association passed a resolution to "withhold cooperation" with ECAPE. Thus, while contractors continued to develop assessment materials and procedures, the political climate for initiating the project appeared to deteriorate.

In 1967, Frank Womer of the University of Michigan was appointed to succeed Jack Merwin as Staff Director. Later that year, ECAPE initiated discussions with the Education Commission of the States (ECS), a newly formed organization of state governors and state education officials. ECS was invited to become the institutional home for NAEP.

In 1968, a successor to ECAPE was established, the Committee for the Assessment of Progress of Education (CAPE), of which George Brain of Washington State University, an active participant in ECS, became Chairman. OE provided a grant of $372,000. Also in 1968, the National Science Foundation (NSF) urged all science teachers to cooperate with CAPE. Encouraged by ECS and NSF, among others, AASA in 1969 altered its position, and agreed to allow each of its members make the decision as to whether or not to cooperate with CAPE. OE then granted an additional $1 million to CAPE.

NAEP UNDER ECS

In the spring of 1969 CAPE moved forward with a successful in-school assessment of 17-year-olds in citizenship, reading, and science. In June of 1969 ECS agreed to assume control of NAEP. Later in the year, the U.S. Office of Education granted $2.4 million to ECS to complete the first-year operation of NAEP. In 1969–70, under the auspices of ECS, assessments in citizenship, reading, and science were conducted in schools of students aged 9 and 13, as well as out of school of 17-and 18-year-olds and young adults.

ECS immediately converted TAC to the Analysis Advisory Committee (ANAC). At the suggestion of TAC, a new Operations Advisory Committee (OPAC) was formed. A National Assessment Policy Committee was appointed, with a membership that included the chairs of CAPE, ANAC, OPAC, Ralph Tyler, and one ECS representative; initially, those members were George Brain, John Tukey, John Letson, Tyler, and Leroy Greene, who was the Chairman of the Education Committee of the California State Assembly.

ANAC turned its attention to the analysis of results and to a framework for reporting assessment findings. To provide a model for reporting, it produced the report of national results for science (Abelson, Cronbach, Jones, Tukey, & Tyler, 1970), which it followed with a report with subgroups comparisons (Abelson,

Coffman, Jones, Mosteller, & Tukey, 1971). The subgroups included four regions of the U.S. (Northeast, Southeast, Central, and West), four community sizes (big cities, urban fringe, medium-size cities, and smaller places), and whether the student was male or female. (Later reports of first-year results also reported findings by race and by level of parental education.) Results were presented in the form of percentages of correct answers (together with standard errors) on individual assessment exercises. Only some of the exercises were released each year. The identity of others was kept confidential to allow them to be used again in later years for the purpose of assessing change over time.

Between 1969 and 1971, Lee Cronbach and Robert Abelson resigned from ANAC; new members were William Coffman, Frederick Mosteller, and John Gilbert. In addition to Jones and Tukey, who remained members of ANAC through 1982, others who served on ANAC were R. Darrell Bock, Lloyd Bond, David Brillinger, James Davis, Janet Dixon Elashoff, Gene Glass, and Lincoln Moses.

Within the OE, oversight for NAEP became the responsibility of the National Center for Education Statistics (NCES) in 1971 and in 1973 funding changed from a grant to a contract. During the mid-1970s, budgetary uncertainties and delays in federal payments to ECS became major difficulties for NAEP. Funding had increased in 1973 from $2 million to $3 million annually. In 1974, President Nixon's budget request for NAEP was $7 million, but only $3 million was appropriated by Congress. Cost considerations led to the elimination of out-of-school sampling, which also meant eliminating the assessment of young adults, and to reducing the frequency of assessment for some learning areas from the schedule that had been envisioned in earlier plans.

Although NAEP had been authorized by Congress, few Senators or House members were familiar with it, and little media attention was given to its reports. ANAC had envisioned possible media interest in the form of daily newspaper coverage, presenting and interpreting student performance on individual exercises, but that proved to have been a naïve expectation. To reduce the information burden on the audience, reporting began to focus on mean or median performance for groups of related exercises, but that too failed to stimulate much attention. It was hoped that more interest would accrue when it became possible to report changes in performance from one assessment to the next. That seemed not be the case, however, perhaps because changes were small in size, because of the inevitable delay in producing reports, and because results were based on a national sample of schools and thus failed to reflect how students performed in a local school or school district or even in a state. The early hopes of some that NAEP findings would impact educational policy were not being realized.

Disappointed that NAEP was having little influence on U.S. education, the Trustees of the Carnegie Corporation in 1972 commissioned an evaluation of the national assessment. The report was completed in 1973 and later was published in book form (Greenbaum, 1977). The Greenbaum critique judged that NAEP had succeeded in meeting some of its objectives: (i) its operational goals of forming educational objectives and launching and maintaining a viable assessment effort,

(ii) developing richer modes of assessment than those of norm-referenced testing, and (iii) providing models for assessments that could be undertaken by states and local communities. It concluded, however, that NAEP had failed to meet its most critical objectives. Greenbaum noted that NAEP was left with

(1) virtually no capacity to answer research questions and even very little capacity to generate significant research hypotheses that could not have been generated more precisely and less expensively by smaller studies;
(2) virtually no capacity to provide the federal government, the lay public, or most educational policymakers with results that are directly useful for decision making; and
(3) most surprising of all, virtually no really significant and supportable new findings with regard to the strengths and weaknesses of American education. (Greenbaum, 1977, p. 169)

The Greenbaum critique elicited a defense in 1975 from ECS/NAEP staff, published as Part 2 in the Greenbaum book. The NAEP staff stated that recent improvements had rendered obsolete some of Greenbaum's criticisms. There nevertheless emerged no substantial changes in the operation of NAEP.

In 1973, contract officers at NCES sought increasing management responsibility for NAEP. That led to heightened levels of conflict between OE and the NAEP Policy Committee at ECS. (The ECS interest in NAEP may have been enhanced by the substantial annual income to ECS in the form of "overhead receipts.")

With encouragement from ECS, Congressional legislation in 1978 served to transfer federal authority for NAEP from NCES to a newly created National Institute of Education (NIE) within OE, and also specified that funding would be provided by a grant or cooperative agreement rather than by contract. This served to restore policy control to ECS rather than to a federal agency. The NIE call for proposals for the five-year continuation of NAEP resulted in only one submittal, from ECS. Following some minor revision, the ECS proposal was funded, and NAEP proceeded much as usual, continuing to disappoint those critics who envisioned that the project would have a greater degree of policy relevance. Among those experiencing continuing disappointment were the staff of the Carnegie Corporation. The initial expectations of Carnegie were not being met. Thus, in 1980, the Corporation, together with the Ford and Spencer Foundations, funded yet another evaluation of NAEP, this time by the consulting firm of Wirtz and Lapointe (1982).

Wirtz and Lapointe appointed a "Council of Seven" to guide the work, Gregory Anrig, Stephen Bailey, Charles Bowen, Clare Burstall, Elton Jolly, Lauren Resnick, and Dorothy Shields. The Council sponsored several special reports and solicited views on how to improve NAEP from more than 150 individuals representing parents, teachers, school administrators, state legislators, organized labor, industry, and measurement professionals. The Wirtz-Lapointe report recommended the continuation of NAEP, but only with numerous important changes. The report emphasized the need for increased funding. It also recommended an increase in the testing time from one to two hours; reporting by grades 4, 8, and 12, rather than by ages 9, 13, and 17; providing results state-by-state and locally within states; reporting by aggregated scores for curriculum domains and sub-domains, rather than reporting by percentages of correct answers to exercises; and several additional changes.

Unlike the response in 1978 to the request for proposal, NIE received five competing proposals to conduct NAEP for the period 1983–1988, including one from ECS. The winning proposal, from ETS, contained essentially all of the changes that were recommended by Wirtz and Lapointe. (By 1983, Gregory Anrig, a member of the Council of Seven, had left his position of Commissioner of Education in Massachusetts to become ETS President. With the award of the grant to ETS, Archie Lapointe moved to ETS as Executive Director of NAEP.)

NAEP UNDER ETS, 1983–1988

The award to ETS ($3.9 million a year for five years) was in the form of a grant rather than a contract. Westat replaced RTI as the organization responsible for sampling and field administration. A new Assessment Policy Committee was formed, as well as a new Technical Advisory Committee (Robert Glaser, Bert Green, Sylvia Johnson, Melvin Novick, Richard Snow, and Robert Linn, Chairman). Other members of this committee through 2001 (later called the Design and Analysis Committee) have been Albert Beaton, Jeri Benson, Johnny Blair, John B. Carroll, Anne Cleary, Clifford Clogg, William Cooley, Jeremy Finn, Paul Holland, Huynh Huynh, Edward Kifer, Gaea Leinhardt, David Lohman, Anthony Nitko, Serge Madhere, Bengt Muthen, Ingram Olkin, Tej Pandey, Juliet Shaffer, Hariharan Swaminathan, John Tukey, and Rebecca Zwick.

Beginning with assessments in 1984, students were sampled by grade as well as by age and, except for reports on achievement change over time, grade became the primary basis for the reporting of findings. Except for the assessment of long-term trend, the administration of items by audiotape was discontinued, students in a single group administration were issued different booklets of exercises (based upon a balanced incomplete "block design"), and "I don't know" was removed as an alternative response in multiple-choice items. Results were no longer reported by percentage of correct responses, exercise-by-exercise; average scaled scores were reported for domains of items, based upon item response theory. NAEP reports were designed to be less confusing to a non-technical audience, and were systematically released at press conferences, with greater attention to obtaining media coverage.

In 1983 *A Nation at Risk*, a publication of the National Commission on Excellence in Education (1983), presented a ringing and influential indictment of the quality of pre-college education in the U.S. At the annual meeting of the Southern Regional Education Board in 1984, several state governors, led by Lamar Alexander of Tennessee and Bill Clinton of Arkansas, called for improved measures of educational achievement, to include comparisons of state with national results. Also that year, the Council of Chief State School Officers (CCSSO) approved plans for cross-state comparisons. Two years later, the National Governors' Association issued a report under the leadership of Lamar Alexander entitled *Time for Results*. The report called for a better national "educational report card," and for report cards to be prepared for individual states. In that same year, Secretary of Education William Bennett appointed a 22-member panel under the chairmanship of Lamar Alexander to make recommendations about the future of NAEP. The panel report was published in March, 1987, and recommended the development by NAEP of a trial state-by-state assessment and the creation of an assessment policy board independent both of the Department of Education and the NAEP contractors (Alexander & James, 1987). A year later, with support from Secretary William Bennett, Congress authorized trial state assessments, sharply increased the funding for NAEP, and established a National Assessment Governing Board (NAGB). Secretary Bennett appointed the members of NAGB in December of 1988.

The Congressional legislation also called for an ongoing evaluation of the state assessments by an impartial panel that was to periodically report its findings to Congress. The 14-member panel was appointed in 1989 under the auspices of the National Academy of Education (NAE), with Robert Glaser and Robert Linn serving as co-chairs.

NAEP UNDER NAGB

NAGB faced major new challenges as it came into being. Entirely new working relations needed to be established among the participant partners on a short-time schedule, especially those involving NCES and the NAEP contractors, ETS and Westat. NAGB was to maintain one historical NAEP project to monitor national achievement trends based on comparable assessment conditions that had been established many years earlier. It was to establish policy for a "new" NAEP, so that assessment items would be matched to newly developing standards for school grades and subject areas. Most notably, it was responsible for developing a trial state assessment, for encouraging participation of the states, and for having the program in operation in 1990, NAGB's very first year of existence. Planning had been underway, of course, by ETS and Westat, with oversight by NCES, and notably by CCSSO under a grant from NSF and the Department of Education. The planning activity was essential to the start of state assessments in 1990.

The Work of CCSSO

An Assessment Steering Committee was appointed by CCSSO from citizens nominated by 18 national organizations, and a Mathematics Objectives Committee was charged with recommending the objectives for the 1990 mathematics assessment. The framework for the objectives was deliberately aligned with the standards for mathematics curricula that had been promulgated in March of 1989 by the National Council of Teachers of Mathematics (NCTM). The draft framework was sent for review to state education agencies in all 50 states as well as to additional mathematics educators. In modified form, it then was approved by the Steering Committee and the Assessment Policy Committee, and ultimately was adopted by NAGB for use again with some extensions, in 1992 and beyond.

CCSSO followed procedures similar to those for mathematics in the areas of reading, science, U.S. history, geography, civics, and the arts. Specialized committees worked with a broad range of organizations and citizens to draft assessment frameworks that then were reviewed by states and finally approved by the Steering Committee and accepted by NAGB and NCES.

In its report to NAGB in January of 1989, CCSSO had presented a series of recommendations, the first of which is:

> An explicit policy is needed by NAGB to direct those developing objectives on the balance of assessing what students do know and can do and objectives that are primarily based on what should be taught students. While "cutting edge" curriculum development should, to some degree, be included in the assessment, if it gets too far outside what schools are currently teaching the willingness to participate will diminish. (National Assessment Governing Board, 1989, Tab 2, p. 14.)

This statement highlights the ever-present tension between those such as Tyler who saw NAEP as a means for describing what students know and can do and others who see NAEP as a means to drive the curriculum to teach what "should be" the objectives of education. The statement also anticipates another recurring problem, namely how to encourage states and school districts to participate in NAEP assessments.

Reporting by "Achievement Levels"

Among NAGB's major innovations was its decision in May of 1990 to report NAEP findings by "achievement level" (basic, proficient, and advanced). NAGB's decision to report results by percentages of children at each of these levels was based on an interpretation of the Congressional mandate for the Board to "identify appropriate achievement goals for each age and grade in each subject area to be tested." In the late 1960s, Lee Cronbach had recognized the desirability of such form of reporting and had urged its consideration by the initial TAC. And in Part 2 of the Alexander-James report, an NAE panel had explicitly supported this kind of reporting:

> We recommend that, to the maximal extent technically feasible, NAEP use descriptive classifications as its principal reporting scheme in future

assessments. For each content area NAEP should articulate clear descriptions of performance levels, descriptions that might be analogous to such craft rankings as novice, journeyman, highly competent, and expert. Descriptions of this kind would be extremely useful to the educators, parents, legislators, and an informed public. (Glaser, 1987, p. 58)

NAGB decided to adopt achievement levels as its primary form of reporting, beginning on a trial basis with the national and state mathematics assessments of 1990, thereby setting the stage for controversies that continued throughout the 1990s as NAGB continued to favor achievement-level reporting and attempted to create "performance standards." Critics of this approach, while generally sympathetic to the intrinsic value of such reporting, remained sharply skeptical of the processes by which performance standards were being established and defined, and thus of the validity of the resulting classification of students by those particular performance standards.

Following its decision in May, 1990, NAGB had immediately instituted a process by appointing a 63-member panel of judges who met on August 16 and 17, 1990 to set standards for the 1990 mathematics assessments. These judges were asked to consider each exercise and to determine the proportion of students at each achievement level (basic, proficient, and advanced) who ought to answer the exercise correctly. Following some revision of procedures by a technical advisory group, 38 of the 63 judges met again on September 29 and 30, 1990, and supplied additional ratings. Later in 1990, a third session was conducted with 11 judges. In May, 1991, NAGB accepted the recommended percentage of correct answers that would serve to distinguish performance at each achievement level.

Recognizing the controversial nature of the process for setting achievement levels, NAGB in 1990 had hired Aspen Systems to conduct an independent evaluation of that process. Daniel Stufflebeam, Richard Jaeger, and Michael Scriven were asked to review all phases of the standard-setting procedures. These investigators filed interim reports in November of 1990 and in January of 1991, each of which suggested improvements of the process. In a third report on May 5, 1991, they advised against releasing results without also providing adequate warning about technical and conceptual shortcomings. They then were asked by NAGB to provide a final "summative" report of their findings.

Stufflebeam, Jaeger, and Scriven prepared a draft final report on August 1 and sent copies on a confidential basis for comment to NAGB members and staff, NCES and contractor personnel, and other leading educational researchers. Their draft final report emphasized that "the technical difficulties are extremely serious," that "these standards and the results obtained from using them should under no circumstances be used as a baseline or benchmark," and that "the procedures used in this exercise should under no circumstances be used as a model." The report went further and questioned the technical competence of NAGB, asserting that "the Board and its Executive Director (were) making technical design decisions that they were not sufficiently qualified to make." The revised final report was submitted to NAGB on August 23, 1991 (Stufflebeam, Jaeger, & Scriven, 1991).

Judging that the draft report included recommendations beyond the charge to the consultants, and discovering that it had been distributed for comment to "outside" individuals without permission from NAGB, the Board was outraged. It sent an official reply to those who had received a copy of the draft report, and took steps to terminate the subcontract with the three researchers. *Education Week* on September 4, 1991, covered the issue under the headline, "NAEP Board Fires Researchers Critical of Standards Process."

The House Education and Labor Committee had been critical of NAGB's efforts to create performance standards from the start. (The House and Senate had disagreed in 1988 on the advisability of setting performance standards.) In October, 1991, the House Committee asked for a review by the General Accounting Office (GAO) of NAGB's efforts to set standards. An interim report was issued by GAO in March of 1992, and its final report was published in June, 1993, under the title, "Educational Achievement Standards: NAGB's Approach Yields Misleading Interpretations" (U.S. General Accounting Office, 1993). The GAO reports essentially supported the earlier advice of Stufflebeam, Jaeger, and Scriven:

> GAO concluded that NAGB's strength lies in its broad representation, not in its technical expertise .... GAO recommends (1) that NAGB withdraw its recommendation to NCES to publish 1992 NAEP results primarily in terms of levels of achievement, (2) that NAGB and NCES review the achievement levels approach, and (3) that they examine alternative approaches. (U.S. General Accounting Office, 1993, pp. 4–5)

On July 13, 1993, *Education Week* covered the story with the headline, "G.A.O. Blasts Method for Reporting NAEP Results."

As noted earlier, a 14-member panel had been appointed in 1989 by NAE to monitor the trial state assessment. In 1992, Commissioner of Education Emerson Elliot asked the panel to evaluate NAGB's standard-setting activities pertaining to the assessments of 1990 and 1992. Already in its first report, the NAE panel had given consideration to the NAGB process for setting standards, and had recommended that:

> Given the problems that occurred with the 1990 assessment and the great importance of the achievement-levels-setting process, the procedures for setting achievement levels should be evaluated by a distinguished team of external evaluators as well as by an internal team. (National Academy of Education, 1992, p. 41)

In its report dedicated to the setting of standards, the panel concluded that the procedure used for establishing achievement levels was "fundamentally flawed because it depends on cognitive judgments that are virtually impossible to make." The report went on to:

> strongly affirm the potential value of performance standards ... as one method for NAEP reporting ... Nevertheless, it is the Panel's conclusion

that the 1992 NAEP achievement levels should not be used. (National Academy of Education, 1993, p. 148)

Once again, *Education Week* reported on the issue; on September 22, 1993, its story was published under the headline, "Yet Another Report Assails NAEP Assessment Methods."

In 1996, responsibility for the Congressionally mandated evaluation of NAEP was transferred from NAE to the National Academy of Sciences (NAS). The first evaluative NAS report recommended that:

The current process for setting achievement levels should be replaced. New models for setting achievement levels should be developed in which the judgmental process and data are made clearer to NAEP's users. (Pellegrino, Jones, & Mitchell, 1999, p. 7).

Of the report's several recommendations, this one received the greatest attention. It followed a conclusion by the NAS Committee that "the current process for setting NAEP achievement levels is fundamentally flawed," thereby echoing the conclusion of earlier panels of evaluators. The Congressional reauthorization of NAEP in 1998 includes a proviso that reports by achievement level be accompanied by a statement "that the achievement levels are to be considered developmental and should be interpreted and used with caution." Four other recommendations in the NAS report also deserve attention and are discussed in a later section of this chapter.

A VOLUNTARY NATIONAL TEST?

NAEP reports of state-by-state achievement in mathematics, reading, and science received increasing attention by state education agencies and by the media in the 1990s. Increasingly, states were creating their own assessment tools, often high-stakes tests designed to determine school promotion from grade to grade and graduation from high school. Many states created state performance standards, loosely analogous to those developed by NAGB. The standards were highly variable among states, however, and calls came from some quarters for uniform national standards and national tests. Indeed, in his State of the Union address in 1997, at the start of President Clinton's second term, the President proposed that all of the nation's fourth graders be tested in reading and that all eighth graders be tested in mathematics. Funding was provided through the Department of Education to develop test materials and plans for a voluntary national test (VNT). NAGB supported these efforts and stood ready to supervise the program, thereby serving to insulate it from the direct control of a federal agency. In late 1997, Congressional legislation gave to NAGB "exclusive authority over all policies, direction, and guidelines for developing voluntary national tests."

Some members of Congress, especially in the House of Representatives and its Committee on Education and Labor, were apprehensive about the idea of a national test. As a consequence, the 1997 legislation provided funding to NAGB only for preliminary test development and planning. The legislation also called for studies to be conducted by the NAS and to be reported to Congress prior to any subsequent legislation. Three NAS reports were completed in 1999 (Feuer, Holland, Green, Bertenthal, & Hemphill, 1999; Koretz, Bertenthal, & Green, 1999; Wise, Noeth, & Koenig, 1999). The reports concluded that it was not feasible to use existing tests for the VNT, that projecting scores from any one test to others was not practical, and that high-stakes testing involved many risks.

In 1999 Congress further restricted the use of funding for VNT, and explicitly prohibited pilot testing of items or the field-testing of item booklets. The Clinton administration failed to press for more funding and no such funding was appropriated for fiscal year 2001.

NATIONAL ACHIEVEMENT TRENDS

Even prior to the first national assessment of 1969–70, planners anticipated that little interest would be generated by results of a single assessment, because there were no firm standards against which to judge the adequacy of measures of student performance. Consequently, it was thought that the primary value of NAEP would be the monitoring of changes in achievement over time. It is a tribute to those responsible for NAEP over its lifetime that maintaining conditions for assessing long-term trends consistently was given high priority. This required not only special sampling by age (9, 13, and 17) but also following procedures that remained unchanged from the earliest assessments, to ensure comparability over time of the results obtained in the special samples.

The most extensive report of achievement trends to date is that of Campbell, Hombo, and Mazzeo (2000), that presents results for reading, mathematics, and science at ages 9, 13, and 17 for each of the national assessments from the early 1970s until 1999. Results for all assessment years have been converted to average scale scores, as established by ETS in 1985. Results from earlier assessments were converted from percentages of correct answers to scale scores, to allow for comparisons.

A rather remarkable feature of national trends for reading, and to a lesser degree for mathematics and science, is the relative stability of average achievement for each subject at each age over three decades. Between 1970 and 1999, the demographics of the nation's school children changed considerably, the country's economy shifted both upwards and downwards, the family status of children's homes was far from stable, and widespread efforts were undertaken to achieve "school reform." Net effects on national achievement scores were minimal, although both mathematics and science achievement show some upward trend from 1986 to 1999.

Reading

For 9- and 13-year-olds, there is a hint of improvement in average reading scores from 1971 to 1980. For both age groups, assessments of reading from 1980 to 1999 (assessments in 1980, 1984, 1988, 1990, 1992, 1994, 1996, and 1999) show essentially no change. At age 17, results show no change for any assessment years from 1971 to 1999.

Mathematics

Mathematics achievement scores at all three ages were essentially the same for the assessments of 1973, 1978, 1982, and 1986. They improved from that level in 1999 by 10 scale points for 9-year-olds, by 8 points for 13-year-olds, and by 6 points for 17-year-olds. These are modest changes, but the consistency of the gains at each age from 1986 to 1999 do support the conclusion that average mathematics performance increased from the late 1980s to 1999.

Science

Science achievement scores declined at all three ages between 1970 and 1982, increased somewhat between 1982 and 1992, and changed little from 1992 to 1999. Average 1999 scores were higher than average 1982 scores by 8 points at age 9, by 6 points at age 13, and by 12 points at age 17 (roughly the same number of points that they had decreased from 1970 to 1982).

SUBGROUP ACHIEVEMENT TRENDS

Campbell et al. (2000) present trends over three decades not only for the nation as a whole, but for subgroups defined by race/ethnicity, gender, level of parents' education, and type of school (public or private).

Trends by Race/Ethnicity

As first reported by Jones (1984), NAEP results for black students in reading, mathematics, and science showed increased achievement relative to whites between the early 1970s and the early 1980s. From the late1980s to 1999, however, average scores for blacks have shown no improvement, even remaining stable for mathematics while average mathematics scores increased for whites. For Hispanic students at each age and subject area, average scores are slightly higher than those for black students (typically by 6 or 7 scale points), but the trends for Hispanics and blacks are quite similar. Public interest in the persistent gap between average scores for black and white children heightened after the appearance of an influential book edited by Christopher Jencks and Meredith Phillips (1998). Increasing media attention has been directed to the persistence of the average white-black gap in NAEP scale scores that in 1999 remained about 30 scale points for reading and mathematics (approximately one within-grade standard deviation) and about 40 points for science.

Trends by Gender

Trends for reading, mathematics and science over three decades of assessments have remained similar for females and males at all three assessment ages. At each age, females have shown an average advantage in reading of roughly 10 scale points, while males display a somewhat smaller average advantage in mathematics (about 3 points) and in science (about 3 points at age 9, 16 points at age 13, and 9 points at age 17).

Trends by Parents' Education

In all assessments, respondents are asked to provide the highest level of education of their parents, and assessment results are reported for the highest level for either parent by four categories, "less than high school graduation," "high school graduation," "some education beyond high school," and "I don't know." For 9-year-olds, about one-third of students report "I don't know." At ages 13 and 17, with much smaller proportions of the "I don't know" response, the distributions of reported levels of parental education have changed dramatically from the early 1970s to 1999: for "less than high school graduation," from about 20 percent to 7 percent; for "high school graduation," from 33 percent to 25 percent; and for "some education beyond high school," from 45 percent to 65 percent. While the distributions of the students' reports of their parents' education shifted in this way, the trends over time in achievement scores for reading, mathematics, and science are quite similar for students in each category, with a single exception. At age 17, average reading scores declined nearly 10 scale points between 1990 and 1999 for students who reported that "high school graduation" was the highest level of a parent's education. This might be related to decreasing rates of high school dropouts in the decade of the 1990s, so that more poor readers (among students whose parents did not attend college) were assessed in 1999 because they remained in high school rather than dropping out.

Trends by Type of School

Quite consistently from the late 1970s until 1999, NAEP results for the three age groups and three subject areas show that average scores for students enrolled in nonpublic schools exceed those for students in public schools, typically by between 10 and 20 scale points. Over that period, the percentage of students enrolled in nonpublic schools increased from about 6 percent to 10 percent of the total at age 17, from about 9 percent to 12 percent at age 13, and remained steady at about 12 percent at age 9. Achievement trends over time are very similar for nonpublic and public school students at each age and for each subject area.

STATE-BY-STATE ACHIEVEMENT TRENDS

From 1990 forward NAEP has reported mean scale scores for public-school students by state for the states that chose to participate in any assessment year, typically about 40 of the 50 states. From 1992 forward state reports also show the percentages of students whose estimated scores place them as below basic, basic, proficient, or advanced. State-level assessments were conducted for mathematics in 1990, 1992, 1996, and 2000; for reading in 1992, 1994, and 1998; for science in 1996 and 2000; and for writing in 1998 (although in some cases prior to 2000, assessments were conducted at grade 4 or 8, but not both). State-by-state results are provided to state education agencies prior to their public release at a national press conference, which then typically is followed immediately by press conferences in the states that participated in an assessment. State results are presented for all public-school students as well as for subgroups, (male-female, ethnic origin, parental education level, and type of community).

More and more states during the 1990s established their own state testing programs in reading and mathematics, and sometimes in science and writing, as well. Increasingly, then, media attention within states has been directed not only to results of annual state testing, often reported district by district or even school by school, but also to the NAEP reports of state-by-state results and especially to a state's changes over time on NAEP assessments, as well as to each state's ranking among all participant states.

The most recent such report is that of August, 2001, a state-by-state report of mathematics achievement for the year-2000 assessment, that also shows results for prior years (National Center for Education Statistics, 2001). At grade 4, the mean national scale score increased between 1992 and 2000 by 7 scale points. However, some states display essentially no change, while others show higher average scores by as much as 19 points. At grade 8, the average national change from 1990 to 2000 is 12 points. All states that participated in both years also show improved average scores at grade 8, ranging from 2 scale points to 30 points (an increase approximately equal to the value of the typical within-state standard deviation for 8th-grade scale scores). In some states, NAEP reports have become "front-page news" and are widely cited in radio and television coverage. Clearly, the NAEP reports are being closely attended to by state education officials.

APPRAISING THE STRENGTHS AND WEAKNESSES OF NAEP

As outlined above, NAEP has succeeded in meeting one of its original objectives by presenting on a regular schedule trustworthy information about changes over time in achievement of U.S. students at ages 9, 13, and 17, especially in the areas of mathematics, reading, and science. For the 1990s, similar trend data have been reported state by state for states (the majority) that chose to participate in the state assessments of NAEP. For both national and state trends, results have been presented also by demographic subgroups. This is a remarkable record for a project that failed to consistently attract either substantial funding or high levels of political support.

Since the 1980s, most states and school districts within states have established educational standards for the public schools within their jurisdiction. To some extent, the NAEP reports have served to stimulate those efforts; especially since 1990, since when state-by-state results have been reported, media coverage of NAEP reports has increased sharply. Most states now have devised their own within-state testing programs, and many have used NAEP as a model, typically after having personnel trained and supported by NAEP staff members. NAEP procedures also greatly influenced the design of international assessments such as TIMSS, the Third International Mathematics and Science Study and national assessments in other countries.

Some important differences, however, distinguish the purposes and the procedures of NAEP from those of the states. The NAEP design focuses on levels of achievement for identifiable groups of students and on achievement trends for those groups over time; it does not provide results for individual students or for schools or classes within schools. Many states have developed high-stakes testing programs that are designed explicitly to decide for individual students whether they are to be promoted to the next grade in school or to be graduated from high school. In some states, student test-score results are also used as a criterion for teacher salary bonuses. In a discussion of differences between NAEP and high-stakes state testing programs, Jones (2001) noted that the latter are beginning to resemble the failed programs of the late 19th century in England and Wales when a system of "payment by results" was employed in a misguided effort to improve public education.

The U.S. Congress mandated an NAS committee study of high-stakes testing practices. Among the recommendations from that committee are several that are critical of basing important educational decisions about individual students on test scores.

> High-stakes decisions such as tracking, promotion, and graduation should not automatically be made on the basis of a single test score, but should be

buttressed by other relevant information about the student's knowledge and skills, such as grades, teacher recommendations, and extenuating circumstances.

In general, large-scale assessments should not be used to make high-stakes decisions about students who are less than 8 years old or enrolled below grade 3. (Heubert & Hauser, 1999, p. 279.)

The extent to which these and related recommendations are being seriously considered by state and local school authorities is not yet known. What is apparent from media reports is that many parents and teachers are echoing these concerns, in some cases effectively, and that some states and localities are reconsidering earlier actions which had mandated that decisions about student progress be based primarily upon test scores.

As noted earlier, the Congressionally mandated evaluation of NAEP conducted by NAS recommended a replacement of NAGB's process for setting achievement levels, and included several additional recommendations:

1. Educational progress should be portrayed by a broad array of education indicators that includes but goes beyond NAEP's achievement results.
2. NAEP should reduce the number of independent large-scale data collections while maintaining trend lines, periodically updating frameworks, and providing accurate national and state-level estimates of academic achievement.
3. NAEP should enhance the participation, appropriate assessment, and meaningful interpretation of data for students with disabilities and English-language learners. NAEP and the proposed system for education indicators should include measures that improve understanding of the performance and educational needs of these populations.
4. The entire assessment development process should be guided by a coherent vision of student learning and by the kinds of inferences and conclusions about student performance that are desired in reports of NAEP results. In this assessment development process, multiple conditions need to be met: (a) NAEP frameworks and assessments should reflect subject-matter knowledge; research, theory, and practice regarding what students should understand and how they learn; and more comprehensive goals for schooling; (b) assessment instruments and scoring criteria should be designed to capture important differences in the levels and types of students' knowledge and understanding both through large-scale surveys and multiple alternative assessment methods; and (c) NAEP reports should provide descriptions of student performance that enhance the interpretation and usefulness of summary scores. (Pellegrino, Jones, & Mitchell, 1999, pp. 4–6).

Steps were taken by NCES and NAGB to respond to Recommendation 3, above, and recent federal legislation now requires that no students be excluded from NAEP based on disability or English-language learning. Recent assessments, both for the nation and the states, have built in investigations of the impact of including more English-language learners and of providing special accommodations during the testing of such children (extra time, reading questions aloud, etc.). For future assessments, testing accommodations are to become standard practice for children who are judged to require them.

Recommendation 4 has received additional attention from yet another study committee at NAS (Pellegrino, Chudowsky, & Glaser, 2001). Among other recommendations, the committee urged more research to improve the validity and fairness of inferences about student achievement, research to better integrate assessment and sound principles of learning, and an increased emphasis on classroom assessment designed to assist learning.

One of the original objectives of NAEP was "to provide ... data to researchers working on various teaching and learning problems, either to answer research questions or to identify specific problems which would generate research hypotheses" (Greenbaum, 1977, p. 13). For most of its history, NAEP results have been available to researchers, but the complexity of the data format and of the procedures needed to access and analyze NAEP findings have discouraged widespread use for secondary data analysis. For the first time in the summer of 2001, access has been rendered more convenient, and researchers are able to interactively organize, download, and analyze NAEP findings on the World Wide Web (NAEP, 2002). It is anticipated that more tools will be added at that site to further facilitate secondary analyses (Cohen & Jiang, 2001).

As emphasized by Greenbaum (1977), NAEP failed to achieve another of its major original objectives, to provide meaningful data "to Congress, the lay public, and educational decision makers so that they could make more informed decisions on new programs, bond issues, new curricula, steps to reduce inequalities, and so on" (p. 160). Greenbaum correctly concluded that this was viewed as an objective of high priority by U.S. Commissioner of Education Francis Keppel, and also by the personnel at the Carnegie Corporation, but that Ralph Tyler was not similarly committed. As a perceptive social scientist, Tyler sensed that NAEP would be unlikely to be capable of providing data that could be used to make decisions about educational policy. Tyler viewed the assessment design to be an appropriate one for providing census-like results, but that other research designs would be required for policy making. On that issue, it seems that history has shown that Tyler was right.

As at earlier key junctures in its history, NAEP again faces an uncertain future. Tensions remain between those who view its appropriate role to be the tracking of changes in educational achievement and those who would convert NAEP into an agent for educational reform. President George W. Bush has proposed to Congress that every student between grades 3 and 8 be tested annually in reading and mathematics, in keeping with his promise, "No Child Left Behind." His plan would require that testing be managed by agencies at the state level. The plan includes financial incentives (and penalties) for schools that report high (or low) test scores or that show (or fail to show) improved scores from year to year. It also recommends that states be required to participate in annual state-level assessments by NAEP for reading and mathematics at grades 4 and 8, so that NAEP would "confirm" findings from the corresponding state tests.

Mark D. Musick, Chairman of NAGB, in testimonies before a subcommittee of the House Committee on Education and the Workforce on March 8, 2001 on President Bush's proposal, stated, "I think that the answer is yes to the question – Could NAEP be used to confirm state results?" (NAGB, 2001). In the same testimony, responding to possible concerns that the activity could lead to a national curriculum (and thereby could threaten state control of curricula), Musick said that, after 30 years of NAEP,

> there is no evidence that we are any closer to a federally directed national curriculum at the beginning of the 21st century than we were at the beginning of the 20th century .... The assertion that the NAEP framework is the basis for a national curriculum just does not withstand scrutiny. (NAGB, 2001).

The NAGB view as presented by Musick seems to present a paradox. If NAEP is to confirm state findings, how can it succeed unless there is a common curriculum, or at least a common set of educational standards, in all the states? As noted earlier, several NAS studies concluded that it is not feasible to equate test findings when tests were designed to meet disparate objectives. Thus, unless all states adopt common standards, and unless those are the same standards that guide NAEP, it is not reasonable to expect that NAEP could meet these demands. And if NAEP is required to take on such new (and high-stakes) responsibilities, will it also be able to effectively monitor the nation's educational progress over time?

ENDNOTE

[1] A far more extensive treatment of the evolution of NAEP soon will be available in an edited book (Jones & Olkin, in press). I am grateful to all of the authors of chapters in that book for providing information that helped me frame this Handbook chapter, and especially to Mary Lyn Bourque, Archie Lapointe, Ina Mullis, and Ramsay Selden. I depended on other sources as well, notably the doctoral dissertations of Fitzharris (1993) and Hazlett (1973) and the history of NAGB by Vinovski (1998). I thank Nada Ballator for her constructive editorial suggestions. My most profound acknowledgements are to Ralph Tyler and John Tukey, who got me into the business of educational assessment in 1965, from which I've never totally extricated myself.

REFERENCES

Abelson, R.P., Cronbach, L.J., Jones, L.V., Tukey, J.W., & Tyler, R.W. (1970). *National Assessment of Educational Progress, Report 1, 1969–70 Science: National results and illustrations of group comparisons*. Denver: Education Commission of the States.

Abelson, R.P., Coffman, W.E., Jones, L.V., Mosteller, F., & Tukey, J.W. (1971). *National Assessment of Educational Progress, Report 4, 1969–70 Science: Group results for sex, region, and size of community*. Denver: Education Commission of the States.

Alexander, L., & James, T. (1987). *The nation's report card*. Stanford, CA: National Academy of Education.

Campbell, J.R., Hombo, C.M., & Mazzeo, J. (2000). *NAEP 1999 trends in academic progress: Three decades of student performance*. NCES 2000-469. Washington, DC: U.S. Department of Education.

Cohen, J., & Jiang, T. (2001). *Direct estimation of latent distributions for large-scale assessments with application to the National Assessment of Educational Progress (NAEP)*. Washington, DC: American Institutes for Research.

Feuer, M.J., Holland, P.W., Green, B.F., Bertenthal, M.W., & Hemphill, F.C. (Eds.) (1999). *Uncommon measures: Equivalence and linkage among educational tests*. Washington, DC: National Academy Press.

Fitzharris, L.H. (1993). *An historical review of the National Assessment of Educational Progress from 1963 to 1991*. Unpublished doctoral dissertation, University of South Carolina.

Glaser, R. (1987). Commentary by the National Academy of Education. In L. Alexander, & T. James, *The nation's report card: Improving the assessment of student achievement*. (pp. 43–61). Stanford, CA: National Academy of Education.

Greenbaum, W. (1977). *Measuring educational progress*. New York: McGraw-Hill.

Hazlett, J.A. (1973). *A history of the National Assessment of Educational Progress, 1963–1973*. Unpublished doctoral dissertation, University of Kansas.

Heubert, J.P., & Hauser, R.M. (Eds.). (1999). *High stakes: Testing for tracking, promotion, and graduation*. Washington, DC: National Academy Press.

Jencks, C., & Phillips, M. (1998). *The black-white test score gap*. Washington, DC: Brookings Institution Press.

Jones, L.V. (1984). White-black achievement differences: The narrowing gap. *American Psychologist*, **39**, 1207–1213.

Jones, L.V. (2001). Assessing achievement versus high-stakes testing: A crucial contrast. *Educational Assessment*, **7**, 21–28.

Jones, L.V., & Olkin, I. (Eds.). The nation's report card: Evolution and perspectives. Bloomington, IN: Phi Delta Kappa International.

Koretz, D.M., Bertenthal, M.W., & Green, B.F. (Eds.) (1999). *Embedding questions: The pursuit of a common measure in an uncommon test*. Washington, DC: National Academy Press.

National Academy of Education. (1992). *Assessing student achievement in the states*. Stanford, CA: Author.

National Academy of Education. (1993). *Setting performance standards for student achievement*. Stanford, CA: Author.

National Assessment of Educational Progress. (2002). *NAEP data*. Retrieved on April 11, 2002 from http://nces.ed.gov/nationsreportcard/naepdata/.

National Assessment Governing Board (1989). *Briefing book, January 27–29*. Washington, DC: Author.

National Assessment Governing Board. (2001). *Testimony of Mark D. Musick, Chairman, National Assessment Governing Board*. Retrieved on August 28, 2001 from: http://www.nagb.org/naep/musick_testimony.html.

National Center for Education Statistics. (2001). *The nation's report card: Mathematics, 2000*. Washington, DC: Author.

National Commission on Excellence in Education. (1983). *A nation at risk: The imperative for educational reform*. Washington, DC: U.S. Government Printing Office.

Pellegrino, J., Chudowsky, N., & Glaser, R. (Eds.) (2001). *Knowing what students know: The science and design of educational assessment*. Washington, DC: National Academy Press.

Pellegrino, J.W., Jones, L.R., & Mitchell, K.J. (Eds.). (1999). *Grading the nation's report card: Evaluating NAEP and transforming the assessment of educational progress*. Washington, DC: National Academy Press.

Stufflebeam, D.L., Jaeger, R.M, & Scriven, M. (1991). *Summative evaluation of the National Assessment Governing Board's inaugural 1990–91 effort to set achievement levels on the National Assessment of Educational Progress*. Washington, DC: National Assessment Governing Board.

Tyler, R.W. (1942). Appraising and recording student progress. In G.F. Madaus, & D.L. Stufflebeam, Ed. (1989). *Educational evaluation: Classic works of Ralph W. Tyler* (pp. 97–196). Boston: Kluwer Academic.

Vinovskis, M.A. (1988). *Overseeing the nation's report card: The creation and evolution of the National Assessment Governing Board (NAGB)*. Washington, DC: National Assessment Governing Board.

U.S. General Accounting Office. (1993). *Educational achievement standards: NAGB's approach yields misleading interpretations*. Report No. 6AO/PEMD-93-12. Washington, DC: Author.

Wirtz, W., & Lapointe, A. (1982). *Measuring the quality of education: A report on assessing educational progress*. Washington, DC: Wirtz & Lapointe.

Wise, L.L. Noeth, R.J., & Koenig, J.A. (Eds.) (1999). *Evaluation of the voluntary national tests Year 2, Final report*. Washington, DC: National Academy Press.

40
Assessment of the National Curriculum in England

HARRY TORRANCE

University of Sussex, Institute of Education, Brighton, UK

Outlining the key features of the national assessment system in England might seem a fairly straightforward task, but the story is a complicated one, and the parameters of the system are constantly changing. The system has its origins in a highly devolved and entirely voluntaristic system of school examinations; has been driven by differing political priorities over a period of 15 to 20 years; and is still evolving as differing priorities interact with implementation difficulties. Moreover, although national assessment was conceived of in the context of a United Kingdom-wide government for implementation across the UK, and at various points in this chapter I shall refer to the UK as if it were a single administrative unit, implementation has differed across England, Scotland, Wales, and Northern Ireland. Scotland and Northern Ireland have always had separate systems of education from England and Wales and, recently, constitutional devolution has placed even more decision making power with the regional parliament in Scotland and regional assemblies in Wales and Northern Ireland. Thus, although the broad thrust of policy is similar across the UK, implementation has differed across the four countries, and hence the detail of the chapter refers only to England. These variations derive at least in part from variation in the strength of the ideological debate underlying national assessment and, although the development of policy has been broadly similar across the UK, it has been implemented in the regions with rather less visceral hatred of the teaching profession than has been manifested by central government in London. Indeed, one of the main tasks in a review such as this is to try to identify what principles of national assessment might be appropriately discussed as policy options elsewhere, shorn of the particular ideological battles which pervaded invention and implementation in England.

The chapter will sketch in a little of the background to the development of national assessment, before identifying its key features and reviewing its costs and benefits. It will outline the debate about evaluation and accountability which led to successive efforts in the 1970s and 1980s to implement some sort of national monitoring and national examination system; identify the key features of the national curriculum and national assessment introduced in 1988; discuss

905

International Handbook of Educational Evaluation, 905–928
T. Kellaghan, D.L. Stufflebeam (eds.)
© 2003 Dordrecht: Kluwer Academic Publishers. Printed in Great Britain.

the issues which arose from its implementation, and modifications that were made; and, finally, review impact on teaching and learning and implications for policy in other contexts.

VOLUNTARISM AND ITS CRITICS

Although only recently acted upon at central policy level, concern about evaluation and accountability in the UK education system has a long history dating back at least 30 years. Although the issues of monitoring national standards and rendering schools more accountable go back to the 1970s, political decisions only coalesced around the creation of a national system relatively recently. Thus the issue of timescale of decision-making and implementation partly revolves around logistics – around the scale and scope of any system – but also must be a function of local political circumstances. While concerns about accountability surfaced in the early 1970s, it was not considered either feasible or desirable to address them through central government intervention in curriculum and testing until the late 1980s. As recently as the mid-1980s, the UK had one of the most decentralized and voluntaristic examination systems, with several examination boards in England and Wales, along with national boards for Scotland and Northern Ireland, setting individual examination papers in individual subjects, to be taken by individual students choosing to sit as many or as few papers as they wished, generally, but by no means exclusively, at ages 16 (the minimum school-leaving age) and 18 (the usual maximum school leaving age prior to university entrance). Now, the UK, and particularly England, has one of the most centrally controlled and extensively tested education systems in the world. This dramatic turnaround has to be understood in the context of the peculiarly ad hoc development of the education system during the twentieth century, so ad hoc, in fact, that it might be argued that the UK system, until very recently, was not a system at all, except in the sense of an administrative entity. It was this lack of any overall plan or direction for education, with its concomitant lack of data on overall performance when politicians faced criticisms about standards, or levers by which government might make a difference, which fuelled the continuing search for mechanisms of accountability and control.

This voluntaristic situation had come about largely because of the enduring influence of Britain's social class system. Up until the 1970s, a high status, academically oriented education had been largely confined to those children attending private fee-paying schools or who passed a selective examination (the 11+) to attend an academic "grammar school" (about 20 percent of the cohort). In turn, a minority of this minority proceeded to university entrance via the secondary school examination system. The examinations themselves had their direct antecedents in the university entrance requirements of the nineteenth century, with the Universities of London (1838), Oxford (1857), and Cambridge (1858) setting up local examination boards to conduct matriculation (entrance) examinations to be taken by external (usually school-based) candidates (see Kingdon and Stobart [1988] for a fuller account).[1]

In effect, a series of ad hoc extensions of educational provision (especially after the second world war) created a very piecemeal educational system in the UK. An academic education was thought appropriate for a small elite likely to progress into social and economic leadership roles, and a non-academic vocationally oriented education appropriate for the rest. Criticisms of the lack of opportunity provided for the majority resulted in the gradual abolition of the 11+ and the creation of comprehensive secondary schools, throughout the late 1960s and 1970s (prompted by the election of a left-of-centre Labour government in 1964), but without an accompanying systematic rethink of curricular provision, accreditation and qualifications, or overall evaluation. These activities were pursued to some degree by individual schools, local education authorities (LEAs), examination boards, and indeed specially constituted government bodies (e.g., the Schools Council which funded curriculum development projects). But there was no overarching monitoring or evaluation of the system as a whole, except for periodic individual inspections of schools by Her Majesty's Inspectors of Schools (HMIs). Furthermore, despite increasingly comprehensive administrative provision, the descendants of the university matriculation examinations, Ordinary (O) level General Certificate of Education (GCE) continued to be taken by around 20 percent of the secondary school population deemed able enough to aspire to higher education, while a parallel system of single-subject Certificate of Secondary Education (CSE) was developed for the next 40 percent of the ability range, with only the highest grade in CSE (grade 1) being considered equivalent to the lowest pass grade in GCE O-level (grade C). Thus, very little coherent policy discussion took place before the late 1970s with respect to what sort of overall curricular provision might be appropriate for a truly comprehensive system of education, far less how this might be assessed at the level of the individual student or evaluated at national level.

In parallel with these developments, the "terms of trade" were turning decisively against Britain's old primary and secondary manufacturing industries (coal mining, steel, shipbuilding, etc.) especially after the so-called "oil crisis" of 1974 when prices were raised significantly. Unskilled jobs began to disappear rapidly and suddenly unemployment, especially youth unemployment, became a major social and political concern. The rise in youth unemployment coincided with the growth of comprehensive education; correlation was interpreted as causation by politicians, and low educational standards were identified as a major part of the problem. Young people needed to leave the compulsory education system with higher (possibly different) levels of achievement if they were to gain more skilled employment. Politicians, however, had no hard evidence about overall educational standards – high, low, or indifferent. Significant comparability studies had been carried out over several years by the Schools Council and the National Foundation for Educational Research (NFER), investigating in particular the comparability of GCE and CSE grades, but these had largely demonstrated what a difficult business conducting such studies was, and it became increasingly apparent that different students took different combinations of examinations, set by different boards in different localities on different syllabuses, while many took no examinations at all, and, of course, even this level of disparate data did not exist for the outcomes of primary schooling.

THE ASSESSMENT OF PERFORMANCE UNIT

The first national attempt to address the issue of national standards came with the setting up of the Assessment of Performance Unit in 1974, again by a Labour government, acting under political pressure to demonstrate that increasing the number of comprehensive schools did not compromise academic standards. Contracts for the development and administration of tests and analysis of results were made with university departments and other agencies such as the NFER. Tests were to be conducted in what were considered to be the "core" subjects of mathematics, English, and science, along with others, subsequently, such as modern languages. They were to be administered to a 2 percent sample of the school population at ages 11 and 15, to find out, essentially, what children of these ages could do in these subjects, with the results being monitored over time to identify a rise or fall in standards.

The APU was met by considerable scepticism and even hostility by many in education at the time, with all the issues of curriculum control and educational values with which we are now so familiar being raised (see MacDonald 1979). Who was to construct the tests? How would appropriate content be selected? If the tests became widely disseminated, might they not effectively begin to define the curriculum? Are not many of the important outcomes of education not susceptible to testing? Since test results are in any case highly correlated with social class, how would this be taken into account? In turn, interest was stimulated in exploring other avenues in school accountability, especially through school self-evaluation and the provision of fuller and more rounded reports to parents and other interested parties (see Becher, Eraut, & Knight, 1981; Elliott, Bridges, Ebbutt, Gibson, & Nias, 1981). The APU, however, turned out to be relatively benign in its influence, perhaps partly because the government of the day recognized the validity of many of these issues and partly because it was still not considered appropriate to take a more interventionist stance. Indeed a government consultative document published in 1977, while arguing that "a coherent and soundly-based means of assessment for the educational system" was necessary, explicitly rejected the production of "league tables" since "test results in isolation can be seriously misleading" (DES, 1977, p.17). Furthermore,

> It has been suggested that individual pupils should at certain ages take external "tests of basic literacy and numeracy," the implication being that those tests should be of national character and universally applied. The Secretaries of State [i.e., the government] reject this view ... the

temptation for schools to coach for such tests would risk distorting the curriculum and possibly lowering rather than raising average standards. (DES, 1977, p.18)

Subsequently, under governments more hostile to the teaching profession and more impatient for change, such well-informed reasonableness was characterized as the "educational establishment" capturing the debate and conspiring against change in its own interests and against the interests of consumers (deemed to be parents and employers).

The APU conducted its work over a ten-year period, taking the issue of producing valid tests of a wide variety of achievements in different subjects very seriously. Many involved the conduct of extended practical and oral work, as well as more traditional paper and pencil tests. They were often developed by leading subject experts and thus the APU developed as more of a research enterprise than an evaluation mechanism, providing considerable evidence about the difficulty of producing good tests, the difficulties children often encountered in test interpretation and response, and the difficulties of measuring changes in standards over time. The Unit also left a legacy of very high quality reports and instruments for LEAs and teachers to use for professional development. However, what it did not do was provide irrefutable evidence of the maintenance (or otherwise) of educational standards. Nor of course, did it provide government with a mechanism to monitor, far less control, what was happening in every school, since it was based from the outset on a very small sample. This was by no means a satisfactory state of affairs for the incoming right-wing Conservative government, led by Prime Minister Margaret Thatcher, in 1979. However, it took her a further eight years, to propose a national curriculum and assessment system.

GCSE: THE TROJAN HORSE FOR A NATIONAL SYSTEM

In essence, the Labour governments of the 1970s tried working with the teaching profession to develop evaluation and accountability procedures to meet political pressures over educational standards. The Conservative governments of the 1980s started out trying to do the same, particularly manifested in the creation of a single system of secondary school examinations – the General Certificate of Secondary Education (GCSE) – in 1986. This amalgamation of GCE and CSE exams at 16+ (school leaving age) had first been recommended by a government committee under Labour in 1978 and can be seen as an obvious development towards a comprehensive system of educational provision. However, the fact that it was finally pushed through by the Conservatives also alerts us to the fact that it allowed central government to take a far more overt role in determining the structure and content of a national system, and provide an ostensibly similar and comparable measure of output, across all schools and candidates, through which an educational market place could be developed. Interestingly, this tension, between central government intervention to restructure and control the system in order to raise standards ("nationalizing" it, as some right wing critics claimed), and the pursuit of measures to facilitate parental choice of schools in order to raise standards by market competition between schools, has remained within the UK and is likely to pervade any debate about the efficacy of a national system.

We will return to these issues later. For the moment it is important to note that many educational ideas and developments also pervaded the debate. The Conservatives first acknowledged the potential of the market place and passed legislation in 1981 making it mandatory for secondary schools to publish their examination results. However, the driving force behind change in the early to mid-1980s was concern about clarity in educational content and outcomes. Educationists were increasingly arguing that clarity of curriculum goals and the creation of a more flexible examining system would benefit students, especially low achievers, by providing clearer curriculum pathways and allowing the accumulation of coursework marks towards final grades (Hargreaves, 1984; Murphy & Torrance, 1988). Considerable developments of this sort were taking place within CSE and it was argued they should be disseminated across the system as a whole and removed from association with a lower status examination (and hence association with lower standards). Industrialists and politicians were similarly interested in the outcomes of education being more clearly described, recorded and communicated. What did a grade 1 CSE or a grade C GCE O-level actually mean? What did secondary school leavers know and what could they actually do? The amalgamation of CSE and GCE meant both agendas could be pursued, and a key defining aspect of the new examination system, proposed with great enthusiasm by the then Secretary of State for Education Sir Keith Joseph, was that it should be based on the principle of reporting positively what each candidate knew, understood, and was able to do, and that syllabuses should be developed in relation to "national criteria" to be developed for each of (initially 20) subjects. Essentially what was proposed was a move from a fundamentally norm-referenced rank-ordered examination system towards one which had at least an aspiration towards criterion-referencing. The technical difficulties of designing and operationalizing such a system were legion, however (Murphy, 1986; Orr & Nuttall, 1983). A lesson of the English experience seems to be that it just is not possible to design a criterion-referenced system at any level of detail. The more clarity one seeks, the more unmanageable the system becomes, as objectives "multiply like vermin" (Brown, 1988).

It is important to note that the development of GCSE provided a key opportunity for government to take a direct role in determining the curriculum of secondary schools and provided a model of potential intervention for the future – a model which was almost instantly seized upon. Sir Keith Joseph gave an influential speech summarizing the essential elements of the new examination in 1984; examination courses were started in 1986; and first examinations were conducted in 1988, by which time legislation creating a national curriculum and assessment system for all schools, primary and secondary, was already on the statute book (Butterfield, 1995; Daugherty, 1995).

THE NATIONAL CURRICULUM AND NATIONAL ASSESSMENT

Even the amalgamated GCSE remained a single-subject examination, taken voluntarily by individual candidates and set by diverse examination boards, albeit following national criteria with syllabuses subject to approval by the Secretary of State, following the recommendation of the Secondary Examinations Council (which had replaced the Schools Council in 1982). It was also, of course, only directly relevant to secondary schools; and it was a development heavily influenced by educational thinking. Many of the innovations initially developed within the lower status and hence less scrutinized CSE system, such as extensive assessment of coursework, practical work and extended project work, were incorporated into GCSE examination syllabuses. Similarly many of the high quality approaches to testing developed by the APU were built on by those setting GCSE examination papers. The arguments deployed paralleled (or perhaps anticipated) those of the American "authentic testing" movement. Modern economies require a highly educated and skilled labor force. Old methods of teaching and testing based on transmission and recall are no longer appropriate. Students have to "learn how to learn" and be capable of acting innovatively and creatively. New curriculum goals involving research, problem solving, and report writing must be pursued, and, in turn, must be underpinned by authentic assessments of these skills and capacities, conducted *in situ*, in the schoolroom or library or laboratory, not under artificial examination conditions.

So GCSE still did not really meet government concerns for the evaluation and accountability of the system as a whole, while, from the point of view of the political right, the new examination suffered from being both too centralized and too controlled by the education profession. Some of these critics also considered it likely to lower standards by employing far too much school-based coursework assessment marked by (untrustworthy) teachers who would have a direct interest in awarding high marks which would reflect well on their teaching (Hillgate Group, 1987; Marks, 1991).[2] What were needed were simple tests of "the basics," coupled with the publication of results in league tables and the exercise of parental market choice. Government funding should, in turn, follow students so that good schools would grow and poor schools close. However, this would be a very high risk strategy for any government to follow and the attraction of raising standards by developing a market *and* controlling the curriculum from the center proved decisive even for the Conservatives under Margaret Thatcher.

Thus the new Secretary of State, Kenneth Baker, announced the intention of "establishing a national curriculum which works through national criteria for each subject area" in January 1987 (quoted in Daugherty 1995, p. 13); a Consultative Document "The National Curriculum 5-16" was published in June 1987; and legislation was passed in time for implementation from September 1988. The consultative document made clear the government's thinking on the matter:

A national curriculum backed by clear assessment arrangements will help to raise standards of attainment by:

(i) ensuring that all pupils study a broad and balanced range of subjects ...
(ii) setting clear objectives for what children ... should be able to achieve ...
(iii) ensuring that all pupils ... have access to ... the same ... programmes of study which include the key content, skills and processes which they need to learn ...
(iv) checking on progress towards those objectives and performance at various stages ... (DES, 1987, pp. 3–4)

The key elements of the new system were that: the National Curriculum would apply to the ages of compulsory schooling (5–16 years); all "maintained" (i.e., government-funded) schools (but not private fee-charging schools) would have to follow its prescriptions; the curriculum would be organized in four "key stages": KS1, ages 5–7 years; KS2, 8–11; KS3, 12–14; and KS4, 15–16; the curriculum would comprise nine "foundation" subjects (mathematics, English, science, technology, history, geography, art, music, a modern foreign language from KS3 (age 11+), plus Welsh in Wales; and be set out, subject-by-subject in terms of "attainment targets," defined in the 1988 Education Act as the "knowledge, skills and understanding which pupils ... are expected to have by the end of each key stage; attainment would be assessed (including by "nationally prescribed tests") and publicly reported at the end of each key stage, i.e., at ages 7, 11, 14 and 16. Thus the bare bones of a criterion-referenced system were laid out, combining the defining of objectives, subject-by-subject, with assessment to measure their attainment at individual student, school, and system level. Translating this into practice was another matter entirely, however, and, in many respects, implementation and concomitant modification have been continuous processes ever since.

A further key "staging post" in the articulation of the new system, though one which turned out to create as many, if not more, problems than it solved, was the report of the Task Group on Assessment and Testing (TGAT), set up as legislation was still being debated in Parliament, and which reported in December 1987. The group accepted as its task that of designing a workable national system of assessment and attempted to combine the government's policy intentions with recent thinking on the role, purpose, and conduct of assessment, arguing that:

> For the purpose of national assessment ...
> assessment results should give direct information about pupils' achievement in relation to objectives: they should be criterion-referenced;
> the results should provide a basis for decisions about pupils' further learning needs: they should be formative;
> the scales or grades should be capable of comparison ... so the assessment should be calibrated or moderated;
> ... the assessments should relate to progression. (TGAT, 1987, para. 5)

Furthermore, the group argued that subject content should be organized progressively, through 10 "levels" of attainment, broadly corresponding to the eleven years of compulsory schooling from 5-16, with the top grades of 7–10 corresponding to GCSE grades A–F (G being the lowest grade awarded in the new GCSE). Thus 7-year-olds would be expected to achieve in the level range 1–3, 11-year-olds in the range 3–5, and 14-year-olds in the range 4–7.

The group summarized the "Purposes and Principles" of the system as being formative, diagnostic, summative, and evaluative (TGAT, 1987, para. 23). In so doing, they accepted that one system, within its constituent parts, could contribute both formatively to student learning and summatively to system evaluation and accountability, and UK teachers and administrators have been struggling to operationalize this combination ever since. However, the political imperative has focused almost exclusively on issues of evaluation and accountability and this has had an inevitable impact on resource allocation and teacher priorities and strategies for improving scores.

IMPLEMENTATION AND MODIFICATION

The essential framework of the new system was that curriculum objectives would be defined in 9 (or in Wales, 10) separate subjects, organized around broad attainment targets (ATs) each of which, in turn, would comprise individual statements of attainment (SoAs). These ATs and SoAs would also be organized sequentially into levels, forming a progressive curriculum "ladder" in each subject, and their attainment assessed and monitored for each individual pupil, with results being reported publicly at the end of each key stage, at ages 7, 11, 14, and 16. For example, "attainment target 3" in English was "writing." At level 2, the statements of attainment were:

a) produce, independently, pieces of writing using complete sentences, some of them demarcated with capital letters and full stops or question marks.
b) structure sequences of real or imagined events coherently in chronological accounts. (Example: an account of a family occasion ... or an adventure story)
c) write stories showing an understanding of the rudiments of story structure by establishing an opening, characters and one or more events.
d) produce simple, coherent non chronological writing. (Example: lists, captions, invitations, greetings cards, notices, posters, etc.)

At level 4, the statements of attainment were that pupils should:

a) produce, independently, pieces of writing showing evidence of a developing ability to structure what is written in ways that make the meaning clear to the reader; demonstrate in their writing generally accurate use of sentence punctuation. (Example: make use of titles, paragraphs or verses, capital letters, full stops, question marks and exclamation marks...)
b) write stories which have an opening, a setting, characters, a series of events and a resolution and which engage the interest of the reader; produce other

kinds of chronologically organised writing. (Example: write, in addition to stories, instructions, accounts or explanations, perhaps a scientific investigation)

c) organise non-chronological writing for different purposes in orderly ways. (Example: record ... an aspect of learning; present information and express feelings in forms such as letters, poems, invitations, etc.)

d) begin to use the structures of written Standard English and begin to use some sentence structures different from those of speech.

e) discuss the organization of their own writing; revise and redraft the writing as appropriate, independently, in the light of that discussion (DES, 1990, pp. 12–13).

As can be seen, the curriculum documents were very detailed, but still largely baffling.

Producing such "programmes of study" across the curriculum was an enormously ambitious undertaking, which both TGAT (para. 13) and subsequent commentators (e.g., Daugherty, 1995) noted had not been attempted anywhere else in the world. Needless to say it has not been implemented in anything like its original form, with an early modification being concentration on implementing and testing what became the *de facto* and later the *de jure* "core curriculum" of English, mathematics, and science. However the process of "slimming down," as it came to be known in the ensuing debate and implementation process, has been a bruising and debilitating business, for politicians and teachers alike, since all complaints about complexity and overload which emerged in the first few years after 1988 were initially dismissed by government as self-interested whining from a profession finally being forced to put the consumers, rather than the producers, first.

Two major problems emerged from 1988 to 1993, when a formal review was instigated. One focused on curriculum content, the other on complexity of the assessment arrangements. These problems interacted since a major element of the complexity of the assessment arrangements was the sheer number of attainment targets and individual statements of attainment that teachers and test producers had to contend with. However, they have tended to be dealt with separately, though in parallel, as first the scope of the assessment arrangements, and second the content of the curriculum, was reduced.

These problems were exacerbated by lack of coherent planning at the center which saw the government replace the Secondary Examinations Council (now outdated since the legislation applied to all maintained schools, not just secondary schools) with two new "arms length" statutory authorities to oversee arrangements for developing the curriculum (the National Curriculum Council [NCC]) and assessment (School Examinations and Assessment Council [SEAC]). In turn, subject groups were set up to write the programs of study without coordination or overlap of membership. A major consequence was that each subject group, working under intense time pressure, included far too much in their program of study, as interest groups within the subject communities argued for inclusion of their particular pet themes and topics. The total curriculum thus became completely unmanageable – a "mile wide and an inch deep" as one common cliché soon had it.

At the same time, consortia of test developers were invited to bid for short-term contracts to develop national tests in subjects at key stages. Different key stages were focused on for the development of the testing arrangements at different times. Key Stage 1 was focused on first, so that a new cohort of pupils could progress through the whole new system, key stage by key stage; KS3 was focused on next, and KS2 after that, since it would take new 5-year-old entrants to "Year 1" six years to reach the end of KS2 (at age 11). Thus subject groups were working to the broad brief outlined by the TGAT report (attainment targets organized into 10 levels of attainment), but had no knowledge of the detailed testing arrangements which might be put in place. And test consortia might win a contract for English but not for maths, and/or for a specific subject at, say KS1, but not KS3, or vice versa. Also there was no guarantee that a contract would be renewed (though those prepared to do the government's bidding, which essentially meant designing simpler and simpler tests, year on year, tended to prosper). How much of this fragmentation came about because harassed civil servants simply dealt with whatever pressing decision was on their desk at a particular time, and how much was a deliberate "divide and rule" strategy by the government, is a moot point. But it certainly did not provide for extensive institutional learning and accumulation of experience across the system. Thus, another lesson from the UK is that taking the political decision to introduce a national curriculum and assessment system is one thing, planning to do it effectively is quite another.

Teachers were the main group who paid the price for lack of coordination; and first in the firing line were teachers of 5- to 7-year-olds (KS1). They had to begin teaching the new programs of study from September 1988, as they came hot off the press; and they had to take part in sample pilot KS1 testing in 1990, with the first full national "run" in 1991. The problems of the sheer speed and scale of the operation were compounded, however, by the attempt of the TGAT report to build on and develop existing good practice in assessment – to attempt to "square the circle" of combining the formative with the summative and evaluative. TGAT argued that "assessment lies at the heart of … promoting children's learning" (para. 3). First and foremost therefore, assessment should be conducted routinely, diagnostically, and formatively by teachers in classrooms to identify student strengths, weaknesses, and progress in order to assist learning. The results of this process, deriving from informal observations and more formal assessment tasks and tests, could then be summarized and reported as part of the overall national system. TGAT called this "teacher assessment" (TA). It could also be combined with formal test results at the end of each key stage to produce an overall summary grade (level 1, level 2, etc.) for each student in each subject. In addition to having the merit of contributing to student learning, TA would also address the issue of the validity and reliability of results by extending the sample of assessment that could be included in the overall national system. Comparability of TA across teachers, schools, and localities would be addressed by extensive moderation procedures which would also contribute to teacher professional development as a whole. Furthermore, however, TGAT argued that the formal external test element of the system should in turn build on best practice and

> employ tests for which a wide range of modes of presentation, operation and response should be used so that each may be valid in relation to the attainment target assessed. These particular tests should be called "standard assessment tasks." (TGAT, 1987, para. 50)

All teachers from September 1988 were expected to start keeping some sort of formal record of their "teacher assessments," though no guidance was issued as to how this should be done. Furthermore, KS1 teachers and students were to be experimental subjects for the development of "standard assessment tasks" (SATs, as they came to be known, rather confusingly for anyone familiar with the abbreviation more usually standing for American Scholastic Aptitude Tests). Without guidance and feeling under intense accountability pressure, teachers started keeping ridiculously detailed TA records, which at their extreme included keeping every piece of work produced by every pupil, annotated to demonstrate which Statements of Attainment had been covered by the work and what level within an overall subject Attainment Target this indicated. Newspapers, prompted by the teacher unions, soon started to report that at KS1, with only the first few SoAs in each subject being taught, and only the "core" subjects of maths, science, and English to be reported on initially, teachers would be dealing with 227 SoAs times c.30 children, totalling 6,810 SoAs per teacher per year (see Daugherty, 1995, p. 117).

Just as problematic, but even more headline-grabbing, were the pilot and first full run of KS1 SATs in 1990 and 1991. They were commissioned from test consortia in maths, English, and science, and were designed to be as "authentic" as possible for an early years classroom. They involved extended tasks, including cross-curricular elements which were intended to assess ATs from across core subjects, usually to be administered to small groups of pupils in order to match the ordinary routines of early years teaching. They could be administered by teachers at any time during the first half of the summer term and, in practice, took about 30 hours of classroom work to complete over a 3- to 6-week period. Class teachers also had to mark the work and report the overall grades awarded. In many respects these SATs represented the zenith of developments which had been started by the APU – a serious attempt to develop authentic standard tasks to test as wide a range of curricular outcomes as possible, administered under ordinary classroom conditions which did not create unnecessary anxiety for pupils. But they certainly created an immense amount of work and anxiety for teachers, because of the overt accountability setting in which they were being implemented. On their own, such tasks might well have become an important resource for teacher development and for further research on the integration of assessment, teaching, and learning, especially if they had been accompanied by the moderation which TGAT originally envisaged. Instead, as essentially evaluative instruments, they were perceived as totally unmanageable and produced results of highly questionable reliability since moderation was never given the policy attention or resources required. The idea that similar instruments might be designed for use at other key stages, and in the other six national curriculum subjects, was soon regarded as wholly unrealistic, by politicians and the teaching profession alike (Torrance, 1993, 1995).

Various agendas were coming into direct conflict to produce enormous system overload. Subject specialists feared that if their particular subject, or approach to a subject, was not included in the statutory orders which defined each National Curriculum subject, then it would quickly disappear from the school timetable. Arts and performing arts teachers were particularly exercised by such a possibility as the government's attention was largely focussed on increasing the proportion of maths, science, and technology in the National Curriculum, along with English (especially spelling and grammar). But the possibility also haunted those who argued that "personal and social education," "citizenship," "health education," and the like, should have a major place in the curriculum. In the absence of such named subjects, English, history, geography, and biology started to expand exponentially to accommodate these topics. Meanwhile, although the political imperative included reorienting the curriculum, especially the primary school curriculum (KS1 and KS2), towards more science and technology, it remained essentially that of producing straightforward results of comparable national assessments at specific points in time so that they could be published and compared across schools and over time as they accumulated. However, the agencies initially charged with developing the national tests saw an opportunity to put the theory of "authentic assessment" and "measurement-driven instruction" into practice: include authentic, integrated, demanding tasks in the national assessment system and you will underpin the development of quality teaching and learning. The result of this clash of competing agendas was that teachers complained about curriculum and assessment overload, while many in the Conservative party saw a conspiracy by the "educational establishment" to undermine the government's basic intention of producing simple tests. "Slimming down" the SATs received the government's initial attention; slimming down curriculum content came next. Following the KS1 piloting, government ministers stated in correspondence with SEAC that they wanted "terminal written examinations" for KS3 (Daugherty, 1995, p. 52) and insisted that similar simplification took place at KS1, albeit tempered by the need to allow early readers and writers to respond appropriately to test stimuli. Thus began the process of moving from Standard Assessment Tasks (SATs), to Standard Tests (STs) to National Tests (NTs) as they are now known. En route, the government insisted that all GCSE examinations should include no more than 20 percent coursework assessment and that a proportion of marks should be allocated in all GCSE subjects for spelling, punctuation, and grammar.

Curriculum content was also recognized as too unwieldy, and a review was set up under Ron Dearing (a former Chairman of the Post Office), who recommended little more than the obvious, but did so after extensive consultations with teacher groups, local authorities, and examination boards, and so appeared to be taking proper account of relevant criticisms and complaints. His report recommended that each National Curriculum subject should be organized in terms of a "core + options," with the total number of ATs and SoAs being significantly reduced. Furthermore, at least 20 percent of the overall timetable should be "free ... for use at the discretion of the school" (Dearing, 1993, p. 7). National testing should be limited to English, maths, and science, which would thus form a core curriculum. GCSE should be retained as is, rather than, as still might have been the case, being completely overtaken and absorbed by the 10-level national system. Effectively therefore, the National Curriculum would now run from ages 5 to 14 years, being assessed and reported through levels 1–8, with the public examination system at KS4 being end-on and, though linked in terms of curriculum progression, no longer fully integrated into a single national system. In particular, subject grading at GCSE would remain reported as grades A–G. Additionally, however, as acknowledgement of arguments about GCSE not stretching the "brightest" and possibly lowering overall standards, Dearing recommended the award of a higher A* (A-star) grade to recognize very high achievement.

While these recommendations were widely welcomed by teachers as helping to reduce their workload, all the essential features of government control of the curriculum and publication of assessment results were retained. The political imperative to produce as simple a set of evaluation and accountability measures as possible had been accomplished. At each successive stage of struggle over curriculum content and scope of the assessment arrangements, "slimming down" has effectively meant simplification of content and procedure. The national curriculum now comprises nine subjects for 5–14-year-olds,[3] organized more as core syllabi plus recommendations for "breadth of study" rather than as detailed lists of objectives (DfEE, 1999). Meanwhile, national testing has become a very narrow exercise indeed: the testing, by externally produced and externally marked paper and pencil tests, of a narrow range of achievements, measurable by such an approach, in three core subjects, English, maths, and science. Subsequently national testing has been further restricted at KS1 to English and maths.

OTHER ASPECTS OF POLICY

The process of slimming down and focussing almost exclusively on the accountability purposes of national assessment has been continued by the most recent Labour governments elected in 1997 and 2001. The emphasis of the new government, however, has been more towards managerial use of the accountability data, rather than simple publication and reliance on market forces to raise standards. Before reviewing this in more detail and bringing the story up to date, so to speak, it is important to recognize the way in which the interaction of policy has reinforced the impact of national testing. Testing and publication of results have never been considered to be an adequate way of raising standards on their own. Giving parents more rights to choose schools, rather than leaving allocation to LEAs, and ensuring that funding followed enrolment, was an integral part of the package. However, popular oversubscribed schools soon began selecting parents/pupils, rather than the other way round, so this was not wholly effective in itself, though it certainly ensured constant pressure on schools to improve results and to "sell" themselves (Gewirtz, Ball, & Bowe, 1995).

Testing was accompanied by the introduction of a National Curriculum, with government approved content (written by co-opted subject experts) in a small range of subjects, which placed particular emphasis on extending the time spent in schools on maths, science, English and, to a lesser extent, technology. Other subjects can still be studied at KS4 and beyond (for GCSE and A-level), but these attract a relatively small number of students[4] and, in any case, still have to meet the general GCSE national criteria for approval by the Secretary of State. A new school inspection regime was instituted to oversee the implementation of the national curriculum and testing arrangements. Hitherto, visits by HMIs to schools, though rigorous, tended to be seen as experienced professionals offering their informed, comparative judgment and advice to fellow professionals. The new regime was based on teams of inspectors, including "lay members" (non-educationists), who were charged with making sure that the national curriculum was being taught, and used uniform, centrally produced observation instruments to measure and report on quality of teaching. Test results would be scrutinized to see how they compared with local and national averages. Reports were (and are) published, and annual summaries by the Chief Inspector of Schools led to headlines such as "15,000 bad teachers should be sacked" (*The Times*, November 3, 1995). This added hugely to the accountability pressures which teachers felt in the early-mid 1990s, and still does.[5]

FROM MARKETS TO MANAGERIALISM

The "New Labour" government has continued this barrage of additional policy implementation to reinforce the accountability "basics" of testing and publishing results. Even more specific content, along with recommended teaching methods, have been introduced to the core subjects of English and maths in conjunction with first a National Literacy Strategy (NLS) and then a National Numeracy Strategy (NNS) at KS1 and KS2. Subsequently, the NLS was extended to KS3. This has been done in tandem with introducing "national targets" for attainment in literacy and numeracy at KS2, which in effect are political objectives which the government has set itself, but then pressurized schools to meet. The targets are, that by 2002, 80 percent of 11-year-olds will reach level 4 or above in English, and 75 percent of 11-year-olds will reach level 4 or above in mathematics (originally deemed by TGAT to be the level which should be attainable by the "average" 11-year-old [TGAT, 1987, para. 104 & 108]). In 2000, 75 percent achieved level 4 in English and 72 percent level 4 in maths (DfEE, 2001).

Even more importantly however, these targets are scrutinized, and target-setting is used as a management tool, at local authority and school level, so that, for example, all schools, but especially those well below the national average (for whatever combination of social and economic reasons), are exhorted to improve year-on-year. This target-setting is now an integral element of government micro-management of the system. Government (through the Office for Standards in Education [OfSTED] which also manages inspections) negotiates/imposes targets on LEAs and they, in turn, negotiate/impose them on individual schools. Target-setting is based on individual Performance and Assessment Reports (PANDAs) produced by OfSTED for each school, in which individual school performance is compared with national and local statistics. Meeting targets is also now attended to in inspections. Furthermore, the government has introduced "performance-related pay" for teachers by which they can cross a threshold to a higher grade. A significant element of the case they must make is the achievement of targets and the raising of "standards" in terms of Key Stage test and GCSE results. Thus evaluation, understood as producing and using test results to further raise test scores, is now an integral part of system management. Accountability is interpreted almost exclusively in terms of published tests scores, but "driving up standards" as the government now puts it, is seen as something which can be accomplished by "performance management" rather than the simple operation of market forces.

WERE STANDARDS FALLING ANYWAY, AND ARE THEY RISING NOW?

When GCSE was first announced, the intention of policy was to bring "the level of attainment of at least 80 to 90 percent of all students up to at least the level currently associated with the average, as reflected in CSE grade 4" (DES, 1985, quoted in Kingdon & Stobart, 1988). Now, of course, "CSE grade 4" means very little in terms of any absolute standard. Similarly, the nature and content of the examination system has changed significantly over time. But insofar as we can make any sort of judgments from the official statistics, in terms of broad equivalences, we can note that successive policy reports have suggested linking the old GCE O-level "pass" (grade C) to CSE grade 1 and GCSE grade C, thus:

GCE	CSE	GCSE
		A*
A		A
B		B
C	1	C
D	2	D
E	3	E
F	4	F
G	5	G

Thus we might imagine that large numbers of students were not achieving at least CSE grade 4 in the early 1980s, and we might look to see how many are achieving at least GCSE grade F today. In fact, official statistics are usually reported in terms of students achieving at least 5 A–Cs and 5 A–Gs, so one would have to go back through individual subject results to calculate the percentage of A–F grades. However, if we note that in 2000, for example, only 4.8 percent of entries in maths were graded "G," and 2.2 percent in English were graded "G," we can probably treat the 5 A–G statistics as accurate to within 2 or 3 percentage points – sufficient to the purpose here.

Thus we can see from Table 1 that considerable progress towards the government's target had already been made between 1975 and 1985, precisely the time when arguments about falling standards started to be heard, and has continued to be made over the years since then. Indeed, the original target has been exceeded for some years now, but this has not stopped continuing complaints about standards being too low, or the need for the new National Assessment targets at KS2 to be met.

Similarly, focusing on English and maths results since the introduction of GCSE we can see pass rates steadily rising (Table 2); likewise the numbers of pupils reaching the "expected" levels of attainment in KS1 & KS2 national assessment tests (Table 3).

Of course, some critics, when results go up, simply complain that the examination(s) have got easier. If results go down, standards are falling; and if results go up … standards are falling. And this was indeed a matter of considerable public debate in the early 1990s, as right-wing critics, wedded to the idea of a normal

Table 1. Percentage of students gaining O-level/CSE/GCSE 1974–1975 to 1999–2000

	% 5 or more A*–C	% 5 or more A*–G
1974–75	22.6	58.6
1984–85	26.9	74.3
1987–88	29.9	74.7
1994–95	43.5	85.7
1999–2000	49.2	88.9

Source: DfES (2001) (results for England)
N.B. 1987/88 is first results of GCSE; Grades A*–C includes O-level A–C, CSE grade 1 & GCSE A*–C; Grades A*–G includes O-level A–E, CSE grades 1–5 & GCSE A*–G

Table 2. Percentage of students gaining GCSE "passes" (Grades A*–C) in English and maths since the introduction of GCSE

	English: A*–C	Maths: A*–C
1987–88	48.9	41.9
1994–95	55.6	44.8
1999–2000	58.6	50.4

Sources: DfEE (1996); DfES (2001) (results for England)

Table 3.   Percentage of students gaining National Curriculum Assessment level 2 or above at KS1 (age 7) and level 4 or above at KS2 (age 11)

| | KS1 | | KS2 | |
	English	Maths	English	Maths
1992	77	78		
1995	76	78	48	44
1996	80	80	58	54
2000	81/84	90	75	72

Sources: *The Times*, 26/1/96; *The Guardian* 18/11/96; DfE (1992); DfEE (2001).

N.B. 1992 is first "full run" of KS1 tests after "slimming down"; 1995 is first full run of KS2 tests; By 2000 KS1 English results were being reported separately in terms of attainment targets (*81 percent gained level 2 in reading, 84 percent in writing). Such details had been available previously but results were routinely reported as "whole subject" levels.

distribution curve of ability, simply could not believe that 40–50 percent (and rising) of the student population could achieve what traditionally had been the preserve of the social elite. In turn, governments can always argue that no matter how high standards are, they need to be higher still, in order to maintain international economic competitiveness in a race which demands eternal vigilance and effort. And certainly, if we assume a reasonable indication of a sound secondary education is 5 GCSE A*–C grades, including English and maths (considerably more demanding than the DES policy announcement of the 1980s), then around 50 percent of the school population is still not achieving this. But these arguments are rarely put positively – standards are always said to be too low – and rarely address the actual evidence of significant progress which successive attempts at developing accountability measures have produced.

SCALE AND COST

Another key issue for the development of a national system is cost-effectiveness. The scale of the enterprise in the UK is enormous. Approximately 605,000 pupils took KS1 tests in England in 2000; 620,000 took KS2 tests; and 580,000 took KS3 tests (DfEE, 2001). Multiply these figures by the number of subjects and the number of papers in each subject and the figures run into millions – all to be set, printed, distributed, collected, and marked annually. At GCSE (KS4), there were 554,000 pupils in 2000, entering a total of 4,744,861 GCSE examinations (DfES, 2001). Every year, therefore, within the compulsory school system (i.e., up to the school leaving age of 16), around 2.3 or 2.4 million students are sitting in excess of 10 million separate national tests and examinations.

Calculating the cost is by no means easy (despite the government's love affair with measurement and statistical "transparency") since national testing is not identified separately in government expenditure figures. At the high end of an estimate, government statistics indicate that 7 percent of the annual primary school budget (£678M) and 8 percent of the annual secondary budget (£660M) is spent on "administration and inspection costs" including "central government expenditure on qualifications" (DfES, 2001, p. 17). Of this, £105M was spent on OfSTED inspections in 2000 (p. 12). At the low end of an estimate we can also note that the Qualifications and Curriculum Authority, now responsible for overseeing the National Curriculum and National Assessment arrangements, had a budget of £68M in 2000, of which £25M was identified as serving "Key Objective 4: Secure a rigorous, consistent and fair system of assessment" (QCA, 2001). This low figure will certainly include QCA staff salaries and may include some of the payments to consortia for producing and marking the tests. So a reasonable guestimate of the direct cost of national assessment might be somewhere between £25M and the £100+M it takes to fund OfSTED. Of course, none of these figures takes into account the indirect costs on local authority and teacher time; nor do they include the cost of GCSE examining, which would have to be calculated from the individual fee income received from candidates by each Examination Board.[6]

IMPACT ON TEACHING AND LEARNING

Evidence from around the world suggests that too narrow a concentration on raising test scores can lead to a narrowing of the curriculum, impoverishment of student learning experience and the possibility of actually lowering educational "standards" as more broadly conceived (Linn, 2000; Shepard, 1990), as indeed was predicted in the government consultative document of 1977 quoted above. Experience confirms this in the UK. Research on the introduction of the National Curriculum and National Assessment has suggested that there have been some benefits, especially in terms of an increase in collegial planning and management of the primary school curriculum (KS1 and KS2), but also many costs. Many primary school teachers reported feeling threatened by the changing emphasis from an arts-based early years curriculum to more of a science-oriented curriculum, but also felt they were becoming more confident over time and thought there were benefits in more collaborative whole-school planning, rather than simply being left to "get on with things" as they had always done in their own individual classrooms (Croll, 1996; Pollard, Broadfoot, Croll, Osborn, & Abbott, 1994). Attention to use of evidence rather than "intuition," when it comes to making classroom assessments and appraising student progress, has also been noted as an outcome of national assessment (Gipps, Brown, McCallum, & McAlister, 1995). Accountability pressures have been severely felt however, and as the national tests have become more and more restricted in scope and allied to target setting, so has the curriculum become narrowed: "Whole class teaching and individual pupil work increased at the expense of group work … [there was] a noticeable increase in the time spent on the core subjects … [and] teachers … put time aside for revision and mock tests" (McNess, Triggs, Broadfoot, Osborn, & Pollard, 2001, pp. 12–13).

Similarly, "in the last two years of primary schooling children encountered a sharp increase in the use of routine tests and other forms of categoric assessment" and pupils became less keen on teachers looking at and commenting on their work (McNess et al., 2001; see also Osborn, McNess, Broadfoot, Pollard, & Triggs, 2000). This latter point, if sustained, will be very counter-productive since it is precisely by looking at and commenting on pupil work that teachers can make a positive difference to pupil learning (Black & Wiliam, 1998) rather than just coaching them to improve test scores.

Coaching also raises issues of instrument corruption, and whether or not increasing test scores mean very much even in their own terms. The APU approach was probably a better way of getting a purchase on "standards," but was far too complex to roll out across the system as a whole, as early experience with the KS1 SATs demonstrated. Interestingly enough, other work on reliability (Wiliam, 2001) suggests that even estimated at around 80 percent, up to 19 percent of pupils would be wrongly graded at KS1, 32 percent at KS2, and 43 percent at KS3 – an extraordinary level of error about which the government seems unconcerned so long as the overall national figures are increasing.

Another puzzling element of government policy in the context of teaching, learning, and standards, is that if quality of curriculum experience and depth of learning is severely compromised over time, this will hardly address the key economic issue of international competitiveness which ostensibly is underpinning government policy on education. As McNess et al. (2001) note: "An increasingly constrained education system focused on 'the basics' and directed by the need to prioritise 'performance targets' is in tension with the discourse of the flexible lifelong learner eager to take risks" (p. 16). One suspicion of course, is that "discourse" (rhetoric) is all it is. Current government policy certainly attends to the issue of globalization and the need to continue to develop a knowledge-based economy. It is also continuing to focus on the consumers of the service, emphasizing transparency of processes and products, and the role that educational achievement can play in individual social mobility and social inclusion. However, as Reich (1991) has noted, "symbolic analysts" are only one of the employable categories that globalization is calling forth, the others being rather less educated "production workers" and "service workers." Were these broad heuristic categories to be found within an economy, as well as across economies, then the fact that none of the current legislation or practice in England applies to independent fee-paying schools, which are free to become exam factories or not, depending on mission and clientele, suggests that most of the "symbolic analysts" in England are already assumed to be continuing to come from this sector. Thirty years on, and the British social class system could be said to be still very firmly in control.

A further consequence of all the changes that have occurred in England since the mid-1980s, but which has grown in severity since the mid-1990s, is a crisis in teacher recruitment and retention. Very large numbers of serving teachers have taken early retirement to escape the overload of the national curriculum and national assessment, and training places are hard to fill. A recent survey indicated that 12% of trainee teachers drop out of training before completion, 30 percent of newly trained teachers never teach, and a further 18 percent of new recruits leave the profession within three years (*Times Educational Supplement*, November 2, 2001, p. 1). Most explanations focus on overwork, linked to the pressure to meet targets, along with relatively low pay for an all-graduate profession. But lack of control over curriculum and teaching methods is also likely to be important. There is simply no scope in the system anymore for innovative educators who might wish to experiment at local level. And, coupled with the immediate crisis of teacher numbers, one wonders where the creative leaders of the profession will come from in five or ten years time.

POLICY LESSONS TO BE LEARNED

What can be learned from the English experience? The most obvious point to note is the continuing tension between the formative and evaluative purposes of a national assessment system and the trade-off between scale and complexity. The larger the system of national assessment envisaged and implemented, the simpler the testing regime must be. And this, in turn, will carry consequences for curriculum focus and quality of educational experience. If policymakers wish to garner some of the more positive elements of "measurement driven instruction" (designing good quality assessments to underpin good quality teaching) and report results nationally, then the system would probably have to operate at no more than two ages/stages (7 & 11? 9 & 14?) to allow sufficient time and resources to be committed to test/task development, teacher development, and the ongoing moderation of teacher judgments which would have to be at the heart of any such system (Khattri, Reeve, & Kane, 1998).

There are also many features of the English system which might be configured in different ways with different emphases. National assessment does not stand alone as a policy option in England. Its peculiarly coercive and corrosive power derives from being linked to a national curriculum; framed by a very mechanistic government view of evaluation and accountability, including the publication of results and target-setting; and further policed by a very punitive inspection regime. All of these elements could be combined in different ways and operationalized with a different emphasis. Thus, one could imagine a national curriculum being implemented without national assessment at all; or without publishing results; or with an element of occasional APU-style sample testing; or with a national assessment system which was more limited in scale but more ambitious in scope. Alternatively, with or without a national curriculum, a national bank of standard assessment tasks could be developed for expected, but nevertheless still voluntary use and modification by teachers, to underpin their own judgments of student progress and school self-evaluation. Similarly, results could be published without being linked to school targets and teacher pay, and set in a more descriptive and explanatory account of what is happening in a particular school and why. Such a description and explanation could be written by the school itself, or be an outcome of a more curious and supportive system of inspection – also indicating what might be done to assist improvement. Elements of these variations have in fact been implemented in the other three countries of the UK, including development of standard assessment task "item banking," and England is now the only country which publishes "performance tables" in overt comparative form.

Nevertheless, the English public and English schools and teachers have become used to seeing annual publication of national assessment and GCSE results. Indeed, unless the press can identify a particular angle (usually involving some blip in the statistics which can be interpreted as yet more evidence of falling standards), their publication can pass almost unremarked. Yet stopping publication in England would be a major and almost unthinkable decision. National testing and the publication of results is here for the forseeable future. The debate about testing continues, however, with considerable unease being expressed about the "over-assessment" of individual students and the system as a whole (e.g., *Times Educational Supplement*, November 23, 2001, p. 19; November 30, 2001, p. 3). Although the current government in England seems immune to such arguments, they ought to be persuasive elsewhere, if the key issue is to develop creative and flexible citizens of the future rather than dutiful drones for today.

ENDNOTES

[1] It should also be noted in this discussion of the fragmented nature of the UK system that the 11+ itself was locally controlled and administered by local education authorities (LEAs, i.e. school districts) and test papers and pass rates varied from one authority to another, with variation usually reflecting the historic provision of grammar school places in each LEA. Indeed one of the factors that led to the demise of the 11+ was precisely this variation, when it became apparent that pass rates varied from as low as 9 or 10 percent of a cohort in some LEAs to over 40 percent in others (see Torrance, 1981).

[2] In fact research on this topic seems to indicate that if anything many teachers' judgments can be harsher than results produced by final papers. Kingdon and Stobbart (1988), reporting on work carried out at the University of London School Examinations Board, note that "we found no support for the claim that coursework would be … a soft option, since in almost half the subjects the mean coursework mark was actually lower than the mean final mark" (p. 121).

[3] Plus physical education (PE) and information and communication technology (ICT) from August 2000. Inclusion of PE responded to concerns about other important subjects being squeezed out of the curriculum and effectively confirmed the place of some physical activity in the curriculum. ICT was similarly thought to be in danger of exclusion if not explicitly recognised, though it is recommended that it is taught across the curriculum within each subject, rather than as a separate subject.

[4] In 2000, for example, there were 554,551 entries in GCSE maths and 533,227 in GCSE English; by contrast there were 81,493 entries in computer studies, 84,670 in drama and 14,835 in social studies (DfES, 2001).

[5] See House of Commons (1999) and Cullingford (1999) for accounts of the impact of inspection.

[6] Personal correspondence with DfES indicates that the direct cost of KS1, 2, and 3 testing for 2001 was £25.6m. (including test development, printing, distribution and marking), but it is not clear what proportion of this figure, if any, overlaps with QCA budget. Further correspondence indicates that £78,000 was spent on "disseminating" the results of the tests through the PANDAs produced for schools. Clearly this figure is a ridiculous underestimate, taking into account little more than the cost of installing the website. The cost of actually producing the statistics has been ignored. Thus even after correspondence it is difficult to know, without asking more and more precise questions, how much is really spent on national testing. None of the figures includes teacher time or LEA adviser time spent administering the tests and/or acting on the results.

REFERENCES

Becher, T., Eraut, M., & Knight, J. (1981). *Policies for educational accountability*. London, Heinemann.

Black, P., & Wiliam, D. (1998). Assessment and classroom learning. *Assessment in Education*, 5, 7–74.

Brown, M. (1988). Issues in formulating and organising attainment targets in relation to their assessment. In H. Torrance (Ed), *National assessment and testing: A research response*. (pp. 15–25). London: British Educational Research Association.

Butterfield, S. (1995). *Educational objectives and national assessment*. Buckingham: Open University Press.

Croll, P. (Ed.). (1996). *Teachers, pupils and primary schooling: Continuity and change*. London, Cassell.

Cullingford, C. (Ed.). (1999). *An inspector calls*. London: Kogan Page.

Daugherty, R. (1995). *National curriculum assessment: A review of policy 1987–1994*. London: Falmer.

Dearing, R. (1993). *The national curriculum and its assessment: Final report*. London: School Curriculum and Assessment Authority.

DES (Department of Education and Science). (1977). *Education in schools. A consultative document*. London: Her Majesty's Stationery Office. (cmnd: 6869)

DES (Department of Education and Science). (1987). *The national curriculum 5-16. A consultation document*. London: Author.

DES (Department of Education and Science). (1990). *English in the national curriculum (No. 2)*. London: Author.

DfE (Department for Education). (1992). *Testing 7-year olds in 1992: Results of the national curriculum assessments in England*. London: Author.

DfEE (Department for Education and Employment). (1996). *Statistics of education: Public examinations: GCSE and GCE in England 1995*. London: Author.

DfEE (Department for Education and Employment). (1999). *The national curriculum for England*. London: Author.

DfEE (Department for Education and Employment). (2001). *Statistics of education: National curriculum assessments of 7, 11 and 14-year olds in England, 2000*. London: Author.

DfES (Department for Education and Skills). (2001). *Statistics of education: Public examinations GCSE/GNVQ and GCE/AGNVQ in England 2000*. London: Author.

Elliott, J., Bridges, D., Ebbutt, D., Gibson, R., & Nias, J. (1981). *School accountability*. London: Grant McIntyre.

Gewirtz S., Ball J., & Bowe, R. (1995). *Markets, choice and equity in education*. Buckingham: Open University Press.

Gipps C., Brown, M., McCallum, B., & McAlister, S. (1995). *Intuition or evidence? Teacher and national assessment of seven-year olds*. Buckingham: Open University Press.

Hargreaves, D. (1984). *Improving secondary schools*. London: Inner London Education Authority.

Hillgate Group. (1987). *The reform of British education*. London: Claridge.

House of Commons. (1999). *Education and Employment Select Committee Fourth Report*. London: Her Majesty's Stationery Office. Retrieved from www.publications.parliament.uk/pa/cm199899/cmselect/cmeduemp/62/6202.htm.

Khattri N., Reeve, A., & Kane, M. (1998). *Principles and practices of performance assessment*. Mahwah, NJ: Lawrence Erlbaum.

Kingdon M., & Stobbart G. (1988). *GCSE examined*. London: Falmer Press.

Linn, R.L. (2000). Assessments and accountability. *Educational Researcher*, 29(2), 4–16.

MacDonald, B. (1979). Hard times – Accountability in England. *Educational Analysis*, 1(1), 23–44.

Marks, J. (1991). *Standards in schools: Assessment, accountability and the purpose of education*. London: Social Market Foundation.

McNess, E., Triggs, P., Broadfoot, P., Osborn, M., & Pollard, A. (2001). The changing nature of assessment in English primary classrooms. *Education 3–13*, 29(3), 9–16.

Murphy, R. (1986). The emperor has no clothes: Grade criteria and the GCSE. In C. Gipps (Ed.), *The GCSE: An uncommon examination*. London: Institute of Education Publications.

Murphy, R., & Torrance, H. (1988). *The changing face of educational assessment*. Buckingham: Open University Press.

Orr, L., & Nuttall, D. (1983). *Determining standards in the proposed single system of examining at 16+*. London, The Schools Council, Comparability in Examinations: Occasional Paper 2, London.

Osborn, M., McNess, E., Broadfoot, P., Pollard, A., & Triggs, P. (2000). *What teachers do: Changing policy and practice in primary education*. London: Continuum.

Pollard, A., Broadfoot, P., Croll, P., Osborn, M., & Abbott, A. (1994). *Changing English primary schools*. London: Cassell.

QCA (Qualifications and Curriculum Authority). (2001). *Annual report*. Retrieved December 2001 from: www.qca.org.uk/annual_report/resourcing.asp.

Reich, R. (1991). *The work of nations*. London: Simon & Schuster.

Shepard, L. (1990). Inflated test score gains: Is the problem old norms or teaching to the test? *Educational Measurement: Issues and practice*, **9**(3), 15–22.

TGAT (Task Group on Assessment and Testing). (1987). *National curriculum: Task Group on Assessment and Testing: A report*. London: DES.

Torrance, H. (1981). The origins and development of mental testing in England and the United States. *British Journal of Sociology of Education*, **2**, 45–59.

Torrance, H. (1993). Combining measurement driven instruction with authentic assessment: The case of national assessment in England and Wales. *Educational Evaluation and Policy Analysis*, **15**, 81–90.

Torrance, H. (Ed.) (1995). *Evaluating authentic assessment*. Buckingham: Open University Press.

Wiliam, D. (2001). Reliability, validity and all that jazz. *Education 3-13*, **29**(3), 17–21.

41
State and School District Evaluation in the United States

WILLIAM J. WEBSTER
Dallas Independent School District, Dallas, Texas, USA

TED O. ALMAGUER
Dallas Independent School District, Dallas, Texas, USA

TIM ORSAK
Dallas Independent School District, Dallas, Texas, USA

The field of educational evaluation developed dramatically over the decades of the 1960s, 1970s, and 1980s. Following a period of relative inactivity in the 1950s, influenced by seminal articles by Cronbach (1963), Scriven (1967), Stake (1967), and Stufflebeam (1966), educational evaluation efforts experienced a period of revitalization in the mid-1960s. Development was further stimulated by the evaluation requirements of the Great Society programs that were launched in 1965; by the nationwide accountability movement that began in the early 1970s; and, most importantly, by the mounting responsibilities and resources that society assigned to educators.

The intent of this chapter is to describe the practice of evaluation among state departments and local school districts in the United States. To accomplish this, the authors draw primarily from studies of local school district evaluation units by Webster (1977), Webster and Stufflebeam (1978), Stufflebeam and Webster (1980), a recent survey of local school districts by the authors, several studies of the characteristics of state accountability systems (Consortium of Policy Research in Education, 2000, Council of Chief State School Officers, 1995, 2000; Education Commission of the States, 1998), and a recent analysis of state accountability systems conducted by the authors. Once the state of educational evaluation is established, some suggestions are offered for future directions.

WHAT IS EVALUATION?

Before attempting to describe the state of evaluation, it is important to reach a suitable definition. For about 30 years educators and other professionals

International Handbook of Educational Evaluation, 929–950
T. Kellaghan, D.L. Stufflebeam (eds.)
© 2003 *Dordrecht: Kluwer Academic Publishers. Printed in Great Britain.*

generally accepted the definition proposed by Smith and Tyler (1942) that evaluation means determining whether or not objectives have been achieved. This definition provided a common view that professionals could use to promote and assess improvements. For example, it was particularly influential in the development of minimum competency testing programs and in the management-by-objectives movement. In general, it focused attention on determining whether intended outcomes were achieved. In the main, however, this definition has been used uncritically and persistently. Undoubtedly, this ritualistic application has limited the usefulness of evaluation services by narrowing their perspectives to concerns evident in specified objectives, by analogously directing attention away from positive and negative side effects, by suggesting that evaluation is applied only at the end of a project or other effort, and by encouraging service providers to define success in terms of objectives without evaluating the objectives.

The objectives-based conception of evaluation still prevails in many organizations and is particularly prevalent as the major part of many state-level accountability systems. On the other hand, most school district evaluation units have moved to a definition based on the view that evaluation should guide decision making. This definition, for example, has been very influential in the evaluation systems of a number of school districts (e.g., Dallas, Fort Worth, and Austin, Texas; Lansing and Saginaw, Michigan; and Cincinnati and Columbus, Ohio). It also has been the dominant approach employed by the United States General Accounting Office. The decision orientation is an improvement over the objectives-oriented definition because it goes well beyond basic accountability in that its thrust is to ensure that evaluation guides a program throughout its development and implementation and because it implies the assessment of a wider range of variables: needs, plans, operations, and results – including side effects. In short, evaluation should aid educators in improving programs in addition to holding them accountable for program outcomes.

The Joint Committee on Standards for Educational Evaluation (1981, 1988, 1994) adopted a third definition for educational evaluation, which is noteworthy because it followed agreement by a national committee, appointed by major national educational, evaluation, and research organizations, to develop standards for educational evaluation. The Joint Committee's definition of evaluation was the basis for its *Standards*, which have become influential in the practice of educational evaluation, and states: "Evaluation is the systematic assessment of the worth or merit of some object." The stipulation calls attention to the importance of clarifying the thing being evaluated, and reflects the truism that an evaluation is an assessment of value. Both points are important, but the latter is especially critical.

For the purpose of reviewing current practices in evaluation, the following definition is offered:

> Evaluation is the process of delineating, obtaining, and applying descriptive and judgmental information about the worth or merit of some object's goals, plans, operations, and results in order to guide decision making,

maintain accountability, and foster understandings. (Stufflebeam et al., 1971, p. 40)

This definition emphasizes that evaluations should assist decision making; it stresses that evaluative inquiries must seek to assess worth and merit; it denotes a wide range of variables to be assessed; it emphasizes that evaluation is an interactive process involving both communication and technical activities; and it points out that, in addition to guiding decisions, evaluations should provide a basis for accountability and should lead to better understanding of the phenomena being studied. Existing evaluation systems are reviewed against this definition as well as five criteria that we believe provide fairness for all stakeholders in the evaluation system. First, the system must include a legitimate value-added component. Second, it must include multiple outcome variables. Third, schools must only be held accountable for students who have been exposed to their instructional program (continuously enrolled students). Fourth, schools must derive no particular advantage by starting with high-scoring or low-scoring students, minority or white students, high or low socioeconomic level students, or limited English proficient (LEP) or non-limited English proficient students. Furthermore, such factors as student mobility, school overcrowding, and staffing patterns over which the schools have no control must be taken into consideration. Finally, the system must be based on cohorts of students, not cross-sectional data.

These five criteria are related to fairness in an evaluation system. Systems must have a value-added component because different students start at different levels and gain must be considered if one is going to give the student and the school credit for improvement. The use of multiple outcome variables is preferred because there are multiple outcomes of education and, to the extent that system stakeholders can agree upon them, they should be included in the system. The inclusion of multiple outcome variables also guards against practitioners focusing on a narrow set of outcomes. Recent criticisms of the Texas State Accountability System have, among multiple other concerns, questioned whether or not the achievement gains measured by one test that the entire state has been drilling on for years are real (Clopton, Bishop, & Klein, 2000).

The issue of holding schools accountable for only the students that they have had the opportunity to teach, although often amazingly controversial, seems logical. "Opportunity to teach" can be defined in a number of ways. In Dallas, it is defined as being continuously enrolled in the same school. This is operationally defined as being enrolled during the first six weeks of the school year and present to take the appropriate test.

The issue of schools deriving no particular advantage by starting with high-scoring or low-scoring students, minority or white students, high or low socioeconomic students, and limited English proficient or non-English-proficient students at either the individual student, classroom, or school level, is one that is a little more difficult to address. Some of the known factors that affect school progress but are outside of the control of the school include, but are not limited to, socioeconomic status, gender, language proficiency, ethnicity, and the existing ability levels of entering students. The criteria by which all systems for evaluating schools need to be judged are the degrees of relationship between these factors and the resulting measures of effectiveness. Using these relationships to adjust the criterion measures for school accountability models is rare based on the author's extensive search of the literature on school effectiveness systems. Because context seems to be so universally ignored, a brief discussion on this issue is presented below.

Systems which employ unadjusted outcomes or testing programs as their basis for evaluation are too highly correlated with the existing factors just delineated. As noted by Jaeger (1992) and Webster, Mendro, Bebry, and Orsak (1995), these types of systems are biased against schools with large proportions of minority and low socioeconomic status students and in favor of schools that contain large proportions of white and higher socioeconomic status students. Thus, when unadjusted outcomes are used, schools are ranked primarily on the types of students that they receive rather than on the education that they provide, and differences in populations of students and how they are selected into their schools and programs are confounded with the difference the schools and programs make. Schools and programs, which draw on higher scoring students, receive the benefits of this bias before their students start their first lesson. Schools and programs that must deal with lower scoring students must overcome this bias before they can begin to show an effect. In short, the worst possible use of evaluative data for public reporting is the presentation of simple averages by districts and schools.

PUBLIC SCHOOL DISTRICT EVALUATION

The information described in this section was collected through surveys in 1978 and 1999 of more than 50 of the largest urban school districts in the United States. The survey conducted in 1978 was mailed to persons having the title of directors of evaluation/research in each of those districts. The 1999 survey was either mailed or faxed to persons responsible for evaluation/research at each of the 56 members of the Council of Great City Schools. The 1978 survey had 35 responses of the 56 surveyed. The 1999 survey had 20 usable responses of 56 surveyed. Nine districts responded to both surveys. Because of the low response rate in 1999 and the fact that only nine districts responded to both surveys, we rely to some extent on previously collected information, some of which is dated.

Pittsburgh and Birmingham reported no formal evaluation or research departments in 1978, while Des Moines and Birmingham responded that they had no formal evaluation or research departments in 1999. Des Moines highlighted the elimination of the district's evaluation unit in 1999 as a result of reorganization. The representatives of some districts were unable to accurately complete the simple questionnaire (three in 1978 and three in 1999), thus their responses were not included in the summarization.

Districts were stratified on the basis of evaluation and research expenditures and questions asked relative to each of three categories. The three categories included large (more than $1,000,000 in research, evaluation, and testing expenditures), medium ($300,000 to $1,000,000 in research, evaluation, and testing expenditures), and small (less than $300,000 in research, evaluation, and testing expenditures). The research expenditure measure was used in an attempt to group departments homogeneously for discussion. Grouping by size of district would have produced extremely heterogeneous groups due to the wide range of evaluation budgets. Thus generalizations are relative to size of evaluation departments.

Expenditures

In the real world of applied evaluation and research, emphasis translates to money. Thus, the relevant question becomes one of the amount of expenditure on evaluation in the districts. Districts in the 1978 study ranged in evaluation and research expenditures from $67,000 to $10,300,000. Federal funds contributed significantly to New York's $10,300,000 research and evaluation department. All other respondents had operating funds comparably distributed between local and state funds and federal funds. In comparison to total expenditure per district, approximately three-tenths of one percent of total expenditures was for evaluation and research. Although many theoretical models suggest a 5 percent expenditure for research and evaluation, these results suggest that, in 1979, school districts generally did not strongly support evaluation and research functions. Nine responding districts did, however, spend more than $1,000,000 on research and evaluation activities (New York, Dallas, Philadelphia, Chicago, Detroit, Boston, Los Angeles, Baltimore, and Atlanta).

Districts in the 1999 study ranged in evaluation and research expenditures from $75,000 to $6,230,922. Of the nine $1,000,000 districts from the 1978 study, New York, Philadelphia, Chicago, and Boston did not respond to the 1999 survey, and Baltimore reported spending only $75,000 in 1999. Available evidence suggests that research and evaluation expenditures in large school districts were not as high proportionally in 1999 as they were in 1978. Only Fresno, Portland, and El Paso incurred increases in purchasing power from 1978 after Consumer Price Index inflation adjustments were calculated. However, ten responding districts did report spending at least $1,000,000 on research and evaluation activities in 1999 (Dallas, Los Angeles, Jefferson County, Fresno, Portland, Atlanta, Houston, Detroit, El Paso, and Sacramento) and three spent over $900,000 (Minneapolis, San Francisco, and Mesa).

Observations regarding funding indicate limited support for evaluation and research functions within public school districts. The 1978 survey reported nine districts classified in the "large" category whereas ten are included in 1999. Of the large districts, local/state funds increased from an average of $840,185 to $1,959,261, while the availability of federal funds decreased from $1,953,518 to approximately one-fifth at $409,041. The thirteen "medium" participants in 1978 reported an average of $280,871 in local/state funds and $198,053 in federal funds. The corresponding "medium" group in 1999 reported an average of $693,298 in local/state funds and $91,200 in federal funds. The five "small" participants in 1978 reported an average of $137,620 in local/state funds and $57,576 in federal funds. The corresponding "small" group in 1999 reported an average of $118,963 in local/state funds and $0 in federal funds. The most obvious change regards reduction of federal funds incorporated into the evaluation and research components of school district operations. Perhaps as local funds are cut, resources are not readily available to write proposals and request federal funds.

Functions

Webster (1977) outlined 16 functions of applied evaluation and research units (Table 1). Respondents were asked to estimate the proportion of evaluation and research resources spent for each function. Once again, data were disaggregated by small, medium, and large evaluation departments. Only 14 functional areas were included in the 1978 survey, with personnel evaluation and value-added evaluation being added in 1999.

A number of generalizations were drawn from the 1978 survey results (Webster & Stufflebeam, 1978). First, the smaller the evaluation unit, the higher the proportion of its resources that were spent on management. Second, the vast majority of evaluation offices controlled the testing function. Third, input evaluation was practically nonexistent in medium and small evaluation units. Fourth, process evaluation was less emphasized as evaluation units became smaller. Fifth, evaluation departments, regardless of size, put most effort into testing, product evaluation, and data processing. Sixth, most evaluation departments, regardless of size, did not control their data processing capability. Seventh, basic research was practically non-existent in public school evaluation. Finally, small evaluation departments spent a comparatively large amount of resources on ad hoc information requirements.

The same basic survey was administered in 1999, yielding similar generalizations. First, medium and large departments allocate a significant portion of resources to testing, whereas small departments no longer appear to either support or be responsible for testing activities. Second, management activities require the greatest allocation in smaller departments. Third, product evaluation retains the most resources of all types of evaluation. Fourth, data processing is not directed/controlled by most evaluation departments. Fifth, personnel evaluation is non-existent in small evaluation departments and receives minimal allocation in large departments. Finally, value-added components were reported from six districts, but received emphasis in only two (Dallas and Minneapolis).

Comparisons regarding the resource allocations to public school evaluation and research departments highlight a disturbing trend towards reduced evaluation services. In the earlier survey, the greatest allocation of funds was

Table 1.   Functions of Public School Evaluation and Research Departments

Function	Description
1. Management	The obtaining, disbursing, and quality control of material and personnel resources necessary to meet the information needs of the district.
2. Assessment	The operation of the basic system-wide data acquisition system to ensure reliable, valid, and objective instrumentation and reporting. This does not include diagnostic testing for special education.
3. Instrument Development	The development and validation of necessary instrumentation.
4. Context Evaluation	The provision of baseline information that delineates the environment of interest, describes desired and actual outcomes, identifies unmet needs and unused opportunities, and diagnoses problems that prevent needs from being met (often called institutional research).
5. Input Evaluation	The provision of information for determining methods of resource utilization for accomplishing set goals.
6. Process Evaluation	The provision of information for determining defects in procedural design or implementation during program implementation stages and for aiding in the interpretation of program evaluation data.
7. Product Evaluation	The provision of information for determining the relative success of educational programs. Product evaluation may be interim or summative and generally addresses the extent to which programs meet their objectives, the relative effects of alternative programs, and/or program cost-effectiveness.
8. Proposal Development	The development of proposals, or the evaluation sections of proposals, for outside funds. In all cases, outside funds should be a means to an end, not an end in themselves.
9. Applied Research	The provision of information pertaining to interaction among student characteristics, teacher characteristics, and/or instructional strategies.
10. Basic Research	The provision of information pertaining to fundamental relationships affecting student learning.
11. Data Processing	The operation of the basic data retrieval and analysis system.
12. Planning Services	The provision of technical assistance to district and project management in planning and managing projects and programs.
13. Ad Hoc Information	The provision of requested information on an ad hoc basis to decision-makers.
14. Research Consultant	The provision of design and analysis help to district personnel in implementing their own research and evaluation projects.
15. Personnel Evaluation	The provision of information for use in personnel evaluation or the management of the personnel evaluation system. Personnel evaluation for this purpose is limited to teacher and principal evaluation.
16. Value-Added Evaluation	The use of measures of adjusted gain in teacher, principal, or school evaluation.

designated for product evaluation for large departments and for testing for medium and small departments. Product evaluation was second highest for the medium and small departments. The 1999 survey indicated that testing was the primary expense of the large and medium departments with approximately 20 to 32 percent of their resources allocated to this area, respectively. The smaller departments indicated a great reduction in testing (down to 2.5 percent), whereas management was their primary expense taking 20 percent of their resources. Overall, the differences between the two surveys indicate shifts away from context evaluation, process evaluation, product evaluation, data processing, and research consultation for the large and medium departments with increases primarily coming in the area of testing. Ad hoc information production also showed increases for the large departments. The small departments indicated a decrease of 16.5 percent in testing and of 7.9 percent in product evaluation with the greatest increases for management (9.3 percent) and research consultation (5.7 percent).

The increases in testing for the large and medium departments can probably be attributed to the additional testing required by state accountability systems. State accountability systems have shifted additional burdens of required testing to local school districts. The most obvious of a school district's departments to assist in implementing the additional testing required by state systems has traditionally been the research and evaluation department. This absorption of additional testing forced resource reallocation from traditional research/ evaluation areas to more management and ad hoc services. In the case of small research departments, the burden of additional testing could not be accommodated by the departments and thus was apparently transferred to another department.

This shift is significant since it signifies a move away from legitimate evaluation activities to assessment. Much of the assessment costs can be attributed to test administration and monitoring activities required by, but not funded by, state agencies. Control of the testing function is essential to operating an efficient evaluation office. To control testing is to control the quality of the majority of research and evaluation product data. Without this quality control mechanism, evaluation is left with the probability of depending on unreliable and invalid data. However, evaluation departments are assuming more and more of the administrative burdens of state testing programs. Rather than increase evaluation budgets to handle these demands, resources are being transferred. Thus, districts are often left spending their sparse evaluation dollars on massive, unwieldy, often invalid assessment programs rather than on legitimate evaluation activities.

Management costs for research and evaluation activities are somewhat high because of the large amount of quality control required of the data and the intensive degree of interaction with decision makers necessary to make evaluation effective. The smaller the department, the greater the amount of time that the department head generally must spend selling evaluation activities to decision makers, including, in many instances, convincing them that they need information to make better decisions.

Input evaluation is an extremely cost-effective form of evaluation. By ensuring that only programs with a high probability of success are adopted, one vastly reduces the probability of costly failure. This process could save millions of dollars in program materials and staff resources. Yet, most evaluation units, whatever their size, did not have input evaluation functions. As a result, it has been the authors' experience that many variables other than program effectiveness contribute to educators' decisions to implement or discontinue programs.

Process evaluation is essential in monitoring programs to ensure that evaluators are not evaluating fictitious events. Furthermore, many changes in instructional delivery can be made during the course of program implementation through the use of process evaluation results. Yet, there is strong evidence that reliance on product evaluation data alone is prevalent among most evaluation units. It is significant to note that one of the major weaknesses of national evaluation studies generally is a lack of adequate documentation of instructional delivery that could be obtained through process evaluation. Over-reliance on product evaluation data alone often leads to extremely misleading results.

Testing, product evaluation, and data processing are extremely important evaluation functions. However, testing without some type of evaluation design is of limited use to decision making. It is, in other words, a necessary but not sufficient tool for evaluation. Product evaluation is the form of evaluation that most Boards of Education support most readily. It is visible, related directly to decision making, and provides information of interest to most laypeople. Questions such as "Did a program meet its objectives?" "Did it meet system objectives better than the competition?" and/or "Was it cost effective?" are of extreme interest to Board members and the public. These are also the kinds of questions asked by federal funding agencies. Yet, even product evaluation activities have declined in the face of demands for increased large-scale assessment programs.

That small evaluation departments spend a comparatively large amount of resources on ad hoc information suggests that they, too, are focused on providing evaluative information for decision making. With a small evaluation budget, inadequate information exists. Thus decision makers usurp a higher proportion of resources to answer the pressing questions of the moment.

Personnel evaluation is a primary means to ensure the quality of education received by students. Indeed, it can be argued that program evaluation in the absence of systematic value-added teacher evaluation is of extremely limited utility. Teacher-proof programs cannot be designed. Competent teachers can make almost anything work, while incompetent ones can ruin even the most brilliant instructional design. Teacher evaluation systems must be outcomes-based, value-added, and must be coordinated with ongoing program and school evaluation. Furthermore, evaluations of principals, support personnel, and administrators must also be outcomes-based and value-added, in most cases including the same outcomes as the teacher system. If funds are limited, systematic outcomes-based, value-added personnel evaluation is much more likely to produce desired results than is program evaluation. Studies of effective and ineffective teachers in Dallas found as much as a 50-percentile point difference in students scores on a norm-referenced test after only three years (Jordan, Bembry, & Mendro, 1998; Jordan, Mendro, & Weersinghe, 1997). (For a discussion of integrating personnel and program evaluation see Webster, 2001b.)

Only 18 percent of the responding districts had any involvement at all in teacher and/or principal evaluation.

Evaluation Models

Stufflebeam's CIPP (Context, Input, Process, Product) was by far the most popular evaluation model employed; six districts reported using it or some form of CIPP. The model was developed based on evaluation experiences in the Columbus, Ohio, public schools, and has been used as the principal evaluation model in Dallas, Cincinnati, Saginaw, Lansing, and Philadelphia. The most operationalized version of the model is in Dallas, where the system is organized to conduct the four kinds of evaluation required by the model. The first is context evaluation, which assesses needs, problems, opportunities, and objectives at different levels of the school district. The second is input evaluation, which searches for alternative plans and proposals and assesses whether their adoption would be likely to promote the meeting of needs at a reasonable cost. The third is process evaluation, which monitors a project or program, both to help guide implementation and to provide a record for determining the extent to which the program or project was implemented as designed. The fourth part of the model calls for product evaluation, which is an attempt to examine the value-added outcomes of a program and the extent to which they meet the needs of those being served. In Dallas, the CIPP model is used both to help implement priority change programs and to provide an accountability record.

Several districts noted various model combinations as their primary evaluation model. Fresno reported using a combination of CIPP, the Discrepancy Model, and General Accounting Office-Yellow Book models. Houston listed Decision Making, Behavioral Objectives, and Systems Analysis models. Detroit, Norfolk, and a number of other districts identified no one specific model.

STATE ACCOUNTABILITY SYSTEMS

In response to public pressure to improve student learning, most states have moved toward enhanced accountability systems, most of which establish standards for instruction, use either norm-referenced or criterion-referenced assessments to measure these standards, rate districts and schools on established standards, provide for some sort of sanctions, and require public reports of the results of the accountability system.

If state accountability systems are to be complete and valid, both content and performance standards must be clear. Moreover, the assessments must be valid measures of the attainment of the standards and especially of student progress. Multiple indicators must be clearly linked to the standards. Rewards must be used only to reinforce valid increases in achievement, and punishments must be used only to negatively reinforce valid decreases in achievement. Moreover, report cards must report valid assessments of school and student progress.

State Departments of Education have taken a leadership role in attempting to develop accountability models, particularly at the school and district level. As of 1995, 46 of 50 states had accountability systems that featured some type of assessment. Twenty-seven of these systems featured reports at the school, district, and state level; three featured school level reports only; six featured reports at both the school and district level; seven featured reports at the district and state level; two featured reports at the state level only; and one was currently under development (Council of Chief State School Officers, 1995). The authors conducted a January, 2002, Internet survey to update these statistics, which are reported later in the chapter.

When one reviews state accountability systems, there is little evidence of valid value-added systems being employed in that apparently only two states, South Carolina (May, 1990) and Tennessee (Sanders & Horn, 1995), have used value-added statistical methodology. North Carolina and Colorado are currently working on value-added components (W. L. Sanders, personal communication, January 2002). Most of the rest tend to evaluate students, not schools or districts, and generally cause more harm than good with systematic misinformation about the contributions of schools and districts to student academic accomplishments. By comparing schools on the basis of unadjusted student outcomes, state reports are often systematically biased against schools with population demographics that differ from the norm. In attempting to eliminate this bias, a number of states (e.g., Texas, California) have gone to non-statistical grouping techniques, an approach that has serious limitations when there is consistent one-directional variance on the grouping characteristics within groups.

In completing the following review, State accountability systems in all 50 states were considered, with a focus on eight states chosen because they had well-developed systems and represented the entire spectrum of accountability at the state level. The eight states were Alabama, California, Georgia, Kentucky, Massachusetts, New York, Tennessee, and Texas. (For more comprehensive examinations of the status of state accountability systems, see the Council of Chief State School Officers, 1995, 2000; Education Commission of the States, 1998; and Consortium for Policy Research in Education, 2000.)

Generally speaking, considerable variability exists in the completeness and validity of the various state accountability systems. The vast majority have an objectives orientation as opposed to a decision-making orientation to evaluation. Furthermore, at the present time, with the exception of Tennessee's accountability system, state accountability systems do not include legitimate value-added evaluation components and generally rely simply on cross-sectional analyses to measure school, district, and teacher impact on student learning.

Standards and Assessments

Many states have developed content and performance standards for each major discipline of instruction offered in their schools. Courses of study define the minimum required subject-area content in terms of what students should know and be able to do at the end of each grade or course. Courses included range from arts education, career/technical education, computer applications, driver education, language arts, foreign languages, health education, physical education, science, and social studies to the basic three Rs. As of 2002, of the 50 states, 45 have developed criterion-referenced tests to measure the attainment of their content standards while 27 use both criterion- and norm-referenced tests to assess school performance. Of the eight states studied in depth, all use criterion-referenced tests to measure at least a subset of developed standards, though six rely primarily on norm-referenced tests.

The State of Alabama relies primarily on a norm-referenced test in its accountability system. In keeping with legislation requiring the use of a norm-referenced test for assessing student achievement, Alabama uses the Stanford Achievement Test (SAT) to assess student achievement in the core subjects, because the test objectives match well its content and performance standards. The test is administered to students in grades 3–11 to assess concepts and skills in reading, mathematics, language, science, and social studies. State-developed tests based on writing standards in grades 5 and 7 are also administered. Moreover, it uses the Alabama High School Graduation Exam, which includes reading comprehension, language, mathematics, and science, to strengthen graduation requirements.

Kentucky uses its Commonwealth Accountability Testing System (CATS) to assess reading and science in grades 4, 7, 11, and 12; writing in grades 4, 7, and 12; and, social studies, mathematics, arts/humanities; and practical living/vocational studies in grades 5, 8, 11, and 12. It assesses proficiency in each of these content areas through various measures including open-response questions, multiple-choice questions, and writing portfolios.

Tennessee is implementing the Tennessee Comprehensive Assessment Program (TCAP), which uses both norm-referenced and criterion-referenced measures. Currently, the TCAP includes the following tests: the Achievement Test (an elementary achievement test), the Writing Test, the Competency Test, and the High School Subject Matter tests. End-of-course tests that will be aligned with specific curriculum objectives are also being developed.

The California Test Bureau developed the achievement test for grades 3–8, which measures basic skills in reading, vocabulary, language, language mechanics, mathematics, mathematics computation, science, social studies, and spelling. The Tennessee Comprehensive Assessment Program Competency Test for ninth-grade students measures skills in mathematics and language arts required for graduation. High school students take the High School Subject Matter Tests at the end of their Algebra, Geometry, and Mathematics for Technology courses. The TCAP Achievement Test is both norm-referenced and criterion-referenced. The TCAP Competency and High School Subject Matter Tests are criterion-referenced.

Classification Systems

Of the 50 states, 27 have a system for classifying schools on the basis of their performance levels. Of the eight states studied in depth, seven use a myriad of systems to classify schools and school systems, while one state has no classification system at this time.

Some examples follow. Schools or school systems in Alabama are classified as Academic Clear, Academic Caution, or Academic Alert. This classification is based on student scores on the *Stanford Achievement Test*. California uses three cut-points to create school, district, county, and state scores: the 25th, 50th, and 75th national percentiles on the Stanford Achievement Test.

With the exception of Title 1, Georgia does not have any set of acceptable levels of performance for schools, districts, or the state on any measures at this time.

Massachusetts reports criterion-referenced results on the Massachusetts Comprehensive Assessment System for individual students, schools, and districts according to four performance levels. The four levels are advanced, proficient, needs improvement, and failed. At the advanced level, students demonstrate a comprehensive understanding of rigorous subject matter and can solve complex problems. At the proficient level, students have full understanding of challenging subject matter and can solve various problems. At the needs improvement level, students have some understanding of the subject matter and can solve simple problems. At the failing level, students demonstrate minimal understanding of subject matter and cannot solve simple problems. School and district success is measured by the percentage of students achieving at each level of performance and by the number of students who move toward a higher level.

In rating school performance, New York identifies only schools that are farthest from state standards. In grades 4 and 8, the criterion for both English language arts and mathematics is 90 percent above the statewide performance benchmark. In grade 11, the criterion is 90 precent of the students in school who have met the graduation requirements in reading, writing, and mathematics. Moreover, a criterion of less than a 5 percent dropout rate is set.

Rewards and Sanctions

Of the 50 states, 17 provide rewards for student performance. Of the eight states studied, five provide rewards for student performance while three do not.

In California, the Governor's Performance Award Program provides monetary and non-monetary rewards to schools that meet or exceed pre-established growth rates and that demonstrate comparable improvement in academic achievement by numerically significant ethnic and socioeconomically disadvantaged subgroups.

Schools that fail to meet annual growth targets must hold a public hearing to announce their lack of progress. The local board of education may reassign staff, may negotiate site-specific amendments, and may opt for other appropriate measures. The Superintendent of Public Instruction (SPI) in California assumes all governing powers for any school that fails to meet performance goals and show significant growth in 24 months. The school's principal must be reassigned. Moreover, the SPI must attend to one of the following. It must allow students to attend other schools or allow the development of a charter school. Alternatively, it must assign the management of the school to another educational institution, reassign certified employees, renegotiate a new collective bargaining agreement, reorganize the school, or close the school.

Georgia has designed a pay for performance program to promote exemplary performance and collaboration at the school level. To attain an award, a school must develop a plan that identifies a comprehensive set of performance objectives in academic achievement, client involvement, educational programming, and resource development. For approval, the performance objectives must be exemplary and must have an impact on a significant portion of the school population.

Georgia's State Board of Education designates schools and school systems as standard, exemplary, and non-standard. It arrives at these designations based on the results of an evaluation of each school and school system conducted at least once every five years by educators from other school systems, universities, and citizens residing within the local system. Each school system that is designated as nonstandard or that operates one or more schools designated as nonstandard must submit a corrective action plan to the State Board of Education. The State Board of Education evaluates each school system designated as nonstandard two years after the Board has approved its plan.

If the Board determines that the system is making unsatisfactory progress, it may increase the school system's local fair share by an amount necessary to finance actions needed to correct identified deficiencies. Or it may require the school system to raise revenue from local sources to finance all actions needed to correct identified deficiencies. In a rather extreme provision, the Board may take civil action to determine whether any local school board member or school superintendent has by action or inaction prevented or delayed implementation of the corrective plan. If the court finds that any of these officials have prevented or delayed plan implementation, it may issue an order requiring the officials to implement the plan. If it finds that its order is not being carried out, the court may remove the official and appoint a replacement until the position can be filled by the normal process. The court also has the authority to appoint a trustee to ensure that its order is carried out.

Texas, in a more conventional approach than Georgia, has implemented the Texas Successful Schools Award System to provide for monetary awards to schools rated exemplary or recognized. A portion also is reserved for schools rated acceptable that have achieved significant gains in student performance, as measured by comparable improvement in the preceding year. Comparable improvement is determined by comparing a school's annual growth for matched students in reading and mathematics to the growth of 40 other schools with similar demographic characteristics.

The Commissioner of Education may take several actions if a district does not meet accreditation criteria. For example, he or she may appoint a management team to direct the operations of the district in areas of unacceptable performance or require the district to obtain such services under contract. The Commissioner may also appoint a board of managers to exercise the powers and duties of the board of trustees if the district has been rated academically unacceptable for at least one year. He or she may also annex the district to one or more adjoining districts, or in the case of home rule, request the State Board of Education to revoke the district's home-rule charter if the district has been rated academically unacceptable for a period of at least two years.

Indicators

Most (43) states use more than one indicator in their accountability system. Nonetheless, various assessments of student performance provide the major accountability indicator in 80 percent of states. Thirty-one of 50 states (62 percent) also use some form of dropout rate in their accountability systems while 27 (54 percent) use attendance rates, 17 (34 percent) consider graduation rates, 16 (32 percent) look at grade transition rates, and 12 (24 percent) look at American College Testing and Scholastic Achievement Test scores. In all cases, these variables are supplementary to various norm-referenced or criterion-referenced assessments. Thirteen states disaggregate data by various school and student demographics.

Report Cards

Of the 50 states, 45 require district level reports. All eight states that were studied in greater detail require districts to report the results of the accountability system to the public. All report cards are at the district or school level. To date, no state requires the public reporting of teacher performance data. Since school and district report cards best represent the products of state accountability systems, eight reporting mechanisms are briefly reviewed.

The Alabama State Superintendent of Education releases annual report cards on academic achievement for each school and school system. The purpose of these is to assess how school systems and individual schools are performing compared to other schools and systems in Alabama and to the national average. The report cards rate schools and school districts on indicators that include achievement, funding, teacher qualifications, and attendance.

California reports student, school, and district scores for subjects tested. It reports the national percentile ranking of the average student, the mean scaled score, and the breakdown of student scores by quartiles. Student, school, and district reports are distributed to districts. Districts must provide individual student reports to parents. Schools must notify parents of the purpose of the report cards and ensure that all parents receive a copy of the report card.

Georgia releases an annual state report card that provides information at the state, local system, and school levels. Test results are disaggregated by grade, school, and school district and are disseminated at the school and district levels. The results of the norm-referenced tests are disaggregated by free or reduced lunch status. The report cards are available on the Internet.

Kentucky requires local boards of education to publish in local newspapers an annual performance report on the district's accomplishments regarding its performance goals, including student performance and retention rates. The State Department of Education also publishes detailed information at the school, district, region, and state levels at the end of each biennium.

Massachusetts posts school and district profile results on its web site. It also provides these profiles to districts that, in turn, provide them to schools, which, in turn, provide them to parents. The profile results are disaggregated by regular students, students with disabilities, and students with limited English proficiency. The profiles include non-cognitive indicators such as pupil/teacher ratios, dropout rates, student exclusions, and the racial compositions of student bodies, special education student populations, limited English proficient student populations, and students eligible for free and reduced price lunch.

The New York State school report card shows how well students in each school and district are performing on state assessments, and provides detailed information on school attendance, suspension, dropout rates, and post-secondary education plans. The card disaggregates test scores for general education students and students with disabilities, and reports performance of LEP students on alternative measures of reading. It includes attendance rates, suspension rates, dropout rates, and total public expenditures per pupil.

Tennessee provides a home report that includes information for parents on their children's performance including percentile ranks, stanines, and mastery of objectives. The scores are broken down by school, grade, and subject, and include overall score and rate of improvement. The District report cards include information on accreditation, personnel data, waivers, class sizes, disaggregated enrollment, attendance rates, promotion rates, dropout rates, and expulsions/suspensions. It also includes competency test passing rates, Comprehensive Assessment results by grade, subject, percentile, and state showing two-year trends, and Comprehensive Assessment Program Value-added three-year average by grade span, subject, and state showing six-year trends in state gains versus national gains.

Texas has designed its Academic Excellence Indicator System (AEIS) to provide reports at the district and school levels on all performance. The base indicators used for accountability ratings are the Texas Assessment of Academic Skills (TAAS) percent passing rates in grades 3–8 and 10 for reading, writing, and mathematics, and dropout rates. A unique AEIS school report card is provided for each school. The school must then provide each student's family with information on TAAS performance, attendance rates, dropout rates, performance on college admissions examinations, end-of-course examination participation, student/teacher ratios, and administrative and instructional costs per student.

Value-Added Components

While a number of states attempt to include improvement statistics in their accountability systems, only one, Tennessee, currently includes a valid value-added component. The Tennessee Value-Added Assessment System (TVAAS) is a statistical process based on mixed model methodology that assesses the impact that districts, schools, and teachers have on student learning indicators (Sanders, 2000; Sanders & Horn, 1995). Through TVAAS, Tennessee attempts to provide unbiased estimates of the impact of district, school, and teacher variables on student achievement while controlling for differences in student context variables. Scale scores of students over a period of three to five years on norm-referenced items on the Tennessee Comprehensive Assessment Program are analyzed. The important idea is that, although students may not achieve at the same levels, districts, schools, and teachers should be, at a minimum, adding value to each student's performance.

Tennessee's TVAAS model is unique in comparison to other state accountability models in that it attempts to measure district, school, and teacher effects on student achievement gains while controlling for context, rather than simply identifying achievement scores at a single point in time, or examining unadjusted gain scores, or comparing "similar" schools and districts. By using adjusted gain scores, the TVAAS attempts to provide an equitable system for measuring district, school, and teacher impact so that teachers, schools, and districts are not penalized for the low academic entry characteristics of disadvantaged students. It makes allowances for teachers who work with low achieving students while still requiring them to help those students achieve.

Other states have attempted to incorporate improvement into their accountability systems. California has developed a new Academic Performance Indicator (API) and has attempted to establish growth targets as the basis of its state accountability system. The API, a composite index of multiple school indicators, is purported to provide a measure to rate the performance of all schools on the academic performance of their students. The indicators include the Stanford Achievement Test, a primary language test results for ESL students, high school exit exams, attendance rates, and graduation rates. Approximately 60 percent of the API is based on test results, while the remaining 40 percent is based on non-cognitive measures.

Kentucky plots average accountability scores against the years 2000 to 2014. The baseline score is the average of the school's accountability scores for years 1998–99 and 1999–2000. The line from the baseline point to the ideal index of 100 in 2014 is designated as the school's goal line. If the school is on or above this goal line every two years, it is eligible for rewards.

Both of these systems, although more sophisticated than other state systems, assume that comparable improvement can be established without going down to the individual student level and that reasonable goals can be established without empirical data.

CONCLUSION

We believe a number of disturbing trends are evident from the various surveys and literature reviews. First, it appears as if public school evaluation units have not prospered during the decade of the 1990s. In fact, evidence from the 1999 survey and from the quality and quantity of professional papers presented at major national research meetings by school district staff suggests that the status of evaluation in the public schools is far worse than it was in the 1980s. Part of this decline is probably due to states having taken over many of the assessment and accountability functions formerly assigned to district evaluation units. This is the second disturbing trend because most state accountability models appear to be extremely Tylerian, and only one features legitimate value-added components. Thus, we would have to conclude that the state of school system and state evaluation in the United States is not unlike the state of an endangered species. Evaluation activities to feed decisions have given way to an almost fanatical emphasis on accountability with little concern for fairness, validity, or professional standards.

At the local school district level, evaluation units have apparently fallen on hard times. Only three districts in the sample have maintained a growth level between 1979 and 1999 that is equivalent to that of the national economy. None of the $1,000,000 spenders in 1979 has done so. This decline in local evaluation efforts has severely hampered efforts to improve education since local evaluation units were the major sources of the vast majority of input and process evaluation that existed. Without adequate input and process evaluation, improvement is unlikely. The only expenditures that consistently increased across evaluation departments that had enough critical mass to accomplish anything were for testing. Thus, despite the fact that six of 20 responding school districts in 1999 stated that their principle evaluation model was CIPP, the evidence suggests that the resources to implement the input and process evaluation components of CIPP are not available. Lack of input and process evaluation would make it difficult to provide a base for understanding and subsequent suggestions for improvement. This, coupled with the almost complete lack of legitimate value-added methodology and the fact that only 18 percent of responding districts had any involvement in personnel evaluation, paints a dismal picture.

But what of state evaluation efforts? While local evaluation units have apparently foundered, state accountability systems have prospered. First, when referring to most existing state accountability systems, evaluation is a misnomer. They are at best accountability systems, and in many cases just assessment systems. If one incorporates the requirement that accountability systems must be fair to all stakeholders, then those systems must include valid value-added components. Incorporating this requirement reduces all state systems but Tennessee to the status of assessment systems.

Most state accountability and/or assessment systems have well developed standards and reporting systems as well as use multiple outcomes. While 80 percent of 50 state systems use assessment scores as a major part of their accountability systems, most (45) use additional indicators. Absolute standards are a necessary part of any accountability system. However, without a legitimate value-added component, these systems are biased against schools that serve high poverty ethnic and/or language minority students. Therefore, the lack of valid value-added components is particularly injurious to schools that serve those student populations when sanctions are applied as part of the system.

Most state systems rely on the definition of like schools in their comparable improvement efforts. Research extending over 12 years by the authors into value-added systems has convinced them that no two schools are exactly alike. In any matched group there are outliers or schools that are closer to schools in one group than in any other group but do not quite match. Matching, if it is to be done, must be done at the student level (Webster et al., 1997).

It would not be very complicated to fix most state systems so that they would meet fairness standards. Value-added systems can be constructed with a variety of similar methodologies, all of which provide preferable alternatives to systems based on unadjusted outcomes or on so-called comparable schools or class-rooms. (For discussions of value-added systems and related methodology see Bryk & Raudenbush, 1992; Darlington, 1990; Dempster, Rubin & Tsutakawa, 1981; Goldstein, 1987; Henderson, 1984; Laird & Ware, 1982; Mendro, Jordan, Gomez, Anderson, & Bembry, 1998; Mendro & Webster, 1993; Sanders & Horn, 1995; Sanders & Rivers, 1996; Webster, 2000, 2001a, 2001b; Webster, Mendro, & Almaguer, 1992, 1993, 1994; Webster, Mendro, Bembry, & Orsak, 1995; Webster, Mendro, Orsark, & Weerasinghe, 1996; Webster & Olson, 1988; Webster et al., 1997; Weerasinghe, Orsak, & Mendro,1997). The essence of all of these systems is to control for factors that are known to affect school outcomes but which are not under the control of the school as well as to focus on improvement. When these systems are designed properly, they offer the best chance of adjusting for effects of variables at the student level that are not explicitly included in the known factors. In other words, they help control to some extent all factors that are not under the control of schools.

During the decades of the 1970s and 1980s there was a great deal of discussion about a code of professional practice for evaluators. We believe that current prac-tice suggests that a code is badly needed, although we suspect that it is already too late. Once states became deeply involved in evaluation and accountability, politics began to play a much heavier role. Concepts such as validity, fairness, and equity have taken a back seat to political expediency. However, these concepts need to be raised to a paramount level so that teachers, students, administrators, and schools are not evaluated unfairly. At this point, this does not appear to be happening.

REFERENCES

Bryk, A.S., & Raudenbush, S.W. (1992). *Hierarchical linear models: Applications and data analysis methods.* Newbury Park: California: Sage.

Clopton, P., Bishop, W., & Klein, D. (2000). *Statewide mathematics assessment in Texas*. Retrieved from http://mathematicallvcorrect.com/lonestar.htm.

Consortium for Policy Research in Education. (2000). *Assessment and accountability in the fifty states: 1999–2000.* Washington, DC: Author.

Council of Chief State School Officers. (1995). *State education accountability reports and indicator reports: Status of reports across the states*. Washington, DC: Author.

Council of Chief State School Officers. (2000). *State education accountability systems*. Washington, DC: Author.

Cronbach, L.J. (1963). Course improvement through evaluation. *Teachers College Record*, **64**, 672–683.

Darlington, R.B. (1990). *Regression and linear models*. New York: McGraw-Hill.

Dempster, A.P., Rubin, D.B., & Tsutakawa, R.V. (1981). Estimation in covariance components models. *Journal of the American Statistical Association*, **76**, 341–353.

Education Commission of the States. (1998). *Accountability indicators*. Denver, CO: Author.

Goldstein, H. (1987). *Multilevel models in educational and social research*. New York: Oxford University Press.

Henderson, C.R. (1984). *Applications of linear models in animal breeding*. Guelph, Canada: University of Guelph.

Jaeger, R.M. (1992). Weak measurement serving presumptive policy. *Phi Delta Kappan*, **74**, 118–128.

Joint Committee on Standards for Educational Evaluation. (1981). *Standards for evaluations of educational programs, projects, and materials*. New York: McGraw-Hill.

Joint Committee on Standards for Educational Evaluation. (1988). *The personnel evaluation standards*. Newbury Park, CA: Sage.

Joint Committee on Standards for Educational Evaluation. (1994). *The program evaluation standards: How to assess evaluations of educational programs*. Thousand Oaks, CA: Sage.

Jordan, H.R., Bembry, K.L., & Mendro, R.L. (1998, April). *Longitudinal teacher effects on student achievement and their relation to school and project evaluation*. Paper presented at the annual meeting of the American Educational Research Association, San Diego, CA.

Jordan, H.R., Mendro, R.L., & Weerasinghe, D. (1997, July). *Teacher effects on longitudinal student achievement: A preliminary report on research on teacher effectiveness*. Paper presented at the CREATE National Evaluation Institute, Indianapolis, IN.

Laird, N.M., & Ware, H. (1982). Random-effects models for longitudinal data. *Biometrics*, **38**, 963–974.

May, J. (1990). Real world considerations in the development of an effective school incentive program. (ERIC Document Reproduction Services No. ED320271.)

Mendro, R.L., Jordan, H.R., Gomez, E., Anderson, M.C., & Bembry, K.L. (1998, April). *Longitudinal teacher effects on student achievement and their relation to school and project evaluation*. Paper presented at the annual meeting of the American Educational Research Association, San Diego, CA.

Mendro, R.L., & Webster, W.J. (1993, October). *Using school effectiveness indices to identify and reward effective schools*. Paper presented at the Rocky Mountain Research Association, Las Cruces, NM.

Sanders, W.L. (2000, July). *Value-added assessment from student achievement data: Opportunities and hurdles*. Paper presented at the CREATE National Evaluation Institute, San Jose, CA.

Sanders, W.L., & Horn, S.P. (1995). The Tennessee Value-Added Assessment System (TVAAS): Mixed model methodology in educational assessment. In A.J. Shinkfield, & D.L. Stufflebeam (Eds.), *Teacher evaluation: A guide to effective practice* (pp. 337–350). Boston: Kluwer Academic Publishers.

Sanders, W.L., & Rivers, J.C. (1996). *Cumulative and residual effects of teachers on future student academic achievement*. Knoxville, TN: University of Tennessee.

Scriven, M.S. (1967). The methodology of evaluation. In R. Tyler, R. Gagne, & M. Scriven (Eds), Perspectives of curriculum evaluation (pp. 39–83). *AERA Monograph Series on Curriculum Evaluation, No. 1*. Chicago, Ill: Rand McNally.

Smith, E.R., & Tyler, R.W. (1942). *Appraising and recording student progress*. New York: Harper.

Stake, R.E. (1967). The countenance of educational evaluation. *Teachers College Record*, **68**, 523–540.

Stufflebeam, D.L. (1966). A depth study of the evaluation requirement. *Theory Into Practice*, **5**, 121–134.

Stufflebeam, D.L., Foley, W.J., Gephart, W.J., Guba, E.G., Hammond, R.L., Merriman, H.O., & Provus, M.N. (1971). *Educational evaluation and decision-making*. Itasca, IL: Peacock.

Stufflebeam, D.L., & Webster, W.J. (1980). An analysis of alternative approaches to evaluation. *Educational Evaluation and Policy Analysis*, **2**, 5–20.

Webster, W.J. (1977, September). *Sensible school district evaluation*. Invited address presented at the evaluation conference of the American Educational Research Association. San Francisco, CA.

Webster, W.J. (2000, July). *A value-added application of hierarchical linear modeling to the estimation of school and teacher effect*. Invited paper presented at the First Annual Assessment Conference of the Council of Great City Schools. Portland, OR.

Webster, W.J. (2001a, April). *An application of two-stage multiple linear regression and hierarchical linear modeling to the estimation of school and teacher effect*. Paper presented at the annual meeting of the American Educational Research Association, Seattle.

Webster, W.J. (2001b, April). *A comprehensive school and personnel evaluation system*. Paper presented at the annual meeting of the American Educational Research Association, Seattle.

Webster, W.J., Mendro, R.L., & Almaguer, T. (1992, April). *Measuring the effects of schooling: Expanded school effectiveness indices*. Paper presented at annual meeting of the American Educational Research Association, San Francisco.

Webster, W.J., Mendro, R.L., & Almaguer, T.D. (1993). *Effectiveness indices: The major component of an equitable accountability system*. ERIC TM 019 193.

Webster, W.J., Mendro, R.L., & Almaguer, T. (1994). Effectiveness indices: A "value added" approach to measuring school effect. *Studies in Educational Evaluation*, **20**, 113–145.

Webster, W.J., Mendro, R.L., Bembry, K.L., & Orsak, T.H. (1995, April). *Alternative methodologies for identifying effective schools*. Paper presented at annual meeting of the American Educational Research Association, San Francisco.

Webster, W.J., Mendro, R.L., Orsak, T.H., & Weerasinghe, D. (1996, April). *The applicability of selected regression and hierarchical linear models to the estimation of school and teacher effects*. Paper presented at annual meeting of the American Educational Research Association, New York.

Webster, W.J., Mendro, R.L., Orsak, T.H., & Weerasinghe, D. (1997). A comparison of the results produced by selected regression and hierarchical linear models in the estimation of school and teacher effect. *Multiple Linear Regression Viewpoints*, **1**, 28–65.

Webster, W.J., & Olson, G.H. (1988). A quantitative procedure for the identification of effective schools. *Journal of Experimental Education*, **56**, 213–219.

Webster, W.J., & Stufflebeam, D.L. (1978, March). *The state of the art in educational evaluation*. Invited address presented at the annual meeting of the American Educational Research Association, Toronto.

Weerasinghe, D., Orsak, T., & Mendro, R. (1997, January). *Value added productivity indicators: A statistical comparison of the pre-test/post-test model and gain model*. Paper presented at 1997 annual meeting of the Southwest Educational Research Association, Austin, TX.

42
International Studies of Educational Achievement

TJEERD PLOMP
University of Twente, Faculty of Educational Science and Technology, Enschede, The Netherlands

SARAH HOWIE
University of Pretoria, Department of Teaching and Training, Pretoria, South Africa

BARRY McGAW
Centre for Educational Research and Innovation, Paris, France

International studies of educational achievements have been conducted since the early 1960s. According to Husén and Tuijnman (1994, p. 6), such an empirical approach in comparative education was made possible by developments in sample survey methodology, group testing techniques, test development, and data analysis. A group of American and European scholars conducted a pilot study from 1959 to 1961 to examine the feasibility of using achievement tests administered to comparable samples of students in cross-national studies to measure the "yield" of educational systems. Key questions were whether it would be possible to develop an appropriate methodology for testing and for processing and analysing data in such a way that meaningful cross national comparisons could be made. Answers from the feasibility study were sufficiently encouraging to lead to the establishment of the International Association for the Evaluation of Educational Achievement (IEA) which conducted the first large-scale international study of educational (mathematics) achievement (Husén, 1967).

Following that study, IEA has conducted surveys in a variety of school subjects (see IEA, 1998). Until the 1980s, the studies were driven by the interest of researchers. However, in the 1980s, as a consequence of the oil crisis and other structural problems in our societies and due to the media attention that comparative studies attracted, policymakers began to develop an interest in, and a concern for, the quality and the cost-effectiveness of education. This can be illustrated by the frequently cited quotation from the report, *A Nation At Risk: The Imperative for Educational Reform* (US National Commission on Excellence in Education, 1983), on the quality of education in the U.S.A. (in which results from the IEA Second International Mathematics Study were used to demonstrate the relatively poor international standing of US school education):

International Handbook of Educational Evaluation, 951–978
T. Kellaghan, D.L. Stufflebeam (eds.)
© *2003 Dordrecht: Kluwer Academic Publishers. Printed in Great Britain.*

> If an unfriendly foreign power had attempted to impose on America the mediocre educational performance that exists today, we might well have viewed it as an act of war. As it stands, we have allowed this to happen to ourselves .... We have, in effect, been committing an act of unthinking, unilateral educational disarmament. (p. 5)

The interest of policymakers in cost-effectiveness and the quality of education (instead of just managing the quantitative growth of educational systems) also became manifest at a meeting of Ministers of Education of Organisation for Economic and Cultural Development (OECD) countries in 1984 (Husén & Tuijnman, 1994; Kellaghan, 1996) following which interest in internationally comparable indicators developed rapidly. Meanwhile, the IEA continued its studies of student achievement levels, and the American National Assessment of Educational Progress (NAEP) extended its activities in two International Assessment of Educational Progress (IAEP) surveys. The OECD commenced more general work on indicators of important characteristics of educational systems, relating to demographic and financial factors as well as educational outcomes, drawing from the IEA surveys and data on various labor market outcomes, in its publication, *Education at a Glance* (OECD, 1992, 1993, 1995, 1996, 1997, 1998, 2000). The increased interest of policymakers is also illustrated in the initiative of a number of Ministries of Education in the Southern African sub-region and of UNESCO in 1991 to establish the Southern African Consortium for Monitoring Educational Quality (SACMEQ), with the purpose of applying survey research techniques to study issues relating to the improvement of the quality of education, as well as by the decision of the OECD, in the second half of the 1990s, to conduct international comparative achievement studies in its Programme for International Student Assessment (PISA) (see, e.g., Schleicher, 2000).

This chapter discusses issues relating to the conceptualization, design, and conduct of international comparative achievement studies. First, a number of purposes and functions of such studies are summarised. This is followed by a description of some organizations that have been active in this area and of their studies. Some conceptual issues related to such studies are then presented, before discussing some important design and methodological issues. The last section of the chapter provides some examples of the impact of this type of study, and also considers some criticisms of the work.

PURPOSES AND FUNCTIONS OF INTERNATIONAL COMPARATIVE ACHIEVEMENT STUDIES

International studies of educational achievement usually have multiple purposes, such as to compare levels of national achievement between countries; to identify the major determinants of national achievement, country by country, and to examine to what extent they are the same or differ across countries; and to identify factors that affect differences between countries (Postlethwaite, 1999, p. 12).

Ways in which the results of international comparative studies might be used and impact on educational policy and practice have been described (Kellaghan, 1996; Plomp, 1998). First, descriptive comparisons with other countries might serve to identify particular aspects of a national system that could be considered problematic because they are out of line with what is found in other countries (e.g., the content of the curriculum, achievement levels of students). This "mirror" function is considered by many to be interesting in itself and may lead to decisions to take some kind of action to remedy a particular deficiency. It can be of particular value when the comparisons are made with other countries of special interest, such as "cultural" neighbours or economic competitors.

Second, and one step further than benchmarking, is monitoring, which involves the assessment of educational processes at different levels in the educational system with the purpose of making informed decisions about change when and where it is needed. A cycle of regular assessments in the subject areas that are being monitored to provide trend data is needed to do this. Both the IEA and the OECD value this function, and are committed to cycles of studies in mathematics, science, and reading literacy.

Third, findings of international studies can contribute to our understanding of differences between or within educational systems, which should be helpful in making decisions about the organization of schooling, the deployment of resources, and the practice of teaching (Kellaghan, 1996). This was an important consideration in discussions of standard setting in education. In the U.S.A. for example, the initiative of the National Council for the Teaching of Mathematics (NCTM) in developing standards for the teaching of mathematics was a reaction to the poor performance of American students in the IEA Second International Mathematics Study (SIMS).

Fourth, variation between educational systems revealed in international comparative studies can be taken as a starting point for research ("the world as a laboratory") leading to a better understanding of the factors that contribute to the effectiveness of education. An example is the analysis by Postlethwaite & Ross (1992) of the IEA Reading Literacy database (for which data were collected in 1990–91) in an effort to find indicators that discriminated between more effective and less effective schools in reading. Keeves (1995) also has identified, on the basis of all IEA studies conducted until 1994, ten key findings with suggested implications for educational planning.

Finally, international, comparative achievement studies also serve to promote general "enlightenment". In this case, there is not a direct link to decisions, but rather a gradual diffusion of ideas into the sphere of organizational decision making (see Kellaghan,1996, with reference to Weiss, 1981). In this view, the findings of international studies may contribute to clarifying policymakers' assumptions about what schools try to achieve, what they actually achieve, and what it is possible to achieve, as well as to enriching public discussion about education (Husén & Tuijnman, 1994). The OECD *Education at a Glance* series has certainly served as a catalyst for such discussion, and Robitaille, Beaton, and Plomp (2000) have reported on the extensive public discussions about the IEA

Third International Mathematics and Science Study (TIMSS) in participating countries.

In addition to the general purposes of international comparative studies, there are some additional benefits that pertain more to developing or less developed countries. These additional benefits may be divided into four areas (see Howie, 2000). First, international studies (e.g., SACMEQ and IEA) contribute substantially to the development of research capacity in developing countries. TIMSS significantly developed the capacity in South Africa (and in other countries) to undertake large-scale surveys involving assessment. In nine African countries, SACMEQ has made a particular contribution to developing the capacity of ministerial staff. Researchers have been introduced to the latest research methods and were provided with substantial training and assistance in their use throughout the research process.

Second, these studies present an opportunity for developing countries to collect baseline data in certain subject areas, where previously there was a vacuum. Third, establishing a national baseline through an international study heightens awareness of what other countries around the world are doing, and points to lessons that can be drawn from them. For example, TIMSS was the first international educational research project in which South Africa participated after years of political and academic isolation, providing the first opportunity to review and compare data from South Africa with those of other countries. The disappointing result of this comparison led the then Minister for Education to announce, during a parliamentary debate, that his department would review the data in order to design new curricula to be introduced by 2005. Finally, education jostles for attention with many other needs in developing countries (e.g., health, poverty, HIV/AIDS, rural development). In this context, the fact that the results of international and not merely national studies are available assists researchers, practitioners, and policymakers to highlight priorities.

ORGANIZATIONS AND STUDIES

Several international organizations publish educational indicators; however, only a few (IEA, OECD, and SACMEQ) actually organize and help manage international comparative achievement studies. All three are described in this section.

International Association for the Evaluation of Educational Achievement (IEA)

The International Association for the Evaluation of Educational Achievement (IEA) is a nongovernmental organization which has conducted international comparative studies of educational achievement in the context of the many variables that determine how teaching and learning take place in schools. Members of the IEA are research institutes and ministries of education. By the year 2000, about 55 countries (or educational systems) were members.

IEA's mission is to contribute through its studies to enhancing the quality of education. Its international comparative studies have two main purposes: to provide policymakers and educational practitioners with information about the quality of their education in relation to relevant reference countries and to assist participating countries in understanding the reasons for observed differences within and between educational systems. In line with these two purposes, IEA strives in its studies for two kinds of comparisons. The first consists of straight international comparisons of the effects of education in terms of scores (or subscores) on international tests. The second focuses on the extent to which a country's intended curriculum (what should be taught in a particular grade) is implemented in schools and is attained by students. The latter kind of comparison focuses mainly on national analyses of a country's results in an international comparative context. As a consequence, most IEA studies are curriculum-driven. An analysis of the curricula of participating countries and the development of achievement tests are the starting points of the design of a study.

Over the years, IEA has conducted studies in major school subjects, such as mathematics, science, written composition, reading comprehension, foreign languages, and civics education. The studies have also covered non-curricular areas, such as classroom environments, preprimary education, and computers in education.

Postlethwaite (1999) has distinguished four phases in IEA's existence up to the year 2000. The first mathematics study in the early 1960s, which was conducted to explore the feasibility of international comparative achievement studies, can be regarded as Phase 1. Phase 2, covering the period until the late 1970s, consists of the six-subject study, a huge endeavor which comprised six parallel surveys in science, literature, reading comprehension, French and English as foreign languages, and civic education. Phase 3, covering the 1980s, consists of a number of single subject studies, two of which were repeat studies in (mathematics and science), and five new studies (classroom environment, computers in education, written composition, reading literacy, and preprimary education). IEA reached its fourth phase at the end of the 1990s with the Third International Mathematics and Science Study (TIMSS), while in the same decade the second civics education study and the Second International Technology in Education Study (SITES) commenced. More information about the IEA can be found in the IEA guidebook (IEA, 1998) and on its Web site: www.iea.nl.

IEA's most prominent study has been TIMSS, which was conducted between 1992 and 1999. The study was designed to assess students' achievements in mathematics and science in the context of the national curricula, instructional practices and social environment of students. It focused on 9-year-old (population 1), 13-year-old (population 2), and final year of secondary school (population 3) students. Data were collected in 1994 and 1995. The achievement testing in populations 1 and 2 and part of population 3 was based on an analysis of the curricula in mathematics and science of participating countries. The other component of the testing in population 3 pertained to mathematical and science literacy of students at the end of secondary education. Data on students, teachers, and schools, as well as on classroom processes, were collected through questionnaires completed by students, mathematics and science teachers, and school principals.

Testing was carried out in more than 40 countries and at five grade levels (3rd, 4th, 7th, 8th, and final year of secondary school). More than half a million of students in more than 15,000 schools responded in more than 30 languages. There were nearly 1,000 open-ended questions, generating millions of student responses in the assessment. Provision was made for performance assessments and for questionnaires containing about 1,500 questions to be completed by students, teachers, and school principals (see, e.g., Beaton, Martin et al., 1996; Beaton, Mullis et al., 1996; Mullis et al., 1997; Mullis et al., 1998; Martin et al., 1997; and International Study Center, 2002).

Students in Asian countries were the highest performers in mathematics and science. In most countries, gender differences in mathematics achievement were minimal or nonexistent, whereas in science boys outperformed girls. Home factors were strongly related to achievement in every participating country.

TIMSS was repeated for population 2 in 1998 and 1999 in 38 countries in Europe, Africa, North and South America, Asia and Australasia (see Martin et al., 2000; Mullis et al., 2000; International Study Center, 2002) and will be continued in a regular cycle as "Trends In Mathematics and Science Education Study," with further data collection in 2002 and 2003.

Organisation for Economic Co-operation and Development (OECD)

The Organisation for Economic Co-operation and Development (OECD) has 30 member countries in Europe, North America, and the Asia-Pacific region, but works in a variety of ways with many other countries. Membership requires a country's commitment to a market economy and a pluralist democracy. OECD provides governments with a setting in which to discuss and develop economic and social policy. In some cases, their exchanges may lead to agreements to act in a formal way but, more often, the benefit lies in national policy development, informed through reflection and exchange with other countries.

In the late 1980s, OECD member countries decided to reorient work on education statistics to build comparative indicators of education systems in the belief that "comparisons of educational indicators can offer information useful for deciding if, and where, educational reform may be needed. In turn, the desire to reform and improve education hinges on perceptions about the economic importance of education and the belief that education is a productive and long-term investment" (Bottani & Tuijnman, 1994, p. 54). The results of this work have been published under the title *Education at a Glance*, the first issue of which appeared in 1992, and the seventh in 2000; it is now established as an annual publication. Indicators in the report focus on system context and performance, and cover the demographic, social, and economic context, financial and human resources invested in education, education participation and completion rates, educational processes, aspects of public expectations, and educational and labor market outcomes.

Indicators of educational achievement included in *Education at a Glance* to date have been drawn from studies of IEA and IAEP (International Assessment of Educational Progress conducted in the 1980s). In the mid-1990s, OECD countries began consideration of managing their own systematic collection of student achievement data and, in 1997, decided to implement the Programme of International Student Assessment (PISA), which is designed to produce policy-oriented and internationally comparable indicators of student achievement on a regular three-year basis. The focus will be on 15-year-olds, which is in many countries the end of compulsory schooling, and the indicators are designed to contribute to an understanding of the extent to which education systems in participating countries are preparing their students to become lifelong learners and to play constructive roles as citizens in society (Schleicher, 2000, pp. 63–64).

PISA covers three substantive domains: reading literacy, mathematical literacy, and scientific literacy. Unlike the IEA surveys, it does not commence with a survey of the curricula in participating countries to identify common components as the focus for assessment. Rather an assessment framework for each domain is structured to reflect important knowledge and skills that students will need in adult life. The primary question is not whether students have learned what the curriculum prescribes but whether they can use it. In the successive three-yearly cycles of PISA, each of these domains will be accorded the major focus, with about two-thirds of the testing time being devoted to it. In the first cycle, for which data were collected in 2000, the major domain was reading (OECD, 2001). In 2003, the major domain will be mathematics, and, in 2006, science. In 2009, the primary focus will return to reading.

PISA also assesses cross-curricular competencies. In the first cycle, assessments of ICT literacy and capacity to self-regulate and manage learning were developed as options for countries. Information on both was obtained by self-reports in questionnaires completed by students. In this cycle, 21 countries took up the option on ICT literacy and 19 the option on self-regulated learning. In the second cycle, problem solving will be added as a broad cross-curricular competence, but also as a special focus in the mathematics assessment. For the third cycle, it is intended to include a more direct assessment of ICT literacy.

The fundamental difference between IEA and OECD studies is in the strength of the focus on national curricula. Both approaches carry risks of the differential validity of their assessment instruments when used across countries. In the IEA approach, there is a risk that the common curriculum components that provide the focus for the tests will be a more substantial part of the curriculum in some countries than in others and, conversely, that what is not assessed, because it is unique to one or more countries, will occupy more of the available curriculum time in some countries than in others. To check on coverage, the IEA typically gathers information from teachers on students' opportunity to learn the material covered in each question and, not surprisingly, the measure is significantly related to students' achievement levels. For OECD, the focus on students' ability by age 15 to use what they have learned in each of the substantive domains runs the risk of advantaging countries for which the curriculum itself contains this kind of emphasis. Many of the OECD countries that collaborated in the design of PISA had substantial prior experience of IEA studies and ongoing involvement in them. They deliberately decided on PISA's focus on "preparedness for adult life" because they believed that:

> a focus on curriculum content would, in an international setting, restrict attention to curriculum elements common to all, or most, countries. This would force many compromises and result in an assessment that was too narrow to be of value for governments wishing to learn about the strengths and innovations in the education systems of other countries (Schleicher, 2000, p. 6).

They believed that a focus on students' capacity to use the knowledge and skills that they have acquired in childhood in situations they could encounter in adult life would provide the kind of outcome measures "needed by countries which want to monitor the adequacy of their education systems in a global context" (Schleicher, 2000, p. 77). Samples of the questions of the kind used in PISA 2000 are provided at http://www.pisa.oecd.org.

Like the IEA studies, PISA is a substantial activity. There were 31 countries involved, three which are not members of OECD. More than 10 additional non-OECD countries are planning to gather data in 2002 with the PISA 2000 instruments. In 2000, more than 180,000 students in over 7000 schools participated, using 26 languages. The assessment included more than 200 items of which about one-third were open-ended. Questionnaire responses were sought from all participating students as well as from participating school principals, on matters relating to family background, familiarity with technology, cross-curricular competencies, and the learning environment at school (OECD, 2001).

Southern Africa Consortium for Monitoring Educational Quality (SACMEQ)

A number of Ministries of Education in the Southern Africa Sub-region have worked together since 1991 to address the need for systematic studies of the conditions of schooling and of student achievement levels. The focus of this work has been to establish long-term strategies for building the capacity of educational planners to monitor and evaluate basic education systems (see Ross et al., 2000).

SACMEQ's mission is to undertake integrated research and training activities that will expand opportunities for educational planners to gain the technical skills required to monitor, evaluate, and compare the general conditions of schooling and the quality of basic education; and to generate information that can be used by decision makers to plan the quality of education in their countries. To meet these aims, the first two SACMEQ projects (SACMEQ I and SACMEQ II) focused on an assessment of the conditions of schooling and the quality of education. SACMEQ I, which commenced in 1995 and was completed in 1998, was the first educational policy research project conducted by the consortium. Seven Ministries of Education participated (Kenya, Malawi, Mauritius, Namibia, Tanzania/Zanzibar, Zambia, and Zimbabwe). Each country prepared a national educational policy report, the final chapter of which provides a meta-analysis of policy suggestions, grouped in five main themes: consultations with staff, community, and experts; reviews of existing planning procedures; data collections for planning purposes; educational policy research projects; and investment in infrastructure and human resources. The first five reports that were published in 1998 have featured in presidential and national commissions on education, education sector studies and reviews of education master plans, and had considerable impact. For example, in Namibia, the SACMEQ project provided the first study of major regional differences in the quality of education across the country, while in Kenya an important impact has been the acknowledgement by the Ministry of Education of the need to employ SACMEQ-style research approaches for databases used for planning purposes (see Ross et al., 2000).

SACMEQ II, for which SACMEQ I will provide baseline information, commenced in mid-1998 and collected data in late 2000.

CONCEPTUALIZING INTERNATIONAL COMPARATIVE ACHIEVEMENT STUDIES

All organizations involved in international comparative achievement studies aim to provide policymakers with data that will assist them in evaluating and monitoring the quality and effectiveness of their educational systems. Typically, all studies collect data about what can be monitored in education: *inputs* into schools, *processes* within schools, and *outcomes* of schooling. Postlethwaite (1994) provides examples of indicators for all three categories that might be of interest to ministries of education.

However, there are also differences between studies. The IEA pursues explicit research goals in addition to its interest in policy issues. In part, this reflects its origins as the creation of a group of researchers seeking to bring a quantitative dimension to comparative educational research. The policy interest in IEA studies reflects both the interest of researchers in policy and the growing engagement of governments in the funding and governance of IEA. The IEA uses an overarching framework for most of its studies, primarily to guide its research goals, including relational analyses.

In contrast, the OECD work on indicators operates with a broader agenda within which the focus of PISA is essentially similar to that of the IEA studies, except for the difference in definition of outcomes already discussed. The general indicator framework provides a logical and sequential arrangement of components without an explicit specification of relational analyses that might be investigated with the indicators, most of which provide information at the level of national systems. With PISA, however, data on both outcomes and context are gathered at the student level to permit extensive exploration of relationships between achievement and contextual conditions which could be altered or have their effects ameliorated by policy changes.

Organizing Framework Proposed by the OECD

For its broad indicator work, the OECD has used an organizing framework for the set of indicators produced for publication in *Education at a Glance* (OECD, 1992 1993, 1995, 1996, 1997, 1998, 2000). The indicators have been organised in three categories, as displayed in Figure 1 (summarized from Bottani & Tuijnman, 1994; Fig. 3.1, p. 53). These categories represent three principal divisions: context information ("contexts of education"), input and process indicators ("costs, resources and school processes"), and outcome indicators ("results of education").

In 1999, in documents adopted by the OECD Education Committee, the framework was expressed in terms of five broad areas: basic contextual variables that can be considered important moderators of educational outcomes; the financial and human resources invested in education; access to education and learning, participation, progression and completion; the learning environment and organization of schools; and the individual, social, and labor market outcomes of education and transition from school to work.

Neither of the frameworks provides a conceptual model that shows or hypothesizes how the components of the educational system (inputs, processes, outputs) are linked or that aims to provide a model for relational analyses between variables (or indicators). What is offered is an array of data agreed by national representatives and readily available for analysis by third parties. In each edition,

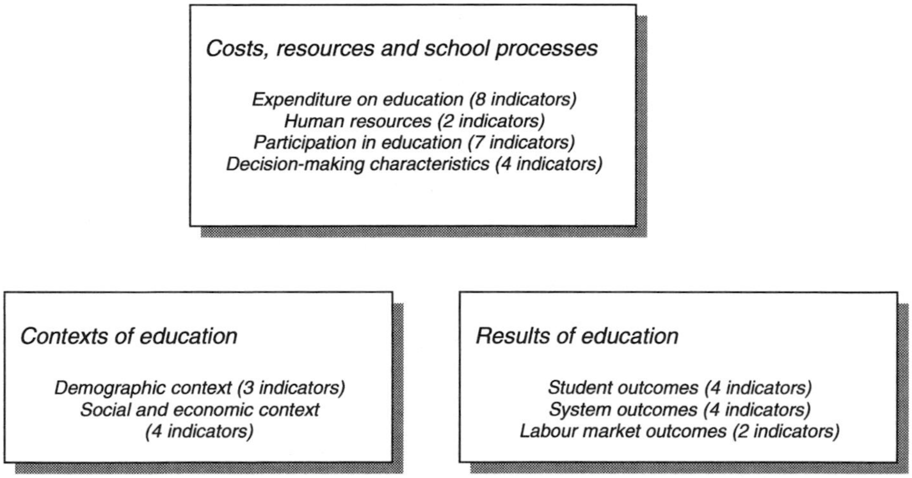

Figure 1:   Organizing Framework for education indicators proposed by the OECD (Bottani & Tuijnman, 1994, p. 53)

about one-third of the indicators are stable over time in content and presentation, about one-third are stable in content but variable in data source, and about a third are new. About half focus on outcomes, including education and labor market outcomes for both young people and adults. About half, particularly among those dealing with outcomes, provide a perspective on in-country variations.

PISA opens a quite different window on educational systems, in much the way that the IEA studies do, with detailed data on student achievement at the individual level, and on background characteristics of home and school with which complex relationships can be explored. The nature of these investigations was planned at the time at which the survey was designed to ensure that relevant information was obtained through the various school and student questionnaires. These reports will explore issues such as the relationship between social background and achievement, with particular attention to ways in which the relationship might vary across countries, gender differences in achievement, attitudes and motivation, school factors related to quality, and equity and the organisation of learning.

Conceptual Framework of the IEA

Over the past 40 years, IEA has applied large-scale research methods through (with a few exceptions) a curriculum-based, explanatory design, that has varied in form and content across studies. The generic IEA conceptual framework is summarized in Figure 2. A difference in research goals becomes apparent when this framework is compared with the indicator-type framework of Figure 1. In IEA, curricula are examined at the system level (intended curricula), school/classroom level (implemented curricula) and at the individual student level (attained curricula). Curricular antecedents (such as background characteristics and school and home resources) can be investigated in relation to curricular contexts to predict curriculum content outcomes. Such a design also enables the development and refinement of predictive models, which utilize data collected at teacher and student level into one conceptual model that includes background influences on schooling, school processes, and student outcomes. Although each individual IEA study develops its own conceptual framework, these typically do not include specifications of indicators, but remain on a more general level directed by the IEA's curriculum-driven underpinning.

To conduct relational analyses, it is necessary to specify explicitly what factors are thought to influence educational achievement. An example of a model that shows how the elements of an educational system are linked, and that provides lists of variables as the basis for operationalizing such factors, is provided by Shavelson, McDonnell & Oakes (1989, p. 14) (see Figure 3). Although the model was not the basis for an international study per se, it was used to inform the conceptualization of relational analyses in studies such as those of IEA.

A further concern regarding the conceptualization and design of indicator frameworks is reflected by Bottani and Tuijnman (1994), when they state that

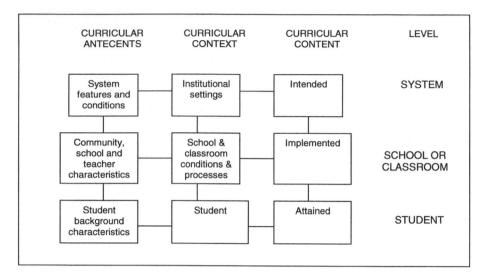

Figure 2:   Model of an IEA Research Study (IEA, 1998, p. 53; Travers & Westbury, 1989)

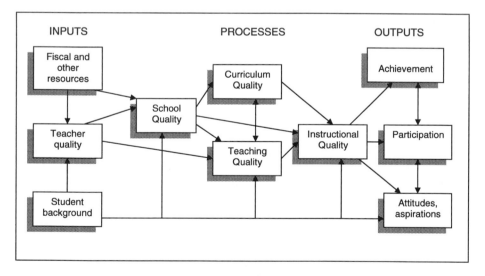

Figure 3:   Linking elements of the educational system (Shavelson et al., 1989, p. 14)

"insufficient attention has so far been paid to the analytical perspective in the design of indicator systems" and that "questions such as how indicators are inter-related and what predictive power they have are rarely addressed systematically" (p. 48). That is largely true of the general OECD indicator work published in *Education at a Glance*, but this is by design. There has been deliberate resistance to the adoption of an overall theoretical framework on the grounds that no adequate framework has been defined, and that to adopt a less than adequate one would unnecessarily and unhelpfully constrain the coverage of the indicators. For large-scale international surveys of student achievement, it is clearly less true, though it can be noted that the general model that has guided IEA studies for more than 30 years has not been much altered by the substantial bodies of evidence generated by successive studies. It would appear that, while great progress has been made in technical and methodological developments, few developments have appeared in the conceptual frameworks that underpin the research being carried out.

Could this stagnation be a result of an increasing pressure for policy-driven research where relatively quick answers are sought to practical questions in preference to reflection on what has already been done and what needs to be in the future to clarify more conceptual and theoretical questions? Howson (1999) claims that most large-scale studies have used an inductive framework, with hypotheses often generated post-hoc for exploration with data already collected, rather then being specified in advance following a "hypothetico-deductive" model. That is not altogether fair with respect to either the IEA studies or PISA, in both of which the design of background questionnaires was guided largely by the research questions to be addressed with the data, in the fashion commended by Shorrocks-Taylor and Jenkins (2000). In the case of PISA, detailed elaborations of planned analytical reports were prepared in advance of the finalization of the background questionnaire to ensure that the required data would be obtained.

DESIGN AND METHODOLOGY

Given their aims and scope, international studies of educational achievement are complex. Kellaghan (1996) specifies a number of conditions for such studies. Next to a number of conditions to increase the relevance of such studies for policy-makers (see below under research questions), he also mentions a few referring to the design of studies such as accurately representing what students achieve, permitting valid comparisons, having clear purposes, and justifying the resources needed to conduct them. To meet these quality demands, careful design, planning and monitoring are needed. This section will first discuss the phases that can be recognized in the design of this type of study, after which a few other conditions for a good study will be addressed.

Design of International Comparative Achievement Studies

IEA (Martin et al., 1999; IEA, 2002) and others (e.g. Westat, 1991) have developed standards for conducting international studies of achievement. These are applied during the study and regular checks are required to ensure that the study proceeds according to the standards. Nowadays, many studies do have well documented and detailed procedures for quality monitoring. For PISA, OECD has produced detailed technical standards, revised for PISA 2003 in the light of experience with PISA 2000 and covering sampling, translation, test administration, quality monitoring, and data coding and entry (see PISA's Web site: http//www.pisa.oecd.org). Other reference works, such as the *International Encyclopedia of Education* (Husén & Postlethwaite, 1994), the IEA technical handbook (Keeves, 1992), and the *International Encyclopedia of Educational Evaluation* (Keeves, 1996) provide many excellent sources for the design and conduct of such studies.

International comparative studies of educational achievement usually comprise a number of phases (see, e.g., Beaton, Postlethwaite, Ross, Spearitt, & Wolf, 2000; Kellaghan & Grisay, 1995; Loxley, 1992; Postlethwaite, 1999; Shorrocks-Taylor & Jenkins, 2000) that constitute a framework for planning and design. In this section, each of the main phases is briefly discussed.

Research Questions and Conceptual Framework

The design of any study will be determined by the questions that it is required to answer. Research questions in international comparative studies often stem from the feeling within some countries that all is not well in education, that quality is a relative notion and that, although education systems may differ in many aspects, much can be learned from other countries ("the world as a laboratory"). The research questions, therefore, should address important policy and theory-oriented issues. For example, in SACMEQ I the research questions were aimed at the interest of policy makers and educational planners, whilst OECD/PISA aims to produce policy-oriented and internationally comparable indicators of student achievement on a regular and timely basis. Within the realm of these policy-oriented aims, such studies need to inform policy makers and educational planners about the "human capital" of a nation as an important determinant of a nation's economic performance (Kellaghan, 1996).

In addition to such policy-related aims, the IEA studies and PISA also include research questions aimed at understanding reasons for observed differences. The general research questions underlying a study are often descriptive in nature. For example, the four major research questions in the IEA TIMSS study are: What are students expected to learn? Who provides the instruction? How is instruction organized? What have students learned? In PISA, one finds descriptive questions about differences in patterns of achievement within countries and differences among schools in the strength of relationships between students' achievement levels and the economic, social, and cultural capital of their families. There are also questions about the relationship between achievement levels and the context of instruction and a variety of other school characteristics.

The first step from the research questions to the design of a study is the development of a conceptual framework. We have already noted that the character of the research questions largely determines this framework, but there are two distinct dimensions to be considered. One is the nature of the outcome measures to be used (e.g., reading literacy, mathematical literacy, and scientific literacy, as defined in PISA). The other is the factors to be studied in relation to the chosen outcome measures (e.g., as specified in the IEA conceptual framework).

Research Design

The research design focuses on the issues that arise from the research questions, and needs to provide a balance between the complexity required to respond to specific questions and the need for simplicity, timeliness, and cost-effectiveness (Beaton et al., 2000). The choice between selecting a design that is cross-sectional (where students are assessed at one point in time) or longitudinal (where the same students are evaluated at two or more points in time) depends on the goals of the study. Most studies have a cross-sectional design in which data are collected from students at certain age/grade levels. However, TIMSS provides an example of a compromise situation. Ultimately, TIMSS's multi-grade design was a compromise between a cross-sectional and longitudinal survey design, as it included adjacent grades for the populations of primary and junior secondary education. This allowed more information about achievement to be obtained (across five grades) and an analysis of variation in cumulative schooling effects.

Both PISA and TIMSS gather data in successive waves with cross-sectional samples at the same age/grade levels several years apart to examine trends, but these are not longitudinal studies. TIMSS offered a further variant by organizing a repeat (TIMSS-R) in which data were gathered for the lower secondary population in the year in which the primary population in the original TIMSS had reached that year of secondary schooling. Again the study was not genuinely longitudinal in the sense of obtaining subsequent measures on the same students. Because of their complexity, international, comparative longitudinal studies are rare. It is not only difficult to retain contact with students over time, but expected high attrition rates have to be reflected in the design, and this adds to the cost of the studies. One example, however, is the sub-study of the IEA Second International Mathematics Study (SIMS), in which eight countries collected achievement data at the beginning and the end of the school year in addition to the main study, as well as data on classroom processes (Burstein, 1992).

A different kind of genuinely longitudinal study is being planned for PISA. Some countries are considering making their PISA 2003 sample the beginning sample for a study in which data on subsequent educational, labor market, and other experiences will be obtained to permit analyses of their relationship with earlier educational achievement levels.

Given the type of research questions that were posed, most IEA studies included *curriculum analysis* as part of the research design. In this, they differ from SACMEQ and OECD studies.

The research design needs to allow for good estimates of the variables in question, both for international comparisons and for national statistics. An important decision in each study relates to the level at which analysis will be focused. If the focus of interest is the school, then it is appropriate to select only one class per school at the appropriate grade level, or a random sample of students. However, if the research questions also relate to class and teacher effects, then more than one class will have to be sampled within each school.

Target Population

An important issue is whether to use a grade or age-based target population. The choice should reflect the underlying question being addressed. If the question concerns what school systems achieve with students at a particular grade level, regardless of how long they have taken to reach the grade, then a grade-based population is appropriate. If, however, the question concerns what school systems have achieved with students of a particular age, or after a given number of years in school, an age-based population is appropriate. In the SACMEQ I study, the question of interest was the former, so a grade-based population (grade 6) was chosen. On the other hand, for OECD/PISA, the question of interest was the latter so an age-based population definition was chosen (15-year-olds, since education is compulsory to this age in most OECD countries).

A grade-based target population is easier to work with. The difficulty with an age-based population is that, due to grade repetition and the timing of the cut-off date for school commencement, students at the target age can be in more than one grade, even in as many as four or more in some countries. The IEA uses a "grade-age" definition as a compromise to reduce the complexity of sampling, while still throwing some light on what systems have achieved with their students by the time they have reached a particular age rather than a particular grade. For example, in TIMSS, where the interest at the junior secondary level was in the achievements of 13-year-olds, the target population was defined as the two adjacent grades where most 13-year-olds could be found at the chosen point in the school year. This approach avoids the additional sampling complexity of a pure, age-based sample such as that used by PISA but, to the extent that there are 13-year-olds in grade levels not sampled, provides only a partial estimate of the achievements of students at the age of interest.

Countries also have to determine whether separate subpopulations need to be identified since an increase in sample size will usually be required to obtain estimates for them. In some countries, there is interest in regional differences, particularly those in which responsibility for education is decentralized to regional (state or provincial) level. In some countries, there is also interest in differences between distinct language or cultural communities.

In any definition of a target population, the possibility of exclusions has to be addressed. For example, it may be extremely expensive to collect data from students in special education schools or in very isolated areas. Normally, the research design indicates that the excluded population in a country should not be more than, for example, 5 percent.

Sampling

In the past decade, considerable attention has been paid to the issue of sampling, which critiques of earlier international studies had highlighted as a problem. International comparative studies need good quality, representative samples. These cannot be obtained without careful planning and execution, following established procedures such as those developed by IEA (IEA, 2002; Martin et al., 1999) or in the PISA technical standards (OECD, 2002). These procedures consist of rules concerning the selection of the samples and the evaluation of their technical precision. For example, IEA standards require (among other things) that the target population(s) have comparable definitions across countries, that they are defined operationally, and that any discrepancy between nationally desired and defined populations is clearly described (Martin et al., 1999). In each participating country, basic requirements have to be met in a number of areas, such as specification of domains and strata, sampling error requirements, size of sample, preparation of sampling frame, mechanical selection procedure, sampling weights and sampling errors, response or participation rates (see also Postlethwaite, 1999).

All samples in large-scale studies involve two or more stages. In a two-stage sample, the first consists of drawing a sample of schools proportional to their size. At the second stage, students within the school are drawn (either by selecting one or more classes at random or by selecting students at random across all classes). In a three-stage sampling, design, the first stage would be the region, followed by the selection of schools, and then students within schools.

The size of sample required is a function of a number of factors, such as the size of sampling error that is acceptable, the degree of homogeneity or heterogeneity of students attending schools, and the levels of analysis to be carried out. Depending on the research questions, researchers may choose one or two classes per school or a number of students drawn at random from all classes at a particular grade level. IEA usually recommends 150 classrooms. The simple equivalent sample size (i.e., if students had been sampled randomly from the total population rather than from schools) should not be less than 400 students (Beaton et al., 2000; Postlethwaite, 1999). PISA requires a minimum national sample of 150 schools and a random sample of 35 15-year-olds from within each school, or all where there are fewer than 35. Replacement schools are also drawn in a sample to enable schools to be substituted in the event that a school in the primary sample declines to participate. In TIMSS, two replacement schools were drawn for each school in the primary sample.

The response rate of the sample is an important quality consideration since non-response can introduce bias. Postlethwaite (1999) says that the minimum acceptable response rate should be 90 percent of students in 90 percent of schools in the sample (including replacement schools where they have been chosen). IEA uses 85 percent after use of replacement schools. PISA requires 85 percent if there is no use of replacement schools, but a progressively higher figure as the proportion of schools drawn from the reserve sample rises. If the response rate from the primary sample drops to 65 percent, the absolute minimum acceptable in PISA, then the required minimum response rate after replacement is 95 percent.

It has become common practice in international comparative studies to "flag" countries that do not meet sampling criteria or even to drop them from the study. In the IEA studies, the results for countries that failed to meet minimum criteria are reported but the countries are identified. In PISA, countries that fail to satisfy sampling criteria are excluded from the report unless they fall only marginally short and can provide unequivocal quantitative evidence from other sources that non-responding schools do not differ systematically from responding schools, thus allaying fears of response bias in their results.

Instrument Development

Another crucial element in international studies is the development of achievement tests, background questionnaires, and attitude scales. In curriculum-driven studies, such as the IEA ones, the first step in test development is to analyze the curricula (analyzing curriculum guides, textbooks, and examinations but also, for example, interviewing subject experts or observing teachers) of participating countries. This forms the basis of a framework or test grid that represents the curricula of the countries involved in the study as much as possible. It usually has two dimensions: content and performance expectations, meaning the kind of performances expected of students (such as understanding, theorizing and analyzing, problem solving). Sometimes more dimensions are added, such as "perspectives" which were included in the TIMSS study to refer to the nature of the presentation of the content in the curriculum materials (e.g., attitudes, careers, participation, increasing interest in the subject). This analysis has to lead to an agreed-upon blueprint for the tests that must cover most of the curricula of participating countries.

In studies that are not curriculum-driven (OECD/PISA, SACMEQ), it is important that the tests reflect the research questions and the practical needs of policy makers (Kellaghan, 1996). In PISA, the assessment frameworks were developed by international expert panels, negotiated with national project managers, and finally approved by a Board of Participating Countries consisting of senior officials from all the countries involved.

Item formats (such as multiple choice, free response, and/or performance items) have to be decided upon, and test items written to cover the cells in the blueprint. Large-scale surveys conducted by IEA and other bodies have traditionally used tests with multiple-choice questions. This type of test is very popular since the conditions of the assessment can be standardized, the cost is low, and they can be machine-scored. However, there has recently been a growing awareness among educators that some important achievement outcomes are either difficult or impossible to measure using the multiple-choice format. Hence, during the development phase of TIMSS, it was decided that open-format questions would be included where students would have to write their answers. In PISA, one-third of the items were open-ended. These items have to be marked manually. TIMSS developed a two-digit coding scheme to diagnose students' answers to the open-ended questions. For example, the first digit registered degree of correctness, while the second was used to code the type of correct or incorrect answer given. The ultimate aim of this scheme was to provide a rich database for research on student's cognitive processes, problem-solving strategies, and common misconceptions (Robitaille & Garden, 1996).

A third type of test item (not often utilized in large-scale studies) involves performance assessment, which consists of a set of practical tasks. Its proponents argue that the practical nature of the tasks permits a richer and deeper understanding of some of the aspects of student knowledge and understanding than is possible with written tests alone. In TIMSS, performance assessment was an option (Harmon et al., 1997).

When student responses are scaled, agreement must be reached on the substantive meaning of the scale in terms of student performance on specified points of the scale (Beaton et al., 2000). There must also be international agreement on the appropriateness of the items, and the reliability of the tests, which requires extensive try-outs, must be established (Beaton et al., 2000). A rotated test design may be applied in which individual students respond to only a proportion of the items in the assessment. This reduces testing time per student, while allowing data to be collected on a large number of items covering major aspects of curricula.

In most studies, questionnaires are used to collect background data about students, teachers, and schools, which are used as contextual information in the interpretion of achievement results. Such data allow researchers to develop constructs relating to the inputs and processes of education, and to address research questions concerning what factors contribute to good quality education (see, e.g., Postlethwaite & Ross, 1992, who concluded that a large number of background variables influenced reading achievement). Another reason to collect such data is that they allow countries to search for determinants of national results in an international context.

A problem with this type of data, however, is that some variables are culturally dependent. Questions that researchers may want to ask about the home environment vary from country to country. For example, when asking about family living in the student's family, interpretation will have to take account of differences in family structure. Questions regarding socioeconomic status raise another set of problems. For example, in countries in Western Europe, televisions, CD players, computers, and motor vehicles are commonplace and so would not be helpful as discriminators of socioeconomic status. They may, however, distinguish status in newly developed countries, but would probably not be very useful in many less developed ones where indicators of wealth (especially in rural areas) could more appropriately be other possessions, such as animals. These issues point to the need in designing questions and in interpreting responses for a thorough understanding of the context in which data are gathered. That is challenging in any international comparative study, but particularly so in ones that cover a diverse range of countries.

In international comparative studies, the translation of instruments is an important and culturally sensitive issue. For example in IEA, participants use a system for translating the test and questionnaires that incorporates an independent check on the translations. All deviations (from the international version of the instruments) in vocabulary, meaning, or item layout are recorded and forwarded to the International Study Center. All translations and adaptations of tests and questionnaires are verified by professional translators, and deviations identified by the translator that may affect results are addressed by the national study centre. Further verification is provided by the International Study Center which also conducts a thorough review of item statistics to detect any errors that might not have been corrected (Martin et al., 1999). In PISA, source tests and questionnaires are provided in English and French. Countries not using these languages are required to produce two independent translations, and strongly urged to produce one from each of the English and French sources. This helps make clear the features of instruments that are essential and those that are unique to a particular language of presentation. The independent translations are checked by a third national translator and all are finally checked by an independent international team. All instruments have to be tried out extensively in each language of testing, which makes instrument development a difficult, time consuming, and complex endeavor.

When attitude scales are used, it is necessary to describe the dimensions. Beaton et al. (2000) indicate that often three times as many items are needed for trial testing as will be required in the final instruments.

Data Collection and Preparation

Data collection requirements need to be specified carefully to ensure the comparability of the procedures that are followed in the data collection. Manuals are generally written for the national centers (or national research coordinators), for the person coordinating the administration of the instruments in each school, and for the persons administering the instruments in each classroom or to a group of students. These are piloted simultaneously with the survey instruments to ensure that stated procedures can be followed or to identify changes that need to be made. In many countries, it is necessary to train the people who will administer the tests. In some developing countries, it is not possible to follow the specification that test materials be sent to schools by post and then administered by the school staff. For a country such as South Africa, that approach has three problems. The first is the fact that many schools do not have functioning postal addresses, or the names of the schools change, or the schools are difficult to locate. Secondly, the postal system is unreliable, which means that it would be almost impossible to ensure that materials would reach their destination safely or in time for the scheduled administration. Finally, there is an overriding need to ensure credibility of the results by employing test administrators who are independent of the participating school. In TIMSS in South Africa, an external field agency was employed to collect data. Out of similar considerations of credibility, PISA required that test administration not be undertaken by any teacher of students in the sample in the subjects being tested, and recommended that the administration not be undertaken by any teacher from the school or any other school in the PISA sample.

Student responses or, in the case of open-ended items, their coded results, are usually transferred on computers at the national center utilizing special data entry software. The data are then sent to the International Study Center for cleaning and file-building. During this time-consuming process there is usually frequent communication between the national and international study centers to deal with problems. Following this, country sampling weights are calculated to account for disproportionate selection across strata, inaccurate sampling frames, missing data, and the like. Advanced psychometric techniques are available to compensate for the effects of a rotated test design and to reduce the effects of missing data.

The results of this phase are data files that are the starting point for the international and national data analyses and reports. Data archives are often made available in the public domain (such as those already available from the IEA TIMSS and SITES studies and are planned for PISA) as the basis for secondary analyses (national and international).

Data Analysis and Reporting

Analyses of data can follow simple or complex procedures. The first international and national reports of a study are usually descriptive, and provide policymakers and educational practitioners with the most relevant outcomes of the study. Such reports have to be clearly written and address the research questions stated at the beginning of the study. It is necessary to reach decisions at an early stage about issues such as units of analysis and the type of analyses to be employed.

After the first report, technical reports covering topics such as the psychometric properties of instruments and the characteristics of the achieved samples are usually prepared. Additional analytic reports explore relationships in the data sets in more detail than can be achieved in the time available for the preparation of the first report. Analyses often use more advanced techniques, such as multilevel analysis (to examine school-level, classroom-level, and student-level variations) and path analysis to test models explaining some of the complex relationships between achievement and its determinants (Lietz, 1996; Vari, 1997). Additional reports can also include more detailed analyses of the errors that students made in incorrect responses to provide teachers and other educational practitioners with insights into the nature of students' misconceptions. Secondary analyses aimed at understanding differences between and within educational systems are also often carried out.

Managing and Implementing Studies

The high stakes and the complexity and costs of international comparative achieve-ment studies make management a fundamental issue. IEA even developed a number of standards for managing and implementing studies (Martin et al., 1999), which are also used in the SACMEQ studies. As well as the design aspects discussed in the previous section, other important components are the selection of an international coordinating center, detailed planning, the development of a quality assurance programme, and technical reports and documentation. Similar issues have to be addressed at national level.

Leadership

Strong leadership is key at both international and national levels in managing and coordinating the design and implementation of international comparative studies. At international level, the need for a center to coordinate and lead the study is obvious. Centers (such as those used in IEA and OECD/PISA studies) require knowledgeable, experienced people in areas such as assessment, psycho-metrics, statistics, and content knowledge of the subjects being studied, as well as others skilled in communication and management.

   At the national level, the center conducting the study requires strong project leadership skills which are both technical and substantive, but which also include management and communication skills. It is essential that national coordinators are knowledgeable about their contexts. They must be able to review the design of the study critically in order to make the necessary adaptations for their country, and to identify the experts that will be required to support the study technically.

Detailed Planning

International comparative studies usually take a number of years to design, implement, analyse, and report. Therefore, detailed short-, medium- and long-term planning is required (see, e.g., Loxley, 1992). This will involve consideration of objectives, methods, time schedule, costs, and outcomes of the study. Data gathering in the northern and southern hemispheres must be undertaken at different times in the calendar year to obtain data at equivalent times in the school year.

Quality Assurance

A quality assurance program is required to ensure that studies are conducted to a high standard. Such a program is particularly important for data collection activities which are often conducted by school personnel or especially appointed data collectors, and so are outside the control of the study staff. In the IEA TIMSS studies, quality control observers in each country made unannounced visits to a sample of schools to check whether data collection followed agreed procedures. In PISA, considerable resources were invested in a similar program of observation by unannounced visits by independent monitors. Guidelines for verification of the translation of instruments are part of such a program.

Technical Reports and Documentation

So that studies can be evaluated and replicated, the study design, instrument development, data collection, and analysis and reporting procedures should be described in technical reports and documentation (see Martin & Kelly, 1996; Martin et al., 1999).

CONCLUSION

Utilization and Impact

It is important that designers, researchers, funders, and policymakers who initiate and conduct international comparative studies should reflect on and assess the extent to which data that are generated and analyses that are undertaken are utilized. They should also monitor the impact of studies on educational systems.

Clear examples of significant impact are available. The results of studies, as well as the more general OECD indicators, have been used in many publications and discussions about the functioning and possible improvement of educational systems. In some cases (e.g., in Australia, Hungary, Ireland, Japan, New Zealand U.S.A.), specific curriculum changes have been attributed to IEA findings (Keeves, 1995; Kellaghan, 1996). The findings of SACMEQ have also been used in educational policy making and reform (Ross et al., 2000). Jenkins (2000, p. 140) cites (amongst others) Hussein (1992, p. 468) who in addressing the question "what does Kuwait want to learn from TIMSS?" responded that he wanted to know whether students in Kuwait are "taught the same curricula as the students in other countries," and whether they "learn mathematics to a level that could be considered of a reasonably high international standard." Similarly, Howie (2000) concludes that the TIMSS results for South Africa not only focused the country's attention on the poor overall performance of South Africa's students, but also identified several other key issues, among them that the Grade 7 and Grade 8 science and mathematics curricula were very different from those of other countries.

Since policy decisions are not normally documented or published, the direct impact of international comparative achievement studies may not be clearly visible (Kellaghan, 1996). This will especially be so if findings serve an "enlightenment" function in discussions about the quality of education. If this is so, international studies will not "necessarily mean supplying direct answers to questions, but rather in enabling planning and decision making to be better informed" (Howson, 1999, p. 166).

International comparative achievement studies can be utilized to place a country's educational practices in an international comparative perspective. One important possibility, often overlooked up till now, is to link national and international assessments. Linking would not only increase the benefits a country can obtain from investments in assessment studies, but also the cost-effectiveness of the operation. The state of Minnesota in the United States provides an interesting example of the use of international data to make comparisons between the performance of students in the state and that of students in the country as a whole, and that of students in other countries (based on their performance on TIMSS) (Sci Math MN, 1998).

Limitations and Criticism

Just as those intimately involved in international studies of achievement reflect on, and evaluate them, so too do external analysts and critics. It is inevitable that external researchers and those in the political arena will critique the studies as part of the academic and political processes related to education. Much of the critique of early studies focused on technical issues relating to sampling and survey design. As the study designers refined their methodologies, assisted by the development of information technology, and improved their quality assurance procedures, these criticisms have largely been dealt with. Flagging the results in international reports of countries with deficient samples has helped, though there remains the risk that the flags and associated footnotes become progressively ignored. The alternative of non-inclusion removes the risk of misinterpretation, but is a harsh penalty after a country has invested considerable resources in gathering its data.

Criticism of the translation of instruments in early IEA studies resulted in the use of more carefully controlled procedures with independent verification. Concerns about the adherence to prescribed data collection methods have also been addressed by more extensive prescription of procedures, increased training of personnel, and stronger quality assurance procedures. Criticism of delays in publishing results has been addressed through ensuring before the study is launched that funds will be available for the whole process, and obtaining a clear commitment to publication of results within two years of data collection.

As is the case with all research, international studies have their limitations. Dissatisfaction with results can be fuelled by unrealistic expectations or even promises. Thus the aspiration of early IEA studies to assess the relative impact of a variety of school resources and instructional processes on achievement proved to be very difficult to realize, as most studies were cross-sectional and provided a limited basis for exploring and testing causal relationships. Another problem arises from the effort that has to be expended in the development of achievement tests. This has often been accompanied by inadequate attention to the development of good quality constructs for the background variables to be used in relational and multi-level analyses.

A pervasive criticism, and it is one that may be applied to any study using educational tests developed and analysed with contemporary psychometric theory, is that the psychometric model imposes unidimensionality on data by eliminating as misfitting items that could contain important information about other dimensions of achievement (Goldstein, 2000). Beaton (2000), on the other hand, emphasizes that items are deleted only when there are clear deficiencies and that the issue of dimensionality is properly addressed in psychometric analyses in the pilot and trial stages of test development.

As technical criticisms have been increasingly addressed, recent critiques have become increasingly political (e.g., Bracey, 1997). Concern has been expressed about the direction, financing, and ownership of the studies and their data. For example, it has been claimed that because the primary responsibility for conducting IEA studies has been with empirical researchers, who are predominantly psychometricians or data analysts, the content area studied (e.g. mathematics and science in TIMSS) has been seen as secondary (Keitel & Kilpatrick, 1999).

This criticism may be addressed at two levels. One is through consideration of the specific personnel involved in each study and the strategies used to engage subject matter experts. Both IEA and OECD/PISA have actively engaged subject-matter experts in the specification of their assessment frameworks and in the design of assessment instruments. In the case of IEA studies, as indicated earlier, the focus is on curriculum content and curriculum coverage and a careful curriculum analysis is one of the pillars of test development. In the case of PISA, the focus is on what students by the time they reach the end of compulsory schooling, should be able to do with what they have learned. The other way in which this criticism can be evaluated is through an analysis of the ways in which the results of studies have been taken up in discussions of curriculum and in curriculum research. It is true that mathematics and science educational research communities, for example, have often paid little attention to the results of international studies. The reason has been largely due to differences in the scale of the issues addressed. The focus of pedagogical research in mathematics and science education has often been on issues which cannot be addressed in large-scale surveys (e.g., the everyday theories of how the world works that young people develop and that science education seeks to modify or displace).

Criticisms of international comparative studies make an important contribution to improving and strengthening the design, development, and implementation of the studies. Among other things, they have resulted in a broadening of the range of people engaged in the work.

Final Word

International, comparative education studies use the world as an educational laboratory to broaden national perspectives and to raise expectations about what might actually be possible. Furthermore, their collaborative processes build national research capacity. This occurs in all countries, but has been particularly important in developing countries, where the enhanced capacity lessens dependence on developed countries in designing and developing interventions in education.

Education systems are embedded in national cultures and histories but, increasingly, they are being subjected to the same global forces that are transforming many other aspects of national life. While exposing national achievements in comparison with others that have done better might bring discomfort, the knowledge can be used constructively for national reforms. Furthermore, the collaborative work that is part and parcel of international assessments can serve to increase the kind of productive exchange of ideas and technologies from which all can benefit.

APPENDIX:

ADDRESSES OF AGENCIES THAT CONDUCT INTERNATIONAL COMPARATIVE ACHIEVEMENT STUDIES

IEA (International Association for the Evaluation of Educational Achievement)
Herengracht 487
1017 BT Amsterdam, Netherlands
tel. +31 20 625 3625; fax: +31 20 420 7136
email: department@iea.nl
Web site: http://www.iea.nl

OECD/PISA (Programme for International Student Assessment)
OECD/CERI
2, rue André-Pascal
75775 Paris 16, France
tel. +33 1 4524 9250; fax: +33 1 4524 1968
Web site: http://www.pisa.oecd.org.

SACMEQ, Southern Africa Consortium for Monitoring Educational Quality
UNESCO Harare Sub-regional Office
P.O. Box HG435
Highlands
Harare, Zimbabwe
tel. +263 4 334 425 -32; fax: +263 4 776 055 / 332 344
email: pfukani@unesco.co.zw

REFERENCES

Beaton, A.E. (2000). The importance of item response theory (IRT) for large-scale assessments. In S. Carey (Ed.), *Measuring adult literacy: The International Adult Literacy Survey (IALS) in the European context* (pp. 26–33). London: Office for National Statistics.

Beaton, A.E., Martin, M.O., Mullis, I.V.S., Gonzalez, E.J., Smith, T.A., & Kelly, D.L. (1996). *Science achievement in the middle school years*. Chestnut Hill, MA: TIMSS International Study Center, Lynch School of Education, Boston College.

Beaton, A.E., Mullis, I.V.S., Martin, M.O., Gonzalez, E.J., Kelly, D.L., & Smith, T.A. (1996). *Mathematics achievement in the middle school years*. Chestnut Hill, MA: TIMSS International Study Center, Lynch School of Education, Boston College.

Beaton, A.E., Postlethwaite, T.N., Ross, K.N., Spearritt, D., & Wolf, R.M. (2000). *The benefits and limitations of international educational achievement studies*. Paris: International Institute for Educational Planning/International Academy of Education.

Bottani, N., & Tuijnman, A.C. (1994). The design of indicator systems. In A.C. Tuijnman, & T.N. Postlethwaite (Eds.), *Monitoring the standards of education* (pp. 47–78). Oxford: Pergamon.

Bracey, G.W. (1997). On comparing the incomparable: A response to Baker and Stedman. *Educational Researcher*, **26**(3), 19–25.

Burstein L. (Ed). (1992). *The IEA study of mathematics III: Student growth and classroom processes*. Oxford: Pergamon.

Goldstein, H. (2000). IALS – A commentary on the scaling and data analysis. In S. Carey (Ed.), *Measuring adult literacy: The International Adult Literacy Survey (IALS) in the European context* (pp. 34–42). London: Office for National Statistics.

Harmon, M., Smith, T.A., Martin, M.O., Kelly D.L., Beaton, A.E., Mullis, I.V.S., Gonzalez, E.J., & Orpwood, G. (1997). *Performance assessment in IEA's Third International Mathematics and Science Study*. Chestnut Hill, MA: International Study Center, Boston College.

Howie, S.J. (2000). TIMSS in South Africa: The value of international comparative studies for a developing country. In D. Shorrocks-Taylor, & E.W. Jenkins (Eds.), *Learning from others* (pp. 279–301). Boston: Kluwer Academic.

Howson, G. (1999). The value of comparative studies. In G. Kaiser, E. Luna, & I. Huntley (Eds), *International comparisons in mathematics education* (pp. 165–181). London: Falmer.

Husén, T. (Ed.) (1967). *International study of achievement in mathematics: A comparison of twelve countries* (2 vols). Stockholm: Almqvist & Wiksell/New York: Wiley.

Husén, T., & Postlethwaite, T.N. (Eds) (1994). *The international encyclopedia of education*. Oxford: Pergamon.

Husén, T., & Tuijnman, A.C. (1994). Monitoring standards in education: Why and how it came about. In A.C. Tuijnman, & T.N. Postlethwaite (Eds.), *Monitoring the standards of education* (pp. 1–22). Oxford: Pergamon.

Hussein, M.G. (1992). What does Kuwait want to learn from the Third International Mathematics and Science Study (TIMSS)? *Prospects*, **22**, 463–468.

IEA (International Association for the Evaluation of Educational Achievement). (1998). *IEA guidebook 1998: Activities, institutions and people*. Amsterdam: Author.

International Study Center. (2002). Retrieved from http://timss.bc.edu/. Chestnut Hill, MA: International Study Center, Lynch School of Education, Boston College.

Jenkins, E.W. (2000). Making use of international comparisons of student achievement in science and mathematics. In D. Shorrocks-Taylor, & E.W. Jenkins (Eds.), *Learning from others* (pp. 137–158). Boston: Kluwer Academic.

Keeves, J.P. (1992). *The IEA technical handbook*. Amsterdam: IEA Secretariat.

Keeves, J.P. (1995). *The world of school learning: Selected key findings from 35 years of IEA research*. Amsterdam: IEA Secretariat.

Keeves, J.P. (Ed) (1996). *The international encyclopedia of evaluation*. Oxford: Pergamon.

Keitel, C., & Kilpatrick, J. (1999). The rationality and irrationality of international comparative studies. In G. Kaiser, E. Luna, & I. Huntley (Eds), *International comparisons in mathematics education* (pp. 241–256). London: Falmer.

Kellaghan, T. (1996). IEA studies and educational policy. *Assessment in Education*, **3**, 143–160.

Kellaghan, T., & Grisay, A. (1995). International comparisons of student achievement: Problems and prospects. In *Measuring what students learn* (pp. 41–61). Paris: Organisation for Economic Co-operation and Development.

Lietz, P. (1996). *Changes in reading comprehension across cultures and over time*. New York: Waxmann.

Loxley, W. (1992). Managing survey research. *Prospects*, **22**, 289–296.

Martin, M.O., & Kelly, D. (1996). *TIMSS technical report. Volume I: Design and development*. Chestnut Hill, MA: International Study Center, Lynch School of Education Boston College.

Martin, M.O., Mullis, I.V.S., Beaton, A.E., Gonzalez, E.J., Smith, T.A., & Kelly, D.L. (1997). *Science in the primary school years*. Chestnut Hill, MA: International Study Center, Lynch School of Education, Boston College.

Martin, M.O., Mullis, I.V.S., Gonzalez, E.J., Gregory, K.D., Smith, T.A., Chrostowski, S.J., Garden, R.A., & O'Connor, K.M. (2000). *TIMSS 1999. International science report*. Chestnut Hill, MA: International Study Center, Lynch School of Education, Boston College.

Martin, M.O., Rust, K., & Adams, R. (Eds) (1999). *Technical standards for IEA studies*. Amsterdam: IEA Secretariat.

Mullis, I.V.S., Martin, M.O., Beaton, A.E., Gonzalez, E.J., Kelly, D.A., & Smith, T.A. (1997). *Mathematics in the primary school years*. Chestnut Hill, MA: International Study Center, Lynch School of Education, Boston College.

Mullis, I.V.S., Martin, M.O., Beaton, A.E., Gonzalez, E.J., Kelly, D.A., & Smith, T.A. (1998). *Mathematics and science achievement in the final year of secondary school*. Chestnut Hill, MA: International Study Center, Lynch School of Education, Boston College.

Mullis, I.V.S., Martin, M.O., Gonzalez, E.J., Gregory, K.D., Garden, R.A., O'Connor, K.M., Chrostowski, S.J., & Smith, T.A. (2000). *TIMSS 1999. International mathematics report*. Chestnut Hill, MA: International Study Center, Lynch School of Education, Boston College.

OECD (Organisation for Economic Co-operation and Development). (1992, 1993, 1995, 1996, 1997, 1998, 2000). *Education at a glance*. Paris: Author.

OECD. (2001). *Knowledge and skills for life. First results from PISA 2000*. Paris: Author.

OECD. (2002). *The OECD Programme for International Student Assessment*. Retrieved from http://www.pisa.oecd.org/.

Plomp, T. (1998). The potential of international comparative studies to monitor quality of education. *Prospects*, **27**, 45–60.

Postlethwaite, T.N. (1994). Monitoring and evaluation in different education systems. In A.C. Tuijnman, & T.N. Postlethwaite (Eds), *Monitoring the standards of education* (pp. 23–46). Oxford: Pergamon.

Postlethwaite, T.N. (1999). *International studies of educational achievement: Methodological issues*. Hong Kong: Comparative Education Research Centre, University of Hong Kong.

Postlethwaite, T.N., & Ross, K.N. (1992). *Effective schools in reading: Implications for planners*. Amsterdam: IEA Secretariat.

Robitaille, D.F., Beaton, A.E., & Plomp, T. (2000). *The impact of TIMSS on the teaching & learning of mathematics & science*. Vancouver: Pacific Educational Press.

Robitaille, D.F., & Garden, R.A. (Eds). (1996). *Research questions and study design*. Vancouver: Pacific Educational Press.

Ross, K.N. et al. (2000). *Translating educational assessment findings into educational policy and reform measures: Lessons from the SACMEQ initiative in Africa*. Paper presented at the World Education Forum, Dakar, Senegal.

Schleicher, A. (2000). Monitoring student knowledge and skills: The OECD Programme for International Student Assessment. In D. Shorrocks-Taylor, & E.W. Jenkins (Eds.), *Learning from others* (pp. 63–78). Boston: Kluwer Academic.

SciMathMN. (1998). *Minnesota 4th grade TIMMS results*. Retrieved from http://www.scimathmn.org/timss_gr4_rpt.htm.

Shavelson, R.J., McDonnell, L.M., & Oakes, J. (1989). *Indicators for monitoring mathematics and science education: A sourcebook*. Santa Monica CA: RAND Corporation.

Shorrocks-Taylor, D., & Jenkins, E.W. (Eds.) (2000). *Learning from others*. Boston: Kluwer Academic.

Travers, K.J., & Westbury, I. (1989). *The IEA study of mathematics I: International analysis of mathematics curricula*. Oxford: Pergamon.

U.S. National Commission on Excellence in Education (1983). *A nation at risk*. Washington, DC: U.S. Government Printing Office.

Vari, P. (Ed.). (1997). *Are we similar in math and science? A study of grade 8 in nine central and eastern European countries*. Amsterdam: IEA Secretariat.

Weiss, C.H. (1981). Measuring the use of evaluation. In J.A. Ciarlo (Ed.), *Utilizing evaluation: Concepts and measurement techniques* (pp. 17–33). Newbury Park, CA: Sage.

Westat. (1991). *SEDCAR (Standards for Education Data Collection and Reporting)*. Washington, DC: US Department of Education.

43
Cross-National Curriculum Evaluation

WILLIAM H. SCHMIDT
Michigan State University, MI, USA

RICHARD T. HOUANG
Michigan State University, MI, USA

This paper is concerned with the measurement of curriculum and its role in cross-national curriculum evaluation studies. The methods developed and the data used to illustrate the procedures are taken from the Third International Mathematics and Science Study (TIMSS).

Before turning to the measurement of curriculum, we examine three types of cross-national curriculum evaluation studies differentiated by the role that curriculum plays in each: the object of the evaluation, the criterion measure for the evaluation, and the context in which to interpret an educational evaluation. These three have their counterparts in within-country educational evaluation studies in the United States. The first is the most common. We bring the three together in a conceptual framework for international research and argue the relevance of curriculum measurement to all three.

CURRICULUM AS THE OBJECT OF AN EVALUATION

The most traditional form of curriculum evaluation is a study in which the curriculum is itself the object of evaluation. In the language of statistics, curriculum is the design variable. Traditionally, such studies are aimed at determining if a curriculum has an effect or if one curriculum is "better" than another. To answer the questions usually requires the specification of criteria against which the curricula are to be evaluated. Criteria are most often defined in terms of learning outcomes, but can also include other kinds of outcomes such as attitudes or behavioral changes. Based on the criteria, instruments such as achievement tests, questionnaires, or attitude inventories are developed and used as the dependent variables in the evaluation study.

In international studies, the comparison is often between the curriculum of one country and that of another. For example, the question might be posed: is

International Handbook of Educational Evaluation, 964–996
T. Kellaghan, D.L. Stufflebeam (eds.)
© *2003 Dordrecht: U.S. Government. Printed in Great Britain.*

the eighth grade curriculum of one country as effective for teaching mathematics as the curriculum in another? Another way the question can be phrased is: is the eighth grade curriculum in mathematics in a particular country effective for student learning when set in an international context? In the latter case, the comparison is not explicitly with the curriculum of another country but rather with principles gleaned from the study of multiple countries implicitly.

This type of curriculum evaluation study can also include an examination of regional differences, or of relationships between curriculum variation and cross-national differences in achievement. The unit of analysis in this case is the country. This was the focus of the Second International Mathematics Study and the Second International Science Study carried out some 20 years ago by the International Association for the Evaluation of Educational Achievement (IEA). In reports of the studies (Burstein, 1993; Garden, 1987; Husén & Keeves, 1991; Keeves, 1992; Kotte, 1992; McKnight et al., 1987; Postlethwaite & Wiley, 1992; Robitaille & Garden, 1989; Robitaille & Travers, 1992; Travers & Westbury, 1989; Westbury & Travers, 1990; Wolf, 1992), the focus was on regional differences in curricula and on the U.S. curriculum as it is related to other countries participating in the study. This was especially the case for mathematics in the U.S. report, *The Underachieving Curriculum* (McKnight et al., 1987).

In such studies, the focus of the evaluation is not on determining the effectiveness of a particular curriculum program with all of its specific activities as contrasted with another program, but on examining structural or systemic features of the various curricula – characteristics such as disciplinary coherence, focus, repetitiveness, the sequencing and selection of topics, and intellectual rigor.

CURRICULUM AS OUTCOME

The second role that curriculum can play in a cross-national evaluation study is as the outcome or criterion (the dependent variable of the study). In this case, the object of the evaluation is more general than the curriculum, most typically the educational system as a whole. The central focus is to determine how educational systems differ with respect to the curriculum that they provide. The curriculum can be thought of as an indication of opportunity to learn (OTL). The use of the concept of OTL as a determinant of learning can be traced back to the First International Mathematics Study (FIMS) (Husén, 1967). Peaker (1975) was the first to incorporate OTL in modeling student achievement in an IEA cross-national study and since then it has become an integral part of most IEA studies.

Curriculum analysis was one of the major purposes of TIMSS, which was designed to explore differences between countries in terms of their definition of school mathematics and science. Two reports provide detailed results pertaining to how the curricula of some 50 countries differ (Schmidt, McKnight, Valverde, Houang, & Wiley, 1997; Schmidt, Raizen, Britton, Bianchi, & Wolfe, 1997).

In this type of evaluation study, the assumption is that the curriculum opportunities (OTL) that are provided are important products of the educational system, and that such opportunities are related to the amount of learning that takes place. The relationship has been examined in numerous studies (see Floden, 2000). Since the choice of how to spend limited resources, such as the total number of hours over a school year, becomes an important policy option for the educational system, consequences of the choices made with respect to such policies are reasonable objects of evaluation.

CURRICULUM AS CONTEXT

The third type of curriculum evaluation in a sense falls between the first two types. In this case, curriculum is neither the object of the evaluation nor the outcome, but represents an intermediate variable, which helps to contextualize the evaluation. The objects of the evaluation are, as in the second case, educational systems, and the criteria against which the systems are to be evaluated are desired outcomes, such as learning. The curriculum is considered an intermediate or moderating variable, through which opportunities to learn are provided to students. In the language of statistics, curriculum becomes a covariate. Its use in this sense would be especially appropriate in a study in which the focus of the evaluation is on some aspect of the educational system other than the curriculum. In comparing an educational system to other systems, this approach recognizes that curriculum opportunities affect the amount of learning that takes place, and so should be controlled for, if one is interested in the role that other systemic features play.

From a cross-national point of view, this is an especially important type of curriculum evaluation. The results of international comparisons permit the rankings of countries, which may be viewed and reported as an indication of the effectiveness of countries' educational systems. In order to make such statements we argue that the OTL provided by each educational system must be taken into account as a context in which to interpret the cross-national differences. Simply stated, if the achievement test focuses only on a limited aspect of mathematics, which is not taught in one country but is taught in another, then to interpret the higher achieving country as having a better educational system is certainly naïve, if not dangerous, without taking into account the fact that the achievement test may simply happen to measure the aspect of mathematics which one country covers and the other does not. Thus, the presence of curriculum as a contextualizing variable is absolutely critical for interpreting any country differences that do not themselves center on the curriculum.

The third type of study includes an examination of the claim that the test is not a fair basis upon which to compare educational systems or countries. This was an issue in TIMSS where some countries claimed that the test did not reflect their curriculum, and hence was unfair when used as a basis for cross-country comparisons. The design principle employed in developing the TIMSS test was to make the test "equally unfair" to all countries. The kind of data that would be collected as a part of this type of curriculum evaluation study could be used to examine this issue.

BACKGROUND ON TIMSS

Given the cross-national focus of this paper, we illustrate the different types of curriculum evaluation studies using curriculum data gathered as a part of TIMSS. In this section we briefly describe TIMSS. It is by far the most extensive and far-reaching cross-national comparative study of education ever attempted, and involves a comparison of the official content standards, textbooks, teacher practices, and student achievements of some 40 to 50 countries. (The actual number of countries varies depending on the number participating in the particular comparison of interest.) More than 1,500 official content standards and textbooks were analyzed. Many thousands of teachers, principals, and experts responded to survey questionnaires, and over half a million students in some 40 countries were tested in mathematics and science.

Tests were administered to 9-year-olds, 13-year-olds, and students in the last year of secondary school. The data focused on in this chapter are drawn from the 13-year-old population (Population 2 in TIMSS). For most countries, including the United States, this population represented seventh and eighth grades. Numerous reports have been released on the international curriculum analysis (Schmidt, McKnight & Raizen, 1997; Schmidt, Raizen et al., 1997; Schmidt, McKnight, & Valverde et al., 1997); on achievement comparisons (Beaton, Martin, Gonzalez, Kelly, & Smith, 1996; Beaton, Martin, & Mullis et al., 1996; Martin et al., 1997; Mullis et al., 1997, 1998); and on the relationship of curriculum to achievement (Schmidt, McKnight, Cogan, Jakwerth, & Houang, 1999; Schmidt et al., 2001). The focus in the study was on the relationship between opportunity to learn (the curriculum) and student learning (see Schmidt & McKnight, 1995).

THE MEASUREMENT OF CURRICULUM

In this section we describe the conceptual issues surrounding the measurement of curriculum and the associated techniques that would be required to conduct the three types of curriculum evaluation studies described above. Many of these methodological issues and innovations were developed as a part of TIMSS. Appropriate references are given with respect to the TIMSS study but are presented here in a more general way, since we believe that the issues would be present in other kinds of curriculum evaluation studies.

What is Curriculum?

If one's concern is in an evaluation study, curriculum must be defined in a way that allows it to be measured. Many have written about the definition of curriculum from a philosophical point of view as well as from a more pragmatic viewpoint (Apple, 1990, 1996; Jackson, 1992; Porter, 1995). We defined curriculum in a way consistent with the IEA tradition as found in international studies.

The IEA tripartite model recognizes three aspects of curriculum (Travers & Westbury, 1989): the intended, implemented, and attained curriculum. The *intended curriculum* is defined in terms of a country's official statement as to what students are expected to learn as a result of their educational experiences. This is the major policy lever available in terms of influencing students' opportunities to learn. The idea of the *implemented curriculum* acknowledges that what teachers teach may or may not be consistent with what is officially intended. The implemented curriculum then is defined in terms of what teachers actually do in the classroom with respect to curriculum. The final aspect of curriculum is the *attained curriculum* which, in IEA parlance, refers to students' actual learning, which is reflected in their achievements.

Operationalization of these three concepts is critical to conducting any of the three types of evaluation studies. In TIMSS, for example, the intended curriculum is represented by the official content standard documents produced by the educational system to inform and to guide instruction, while the implemented curriculum is represented by the teacher's indication of the number of lessons in which they dealt with specific topics.

The curriculum can also be defined in terms of textbook coverage. Textbooks can be considered as part of the intended curriculum since they often embody specific academic goals for specific sets of students. However, from a practical perspective, textbooks can be thought of as representing the implemented curriculum since they are employed in classrooms to organize, structure, and inform students' learning experiences. The extent to which textbooks actually represent the curriculum as implemented in the classroom is very much dependent on both the nature of the textbook and how the teacher chooses to use it. These considerations led to a definition of the textbook as the potentially implemented curriculum, recognizing that it serves as a bridge between the official declarations of content standards and the actual activities undertaken in the classroom (Schmidt, McKnight, & Raizen, 1997; Schmidt, Raizen et al., 1997).

In summary, curriculum evaluation studies should define curriculum in some way, and we recommend one of three ways or, as done in TIMSS, all three ways. How to measure the content standards or the textbook will be considered in a later section. To measure teacher implementation, teachers were asked to indicate the total number of periods they allocated over the academic year to the coverage of a given topic. Our experience in TIMSS is that the teachers in general take this seriously and, as a result, their responses provide a fairly reliable indicator of the amount of time, at least in a relative sense, allocated to the study of topic areas. The measurement of curriculum from documents, such as content standards and textbooks, is more difficult to achieve.

The Need for a Curriculum Framework

In measuring any of the three aspects of curriculum (intended, potentially implemented, and implemented), the methodological issue that must be addressed is how to quantify data that are essentially qualitative in nature. In TIMSS, a procedure was developed for doing this based on a curriculum framework. The framework is a qualitative listing of all of the topic areas within the discipline being studied. This common category framework, with its associated descriptive language, allows for the measurement of all aspects of the curriculum. This is true whether one is characterizing part of a curriculum document or defining the list of topics to which teachers are expected to attend. Such descriptions have to be qualitatively distinct and clear, using common terms, categories, and standardized procedures, so that codes can be unambiguously assigned to any portion of a document.

In the TIMSS study, as well as in other studies (see for example, Porter, 1989, 1995) this common language is provided by a framework for the subject area being considered. The TIMSS study had two such documents, one for mathematics and one for science (Robitaille et al., 1993). Each covered the full range of years of schooling in a unified category system. In the development of the frameworks, it was recognized that methodologically it would be best if they were defined as multifaceted and multilayered.

The frameworks developed as part of TIMSS covered three aspects of subject matter: content, performance expectation, and perspective. *Content* referred to the subject-matter topic; *performance expectation* to what students are expected to do with the particular content; and *perspective* to any over-arching orientation to the subject matter.

It was not necessary to conceive of the framework as a matrix in which a given part of a curriculum document was classified as having a particular topic, together with a particular performance expectation. This has traditionally been the case for item classification or test blueprints where an item is placed in a cell of a matrix, in which the rows represent the topics and the columns the performance expectations. The TIMSS procedures produced a signature in which a segment of the curriculum document was identified as covering as many topic areas as appropriate, and as many performance expectations as needed. This approach allows greater flexibility when identifying curriculum content, while recognizing that curriculum is often designed to cover multiple topics with multiple expectations through the same material.

The data used in the following sections to illustrate the three approaches were taken from the mathematics portion of TIMSS, which contains 44 topic areas and 21 performance expectations. Each aspect of the framework is organized hierarchicly using nested subcategories of increasing specificity. Within a given level, the arrangement of topics does not reflect a particular rational ordering of the content. Each framework aspect was meant to be encyclopediac in terms of covering all possibilities at some level of specificity. No claim is made that the "grain size" (the level of specificity for each category) is the same throughout the framework. Some sub-categories are decidedly more inclusive and commonly used than others (Schmidt, McKnight, Valverde et al., 1997).

For other subject-matter areas, such a framework would need to be developed in order to carry out the kind of curriculum measurement that we are proposing and illustrating in the following sections. TIMSS has done it for science as well. For curriculum evaluation of any of the three types, we recommend that subject matter experts be convened to develop a framework along these lines.

How to Measure Curriculum?

In this section, we describe how to measure each of the three aspects of curriculum described above, taking into account the common definition of the subject matter area as reflected in the frameworks. The TIMSS study developed a document-based methodology to allow for the analysis of the content standards and textbooks according to the mathematics framework.

This methodology has been described in great detail elsewhere (Schmidt, McKnight, & Raizen, 1997; Schmidt, Raizen et al., 1997). The basic approach worked fairly well and exhibited the desirable characteristics of validity and reliability (see Appendix E: Document Analysis Methods in Schmidt, McKnight, Valverde et al., 1997). The amount of training and quality control involved, however, was extensive, and whether reliable methods which are less labor intensive can be developed needs further study.

The basic methodological approach involved subdividing the content standards or textbooks into smaller units, which are termed blocks, and can be described as relatively homogeneous segments of the curriculum document. Each segment was then given a signature, which is represented by a series of codes on each of the two aspects of subject matter: topic (content) and performance expectation. (In TIMSS, perspective was also coded, but is not considered here.)

As already suggested, these signatures, although often represented by a single topic code and a single performance expectation code, could be more complex, and reflect several topics and/or several performance expectations. Coding was completed for all blocks within a curriculum document. The quantification of the qualitative specifications was accomplished by aggregating similarly coded blocks over the document to represent in relatively simple terms the proportion of a book or a content document that focused on a particular topic. The subtleties involved in this process, including the rules for segmenting or blocking the document, and the methodological issues are discussed in the above-cited references and need not concern us here. The major point to be made is that some methodology, such as the one used in TIMSS seems promising as a way of turning qualitative information about curriculum into quantities which can be used analytically as a part of a curriculum evaluation study.

In mathematics and science education, subject-matter specialists emphasized the importance of the performance expectation as it pertains to the coverage of various topics, considering it as important as coverage when characterizing a curriculum. For example, it is not enough to know whether a topic in mathematics was covered; one also needs to know if it was covered with the expectation that students would go beyond merely knowing and being proficient in the use of

algorithms to being able to solve mathematical problems and engage in mathematical reasoning. Because the frameworks allow for such coding of textbooks
and content standards, they permit characterization of the percentage of the
document that was focused on more complex cognitive demands as well the
content that was covered.

The measurement of the teacher implementation variable is much more
straightforward. If the topics listed in the questionnaire to which the teacher
responds in terms of his or her coverage of topics over the school year are those
specified in the framework, or are some aggregation of those topics, teachers
simply indicate the number of periods they spent covering a given topic, which
then is directly quantifiable and can be used as a means of characterizing the
teacher implemented curriculum.

A thorough curriculum evaluation study of any of the three types of curriculum evaluation discussed above would demand attention to each of the following
issues. First, it is necessary to determine which aspect(s) of curriculum is critical
to the study, and then to define the means by which it will be measured. Second,
the measures should be based on a common definition or framework. Also the
methodology employed should recognize the qualitative nature of curriculum,
but in a way that allows for quantification for statistical analysis.

The Attained Curriculum

The IEA concept of the attained curriculum is what most would simply refer to
as achievement or the outcome measure. There is a long-standing tradition of
measuring achievement, which need not be considered here. What will be considered are several issues that are critical to the first and third type of curriculum
evaluation study in which the outcome is achievement.

One issue that arises is whether achievement is to be defined in terms of the
status of the individual at a given point in time or in terms of what has been
learned over a period of time such as during eighth grade. Status is a measure of
what students know at a given point in time and represents an accumulation of
all that has been learned up to that point. Given that the typical focus of a cross-
national curriculum evaluation study is on the effect on learning of a curriculum
associated with a particular grade, status is not the appropriate measure in most
cases. If the curriculum evaluation is designed to determine the effectiveness of
different educational systems up to some grade level, such as grades one through
eight, then a status measure collected at the end of grade eight, might be
appropriate.

However, in most cases the focus is on particular curricular experiences gained
as part of a specified school year. Under these circumstances, status is not
the appropriate measure as it reflects experiences gained outside the specified
year's curriculum. Therefore, achievement gain which takes into account the
achievement level before and after the curricular experience would be more
appropriate.

In TIMSS it was not possible to obtain achievement data on students at both the beginning and end of the school year. However, the design incorporated the two adjacent grades containing 13-year-olds (in most countries, seventh and eighth grades). Making certain assumptions, the seventh grade, at least in terms of country-level differences, could be used as a surrogate to reflect students' achievements going into the eighth grade. Thus, it was possible to report results pertaining to the first type of curriculum evaluation study dealing with achievement gains and not status (Schmidt et al., 1999; Schmidt et al., 2001).

The second issue is whether the achievement measures have been designed to be "curriculum sensitive," that is, if the nature of the test, as well as the scaling employed, is sensitive to the curriculum experiences of students. Measures based on a test that covers a broad spectrum of the topics within a discipline, such as mathematics and the resulting scaling that combines all those items (either as a simple total number correct or a scaled score based on some Item Response Theory model), will reflect what is common across disparate items. When the items are based on many different topics, what is common will essentially reflect a general propensity or ability to do mathematics problems. Such a measure will not be particularly sensitive to curriculum differences, and it is likely that it will reflect other factors such as general ability, reading ability, social class, and general motivational level. When this issue was examined using TIMSS data, country rankings based on scaled scores were found to change very little even when it was clear from other data that curriculum differences among countries were pronounced (Schmidt, Jakwerth, & McKnight, 1998). When the measures were more aligned with curricula and based on items that focused on a specific part of mathematics rather than on mathematics as a whole, differences in country rankings were quite evident. This led to the development of 20 subtest areas for mathematics. This indicates that when scales used in curriculum evaluation studies are designed to be specific to topic areas rather than generic (generalizing over multiple topic areas within the discipline), they will be more sensitive to curricula.

EXAMPLES OF THE THREE TYPES OF CURRICULUM EVALUATION STUDIES USING THE TIMSS DATA

Curriculum as the Object of the Evaluation: Curriculum as a Design Variable

When curriculum is the object of an evaluation, the major question is: is curriculum related to achievement gain? The question of why one would need to measure curriculum by the methods described in the previous section for this type of study is important to address. Two answers arise, but for very different reasons.

In international studies, unlike many within-country curriculum evaluation studies, no two countries have exactly the same curriculum. In such a situation, even slight variations among countries would need to be taken into account in examining the relationship between curriculum and achievement gain. Hence, in any curriculum evaluation study of this type, the need to measure the curriculum, either in terms of emphasis or in terms of degree of implementation, is indicated.

When such measures are used, an analysis of variance model with curriculum as the design variable may not be the most appropriate. When quantitative measures of the degree of implementation of the curriculum or of the degree of emphasis allocated to different topics are available for each country, the resulting data could be used in a regression model with achievement gain as the dependent variable and curriculum as the quantitative independent variable(s). This, in fact, was done with TIMSS data, for which a series of regression analyses were carried out for 20 sub-areas of mathematics in which all three aspects (intended, potentially implemented, and implemented) of curriculum were used as independent variables (Schmidt et al., 2001).

This approach may be illustrated using three variables. Table 1 presents the results for four subtest areas: measurement units, common fractions, congruence and similarity, and equations and formulas. Do the results indicate that curriculum impact varies by topic? In one case, measurement units, the answer appears to be no: curriculum differences between countries do not seem to be related to learning differences between countries. For the other three areas, the answer is, yes, but the aspect of curriculum that is related to learning varies. In the case of common fractions and equations and formulas, it is not the amount of space in textbooks, nor the amount of time spent by teachers on the subject, that makes a difference. Rather, it is the extent to which the percentage of textbook space covered is allocated to more complex cognitive demands associated with a topic. In the case of congruence and similarity, measures of the amount of textbook space and the amount of time teachers allocate to the topic are related to the amount of learning. These results suggest that the answer to the question, is curriculum related to learning, is complex; it depends on topic area and aspect of the curriculum. They also suggest that, even within countries, when various curriculum approaches are being evaluated, the answers may be much more complex than has traditionally been thought to be the case. Cross-national results clearly support the need for achievement measures that reflect small areas of the curriculum rather than a general overall total score. Analyses using a total score often result in the conclusion that curriculum really does not matter. However, it is clear that when topics are defined at a more specific level, curriculum does have an impact on student learning.

Curriculum as the Criterion for an Evaluation Study: Curriculum as the Dependent Variable

Do educational systems provide different curriculum opportunities for students? This question could also be phrased in terms of the extent to which different curriculum opportunities to learn are provided by different educational systems or countries. In this case, opportunity to learn or the curriculum measures become the dependent variables.

Table 1.   **Using Curriculum Variables to Predict Achievement Gains in Eighth Grade Mathematics in 31 TIMSS counties**

TIMSS 8th Grade Mathematics Subtest Areas	*Amount of coverage of topics in textbook (% of book)*			*Amount of textbook allocated to complex cognitive demands for the topics (% of book)*			*Amount of time teachers allocate to the topics (% of time)*		
	Reg. Coef.	*Std. Errors*	*p*	*Reg. Coef.*	*Std. Errors*	*p*	*Reg. Coef.*	*Std. Errors*	*p*
Common Fractions	0.254	0.181	0.172	0.405	0.170	0.025	0.206	0.183	0.267
Measurement Units	0.288	0.181	0.119	0.194	0.184	0.296	0.208	0.182	0.265
Congruence & Similarity	0.434	0.168	0.015	0.227	0.184	0.218	0.620	0.147	0.000
Equations & Formulas	−0.203	0.177	0.262	0.388	0.168	0.029	−0.082	0.181	0.654

31 Countries Included: Australia, Austria, Belgium-Flemish, Belgium-French, Canada, Colombia, Cyprus, Czech Republic, Slovak Republic, Denmark, France, Germany, Greece, Hong Kong, Hungary, Iceland, Ireland, Japan, Korea, Netherlands, New Zealand, Norway, Portugal, Romania, Russian Federation, Singapore, Spain, Sweden, Switzerland, USA, Slovenia

Two volumes characterizing differences in both the characteristics of the curriculum and the substance of the curriculum are available for TIMSS (Schmidt, McKnight, Valverde et al., 1997; Schmidt, Raizen et al., 1997). Different findings emerge in a study reported by Schmidt et al., 2001. For purposes of illustration, one aspect of the curriculum (textbooks) will be considered here. The profile of coverage for the 44 topics covered in the mathematics framework is examined for 32 countries. Data for analysis are the percentage of each country's textbook that covers each of the mathematics topics. The results summarized in Table 2 indicate that there are substantial differences in topic coverage across countries. While the top five topics across all countries are equations and formulas; polygons and circles; functions and relations; 3-D geometry; and perimeter, area, and volume, there is substantial variation on each.

One way to examine between-country variations is to perform a median polish analysis (Mosteller & Tukey, 1977, p. 178). The analysis identifies countries which give more or less attention to topics in their textbooks than is given in other countries, or indeed to other topics in the country itself. Using the criterion of an absolute difference of 10 percent, large country-by-topic interactions were found for approximately two-thirds of topics in terms of textbook coverage. (see Table 3). Textbooks varied in their coverage of topics, both across countries and within countries. Thus, it may be inferred, countries vary in the opportunities to learn that they provide.

The topic for which the greatest variation in textbook coverage was found was equations and formulas. In Japan, for example, more textbook space was devoted to this topic than would be predicted from the typical amount of space devoted to topics in that country, as well as from the amount devoted to the topic in other

Table 2.   Percent of Textbook Space Devoted to TIMSS Mathematics Framework Topics

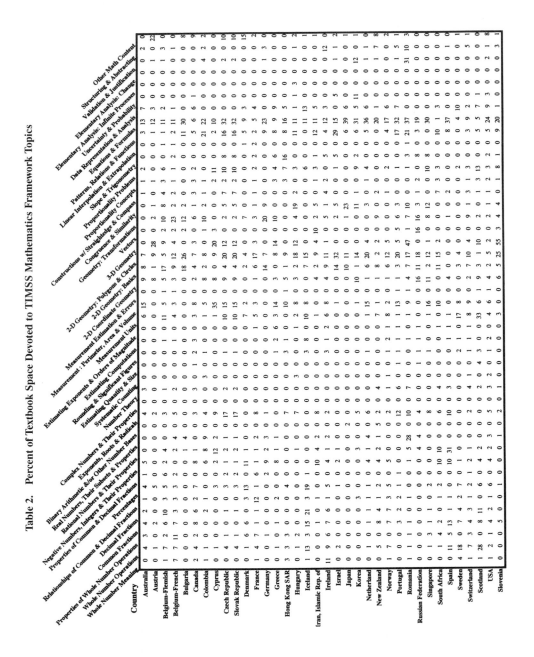

Table 3. Mased Median Polish Unique Effect of Textbook Space Devoted to TIMSS Mathematics Framework Topics (Magnitude of 10% or greater)

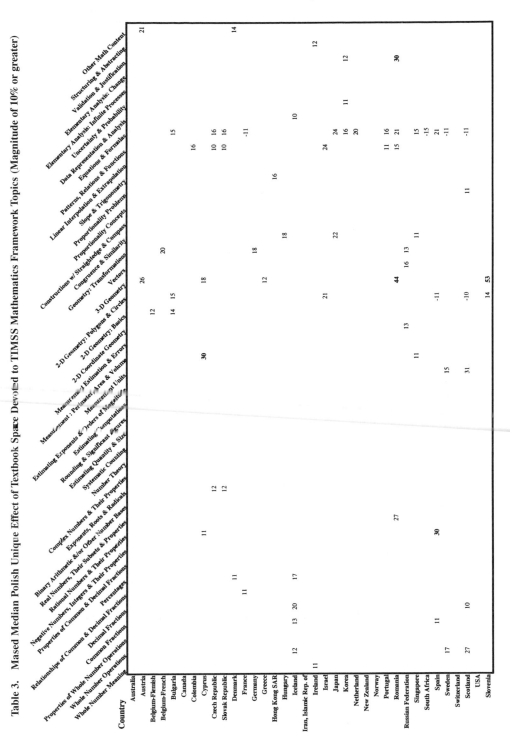

countries. The results of analyses of other aspects of the curriculum are provided in Schmidt et al. (2001).

Curriculum as the Context for a Curriculum Evaluation Study: Curriculum as a Nuisance Variable

The results of international studies are often used to conclude that some educational systems are better than others. Policy decisions may follow. For example, on the basis of the findings of the Second International Mathematics Study, teachers in the United States were exhorted in the 1980s and 1990s to model their teaching on Japanese practice. Some now suggest that since Singapore performed so well in TIMSS that it is the country to emulate.

The use of the results of an international assessment in this way brings us to the third type of curriculum evaluation study. Is it a reasonable conclusion that the educational system in Singapore at the eighth grade is better than those of other countries that participated in TIMSS? The answer can only begin to be addressed (putting aside the folly of even asking it, or of reaching such conclusions on the basis of this kind of a cross-national study) by taking into account the curriculum of that country compared to the curricula of other countries. To accomplish this, not only would achievement have to be measured in the way described previously but curriculum measures would also have to be obtained so that they could be entered into analyses as control or conditioning variables. Since we do not believe this to be an appropriate use of international data, we will not illustrate the kind of analysis that would use opportunity to learn as a covariate in examining the relative merits of educational systems.

However, it would be reasonable to ask whether the TIMSS test was equally fair or unfair to countries. To explore this issue, each country could be represented on each aspect of the curriculum as a point in a 44-dimensional space, each dimension representing one of the 44 topics of the mathematics framework. The TIMSS test could similarly be represented. The distance between those points within the 44-dimensional space would provide an indication of fairness.

This makes the assumption that the space is Euclidean, which was accepted in the absence of evidence to the contrary. Using the standard definition of distance within a Euclidean space, the distances between the TIMSS test and each of the countries on each of the various aspects was tabulated (Table 4). It is clear from the data that the TIMSS test was not equally unfair to all countries and, in fact, was much closer to the curriculum of some countries than to the curricula of others.

CONCLUSION

A common thread through each of the three types of curriculum study evaluations considered in this paper is that the curriculum needs to be measured in

Table 4.   **Alignment (Measured by Distance) between Coverage in Textbook and in TIMSS Eighth Grade Mathematics Test**

Country	Distance^2	Distance
Australia	591	24
Austria	1907	44
Belgium-Flemish	780	28
Belgium-French	1112	33
Bulgaria	1806	42
Canada	517	23
Colombia	1136	34
Cyprus	2060	45
Czech Republic	1885	43
Slovak Republic	1885	43
Denmark	1014	32
France	966	31
Germany	1280	36
Greece	882	30
Hong Kong SAR	837	29
Hungary	1224	35
Iceland	994	32
Iran, Islamic Rep. of	883	30
Ireland	805	28
Israel	2147	46
Japan	1609	40
Korea	1176	34
Netherlands	1247	35
New Zealand	683	26
Norway	443	21
Portugal	1293	36
Romania	5548	74
Russian Federation	1657	41
Singapore	1178	34
South Africa	1238	35
Spain	2123	46
Sweden	853	29
Switzerland	608	25
Scotland	1903	44
USA	500	22
Slovenia	3895	62
Average	1407	36
Standard Deviation	975	11
Minimum	443	21
25%ile	849	29
Median	1177	34
75%ile	1826	43
Maximum	5548	74

quantifiable ways that allow for appropriate kinds of statistical analysis. This is so whether curriculum is the object of an evaluation, the criterion for it, or the context in which an evaluation is interpreted. Furthermore, on the basis of the experience of TIMSS, it is reasonable to conclude that curriculum can be measured both validly and reliably. This is not to say that the methods and the procedures developed for TIMSS are perfect. However, they do serve to illustrate that curriculum can be measured and portrayed as an interesting outcome in itself, and in relation to achievement gain. A final point is that given the diversity of curricula, some way of measuring them is an essential component of an international study. The methodologies and issues discussed in this chapter would also appear relevant when curricula are being evaluated in countries which do not have a national curriculum.

REFERENCES

Apple, M.W. (1990). *Ideology and curriculum*. New York: Routledge.

Apple, M.W. (1996). Power, meaning, and identity: Critical sociology of education in the United States. *British Journal of Sociology of Education*, **17**, 125–144.

Beaton, A.E., Martin, M.O., Gonzalez, E.J., Kelly, D.L., & Smith, T.A. (1996). *Mathematics achievement in the middle school years. IEA's Third International Mathematics and Science Study*. Chestnut Hill, MA: TIMSS International Study Center, Boston College.

Beaton, A.E., Martin, M.O., Mullis, I.V.S., Gonzalez, E.J., Smith, T.A., & Kelly, D.A. (1996). *Science achievement in the middle school years: IEA's Third International Mathematics and Science Study*. Chestnut Hill, MA: TIMSS International Study Center, Boston College.

Burstein, L. (Ed.). (1993). *The IEA study of mathematics III: Student growth and classroom processes*. Oxford: Pergamon.

Floden, R.E. (2000). *The measurement of opportunity to learn*. Methodological advances in large-scale cross-national education surveys. Paper presented at a symposium sponsored by Board on International Comparative Studies in Education.

Garden, R.A. (1987). The second IEA mathematics study. *Comparative Education Review*, **31**, |47–68.

Husén, T. (Ed.). (1967). *International study of achievement in mathematics: A comparison of twelve countries*. (2 vols). Stockholm: Almqvist & Wiksell.

Husén, T., & Keeves, J.P. (Eds). (1991). *Issues in science education*. Oxford: Pergamon.

Jackson, P.W. (Ed.). (1992). *Handbook of research on curriculum*. New York: Macmillan.

Keeves, J.P. (Ed.). (1992). *The IEA science study III: Changes in science education and achievement 1970 to 1984*. Oxford: Pergamon.

Kotte, D. (1992). *Gender differences in science achievement in 10 countries*. Frankfurt: Lang.

Martin, M.O., Mullis, I.V.S., Beaton, A.E., Gonzalez, E.J., Smith, T.A., & Kelly, D.A. (1997). *Science achievement in the primary school years. IEA's Third International Mathematics and Science Study*. Chestnut Hill, MA: TIMSS International Study Center, Boston College.

McKnight, C.C., Crosswhite, F.J., Dossey, J.A., Kifer, E., Swafford, J.O., Travers, K.J., & Cooney, T.J. (1987). *The underachieving curriculum: Assessing U.S. school mathematics from an international perspective*. Champaign, IL: Stipes.

Mosteller, F., & Tukey J.W. (1977). *Data analysis and regression: A second course in statistics*. Reading, MA: Addison-Wesley.

Mullis, I.V.S., Martin, M.O., Beaton, A.E., Gonzalez, E.J., Kelly, D.A., & Smith, T.A. (1997). *Mathematics achievement in the primary school years. IEA's Third International Mathematics and Science Study*. Chestnut Hill, MA: TIMSS International Study Center, Boston College.

Mullis, I.V.S., Martin, M.O., Beaton, A.E., Gonzalez, E.J., Kelly, D.A., & Smith, T.A. (1998). *Mathematics and science achievement in the final year of secondary school. IEA's Third International Mathematics and Science Study*. Chestnut Hill, MA: TIMSS International Study Center, Boston College.

Peaker, G.F. (1975). *An empirical study of education in twenty-one systems: A technical report*. Stockholm: Almqvist and Wiksell.

Porter, A. (1989). A curriculum out of balance: The case of elementary school mathematics. *Educational Researcher*, **18**(5), 9–15.

Porter, A.C. (1995). The uses and misuses of opportunity to learn standards. In D. Ravitch (Ed.), *Debating the future of American education: Do we need national standards and assessments?* (pp. 40–65). Washington, DC: Brookings Institution.

Postlethwaite, T.N., & Wiley, D.E. (1992). *The IEA study of science II: Science achievement in twenty-three countries.* Oxford: Pergamon.

Robitaille, D.F., & Garden, R.A. (1989). *The IEA study of mathematics II: Contexts and outcomes of school mathematics.* Oxford: Pergamon.

Robitaille, D.F., Schmidt, W.H., Raizen, S., McKnight, C., Britton, E., & Nicol, C. (1993). *Curriculum frameworks for mathematics and science.* Vancouver: Pacific Educational Press.

Robitaille, D.F., & Travers, K.J. (1992). International studies of achievement in mathematics. In D.A. Grouws (Ed.), *Handbook of research on mathematics teaching and learning* (pp. 687–709). New York: Macmillan.

Schmidt, W.H., Jakwerth, P.M., & McKnight, C.C. (1998). Curriculum-sensitive assessment: Content *does* make a difference. *International Journal of Educational Research, 29*, 503–527.

Schmidt, W.H., & McKnight, C.C. (1995). Surveying educational opportunity in mathematics and science: An international perspective. *Educational Evaluation and Policy Analysis, 17*, 337–353.

Schmidt, W.H., McKnight, C.C., Cogan, L.S., Jakwerth, P.M., & Houang, R.T. (1999). *Facing the consequences: Using TIMSS for a closer look at U.S. mathematics and science education.* Boston: Kluwer Academic.

Schmidt, W.H., McKnight, C.C., Houang, R.T., Wang, H., Wiley, D.E., Cogan, L.S., & Wolfe, R.G. (2001). *Why schools matter: A cross-national comparison of curriculum and learning.* San Francisco: Jossey-Bass.

Schmidt, W.H., McKnight, C.C., & Raizen, S.A. (1997). *A splintered vision: An investigation of U.S. science and mathematics education.* Boston: Kluwer Academic.

Schmidt, W.H., McKnight, C.C., Valverde, G.A., Houang, R.T., & Wiley, D.E. (1997). *Many visions, many aims. Volume 1: A cross-national investigation of curricular intentions in school mathematics.* Boston: Kluwer Academic.

Schmidt, W.H., Raizen, S.A., Britton, E., Bianchi, L.J., & Wolfe, R.G. (1997). *Many visions, many aims. Volume 2: A cross-national investigation of curricular intentions in school science.* Boston: Kluwer Academic.

Travers, K.J., & Westbury, I. (1989). *The IEA study of mathematics I: Analysis of mathematics curricula.* Oxford: Pergamon.

Westbury, I., & Travers, K.J. (Eds). (1990). *Second International Mathematics Study.* Urbana IL: University of Illinois.

Wolf, R.M. (Ed.). (1992). The Second International Science Study. *International Journal of Educational Research, 17*, 231–397.

List of Authors

Lisa M. Abrams, Boston College, Center for the Study of Testing, Evaluation and Educational Policy, 323 Campion Hall, Chestnut Hill, MA 02467, USA. E: abramsli@bc.edu.

Peter W. Airasian, Boston College, School of Education, Campion 336D, Chestnut Hill, MA 02167, USA. E: airasian@bc.edu.

Marvin C. Alkin, University of California at Los Angeles, Department of Education – Moore 230, 405 Hilgard Avenue, Los Angeles, CA 90024-1521, USA. E: alkin@gseis.ucla.edu.

Ted O. Almaguer, Dallas Independent School District, 6741 Alexander Drive, Dallas, TX 75214, USA.

H. S. Bhola, Indiana University (retired), 3537 East Nugget Canyon Place, Tucson, AZ 85718, USA.

William Bickel, University of Pittsburgh, Learning Research and Development Center, 740 LRDC Building, 3939 O'Hara Street, Pittsburgh, PA 15260, USA. E: bickel@pitt.edu.

Robert F. Boruch, University of Pennsylvania, 6417 Wissahickon Avenue, Philadelphia, PA 19119, USA. E: robertb@gse.upenn.edu.

Carl Candoli, University of Texas (retired), 8103 East Court, Austin, TX 78759-8726, USA. E: candoli@mail.utexas.edu.

Naomi Chudowsky, National Research Council, 2101 Constitution Ave., NW Washington, DC 20418, USA. E: nchudows@nas.edu.

Marguerite Clarke, Boston College, Lynch School of Education, CSTEEP 332G, Chestnut Hill, MA 02467, USA. E: clarkemd@bc.edu.

J. Bradley Cousins, University of Ottawa, Faculty of Education, 145 Jean Jacques Lussier, Ottawa ON K1N 6N5, Canada. E: bcousins@uottawa.ca.

Lois-ellin Datta, Datta Analysis, P.O. Box 383768, Waikoloa, HI 96738, E: datta @kona.net.

E. Jane Davidson, Western Michigan University, The Evaluation Center, Kalamazoo, MI 49008, USA. E: jane. davidson@wmich.edu.

Alice Dignard, Ministry of Natural Resources, Quebec, Direction de la Planification Strategique, 5700, 4e Avenue Ouest, Bureau A-313, Charlesbourg Quebec G1H 651, Canada. E: alice.dignard@mrn.gouv.qc.ca.

Elliot Eisner, Stanford University, School of Education, 485 Lausen Mall, Stanford, CA 94305-3096, USA. E: eisner@leland.stanford.edu.

International Handbook of Educational Evaluation, 997–1000
T. Kellaghan, D.L. Stufflebeam (eds.)
© *2003 Dordrecht: Kluwer Academic Publishers. Printed in Great Britain.*

Kadriye Ercikan, University of British Columbia, Faculty of Education, 2125 Main Mall, Vancouver BC V6T 1Z4, Canada. E: kadriye.ercikan@ubc.ca.

Gila Garaway, Moriah Africa, P.O. Box 22, Poriya Ilit 15208, Israel. E: ggaraway @moriahafrica.org.

Caroline Gipps, Kingston University, 53–57 High Street, Kingston upon Thames, Surrey KT1 1LQ, United Kingdom. E: C.Gipps@kingston.ac.uk.

Naftaly S. Glasman, University of California at Santa Barbara, Department of Education, Santa Barbara, CA 93106-9490, USA. E: glasman@education. ucsb.edu.

Ronald H. Heck, University of Hawaii at Manoa, Department of Educational Administration, 1776 University Avenue, Honolulu, HI 96822, USA. E: rheck @hawaii.edu.

Carolyn Huie Hofstetter, University of California at Berkeley, 717 Hillside Ave., Albany, CA 94706, USA. E: chofstet@uclink4.berkeley.edu.

Richard T. Houang, Michigan State University, 458 Erickson Hall, East Lansing, MI 48824, USA. E: houang@msu.edu.

Ernest R. House, University of Colorado, School of Education, P.O. Box 249, Boulder, CO 80309-0249, USA. E: ernie.house@colorado.edu.

Kenneth R. Howe, University of Colorado, School of Education, 249 UCB, Boulder, CO 80309-0249, USA. E: ken.howe@colorado.edu.

Sarah Howie, University of Pretoria, Department of Teaching and Training, 0002 Pretoria, South Africa. E: sjhowie@mweb.co.za.

Robert Johnson, University of South Carolina, Department of Educational Psychology, 261 Wardlaw Hall, Columbia, SC 29208, USA. E: RJOHNSON @gwm.sc.edu.

Lyle Jones, University of North Carolina at Chapel Hill, Department of Psychology, CB 3270, Chapel Hill, NC 27599, USA. E: lvjones@email.unc.edu.

Ove Karlsson, Mälardalen University, Mälardalens högskola, ISB, Box 325, 631 05 Eskilstuna, Sweden. E: ove.karlsson@mdh.se.

Thomas Kellaghan, St. Patrick's College, Educational Research Centre, Dublin 9, Ireland. E: tkellaghan@erc.ie.

Jean King, University of Minnesota, Department of Educational Policy and Administration, 330 Wulling Hall, 86 Pleasant St SE, Minneapolis, MN 55455, USA. E: kingx004@maroon.tc.umn.edu.

Henry M. Levin, Columbia University, Teachers College, Box 181, 525 W. 120th Street, New York, NY 10027-6696, USA. E: levin@exchange.tc.columbia.edu.

Yvonna S. Lincoln, Texas A&M University, Department of Educational Administration, 222 M. T. Harrington Education Center, College Station, TX 77843-4226, USA. E: ysl@tamu.edu.

Linda Mabry, Washington State University at Vancouver, Education and Human Development 217, 14204 NE Salmon Creek Avenue, Vancouver, WA 98686-9600, Canada. E: mabryl@vancouver.wsu.edu.

George Madaus, Boston College, Center for the Study of Testing, Evaluation and Educational Policy, 321 Campion Hall, Chestnut Hill, MA 02167-3807, USA. E: madaus@bc.edu.

Patrick J. McEwan, Department of Economics, Wellesley College, 106 Central Street, Wellesley, MA 02481, USA. E: pmcewan@wellesley.edu.

Barry McGaw, Centre for Educational Research and Innovation, Organisation for Economic Co-operation and Development, 2 rue André-Pascal, 75775 Paris 16, France. E: Barry.MCGAW@oecd.org.

Gary Miron, Western Michigan University, The Evaluation Center, Kalamazoo, MI 49008, USA. E: gary.miron@wmich.edu.

Robert J. Mislevy, University of Maryland, Measurement, Statistics, and Evaluation, 1230C Benjamin Building, College Park, MD 20742-1115, USA. E: rmislevy @ets.org.

Michael Morris, University of New Haven, Department of Psychology, West Haven, CT 06516, USA. E: MMorris@newhaven.edu.

Catherine Awsumb Nelson, Evaluation Consultant, 55898 Cedar Lane, Paw Paw, MI 49079, USA. E: awsumb@kalnet.net.

Michael Abiola Omolewa, Nigerian Permanent Delegation to UNESCO, 1 Rue Miollis, 75015 Paris, France. E: M.Omolewa@unesco.org.

Tim O. Orsak, Dallas Independent School District, 6741 Alexander Drive, Dallas, TX 75214, USA.

John M. Owen, The University of Melbourne, Centre for Program Evaluation, Parkville, Victoria 3052, Australia. E: j.owen@edfac.unimelb.edu.au.

Michael Quinn Patton, Union Institute and University, 3228 46th Avenue, South, Minneapolis, MN 55406, USA. E: MQPatton@prodigy.net.

Mari Pearlman, Educational Testing Service, 39-L, Rosedale & Carter Roads, Princeton, NJ 08541, USA. E: mpearlman@ets.org.

Tjeerd Plomp, University of Twente, Faculty of Educational Science and Technology, P.O Box 217, 7500 AE Enschede, Groningen, The Netherlands. E: plomp@edte.utwente.nl.

Jennifer Post, University of Pittsburgh, Learning Research and Development Center, 2511 Chestnut Ridge Drive, Pittsburgh, PA 15205, USA. E: jenniferepost@netscape.net.

Hallie Preskill, University of New Mexico, 7112 Staghorn Dr., Albuquerque, NM 87120, USA. E: hpreskil@unm.edu.

Fernando Reimers, Harvard University, Graduate School of Education, Gutman 461, Cambridge, MA 02138, USA. E: fernando_reimers@ harvard.edu.

James R. Sanders, Western Michigan University, The Evaluation Center, Kalamazoo MI 49008, USA. E: james.sanders@wmich.edu.

William H. Schmidt, Michigan State University, 463 Erickson Hall, East Lansing, MI 48824, USA. E: bschmidt@msu.edu.

Michael Scriven, Claremont Graduate University, P.O. Box 69, Point Reyes, CA 94956, USA. E: scriven@aol.com.

M. F. Smith, University of Maryland, The Evaluators' Institute, DE (Emerita), 116 Front Street, Federal Building, Rm 236, Lewes, DE 19958, USA. E: evalinst@erols.com.

Robert Stake, University of Illinois at Champaign-Urbana, CIRCE, 190 Children's Research Center, MC-670, 51 Getty Drive, Champaign, IL 61820, USA. E: r-stake@uiuc.edu.

Gordon Stobart, University of London, Institute of Education, 20 Bedford Way, London WC1H 0AL, United Kingdom. E: g.stobart@ioe.ac.uk.

James Stronge, College of William and Mary, School of Education, Jones Hall – P.O. Box 8795, Williamsburg, VA 23187-8795, USA. E: jhstro@facstaff.wm.edu.

Daniel L. Stufflebeam, Western Michigan University, The Evaluation Center, Kalamazoo MI 49008, USA. E: daniel.stufflebeam@wmich.edu.

Richard Tannenbaum, Educational Testing Service, Rosedale & Carter Roads, Princeton, NJ 08541, USA. E: rtannenbaum@ets.org.GWIA.WMU.

Harry Torrance, University of Sussex, Institute of Education, EDB 333, Falmer, Brighton BN1 9RH, United Kingdom. E: h.torrance@sussex.ac.uk.

William J. Webster, Dallas Independent School District, 6741 Alexander Drive, Dallas, TX 75214, USA. E: wwebster2@mindspring.com.

Mark R. Wilson, University of California at Berkeley, Graduate School of Education, Berkeley, CA 94720, USA. E: mrwilson@socrates.Berkeley.edu.

Lori A. Wingate, Western Michigan University, The Evaluation Center, Kalamazoo, MI 49008, USA. E: lori.wingate@wmich.edu.

Richard M. Wolf, Columbia University, Teachers College, Box 165, New York, NY 10027, USA. E: rmwolf@westnet.com.

Blaine R. Worthen, Utah State University; Western Institute for Research and Evaluation, Department of Psychology, 2810 Old Main Hill, Logan, UT 84322-2810, USA. E: Blaine@coe.usu.edu.

Index of Authors

Abbott, A. 923
Abelson, Robert 884, 886–7
Abma, Tineke 69, 70, 72, 178, 259
Abrams, Lisa M. 5, 485, 486, 533–48
Abt, Clark 351, 356
Achilles, C.M. 109, 113, 114, 833
Ackland, J.W. 812
Adams, J.E. 650
Adams, K.A. 305, 320
Adams, R. 525
Afemikhe, O.A. 478
Aguilera, D. 172
Ahmann, J.S. 541
Ahuja, R. 456
Ahuja, Sanchez R. 457
Ai, X. 211
Airasian, Peter W. 5, 485, 486, 533–48, 878
Aitken, R. 811
Akpe, C.S. 478
Akubue, A. 473
Alexander, D. 49
Alexander, Lamar 536, 889, 890
Ali, A. 473
Alkin, Marvin C. 4, 9, 189–95, 197–222, 226,
  237–9, 242, 247, 263n1, 661, 724
Allan, J. 172
Allen, M. 615
Allen, R. 567, 570
Almaguer, Ted O. 6, 51, 881, 929–49
Almond, R.G. 489, 502, 505, 528
Altschuld, James W. 335–6, 338
Alvarez, B. 470
Amano, I. 578
Ames, C. 592
Anderson, J.O. 569
Anderson, John R. 228, 526
Anderson, L.W. 526
Anderson, M.C. 947
Anderson, Scarvia B. 291
Angrist, J. 142
Anrig, Gregory 888, 889
Apling, R. 207, 725
Apple, M.W. 982
Archer, J. 592

Arends, R.I. 538
Argyris, C. 812, 814
Arkes, J. 613
Armstrong, I. 410
Arnheim, R. 154
Arregui, P. 442, 453
Arter, J. 541
Arthur, G. 452
Arubayi, E. 478
Asamoah, Y. 411
Asayesh, G. 848
Atkin, Mike 67
Au, K.H. 631
Ausubel, D. 536
Avalos, B. 443
Awsumb Nelson, Catherine 773

Bachman, J. 631
Bachor, D.G. 569
Backhouse, J.K. 588
Backus, C.A. 75
Bailey, Stephen 888
Bajah, S.T. 478
Baker, Eva L. 333, 334
  alternative assessment 550, 557, 567, 571
  teacher evaluation 616, 631, 632
  US program evaluation 723, 724, 726–7,
    728–9, 730
Baker, Kenneth 911
Baker, W.K. 633
Balistrieri, M. 71
Ball, J. 919
Ballator, Nada 902n1
Ballou, D. 657, 660
Bamberger, M. 320, 411, 711
Barkdoll, Gerald 235
Barnes, H.V. 118
Barnett, B. 657
Barnett, W.S. 109, 135, 137, 140, 141, 145, 146
Barone, Tom 155
Barrington, G.V. 255
Bartell, C. 656
Bartell, E. 135
Barth, P. 626

International Handbook of Educational Evaluation, 1001–1020
T. Kellaghan, D.L. Stufflebeam (eds.)
© *2003 Dordrecht: Kluwer Academic Publishers. Printed in Great Britain.*

Subject Index

International Handbook of Educational Evaluation, 1021–1062
T. Kellaghan, D.L. Stufflebeam (eds.)
© *2003 Dordrecht: Kluwer Academic Publishers. Printed in Great Britain.*

Kluwer International Handbooks of Education